I0882653

AI as Help and Hindrance in Education

Alexandre Duarte
NOVA University of Lisbon, Portugal

José Gabriel Andrade
University of Minho, Portugal

Patricia Dias
Catholic University of Portugal, Portugal

IGI Global
Scientific Publishing
Publishing Tomorrow's Research Today

Vice President of Editorial — Melissa Wagner
Director of Acquisitions — Mikaela Felty
Director of Book Development — Jocelynn Hessler
Production Manager — Mike Brehm
Cover Design — Jose Rosado

Published in the United States of America by
IGI Global Scientific Publishing
701 East Chocolate Avenue
Hershey, PA, 17033, USA
Tel: 717-533-8845
Fax: 717-533-7115
Website: https://www.igi-global.com E-mail: cust@igi-global.com

Copyright © 2026 by IGI Global Scientific Publishing. All rights reserved. No part of this publication may be reproduced, stored or distributed in any form or by any means, electronic or mechanical, including photocopying, without written permission from the publisher.

Product or company names used in this set are for identification purposes only. Inclusion of the names of the products or companies does not indicate a claim of ownership by IGI Global Scientific Publishing of the trademark or registered trademark.

Library of Congress Cataloging-in-Publication Data

Names: Duarte, Alexandre editor | Andrade, Jose Gabriel, 1983- editor | Dias, Patricia editor
Title: AI as help and hindrance in education / [edited by] Alexandre Duarte, José Gabriel Andrade, Patrícia Dias.
Description: Hershey, PA : IGI Global Scientific Publishing, [2026] | Includes bibliographical references and index. | Summary: "This book explores the use of AI in learning platforms. It comprehensively discusses both the opportunities and challenges to the integration of AI in education"-- Provided by publisher.
Identifiers: LCCN 2025031530 (print) | LCCN 2025031531 (ebook) | ISBN 9798337360195 paperback | ISBN 9798337360188 hardcover | ISBN 9798337360201 ebook
Subjects: LCSH: Artificial intelligence--Educational applications | Educational technology
Classification: LCC LB1028.43 .A3775 2026 (print) | LCC LB1028.43 (ebook)
LC record available at https://lccn.loc.gov/2025031530
LC ebook record available at https://lccn.loc.gov/2025031531

British Cataloguing in Publication Data
A Cataloguing in Publication record for this book is available from the British Library.

All work contributed to this book is new, previously-unpublished material.
The views expressed in this book are those of the authors, but not necessarily of the publisher.
This book contains information sourced from authentic and highly regarded references, with reasonable efforts made to ensure the reliability of the data and information presented. The authors, editors, and publisher believe the information in this book to be accurate and true as of the date of publication. Every effort has been made to trace and credit the copyright holders of all materials included. However, the authors, editors, and publisher cannot assume responsibility for the validity of all materials or the consequences of their use. Should any copyright material be found unacknowledged, please inform the publisher so that corrections may be made in future reprints.

Table of Contents

Detailed Table of Contents

The intersection of artificial intelligence (AI) and bilingualism represents a rapidly evolving field with far-reaching implications for language education and global communication. Adaptive learning systems powered by AI algorithms transform the way individuals acquire new languages by tailoring instructions to each learner's unique needs, pace, and learning style. These systems analyze user performance in real time by adjusting the difficulty and content of lessons to optimize the learning outcomes. Concurrently, natural language processing (NLP) and speech recognition technologies are enhancing the accuracy and efficiency of language translation tools, breaking down the communication barriers between speakers of different languages. As AI continues to advance, its impact on bilingualism extends beyond traditional language learning environments. AI-powered chatbots and virtual language partners provide learners with opportunities for immersive real-time conversational practices that simulate authentic language interactions.

This chapter explores the transformative role of artificial intelligence (AI) in current education, highlighting its potential to democratize learning through personalization, inclusivity, and interdisciplinary collaboration. It examines both opportunities and challenges, including equity, ethics, and the shifting roles of educators and students. By integrating AI into curricula, the chapter demonstrates how educators can foster critical thinking, engagement, and creativity while addressing practical and ethical complexities. A key case study details an AI-supported experiment on creativity and motivation in a university course. Students designed and analyzed a randomized controlled experiment assessing the effect of financial incentives on creative performance, showcasing digital tools' and AI's role in experimental design,

In today's fast-paced work environment, L&D teams face pressure to train employees within tight schedules. AI is automating content curation and implementing microlearning approaches to provide short, relevant, and easy-to-access learning resources. Smart content solutions gather information from various sources and evaluate it, relating it to the knowledge needed. They categorize content into microlearning sections, allowing for easy access and improved learning outcomes. This approach enhances focused adaptation and prolonged memory, allowing learners to improve their knowledge and skills in new market trends. AI-driven content curation and microlearning are a breakthrough in the L&D field, offering personalized learning progression for different levels of employees.

This study aims to explore the impact of Generative AI on communication in higher education from two key perspectives: those of students and teachers. As technology often drives development and innovation, our central research question is how AI influenced students' behavior, their expectations, and teachers' approaches to education. Initially, AI was viewed negatively due to concerns about controlling or certifying knowledge. However, students have become increasingly fascinated by it, prompting teachers to reconsider their initial opinion. The main hypothesis of this research is that AI introduces new strategies for academic work, simultaneously updating traditional methods and transforming the teacher-student relationship. This shift fosters greater student engagement and encourages innovative approaches to communication in various contexts. This study investigates both students' and teachers' perspectives on AI's role in higher education. Both groups play essential roles in education, striving to find the most effective ways to absorb knowledge and achieve personal goals.

This study explores the perception of Artificial Intelligence (AI) in an educational setting through the perspective of university students – focusing on students' attitudes

Artificial intelligence has transformed higher education by improving academic efficiency and delivering personalized learning experiences; yet, it raises concerns about data security and algorithmic bias. This study explores how undergraduate and graduate students in journalism, media, and communication perceive AI-driven educational systems, focusing on data privacy, ethical challenges, and algorithmic inequalities. We gathered insights through semi-structured interviews with students of varying academic abilities, using a phenomenological approach, and thematic analysis. Findings reveal limited awareness of data management processes, fears of misuse, and concerns about AI biased feedback. The study emphasises the need for greater transparency, inclusive AI development, and educational initiatives to address these ethical issues. By amplifying student perspectives, it contributes to the conversation on ethical AI practices, offering actionable recommendations for policymakers, educators, and developers to promote trust, equity, and accountability in AI-integrated education.

This chapter explores the use of AI for teaching and learning among students studying public relations. In particular, it focuses on the reception by students taking a module (course) designed for first year students at a university in the UK. The module has run for a number of years but for the 2023/4 academic year students were allowed to use generative AI tools for their assessed work, which took the form of a public relations plan and a creative portfolio. Taking a reflective case study approach, this chapter explores the student experience of this module, focusing in particular on the themes of student fear and resistance to using AI in the classroom.

This study examines the users' perspective on the opportunities, challenges and implications related to artificial intelligence technologies such as ChatGPT in the context of scientific writing. To achieve the research objective, the study adopts an inductive exploratory study, carried out through a qualitative approach and based on 15 in-depth interviews with researchers analyzed using QDA-miner software. The respondents perceive ChatGPT as a useful tool that simplifies activities and reduces time and human errors. However, risks associated with the use of this tool have been identified, such as the reliability of the information provided, superficiality, redundancy, misinformation, the need for more confidentiality for the personal data requested and the risk of human extinction.o the authors' knowledge, this is the first study to examine a holistic perspective containing both the benefits and challenges of the AI ChatGPT tool in the context of research publication from the researchers' perspective.

The integration of generative AI into creative fields is transforming education and professional environments. However, this shift raises concerns about the potential loss or dilution of human skills in favor of faster AI-driven solutions. This study explores how communication students specializing in advertising and public relations perceive and use generative AI in their higher education context, as well as the skills they believe are at risk due to AI integration. Based on semi-structured interviews, the findings reveal that while AI enhances soft skills like creativity and critical thinking, these abilities are paradoxically at risk of diminishing in importance. Among hard skills, writing and content creation are heavily impacted, with AI improving but simultaneously devaluing their relevance. Respondents emphasize the need for ethical AI use, highlighting the importance of transparency and guidance. They call on educators to address these challenges, promoting responsible and balanced use of AI in academia.

Digital technologies have created dynamic, cutting-edge learning settings that emphasise communication and cooperation. Communication is crucial to improve education in digital contexts, as discussed in this chapter. First, we analyse how internet platforms and technologies alter traditional teaching and learning paradigms. This chapter explores AI's growing importance in education, identifying key ideas and current AI application directions. Recently, AI technology has made significant advances. AI-powered chatbots let students and teachers communicate, and adaptive learning systems personalise instruction. These innovations boost learner engagement and assistance and reveal communications that might inform pedagogy. The chapter explains how AI and communication tactics create effective digital learning experiences. AI can make education more accessible, interactive, and personalised, preparing students for a digital future.

This research explores digital transformation within the educational sector, with a specific focus on how Generative Artificial Intelligence (GenAI) is reshaping the educational landscape. The purpose of this case study is to assess the perceptions of students and educators within the field Media and Communication, focusing on potential benefits and risks associated with GenAI usage. A special attention was given to ethical considerations arising from utilizing these new tools in higher education. We used a survey performed on Media and Communication students and a focus group with faculty members specialized on Media, Communication and Digital Pedagogy at the University of Bucharest (our case study). We identified two different approaches to GenAI: enthusiasm among students and cautiousness among educators. Students have largely adopted GenAI tools in academic tasks while for educators the effective integration of AI into educational practices is still at the beginning. Both students and teachers are in favour of regulating the use of AI in universities.

Education in the 21st century has moved beyond traditional classrooms, powered by technologies like the Internet of Things (IoT). IoT connects devices globally, enabling students and teachers to share resources and communicate anytime, fostering seamless interaction and expanding learning networks. Digital natives, familiar with smartphones and apps, benefit from IoT tools like smartboards, which offer interactive displays, cloud-based lessons, and multi-touch functionality. Beyond classrooms, IoT applications include video creation, automated payments, and smart school buses, enhancing overall efficiency. Parents also gain real-time insights into their children's academic performance. This integration of IoT and Machine Learning redefines education, making it more efficient, interactive, and accessible for all stakeholders while shaping its future. This chapter delves into global IoT and Machine Learning use cases, showcasing their advantages for students, educators, and parents, and how they shape the future of education.

In recent years after post covid, students have struggled with learning and faced difficulties in meeting the challenges confronted before them to meet the demands of society. It is essential to make a revolution in teaching methodologies to assist students to improve their learning process motivating them to achieve their goals. This chapter deals with the methodologies that help the students to understand the concept in the subject and keep them focused on the subject reducing the negative stress level. It also discusses the impact of motivation, lack of motivation, and ways to deal with the student with motivational factors that help the facilitator to create an effective Teaching-Learning (TL) environment for the students to accomplish their goals. It also guides the facilitator to direct the students towards a stress-free learning process with better academic achievements.

Preface

We are living through an era of accelerated transformation in which artificial intelligence (AI) is profoundly reshaping the landscape of contemporary education. The integration of digital technologies and automated systems into teaching and learning is no longer a future promise — it is a present reality that is fundamentally altering how we communicate, instruct, and engage with knowledge. Within this context, AI as Help and Hindrance in Education emerges as a timely and critical volume, bringing together diverse international voices to explore the dual role of AI as both an ally and a challenge in education today.

This book serves a dual purpose: to examine effective communication strategies in the context of digitally mediated education and to analyze the broad array of opportunities and tensions created by AI in academic environments. It seeks to contribute to the global conversation on how digital tools, particularly AI, are reshaping pedagogical practices, assessment systems, learner engagement, and even mental health in educational settings.

In Chapter 1, Emerging Trends and Technologies in AI and Bilingualism, Aqsa Anwar and Sanjeev Kumar delve into the intersection between language education and AI, highlighting how bilingualism and digital tools can shape global communication and inclusive learning. Moving forward, Chapter 2, by Hana Moravcová and Tereza Klabíková Rábová, explores the challenges and opportunities posed by AI in interdisciplinary education, emphasizing the importance of navigating complexity across domains.

Chapter 3, by Menard Musendekwa, proposes a paradigmatic shift in learning — from an answer-seeking model to one driven by inquiry and critical thinking, catalyzed by the capabilities of AI. In Chapter 4, K. Fouzia Sulthana and colleagues raise concerns about fairness and bias in AI-driven university assessments, offering insights into how these systems might reproduce inequality if not carefully designed and evaluated.

The role of AI in workplace learning is taken up in Chapter 5, where Arpita Nayak and Ipsita Mohapatra explore AI-based content curation and microlearning strategies that promote flexible, just-in-time education for modern professionals. In Chapter 6, Mădălina Moraru presents findings from Romania, where students and faculty reflect on the future labor market and how AI is influencing academic preparation and job readiness.

Turning to students' direct experiences, Chapter 7 by Mayyer Ling captures learners' perspectives on AI use in educational contexts — oscillating between excitement, skepticism, and uncertainty. Chapter 8, a featured contribution by Sónia Pedro Sebastião and David Dias, offers a comprehensive mapping of Portugal's higher education landscape, analyzing both institutional practices and regulatory frameworks surrounding AI-based educational training.

In Chapter 9, Aftab Hossain and collaborators apply a phenomenological lens to the experiences of Bangladeshi university students, questioning whether AI genuinely supports student learning or complicates it further. Chapter 10, by Elizabeth Bridgen and Sarah Williams, explores emotional reactions such as fear, resistance, and creative response to AI within public relations education — a field centered on human communication.

The tension between human agency and technological automation is brought into sharp focus in Chapter 11, where Arij Jmour asks whether humanity still holds a place in the age of AI, contrasting positive and negative perceptions of tools like ChatGPT. A related concern is raised in Chapter 12 by Ioana Iancu, who examines how generative AI may undermine students' development of communication skills — particularly in fields where originality and articulation are core.

Broader technological trends are addressed in Chapter 13, where Saritha Peddi and Geetha Manoharan present a panorama of emerging AI tools in education, while Chapter 14 by Camelia Cusnir and Romina Surugiu stresses that generative AI is now a social practice that higher education — particularly in media and communication — can no longer ignore.

Expanding beyond AI alone, Chapter 15, by Narayanaswamy T. and colleagues, explores the combined use of Internet of Things (IoT) and machine learning in educational contexts, envisioning more interconnected and adaptive learning systems. In Chapter 16, Magdalene Delighta Angeline D. and Samuel Peter James I. use machine learning algorithms to evaluate the effectiveness of different teaching methodologies and motivational techniques on student outcomes.

Finally, Chapter 17, by Goh Yingsoon, Zhang Suyan, and co-authors, closes the volume by focusing on the transformation of digital classrooms and the importance of fostering trust, communication, and empowerment in hybrid and virtual learning environments — an essential consideration for the post-pandemic academic world.

This book is not merely a catalog of technological innovation, but a critical inquiry into how AI is redefining the educational experience. It offers a rich tapestry of perspectives from across the globe, balancing optimism with caution, and theory with practice. From regulatory frameworks and student emotions to emerging tech trends and pedagogical paradigms, AI as Help and Hindrance in Education provides a much-needed compass for navigating the complexities of 21st-century learning.

May this volume inspire thoughtful innovation, inclusive transformation, and the ethical use of AI — with technology serving not as a substitute for human connection, but as a tool to enhance it. In doing so, we hope to contribute to a more equitable, dynamic, and human-centered future for education.

José Gabriel Andrade
University of Minho, Portugal

Patrícia Dias
Catholic University of Portugal

Alexandre Duarte
University of Minho, Portugal

Chapter 1
Emerging Trends and Technologies in AI and Bilingualism:
Shaping the Future of Language Education and Global Communication

Aqsa Anwar
https://orcid.org/0009-0004-4315-3776
GIFT University, Pakistan

Sanjeev Kumar
https://orcid.org/0000-0002-7375-7341
Lovely Professional University, India

ABSTRACT

The intersection of artificial intelligence (AI) and bilingualism represents a rapidly evolving field with far-reaching implications for language education and global communication. Adaptive learning systems powered by AI algorithms transform the way individuals acquire new languages by tailoring instructions to each learner's unique needs, pace, and learning style. These systems analyze user performance in real time by adjusting the difficulty and content of lessons to optimize the learning outcomes. Concurrently, natural language processing (NLP) and speech recognition technologies are enhancing the accuracy and efficiency of language translation tools, breaking down the communication barriers between speakers of different languages. As AI continues to advance, its impact on bilingualism extends beyond traditional language learning environments. AI-powered chatbots and virtual language partners

DOI: 10.4018/979-8-3373-6018-8.ch001

Copyright © 2026, IGI Global Scientific Publishing. Copying or distributing in print or electronic forms without written permission of IGI Global Scientific Publishing is prohibited.

provide learners with opportunities for immersive real-time conversational practices that simulate authentic language interactions.

INTRODUCTION

The convergence of artificial intelligence (AI) and bilingualism is a rapidly developing area with significant consequences for language learning and worldwide communication. AI-driven adaptive learning platforms are revolutionizing language acquisition by customizing lessons to suit individual learners' specific requirements, speed, and preferred learning methods. These platforms continuously evaluate user progress and modify lesson complexity and subject matter to maximize learning effectiveness (Boothe & Caspary, 2018). Simultaneously, advancements in natural language processing (NLP) and speech recognition technologies have improved the precision and speed of language translation tools, helping eliminate communication obstacles between individuals who speak different languages. The combination of AI and language technologies not only improves individual learning experiences but also promotes greater intercultural understanding worldwide (J. Chen et al., 2020). As AI progresses, we can expect even more advanced language-learning tools that can replicate immersive settings and offer instant feedback on pronunciation and grammar. Moreover, these innovations may result in the creation of universal translation devices capable of effortlessly enabling multilingual discussions in various contexts, ranging from global business meetings to informal tourist interactions (X. Chen et al., 2021).

As AI technology progresses, the influence of artificial intelligence on bilingualism is expanding beyond conventional language-learning settings (Woo & Choi, 2021). Learners can now engage in immersive, real-time conversational practice through AI-driven chatbots and virtual language companions that replicate genuine linguistic exchanges. Furthermore, AI enhances cross-cultural communication by delivering more sophisticated and context-sensitive translations, maintaining cultural subtleties and idiomatic expressions that are typically lost in conventional machine-translated content (Graf et al., 2014). Artificial intelligence is transforming bilingualism, going well beyond conventional language learning techniques, and reshaping how people acquire and communicate across different languages (Jia et al., 2022). Advanced AI-driven language learning tools now create customized learning plans that adjust to individual students' progress, capabilities, and areas for improvement, delivering specific exercises and inputs to enhance language acquisition. These technologies can instantly evaluate speech patterns, pronunciation, and grammatical usage, thereby providing prompt corrections and recommendations for enhancement (Kamalov et al., 2023). Furthermore, AI systems can examine extensive linguistic datasets to recognize patterns and subtleties in language use, assisting learners in grasping the contextual and cultural elements of a language that are typically difficult to master through traditional learning methods (Kannan & Munday, 2018).

The influence of artificial intelligence on bilingualism is becoming increasingly apparent in work and educational environments (C. Lai, 2019). Language tools powered by AI are now being incorporated into collaborative workspaces, enabling smooth communication among team members who speak different languages. These applications not only provide on-the-spot translation, but also offer insights into cultural norms and etiquette, promoting more productive cross-cultural exchanges. In the realm of academic research, AI allows researchers to examine multilingual texts and datasets more efficiently, revealing linguistic trends and cultural insights that were previously challenging to identify (Liang et al., 2023). This technological progress dismantles language obstacles in scientific cooperation and information sharing, potentially accelerating the rate of worldwide research and innovation (Liang et al., 2023).

REVIEW OF LITERATURE

AI's influence reaches beyond educational settings, revolutionizing worldwide communication by eliminating language obstacles. Neural machine translation models have enabled accessible and efficient cross-language interactions through instant translation and interpretation services. These technologies are increasingly being incorporated into various platforms, including business meeting software and social networking sites, to enable smooth international cooperation and cultural interchange (Melkonyan & Matevosyan, 2020).

The increasing use of AI in bilingual settings has brought forth significant ethical issues that require attention. Concerns include the protection of personal data, the risk of AI misinterpreting cultural nuances in automated translations, and the growing gap between those who can access these technologies and those who cannot (Woo & Choi, 2021). These challenges are substantial and must be addressed. As artificial intelligence continues to advance, it is essential to tackle these ethical dilemmas and ensure that AI-powered language tools are accessible (Zhao & Gallant, 2012). This approach is critical for maximizing the advantages of AI technology in both bilingual and worldwide communications.

Advancements in AI Technology Revolutionized Bilingual Education

It offers innovative tools that significantly enhance language acquisition processes. AI-powered language learning platforms now provide personalized learning experiences and can adapt to individual students' needs and learning styles (Bian et al., 2022). These systems utilize natural language processing and machine-learning algorithms to offer real-time feedback on pronunciation, grammar, and vocabulary usage. Additionally, AI-driven virtual reality and augmented reality applications create immersive language-learning environments that allow students to practice their skills in simulated real-world scenarios (Anand et al., 2010). This technology not only accelerates language acquisition but also fosters greater cultural understanding by exposing learners to authentic contexts and interactions (Kanglang, 2021).

Information and Communication Technology (ICT)

The incorporation of digital tools and platforms has transformed traditional language classrooms and created novel opportunities for dynamic and captivating instruction (Nath & Liu, 2017). These technological innovations have provided language learners with unprecedented access to genuine linguistic materials, allowing them to hone their abilities in lifelike digital settings and facilitating connections with fluent speakers worldwide (Al-Rahmi et al., 2020). Consequently, language instructors now face the task of seamlessly integrating these digital resources into their teaching approaches while ensuring that the core principles of language acquisition are not eclipsed by the allure of new technologies (K. Lai & Pratt, 2004).

Computer-Assisted Language Learning (CALL)

Computer-Assisted Language Learning (CALL) has progressed in three distinct phases: structural, communicative, and integrative. The initial structural phase uses basic computer technology to deliver repetitive language drills and grammar exercises (Garrett, 2009). As technology advanced, the communicative phase emerged, emphasizing interactive language use and task-oriented activities. Currently, CALL is in its integrative phase (Davies & Elder, 2004), which combines multimedia resources, authentic materials, and online communication tools to create a comprehensive language learning environment (Higgins, 1983).

Mobile-Assisted Language Learning (MALL)

The advent of mobile technology has resulted in Mobile-Assisted Language Learning (MALL), which is a method that facilitates learning without boundaries. MALL provides students with the opportunity to access language learning resources at any time and place, thereby overcoming the limitations of conventional classroom environments (Liu & Chen, 2015). This methodology utilizes various portable devices, including smart-phones and tablets, to deliver customized and interactive language learning sessions. With ongoing advancements in mobile technology, MALL is incorporating more advanced features such as artificial intelligence and augmented reality, thereby improving its efficacy in language acquisition (Nuraeni et al., 2020).

Networked Learning (NL)

It provides students with global connectivity and access to Open Educational Resources. This interconnected system allows learners to work together across geographical boundaries and time differences, thereby encouraging a variety of viewpoints and intercultural exchanges. NL offers students the opportunity to interact with diverse digital content ranging from hands-on simulations to video lectures by experts, which deepens their understanding of intricate subjects. Furthermore, NL encourages independent learning, enabling students to customize their educational journey according to their specific requirements and areas of interest. This approach ultimately equips them with the challenges of an increasingly digitized and globalized job market.

Language Education Experiencing a Renaissance through Artificial Intelligence (AI)

Modern AI-driven language learning platforms can customize their approach for each student, offering personalized exercises and instantaneous feedback (Goyal, 2023). These intelligent systems examine data on learner performance to pinpoint areas of strengths and weaknesses, thereby enabling more focused instruction and practice sessions. Consequently, learners can advance at a pace that suits them, concentrating on aspects that need improvement while remaining motivated through individualized content and tasks (Anderson, 2015). The results in a more efficient and engaging language-learning experience tailored to each student's unique needs.

Intelligent Computer-Assisted Language Learning (ICALL)

The development of Intelligent Computer-Assisted Language Learning (ICALL) is significantly influenced by Natural Language Processing (NLP). ICALL platforms use NLP methodologies to deliver customized language-learning experiences that cater to each student's specific requirements (Amaral & Meurers, 2011). These advanced systems can be used to examine learners' responses, identify mistakes, and provide specific suggestions for enhancing their language skills. Additionally, NLP-enhanced ICALL tools can create dynamic exercises, replicate authentic dialogues, and evaluate student advancement with higher precision than conventional CALL programs (Lu, 2018).

Language Learning

This is being transformed by artificial intelligence applications, such as machine translation and speech recognition. These AI-driven tools provide language learners with more opportunities to enhance their abilities outside conventional classroom environments (Norton & Toohey, 2011). As AI technology progresses, we may witness increasingly customized and flexible language-learning experiences that cater to specific individual requirements and learning approaches. Nevertheless, it is crucial to evaluate potential negative aspects, including excessive dependence on technology and diminishing human interaction in the process of acquiring language skills (Wenden, 2002). .

Issues regarding privacy and the need for openness in AI-powered educational systems are among the obstacles faced. To safeguard individual privacy rights, educators and policymakers must carefully consider methods for collecting, storing, and utilizing student information (Cotterall, 1999). There is also an urgent need to establish explicit guidelines and regulations governing the application of AI in educational environments, to ensure equity and responsibility. Furthermore, it is crucial to inform students, parents, and educators about the potential and constraints of AI systems, promoting well-informed decision making and the proper use of these technologies in learning spaces (Svalberg, 2007).

Educator's transition into facilitators of distributed expertise as educational landscapes evolves. With the advancement of technology in learning environments, teachers have become knowledge organizers, rather than exclusive information providers. They assist students in exploring vast information resources and fostering the development of the analytical skills necessary for evaluating and integrating diverse sources (Elley & Mangubhai, 1983). This transformation has enabled students to become more self-reliant and flexible, equipping them with a dynamic world in which lifelong learning is crucial.

This could encompass the use of AI-driven conversational agents or immersive virtual environments to complement in-person language instruction. By leveraging the advantages of both artificial intelligence and human-to-human interaction, students may gain access to individualized feedback and supplementary practice sessions beyond the classroom. Furthermore, researchers must investigate the most efficacious methods for integrating AI-enhanced learning with traditional face-to-face approaches to optimize language learning outcomes (Levy, 2009). The objective is to achieve an optimal equilibrium between these two modalities for the most effective language acquisition process.

A holistic approach to language acquisition encompassing the cognitive, metacognitive, affective, and social dimensions of the learning process is gaining prominence (Benson & Lor, 1999). This integrated perspective acknowledges that language acquisition involves more than just cognitive processes, and is significantly influenced by affective factors, social interactions, and metacognitive awareness. Educators are now implementing methodologies that address these dimensions such as fostering supportive learning environments, facilitating collaborative learning, and developing metacognitive strategies. By recognizing the interrelationships among these elements, language pedagogy can be optimized and tailored to meet the diverse needs of individual learners.

IMPACT OF AI TOOLS TO IMPROVE BILINGUAL PROFICIENCY

AI tools help increase the proficiency of learning bilingual communication skills, and various tools also have a positive impact on bilingual communication. Some tailored content platforms analyze individual learners' strengths, weaknesses, and preferences to deliver customized lessons (Ling et al., 2008). This ensures that learners engage with materials most relevant to their current proficiency levels. Adaptive AI algorithms adjust the difficulty of exercises based on real-time performance, helping learners progress at their own pace while appropriately challenging them. Many new platforms have incorporated (Kuddus, 2022) game-like elements to motivate learners, making the process more engaging and enjoyable. Through intelligent tutoring systems, chatbots simulate real-life conversations, allowing learners to practice speaking and listening skills in a low-pressure environment. It can also access a learner's proficiency through various metrics, providing insights into areas that need improvement. It can be integrated in two ways: videos, audio clips, and text, to cater to different learning styles and enhance comprehension. Some contexts use cultural nuances and idiomatic expressions for a better understanding (Ma, 2024). AI-driven personalized learning platforms and intelligent tutoring systems enhance bilingual proficiency by offering tailored experiences, immediate feedback, and engaging content, ultimately making language learning more effective and accessible.

NEW EMERGING AI TECHNOLOGIES TO RESHAPE BILINGUALISM

New emerging AI technologies play a crucial role in the development of significant reshaping of bilingualism by enhancing language learning experiences and providing innovative tools for communication (Salas-Pilco et al., 2022). The advancement of NLP enables seamless real-time translation through applications such as Google Translate and translation devices, facilitating communication across languages, and encouraging bilingual interactions (Jones et al., 2022). The NPL tool helps learners to understand different languages beyond literal translations. The new IA tool also has the features of a speech recognition system and helps to improve the pronunciation that helps the learners while speaking. Machine learning algorithms analyze learner data to adapt content and teaching methods, ensuring a more effective learning path tailored to individual needs. The content creation tool used to generate personalized reading materials, quizzes, and exercises can enhance exposure to diverse vocabulary and grammar structures, supporting bilingual development (Stone, 2014). AI will help educators curate relevant content that interests and proficiency levels, making learning more relatable and effective. These emerging AI technologies continue to develop, and have the potential to make bilingualism more accessible, engaging, and effective.

By personalizing learning experiences, enhancing communication, and immersing learners in cultural contexts, AI can significantly reshape how individuals approach language learning and usage, ultimately fostering greater bilingual proficiency in an interconnected world. Advanced AI voice synthesis technologies produce lifelike speech, allowing learners to hear accurate pronunciation and intonation, which can help mimic native speakers more effectively. AI can analyze user input in real-time, offering corrections and suggestions that consider context and intended meaning, thus enhancing conversational skills. To gain cultural insights for new learners, they interact with virtual characters. AI powered language mixtures and immersive learning environments create energetic and engaging opportunities for language acquisition. By leveraging these technologies, learners can experience personalized, contextualized, and interactive language learning that not only enhances proficiency, but also fosters a deeper appreciation of cultural nuances.

Technologies Change Societal Attitudes towards Language Learning and Bilingualism

I. **Increased Accessibility:** The new application of technologies that include mobile apps, online courses, and AI-driven language tools make language learning accessible to diverse populations, including those in remote or underserved areas. It is a more affordable and user-friendly resource, where everyone encourages pursuing bilingualism without financial or logistical barriers.
II. **Enhanced Motivation:** Gamification is a new tool for language learning and immersive environments, which includes VR and AR, to make learning effective and engaging, motivating more people to embark on language journeys.
III. **Normalization of Bilingualism:** The use of new technologies has a greater impact on communication skills, especially in social media, content sharing, and so on. Bilingualism requires more practical skills, and it is also a diverse communication tool used for translation, and global communication and understanding tools for better understanding.

Global Collaboration and Understanding

The importance of bilingualism in professional life has become more important in different workplace technologies and languages working together. Exposure to multiple languages creates a positive culture and leads to greater appreciation. Bilingualism, which increases their daily value in terms of soft skills, enhances employability and interpersonal communication. As technology continues to develop, it plays a crucial role in reshaping societal attitudes towards language learning and bilingualism (Luukkonen et al., 1992). By enhancing the accessibility, motivation, and normalization of bilingualism, these technologies can foster a more inclusive and culturally aware society that values linguistic diversity as an asset.

AI TOOLS AND OTHER PLATFORMS FOR BILINGUAL EDUCATORS & DEVELOPERS

The various applications are used to learn a new language, and all language application apps provide basic information on how to learn a new language and can be used in professional life.

Language Learning Apps

Duolingo

Offers gamified language courses with a focus on vocabulary and grammar using AI to personalize learning paths.

Babbel

Tailors lessons for specific learning goals and incorporates real-life conversations.

Translation Tools

Google Translate

Provides instant translations and supports voice recognition in pronunciation practice.

Microsoft Translator

Features real-time translation and conversation mode for bilingual communication.

Chatbots and Conversational AI

Replika

An AI companion that allows users to practice conversational skills in a safe environment.

HelloTalk

Connects users with native speakers for language exchange, incorporating text and voice messaging.

For Educators: Adaptive Learning Platforms

Knewton

Offers personalized learning experiences by adapting content to student needs, helping educators tailor their instruction.

DreamBox

Focuses on math, but provides insights into adaptive learning strategies applicable to language education.

AI-Powered Assessment Tools

Gradescope

Helps educators evaluate assignments efficiently by using AI for grading and feedback.

Edulastic

Provides formative assessment tools that adapt based on student performance.

Professional Development Resources

ACTFL

The American Council on the Teaching of Foreign Languages offers resources and training to language educators, including digital tools.

Teacher Training Videos

Platforms like Edutopia feature videos of best practices in language teaching and the use of technology.

For Developers: Natural Language Processing (NLP) APIs

Google Cloud Natural Language API

Enables developers to analyze text, providing insights into sentiment, entities, and syntax.

IBM Watson Language Translator

Offers translation services and language detection capabilities for integration into applications.

Machine Learning Frameworks

TensorFlow

An open-source platform for building machine-learning models that is useful for developing language-related applications.

PyTorch

Another popular framework for machine learning that supports NLP projects.

Open-Source Language Resources

Hugging-face transformers

Provide pre-trained models for various NLP tasks, enabling developers to quickly build language applications.

SpaCy

A fast and efficient NLP library for Python that supports multiple languages and is useful for developing bilingual applications.

AI AND MULTIMODAL BILINGUAL COMMUNICATION

AI is transforming multimodal bilingual communication, allowing for richer and more effective interactions that leverage various modes of communication, such as text, audio, visual, and gestural elements.

I. **Multimodal Interfaces:** AI-driven platforms combine text, voice, and visual elements, allowing users to communicate simultaneously in multiple formats. For example, chat applications may support text alongside emojis, images, or voice messages to convey meaning more effectively. Tools such as Google Translate can convert spoken language into text while translating it into another language, thereby facilitating real-time bilingual conversations across various modalities.
II. **Contextual Understanding:** Advanced natural language processing allows AI to analyze contexts more effectively, thereby improving the interpretation of mixed-language inputs. The crucial aspect of bilingual communication is that idiomatic expressions and cultural references may vary significantly (Kuddus, 2022). AI can assess emotional tone through voice modulation and facial expres-

sions in video communication, providing richer insights into the communicative context.

III. **Interactive Language Learning:** AI-powered platforms can create immersive, interactive scenarios, in which learners engage with language through multiple modalities, including "text, speech, and visual cues." Tools that analyze learners' pronunciation and context-based usage in real time provide immediate, multimodal feedback, enhancing the learning experience (Kumar, 2024).

IV. **Assistive Communication Technologies:** AI tools that convert speech to text and vice versa allow users to communicate in their preferred language while accommodating those who may prefer a different mode. This is particularly helpful for individuals with disabilities. AR can overlay translations or contextual information onto real-world objects, enabling visually enhanced and contextually rich bilingual communication.

V. **Cross-Cultural Communication:** AI can incorporate cultural elements into language translation and communication, making it easier for users to understand "social cues, body language, and cultural norms," which are crucial in bilingual interactions (Kumar et al., 2023). AI-driven virtual reality platforms can simulate real-life interactions in bilingual contexts, helping users to practice communication skills while experiencing cultural nuances.

VI. **Collaboration and Networking:** AI tools can facilitate multilingual teamwork by providing real-time translation and transcription during meetings, allowing participants to contribute their preferred language and mode. AI can enhance bilingual communication on social media by analyzing and promoting multilingual content, thus enabling users to engage with diverse audiences. AI's impact of AI on multimodal bilingual communication is profound, offering new ways to engage, learn, and connect across languages and cultures (Talukder & Kumar, 2024). As technology continues to evolve, it is essential to focus on inclusivity and accessibility to ensure that these advancements benefit all users, fostering effective communication and understanding in our increasingly interconnected world.

This study delves into the potential future development of artificial intelligence and its impact on bilingualism and linguistic diversity. It explores how AI technologies may shape language learning, communication, and cultural exchange in the coming years. The analysis considered various scenarios such as the widespread adoption of real-time translation tools, AI-powered language tutors, and advanced natural language processing systems. These advancements can potentially bridge language barriers, facilitate cross-cultural understanding, and support the preservation of endangered language.

FUTURE PROSPECT OF EXPLORING AI AND BILINGUALISM

Exploring the intersection of AI and bilingualism presents exciting prospects that can shape the future of language learning, teaching, and communication. The impact of AI is the advanced process and great learning experience, learning style preferences, and progress to create highly customized learning paths that optimize engagement and retention. This increases language proficiency, and AI leads to more sophisticated assessment tools that accurately gauge language proficiency through spoken and written tests, providing real-time feedback and suggestions for improvement. AI might track language gain over time, identifying trends and areas of struggle to offer targeted support. AI can integrate cultural elements into language instruction, helping learners understand contexts, idioms, and cultural references, thus fostering deeper bilingual proficiency. Future technologies may allow users to navigate cultural differences more efficiently, thereby enhancing bilingual communication in diverse environments. AI facilitates connections between language learners and native speakers through smart matchmaking, thereby promoting collaborative learning experiences and cultural exchanges. VR and AR have become main-stream, allowing learners to practice languages in realistic, interactive settings that replicate real-world interactions.

Ongoing professional development can be supported by AI, encouraging lifelong learning and adaptability in an increasingly global job market. AI can facilitate the creation of global language communities where users share resources, tips, and practice opportunities, fostering a sense of belonging and support among bilingual learners. As bilingual individuals share content online, AI tools can help curate and promote multilingual content, encouraging a wider appreciation and understanding of different languages and cultures. Future research could focus on ensuring that AI tools are free from bias, promoting equitable access to language learning resources for all individuals, regardless of the background. Addressing the disparities in access to technology will be crucial in ensuring that advancements in AI benefit diverse populations and promote bilingualism across different communities. The intersection of AI and bilingualism holds transformative potential for individuals, educators, and society. By leveraging AI advancements, we can create more effective, engaging, and inclusive language learning experiences that not only enhance proficiency, but also foster cultural understanding and global communication. As we explore these prospects, ongoing collaboration among technologists, educators, and linguistic experts is essential to realize this vision.

CONCLUSION

This study offers a thorough analysis of the convergence between artificial intelligence and bilingualism, uncovering notable ramifications in language instruction and worldwide communication. The findings indicate that AI-driven adaptive learning systems can transform bilingual education by delivering customized learning experiences adapted to individual requirements, learning speeds, and favored methods. These platforms have the potential to boost student participation, enthusiasm, and language acquisition. The exploration of AI-enhanced virtual and augmented reality technologies has emphasized their ability to generate immersive language learning settings that provide contextually rich, interactive experiences for bilingual students. These innovations offer prospects for cultural immersion and instantaneous feedback, potentially expediting language acquisition and enhancing retention.

Nevertheless, this research has also revealed crucial ethical considerations that must be tackled as AI becomes more widespread in multilingual contexts. Concerns regarding data privacy, cultural misinterpretation in AI-powered translations, and disparate access to AI-enhanced language-learning tools across socioeconomic groups present significant hurdles. These discoveries underscore the necessity of responsible AI implementation and the establishment of ethical guidelines to ensure fair access and cultural sensitivity in AI-driven language tools. This study has pinpointed several areas for future research, including long-term investigations into the efficacy of AI in bilingual education, comparative studies of AI-enhanced immersive technologies versus conventional methods, and approaches to mitigate ethical concerns. As AI continues to progress, it is vital to weigh the potential advantages of these technologies, with careful consideration of their societal impact.

This research contributes valuable insights to the field of AI and bilingualism, establishing a foundation for educators, policymakers, and technology developers to make well-informed decisions about incorporating AI into language learning and communication platforms. By addressing the challenges and capitalizing on the opportunities presented by AI, we can strive towards a future where technology enhances bilingual education and promotes global communication while preserving cultural nuances and fostering equitable access to these transformative tools.

REFERENCES

Al-Rahmi, W. M., Alzahrani, A. I., Yahaya, N., Alalwan, N., & Kamin, Y. B. (2020). Digital Communication: Information and Communication Technology (ICT) Usage for Education Sustainability. *Sustainability*, *12*(12), 5052. DOI: 10.3390/su12125052

Amaral, L. A., & Meurers, D. (2011). On using intelligent computer-assisted language learning in real-life foreign language teaching and learning. *ReCALL*, *23*(1), 4–24. DOI: 10.1017/S0958344010000261

Anand, M. O., Krishnaswamy, J., Kumar, A., & Bali, A. (2010). Sustaining biodiversity conservation in human-modified landscapes in the Western Ghats: Remnant forests matter. *Biological Conservation*, *143*(10), 2363–2374. DOI: 10.1016/j.biocon.2010.01.013

Anderson, M. (2015). Renaissance Language and Memory Forms. In M. Anderson, *The Renaissance Extended Mind* (pp. 116–144). Palgrave Macmillan UK. https://doi.org/DOI: 10.1057/9781137412850_4

Benson, P., & Lor, W. (1999). Conceptions of language and language learning. *System*, *27*(4), 459–472. DOI: 10.1016/S0346-251X(99)00045-7

Bian, J., Al Arafat, A., Xiong, H., Li, J., Li, L., Chen, H., Wang, J., Dou, D., & Guo, Z. (2022). Machine learning in real-time internet of things (iot) systems: A survey. *IEEE Internet of Things Journal*, *9*(11), 8364–8386.

Boothe, D., & Caspary, M. (2018). Critical Issues and Practices for Hybrid and Online Teaching and Learning: Building Improved Models for 21st Century English Language Learning. *Cognitive Science – New Media – Education,* *2*(1), 99. https://doi.org/DOI: 10.12775/CSNME.2017.006

Chen, J., Zhang, M., Xu, B., Sun, J., & Mujumdar, A. S. (2020). Artificial intelligence assisted technologies for controlling the drying of fruits and vegetables using physical fields: A review. *Trends in Food Science & Technology*, *105*, 251–260. DOI: 10.1016/j.tifs.2020.08.015

Chen, X., Zou, D., Cheng, G., & Xie, H. (2021). Artificial intelligence-assisted personalized language learning: Systematic review and co-citation analysis. *2021 International Conference on Advanced Learning Technologies (ICALT)*, 241–245. https://doi.org/DOI: 10.1109/ICALT52272.2021.00079

Cotterall, S. (1999). Key variables in language learning: What do learners believe about them? *System*, *27*(4), 493–513. DOI: 10.1016/S0346-251X(99)00047-0

Davies, A., & Elder, C. (Eds.). (2004). *The Handbook of Applied Linguistics* (1st ed.). Wiley., DOI: 10.1002/9780470757000

Elley, W. B., & Mangubhai, F. (1983). The Impact of Reading on Second Language Learning. *Reading Research Quarterly*, *19*(1), 53. DOI: 10.2307/747337

Garrett, N. (2009). Computer-Assisted Language Learning Trends and Issues Revisited: Integrating Innovation. *Modern Language Journal*, *93*(s1), 719–740. DOI: 10.1111/j.1540-4781.2009.00969.x

Goyal, I. (2023). AI Renaissance, artificial intelligence, information overload, human-computer interaction, decision-making. *Review of Artificial Intelligence in Education*, *4*(00), e012. DOI: 10.37497/rev.artif.intell.educ.v4i00.12

Graf, S., Chang, T.-W., Kersebaum, A., Rath, T., & Kurcz, J. (2014). Investigating the Effectiveness of an Advanced Adaptive Mechanism for Considering Learning Styles in Learning Management Systems. *2014 IEEE 14th International Conference on Advanced Learning Technologies*, 112–116. https://doi.org/DOI: 10.1109/ICALT.2014.41

Higgins, J. (1983). Computer assisted language learning. *Language Teaching*, *16*(2), 102–114. DOI: 10.1017/S0261444800009988

Jia, F., Sun, D., Ma, Q., & Looi, C.-K. (2022). Developing an AI-Based Learning System for L2 Learners' Authentic and Ubiquitous Learning in English Language. *Sustainability*, *14*(23), 15527. DOI: 10.3390/su142315527

Jones, L., Smith, S. L., & Durham, C. (2022). Teachers as digital composers: Designing digital jumpstarts to scaffold for emerging bilingual learners. *Computers & Education*, *189*, 104592. DOI: 10.1016/j.compedu.2022.104592

Kamalov, F., Santandreu Calonge, D., & Gurrib, I. (2023). New Era of Artificial Intelligence in Education: Towards a Sustainable Multifaceted Revolution. *Sustainability*, *15*(16), 12451. DOI: 10.3390/su151612451

Kanglang, L. (2021). Artificial Intelligence (AI) and Translation Teaching: A Critical Perspective on the Transformation of Education. *International Journal of Educational Sciences*, *33*(1–3). Advance online publication. DOI: 10.31901/24566322.2021/33.1-3.1159

Kannan, J., & Munday, P. (2018). New Trends in Second Language Learning and Teaching through the lens of ICT, Networked Learning, and Artificial Intelligence. *Círculo de Lingüística Aplicada a la Comunicación*, *76*, 13–30. DOI: 10.5209/CLAC.62495

Kuddus, K. (2022). Artificial Intelligence in Language Learning: Practices and Prospects. In Mire, A., Malik, S., & Tyagi, A. K. (Eds.), *Advanced Analytics and Deep Learning Models* (1st ed., pp. 1–17). Wiley., DOI: 10.1002/9781119792437.ch1

Kumar, S. (2024). The Role of Digital Marketing on Customer Engagement in the Hospitality Industry. In Bansal, R., Ngah, A. H., Chakir, A., & Pruthi, N. (Eds.), (pp. 177–191). Advances in Business Information Systems and Analytics. IGI Global., DOI: 10.4018/979-8-3693-0815-8.ch010

Kumar, S., Dhiraj, A., Shah, M. A., & Rani, D. (2023). Application of Metaverse in the Hospitality Industry. In *Influencer Marketing Applications Within the Metaverse* (pp. 178–194). IGI Global.

Lai, C. (2019). Technology and Learner Autonomy: An Argument in Favor of the Nexus of Formal and Informal Language Learning. *Annual Review of Applied Linguistics*, *39*, 52–58. DOI: 10.1017/S0267190519000035

Lai, K., & Pratt, K. (2004). Information and communication technology (ICT) in secondary schools: The role of the computer coordinator. *British Journal of Educational Technology*, *35*(4), 461–475. DOI: 10.1111/j.0007-1013.2004.00404.x

Levy, M. (2009). Technologies in Use for Second Language Learning. *Modern Language Journal*, *93*(s1), 769–782. DOI: 10.1111/j.1540-4781.2009.00972.x

Liang, J.-C., Hwang, G.-J., Chen, M.-R. A., & Darmawansah, D. (2023). Roles and research foci of artificial intelligence in language education: An integrated bibliographic analysis and systematic review approach. *Interactive Learning Environments*, *31*(7), 4270–4296. DOI: 10.1080/10494820.2021.1958348

Ling, Y., Simsek, Z., Lubatkin, M. H., & Veiga, J. F. (2008). Transformational Leadership's Role in Promoting Corporate Entrepreneurship: Examining the CEO-TMT Interface. *Academy of Management Journal*, *51*(3), 557–576. DOI: 10.5465/amj.2008.32626023

Liu, P.-L., & Chen, C.-J. (2015). Learning English through actions: A study of mobile-assisted language learning. *Interactive Learning Environments*, *23*(2), 158–171. DOI: 10.1080/10494820.2014.959976

Lu, X. (2018). Natural Language Processing and Intelligent Computer-Assisted Language Learning (ICALL). In Liontas, J. I. (Ed.), *The TESOL Encyclopedia of English Language Teaching* (1st ed., pp. 1–6). Wiley., DOI: 10.1002/9781118784235.eelt0422

Luukkonen, T., Persson, O., & Sivertsen, G. (1992). Understanding Patterns of International Scientific Collaboration. *Science, Technology & Human Values*, *17*(1), 101–126. DOI: 10.1177/016224399201700106

Ma, A. (2024). AI vs. human translation: Shaping the future of language learning through AI-generated bilingual captions. *SHS Web of Conferences, 199*, 01023. https://doi.org/DOI: 10.1051/shsconf/202419901023

Melkonyan, A., & Matevosyan, A. (2020). Technology-assisted foreign language learning (TALL) in the digital age. *SHS Web of Conferences, 88*, 02005. https://doi.org/DOI: 10.1051/shsconf/20208802005

Nath, H. K., & Liu, L. (2017). Information and communications technology (ICT) and services trade. *Information Economics and Policy*, *41*, 81–87. DOI: 10.1016/j.infoecopol.2017.06.003

Norton, B., & Toohey, K. (2011). Identity, language learning, and social change. *Language Teaching*, *44*(4), 412–446. DOI: 10.1017/S0261444811000309

Nuraeni, C., Carolina, I., Supriyatna, A., Widiati, W., & Bahri, S. (2020). Mobile-Assisted Language Learning (MALL): Students' Perception and Problems towards Mobile Learning in English Language. *Journal of Physics: Conference Series*, *1641*(1), 012027. DOI: 10.1088/1742-6596/1641/1/012027

Salas-Pilco, S. Z., Xiao, K., & Oshima, J. (2022). Artificial Intelligence and New Technologies in Inclusive Education for Minority Students: A Systematic Review. *Sustainability*, *14*(20), 13572. DOI: 10.3390/su142013572

Stone, A. (2014). New Directions in ASL-English Bilingual Ebooks. *Critical Inquiry in Language Studies*, *11*(3), 186–206. DOI: 10.1080/15427587.2014.936242

Svalberg, A. M.-L. (2007). Language awareness and language learning. *Language Teaching*, *40*(4), 287–308. DOI: 10.1017/S0261444807004491

Talukder, M. B., & Kumar, S. (2024). The Development of Human Capital in The Hospitality Business. In S. Taneja, P. Kumar, Reepu, B. Balusamy, K. Sood, & S. Grima (Eds.), *Contemporary Studies in Economic and Financial Analysis* (pp. 21–38). Emerald Publishing Limited. https://doi.org/DOI: 10.1108/S1569-375920240000114002

Wenden, A. L. (2002). Learner Development in Language Learning. *Applied Linguistics*, *23*(1), 32–55. DOI: 10.1093/applin/23.1.32

Woo, J. H., & Choi, H. (2021). *Systematic Review for AI-based Language Learning Tools* (Version 1). arXiv. https://doi.org/DOI: 10.48550/ARXIV.2111.04455

Zhao, J., & Gallant, D. J. (2012). Student evaluation of instruction in higher education: Exploring issues of validity and reliability. *Assessment & Evaluation in Higher Education*, *37*(2), 227–235.

Chapter 2

Navigating the Impact of AI in Interdisciplinary Education:

Challenges and Opportunities

Hana Moravcová
https://orcid.org/0000-0002-5853-430X
Charles University, Czech Republic

Tereza Klabíková Rábová
https://orcid.org/0000-0001-6970-3511
Charles University, Czech Republic

ABSTRACT

This chapter explores the transformative role of artificial intelligence (AI) in current education, highlighting its potential to democratize learning through personalization, inclusivity, and interdisciplinary collaboration. It examines both opportunities and challenges, including equity, ethics, and the shifting roles of educators and students. By integrating AI into curricula, the chapter demonstrates how educators can foster critical thinking, engagement, and creativity while addressing practical and ethical complexities. A key case study details an AI-supported experiment on creativity and motivation in a university course. Students designed and analyzed a randomized controlled experiment assessing the effect of financial incentives on creative performance, showcasing digital tools' and AI's role in experimental design, data analysis, and collaborative learning. The chapter concludes by emphasizing the need for AI literacy, ethical practices, seeking multifaceted explanations, and interdisciplinary strategies to ensure its integration in education, empowering all learners.

DOI: 10.4018/979-8-3373-6018-8.ch002

Copyright © 2026, IGI Global Scientific Publishing. Copying or distributing in print or electronic forms without written permission of IGI Global Scientific Publishing is prohibited.

INTRODUCTION

This chapter explores the transformative role of artificial intelligence (AI) in education, emphasizing both the immense opportunities and the nuanced challenges that accompany its integration into learning environments. It advocates for the open and fearless adoption of AI tools within university courses, underscoring their potential to enhance inclusivity, personalization, and the adaptability of educational practices. Simultaneously, it acknowledges the pressing need for students and educators to develop proficiency with these innovative tools, balancing the democratization of access against the demands of fostering realistic expectations. A critical question emerges: How can these tools best be integrated to support and strengthen participatory engagement in the educational process?

The era of widespread online educational resources has already generated significant expectations regarding positive externalities, democratization of access, and spillover effects in education (Acemoglu et al., 2014). With the advent of AI tools, these expectations are magnified further. However, new and complex questions arise: Will AI replace underperforming teachers, or will it universally empower teachers by complementing their pedagogical and andragogical practices? Will students around the world benefit from the fact that they can reach the same level of guidance on how to cope with difficult tasks (Li & Zhao, 2024), or will the digital divide widen or even worsen (Ahmed & Wahed, 2020), leaving only technologically proficient learners and professionals equipped to leverage AI effectively? Addressing these challenges necessitates a broadening of media and digital literacy to include AI literacy (Eurostat, n.d.).

A pivotal question centers on the responsibility of cultivating AI literacy (Walczak & Cellary, 2023). Should it be the role of the state, educators, or AI providers to ensure purposeful and responsible use of these tools by students, teachers, and the broader populace? The European Union provides a partial answer through its regulations, emphasizing the shared responsibility of AI system providers and deployers. As stated in Regulation (EU) 2024/1689, Article 4: "*Providers and deployers of AI systems shall take measures to ensure, to their best extent, a sufficient level of AI literacy of their staff and other persons dealing with the operation and use of AI systems on their behalf, taking into account their technical knowledge, experience, education, and training and the context the AI systems are to be used in, and considering the persons or groups of persons on whom the AI systems are to be used.*" This regulation reflects a recognition that the integration of AI requires an ecosystem of knowledge-sharing and capacity-building across all stakeholders. If there is a milestone in the history when the digital divide (studied for the case of higher education e.g., by Legowo et al., 2024) could be a crucial disintegrative power for the society, it is now.

We believe that rather than passively awaiting the outcomes of AI companies' educational endeavors, educators must adopt a proactive stance, collaborating with these entities to shape the future of learning. This approach prioritizes inclusion and emphasizes the role of public institutions, particularly universities, in fostering non-discriminatory environments. By doing so, they can ensure equitable access to the benefits of AI advancements and maximize the opportunities these tools present (Cazzaniga, 2024). For example, the incorporation of AI systems into educational curricula can be strategically aligned with efforts to enhance personalization and efficiency in learning. This includes not only tailoring educational content to individual needs but also enabling students to actively participate in shaping their learning journeys (Rane, 2024). The proposed approach thus stresses the importance of inclusion – as we are convinced that the state, which is, in many countries, the ultimate source of financing for universities, should ensure a non-discriminative environment that equalizes access to the best way to benefit from the advancements and opportunities provided by artificial intelligence.

Moreover, the iterative process of testing and refining these systems in collaboration with students provides an additional layer of empowerment. By involving learners directly in evaluating and improving AI applications, educators can amplify their sense of agency and ownership over their educational experiences.

In the next chapter, which focuses on the practical implications and real-world analysis of specific university teaching experiences with AI integration, we share insights and recommendations drawn from our teaching and learning experiences, as well as the limited evidence gathered to date. The aim of this paper is not to present all extant approaches - from now on, we are convinced that each interested reader could gather the information she needs via new tools like Elicit or Google NotebookLM – instead, we would like to offer our point of view supported by several case studies. Our approach also strengthens multidisciplinary learning by fostering connections across various fields of study, like sociology, media studies, economics, and behavioral studies.

SUBCHAPTER 1: EMBRACING AI IN EDUCATION

This subchapter explores the reasons why contemporary university courses are uniquely suited environments for the thoughtful and critical integration of AI tools. By incorporating AI into assignments and projects, students can tackle educational challenges in fresh and innovative ways, broadening accessibility and creating new opportunities for engagement. AI-assisted learning allows individuals, regardless of their initial skill level, to approach tasks on a more equitable footing. Our discussion centers specifically on scenarios where AI tools, particularly large language models (LLMs) such as Generally Pre-trained Transformers, are used to enrich both teaching and learning practices. We aim to present concepts, considerations, and practical guidelines that support educators in collaboratively and responsibly navigating AI's capabilities alongside their students. This approach emphasizes accountability, transparency, and partnership.

In traditional educational systems, students' chances of success often depended heavily on their access to institutional resources, financial backing, and previous investments in human capital. AI tools, however, significantly lower the barriers to these supports (Choi & Schwarcz, 2023), reducing the time, money, and effort required to acquire them. As a result, AI is challenging the historical dominance of students from elite universities by leveling the playing field and offering similar advantages to a broader audience (Kamalov, 2023). This subchapter critically examines whether AI's potential to democratize education might disrupt the long-held comparative advantage of prestigious institutions as the technology begins to diminish disparities in the skills and knowledge traditionally valued by the global labor market.

At least, the concept of democratization is increasingly visible in the public discourse, represented by e.g., Whittaker, T., & Jenkins, R. (2024, September 12), Erasmus Nostrum (2024, July 20), or University of Sydney. (n.d.). However, this democratizing effect is not automatic. While AI tools can mitigate many barriers to learning (Chadha, 2024), they also introduce new challenges. The expectation that students must be able to effectively use AI places a burden on them to quickly develop proficiency in these technologies. The belief that students can independently produce solutions using AI-generated methods, techniques, or programming introduces significant pressure to continuously adapt to rapidly evolving tools.

The discussion focuses on the tension between an optimistic view—where AI empowers all students to tackle complex tasks—and a pessimistic view, which sees both students and educators struggling under the weight of the expectation to master every new tool. The dual impact of increased inclusivity and democratization, along with a growing demand for high-quality results, highlights the necessity for educational practices that actively balance these opposing forces.

The tension we are focusing on is not the only sensitive area to which both researchers and practitioners should turn their attention. The ongoing process of embracing AI tools in education must comprise systematic and proactive evaluation of whether it is safe to use it in terms of protection of personal data, including compliance with non-disclosure agreements, and whether the AI-generated content does not reinforce biases due to the substance of data on which it is trained (Barnes & Hutson, 2024). Such a strategy requires employing the interdisciplinary approach, which we illustrate in our chapter as well.

Even though we believe, based on the case studies we present, that following certain principles might help mitigate the risks of cheating, any design of educational program should be aware of the possibility that students might present the results generated by AI as their own. With AI technologies, cheating is less and less costly, creating greater and greater temptation to engage in unethical practices (as documented, e.g., by Dakakni & Safa, 2023). As the detection of AI-generated content is so far imperfect, the design of courses could be sustainably immune to the detrimental effect of AI only when it inherently makes cheating useless and obsolete.

In a supportive environment with a robust institutional framework (as stressed by Chadha, 2024) academics, educators, and students can transparently conduct a dialog, sharing data about the effects of introducing AI on their learning experience and thus contributing to the evolving scientific consensus about the impact of such structural break. Even if we collect and share the data for the purpose of managing AI-related risks, we must insist on the protection of privacy and remember that each data point represents a unique human experience. Careful interpretation and respect for humanistic values (Bai, 2024) are possible safeguards against the non-critical adoption of biased outcomes of LLMs; thus, educators stand at the center of this process, bearing responsibility for future generations' equipment for such crucial competence.

SUBCHAPTER 2: STRATEGIES FOR MANAGING AI INTEGRATION IN LEARNING

The successful integration of AI into modern education requires well-thought-out strategic approaches to effectively manage the complex balance of associated risks and rewards. According to the whitepaper of Cengage (2024), instructors within academia continue to seek more comprehensive and nuanced guidance on how to leverage AI tools in their teaching practices both effectively and ethically. That is why this subchapter offers a range of practical strategies for educators to support students in navigating and adapting to the increasingly AI-driven learning environment. In the same vein, the proposed approach would like to contribute to raising the self-confidence of educators who might, due to several reasons, feel distressed connected with a new era when AI threatens to replace some of their unique capacities and leave behind those that do not catch the unprecedented pace of AI development (as identified by Slimi et al., 2023).

The Role of the Teacher as a Facilitator

In an AI-enhanced educational setting, teachers should assume the role of facilitators working alongside their students toward a shared goal of meaningful learning. Rather than simply assigning tasks that AI could quickly complete, educators should prioritize cultivating students' ability to critically assess AI-generated responses in the first step. By guiding students through this evaluative process, teachers not only deepen their understanding of the subject matter but also nurture essential critical thinking skills.

The next phase calls for a collective shift in perspective—acknowledging that the emergence of AI necessitates tackling a broader and more complex range of challenges than ever before. This expanded scope offers an opportunity to prepare students to navigate and utilize AI tools effectively while simultaneously recognizing their limitations. Teachers play a crucial role in helping students identify areas for skill improvement, fostering a balance between human ingenuity and AI's capabilities. This approach enhances academic growth and equips learners with the adaptability and analytical mindset required for a future shaped by evolving technologies.

Certainly, it is crucial for everyone to grasp the inherent limitations of the functioning of large language models (LLMs) (Ferrara, 2023). Without such understanding, their uncritical use could result in significant and far-reaching damage. The legal system is adapting to this new technological landscape (Świerczyński & Więckowski, 2023), yet litigation concerning accountability for damages and the mechanisms for compensation is likely to be protracted, complex, and prohibitively expensive. This underscores the necessity for educators at all levels of the educational system to instill in students a critical approach to using AI tools. However, this responsibility should not be seen as an endpoint but rather as a foundational step.

In this context, we propose an elevation of our educational goals—reframing the way we teach and learn to maximize the benefits of these tools while minimizing redundant effort. Such an evolution involves transforming expectations placed on both educators and students, fostering a mindset where AI tools are seamlessly integrated into the learning process. With LLMs readily accessible, they can deliver precise and relevant information tailored to virtually any need.

But does this newfound capability risk undermining essential intellectual practices, such as conducting literature reviews or rigorously validating facts against credible sources? Will the countless hours we've spent on traditional homework tasks now seem irrelevant or outdated? These questions compel us to reflect not only on the practical applications of AI but also on the broader implications for cognitive development and intellectual autonomy in an era where information is effortlessly at our fingertips.

The answer to all these questions is relatively straightforward – we will not ask these questions anymore. Instead, we will change the modus operandi, starting with training on how to broaden our horizons and rethink our approaches. First, we need to adjust to the new expectations that our peers and collaborators will place upon us. Any task we are required to accomplish may probably be solved more elegantly and efficiently, pushing us to embrace a mindset of continuous adaptability. LLMs might help us to discover new tools, whether a service provider, a technique, a method, or an application – tools that were once beyond our imagination or knowledge (Woerner et al., 2024). Second, we need to internalize the reality that we are now expected to be more empowered and resourceful so that we can tackle a range of genuinely novel and complex tasks with confidence. This shift challenges us to rethink not only our workflows but also the fundamental ways in which we learn, innovate, and contribute in a rapidly evolving landscape.

We propose that critical issues of social sciences from now on should be automatically considered from the point of view of theories of all social sciences branches – economics, political science, sociology, and communication science. Why? Just because we can. Even if we are specialists in a particular field, this does not give us the right to limit the explanation of the observed phenomena just by one theory. But it also means that, given the fact that we are not experts in all subjects, we have to cope with the changing positions of teachers who do not know everything. Rather, we propose that teachers and students should be in a team of equally weighted seekers of explanations of diverse phenomena.

Moreover, not only should we adopt broader perspectives more readily, but we must actively encourage students to embrace technical solutions boldly, exploring and experimenting with the tools at their disposal. It is often through meticulous scrutiny of data that we uncover answers to the questions we pose. Yet, for many students with limited backgrounds in data analysis—whether in sociology, economics, or other fields—it remains challenging to envision how effectively data from their surveys or experiments can be leveraged to yield statistically significant and meaningful results. This difficulty stems from a twofold problem: either they fail to recognize when and how theoretical principles they've learned should be applied, or they struggle to manage the practical aspects of analysis itself.

It is up to educators to show students that every single step of their analysis might be supported, explained, and interpreted with LLMs. The point is that without understanding what they are doing and why, they will not succeed at all. AI could dramatically develop the applicability of a basic understanding of statistics and data analysis so that the students who did not feel confident enough to run would dare to try. We are convinced that such an approach should be supported as much as possible because it will narrow the opportunities for all kinds of students, regardless of their initial skill and knowledge.

AI tools are not magical panaceas capable of solving every problem we encounter or saving us from all challenges with a single click. We believe that their true value lies in how we use them to enhance our thought processes and decision-making skills while maintaining our integrity and a clear conscience (Sok & Heng, 2023). The goal is not to outsource our intelligence but to refine it—to cultivate a way of thinking that allows us to harness these tools effectively, without feeling as though we're cheating or undermining our own efforts. At the heart of this lies a critical skill: the art of asking the right questions. This is where *prompting* becomes indispensable.

Prompting is more than just a technical task; it's a cognitive discipline that unlocks the potential of AI tools to serve as extensions of our reasoning, creativity, and problem-solving capabilities. By mastering this skill, we can guide AI systems to deliver insights, generate solutions, or illuminate paths forward that align with our goals and values. The aim is not merely to teach students how to interact with technology but to embed prompting into the very fabric of their learning processes. It should be a natural and integral part of their approach to tackling challenges—an enabler that empowers them to think critically and act decisively.

As educators, we should strive to shift the focus away from displaying our own knowledge of specific facts or solutions. Instead, we must inspire a mindset in students where they realize that they already possess the latent potential to solve problems. Our role is to help them activate this potential. When students learn to frame questions effectively and apply prompting as part of their problem-solving toolkit, an automatic and self-sustaining process begins to take shape.

This approach equips students not only to handle real-time, high-pressure situations but also to collaborate meaningfully with peers and engage constructively with the broader world. It emphasizes adaptability, resilience, and critical thinking, laying the foundation for lifelong learning. By embracing and promoting the art of prompting as a core skill, we prepare students to navigate complex challenges confidently and creatively, transforming AI tools from mere utilities into catalysts for human ingenuity and growth.

Here, we propose several practical tools for approaching the teaching/learning process.

Many institutions have their internal rules on how to use AI tools ethically (Luo, 2024). We believe that many ethical dilemmas may capture instructors and students. The only way out is not to demand an output that LLMs could easily accomplish as a graded task. Furthermore, if AI could do a particular task, remember that what counts is the result. Is it perfect and sufficiently practically applicable? Well, where is the problem? Still, the burden lies on students, who must apply their capacities when prompting and checking whether the solution makes sense. What is the cutting edge of how to resolve the dilemma? Let us explain it using the ad absurdum method. We certainly do not want people to consult LLMs in cases where their inner memories and knowledge should work automatically. Doctors must save lives quickly, lawyers must reply eloquently, and communication professionals must react wittily. Thus, the time perspective might be one of the factors when we should insist on presenting results without the help of AI.

If one wants to be sure that students are ready to use LLMs in an ethical way, prepare a model example and go through it together. Where questions arise and answering them becomes an unsurmountable issue, take your time and share the case with other colleagues and bodies responsible for ethical AI applications in your institution. The key is to insist on transparency and framing the whole project as an activity of continuous searching for an acceptable outcome that is welcome by all parties. Only in a safe environment, when students are sure that empowering their abilities and knowledge with AI will not be punished, will transparency and mutual trust be fostered, and will the scope and the level of accomplished tasks be pushed to a higher level. AI tools presented as a shady activity might have a dangerous side effect: Students might hold back, developing only a fragment of possible knowledge, expertise, and experience.

Map together how a task could be accomplished. This approach seems, at first glance, self-evident. Nevertheless, this is the teacher's key role in managing the whole process of being advised by LLMs. This is the moment when education and bare cheating clash. Without explaining the substance of a phenomenon we strive to master, there is no chance the LLM would be asked purposefully. Moreover, this is the phase when all participants of a course receive input from a teacher and when one can observe how the gap between the knowledge of those who are more familiar with the topic and those for which it is entirely new is narrowing.

It is crucial for those with a high initial knowledge gap to understand the extent to which LLMs could provide advice. Inducing students to start with a blank paper and build their projects from the beginning must be carefully overseen by teachers. Classroom management, thus, is starting to be more challenging than ever before. At the same time, teachers are expected to follow who and how they are thinking about the problem and topic and softly but firmly induce people to focus on acquiring the body of knowledge defined in advance. Thus, the design of the class has to be built on structured self-reporting and formative evaluation of whether students understand the problem or whether they still struggle even to understand the purpose of an activity (Baïdoo-anu & OWUSU ANSAH, 2023).

Map together whether it helped to remember and learn more or whether LLMs demotivated students. Collect feedback about the learning experience. It seems like an unsurmountable task; however, remember that the teachers may also be equipped with LLMs and other digital platform tools that help to evaluate and map the progress of each student individually. Here, the adherence to the rule that the final evaluation must be the teacher's responsibility is crucial. When we define our goal as "a reasonable expectation that in the head of each student, there is a critical package that once opened, the automatic process starts and the problem-solving in real-time, stressful conditions and cooperation with the rest of the world will run" – as mentioned before in this chapter – then each lesson should have its own description of objectives. Before any formal exams, let students self-report in a safe and non-judgmental environment to what extent they achieved this specific goal. Without AI tools, the evaluation would be highly burdensome. However, once we can cope with mastering those tools, again using LLM's advice to design them, we have no excuse but to implement the individual approach as a new normal.

Consider the privacy of personal data, research data, original ideas, etc., that teachers and students may not entrust any LLMs tool (Firat, 2023). Remember that a non-disclosure agreement is valid even when the data is used for prompting. The cost of compensating for damages for leaking key information about partners might be much higher than saving time, money, and effort for smoothing our process of creating the output. The feasible way to cope with that risk might be to use the LLM as a consultant who will work in the regime of a generalized example. Thus, the emphasis is not on the output but on the method to reach it. Then, the private data that must not be shared remains in the domain of your own devices or digital spaces with limited and controlled access.

Embracing Multiple Approaches to Learning

AI integration offers diverse ways to achieve learning outcomes, encouraging a mindset where there are no absolute right or wrong answers. Instructors should foster an environment where students can explore various methods to solve problems and learn from their interactions with digital technologies. This flexibility not only accommodates different learning styles but also encourages creativity and innovation.

Experimentation as a Learning Tool – a Case Study

Digital technologies make it easier than ever to conduct experiments in the classroom, allowing both students and educators to gain insights into learning behaviors. This subchapter illustrates how theoretical concepts can be tested in a practical setting, enhancing students' understanding through hands-on involvement in designing and running the experiment.

Higher education's[1] curriculum for marketing communication studies necessarily includes creative thinking courses. This subchapter presents the case study of the project of running an experiment within such a course. The aim of the project was twofold. First, change the learning process. The knowledge about creative thinking from the considerable body of literature[2] was not predominantly presented by the teacher. Instead, students themselves decided which ideas they deemed crucial to be presented and worthy of remembering. And they presented them on their own by the means they perceived to be creative. Second, the whole learning process was wrapped up in the framework of an experiment. This experiment was codesigned by students who decided which parameters it should have to deliver a valid and convincing outcome. Thus, thanks to the experiment, students got learning-by-doing experience on how they can draw conclusions based on inferential statistics and what is the role of randomization in it.

The intrinsic part of the creative thinking course is the phenomenon of individual creativity. Therefore, the lectures included the presentation of how state-of-the-art literature contributes to the never-ending and lively debate on whether financial incentives spur creativity. This particular puzzle was the central topic of the project. Hence, students were encouraged to figure out how they would design an experiment to statistically assess whether the effect of financial incentives exists or not. The experiment took the form of a tournament. During this tournament, we aimed to reach two goals: 1) to learn the basic ideas from the field of creative thinking, using the students´ evaluation of their relevance; 2) to learn how to design an experiment to assess the effect of financial incentives on creativity.

This competition ran during the whole semester. The task for each individual student was to perform a 2-minute piece of work in any form, digitally, personally, visually, etc. The assignment for each student was different – they presented a different paper, part, or a chapter of the literature from the course´s syllabus. Which ideas they decided to present had been up to them. The point of the experiment was that only half of them were eligible to participate in the competition. Which half, it was a secret. The students competed about whose contribution would be perceived by their peers as the most creative.

First, let us summarize the literature's key findings that are the most relevant for discussing which factors shape individual creativity[3]. As a next step, we propose a methodologic framework for running an experiment in a feasible and educative way, explaining which capacities and key competencies are developed. The results of the experiment, accompanied by an explanation of how the results formed students' attitudes toward the phenomenon of individual creativity and how students learned about statistical inference, follows.

To our knowledge, this contribution is unique in being the first to demonstrate the combination of two principles that go against each other, at least at first sight[4]. At the same time, it presents an andragogic approach leading to the engagement in scientific thinking about inference on the one hand; on the other hand, it practically implements the methods and elements that spur creativity according to the literature studied and presented by students. It comprises elements such as a democratic atmosphere, a secure environment, and a high degree of autonomy as the key factors promoting creativity (Franková, 2011; Whitaker, 2016). Literature used by students for presentations comprised some of the most important scientific papers and monographs, as well as popular books about creativity. The list is Appendix A.

Literature on incentives for creation

A huge repository of papers discusses different factors that contribute to creativity. The whole body of knowledge has already been presented by, e.g., Charness and Grieco (2019) or Attanasi (2021). To run the experiment, students received basic information that existing approaches generated mixed results due to different conditions and employed methods (Attanasi, 2021; Byron, K., & Khazanchi, S., 2012). Nevertheless, several principles seem consistent across time and with the authors, as discussed by Charness and Grieco (2019). These authors offer a brief explanation of the evolution of the notion of creativity (defined as the production of novel and useful ideas), pointing to crucial psychology literature (e.g., Guilford, Torrance, etc.). They also discuss the issue of internal motivation, which has been proven to be a decisive driving force of creativity, while the role of external motivation is perceived as minor. According to Charness and Grieco, financial motivation is important only for closed tasks requiring a convergent thinking style, confirmed by Kun (2020). Financial incentives for open creativity may even hinder inner motivation. Experiments by Charness and Grieco (2019) show that open creativity (a task with no restrictions to complete) is not enhanced by external financial motivation, namely by participating in the tournament. They prove that the evaluation given by peers is a substantial motivating factor for both (closed and open) types of creativity.

The lecturer framed the whole discussion about the literature as the process of clarification of what the literature expects about the future outcome of the experiment. What was specific to our experiment was the task. It required a high degree of open creativity. In contrast to it, Xu and Hamari (2022) employed Alternative Uses Task subject to different incentivizing schemes. One of their incentive schemes was gamification. Gamification also provides a powerful way to motivate people. Therefore, we discussed whether the financial prize in the tournament or the participation in our experiment mimicking the game regime would be the driving force behind our effort to come up with the most creative piece.

There is a variety of research on the difference between the creativity of genders, as summarized by Taylor et al. (2023), who explained that their meta-analysis does not prove the existence of greater differences in the creativity of males and females. Thus, students did not expect the results for the two groups to differ.

Design – Competence 1: Recognition of the importance of random selection of the treatment group

Step one introduces how psychologists, economists, and other relevant social scientists studied individual creativity. Students were encouraged to consider whether they personally react to financial motivation when engaging in open creativity tasks. In the case of the experiment presented here, only a basic framework extracted from the literature was provided for the sake of simplicity.

Step two can be described as a lecturer's task to facilitate the discussion of designing the experiment to receive the most relevant and non-biased answer to the question. An important aspect was to engage students in formulating the question as such. We frame the whole problem as something the researchers have not resolved so far and is thus worthy of examination. The lecturer provided a framework for the experimental design with posttest-only analysis of a randomized experiment. The lecturer explained that students had been randomly assigned to two groups. Everybody participated in the tournament, but only the second (treatment group) could have gotten a financial prize.

The students were confronted with the question of why people who participated in the competition should be chosen randomly. The basic idea that the treatment variable must not be correlated with the expected creativity and motivation of students was presented intuitively. The teacher explained that, e.g., self-selection of students for being members of the competing group would bias the results. Thus, the observed difference between the perceived level of creativity of the two groups would be overestimated. In the case of self-selection, the competing group yielding a higher perceived level of creativity would not signal the actual effect of financial incentives. Instead, it would reveal that a group of students with higher inner motivation would prepare and present pieces of work that are perceived as more creative.

The result of this stage of the learning process was that students understood that dividing them randomly causes that, on average, the characteristics of the two halves would be comparable to each other. Thus, the only reason why the observed difference in the perceived level of creativity between the two groups is different is just the treatment. In the design with random selection, just participation in the competing group should reveal whether it is or it is not a sufficient incentive to raise the perceived creativity.

Consequently, the lecturer explained to students what the task was. Each student (n = 63) presented a specific part (chapter, scientific paper) of the compulsory or recommended literature from the course syllabus. This presentation had to be a creative work in any form presented by the students personally or by technical means. The duration had to be less than two minutes.

The students proposed and then voted for pay-off schemes that could most efficiently motivate the treatment group to win the creativity contest. Thus, they voted and chose the option where the first won 1500 CZK (approx. 60 EUR[5]), the second 1000 CZK (approx. 40 EUR), and the third 500 CZK (approx. 20 EUR). Students believed that this was the combination that would lead to the most significant difference between the level of creativity of the control and treatment groups. Of course, the fact of being in the treatment group was a secret and had to be kept confidential for the semester when the experiment was running.

Each student had his/her own online template where he/she filled out the evaluation of the peers' creativity level just after the presentation of an individual had finished. Their rating was not available to peers to ensure the maximum level of independence and to minimize the attempt to strategize. An important stage in the whole educational process was a moment of collective reflection about what students themselves perceived to be decisive components of creativity and evaluation of whether it fits in with the definition established in the literature. Students themselves proposed and agreed by voting on the three criteria of the level of creativity: Ability to attract attention, originality, and comprehensibility. We explicitly stated that we would not evaluate whether the literature was interpreted correctly, assuming their general ability to transfer the content without substantial flaws and discrepancies.

In the end, each student received one final grade expressing the level of creativity of their performance, which was calculated as a simple average of the evaluation given by peers. The scale was from 0 to 10 points, allowing half-points, e.g. 8.5 points. 10 meant the highest level of evaluation.

Results – Competence 2: using OLS for measuring the difference in means and evaluating its statistical significance

Relying on the random assignment that allowed us to observe the causality, we ran a simple OLS. The dependent variable was the level of creativity students exhibited during presentations or performances, as perceived by their peers (0 – 10 points)[6]. The criteria for evaluation were ability to attract attention, originality, and comprehensibility. The score of each student was calculated as a simple average of the evaluations of the peers. The treatment variable was the dummy, where 0 was the value for a noncompeting student and 1 for a competing student. The OLS yielded results showing that there was no statistical difference if we compared the two averages of perceived creativity between the control and treatment groups. The proportion of male and female participants was the same in both treatment and control groups. Those that competed had, on average, higher evaluation of creativity, but only by 0.16 points, with st. error of 0.33 and $p = 0.6362$. That means that the coefficient of 0.16 is not statistically significant. For the sake of comprehensibility for the students of the bachelor level of studies, the statistical analysis did not go further; moreover, n = 63 set certain limitations as well.

Figure 1. Presenting the results of the experiment by depicting linear regression. The dots are for female participants, whereas the crosses are for male participants.

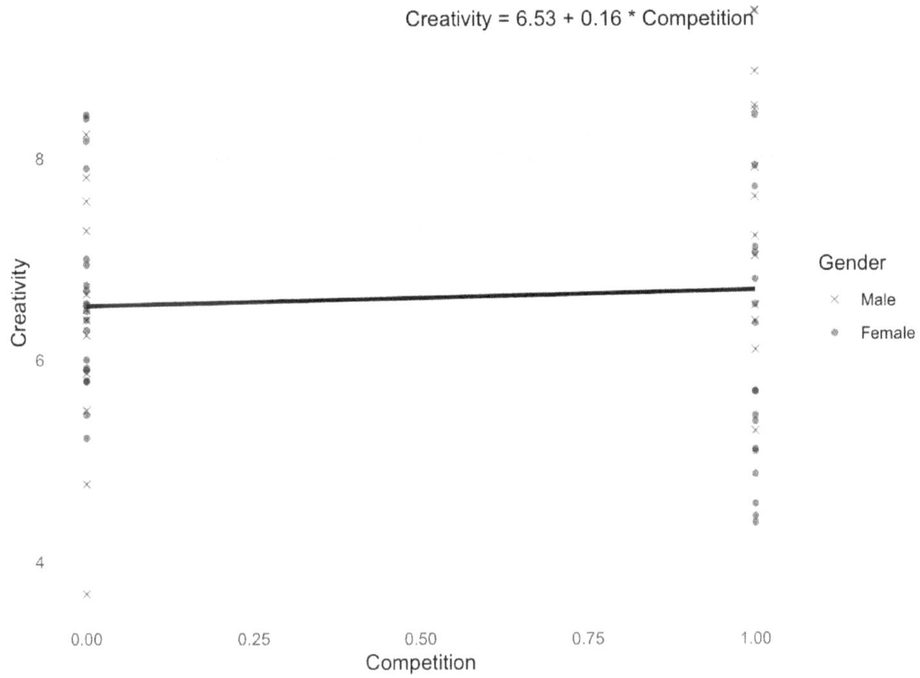

The presentation of the results in Figure 2 comprised the explanation of how calculations of a t-test for assessing whether the difference between the two means is statistically significant and running simple linear regression (OLS) with the dum my explanatory (in Figure 1) variable yields the same results. Looking at the same problem via the two techniques that seemed at first glance as different revealed to students the design of linear regression and deepened understanding of its functioning.

The cornerstone of the learning process stressed that the means per se are not subject to comparison. The distribution of the outcome variables of the two groups matters as well. To illustrate this principle, the lecturer presented a histogram of the frequency of the level of creativity showing how it is distributed in the class, conditionally to the control and treatment group. The graph shows the means as well, but students observed that the distribution of the creativity of the control group overlapped the distribution of the creativity of the treatment group. Thus, this graphical representation of results helped to understand that both groups had relatively high standard deviations compared to the absolute difference between the two means.

The results of the t-test are naturally almost the same as the p-value for the estimated parameter from OLS where the regressor is the dummy variable (t = -0.47304, df = 54.73, p-value = 0.6381, H0: true difference in means is equal to 0. Sample estimates: mean of non-competing = 6.534880; mean of competing = 6.690231). Again, students obtained another type of confirmation that the difference of approx. 0.16 points (as in OLS) is not statistically significant, as we cannot reject the null hypothesis about equality of means.

Figure 2. The frequency of ratings. The light grey is for competing students, and the dark grey is for non-competing students. The illustration of the distribution (apparently with very high standard deviations) and the two depicted averages help us understand why the difference between the two means is not statistically significant. The bars are transparent; thus overlapping results in darker areas.

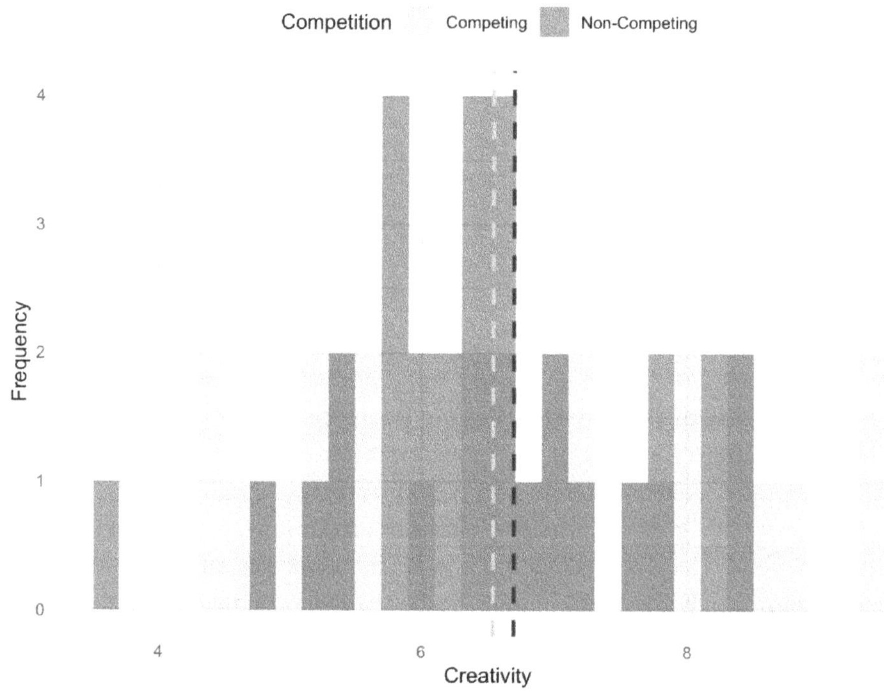

Discussion and Limitations – Competence 3: Identifying the caveats of the experimental design

The discussion about results between the lecturer and students highlighted that even though there are no statistically significant differences between the two groups, this is a result per se. Students aligned it with the existing debate stressing the importance of inner motivation. On the one hand, the tournament might be a good motivator, accompanied by the need for recognition (Kun, 2020). On the other hand, many studies have revealed that external motivation, especially monetary motivation, is not proven to be a decisive power that spurs open creativity, and our experiment is in line with this idea.

Nevertheless, students themselves observed interesting patterns in the data. They expressed an opinion that gender[7] might have played an important role as a predictor of creativity, but only for the group of treated, competing male students. Due to a small sample, we cannot assess whether their intuition was right, as the t-test is not reliable in such cases.

Students were aware that the random assignment of the treatment might not ensure the equivalence due to a small sample (n=63). They pointed to the fact that in such a small sample, the characteristics of several personalities might lead to the situation that random assignment of the treatment is not a sufficient tool to ensure that both groups would have, on average, the same characteristics.

The other concerns about the experiment's internal validity came from the fact that the students presented their creative works or performances on four different dates. They were not evaluated under the exact same conditions, and naturally, order had to play an important role. The question of whether it substantially impacted the result and causal inference was another occasion for discussing the role of random assignment, as the time slots for different students were chosen randomly. Thus, we summarized that the conditions were not even, but the unevenness was randomly distributed, and there was no reason why one group suffered systematically worse conditions than the other. Similarly, we discussed that the distribution of papers and chapters could have been uneven. Some texts were more difficult to comprehend and not so inspiring. Again, we concluded that there was no reason why the treatment group should have had systematically different conditions than the control group.

A limitation of this case study might be identified as a lack of evaluation of the learning process and its outcomes from the perspective of all participants, as only the most active ones expressed their opinions about the project. Moreover, we did not test the acquired knowledge and ability in a systematic way that would compare the evolution of the competencies of different cohorts of students over the years.

The conclusion From The Experiment – would it be feasible without AI and digital tools?

This subchapter shows how to employ digital technologies for running an experiment with a double purpose: to learn about creativity and experimental design at the same time. We believe this puzzle, still unresolved by economists and psychologists, can be a unique opportunity to engage students' interest. Thus, we introduced the experimental design and the causal inference to students with the help of a posttest-only analysis of a randomized experiment. The study was designed by the students themselves with the aim of enhancing the following competencies: recognition of the importance of the random selection of the treatment group, using OLS for measuring the difference in means and evaluating its statistical significance, and identifying the caveats of the experimental design. The whole experiment process and how we obtained the result was a practical exercise for students on concluding causality thanks to a randomized experiment. Thus, students learned how to use post-test only analysis and when the results of the OLS model imply a causal effect.

We have no statistically significant treatment effect for the treatment being the participation in the competition for monetary prizes. This result is in line with the current stream of literature stressing the importance of intrinsic motivation as a critical determinant of open creativity. However, contributing to answering this question was not the goal per se; rather, the process was important. An essential aspect of this teaching style is the element of democracy and the considerable autonomy of students. During the semester, students presented ideas from the literature about how individuals, teams, and organizations should contribute to a more creative environment. The intrinsic part of the course was a practical demonstration of introducing some of these important principles recommended by literature. Finally, it was not the teacher but the students who creatively contributed to understanding the basic concepts of creative thinking, design thinking, and pro-creative management strategies.

AI and digital tools were crucial to the feasibility of the experiment. First, administering the whole process would not be possible without sharing the sheets for evaluations of peers online. Then, of course, the data had to be gathered and statistically processed via specialized software, be it Gretl or R studio, for better visualization. And what about AI assistance? LLM might be helpful in each stage of the project – gathering references to the most important scientific resources, considering the most suitable experimental design, and how to measure and detect a difference between the two groups. Even each step of technically mastering the statistical software could be AI-assisted. All the students needed was one guide who gave them sufficient incentives. It is not surprising that many creative outputs that presented ideas about creativity were in the digital format, enhanced often by AI techniques (voice and video generators), be it short, animated videos, games, quizzes, live-action short videos, remakes of famous songs, parodies of notorious ads, etc.

SUBCHAPTER 3: EVALUATING LEARNING OUTCOMES IN THE AI ERA

Evaluating student performance in an AI-driven educational landscape requires a shift in perspective (Corsten & Skousen, 2023). This subchapter explores how to effectively assess learning outcomes when AI tools are part of the learning process. So far, we have tackled several topics and principles we may apply during the phase of teaching and learning. But what about objectivity in evaluating whether we, together with students in a managed, transparent, and safe environment, reached a common goal of "a reasonable expectation that in the head of each student, there is a critical package that, once opened, the automatic process starts and the problem-solving in real-time, stressful conditions and cooperation with the rest of the world will run"? At first glance, one may argue that training using AI tools is perfectly OK, but students' examinations should be strictly closed-book exams with no access to AI tools like LLMs. However, we would like to provide preliminary evidence that even in open books and AI-assisted exams, students' outputs clearly reveal who comprehended the substance and who did not.

What Should Be Learned and Evaluated?

The focus should not only be on students' final results but also on their engagement, comprehension of fundamental principles, and the ability to apply knowledge in practical settings. Evaluation should account for the process, including students' abilities to critically analyze AI-generated content and adapt their understanding accordingly. However, as we pointed out, this can be challenging, as educators' capacity for individualized assessment is limited. The section discusses the development of evaluation procedures that balance individualized approaches with standardized measures, ensuring transparency and consistency in the assessment process.

In this place, we would like to offer an uncommon approach to the question of evaluation. It comprises attitudes based on transparency, cooperation, and, of course, digital tools enhanced by LLMs. Let us start by explaining how we can use LLMs. The most straightforward answer is – to use it as a student. Then, after receiving the most commonly generated text for commonly phrased questions, you will receive a benchmark to which one can compare an answer based on AI tools and an answer including inputs originating in the mind of a student who understands well the substance of the problem. We would like to stress that even a more elaborated answer that was generated by AI is counting as better. And why? It must have been prompted by a student who masters the topic and thus knows how to ask an LLM to obtain an answer that is a contribution.

The reason why we must include transparency and cooperation in this process is that we should evaluate not just the bare output. We should evaluate the whole process. With large courses, when teaching typically hundreds of students, again, we call for action the tools of digital tools enhanced by LLMs as the amount of data to process might be overwhelming.

The Dual Role of AI: Good Servant but Poor Master

This section examines whether AI tools enhance students' ability to grasp and apply core concepts, or if they simply provide an easy shortcut that discourages genuine learning effort. It explores the delicate balance between using AI as an enabler of learning and avoiding an over-dependence on technology, which could impede the development of independent problem-solving skills.

How do we resolve this dilemma? We propose a solution that takes a lot of energy from students and teachers, but we are convinced that, in the long term, it will bring its fruit. It is time to admit that students are not only the subject of education but should be responsible for defining what to do and how to do it. The expertise of teachers should be like that of a navigator, as one of the most experienced in the team, ensuring that the whole boat will not miss the continent while it discovers the nearby island. Communication that functions well is crucial, like in many other cases of human actions. Thus, any tool that facilitates the exchange of information between students and teachers and helps gather the most important messages should be welcomed and included in the daily routines of educational institutions.

If we ask bachelor students (n = 29) how they perceive current threats, the most common answer is that they deem it dangerous in relation to authenticity – they worry that people will not recognize reality and fiction and that the phenomenon of deepfakes will evolve dramatically (Figure 3). They have no concerns that AI may endanger the quality of education. Specifically, there was a fear of social engineering, using AI technologies to limit purchasing certain types of allegedly harmful or nonecological food. These concerns arise from the fact that the students were aware of the current extensive collection of personal data used for personalization of the displayed content, which are now standardly powered by AI-assisted tools. Some students expressed fear that people might use LLMs in an inappropriate way, not exactly understanding the principles behind LLMs that shape how they generate text, and the character of existing biases and limitations - students were afraid that people would use the output of LLMs as it was a human entity with moral scruples.

Figure 3. The most common AI-related concerns

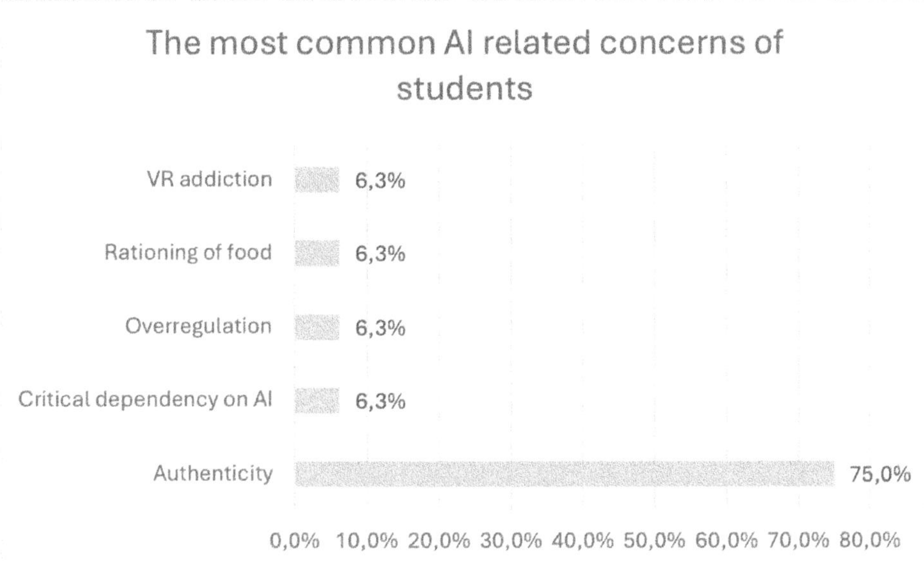

Figure 4. The most common improvements for studies

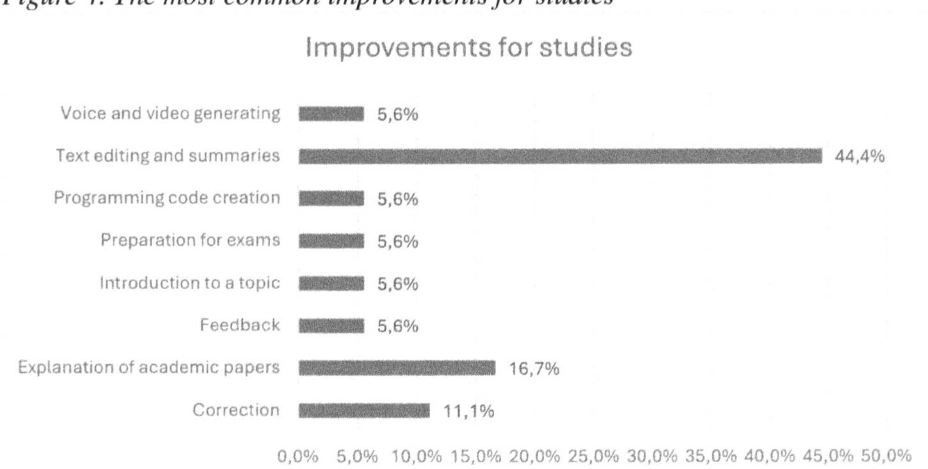

Among the most elegant and helpful tools (Figure 4) several students are used to employ, we can name Questions and Answers GPT - Exam Prep Assistant or Notebook LM. This tool, Notebook LM, enables students to extract the most important, structured, and well-comprehensible ideas from many resources, like PDF files with academic papers, their own text notes, videos on YouTube, presentations, etc. All results are cited. They also use the service Elicit to mine knowledge from different research papers. Moreover, they search for the most relevant papers for the topic of their interest. Some students use ChatGPT to check the mistakes in the programming code. Another student` hack is transmitting their study notes to a podcast.

SUBCHAPTER 4: CASE STUDY – AI-ENHANCED OPEN BOOK TEST IN STATISTICS

This subchapter presents a case study focused on an AI-enhanced open-book test in a statistics-related course (data available on request in an anonymized form). Students with limited prior knowledge of statistical inference were tasked with evaluating the effect of an intervention on an outcome variable. The assignment was designed to introduce counterfactual thinking in the analysis of marketing data, emphasizing the importance of understanding the assumptions required for robust and unbiased statistical inference.

The case study investigates whether the use of AI-assisted tools helped students understand the underlying statistical concepts or whether it merely provided a crutch that limited their mental effort. What did the results show? The data suggests that the educational process and face-to-face interaction are irreplaceable. If we can generalize the case study of one course with approximately 50 students – even if there was teaching support during the semester, common calculating of an analogical case during the lesson, all teaching materials, books, and AI assistance available during the exam – the distribution of the results in Figure 5 shows that AI assistance did not provide any substantial advantage. Students who could not comprehend the ideas were not saved by simple LLM usage. The time window to complete the task was 48 hours. Thus, we can exclude the factor of time pressure as being a determinant of the results. 15% of the students reached much worse grades for the statistics task than expected according to the outcomes from other parts of the test. If the AI tools were an omnipotent tool for universal cheating, all students would reach 100% points for each of the tasks, but it apparently did not happen.

Figure 5. The histogram of the distribution of the results of statistic tasks. The numbers around 1 mean that for the given student, her grading of the statistical task contributed relatively equally to the final grade as the rest of the tasks in the test. The numbers below 1 represent situations when the statistic task was graded much lower than the rest of the test. 8 students out of 53 were far below the expected outcome given their results in other parts of the test.

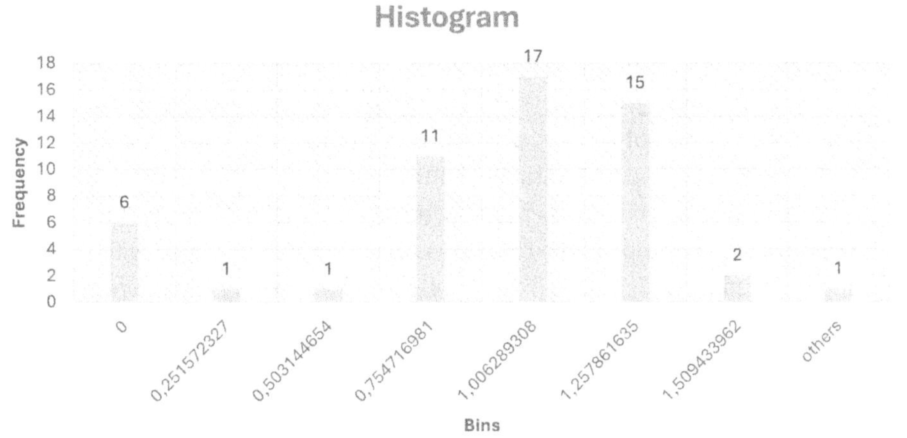

The findings reveal both the potential advantages and limitations of using AI during the exams. The main insights into how educators can design AI-inclusive assignments that encourage deep learning and critical thinking are twofold: AI tools like LLMs are an element that provides more support to everybody. However, it is not an omnipotent tool, and when we ask good questions, it is impossible to use it for cheating.

CONCLUSION

The actual integration of artificial intelligence (AI) into education holds significant promise, offering new ways to personalize learning, foster inclusivity, and encourage interdisciplinary collaboration. Rather than replacing human creativity and expertise, AI is a tool to enhance them, creating opportunities for environments that prioritize collaboration, critical thinking, and adaptability. To achieve this, both technical skills and a strong ethical foundation are essential, ensuring that AI is applied with fairness, transparency, and clear purpose.

A major challenge for educational systems, particularly universities, lies in navigating AI's dual impact: its potential to equalize access to learning while simultaneously demanding new levels of technological proficiency and adaptability. In this context, educators take on the role of facilitators and co-learners, guiding students to experiment, ask critical questions, and develop problem-solving abilities. This approach shifts education from rote memorization to a dynamic, participatory model that actively engages learners.

An interdisciplinary perspective further enriches the integration of AI, bridging disciplines such as sociology, economics, and media studies to address complex, real-world problems. As demonstrated in our experiment, the integration of insights from diverse disciplines is not only possible but essential, thanks to the capabilities of AI—provided it is accompanied by appropriate guidance and critical understanding. This approach underscores the need for collaboration across fields to fully harness AI's potential while addressing ethical and logistical issues, including privacy concerns and the risk of over-reliance on AI. A balanced approach is key to ensuring that AI serves as an aid rather than a barrier to learning, fostering deeper insights and meaningful connections across disciplines.

The chapter offers practical insights and strategies to help both students and educators effectively navigate the opportunities and challenges posed by AI. By emphasizing thoughtful implementation, it ensures that technology supports rather than disrupts the learning process. However, we must insist on being very careful about being rigid in the era of AI – it might happen in the near future that our recommendations will not be valid anymore. We assume that we will need to adjust our strategies, following the current trends, new products and their opportunities and threats. It seems that a new product that competes for our attention, data, and, most importantly, financial and time resources appears almost every week.

It is up to instructors to discover and help understand how new tools could be used and help students to grasp the maximum, while not being overwhelmed. In summary, one only long-lasting advice for the university communities is to remain curious but still skeptical. Remember, that the AI is just a tool, and what matters is the interaction with students and the learning outcome as such. Even though the providers of AI tools might compete for our attention, the world of higher education needs as much as cooperation as possible, to tackle all the AI challenges.

REFERENCES

Acemoglu, D., Laibson, D. I., & List, J. A. (2014). Equalizing superstars: The internet and the democratization of education. *The American Economic Review*, *104*(5), 523–527. DOI: 10.1257/aer.104.5.523

Ahmed, N., & Wahed, M. (2020). The De-democratization of AI: Deep Learning and the Compute Divide in Artificial Intelligence Research. ArXiv (Cornell University). https://doi.org//arxiv.2010.15581DOI: 10.48550

Attanasi, G., Chessa, M., Gil-Gallen, S., & Llerena, P. (2021). A survey on experimental elicitation of creativity in economics. *Revue d'Economie Industrielle*, *174*, 273–324. DOI: 10.4000/rei.10448

Bai, X. (2024). THE ROLE AND CHALLENGES OF ARTIFICIAL INTELLIGENCE IN INFORMATION TECHNOLOGY EDUCATION. *Pacific International Journal*, *7*(1), 86–92. DOI: 10.55014/pij.v7i1.524

Baídoo-anu, D., & OWUSU ANSAH, L. (2023). Education in the Era of Generative Artificial Intelligence (AI): Understanding the Potential Benefits of ChatGPT in Promoting Teaching and Learning. Journal of AI, 7(1), 52-62. https://doi.org/DOI: 10.61969/jai.1337500

Barnes, E., & Hutson, J. (2024). Navigating the ethical terrain of AI in higher education: Strategies for mitigating bias and promoting fairness. *Forum for Education Studies*, *2*(2), 1229. DOI: 10.59400/fes.v2i2.1229

Byron, K., & Khazanchi, S. (2012). Rewards and creative performance: A meta-analytic test of theoretically derived hypotheses. *Psychological Bulletin*, *138*(4), 809–830. DOI: 10.1037/a0027652

Cazzaniga, M. (2024). *Gen-AI: Artificial Intelligence and the Future of Work*. International Monetary Fund., DOI: 10.5089/9798400262548.006

Cengage. (2024). Exploring AI in higher education. Cengage. https://cengage.widen.net/s/wmnqhdkqwx/genai-report-2024?j=2122864&sfmc_sub=926794796&l=6504_HTML&u=44990356&mid=515011284&jb=225&utm_source=marketing&utm_medium=email&mid=515011284&utm_campaign=Gen-AI-report&utm_content=Gen-AI-report&segment=Faculty&region=HED_EMEA

Chadha, A. (2024). Transforming Higher Education for the Digital Age: Examining Emerging Technologies and Pedagogical Innovations. *Journal of Interdisciplinary Studies in Education*, *13*(1), 53–70. DOI: 10.32674/em2qsn46

Charness, G., & Grieco, D. (2019). Creativity and Incentives. *Journal of the European Economic Association*, *17*(2), 454–496. DOI: 10.1093/jeea/jvx055

Choi, J. H., & Schwarcz, D. B. (2023). AI Assistance in Legal Analysis: An Empirical Study. SSRN Electronic Journal. https://doi.org/DOI: 10.2139/ssrn.4539836

Corsten, D., & Skousen, B. (2023). 'Get AI Answer?' – Exploring the Effects of Embedding ChatGPT in Exams to Improve Student Learning Outcomes. SSRN Electronic Journal. https://doi.org/DOI: 10.2139/ssrn.4409035

CZSO. (2023). Evropský srovnávací program. Český statistický úřad. Retrieved January 11, 2024, from https://www.czso.cz/csu/czso/evropsky_srovnavaci_program

Dakakni, D., & Safa, N. (2023). Artificial intelligence in the L2 classroom: Implications and challenges on ethics and equity in higher education: A 21st century Pandora's box. Computers and education. *Artificial Intelligence*, *5*, 100179. DOI: 10.1016/j.caeai.2023.100179

Nostrum, E. (2024, July 20). AI tools democratizing education for less privileged students. https://erasmusnostrum.org/ai-tools-democratize-education/

Eurostat. (n.d.). Individuals' level of digital skills. European Commission. Retrieved December 19, 2024, from https://ec.europa.eu/eurostat/databrowser/view/ISOC_SK_DSKL_I21/default/table

Ferrara, E. (2023). Should ChatGPT be biased? Challenges and risks of bias in large language models. *First Monday*, *28*(11), 1. DOI: 10.5210/fm.v28i11.13346

Firat, M. (2023). What ChatGPT means for universities: Perceptions of scholars and students. *Journal of Applied Learning & Teaching*, *6*(1), 57–63. DOI: 10.37074/jalt.2023.6.1.22

Franková, E. (2011). *Kreativita a inovace v organizaci* (1st ed.). Grada.

Xu, H., & Hamari, J. (2022). How to improve creativity: A study of gamification, money, and punishment. *Behaviour & Information Technology*. Advance online publication. DOI: 10.1080/0144929X.2022.2133634

Kamalov, F., Santandreu Calonge, D., & Gurrib, I. (2023). New Era of Artificial Intelligence in Education: Towards a Sustainable Multifaceted Revolution. *Sustainability*, *15*(16), 12451. DOI: 10.3390/su151612451

Kun, H. (2020). Performance incentives, divergent thinking training, and creative problem solving. *Journal of Management Accounting Research*, *32*(1), 159–176. DOI: 10.2308/jmar-52479

Legowo, B., Nurhasanah, F., Saddhono, K., Budiastuti, V. I., Sutomo, A. D., & Murwaningsih, T. (2024). *Enhancing Educational Outcomes Through Exploring the Optimized Options Artificial Intelligence and Deep Learning*. IEEE., DOI: 10.1109/ICACITE60783.2024.10616772

Li, Y., & Zhao, Z. (2024). The Role of Education in the Era of AI: Challenges Along with Opportunities. Journal of Humanities. *Arts and Social Science*, *8*(4), 1034–1039. DOI: 10.26855/jhass.2024.04.039

Luo, J. (2024). A critical review of GenAI policies in higher education assessment: A call to reconsider the "originality" of students' work. *Assessment & Evaluation in Higher Education*, *49*(5), 651–664. DOI: 10.1080/02602938.2024.2309963

Rane, N. (2024). Enhancing the quality of teaching and learning through ChatGPT and similar large language models: Challenges, future prospects, and ethical considerations in education. *TESOL and Technology Studies*, *5*(1), 1–6. DOI: 10.48185/tts.v5i1.1000

Slimi, Z., & Carballido, B. V. (2023). Navigating the Ethical Challenges of Artificial Intelligence in Higher Education: An Analysis of Seven Global AI Ethics Policies. TEM Journal, 12(2), 590-602. https://doi.org/DOI: 10.18421/TEM122-02

Sok, S., & Heng, K. (2023). ChatGPT for education and research: A review of benefits and risks. *Cambodian Journal of Educational Research*, *3*(1), 110–121. DOI: 10.62037/cjer.2023.03.01.06

Świerczyński, M., & Więckowski, Z. (2023). Liability for damages caused by artificial intelligence systems – main challenges to be addressed by the European Union conflict-of-laws regulations. *Prawo w Działaniu*, *54*, 200–216. DOI: 10.32041/pwd.5407

Taylor, C. L., Said-metwaly, S., Camarda, A., & Barbot, B. (2023). Gender differences and variability in creative ability: A systematic review and meta-analysis of the greater male variability hypothesis in creativity. *Journal of Personality and Social Psychology*, •••, 1–19. DOI: 10.1037/pspp0000484

University of Sydney. (n.d.). Artificial intelligence in education: Democratising policy. https://www.sydney.edu.au/arts/our-research/research-projects/artificial-intelligence-in-education-democratising-policy.html

Yang, X., Zhang, M., Zhao, Y., Wang, Q., & Hong, J.-C. (2022). Relationship between creative thinking and experimental design thinking in science education: Independent or related: Independent or related. *Thinking Skills and Creativity*, *46*, 101183. https://doi.org/https://doi.org/10.1016/j.tsc.2022.101183

Walczak, K., & Cellary, W. (2023). Challenges for higher education in the era of widespread access to generative AI. Economics and Business Review/The Poznań University of Economics Review, 9(2), 71-100. https://doi.org/DOI: 10.18559/ebr.2023.2.743

Whitaker, A. (2016). *Art Thinking: How to Carve Out Creative Space in a World of Schedules, Budgets, and Bosses* (1st ed.). HarperBus.

Whittaker, T., & Jenkins, R. (2024, September 12). AI literacy on the agenda: EU, UK and US. Society for Computers and Law. https://www.scl.org/ai-literacy-on-the-agenda-eu-uk-and-us/

Woerner, J. H. R., Turtova, A. P., & Lang, A. S. I. D. (2024). *Transformative Potentials and Ethical Considerations of AI Tools in Higher Education: Case Studies and Reflections*. IEEE., DOI: 10.1109/SoutheastCon52093.2024.10500042

ADDITIONAL READING

Charness, G., & Grieco, D. (2019). Creativity and Incentives. *Journal of the European Economic Association, 17*(2), 454–496. DOI: 10.1093/jeea/jvx055

De Bono, E., & Jansa, P. (2020). Šest klobouků, aneb, Jak myslet. Dobrovský s.r.o.

Darley, W. K., & Lim, J. -su. (2023). Advertising creativity and its effects: A meta-analysis of the moderating role of modality. *Marketing Letters*, *34*(1), 99–111. DOI: 10.1007/s11002-022-09627-6

Fichnová, K. (2013). *Psychology of creativity for marketing communication: selected aspects*. Association Amitié Franco-Sovaque.

Field, S., & Houdek, L. (2007). *Jak napsat dobrý scénář: základy scenáristiky*. Rybka.

Franková, E. (2011). *Kreativita a inovace v organizaci* (1st ed.). Grada.

Harford, T. (2019). *A powerful way to unleash your natural creativity*. TED.

Horňák, P. (2014). Kreativita v reklamě. *Verbum*.

Kleon, A. (2019). *Keep Going*. Workman Publishing Company, Incorporated.

Kleon, A. (2014). *Show your work!: 10 ways to share your creativity and get discovered*. Workman Publishing Company.

Knapp, J., Zeratsky, J., Kowitz, B., & Mohelská, L. (2017). *Sprint: jak vyřešit velké problémy a otestovat nové myšlenky v pouhých pěti dnech.* Jan Melvil Publishing.

Lehnert, K., Till, B. D., & Ospina, J. M. (2014). Advertising Creativity: The Role of Divergence Versus Meaningfulness. *Journal of Advertising, 43*(3), 274–285. DOI: 10.1080/00913367.2013.851630

Norman, D. A. (2013). *The design of everyday things (Revised and expanded edition).* MIT Press.

Nyilasy, G., Canniford, R., & Kreshel, J., P. (2013). Ad agency professionals' mental models of advertising creativity. *European Journal of Marketing, 47*(10), 1691–1710. DOI: 10.1108/EJM-11-2011-0651

Vysekalová, J., & Mikeš, J. (2018). *Reklama: jak dělat reklamu (4., aktualizované a doplněné vydání).* Grada.

Whitaker, A. (2016). *Art Thinking: How to Carve Out Creative Space in a World of Schedules, Budgets, and Bosses* (1st ed.). HarperBus.

ENDNOTES

1 This subchapter concerns a course in the bachelor study program.

2 The list of the literature students interpreted is in Appendix A.

3 The notion of creativity discussed within this subchapter is limited to the definition formulated by the students' discussion during the classes. In line with existing concepts summarized by e.g. Charness and Grieco (2019), they specified the perceived level of creativity as a mix of three attributes: the ability to attract attention, originality, and comprehensibility.

4 Creative thinking and experimental design thinking were theoretically rooted in Yang et al. (2022).

5 The price level of actual individual consumption in the Czech Republic, where the experiment was conducted, is according to CZSO 28 p.p. lower than the average of the EU. (CZSO, 2023)

6 The interrater reliability was not possible to calculate because not all raters did rate each colleague (competing subject). Thus, we have checked for the distribution of the standard deviation of the ratings that each participant received from all the raters. Given that the median of the standard deviation of

the rating was 1.72 points (with minimum of 1.2 and maximum 2.4 points) the raters proved to be satisfactorily consistent.

7 In this study, we attribute gender simply according to the names of the students.

Chapter 3

Redefining Learning: The Shift From Answer-Seeking to Inquiry in the Age of AI

Menard Musendekwa
https://orcid.org/0000-0002-6644-8727
Reformed Church University, Zimbabwe

ABSTRACT

Critical inquiry has replaced knowledge acquisition as the main goal of education since artificial intelligence (AI) was introduced. The role of education has changed to stress the capacity to pose important, thought-provoking questions in light of AI's ability to provide immediate answers. This study promotes the importance of inquiry in curriculum by examining how AI changes teaching approaches. The ability to critically connect with knowledge through good questioning is crucial as information becomes more widely available. In order to promote higher-order thinking, problem-solving, and moral decision-making, this study suggests an educational framework that places a strong emphasis on questioning. By doing this, it equips kids to handle difficult situations with imagination, judgment, and intellectual curiosity.

INTRODUCTION

The digital transformation of education, which has been predominantly driven by the advancement of artificial intelligence (AI), has fundamentally altered the way that teaching and learning are conducted. Traditional educational approaches, which usually gave more weight to rote memorization and material delivery, are currently being redefined by the arrival of technology that enables individualized, adaptive, and inquiry-based learning. AI has made it possible for pupils to obtain vast amounts of information quickly, therefore educators' duties now mostly involve

DOI: 10.4018/979-8-3373-6018-8.ch003

Copyright © 2026, IGI Global Scientific Publishing. Copying or distributing in print or electronic forms without written permission of IGI Global Scientific Publishing is prohibited.

fostering intellectual curiosity and critical thinking rather than providing answers. This paradigm shift highlights how crucial it is for students to be able to ask relevant and thought-provoking questions in order to stimulate creativity and promote deeper learning. This chapter examines how artificial intelligence (AI) is transforming education while also encouraging the development of critical thinking, problem-solving, and ethical decision-making skills—all of which are essential for navigating the complexity of today's world. In order to prepare students for challenges both inside and outside of the classroom, this chapter explores the shift from answer-seeking to inquiry-based learning, highlighting the importance of integrating questioning strategies into the curriculum. In a time where knowledge is almost limitless, it also examines how AI technologies could be utilized to assist these skills and improve learning outcomes while ensuring that students develop an ethical and just mindset toward the use of information.

Problem Statement

Even though artificial intelligence (AI) offers tailored learning experiences and fast access to information, many educational institutions continue to rely on traditional methods of content distribution that emphasize memorization and passive learning. The limitations of this approach have been made clear by the broad availability of AI, as it does not foster critical engagement with knowledge or the development of critical thinking and problem-solving skills in pupils. The true challenge for educators is to create an atmosphere where kids not only absorb material but also learn how to ask the correct questions that will help them navigate complex concepts and global concerns, given AI's ability to provide instant solutions.

The capabilities of AI and the approaches now used in the majority of educational institutions differ significantly. Although there are more and more resources available to support inquiry-based learning, educational frameworks have not yet completely adjusted to this change. Consequently, kids may miss the opportunity to develop vital cognitive skills such as critical thinking, creative problem-solving, and intellectual curiosity, which are required for prospering in the digital era. In order to enable students to become active learners rather than passive information consumers, there is a need for a more deliberate integration of AI technology into curricula that prioritizes inquiry, questioning, and interaction with knowledge.

Objectives

1. **Examine the Impact of AI Technologies on Traditional Educational Models:** Investigate how AI has shifted the focus of education from content delivery to inquiry-based learning, and its implications for teaching and learning practices.

2. **Explore the Role of Questioning Skills in Modern Education:** Analyze how fostering the skill of asking meaningful and thought-provoking questions can enhance critical thinking, problem-solving, and creativity among students.
3. **Propose a Framework for Integrating AI-Driven Inquiry-Based Learning:** Suggest strategies for effectively incorporating AI technologies into educational systems to cultivate inquiry-based learning, preparing students to engage with global challenges and develop ethical decision-making skills.

BACKGROUND

Due in major part to technology improvements, the educational landscape has changed significantly over the last few decades. New pedagogical techniques that prioritize active learning and critical thinking are posing a growing threat to the old educational model, which views teachers as the main knowledge providers and students as passive recipients of information. The way that knowledge is imparted, absorbed, and used has further changed with the advent of computers, the internet, and, more recently, artificial intelligence in the classroom. Teaching as a one-way information transfer has given way to a more dynamic, interactive learning environment thanks in large part to artificial intelligence.

This change has been accelerated by the development of AI technology. Students can learn at their own pace with the help of AI tools like chatbots, automated tutors, and personalized learning systems, which give them instant feedback and customized information (Baker & Siemens, 2014). These tools facilitate a more individualized and inquiry-driven learning experience, where students are not simply passive consumers of knowledge but active participants in their learning process.

But since AI makes factual knowledge easily accessible, teachers must push students to use higher-order cognitive processes like analysis, synthesis, and assessment to engage with the content profoundly rather than just memorize it (Anderson & Krathwohl, 2001). Therefore, AI's function in education needs to change to support students in becoming more capable of conducting research, coming up with original questions, and using knowledge in new ways. Once a secondary ability in conventional classrooms, questioning is now essential for negotiating the complexity of contemporary learning contexts.

There are difficulties associated with the transition to inquiry-based learning. Many educational institutions are still firmly rooted in conventional methods that place more emphasis on mastering the material than on critical engagement, and many teachers are still getting used to using AI technologies in the classroom. Additionally, there are worries about the ethical application of AI, such as concerns about algorithmic bias, data privacy, and how AI affects student agency (Zawacki-

Richter, 2019). Therefore, creating a framework that integrates AI into curriculum while encouraging the growth of critical thinking, ethical reasoning, and questioning abilities is crucial.

Teachers may better prepare children to succeed in an information-rich environment where the capacity to critically assess and interact with knowledge is more crucial than ever by incorporating AI into curricula in a way that prioritizes inquiry and questioning. In order to create an educational atmosphere that encourages critical thinking, creativity, and moral decision-making, this chapter attempts to offer insights on how these frameworks might be created and put into practice.

THEORETICAL FRAMEWORK: INQUIRY-BASED LEARNING AND ITS RELEVANCE

This chapter examines the theoretical underpinnings of Socratic questioning, inquiry-based learning (IBL), and problem-based learning (PBL), evaluating their applicability in promoting an educational approach that is question-centric. The frameworks covered in this chapter highlight the value of inquiry as a key teaching strategy for fostering metacognition, critical thinking, and problem-solving skills. The expanding significance of AI in education has made these frameworks more relevant than ever, as they foster the active engagement of students with knowledge, empowering them to traverse complicated situations through inquiry rather than merely retaining facts.

Inquiry-Based Learning (IBL)

The idea that students learn best when they actively participate in the process of discovering knowledge rather than passively absorbing it is at the core of inquiry-based learning, or IBL. IBL encourages students to conduct investigations that are pertinent to real-world issues, investigate answers, and pose questions. IBL, which has its roots in constructivist learning theories, asserts that rather than just memorization of facts, students build knowledge via inquiry and reflection (Piaget, 1970; Vygotsky, 1978). IBL's primary feature is its focus on student-driven inquiry, which inspires students to interact critically with the material and promotes intellectual curiosity and deeper comprehension.

In the student-centered learning environment that IBL promotes, students are encouraged to recognize their knowledge gaps and use critical questioning to find information. This process helps individuals become lifelong learners who can handle complexity and ambiguity by improving both their comprehension of the material and their capacity to interact with the larger learning environment. Because IBL requires students to critically assess circumstances and synthesize information, research indicates that it improves their problem-solving skills (Blumenfeld et al., 1991). As information becomes more widely available in the AI era, IBL assists students in making the shift from passive information consumers to active knowledge creators.

Socratic Questioning

Another critical teaching strategy that fits with IBL is Socratic inquiry, which was created by the ancient Greek philosopher Socrates. Through discussion, this method promotes in-depth investigation and challenges students to consider their presumptions, convictions, and logic critically. By posing thought-provoking queries that spark debate, test students' preconceptions, and guide them toward more profound understandings, socratic questioning encourages a reflective mentality (Paul & Elder, 2014). The foundation of socratic questioning is the notion that students can clarify ideas, reveal presumptions, and improve their thinking by asking probing questions.

Socratic inquiry has been modified in contemporary education to foster meta-cognitive awareness, critical thinking, and problem-solving skills. Incorporating Socratic inquiry into the curriculum fosters students' ability to think critically and reason on their own, two abilities that are critical in the digital age. The ability to critically interact with content by asking questions, evaluating, and understanding it is becoming increasingly important as AI tools make information instantly accessible. In order to help students build their understanding of complex subjects in collaborative, reflective, and dynamic ways, the educator's role changes to that of a facilitator who leads students via questioning (McTighe & Wiggins, 2013).

Problem-Based Learning (PBL)

Another strategy that supports IBL is Problem-Based Learning (PBL), which centers the learning process around real-world issues. PBL entails posing challenging, open-ended challenges to students and asking them to collaborate to discover answers. The purpose of this teaching approach is to foster problem-solving, collaboration, and critical thinking skills. PBL requires students to apply their knowledge in real-world situations by posing both theoretical and practical questions. Students must challenge presumptions, consider several viewpoints, and synthesize data from a variety of sources in order to solve these challenges, which promotes deep learning (Barrows & Tamblyn, 1980).

In the domain of AI, PBL is quite relevant. The capacity to ask the proper questions and approach problems with an open, investigative mindset is crucial as kids face more complicated difficulties in the digital era. By offering real-time data and facilitating cooperative problem-solving, AI systems can improve PBL. But for PBL to be successful, students must be able to create questions that direct their research and motivate them to find answers. In this way, PBL fosters inquiry, teamwork, and critical thinking abilities—all of which are necessary for lifetime learning—in addition to subject-specific information.

Contemporary Theories on Questioning in Education

The importance of inquiry in the learning process is becoming more widely acknowledged in modern educational philosophies. Dewey (1933) asserts that a key component of reflective thinking is the inquiry process. Dewey stressed that in order for pupils to develop critical thinking and problem-solving abilities, they must inquire about and investigate their surroundings. The role of educators in developing the capacity to ask the proper questions becomes increasingly more important in the digital age, when artificial intelligence (AI) systems can respond to factual inquiries. This is consistent with Bloom's (1956) Taxonomy of Educational Objectives, which grouped higher-order thinking abilities like assessment, synthesis, and analysis—all of which are closely linked to the ability to ask questions.

Furthermore, metacognitive theories emphasize the significance of being conscious of one's thought process, as outlined by Flavell (1979). Metacognition in the context of AI and education entails critically analyzing the implications of learned information, assessing the sources of information, and reflecting on how one arrives at answers. The foundation of metacognitive awareness is effective questioning, which pushes students to evaluate the applicability, correctness, and relevance of their knowledge. According to research, students are more likely to retain material and get a better understanding when they participate in metacognitive activities including asking questions and reflecting on their learning processes (Schraw, 1998).

The importance of questioning in education is emphasized by the pedagogical frameworks of inquiry-based learning, problem-based learning, and socratic questioning. By encouraging students to ask and investigate questions that result in a greater knowledge, these methods foster active, student-centered learning. These frameworks are becoming more and more important in helping students develop their critical thinking, creative problem-solving, and critical engagement skills as AI continues to influence the educational landscape. Incorporating these methods into the curriculum not only encourages kids to be curious but also equips them to succeed in a world that is becoming more linked and complex.

FROM KNOWLEDGE ACQUISITION TO INQUIRY-BASED LEARNING: THE CHANGING ROLE OF EDUCATION

Over the past century, the educational environment has changed dramatically, shifting from a concentration on information acquisition and rote memorization to one that emphasizes inquiry-based learning (IBL), critical thinking, and problem-solving. In the past, the foundation of educational systems was the dissemination of knowledge, and students' main responsibility was to take in and remember knowledge. The demand for a workforce with specialized skills for factory-based labor throughout the industrial era had a significant impact on this paradigm (Tyack & Cuban, 1995). But the speed at which technology is developing, especially with the introduction of artificial intelligence (AI), has put traditional educational paradigms to the test. As a result, the emphasis has shifted from content-heavy curricula to inquiry-driven models that prioritize the development of higher-order cognitive skills.

Historical Evolution of Educational Priorities

Education's historical emphasis, especially in Western societies, was on passive learning as a means of knowledge acquisition. Education systems in the early 20th century were created to impart a set of knowledge to pupils, frequently with little focus on critical thinking or problem-solving techniques. According to Lagemann (2000), this paradigm was predicated on the idea that knowledge could be categorically packed and passed from instructor to pupil. Teachers were seen as the ultimate knowledge providers in these systems, and students were supposed to learn and replicate the material via assignments and tests.

But by the middle of the 20th century, this strategy's shortcomings became apparent. According to educational theorists like John Dewey, education should include pupils in active learning that fosters their capacity for critical thought and problem-solving rather than just imparting knowledge (Dewey, 1938). The foundation for what is now known as inquiry-based learning (IBL) was established by Dewey's support of experiential learning and his focus on the value of inquiry in the learning process. According to Dewey (1938), learning is most successful when it is based on problems and questions that students actively try to understand rather than just passively absorbing knowledge.

As the 20th century went on, education began to emphasize the development of abilities that would be useful in the information era, like critical thinking, logical reasoning, and problem-solving. The growing use of technology in the classroom, which began to create new opportunities for instruction and learning, hastened this change even more. Traditional means of delivering content were increasingly viewed as antiquated as digital technology and the internet made knowledge almost infinitely accessible. Inquiry-driven learning approaches became widely adopted as a result of educational goals shifting to prioritize abilities that may assist students in navigating and making sense of an ever-increasing volume of knowledge.

The Impact of Artificial Intelligence on Education

The development of artificial intelligence (AI) has significantly sped up the process of educational change by transforming the way that knowledge is acquired, digested, and applied. Large volumes of information are now easily accessible at the touch of a button thanks to artificial intelligence (AI) technologies like machine learning, data analytics, and natural language processing. In a world where information can be rapidly retrieved from databases, search engines, and AI-driven platforms, this change has made old educational methods—which frequently centered on rote memory and recall—less applicable.

In this new environment, education's function extends beyond simply imparting knowledge to include helping students become capable of interacting with it in a meaningful way. The focus has switched from learning facts to developing the abilities required for inquiry due to AI's capacity to deliver immediate answers to factual questions. Students now need to learn how to critically assess information, ask the proper questions, and do in-depth research instead of concentrating on memorization of large amounts of knowledge (Baker et al., 2020). Because of this, education has changed from being centered on acquiring knowledge to being centered on inquiry, where students are urged to ask questions, look for resources, and investigate answers by actively engaging with the subject matter.

Inquiry-Based Learning (IBL) and Its Relevance in the AI Era

A teaching strategy known as inquiry-based learning (IBL) encourages students to actively participate in their education by posing queries, carrying out research, and resolving real-world issues. IBL's core belief is that learning occurs most effectively when students are actively involved in the inquiry process—posing queries, looking for solutions, and critically assessing the data they come across (Bransford et al., 2000). The demands of the digital age, where knowledge is plentiful but requires critical thinking and problem-solving abilities to make sense of it, are closely met by this method.

IBL becomes much more important in the AI era. The cognitive processes required to formulate meaningful, pertinent, and perceptive inquiries cannot be replaced by AI technologies, notwithstanding their growing ability to provide factual answers. The capacity for self-directed inquiry—skills necessary for fostering learning autonomy and equipping students for lifelong learning—is a crucial element of IBL, according to Tharp (2008). Additionally, while AI systems can support the inquiry process by giving students tailored learning experiences, recommending pertinent materials, and providing feedback, they are unable to fully replace humans' ability to pose thoughtful, nuanced questions.

IBL encourages students to view learning as an active process of inquiry and discovery rather than as a passive act of taking in information. It encourages critical thinking, creativity, and teamwork—all of which are vital abilities in the AI-driven, information-rich world of today. Students gain metacognitive abilities that allow them to assess and modify their learning processes as they improve their questioning and thinking (Anderson & Krathwohl, 2001). They will be able to prosper in a world that is becoming more interconnected and sophisticated because of these very abilities.

Moving Beyond Traditional Learning Outcomes

The need to go beyond traditional learning outcomes—which have traditionally concentrated on material mastery and factual recall—has been brought to light by the development of AI. It is no longer enough for students to simply recall facts or replicate information in a world where information is more readily available than ever. Developing students' capacity to interact critically with information, pose insightful queries, and apply what they have learned to real-world problems should be the aim of education instead (Vygotsky, 1978).

This change necessitates reconsidering assessment techniques as well. It's possible that rote memorization tests and other traditional evaluations are no longer the best approach to gauge students' learning outcomes. Assessments ought to instead concentrate on students' capacity for critical thought, investigation, and knowledge application in new situations. As a way to measure learning in the AI era, authentic assessments—which ask students to solve real-world problems and show their inquiry skills—are growing in popularity (Darling-Hammond et al., 2017).

In conclusion, a fundamental change in the function of education is represented by the move from content-heavy curriculum to inquiry-driven approaches. AI has sped up this shift by making knowledge more widely available than ever before. As a result, the focus in education is moving from acquiring knowledge to developing inquiry skills, where students are encouraged to think critically, ask questions, and solve problems in addition to seeking answers. A key component of this change is inquiry-based learning (IBL), which gives students the tools they need to function in a world that is getting more complicated and information-rich by the day. Students can be better prepared for the potential and difficulties of the AI-driven future through education that promotes inquiry, critical thinking, and metacognitive abilities.

ARTIFICIAL INTELLIGENCE AS AN ANSWER PROVIDER: OPPORTUNITIES AND CHALLENGES FOR EDUCATORS

As a potent instrument that can offer immediate access to a wealth of knowledge, artificial intelligence (AI) has quickly changed the face of education. AI has completely changed how knowledge is accessible and processed, from basic search engines to sophisticated models that can produce in-depth evaluations. These advancements present educators with important chances to abandon conventional approaches to content distribution and concentrate on encouraging inquiry, critical thinking, and the moral use of AI-generated knowledge. To optimize AI's advantages in the classroom, educators must overcome a number of obstacles and constraints that come with its enormous potential.

AI as a Provider of Knowledge: Opportunities for Educators

The role of educators has been significantly altered by AI's capacity to instantaneously deliver answers to factual queries. In the past, teachers were in charge of imparting knowledge and making sure that students learned a certain body of knowledge. However, the role of the educator is changing from delivering knowledge to teaching students how to evaluate, analyze, and critically interact with AI-generated information, as AI systems can now retrieve and even generate thorough answers across a wide range of subjects.

Artificial intelligence (AI) techniques, like machine learning algorithms and natural language processing models, have made it possible to develop educational platforms that can produce customized answers to student questions. AI-powered tutoring programs, for instance, can provide students immediate feedback on their work, recommend additional reading, and even involve them in interactive problem-solving exercises (Zawacki-Richter, 2018). These features provide a more individualized and learner-centered educational experience by enabling students to investigate subjects more thoroughly and at their own speed.

Furthermore, by giving students insights that might be challenging to find using conventional techniques, AI's capacity to evaluate enormous datasets and spot patterns might improve the learning process. AI systems, for example, are able to compile information from multiple sources, providing pupils with a thorough rundown of intricate subjects (Brynjolfsson & McAfee, 2014). In this situation, teachers can concentrate on helping students understand and synthesize AI-generated content while pushing them to challenge preconceptions and consider different viewpoints.

The Shift in Educators' Roles: From Delivering Content to Guiding Inquiry

The role of educators must change from one of knowledge provider to one of facilitator and guide as AI gets better at providing factual answers. This change highlights how crucial it is to foster critical thinking and inquiry-based learning (IBL), where students are taught to think critically about the information they come across rather than just memorize facts.

It is now the responsibility of educators to guide students through the complexity of AI-generated content, especially by urging them to consider the veracity, context, and possible biases of the information they are exposed to. In order to do this, educators must help students develop critical assessment abilities, which enable them to evaluate the origins, approaches, and constraints of AI-driven replies. By doing this, teachers enable students to have a deeper comprehension of the subject matter and go beyond passively consuming knowledge (Winkler & Söllner, 2020). Teachers may prepare children for a future in which artificial intelligence (AI) is a ubiquitous tool, but human judgment is still essential for properly interpreting and using knowledge, by encouraging these inquiry-based abilities.

The Limitations of AI: Biases and Data Dependence

Although artificial intelligence (AI) presents many chances to improve education, it's critical to understand its drawbacks, including its dependence on preexisting data and its biases. Large datasets can be analyzed by AI systems, which then produce answers based on patterns found in the data. These systems, however, can unintentionally reinforce preexisting biases or inaccuracies because they are only as good as the data they are trained on (O'Neil, 2016). An AI model trained on biased historical data, for instance, can reinforce similar biases in its answers, producing information that is skewed or uneven.

These drawbacks highlight how crucial it is to evaluate AI-generated knowledge critically and with questions. Teachers need to push pupils to challenge the presumptions that underlie AI systems as well as the content that these systems give. This entails raising students' understanding of the ethical ramifications of AI in education as well as teaching them how to identify and challenge biases in AI responses. By tackling these problems, teachers can assist students in gaining a more sophisticated comprehension of the function of artificial intelligence in education as well as the possible dangers of depending solely on AI-generated content without conducting critical analysis.

AI and the Future of Education: A Balanced Approach

It is crucial for educators to combine utilizing AI's potential with upholding the integrity of human-driven inquiry and critical thinking while weighing the opportunities and difficulties it offers. It is imperative that educators continue to support the development of skills like questioning, problem-solving, and ethical reasoning, even while AI can improve educational experiences by offering tailored learning routes, fast access to knowledge, and data-driven insights. Students need these abilities to succeed in a world where artificial intelligence (AI) is becoming more and more important in the sharing of knowledge.

Teachers must take advantage of professional development opportunities that give them the tools they need to successfully incorporate AI into their teaching methods in order to strike this balance. This entails being aware of AI's limitations, comprehending how it might enhance inquiry-based learning, and creating plans to guarantee that students can interact critically with content produced by AI. The strategies used by educators to help pupils navigate the intricacies of this new educational paradigm must also advance along with AI.

In conclusion, educators face both tremendous potential and difficulties as a result of AI's function as a knowledge provider. Artificial intelligence (AI) systems can improve learning by providing immediate access to information and tailored feedback, but they also need a change in the role of educators, who must concentrate on helping students understand and interact critically with AI-generated content. The drawbacks of AI, namely its reliance on preexisting data and its biases, also emphasize the necessity for students to take a critical stance that questions the presumptions that underlie knowledge produced by AI. By encouraging inquiry-based learning and critical thinking, teachers can make sure that students are prepared to handle the challenging terrain of AI-driven education.

The Art of Question Formulation: Teaching Students to Ask the Right Questions

In the era of artificial intelligence, when students have access to a wealth of knowledge, the capacity to formulate insightful and pertinent questions is a critical aptitude. This section looks at useful methods for instructing students on how to create compelling questions, which encourages deeper engagement with the material and critical thinking. We present frameworks and classroom activities that can be used to build a variety of question kinds, from simple comprehension to more complex analytical and evaluative questions, by drawing on Bloom's Taxonomy and critical inquiry models. This section provides ways to help students become excellent questioners in academic and real-world contexts by highlighting curiosity, context awareness, and iterative question refinement.

Bloom's Taxonomy: A Framework for Question Development

A well-known framework in educational theory, Bloom's Taxonomy (1956) offers an organized method for classifying cognitive abilities and aids teachers in comprehending the kinds of questions that can encourage different levels of thinking. From lower-order thinking (like remembering and understanding) to higher-order thinking (like analyzing, evaluating, and producing), the taxonomy is separated into six levels. According to Anderson and Krathwohl (2001), each level can help students ask increasingly difficult questions that call for a deeper understanding of the subject matter.

For instance, students may pose simple comprehension-focused queries at the lowest level of Bloom's Taxonomy, like "What is the main idea of this passage?" or "What are the most important facts?" These fundamental questions aid students in developing a fundamental comprehension of the subject matter. Students can start posing increasingly complex queries as their cognitive abilities advance. Questions might change to, for example, "What are the causes and effects of this event?" or "How does this concept relate to other ideas in the text?" at the analytical level. Students may inquire, "What are the strengths and weaknesses of this argument?" at the evaluation level. or "How would you evaluate this information's applicability in a modern setting?" Teachers can gradually advance their students' question-formulation skills from basic understanding to sophisticated analysis and evaluation by utilizing Bloom's Taxonomy.

Developing Critical Inquiry Skills through Questioning

In addition to Bloom's Taxonomy, critical inquiry models enable teachers help students become better questioners. Approaching issues with an open mind, challenging presumptions, and taking into account many viewpoints are all components of critical inquiry (Paul & Elder, 2014). By encouraging students to challenge the veracity, applicability, and ramifications of the information they come across, educators can promote critical inquiry. Asking students to think critically about the context in which material is provided by asking them questions like "Who is the author of this text, and what is their perspective?" or "What are the potential biases in this argument?" is one useful tactic.

Teachers can use the "questioning triangle" technique, which asks students to formulate questions at various depths, to help students further develop critical inquiry (McTighe & Wiggins, 2013). Along with factual questions like "What happened in this chapter?" this model encourages students to come up with conceptual questions like "Why is this idea important in the context of this theme?" and even metacognitive questions like "How does my understanding of this topic change after considering different perspectives?" respectively. By encouraging students to pose a range of questions, teachers can foster more complex and nuanced methods of inquiry.

Classroom Exercises for Question Development

The "Question Formulation Technique" (QFT), created by the Right Question Institute, is a useful teaching tool for students to learn how to formulate inquiries. Students are encouraged to create their own questions and develop them through a series of processes in the QFT, which is an organized procedure. Students start the process by coming up with as many questions as they can regarding a certain subject. Students are expected to classify their questions after coming up with a list of them, with an emphasis on refining or extending them. Students might take a topic like "What is the main idea of the text?" and turn it into something more detailed and intricate, like "How does the main idea of the text relate to contemporary issues in society?" because of this. Students learn the importance of iterative asking with this practice, which helps them refine their initial inquiries to promote deeper comprehension.

Using "think-pair-share" exercises, in which students first jot down any questions they may have about a certain subject before discussing them with a partner, is another helpful tactic. Through peer engagement, students can hone their inquiries and take into account fresh viewpoints, assisting them in moving from straightforward factual inquiries to more intricate ones. Students are taught to think critically and have fruitful conversations by routinely practicing question formation in a group environment.

Curiosity, Context Awareness, and Iterative Question Refinement

Cultivating curiosity is essential to the skill of question formulation. Students need to be encouraged to perceive asking questions as a continuous process of inquiry and discovery rather than just a way to get information. By structuring assignments and class discussions around open-ended questions that encourage investigation rather than a single correct response, educators can foster curiosity (Harvard, 2020). For example, teachers could question, "What do you think were the key turning points in history, and why?" instead of having pupils remember historical facts.

Furthermore, when formulating questions, context awareness is crucial. It is necessary to teach students how to formulate their inquiries in light of the subject matter, taking into account social, cultural, and historical elements that might affect their way of thinking. Students must understand the sources of information and the viewpoints that are used to portray it in order to accomplish this. By posing questions like "In what ways might the question change if we approached it from a different cultural or historical perspective?" teachers can help students develop this insight.

Lastly, one of the most important aspects of creating good questions is iterative question refinement. Over time, students should be encouraged to go back and rework their questions, making adjustments in light of new knowledge or evolving circumstances. Students have a deeper comprehension of the subject matter and are inspired to see learning as a dynamic, ever-evolving process as a result of this iterative approach.

To sum up, teaching children how to ask insightful questions is a crucial ability that fosters critical thinking, intellectual curiosity, and deeper learning. Teachers can help students create a variety of question kinds, from straightforward comprehension questions to more intricate, evaluative ones, by using frameworks like Bloom's Taxonomy and critical inquiry models. Think-pair-share activities and the Question Formulation Technique are two examples of classroom exercises that provide useful methods for developing these abilities. In the end, encouraging students' curiosity, context awareness, and iterative question refining enables them to go beyond passive learning and adopt a more active, deliberate approach to their education.

Assessment and Feedback in a Question-Centric Curriculum

Assessments in the traditional educational model have frequently been created to gauge students' capacity for fact recall, comprehension, and application of particular knowledge. However, the emphasis moves from evaluating students' knowledge to evaluating their problem-solving, question-generating, and critical engagement with content in a question-centric curriculum that emphasizes inquiry-based learning. This section looks at how tests can be redesigned to place more emphasis on the breadth, originality, and applicability of the questions students ask than merely the correctness of their responses. Along with providing case studies of organizations that have effectively adopted question-based assessments, it also looks at alternative assessment models that promote a more comprehensive understanding of student learning. There is also discussion of useful recommendations for implementing these principles in various educational contexts.

RETHINKING ASSESSMENT: FROM RECALL TO INQUIRY

Conventional evaluations frequently gauge a person's capacity to remember facts and apply them to pre-established situations. Although this kind of evaluation is useful for gauging the acquisition of fundamental knowledge, it is unable to capture the critical thinking and problem-solving skills necessary for handling challenging, real-world situations (Black & Wiliam, 1998). Assessment should move toward gauging students' capacity to pose insightful queries, carry out careful analysis, and exhibit intellectual curiosity in an inquiry-based curriculum. In addition to promoting higher-order thinking, this method develops abilities more suited to the contemporary, information-rich environment, where instantaneous access to facts is made possible by technological developments like artificial intelligence (Jonassen, 2003).

Teachers can gauge students' level of engagement with the subject matter and their ability to view learning as an active process by assessing the caliber of the questions they pose rather than just the accuracy of their responses (Harvard, 2020). For instance, students may be required to formulate a research question on a specific subject and create a strategy for examining it as part of inquiry-based exams. With the use of this assessment paradigm, students can show that they can think critically, recognize knowledge gaps, and solve problems using multidisciplinary techniques.

Alternative Assessment Models

A number of different evaluation approaches place more emphasis on question framing and inquiry than on factual memory. Portfolio-based evaluation is one such paradigm in which students gather a variety of their work over time, including iterative versions of their inquiries, drafts of research questions, and reflective pieces (Arter & Spandel, 1992). This method provides a more comprehensive view of how students learn and how their thinking changes as a result of inquiry and questioning. Additionally, portfolios offer a forum for peer and self evaluation, empowering students to take charge of their education and consider their own development.

Project-based learning (PBL), which entails students working on challenging, real-world issues that call for them to formulate questions, do research, and cooperatively create solutions, is another promising strategy. In PBL, evaluation is centered on the process as well as the outcome, emphasizing students' capacity for research, problem-solving, and productive teamwork (Thomas, 2000). Because students are continuously honing their questions and hypotheses throughout the project, this model highlights the value of inquiry and enables teachers to evaluate students' critical thinking and problem-solving abilities in addition to the final product.

In question-centric courses, formative assessments—which are carried out during the learning process rather than at the conclusion—are very helpful. Regular chances for students to ask questions during lectures or discussions and get feedback on the caliber and applicability of their queries may be part of these evaluations. Teachers can direct students' thinking, promote deeper inquiry, and cultivate a growth mindset by providing regular feedback on their questions (Black & Wiliam, 1998). By allowing students' questions to direct the learning process, formative evaluations establish an ongoing learning loop that helps teachers spot areas of misunderstanding or confusion before they become deeply ingrained.

CASE STUDIES OF SUCCESSFUL IMPLEMENTATIONS

The success of this strategy has been demonstrated by the several institutions that have effectively incorporated question-based exams into their courses. Harvard University is one example, as many of their graduate-level programs use inquiry-based examinations. Students are evaluated on the uniqueness and profundity of their questions as well as the correctness of their answers in classes like Critical Thinking and Problem Solving (Harvard, 2020). These courses' focus on question formulation inspires students to interact critically with difficult texts and problems, fostering the analytical abilities required for success in both the classroom and the workplace.

In its undergraduate programs at The University of Sydney, faculty members have adopted an inquiry-based assessment paradigm, especially in fields like the social sciences, philosophy, and history. According to Boud and Falchikov (2006), these programs require students to formulate a research question at the start of the semester and then refine it through iterative revisions and peer review. The final evaluations of the students are determined by how well they have honed their research question and how well they can use critical thinking and evidence-based reasoning to tackle the subject from several perspectives. This approach encourages students to view learning as a dynamic, continuous process rather than a fixed result by moving the emphasis from the ultimate solution to the inquiry process itself.

In a similar vein, The University of California, Berkeley has integrated question-driven evaluations into their multidisciplinary curricula, especially when it comes to tackling global issues like climate change. Students in these programs are evaluated on their ability to formulate questions that take into account social, economic, and environmental aspects as well as their ability to solve problems using a multidisciplinary approach (Glesne, 2016). Through the integration of many viewpoints and methodologies, this process-based model promotes critical thinking and teamwork among students.

Guidelines for Implementing Question-Based Assessments

Teachers need to use a few crucial tactics in order to successfully conduct question-based assessments:

1. Establish Specific Learning Objectives: Teachers should be clear about the kinds of questions they want their students to come up with. Do they want pupils to answer simple comprehension questions or do they want them to undertake more in-depth, critical thinking? Students will be better able to formulate their questions if these expectations are clearly stated up front (Anderson & Krathwohl, 2001).
2. Give Feedback on Questions: Rather than concentrating only on the correctness of students' responses, feedback should also address the caliber of the questions they pose. Teachers can comment on whether students' inquiries are clear, pertinent, and apt to inspire more research. Students should be encouraged to improve their inquiries and create new lines of investigation by receiving constructive criticism (Sadler, 1989).
3. Promote Peer Review and Collaboration: Teachers can foster a collaborative learning environment where students can improve their own questions and learn from one another's by introducing peer review into question-based exams (Topping, 2009). Peer review also helps students see questioning as a collaborative, iterative process and cultivates a sense of shared responsibility for learning.
4. Use Iterative Processes: Encourage students to continuously improve their questions in light of feedback, fresh data, and developing understandings as part of formative assessment. Students gain a deeper understanding of the subject matter and the need of continuous inquiry thanks to this iterative approach.

In conclusion, assessment procedures need to adapt as the educational landscape moves toward inquiry-based learning. By emphasizing the caliber of students' inquiries rather than their responses, teachers can encourage greater participation, critical thinking, and problem-solving abilities. The potential for these models to promote more dynamic, inquiry-driven learning environments is demonstrated by the instances of institutions that have effectively adopted question-based evaluations. Teachers can better prepare children for the complex, information-rich world they will traverse by implementing frameworks that place a higher priority on the inquiry process.

CULTIVATING A QUESTIONING MINDSET FOR LIFELONG LEARNING

The function of education has changed dramatically in a time of swift technological development and the spread of artificial intelligence (AI). Even though AI is capable of answering a wide variety of queries, asking perceptive, important inquiries is still a skill that only humans possess. Effective questioning techniques are crucial for kids' academic achievement as well as their capacity to adjust to an uncertain future. This last section positions inquiry as the cornerstone of lifelong learning by examining the long-term advantages of helping students develop a questioning attitude. It highlights how question-based learning gives students the tools they need for critical thinking, career advancement, and active civic engagement and explores methods for promoting this mentality outside of the classroom.

The Importance of Questioning in Lifelong Learning

Critical thinking is characterized by the capacity to pose meaningful, pertinent questions, which forms the basis of lifelong learning. The focus of education needs to change from learning facts to developing critical thinking abilities at a time where knowledge is readily available through artificial intelligence (AI) and other digital tools. Individuals must continue to be inquisitive, flexible, and able to challenge the status quo in order to engage in lifelong learning, which is described as the continuous, voluntary, and self-motivated pursuit of knowledge for personal or professional development (Knowles, 1980). In order to survive and thrive in a world that is constantly changing, people must engage in this process of constant questioning and investigation.

Metacognition, or the capacity to reflect on one's own thinking, is emphasized in research on lifelong learning as a crucial element in cultivating a questioning mentality. Students are better prepared to create questions that are both pertinent to the activity at hand and supportive of deeper comprehension when they learn to reflect on their own thought processes (Flavell, 1979). Therefore, fostering a mindset that sees learning as a lifetime endeavor requires inquiry-based learning, which promotes the continuous creation and improvement of questions. We establish a framework that promotes curiosity, self-directed learning, and flexibility by placing questions at the core of education.

Strategies for Fostering a Questioning Mindset Beyond the Classroom

Teachers need to encourage students to participate in reflective techniques that promote inquiry in order to develop a questioning mindset that transcends the classroom. After formal education is over, students can use a variety of techniques to continue and improve their questioning abilities:

1. Modeling asking Behavior: During lectures, conversations, and feedback, educators should set an example for successful asking by regularly exhibiting how to ask insightful questions. Students are more likely to absorb these techniques and use them in their own learning when teachers clearly explain how they formulate questions (Paul & Elder, 2014). Instead of viewing asking as a simple task of determining the "right" response, this modeling helps children see it as an important tool for understanding.
2. Promoting Self-Reflection: One of the most important techniques for developing a questioning mentality is self-reflection. Teachers can encourage students to analyze their learning processes and the questions they have investigated by incorporating reflective journaling or other self-assessment techniques. Because reflective techniques force students to critically examine how they approach problems and formulate questions, research indicates that they enhance metacognition (Boud, Keogh, & Walker, 1985).
3. Fostering Curiosity in Daily Life: Students need to be inspired to use their inquiry abilities in practical contexts in order to take questions outside of the classroom. Promoting interest in social, political, environmental, and cultural issues is part of this. Teachers can help students understand that inquiry is not limited to academic settings but is a crucial ability in both personal and professional life by highlighting the importance of questioning in daily decision-making and civic involvement (Bransford, Brown, & Cocking, 2000).
4. Offering Problem-Solving Opportunities: Giving students the chance to solve problems in real-world settings through internships, volunteer work, or professional experiences allows them to practice their questioning techniques. Students learn to ask questions that result in original ideas and fresh perspectives when they are given the opportunity to tackle difficult, unsolved problems. The importance of inquiry as a lifetime tool for both professional and personal development is reinforced by these possibilities (Bielaczyc & Collins, 1999).

Preparing Students for the Future Through Question-Based Learning

The capacity for critical thought, questioning, and change adaptation will become even more crucial as we turn to the future. The ability of humans to ask meaningful, ethical, and sophisticated questions will be crucial for navigating the opportunities and problems of the future in a world where artificial intelligence can deliver rapid answers to almost any query. By encouraging children to ask questions, we are equipping them to think critically about new knowledge, adjust to a world that is changing quickly, and participate actively in societal challenges. Additionally, students that receive inquiry-based training will be more prepared to spearhead innovation in domains like technology, healthcare, education, and the arts, where challenging presumptions frequently serves as the foundation for ground-breaking concepts (Willingham, 2007).

It is possible to see this emphasis on inquiry as a reaction to the difficulties presented by a quickly changing technology environment, where human creativity and critical thinking are more important than ever. The ability to critically think and reason ethically will set humans apart from computers as AI continues to automate repetitive tasks (Brynjolfsson & McAfee, 2014). As a result, question-based learning becomes a crucial instrument for giving pupils the mental adaptability and analytical abilities they need to prosper in an uncertain future.

CONCLUSION

To sum up, the focus on inquiry-based learning is a deliberate and essential reaction to the quickening pace of technological development reshaping the contemporary world. In a time where routine, repetitive jobs may be handled more and more by automation and artificial intelligence, human potential truly shines through in creativity, critical thinking, and ethical reasoning. These abilities are essential for succeeding in a complicated and uncertain global world; they are not only supplemental.

A revolutionary educational strategy, inquiry-based learning gives students the mental flexibility they need to deal with uncertainty and adjust to changing paradigms. It pushes students to actively interact with questions that cast doubt on presumptions, pique curiosity, and necessitate more in-depth research, going beyond passively absorbing information. Along with developing analytical skills, this method cultivates a lifelong learning mindset, which is crucial for success in the future.

Furthermore, humanity needs people who can make logical decisions and exercise moral leadership as we confront more interrelated global issues, such as climate change and moral conundrums in the development of AI. By putting questions at the center of education, we develop a generation that is ready to face these challenges, equipped with the courage to be creative and the discernment to behave responsibly.

In the end, question-based learning is a philosophy that adapts education to the needs of a quickly evolving technological age rather than only being a pedagogical tool. It gives pupils the ability to think critically, act morally, and react creatively, ensuring that they are not only ready for the unknowns of the future but also in a position to lead and influence it.

REFERENCES

Anderson, L. W., & Krathwohl, D. R. (Eds.). (2001). *A taxonomy for learning, teaching, and assessing: A revision of Bloom's taxonomy of educational objectives*. Pearson Education.

Arter, J. A., & Spandel, V. (1992). *Creating a framework for classroom assessment: Guidelines for teachers*. ERIC Clearinghouse on Assessment and Evaluation.

Baker, R. S.. (2020). *Artificial Intelligence in education: Promise and implications for teaching and learning*. Taylor & Francis.

Baker, R. S., & Siemens, G. (2014). *Educational data mining and learning analytics*. In R. K. M. K. L. E. A. G. S. (Ed.), *Handbook of learning analytics* (pp. 61-72). Society for Learning Analytics Research.

Barrows, H. S., & Tamblyn, R. M. (1980). *Problem-based learning: An approach to medical education*. Springer Publishing Company.

Bielaczyc, K., & Collins, A. (1999). Design research: An emerging paradigm for transforming the practice of teaching. *Yearbook of the National Society for the Study of Education*, *98*(1), 44–62.

Black, P., & Wiliam, D. (1998). Assessment and classroom learning. *Assessment in Education: Principles, Policy & Practice*, *5*(1), 7–74. DOI: 10.1080/0969595980050102

Blumenfeld, P. C., Soloway, E., Marx, R. W., Krajcik, J. S., Guzdial, M., & Palincsar, A. S. (1991). Motivating project-based learning: Sustaining the doing, supporting the learning. *Educational Psychologist*, *26*(3-4), 369–398. DOI: 10.1080/00461520.1991.9653137

Boud, D., & Falchikov, N. (2006). *Rethinking assessment in higher education: Learning for the longer term*. Routledge.

Boud, D., Keogh, R., & Walker, D. (Eds.). (1985). *Reflection: Turning experience into learning*. Kogan Page.

Bransford, J. D., Brown, A. L., & Cocking, R. R. (2000). *How people learn: Brain, mind, experience, and school*. National Academy Press.

Brynjolfsson, E., & McAfee, A. (2014). *The second machine age: Work, progress, and prosperity in a time of brilliant technologies*. W.W. Norton & Company.

Darling-Hammond, L.. (2017). *Using assessment to improve learning in schools*. Harvard Education Press.

Dewey, J. (1933). *How we think*. D.C. Heath & Co.

Dewey, J. (1938). *Experience and education*. Kappa Delta Pi.

Flavell, J. H. (1979). Metacognition and cognitive monitoring: A new area of cognitive-developmental inquiry. *The American Psychologist, 34*(10), 906–911. DOI: 10.1037/0003-066X.34.10.906

Glesne, C. (2016). *Becoming qualitative researchers: An introduction* (5th ed.). Pearson.

Harvard Graduate School of Education. (2020). *The art of asking questions: How inquiry-driven education promotes critical thinking*. Harvard University Press.

Jonassen, D. H. (2003). *Learning to solve problems: A handbook for designing problem-solving learning environments*. Educational Technology Publications.

Knowles, M. S. (1980). *The modern practice of adult education: From pedagogy to andragogy* (2nd ed.). Cambridge Books.

Lagemann, E. C. (2000). *An elusive science: The troubling history of education research*. University of Chicago Press.

McTighe, J., & Wiggins, G. (2013). *Essential questions: Opening doors to student understanding*. Association for Supervision and Curriculum Development.

O'Neil, C. (2016). *Weapons of Math Destruction: How Big Data Increases Inequality and Threatens Democracy*. Crown Publishing Group.

Paul, R., & Elder, L. (2014). *The miniature guide to critical thinking concepts and tools* (7th ed.). Foundation for Critical Thinking.

Piaget, J. (1970). Piaget's theory. In Mussen, P. (Ed.), *Carmichael's manual of child psychology* (3rd ed., pp. 703–732). Wiley.

Right Question Institute. (n.d.). *Question formulation technique (QFT)*. Retrieved from https://rightquestion.org/qft/

Sadler, D. R. (1989). Formative assessment and the design of instructional systems. *Instructional Science, 18*(2), 119–144. DOI: 10.1007/BF00117714

Tharp, R. G. (2008). Effective pedagogy in culturally responsive classrooms. *International Journal of Educational Development*.

Thomas, J. W. (2000). *A review of research on project-based learning*. Retrieved from https://www.bie.org/files/researchreviewPBL_2000.pdf

Topping, K. J. (2009). Peer assessment. *Theory into Practice*, *48*(1), 20–27. DOI: 10.1080/00405840802577569

Tyack, D., & Cuban, L. (1995). *Tinkering toward Utopia: A century of public school reform*. Harvard University Press.

Vygotsky, L. S. (1978). *Mind in society: The development of higher psychological processes*. Harvard University Press.

Willingham, D. T. (2007). Critical thinking: Why is it so hard to teach? *American Educator*, *31*(1), 8–19.

Winkler, R., & Söllner, M. (2020). *Personalization in Artificial Intelligence: How the AI Revolution is Reshaping Education and Learning*. Springer.

Zawacki-Richter, O. (2018). *Theories of Distance Education and AI in Learning*. Routledge.

Zawacki-Richter, O. (2019). The role of artificial intelligence in education: Current insights and future research directions. *Educational Technology Research and Development*, *67*(4), 745–773. DOI: 10.1007/s11423-019-09764-7

Zohar, A., & Dori, Y. J. (2003). Higher order thinking skills and low-achieving students: Are they mutually exclusive? *Journal of the Learning Sciences*, *12*(2), 145–181. DOI: 10.1207/s15327809jls1202_1

Chapter 4
Ensuring Fairness in AI-Driven University Assessments:
Addressing Bias in Online Course Evaluations

K. Fouzia Sulthana
https://orcid.org/0009-0006-5014-6026
Rajalakshmi Institute of Technology, India

B. Sandhiya Rajeshwari
Rajalakshmi Institute of Technology, India

M. Ashok
https://orcid.org/0000-0002-2868-864X
Rajalakshmi Institute of Technology, India

M. Robinson Joel
https://orcid.org/0000-0002-3030-8431
KCG College of Technology, India

ABSTRACT

The growing concern over bias in AI systems, particularly in high-impact areas like healthcare, hiring, criminal justice and education emphasizes the need for ethical implementations to ensure fairness. To address bias, indicators such as demographic parity, equalized odds, calibration, and disparate impact measurement are crucial in monitoring and reducing biased outcomes across different demographic groups. In a scenario of university students taking online courses, where the exams were

DOI: 10.4018/979-8-3373-6018-8.ch004

Copyright © 2026, IGI Global Scientific Publishing. Copying or distributing in print or electronic forms without written permission of IGI Global Scientific Publishing is prohibited.

evaluated by an AI system, raising concerns about potential bias in the evaluation process. The key problem identified is ensuring that AI-driven assessments fairly evaluate students from diverse backgrounds, without disproportionately favoring or penalizing certain groups. Bias detection and mitigation efforts are essential to foster trust, fairness, and consistency in AI-based evaluations.

1.INTRODUCTION

Depending on the assessment style, topic content, and university strategy, AI-driven university evaluations are becoming increasingly widespread and can take many different forms. In these evaluations, artificial intelligence's primary characteristic is its application to improve productivity, equity, and customization. These systems leverage AI algorithms to assist in tasks such as grading, feedback provision, proctoring, and personalized learning. Here's an overview of how AI is transforming university assessments. An outline of how they are usually carried out is provided below.

2. AUTOMATED GRADING AND FEEDBACK

Multiple-Choice Questions (MCQs) are frequently graded instantaneously by AI systems. The system can process a lot of entries fast, giving pupils results right away.AI-driven systems can automatically grade assignments, quizzes, and even essays using advanced algorithms like natural language processing (NLP)(Shaik et al 2022). These systems are particularly effective for objective questions (e.g., multiple-choice), but advancements are also being made in assessing subjective responses (e.g., essays).

Figure 1. Element of AI Based Exams

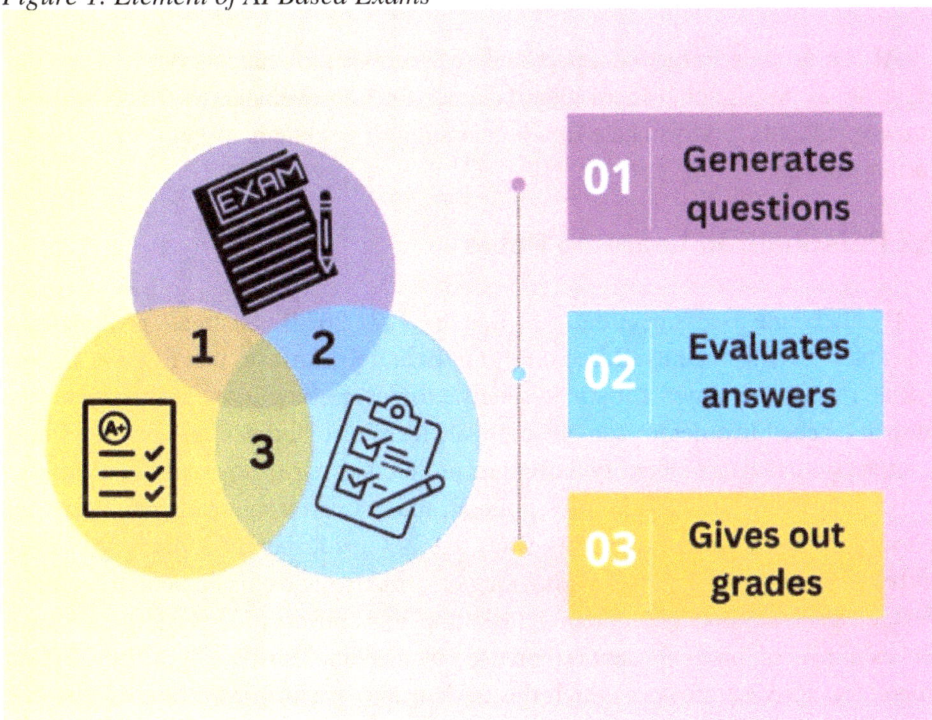

As shown in Figure 1, represents the three core functions of an automated assessment system using a Venn diagram and a step-by-step breakdown. The three overlapping circles symbolize the interconnected tasks involved in the educational evaluation process. The purple circle represents "Generates questions" (Step 1), indicating the system's ability to create exam questions. The blue circle signifies "Evaluates answers" (Step 2), reflecting the system's role in checking and analyzing student responses. The yellow circle stands for "Gives out grades" (Step 3), highlighting the final step where the system assigns grades based on performance. The central area, marked with the number 3 where all circles intersect, symbolizes a comprehensive system that integrates all three capabilities—question generation, answer evaluation, and grading. This visualization emphasizes how these individual components work together to form a cohesive, automated educational assessment tool.

2.1 AI-Powered Feedback

AI can provide immediate, personalized feedback to students on their assignments or exams, helping them identify areas for improvement. Some AI systems analyze students' performance trends and suggest resources to help them master certain concepts.

2.2 Personalized Learning Paths

By analyzing assessment data, AI(Sriram et al., 2024) can create personalized learning paths for students. Based on strengths and weaknesses identified in assessments, the system may recommend specific topics, resources, or courses to help a student succeed.In order to promote improved learning outcomes, AI-driven systems evaluate student data to identify individual preferences, strengths, and shortcomings before suggesting tailored activities, content, and tests. AI techniques enable tailored learning pathways in the following ways. AI systems for learning analytics gather and examine information on the behavior, performance, and engagement of students. Test results, assignment completion, task time, and conversation participation are a few examples of this. This data is then used by machine learning algorithms to find trends and forecast areas in which the student may perform well or struggle. For instance, remedial activities and videos centered on specific math subjects can be recommended to a student who consistently has difficulties with them.

2.3 Adaptive Assessments

AI-driven adaptive assessments change in real time based on student responses. For example, if a student answers a question correctly, the system may offer a more challenging question next, and vice versa. This personalizes the difficulty level to match a student's capabilities. Adaptive learning technologies adjust the pace and difficulty of lessons based on real-time student performance. As the student progresses, the system dynamically alters the content to match their learning speed and ability.

2.4 Accessibility and Inclusivity

AI-driven assessments can be designed to accommodate diverse student needs. For example, adaptive interfaces or voice-activated systems may assist students with disabilities, ensuring assessments are accessible to all learners. AI can read exam questions aloud to students who have visual impairments, learning disabilities (such as dyslexia), or reading difficulties using text-to-speech (TTS)(Ren et al., 2019). For improved comprehension, TTS systems can be tailored to change the voice, tone, and pace. Text-to-Speech (STT) where the AI-powered speech recognition enables students who struggle with writing or motor impairments to speak their answers and turn them into written text. Physical writing and typing are no longer necessary as a result.

2.5 Intelligent Tutoring Systems

Intelligent tutoring systems (ITS) (Lin et al., 2023). offer real-time, individualized advice and feedback, simulating one-on-one tuition. Using natural language processing (NLP), these systems can communicate with students to respond to inquiries, clarify ideas, or offer guidance when a student is having trouble. An AI instructor on a coding platform, for instance, may provide recommendations when a student types a mistaken line of code, helping them to repair it step-by-step. Improves student interest and comprehension by providing tailored assistance akin to that of a real instructor.

2.6 Emotional and Behavioural Perspectives

Many AI systems use sentiment analysis(Joel et al 2023), often known as emotional AI, to ascertain a student's emotional state during study sessions. This allows the system to adjust the learning path based on how frustrated, confused, or disengaged the student is. Example like to keep a student interested, the system may reduce the difficulty level, recommend a break, or provide encouraging feedback if they show signs of irritation (such as repeatedly giving the wrong answer). Benefit like improves students' emotional health and motivation, which leads to better learning opportunities.

2.7 Cooperation and Learning from Peers

AI systems can also give students opportunities to engage in collaborative learning based on their own learning preferences and needs. Through the evaluation of student data, the system can combine students who can benefit from working together because they are working at similar levels or have complementary talents. An AI system might, for example, recommend a peer study group to a student who is struggling to understand a concept that others have just mastered in order to promote group problem-solving. Benefit are like encourages social learning and peer interaction, two things that are essential for developing communication and collaborative skills.

2.8 Motivation and Gamification

In order to incentivize students according to their performance and engagement levels, AI systems can implement gamified components like leader boards, badges, and awards. These components can be changed to accommodate unique tastes or habits. As an illustration, a student who thrives on difficulties can be inspired by levelling up or receiving points for finishing challenging tests, but a student who need encouragement might be rewarded with badges for consistent advancement. Benefit are like makes studying more pleasurable and effective by raising student motivation and engagement.

2.9 Tracking Progress in Real Time

Dashboards with AI capabilities let teachers and students monitor progress in real time. Pupils are able to recognize their progress, pinpoint areas for improvement, and acknowledge their accomplishments. Teachers can then keep an eye on their students'

3. THE ROLE OF AI IN UNIVERSITY ASSESSMENTS

AI has brought numerous advantages to education, such as personalized feedback(Athinarayanan et al., 2024), streamlined grading, and large-scale data analysis. In online course evaluations, AI systems analyze student feedback to assess instructors, curricula, and overall course effectiveness. These evaluations are often crucial for tenure decisions, promotion reviews, and funding allocation. While AI can provide efficiency and scalability, it is essential to ensure these systems operate fairly.

3.1 Bias in Online Course Evaluations

AI-driven systems may inherit biases from various sources, which can lead to skewed or unjust outcomes. Key sources of bias include the following like Historical Data Bias AI systems are trained on historical data, which may already contain biases related to gender, race, or other demographic factors as shown in Figure 2. For example, past evaluations might reflect societal prejudices, leading the AI to continue perpetuating unfair assessments.

Figure 2. Elements of Bias in Online Course Evaluations

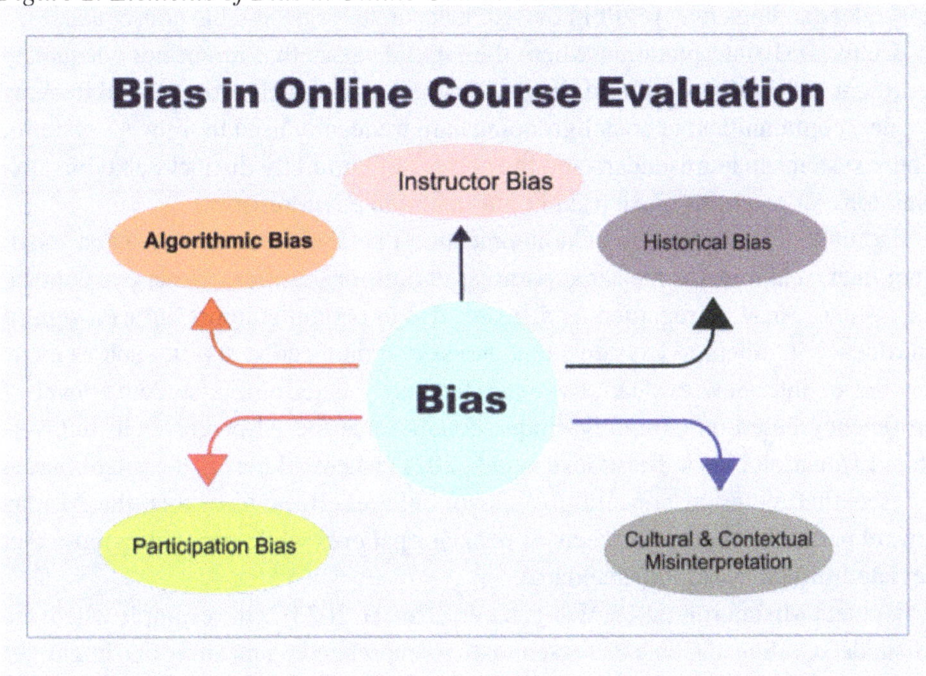

A visual representation of historical data bias in online course evaluations. The image shows a stack of digital data files, with a magnifying glass highlighting biased data points. The data is displayed as charts and graphs, where certain demographic groups are disproportionately represented with negative evaluations (red) compared to others (green). The background shows AI algorithms processing(Athinarayanan et al., 2024) these evaluations, with symbols of inequality like unbalanced scales. The overall tone conveys concern about fairness and bias in the data.

3.2 Cultural and Contextual Misinterpretation

Online students come from diverse cultural backgrounds, and their feedback may be misinterpreted by AI models not designed to account for these variations. Terms and expressions may carry different meanings in different cultures, leading to inaccurate assessments. In AI evaluation, cultural and contextual misunderstanding describes situations in which AI systems are unable to comprehend or evaluate inputs correctly because of variations in cultural norms, practices, or contextual subtleties that the AI model does not adequately reflect or comprehend. In a variety of contexts, such as social media moderation, employment, healthcare, and education, these misunderstandings may result in biased, inaccurate, or unsuitable consequences.

Cultural Misinterpretation where the large datasets that might not adequately represent the variety of cultural customs, languages, and behaviours found in many locales, communities, or social groupings are frequently used to train AI systems. These systems may misunderstand the context of culturally distinct behaviors, expressions, or reactions when used in multicultural environments.

Example in Language and Communication like distinct cultures may have distinct interpretations for the same phrases, idioms, or gestures. Direct eye contact, for instance, may be regarded as disrespectful in certain cultures but as a sign of confidence in others. AI systems that assess communication styles, such as essay scoring or interview evaluations, may incorrectly determine a student's level of proficiency based on culturally unique conduct that the AI perceives as unfavorable. Evaluation Metric Bias(Gezici et al., 2021) where AI may make use of biased datasets that represent prevailing values or cultures. Because of this, the AI may reward particular thought, speech, or behavior patterns while penalizing those that deviate from other cultural standards.

Context Misinterpretation(Wang, R., & Zhan, H. 2023) is the example where the Misunderstanding of Context is essential for comprehending meaning and intent, yet AI systems may find it difficult to take it into consideration. Context misinterpretation happens when an AI evaluates input without taking into account the environment, social dynamics, or surrounding situations, which results in incorrect conclusions or judgments. Example in Social Behavior are the AI systems that are meant to assess emotional or social intelligence may misunderstand context-dependent behaviors like irony, sarcasm, or humor. For instance, a joke or a way to vent displeasure could be considered improper in one situation but totally acceptable in another. Local Contexts in Education where Students from various geographical locations may approach problem-solving in a way that is representative of their cultural backgrounds or local experiences in an educational setting. Even though a student's comments might be appropriate in their cultural or regional context, AI systems that fail to take this context into consideration may mark them as inaccurate or irrelevant.

3.3. Algorithmic Bias

The possibility of biased results when utilizing AI-based systems to assess students' academic achievement or associated activities in an educational setting is known as algorithmic bias in AI assessment evaluation in universities. For a variety of assessment-related tasks, such as grading, admissions, learning analytics, and even individualized education, universities are depending more and more on AI systems. But if fairness isn't properly considered, these AI systems may reinforce prejudices that disproportionately impact particular student groups, producing unfair results. The algorithms themselves can introduce bias based on how they are designed. If AI systems prioritize certain kinds of feedback (e.g., negative comments or specific phrases), they may over represent certain perspectives while underrepresenting others.

3.3.1 Important Elements of Algorithmic Bias in University AI Assessments

Training Data Bias that the Historical Academic Performance by giving preference to some student groups over others, an AI system trained on data reflecting historical disparities (such as performance data from kids who had access to greater resources) may reinforce existing prejudices. Demographic Disparities(Omar, M et al., 2025) where the AI system may perform better for students from majority groups if the data used to train AI models for academic assessment is not representative of the diversity of the student body. This could result in biased assessments for underrepresented groups (such as women in STEM fields or members of racial minorities). Bias in Grading Schemes where the Automated Essay Grading works on the AI programs that score written assignments automatically could give preference to particular linguistic patterns, cultural allusions, or writing styles that fit the dominant group. For example, if the AI is prejudiced toward particular linguistic standards, pupils from diverse cultural backgrounds or non-native speakers of a language may obtain poorer grades. Similarly the Subjective Evaluation that the AI systems may unintentionally benefit students from specific backgrounds or educational institutions that conform to historical standards when they are employed for subjective evaluations, such as assessing originality, participation, or presentations.

Admissions AI Bias where the AI systems rely on historical data that reflects current inequities (such as socioeconomic background or standardized test scores), they may be prejudiced when predicting student success for admissions choices. Students from affluent families may receive unfair advantages as a result, which could distort the results of university admissions. Standardized Test Results that the exams are frequently criticized for favoring students from higher socioeconomic backgrounds, AI systems that use them to determine admissions may reinforce bias.

Learning Analytics Bias(Uttamchandani, S., & Quick, J. 2022) where the students who follow conventional learning techniques may be given preference by AI systems that monitor their progress and offer suggestions. If the system does not acknowledge varied learning styles, students with different learning requirements or approaches may be at a disadvantage. Personalized Feedback for the Learning styles, cultural backgrounds, and resource accessibility may not be taken into consideration by systems intended to provide tailored feedback. As a result, biased data may be used to provide some students with less helpful feedback or guidance.

Predictive Student Success Models with Bias of the AI is occasionally used by universities to forecast which students are most likely to drop out. These models may disproportionately identify minority or low-income pupils if they are based on skewed historical data (such as socioeconomic characteristics), which could result in initiatives that stigmatize particular groups or limit their chances. Academic Intervention are the Disparities in educational achievements can be sustained when predictive algorithms that use biased data to trigger academic support services either over-intervene with some groups or under-serve others.

Automated Proctoring Bias(Yoder-Himes et al., 2022) where the problems with Facial Recognition. Racial and gender biases may be present in AI-based proctoring systems, which are being utilized more and more in online tests, particularly in facial recognition software. Students with darker skin tones may not be correctly detected by these systems, which could result in unjustified charges of cheating or technical issues during tests. Disability Discrimination where the automated proctoring systems' algorithms do not take into consideration the variety of physical or cognitive variations in how students use technology during tests, they may also be unable to accommodate students with impairments.

3.3.2 Algorithmic Bias's Effects on University AI Assessments Include Unfair Grading

Certain student groups may receive unduly low grades as a result of bias in AI grading systems, especially those from non-dominant linguistic or cultural backgrounds. Students' academic achievement and their chances of receiving scholarships, internships, or continuing their education may be impacted by this. Disparate Admissions preferentially favoring students from affluent backgrounds, biased AI admissions algorithms have the potential to worsen already-existing disparities and reduce diversity in the student body. This can restrict access for underrepresented groups and maintain systemic educational disparities.

Inequities in Learning when AI systems exclusively support specific learning styles or give biased feedback, students who don't follow the system's recommended method may find it difficult to keep up. This may lead to unequal access to scholarly materials. Stereotype Reinforcement (G. Manikandan et al., 2023) where the predictive models that incorrectly identify particular groups as being at risk—such as students from particular racial or socioeconomic backgrounds—can stigmatize students and promote unfavorable preconceptions, which may cause disengagement or dropout. Privacy Issues and Mental Health also Biased automated proctoring systems can put students under unnecessary stress, particularly if they are mistakenly marked for suspicious behavior or have technological difficulties because of biases in facial recognition. Students' mental health may suffer as a result, and privacy issues may arise.

3.3.3. Utilize Representative and Diverse Training Data to Reduce Algorithmic Bias in AI Evaluation at Universities

Make ensuring that a varied range of student demographics, learning preferences, and cultural backgrounds are represented in the data utilized to train AI systems for evaluation. This can lessen the possibility that one group will be disproportionately favored over another by the AI system. Fairness-Conscious AI Systems(Jin et al., 2023) that put into practice fairness-aware algorithms that minimize discriminatory impact and account for demographic parity. By ensuring that AI systems operate fairly across various student populations, these algorithms can lessen the likelihood of biased results in admissions, grading, and other evaluations.

AI that is transparent and explicable make sure AI evaluation systems produce outcomes that are easy for teachers and students to understand and can be interpreted. This can assist in detecting biases and enabling human involvement when required, particularly when the AI system's judgments appear unjust or problematic. Fairness metrics and bias audits make that AI systems used for evaluation are equitable for all groups by conducting routine bias audits. Incorporate fairness indicators into AI system evaluations to track student success across various ethnicities, socioeconomic backgrounds, and learning styles.

Human Monitoring and Assistance that the AI-powered evaluation tools must always be used in tandem with human supervision. Teachers should be able to examine grades, predictions, or feedback produced by AI and take action if they see bias or mistakes in the assessment. Practices for Inclusive Design where the involve a range of stakeholders in the planning, creation, and testing of AI evaluation tools. To guarantee that the AI system is created to satisfy the demands of every student, this group consists of educators, students from various backgrounds, and specialists in justice and ethics. Disabilities accommodations make sure AI systems are made to accommodate students with disabilities, particularly those utilized for proctoring or tailored learning. This involves making certain that systems for behavior analysis and facial recognition are trained on a variety of data and are able to take into account for a range of physical and cognitive differences.

Security and Privacy using AI assessment tools, give students' privacy and data protection top priority. Students should be able to choose not to participate in AI-driven tests if they have privacy or fairness concerns, and clear regulations should be in place to guarantee that their academic and personal information is safeguarded. Stereotyping interpreting data in ways that support pre-existing biases in the dataset, AI systems devoid of cultural context may reinforce stereotypes. For instance, because AI links success to particular traits associated with the dominant culture, certain cultural experiences or educational backgrounds may be discounted in hiring algorithms.

Language models may not function as effectively in non-Western languages or dialects if they were predominantly trained on English data from Western contexts. This may cause culturally unique phrases, idioms, or tones to be misunderstood, which could impair sentiment analysis or language competence assessments. The diversity of the academic community, educational equity, and students' academic careers can all be significantly impacted by algorithmic bias in AI assessment evaluation in higher education. By utilizing a variety of datasets, implementing fairness-aware algorithms, and guaranteeing openness in AI-based decision-making, universities may proactively address potential biases in AI systems. Universities can reduce the possibility of prejudice and guarantee that AI technologies are applied to improve educational fairness rather than impede it by putting protections in place and maintaining human monitoring.

3.4 Participation Bias

Online evaluations often suffer from voluntary response bias, where only a subset of students participates. If certain groups of students (e.g., those who are more engaged or those with stronger opinions) are more likely to complete evaluations, AI-driven systems may produce results that do not accurately reflect the full student body. The distortion that occurs when the sample of individuals assessing or interacting with an AI system is not representative of the larger population for which the AI system is designed is known as participation bias in AI evaluation. This may distort the evaluation's findings, making it challenging to gauge how well the AI functions in practical situations. Participation bias in the context of AI might arise for a number of reasons.

Non-representative User Groups where the results could overstate or underestimate the AI's effectiveness if the people assessing it don't represent the variety of the system's real users (for example, in terms of demographics, location, or technical proficiency). Voluntary Participation that the people who have more strong views (whether favorable or unfavorable) regarding AI are more likely to take part in an AI evaluation, whereas people who are less involved or more neutral may choose not to. This may result in a skewed perception of system efficacy or user happiness.

Demographic Skew(Vettleson-Trutza et al., 2023) where AI systems may be optimized for a certain age group, gender, socioeconomic class, or cultural background at the expense of other groups if the evaluators are primarily from that group. For instance, an AI may function effectively for youthful, tech-savvy users but poorly for elderly or less tech-savvy people if it is evaluated mostly on these users. Geographical or Cultural Bias where the AI systems tested by individuals from a certain area or culture could not translate effectively to users from other countries. Bias may be introduced into the appraisal process by linguistic, social, or internet-based differences.

Self-Selection of Participants that the people who are more tech-savvy or who have particular expectations about AI systems may be more inclined to take part in user studies or crowdsourced reviews. This biases the findings in favor of some user types while ignoring others who would find the system unusable or challenging. Platform-Specific Bias that the users of particular platforms (such as smartphones, particular software environments, etc.) may not accurately reflect the entire spectrum of users who will eventually use the AI system when it is tested on those platforms. As a result, assessments may not accurately reflect usability across settings and devices.

Implications of Participation Bias in AI Assessment that the Overestimation or Underestimation of Performance. Because AI systems are only tested on a limited set of users, they may appear more precise, quick, or user-friendly than they actually are Bias Amplification that when an AI model is trained on non-representative data and then assessed by a similarly biased group of participants, participation bias can intensify preexisting biases in AI systems. Lack of Generalizability that the AI systems tested in biased environments might not function well in real-world situations involving a wider range of users.

Reducing Participation Bias which used to guarantee a representative assessment, actively seek out participants with a range of demographics, geographic locations, technical specialties, and socioeconomic backgrounds. Stratified Sampling Techniques(Pandey, K. K., & Shukla, D. 2020) that guarantee that various demographic groups are fairly represented during the assessment process, employ stratified sampling techniques. Paying for Voluntary Bias which make sure that evaluation techniques are available to all user types and promote or reward involvement from underrepresented groups. Post-Adjustment which use statistical methods to correct for sample biases that are known to exist, such as giving underrepresented groups a higher weight in the final assessment. Longitudinal Studies fully capture the range of user interactions and performance outcomes, conduct long-term evaluations across different locations, user bases, and situations.

3.5 Instructor Bias

Gender, race, and other attributes of instructors may affect student evaluations. Studies have shown that women and minority faculty members often receive lower evaluations than their counterparts, despite comparable teaching performance. AI systems trained on such biased evaluations risk reinforcing these disparities. The impact that evaluators or instructors—those who direct, carry out, or oversee the assessment process—may have on the results of an AI system's performance testing is known as instructor bias in AI evaluations. This kind of bias occurs when an AI model's evaluation or presentation is inadvertently (or occasionally purposefully) influenced by the preferences, expectations, or subjective assessments of teachers. The evaluation findings may be skewed by instructor bias, which could distort how well the AI system performs in real-world scenarios.

3.4.1. Reasons for Instructor Bias in AI Assessments

Subjective Interpretation of outcomes where the teachers may interpret unclear outcomes in ways that support their preconceived notions or expectations about how well the AI system is performing. As a result, some aspects of the AI's output may be overrated or underrated. Leading Instructions or Questions that in an AI evaluation, the way an instructor presents tasks, questions, or instructions to participants might influence their answers or choices in ways that favor particular results. Leading instructions, for instance, may gently encourage participants to concentrate on particular features of an AI system, producing biased feedback.

Confirmation Bias that the teachers who have high expectations for the AI system's performance may unintentionally look for or highlight data that confirms their expectations while downplaying or disregarding contradicting data. Instructor Bias's Effects where the False Performance Measures of the instructor bias can produce erroneous performance data, developers and stakeholders may conclude that an AI system is more dependable or effective than it actually is. Overfitting to Instructor Expectations that the AI systems are assessed via a biased lens, they may be excessively adjusted to satisfy the instructors' tastes or expectations, which can lead to models that are not very generalizable to larger user bases. Biased Model Development when evaluations are influenced by instructor bias, developers may receive biased feedback, which causes them to modify models to accommodate biased assessments rather than fixing actual system flaws. Persistence of Bias in AI Models that if an instructor's prejudices coincide with cultural or societal norms, the assessment procedure may strengthen these prejudices, thus leading to detrimental outcomes.

3.4.2.Instances of Instructor Bias in AI Assessment

Bias of Humans in the Loop where the decisions made by instructors over when to step in might generate bias in systems where they guide or intervene during the evaluation (e.g., reinforcement learning with human oversight). To artificially improve the AI's apparent performance, they might, for instance, only step in when the system is about to make a mistake. Bias in Ground Truth where during training or assessment, instructors are crucial in determining the "ground truth" or right responses. System development and evaluation outcomes may be skewed if its labeling or judgment is biased (for instance, in sentiment analysis or picture classification tasks).

Cultural Assumptions in Task Design(Matthiesen, S., & Nelius, T. 2018) where the teachers may create assessment items that represent their own cultural standards, but they may not be broadly applicable. Reducing Instructor Prejudice in AI Assessments to standardization of Protocols for Evaluation. Provide standardized, objective, and transparent evaluation processes that restrict room for teachers' subjective interpretations. This could use formal feedback forms, pre-established parameters, and, if practical, blind evaluations. Varied Evaluation Teams likelihood of individual biases affecting the evaluation can be decreased by assembling a varied group of instructors and assessors. Diversity in background, gender, culture, and technical proficiency can contribute to the assessment process by bringing a variety of viewpoints.

Blind Testing means that whenever possible, carry out double-blind assessments in which participants and instructors are not aware of important information that can induce bias (e.g., the expected outcome or the origin of the AI system). This lessens the possibility of prejudice stemming from stereotypes. Automated and Objective measures done in situations where subjective judgment may generate bias, use automated, objective measures to augment human evaluations. These measurements can offer a more trustworthy standard by which human assessments can be evaluated. Transparency and Documentation will use to promote openness in the assessment procedure by keeping records of all judgments, interpretations, and departures from accepted evaluation practices. This improves accountability and enables a more in-depth examination of any biases.

Several teachers in the assessment procedure and contrasting their evaluations can assist in spotting discrepancies and possible prejudices. Analyzing evaluation discrepancies can help identify potential sources of bias. The perceived fairness and performance of AI systems can be significantly impacted by constructor bias in AI evaluations. Recognizing and reducing this kind of prejudice is crucial to ensuring more accurate, trustworthy, and equitable assessments. AI researchers and developers may reduce the impact of instructor bias and create more reliable AI systems by employing objective criteria, standardizing review procedures, and enlisting diverse evaluation panels.

4. PROCTORING AND SECURITY

In order to preserve the integrity of exams, the growth of online learning has made the creation of advanced AI-driven proctoring systems (Muncey et al.,2024). necessary. These platforms use cutting-edge technology to establish a safe evaluation setting. Webcams and microphones are used by the proctoring software to track students' movements during an exam in real time. The AI systems are made to identify a range of actions that might be signs of cheating. To make sure students are concentrating on their screens and not looking at unapproved materials or getting outside help, for instance, the technology tracks eye movements. The AI has the ability to send out a warning for additional research if it detects excessive glancing away from the computer.

Another important consideration is background noise; the program can identify sounds that indicate another person is in the room. Conversations, rustling papers, or even noises from non-exam technological gadgets could fall under this category. This kind of oversight helps guarantee that the test is administered in a way that reduces the possibility of cheating.

Key features of AI-based proctoring tools are Facial Recognition. How Facial Recognition Operates matches the test-taker's face with the photo ID they provided at registration using AI algorithms to confirm their identity. It assures that the registered student is the one taking the test and helps avoid impersonation. Behaviour Analysis Operates is it throughout the test, AI keeps track of the test-taker's motions and looks for patterns that could indicate cheating, including frequent head movements or frequent looks away from the screen. Its significance is it recognizes questionable actions that might point to unethical behaviour.

Behavioural Analysis(Sivakumaran, et al., 2024) in Recruitment and Hiring Based on patterns, interactions, and answers, artificial intelligence (AI) systems are used to assess individuals' behavioral characteristics(Selvi et al., 2024) and forecast their fit for particular job jobs. HireVue is AI-powered tool analyzes video interviews by looking at body language, speech patterns, tone of voice, and facial expressions. It is able to identify emotional stability, excitement, and stress levels. Skeeled is used to assists recruiters with determining whether a prospect is compatible with the corporate culture by analyzing behavioral(Joel et al., 2024) and personality features during interviews.

Screen Monitoring Operates is it captures the test-taker's screen activity during the exam, frequently taking screenshots or video recordings. Its significance is it prevents accessing other websites or using illegal materials while taking the test. Audio Monitoring Operates is it uses the microphone on the device to listen for conversations or background sounds that can point to cheating or collusion. Its significance is it assists in maintaining a peaceful and unaided testing environment.

Browser Lockdown Operates is it limits the test-taker's ability to leave the exam interface, frequently by preventing access to other websites and programs. Its significance is it lowers the possibility of utilizing unapproved resources or asking for outside assistance.

Post-Exam Analytics Operates is the proctoring technology creates reports following the test that contain metrics on test-taker behavior, including the amount of time spent on questions, the frequency of the student's eye movements, and incidents that were reported. Its importance is it gives teachers information on the integrity and engagement of their students, allowing them to make well-informed decisions regarding the legitimacy of exams.

5. RELATED APPLICATIONS AND SERVICES

5.1 Respondus Monitor

Developed to improve the integrity of online tests, Respondus Monitor is a popular online proctoring tool. When used with the Respondus LockDown Browser, it gives pupils a safe testing environment. Here is a detailed examination of its attributes, capabilities, and factors. Respondus Monitor records students using a webcam and analyzes their behavior during the test, enabling institutions to administer safe online exams. It is mostly employed in higher education environments to guard against cheating and guarantee that tests are administered equitably. Respondus Monitor's primary features include integration with the LockDown browser(Ruzgar, N. S., & Chua-Chow, C. 2023).

Figure 3. Elements of Behavioural Analysis

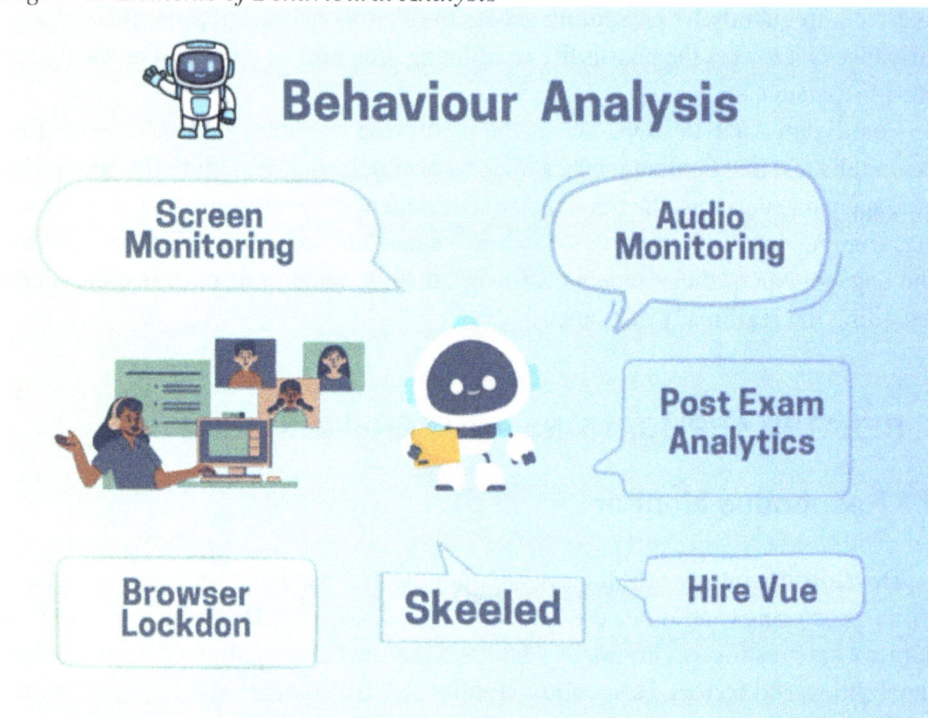

Secure Environment where the LockDown Browser, which is necessary to use Respondus Monitor, shuts down the testing environment by prohibiting access to other programs and websites while the test is being administered. Improved Security is a combination makes it more difficult for students to obtain unapproved resources or get aid during tests. Webcam Monitoring is a spot any possible instances of cheating, the application records the test-taker's face and surroundings on camera as they complete the exam. Storage and Access is the test, instructors can check the recordings, which are safely kept. Figure 3 explained about the Behavioural Analysis. Analysis of Behavior to AI Flagging that the system makes use of artificial intelligence to identify odd behavior, such turning away from the screen, moving out of the camera's field of vision, or having other persons in the room. Incident Reports is that the following the test, teachers get a report outlining any occurrences that were flagged. These can be examined for possible infractions of exam integrity. Verification of Identity Photo ID Requirement before beginning the test, students must show a valid photo ID, which will be compared to their profile picture. Facial Recognition that the throughout the test, the system can verify the test-taker's identity by using facial recognition technology. Customizable Settings where the teachers have the ability to alter the parameters for every test, including the degree of surveillance, the duration of the video, and the particular actions to report. Features of Respondus Monitor like User-Friendly Interface with clear instructions on how to set up and take tests, the platform is made to be easy to use for both students and teachers. Respondus Monitor's smooth integration with well-known learning management systems (LMS) such as Canvas, Blackboard, and Moodle makes it simple to administer and access online tests.

Support Materials is to assist instructors and students in navigating the proctoring process, Respondus provides a number of materials, such as manuals and video tutorials. Respondus Monitor Privacy and Data Security Considerations. Data protection is an organizations need to make sure that privacy laws, such as FERPA(Parks, C. 2017), are followed and let students know how their data will be handled and kept safe. Recording Awareness where in order to allay any privacy concerns, students should be made aware of the recording procedure and the goal of the monitoring. Technical specifications and System Compatibility where the students must confirm that their gadgets have the required technological features, such as a webcam, microphone, and dependable internet access.

Pre-Exam Checks is to find any possible problems, it is helpful for students to run system checks before the test. Cost means Pricing Structure where the depending on the number of users and the institution's licensing agreements, Respondus Monitor may have different prices. Institutions ought to weigh the advantages of preserving exam integrity against this expense. Experience of the User relay on Possible Stress where some students may become more anxious due to the monitoring component of proctoring. Institutions ought to offer assistance and process assurance.

Accessibility is based on consideration for All Students. Respondus Monitor is a strong solution for online proctoring, effectively combining the security of the LockDown Browser with sophisticated monitoring features. It allows institutions to uphold academic integrity in remote assessments while providing a user-friendly experience. However, attention to privacy, technical requirements, and accessibility is crucial to ensure a fair and supportive environment for all students. Familiarization providing practice exams or mock proctoring sessions can help students become comfortable with the technology and process.

5.2 ExamSoft

ExamSoft provides tools for creating, administering, and grading exams in a secure environment. It is particularly popular in professional schools, such as law, medical, and nursing programs, due to its robust security measures and detailed analytics. The Key Features of ExamSoft are Secure Exam Delivery like Lockdown Browser where the ExamSoft uses a secure exam environment that restricts access to other applications, websites, and functions on the test-taker's device during an exam. Offline Capabilities: Exams can be downloaded and completed offline, which is beneficial for students with unstable internet connections.

Comprehensive Exam Creation where the instructors can create a library of questions and organize them by subject, difficulty, and other criteria. Variety of Question Types can supports multiple-choice, essay, and performance-based questions, allowing for diverse assessment formats. Options for Proctoring where the ExamSoft can be set up with proctoring tools that keep an eye on students' conduct during tests, albeit they might not have as much real-time monitoring as some specialized proctoring programs. Integration with Third-Party Proctoring for improved monitoring capabilities, educational institutions can combine ExamSoft with other proctoring programs.

Strong Reporting and Analytics where the ExamSoft offers thorough insights on item analysis, exam statistics, and student performance following tests. Teachers can use data analysis to spot patterns and areas that need work. Feedback Mechanism where it enables teachers to comment on each student's performance as well as on specific questions. User-Friendly Interface with easy-to-follow directions for administering and participating in exams, the platform is made to be user-friendly for both teachers and students. Assistance and Instruction Extensive Resources to assist institutions in successfully implementing and utilizing the platform, ExamSoft provides a variety of training materials, webinars, and customer assistance. ExamSoft's ability to link with well-known learning management system (LMS) platforms(Bradley, V. M. 2021) makes it possible for data sharing and exam administration to run smoothly. Accessibility features, such as longer time and alternate formats, are intended to accommodate students with disabilities.

Customizable Options where the teachers have the ability to alter the time limitations, proctoring choices, and grading standards for every exam. ExamSoft Privacy and Data Security Considerations. Regulation Compliance where the Organizations need to make sure they abide by data protection rules (like FERPA) and let students know exactly how their data will be used. Data Storage and Access where the ExamSoft employs safe data storage procedures, yet trust-building requires openness about data use. Technical specifications like

Device Compatibility. In order to operate the ExamSoft program, students must make sure their devices fulfill the required technical criteria. online connectivity where there are offline options, downloading tests and posting finished assessments require a steady online connection. Price for the device meant for fees for licensing. The size and requirements of the institution can affect the pricing structure. Institutions ought to weigh the costs of using the platform against its advantages.

User Experience also means of Stress Management. Institutions should take into account how the exam style may impact students' anxiety and offer support resources, even though secure testing is crucial. Student training: Providing mock tests and orientation sessions might help students get comfortable with the platform and feel less nervous on test day. Accessibility where the Organizations need to make that ExamSoft complies with accessibility guidelines and provide the required modifications to students who need them. ExamSoft is an effective tool for educational institutions wishing to administer safe online tests and obtain insightful data about student performance. It is especially well-suited for professional education settings because of its user-friendly interface, analytics capabilities, and security measures. However, to create a fair and efficient assessment experience, careful consideration of privacy, technical needs, and accessibility is essential.

6. CHALLENGES FACED IN USING AI PROCTORING TOOLS IN EDUCATIONAL INSTITUTIONS

To guarantee the integrity of online tests, educational institutions frequently use online proctoring systems like ExamSoft and Respondus Monitor. Both platforms, however, have a lot of problems, especially when it comes to privacy, fairness, and technical difficulties that can impact both teachers and students. The following are some of the main issues these tools face. Proctoring Algorithmic Bias where the problems with Face Recognition ExamSoft and Respondus Monitor employ AI to track students' eye movements and facial recognition. But when it comes to women, people with darker skin tones, and other underrepresented groups, facial recognition algorithms frequently do poorly. As shown in Figure 4, Challenges faced in using ai proctoring tools in Educational Institutions are explained one by one. This may result in unfair sanctions due to improper flagging or failing to identify students. Cultural and Physical Differences is the Bias in these systems is further highlighted by the possibility that students from diverse cultural backgrounds or with particular physical traits (such as wearing religious clothing like hijabs) could be mistakenly tagged for "suspicious" conduct or as unrecognized.

Figure 4. Challenges faced in using ai proctoring tools in Educational Institutions

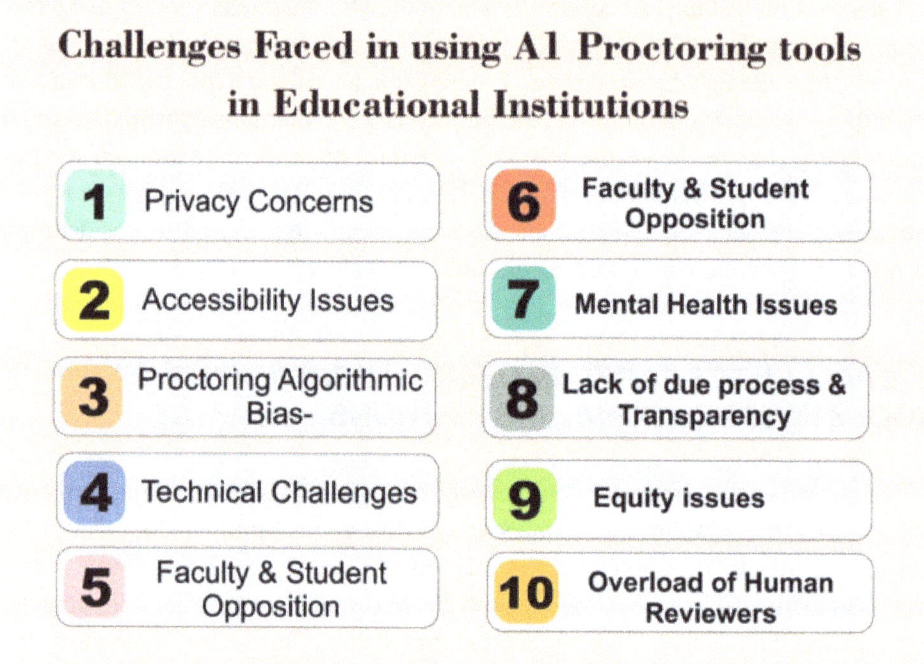

6.1. False Positive Results

Unusual Movements where the artificial intelligence (AI) technologies in these tools are made to recognize odd behaviors or movements that could be signs of cheating. Students with disabilities, those who fidget, or those who need adjustments (such extra time or helpful technology) can be mistakenly detected, which would be stressful and necessitate human review. Environmental Factors where the algorithm may mistakenly alert students for anomalies like several people in the frame or poor camera visibility if they take tests in less-than-ideal settings (such as shared places, dim lighting, or inadequate bandwidth).

6.2. Privacy Concerns

Data collection and surveillance where the Respondus Monitor and ExamSoft's level of surveillance, which includes ongoing audio and video recording, keystroke tracking, and data collecting on personal devices, frequently makes students uneasy. Concerns about data privacy may arise from this feeling of intrusion, particularly in relation to the duration of data storage and the individuals who have access to it.

Privacy of the Home Environment where Access to students' cameras and microphones is necessary for proctoring systems, which may encroach on their privacy. Some students might not have a suitable private area to take the exam without interruptions or privacy concerns,(Kovba et al.,2024) and others could feel uneasy about being watched in their homes.

6.3. Accessibility Issues

Providing for Students with Disabilities The fact that both systems are less accessible to students with impairments has drawn criticism. Strict proctoring criteria, such keeping eye contact with the computer or remaining still for extended periods of time, may be challenging for students with physical disabilities, learning disabilities, or mental health issues to meet. Although certain accommodations, such as additional time, can be manually entered, many students believe that the systems do not sufficiently take into account their particular needs or circumstances, and that the default settings may penalize them for actions that stem from their disability.

6.4.Technical Challenges

Stable internet connections are necessary for Respondus Monitor and ExamSoft to work properly. Exams may be invalidated or marked for review if students in remote locations or those with inadequate internet connectivity encounter lags, dropped video feeds, or disconnections. These platforms do not support every device or operating system. For example, during tests, certain students may encounter lags, crashes, or incompatibilities if they are utilizing outdated devices or less popular operating systems. For students who do not have access to more recent technologies, this results in an unfair testing atmosphere.

6.5. Stress and Issues with Mental Health

According to numerous students, these instruments' stringent behavioral monitoring (Destefani et al.,2024). and surveillance greatly raise their anxiety levels during tests. It can be mentally exhausting for children to know that every step they make is being monitored, particularly if they already experience test anxiety or other mental health issues. Students may perform worse on tests or become less focused as a result of the fear of being wrongly accused of cheating because of AI flagging and the knowledge that every action is being observed.

6.6. Lack of Due Process and Transparency

Imprecise AI Decision-Making Students and teachers frequently lack a thorough understanding of how Respondus Monitor's or ExamSoft's AI algorithms decide which conduct to identify as suspicious. Students find it challenging to refute claims of cheating because of this lack of openness, particularly if they are unaware of the reasons for their initial warning.

Even while flagged occurrences are frequently reviewed by human reviewers, the process can be sluggish and uneven, leaving students unsure if their actions will result in disciplinary action. Students sometimes complain that they were punished without being given a thorough explanation or a chance to appeal.

6.7. Equity Issues

Students from lower-income families could not have access to fast internet connections, quiet, private areas, or high-quality cameras, which could result in unfair exam flagging. Students who have fewer resources confront more difficulties as a result of these unfair circumstances. AI systems are ill-prepared to manage the differences in living conditions experienced by some students, who reside in multi-person families or other settings where disruptions are unavoidable. Technical issues could cause these pupils to get undeserved punishments that are out of proportion to their academic performance.

6.8. Faculty and Student Opposition

Concerns have been raised by certain academics regarding the moral ramifications of employing AI-based proctoring systems, specifically with regard to student autonomy, privacy, and mental health. To get around these problems, teachers frequently choose to employ different assessment techniques. Concerns about privacy, fairness, and the additional stress of being continuously monitored have led to student protests against Respondus Monitor and ExamSoft in numerous colleges. There have been lawsuits or petitions against certain colleges urging them to stop using these proctoring technologies.

6.9. Overload of Human Reviewers

The number of cases that human reviewers must look into may be too much for them to handle because AI algorithms frequently flag many incidents as possibly suspicious. Exam results may be delayed as a result, reviews may be inconsistent, and there may even be a higher chance of unfounded charges of cheating. ExamSoft and Respondus Monitor provide useful resources for upholding academic integrity in online tests, but they also pose serious problems with regard to equity, privacy, bias, and technical difficulties. Universities must carefully analyze these issues, think about taking steps to reduce the dangers, and investigate alternate evaluation techniques that support equity and the welfare of students.

7. OVERVIEW OF THE PROPOSED SYSTEM

7.1. Human Supervision and Hybrid Proctoring

The system reviews identified instances by combining real-time human proctors with AI-based monitoring, rather than depending solely on AI. In order to reduce prejudice and false positives, AI would help by automating repetitive jobs (such identifying odd behaviors) while allowing human intervention to analyze and evaluate flagged behaviors. During tests, students would be able to interact with proctors in real time, which would enable them to explain any interruptions (such as technological difficulties or a child entering the room) and prevent needless flagging.

7.2. AI Fairness Algorithms for Reducing Bias

To reduce performance gaps across various demographic groups, the system would make use of fairness-aware AI algorithms. The problem of facial recognition bias and other types of algorithmic bias would be addressed by training these algorithms on diverse datasets that comprise students from a range of racial, ethnic, gender, and socioeconomic backgrounds. To make sure AI models don't unfairly flag kids from particular groups, the system would regularly evaluate them. This would entail looking for bias tendencies in the highlighted occurrences and modifying the algorithms accordingly.

7.3. AI Decision-Making That Is Transparent

The AI system would have models that could explain why some behaviors were deemed suspicious in an easy-to-understand manner. This would guarantee that decisions are just and comprehensible and enable students to contest flags based on clear criteria.

Students would be able to observe highlighted instances, the cause behind the flag, and the steps taken by human reviewers through a review site. Students would be able to challenge unjust accusations of cheating and gain more trust in the process thanks to this open method.

7.4. Design with Privacy in Mind

By collecting as little data as possible, the system would put privacy first. Instead of continuously monitoring during the exam, it would simply record the crucial information needed to guarantee exam integrity (such as brief video clips or pictures taken when situations that were highlighted). To guarantee that all recorded data is erased within a given time frame (such as 30 days following the test review), strict data deletion procedures would be in place. This would solve privacy issues and guarantee that pupils' private data isn't kept forever. If students feel uneasy about their personal devices being watched, they can choose to use secure testing facilities, which lessens the invasion of their privacy at home.

7.5. Enhancements in Equity and Accessibility

Students with disabilities would have the option to customize the system's settings. For instance, proctoring procedures would be customized for students who require accommodations (such as extra time or the use of assistive technology). Turning off specific behavioral tracking tools that would otherwise penalize children with disabilities is one way to do this. Various living situations would be supported by the system's architecture. To prevent unfair flagging, it would, for instance, enable students to identify possible distractions (such as roommates or family members present) prior to the start of the exam.

7.6. Strong Technical Framework

For students with inadequate internet connections, the system would provide a low-bandwidth mode. Instead of continuously streaming HD video, this would entail taking snapshots or smaller data packets. Additionally, it would lessen the possibility of disqualification by enabling students to continue the test in the event of brief internet interruptions. Students can utilize older or non-standard devices without encountering technical issues because the system is made to function flawlessly across a variety of devices and operating systems. Additionally, the platform would offer offline exam features that would synchronize with the restoration of internet access.

7.7. Alternate Methods of Assessment

Universities should use alternate assessment techniques that prioritize comprehension and learning over high-stakes tests in order to lessen their dependency on AI proctoring. Among the examples are Open-Book or Take-Home Exams these tests eliminate the need for rigorous proctoring by emphasizing critical thinking and problem-solving skills over memory. Projects give students the chance to show off their abilities and knowledge throughout time, giving teachers a more complete picture of their students' performance. To assess students, video conferences with human examiners can be used for oral exams or presentations. This eliminates the requirement for automated proctoring.

7.8. Students' Real-Time Support

Students who encounter technological issues during exams will have access to a dedicated, round-the-clock support staff through the system. This would guarantee that students who experience gadget malfunctions, internet problems, or other technological difficulties get help right away, avoiding punishment for uncontrollable conditions.

To make sure they meet the requirements, the system would ask students to perform a pre-exam check of their surroundings, internet connection, and device configuration before to the start of the exam. This lowers the possibility of technical issues during the test.

7.9. Human Review and Appeal Procedure

To make sure that suspicious behavior is not solely determined by AI-generated flags, human proctors or faculty would assess each highlighted incident. Context, including technical challenges or environmental factors, would be taken into consideration during the human review. Students could challenge any choices made by AI or human proctors through a formal appeal procedure. Students would have the chance to defend their behavior and offer more proof (such as a medical ailment or technical problem) that could have contributed to their behavior being reported, and the process would be transparent.

7.10. Integrity in Education

Students would be trained on the proctoring system, including how the AI functions, which behaviors are flagged, and how to steer clear of unneeded flags. Since students will know exactly what to expect on the test, this could help reduce anxiety and confusion. Universities should teach students about academic integrity and the value of honest work in addition to using proctoring technologies. The goal of this strategy is to promote an integrity-based culture (Ashalatha et al.,2024) which could lessen the need for intrusive proctoring techniques.

8. BENEFITS OF THE PROPOSED SYSTEM

All students would be treated equally regardless of their history or personal traits thanks to the system's implementation of fairness-aware AI algorithms, human monitoring, and frequent audits, which would lower the possibility of biased results. Students' fears about privacy could be allayed and their trust in the system increased by minimizing data gathering, enforcing stringent deletion regulations, and offering other assessment venues to students who are uneasy with home monitoring. Flexible accommodations for various living situations and locations that may be tailored for students with disabilities would guarantee that no student is unjustly disadvantaged because of their physical or personal circumstances.

By ensuring that students with limited resources or technical difficulties are not penalized, real-time technical help, low-bandwidth alternatives, and offline capabilities would create a more inclusive and dependable system. Explainable AI and an easy-to-use student review site would improve openness by enabling students to comprehend and challenge behaviors that have been highlighted, guaranteeing that the proctoring procedure is impartial and reliable. Students' academic performance and general well-being would improve as a result of the hybrid proctoring approach, real-time communication with proctors, and alternate assessment techniques.

9. CONCLUSION

AI-driven university assessments are becoming more and more common and can take many various shapes, depending on the assessment style, issue content, and institution strategy. The main feature of artificial intelligence in these assessments is its use to increase customisation, equality, and productivity. These systems use artificial intelligence (AI) algorithms to help with proctoring, grading, feedback providing, and personalised learning. An outline of how AI is changing university exams may be found here. Below is a summary of how they are typically performed. It will need a mix of technology advancements, regulatory changes, and alternative evaluation techniques to overcome the obstacles presented by the above services and Application Tools. The suggested solution below aims to preserve the integrity of online tests while addressing concerns about algorithmic bias, privacy, accessibility, and fairness.

REFERENCES

Ashalatha, K., & Narasimhulu, K. (2024). Enhancing concrete durability: Structural health monitoring of polypropylene fiber-reinforced concrete with accelerometer sensors. *E3S Web of Conferences, 591*, 09003.

Athinarayanan, S., Navaz, K., & Joel, M. R. (2024, January). Analysing various algorithms applied to Alzheimer's disease dataset to help the future generation. In *2024 International Conference on Intelligent and Innovative Technologies in Computing, Electrical and Electronics (IITCEE)* (pp. 1–5). IEEE.

Bradley, V. M. (2021). Learning management system (LMS) use with online instruction. *International Journal of Technology in Education*, *4*(1), 68–92.

Gezici, G., Lipani, A., Saygin, Y., & Yilmaz, E. (2021). Evaluation metrics for measuring bias in search engine results. *Information Retrieval Journal*, *24*, 85–113.

Jin, D., Wang, L., Zhang, H., Zheng, Y., Ding, W., Xia, F., & Pan, S. (2023). A survey on fairness-aware recommender systems. *Information Fusion*, *100*, 101906.

Joel, M. R., Ebenezer, V., Jeyaraj, K. A., Navaneethakrishnan, M., Arunadevi, R., & Jenifa, D. R. (2023, February). Decoding and analysing consumer feedback for companies and goods using machine learning. In *2023 Third International Conference on Artificial Intelligence and Smart Energy (ICAIS)* (pp. 1085–1091). IEEE.

Joel, M. R., Rajakumari, K., Priya, S. A., & Navaneethakrishnan, M. (2024). Big data classification using SpinalNet-Fuzzy-ResNeXt based on spark architecture with data mining approach. *Data & Knowledge Engineering*, *154*, 102364.

Lin, C. C., Huang, A. Y., & Lu, O. H. (2023). Artificial intelligence in intelligent tutoring systems toward sustainable education: A systematic review. *Smart Learning Environments*, *10*(1), 41.

Manikandan, G., Bhuvaneswari, G., & Joel, M. R. (2023). Artificial intelligence to the assessment, monitoring, and forecasting of drought in developing countries. In *2023 International Conference on Circuit Power and Computing Technologies (ICCPCT)* (pp. 886–892). IEEE. https://doi.org/DOI: 10.1109/ICCPCT58313.2023.10245072

Matthiesen, S., & Nelius, T. (2018). Managing assumptions during analysis-study on successful approaches of design engineers. In *DS 91: Proceedings of NordDesign 2018*, Linköping, Sweden, 14th–17th August 2018.

Omar, M., Sorin, V., Agbareia, R., Apakama, D. U., Soroush, A., Sakhuja, A., & Klang, E. (2025). Evaluating and addressing demographic disparities in medical large language models: A systematic review. *International Journal for Equity in Health, 24*(1), 57. PMID: 40011901

Pandey, K. K., & Shukla, D. (2020). Stratified sampling-based data reduction and categorization model for big data mining. In *Communication and Intelligent Systems* [Springer Singapore.]. *Proceedings of ICCIS, 2019*, 107–122.

Parks, C. (2017). Beyond compliance: Students and FERPA in the age of big data. *Journal of Intellectual Freedom & Privacy*, *2*(2), 23–33.

Ren, Y., Ruan, Y., Tan, X., Qin, T., Zhao, S., Zhao, Z., & Liu, T. Y. (2019). Fastspeech: Fast, robust and controllable text to speech. In *Advances in Neural Information Processing Systems, 32*.

Ruzgar, N. S., & Chua-Chow, C. (2023). Perception of students on online exams and how sequential exams and the lockdown browser affect student anxiety and performance. *WSEAS Transactions on Computer Research*, *11*, 92–110.

Selvi, R., Athinarayanan, S., Devi, V., Gobinath, M., & Shanthakumar, P. (2024). Combining neural and semantic features in the analysis of being supportive in online feedback from customers. *ITEGAM-JETIA*, *10*(48), 8–13.

Shaik, T., Tao, X., Li, Y., Dann, C., McDonald, J., Redmond, P., & Galligan, L. (2022). A review of the trends and challenges in adopting natural language processing methods for education feedback analysis. *IEEE Access : Practical Innovations, Open Solutions*, *10*, 56720–56739.

Sivakumaran, A. R., Shanthakumar, P., & Joel, M. R. (2024). IoMT-based smart intelligent healthcare system using optimization-driven deep residual network for brain tumor detection. *International Journal of Pattern Recognition and Artificial Intelligence*, *38*(15), 2457011.

Sriram, K. P., Sujatha, P. K., Athinarayanan, S., Kanimozhi, G., & Joel, M. R. (2024, July). Transforming agriculture: A synergistic approach integrating topology with artificial intelligence and machine learning for sustainable and data-driven practice. In *2024 2nd International Conference on Sustainable Computing and Smart Systems (ICSCSS)* (pp. 1350–1354). IEEE.

Uttamchandani, S., & Quick, J. (2022). An introduction to fairness, absence of bias, and equity in learning analytics. In *Handbook of Learning Analytics* (pp. 205–212).

Vettleson-Trutza, S., Yang, Y., Snyder, M., & Jazdzewski, D. (2023). B-138 Skewed demographics of patient population contributes to selection biases in clinical study population. *Clinical Chemistry*, *69*(Supplement_1), hvad097–472.

Wang, R., & Zhan, H. (2023). Deliberate misinterpretation from the perspective of socio-cognitive pragmatics. *Humanities & Social Sciences Communications*, *10*(1), 1–8.

Yoder-Himes, D. R., Asif, A., Kinney, K., Brandt, T. J., Cecil, R. E., Himes, P. R., & Ross, E. (2022, September). Racial, skin tone, and sex disparities in automated proctoring software. [). Frontiers Media SA.]. *Frontiers in Education*, *7*, 881449.

Chapter 5
Artificial Intelligence (AI)-Driven Content Curation and Microlearning:
Revolutionizing On-the-Go Learning in Modern Workplaces

Arpita Nayak
https://orcid.org/0000-0003-2911-0492
KIIT School of Liberal Studies, KIIT University, India

Ipsita Mohapatra
https://orcid.org/0009-0009-1867-519X
KIIT School of Liberal Studies, KIIT University, India

ABSTRACT

In today's fast-paced work environment, L&D teams face pressure to train employees within tight schedules. AI is automating content curation and implementing microlearning approaches to provide short, relevant, and easy-to-access learning resources. Smart content solutions gather information from various sources and evaluate it, relating it to the knowledge needed. They categorize content into microlearning sections, allowing for easy access and improved learning outcomes. This approach enhances focused adaptation and prolonged memory, allowing learners to improve their knowledge and skills in new market trends. AI-driven content curation and microlearning are a breakthrough in the L&D field, offering personalized learning progression for different levels of employees.

DOI: 10.4018/979-8-3373-6018-8.ch005

Copyright © 2026, IGI Global Scientific Publishing. Copying or distributing in print or electronic forms without written permission of IGI Global Scientific Publishing is prohibited.

I. INTRODUCTION

Owing to increased use of digital technologies and constantly changing requirements in the workplace, the organization learning and development L&D is changing at a fast pace. While previously individuals were supposed to update their knowledge and acquire new skills in order to perform a certain job, today's employees, in addition, have to undergo constant change that entails flexibility, tempo, and accuracy. Conventional training approaches, conventional training paradigms where training is typical accustomed to meetings at a fixed interval like regular workshops or certified courses (Alias & Razak, 2025).

AI has brought revolutionary changes in almost every field and learning and training at workplace and education is no exception. Using data processing and future analysis techniques, machine learning, and customization, AI provides organizations with the ability to offer better and more relevant training programs to employees. AI curation goes a step above that by sorting the information to determine which of the content is most helpful and credible for each consumer. Through an understanding of the learner's preferences, their roles within organizations, and past learning behaviors AI adapts the respective learning model. This helps employees to get exactly what they need whenever they need it so that the content is as timely and relevant as it can be not to mention the time factor (Omona,2024).

When integrating AI in the workplace learning process, it is more effective when paired with microlearning that involves the passaging of information in short, teachable moments. Microlearning caters to the fact that people cannot spend a lot of time and or attention at their workplace due to numerous challenges. Rather, microlearning allows student to access highly focused workshops that take anywhere between five to thirty minutes, or thereabout, to complete. When AI is added to the mix and makes microlearning its focus, a flexible and customised mobile learning platform that can be used anytime, anywhere, is developed with its effectiveness being amplified for workers to upskill and reskill in real time (Swargiary,2024).

People also spend more time interacting with their workplaces digitally, and have less attention spans and time for focused work. Recent studies has suggested that learner preferences today are in a direction of continuing learning approaches that enable the worker to learn skills and knowledge but not to be out of the work environment. Microlearning can be executed in this setting by offering short intensive learning breaks that are easily digestible into working hours. Since the tasks are designed in short modules with the focus on particular efficient skills, microlearning helps avoid an overload of information and lets learners get real value from the materials. Microlearning fits the workplace needs perfectly, as people at work do not have large chunks of time to devote to learning (Viterouli et al.,2024).

One of the major issues with microlearning is how to make every individual learning event truly meaningful for the learner at that given time. However, AI-voice based content aggregation is a boon during such time. AI can sift through volumes of data available from different sources including content on learner performance, history and the current job role, to provide learners with personalized content. Since content is adapted and improved continuously according to what is obtained from real-time feedback, AI serves to keep microlearning modules relevant to the learner's needs. Hence, it serves well as a learning content recommence system, whose main function is to deliver the right material on the specific topic that each employee needs to learn, at the right time, with no extraneous distractions and noise . The Global EdTech Market is expected to grow to USD 810.3 billion in the year 2033 – up from USD 220.5 billion in the year 2023, with a CAGR of 13.9% between 2023 and 2033. Looking at the data in 2023, North America led the capturing of the market with more than 37.3% of the total share and a revenue of 82.24 US billion dollars.When simplified, EdTech means embracing technology elements and tools used to improve and advance teaching and learning processes. Thus, EdTech breaks the silos of hardware and software and educational methodologies to provide better and learner-centric learning environments. Sub-sector of this sector includes web-based learning interface, virtual classes, web-based learning modules, digital text and knowledge enhancing applications where new mode of delivering education in an efficient way is beneficial as shown in fig 1.

Figure 1. Global Ed Tech Market, Size Deployment Mode, 2024-2033(USD Billion)

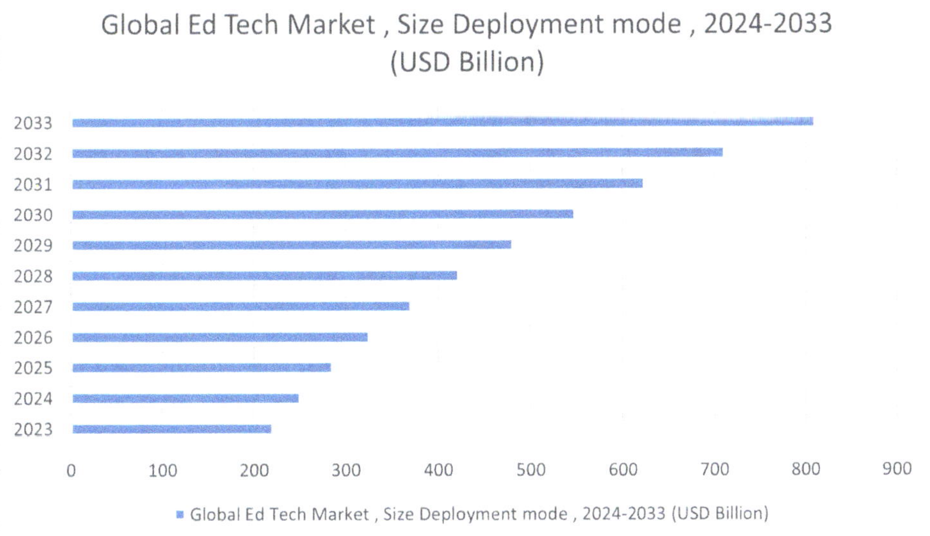

Source: https://market.us/report/edtech-market/

In today's world, when any learner is exposed to a flood of content available on the internet, it becomes extremely difficult to search for good quality and course relevant materials for learning. AI systems can help automate this process in the view to providing learners only with what they are interested in and based on organization goals and policies, up-to-date information only. This refined approach also brings about better learning effectiveness that is complemented by a concept of progressive learning championed by the organization as the employees are given the autonomy to manage their training needs (Carson,2017).

II. RESEARCH QUESTION

- How might AI assist with improving the microlearning delivered through concise content packages accessible in on-the-go mobile workplace environments?
- To what extent does the use of AI microlearning improve and enhance, the present-day employee engagement as well as their knowledge as well as skill training?

III. RESEARCH OBJECTIVES

- To assess the way AI can support the facilitation of relevant and engaging learning content to and for the needs, positions, and immediate requirements of the employee in a dynamic workplace.
- To assess the research question as to whether the implementation of the proposed AI-driven microlearning approach enhances learning outcomes such as employee engagement, learning and knowledge retention, and skills application across different organizations.

IV. REAL-TIME RELEVANT ASSESSMENT

In the modern world where information is easily available, content must be relevant and should be in concordance with organizational objectives and trends of the market. Standard practices of content selection for consumption can be helpful, but do not scale well to the constant shifts in knowledge, skill, and technology demands in different disciplines. This is where Artificial Intelligence (AI) and relevance as you go assessment come in to redesign how learning contents are selected and delivered. Specifically, AI real-time relevance evaluation with the help of sophisticated algorithms defines priorities of materials according to the current relevance to the needs of an organization and continuous changes in the field of industry. This way they not only guarantee that employees have the latest content of learning but also provide a sense of direction to learning for better prepared and more adaptive workforce (Vetrivel & Arun, 2024).

Credit calculation in real time is an AI-based process of categorizing what has been learned into how useful it will be to the learner and his or her organization at the time it is being learned. This approach involves compiling information about skill needs of the employees, trends within the industry and new organizational learning objectives to sort and suggest relevant material to learners. This particular method referred to as the relevance-oriented approach works as the response to the more conventional approach of mass customization of theoretical knowledge that are not suitable for the needs of professions in the modern, fast-growing fields. Machine learning techniques do relevance analysis of a large number of these elements, and compare the results with the content in the learning library in real time. Such data may encompass shift in job description, project demands, estimated performance of the employees, and emerging trends. Thus, by performing such evaluations on a constant basis, AI will not only determine what kind of content is most appropriate for use but also what learning materials may be useful in the upcoming period. It is always useful to predict these changes due to highly dynamic knowledge factors especially in information related fields such as information technology, medicine, finance and engineering (Porter & Grippa,2020).

ML helps the algorithm evolve with the use and choice history of the users so the algorithm can keep improving its results. Some of the key objectives of this approach are as follows: Learning behavior patterns are trends that based on which ML algorithms can self-develop what can be considered relevant content Implementing NLP enable AI systems to read and comprehend learning content in natural languages. This component is also prospective for the content scanning and indexing for without understanding of the context of a certain text, it would be challenging for the algorithm to describe the topics spreading through the available sources. To determine real-time relevance of content, NLP also helps the algorithm compare the content against the current trends and news within the industry to prioritise materials that are relevant to current trending topics or newly developed skills. Relevance at real time is calculated based on factors that include performance, project requirements, proficiency tests, and user reviews. These integrated approaches enable the connections between learner needs and the organisational objectives in order to align the suggested learning approaches and pipe content (Ahmed et al.,2024)

Real-time relevance assessment means that the learning that is recommended has to do with an employee's position, aspirations as well as the current tasks they are handling. With the help of the skills, learning history and performance data constantly evaluating an individual, AI offers meaningful and informative content. This approach saves much of the employees' time that could otherwise be spent on filtering learning content that is not useful immediately in their work as organizations grow, the requirements of their L&D change as well. Learnability and AI discourse enables relevance assessment to maintain the orientation of learning initiatives to such emerging goals through constant change of content relevance assessments to organisational changes. An example of such fields is technology and financial industries changing regularly by new regulation, innovations and market shifts. Through an AI relevance assessment, organizations maintain competitiveness because the staff is regularly updated on the latest information. It does this through routine use of Industry, Research Articles and News which the AI algorithm feeds into the work force focusing on Articles that depicts emerging trends in the markets and skills within the industry to keep the workforce as active as needed (Yusuf et al.,2024).

The prospect of AI-supported computation of real-time relevance is exciting for workplace learning; however, concerns arise. Data protection is one of those important concerns together with the power to understand the details of the algorithms that are giving recommendations, and fighting against possible prejudices. With the progress of AI, organisations have to counter these issues and optimise the results of relevance assessment as well as develop the trust of employees. In the future, using personal information of learners along with other real-time collected data that can indicate the extent of the learner engagement in the learning process as wearable devices, the emotional analytics data, the assessment of the relevance of the content in real time and its immediacy may constructively complement the proposed real-time relevance assessment mechanism and contribute to personalization and effectiveness of learning.

V. AUTOMATED CONTENT SOURCING

In today wet working environment, where knowledge demands and qualification expectations are systematically changing not seldom, the challenges of finding and aggregating appropriate learning content play a critical role. Conventionally, the L&D teams compile these sources and while this practice serves adequate purpose in some situations it isn't capable of thriving in the growing information era and encompassing learning requirements. This challenge can be addressed by new trends in content acquisition — automated content sourcing with the help of Artificial Intelligence (AI) technology that offers a unique opportunity to find current and relevant learning material virtually, including internal databases, articles, videos and other multimedia sources. Not only is AI capable of diversification of content but is also able to automate the process by which employees are presented with a wide assortment of options to learn from. This capability has indeed proved to be rather important as organisations attempt to design sustainable training ecosystems that are capable of supporting lifelong learning for employees (Karlsson,2020).

By means of automated content sourcing, an organization applies the cognitive AI tools and algorithms enabled with the ability to conduct the bulk of content sourcing and curation processes in a self-directed manner while also matching the Content Curriculum to the organization's as opposed to content acquisition being driven primarily by people, recommenders use artificial intelligence and NLP techniques to present usable information from unending feeds all the time. But it is not a random acquisition of information, it filters and categorizes information according to topics, skills, competencies, or learning types, which reading systems available to learners makes learning materials organized and systematic. The kind of learning content that is developed can be automatically sourced so that the learning platform always has fresh material to deliver, and such content can be standardized to conform to the latest industry or field norms and guidelines (Dolle et al., 2019).

Web crawling technique is employed where the AI algorithm searches information from standard websites, scholarly articles and journals, and trades magazines. AI content sourcing is incomplete without NLP since it helps the tool to comprehend, analyze and categorize articles by topics or skills in an article, white papers or current research readily available for learners. NLP analyses the textual content of articles, videos, and other media and then recommends the users learning material based on keywords and topics instead of a simple tags and metadata copying. Content mining gathers information from multiple sources leading to the redundancy. The deduplication is a common technique employed in the development of AI algorithms employed in sourcing to exclude similar content or to group similar content and forward it to the employees as unique content. Automated content sourcing guarantees that the learning material is always relevant and relevant to the need of the employees and the organization. With new content acquisition possible around the clock, the AI tools can filter new content sources based on topics that surface new trends, new technologies, and new market configurations. (Pavlova,2024).

AI tools may be used for sourcing of numerous forms of knowledge and types of content that means that employees can update their insight through videos, articles, podcasts or even interactive courses. This multimedia strategy covers all the gaps of physical and electronic learning preferences at a single place thus making the learning process more effective, interesting and productive (Cui et al.,2022).

The continuous availability of content sourcing using AI enhances the learning and development in the organization. Every hour, day, week and month, the employees would be able to get updated information, research and best practices thus making the employees up to date in the field of specialized knowledge. This feature is especially helpful in knowledge-intensive industries including but not limited to;

finance, technology, and health sectors because the knowledge needed often changes over time, and the employees must adapt (Hoffreumon, et al.,2024).

In the future the automated content sourcing may be even more complex, as algorithms take into account real-time feedback from the employees to tailor the learning process as well as the content being recommended. With the help of contemporary intelligent technologies, it was possible to identify learning needs before they arise because of shifts in roles or shifts in projects. Hence, the technology of the AI-based automated content sourcing is in the process of redefining Workplace Learning by sourcing and filtering the content organically that is of high interest and relevance to the learners across various sources. It's this capability that allows organizations to deliver to their employees great learning programs that increases their knowledge and engagement to aid in, improve and advance skills to achieve organizational strategic goals and mission. Hence, the automated content sourcing can be said to enhance the ability of organizations to deliver for the modern day, knowledge based, dynamic workplace

VI. PROGRESS TRACKING AND ANALYTICS

In today's dynamic and ever-evolving workplace progress and analytics has become critical to every corporate learning and development (L&D) program. There are two sides to worry about in microlearning: It's not only important that appropriate and motivating content is made available to employees but also that the training's effectiveness in terms of knowledge acquisition can be assessed. Such AI management of learning progress and performance assessments aimed at making a notable contribution by furnishing the L&D teams with invaluable data on the ways and means of learners' activity, the second birthdays, overall effectiveness of retention and utilization of precious feedbacks. In this way, AI helps L&D teams collect and distill these data points, so they can adjust their learning programs in line with the learners and the organization's needs (Allam et al.,2023).

Employer and employee management indicators enforced by progress tracking AI applications and analytics reflect different aspects of how employees engage with microlearning Processed and synthesized separately, often as shorter flash-based learning segments, microlearning delivers information in brief sequences. Thanks to machine learning algorithms AI is able to accumulate and analyze not only the distinctive rates of each separate module, the time spent on each segment, quiz results, and even click-through rates. Such statistics are highly beneficial for the evaluation of particular learning modules, employee interest levels, as well as the general success of the microlearning concept. Also, the AI system can produce insights into how the employees is interacting with the learning assets once deployed, and where they are likely to encounter challenges (Halper,2017).

Self-improvement systems can then recommend the appropriate learning trajectories based on the patterns of progress data that the AI systems can examine and provide. Having the information about employees' strengths and deficiencies the AI tool can propose to choose different modules of the course, quizzes, and even useful materials that will help to reinforce knowledge. This befitting approach enhances interaction and empowers workers to build their aptitudes as per their abilities and convenience. Among the priorities of AI- based analytics, there stands the flexibility to adjust learning content in real-time. Through statistics such as completion rates, engagement, and feedback, L&D teams can better understand deficiency areas to include tweaking the length of the modules, changing the format of their content presentation, or even improving the content's applicability in real life. The cyclic nature of updating the content guarantees that knowledge updates remain helpful, timely, and interesting to learners over time. Driven by AI analytics, knowing how well the employees retain the information after going through microlearning modules is beneficial. Based on quizzes taken as well as subsequent checks, AI can find out trends concerning the retention rate and those subject matters that require further coverage with employees. This approach to retention and reinforcement is more target and is more effective for knowledge transfer and ensures that the employee applies what has been learnt on the job (Collins,2021).

With AI the advancement, organizations can start measuring the percentage to determine the actual ROI of microlearning programs. Thus, learning engagement rates, completion statistics, and retention metrics let L&D teams evaluate learning initiatives to see how they can contribute to the achievement of the organization's strategic objectives. This data orientation when it comes to ROI measurement will enable organisations to effectively plan and justify for investment in learning and development (Schweyer,2018).

All in all, AI solutions are instrumental in monitoring and evaluating the trends and improvement of microlearning in the working setting. Making the data output of the L&D teams clearer about the level of engagement to completion rates, retention rates, and user feedback, AI helps organizations to keep improving their learning programs. Besides, this evidence-based approach contributes to the enhancement of practically all aspects of microlearning and helps employees to enhance their professional experience and competencies as well as supports organizational culture promoting constant and progressive learning.

CONCLUSION

The study emphasises on how artificial intelligence has changed the way people learn and train their staff in the contemporary workplace. Through smart acquisition of content, evaluating its timeliness in real time, and designing learning paths at the specifically micro level, AI ensures not only that the learning process is fun, but also correspondingly relevant to the organizational requirements, as well as the learners' aspirations. AI's progression tracking also helps L&D teams to keep the pulse of the employees' interaction, duration session, and other forms of feedback while enhancing responsiveness. Due to the constant changes in the conditions and requirements of work, applying AI in microlearning becomes a valuable experience for improving the qualifications of employees.

REFERENCES

Ahmed, N., Saha, A. K., Al Noman, M. A., Jim, J. R., Mridha, M. F., & Kabir, M. M. (2024). Deep learning-based natural language processing in human–agent interaction: Applications, advancements and challenges. *Natural Language Processing Journal*, *9*(100112), 100112. DOI: 10.1016/j.nlp.2024.100112

Alias, N. F., & Razak, R. A. (2025). Revolutionizing learning in the digital age: A systematic literature review of microlearning strategies. *Interactive Learning Environments*, *33*(1), 1–21. DOI: 10.1080/10494820.2024.2331638

Allam, H., Khan, Z., Letsholo, K., Pandya, B., Shah, K., & Ahamed, J. (2023). A Proposed AI Method for Tracking College Students' Academic Progress. In *2023 9th International Conference on Information Technology Trends (ITT)* (pp. 215–219). IEEE.

Carson, B. (2017). *Learning in the Age of Immediacy: 5 Factors for How We Connect, Communicate, and Get Work Done*. Association for Talent Development.

Collins, C., Dennehy, D., Conboy, K., & Mikalef, P. (2021). Artificial intelligence in information systems research: A systematic literature review and research agenda. *International Journal of Information Management*, *60*(102383), 102383. DOI: 10.1016/j.ijinfomgt.2021.102383

Cui, R., Li, M., & Zhang, S. (2022). AI and procurement. *Manufacturing & Service Operations Management*, *24*(2), 691–706. DOI: 10.1287/msom.2021.0989

Dolle, N., Wilhelm, C., & Rössle, M. (2019, October). Applying modern text processing technologies to implement a self-learning marketplace by using cloud services as an example. In *International Conference on Reliability and Statistics in Transportation and Communication* (pp. 450-459). Cham: Springer International Publishing.

Halper, F. (2017). *Advanced analytics: Moving toward AI, machine learning, and natural language processing*

Hoffreumon, C., Forman, C., & van Zeebroeck, N. (2024). Make or buy your artificial intelligence? Complementarities in technology sourcing. *Journal of Economics & Management Strategy*. Advance online publication. DOI: 10.1111/jems.12586

Karlsson, F. (2020). The opportunities of applying artificial intelligence in strategic sourcing.

Market. us. (2024). *EdTech market size, share, trends | CAGR of 13.9%* [Data set].

Omona, K. (2024). *Global Perspectives on Micro-learning and Micro-credentials in Higher Education*. IGI Global.

Pavlova, O., & Kuzmin, A. (2024). Analysis of artificial intelligence based systems for automated generation of digital content.

Porter, B., & Grippa, F. (2020). A platform for AI-enabled real-time feedback to promote digital collaboration. *Sustainability*, *12*(24), 10243. DOI: 10.3390/su122410243

Schweyer, A. (2018). Predictive analytics and artificial intelligence in people management. Incentive Research Foundation, 1–18.

Swargiary. (2024). *Navigating the Digital Frontier: Case Studies in Online Learning for Career Advancement*. Scholars' Press

Vetrivel, V. P., & Arun. (2024). The role of AI in transforming assessment practices in education. In *Advances in Educational Marketing, Administration, and Leadership* (pp. 43–70). IGI Global

Viterouli, M., Belias, D., Koustelios, A., Tsigilis, N., & Papademetriou, C. (2024). Time for Change: Designing Tailored Training Initiatives for Organizational Transformation. In *Organizational Behavior and Human Resource Management for Complex Work Environments* (pp. 267–307). IGI Global

Yusuf, S. O., Abubakar, J. E., Durodola, R. L., Ocran, G., Paul-Adeleye, A. H., & Yusuf, P. O. (2024). Impact of AI on continuous learning and skill development in the workplace: A comparative study with traditional methods.

Chapter 6
Integrating AI Into Academic Education:
Romanian Students' and Professors' Perspectives on the Future Labour Market

Mădălina Moraru
https://orcid.org/0000-0001-5976-7968
University of Bucharest, Romania

ABSTRACT

This study aims to explore the impact of Generative AI on communication in higher education from two key perspectives: those of students and teachers. As technology often drives development and innovation, our central research question is how AI influenced students' behavior, their expectations, and teachers' approaches to education. Initially, AI was viewed negatively due to concerns about controlling or certifying knowledge. However, students have become increasingly fascinated by it, prompting teachers to reconsider their initial opinion. The main hypothesis of this research is that AI introduces new strategies for academic work, simultaneously updating traditional methods and transforming the teacher-student relationship. This shift fosters greater student engagement and encourages innovative approaches to communication in various contexts. This study investigates both students' and teachers' perspectives on AI's role in higher education. Both groups play essential roles in education, striving to find the most effective ways to absorb knowledge and achieve personal goals.

DOI: 10.4018/979-8-3373-6018-8.ch006

Copyright © 2026, IGI Global Scientific Publishing. Copying or distributing in print or electronic forms without written permission of IGI Global Scientific Publishing is prohibited.

INTRODUCTION

In the last century, educational development strategies focus on creating programs that not only meet national standards but also align with global trends. These strategies recognize digitalization as a fundamental aspect of both learning and management across all areas of modern life (Glatthorn et al., 2018). Although both teachers and students struggle to keep up with technology integrated into the academic context, they must not forget the primary teaching tool that ensures success in higher education: communication, both in its traditional and innovative forms. In this sense, Crowley and Mitchell consider that "Communication is a flow concept, reflecting the process of transmission and exchange of knowledge and values, which itself creates information influencing knowledge and values" (1994, p. 255). Communication through technology in educational environments has become essential to meet the demands of labor market performance. Education inherently involves communication, but today, scholars address this issue by focusing not only on the subject itself but also on the tools used. Therefore, understanding the role of virtual communication is a crucial aspect of higher education, regardless of the type of courses. The use of artificial Intelligence (AI) should be seen as a new era of integrating knowledge into learning environment and developing skills to achieve higher performance in education.

A suitable definition of AI is "computing systems that are able to engage in human-like processes such as learning, adapting, synthesizing, self-correction and the use of data for complex processing tasks" (Popenici et al., 2017, p. 2) In other words, AI stands for a method of absorbing knowledge and performing complex activities by involving learning machines. As the impact of AI continues to grow, it is essential to understand the extent to which education can benefit from such emergence.

The use of technology as a tool promotes student engagement and, according to Chen et al. (2010), enhances the achievement of educational goals. Once they enter higher education, Gen Z students must learn to integrate into a new community and navigate competitive demands. Chatbots and online platforms help young students identify their reference groups and sense of belonging, as Pérez states, "They (chatbots) can function as service assistants or as educational agents" (2020, p. 1). The most significant aspect is the interactivity provided by various tools, which empowers students to become active partners in own learning.

The purpose of this research is to understand whether students believe AI should be utilized in academia, during classes, for assignments, immediate feedbacks and other educational activities, delivered in a virtual environment. Additionally, the study will explore teachers' perspectives on using generative artificial intelligence (GenAI) to improve their methods of sharing knowledge.

The expected outcome of this research is that teachers view AI more as an enemy than a partner, primarily because they find it challenging to control. Older teachers tend to have less trust in chatbots, online platforms, and AI. In contrast, future employees—students—are more likely to embrace AI, believing that academia should leverage its resources and efficiency. As it is, while AI poses a source of pressure for many teachers, it represents a real opportunity for students.

THEORETICAL BACKGROUND

Learning Experiences Provided by AI

In the last five years, AI has emerged as a significant challenge in higher education, with both teachers and students becoming increasingly engaged in making use of its tools across various contexts. However, concerns have arisen regarding ethical use of AI, along with its limitations and the difficulty of controlling its capabilities. Consequently, the decision to employ AI tools for crucial academic tasks presents a real dilemma for teachers and mentors on one side, and for students and mentees on the other.

ChatGPT represents one of the most often used tools considering that it offers the chance to initiate dialogue generating useful content. ChatGPT was launched in November 2022, and from the very first moment it was tested, it has been associated with higher education. This system generates a network of communication based on a wide range of text inputs. Bearing in mind Chan and Hu' s approach, ChatGPT was perceived as it follows: "It is a conversational AI system developed by OpenAI, an autoregressive large language model (more than 175 billion parameters) has been pre-trained on a large corpus of text data." (2023, p. 2) From the very beginning, ChatGPT was associated with communication and education, but it was mostly used individually and not easily integrated into the curriculum.

According to some scholars (Azaiz, Deckarm & Strickroth, 2023; Lee, 2023) ChatGPT provides personalized learning experiences adapted to individual students' needs and abilities. This represents a significant advancement over traditional educational tools, which generally offered non-specific content. Lot of research focuses on the way AI influences learning process in different areas of education, such as engineering, maths, medical issues, physics etc. For example, Liang et al. (2021) conducted a systematic review and bibliographic analysis on the role and research of AI in language education. According to Zawacki-Richter et al. (2019), the main purposes of using AI tools in higher education are the following: (1) profiling and prediction, (2) assessment and evaluation, (3) adaptive systems and personalization, and (4) intelligent tutoring systems. Significant is the fact that AI tools encourages research experiences at different levels, while saving time. Crompton and Burke (2023) added other issues to this list, or better said, even approaching them separately. The list encompasses the following activities that can be done easier with AI tools: (1) Assessment/Evaluation, (2) Predicting, (3) AI Assistant, (4) Intelligent Tutoring System (ITS), and (5) Managing Student Learning.

This study highlights the differing attitudes of students and teachers toward ChatGPT's role in academic practice. As Chan and Hu (2023) state "One of the key uses of GenAI in higher education is for enhancing students' learning experience through its ability to respond to user prompts to generate highly original output." (p. 1) Students recognized and appreciated the potential for personalized learning support, writing and brainstorming assistance. Obviously, in the above-mentioned article there are concerns about accuracy, privacy, ethical issues, and the impact on personal development, career prospects, and societal values.

The learning environment, technological approach in academia, and specific, high-quality feedback motivate students to use ChatGPT as they gather knowledge over the years. The more innovative the learning environment, the more willing students are to use AI tools in developing academic activities. This idea involves a modern curriculum, advanced technology, well-organized spaces, and, last but not least, effective time management. If the learning environment requires significant improvements, AI means may be perceived as effective replacements for various other means, such as digital platforms, time management tools, applications, rapid research methods, and diverse feedback mechanisms.

When it comes to technological way, academia engages in a variety of activities aimed at ensuring relevance to the future labour market. However, the extent to which technology can be efficiently applied cannot always be controlled by GenAI. As a result, technology is often viewed as a tool that fosters trust in the new era of AI, yet its success ultimately depends on the development and adaptability of the higher education system. AI means offer students interactive feedback, empowering them to elevate their results and overall performance. Although assessments conducted using AI tools may sometimes seem superficial, the process ultimately fosters student growth, as they view the feedback as an opportunity to refine and improve their work.

The Chatbot as an Active Friend

As Abu Shawar and Atwell argue, "the chatbot architecture integrates a language model and computational algorithms to emulate informal chat communication between a human user and a computer using natural language." (2007, pp. 29-30). This is why, initially, the use of chatbots was primarily associated with learning foreign languages or facilitating communication in a specific language to interact with human-computer users. Researchers have employed various terms to capture the features of machine learning systems designed for communication: machine conversation system, virtual agent, dialogue system, and chatterbot (Shawar & Atwell, 2007, p. 29). It is essential to mention that chatbots have been progressively developed since the 1960s and 1990s, when a range of machine learning systems entered the market, including MegaHAL (Hutchens, 1996), CONVERSE (Batacharia et al., 1999), ELIZABETH (Abu Shawar and Atwell, 2002), HEXBOT (2004), and ALICE (2007). The earliest effort to create chatbots was ELIZA, developed by Joseph Weizenbaum in the 1960s to simulate a psychotherapist during clinical sessions (Weizenbaum, 1966, 1967). However, ELIZA was unable to provide in-depth responses designed to encourage patients to engage in self-analysis. The chatbot quickly reached its limitations because it relied on pre-programmed, monotonous, and predictable phrases.

Nowadays, the chatbot's role is particularly relevant from at least two perspectives: an educational and a psychological one. A chatbot is perceived as a machine learning facility capable of stimulating human interaction through guided conversations on various topics. Iku-Silan, Hwang, and Chen (2023) underline the role of chatbots as a promising item for delivering instant feedback and personalized guidance in educational settings. Therefore, motivation to delve into new information, validate recent outcomes or look for unconventional ways of solving problems become stronger while using a Chatbot as a quick landmark. With their interactive and user-friendly interfaces, chatbots hold significant potential to enhance students' classroom engagement while alleviating their cognitive load in interdisciplinary or cross-disciplinary learning. Students require quick and comfortable access to data and information to satisfy their curiosity through machine learning tools. Without such facility, they may abandon the effort or become less engaged. Over the years, many chatbots demonstrated their relevance regardless the fields in education. For instance, Gibbs et al. (2004) implemented a chatbot conversation to improve the understanding of social theory. They use an ALICE chatbot to create a base of knowledge that responded to inquiries of the type "tell me more about...". The model was tested with sociology undergraduates enrolled in a natural theory course. Sofia was created to assist while teaching maths and it was used at Harvard Mathematics Department.

As Nusivera et. al. (2024) state regarding AI, "Chat-GPT will produce a dialogue that encourages students to analyze, evaluate, and synthesize information, which is a major component in critical thinking skills" (p. 375). This is thc highly desired goal of communication in education, provided that ChatGPT is personalized and students are taught to use it in accordance with ethical standards and academic requirements. By learning how to communicate argumentatively and how to formulate and demand well-reasoned answers from all actors involved in the educational process, students are taught to gather more information using ChatGPT. As Loyens et al. (2023) state, AI provides an opportunity to validate communication during debates by relying on arguments sometimes generated through ChatGPT research.

The conclusion suggests that a chatbot can be highly effective in the educational process if students recognize both the advantages and disadvantages of using it in various contexts. It serves as a source of building trust—from a psychological perspective—and offers rapid feedback.

Teachers' Awareness of AI Assistance During Classes

ChatGPT encourages teachers to elevate the level of interactivity in their courses by fostering creative involvement, challenging students' progress, and encouraging them to take risks in expressing their ideas. It enables teachers to ask thought-provoking questions, seek clarifications, explore new topics or areas of interest, and enhance communication with students. In essence, ChatGPT serves as a robust bridge, connecting teaching methods with students' interests and priorities. In their 2024 research study, Al-Mughairi and Bhaskar identified four key motivational themes that drive the use of ChatGPT to achieve optimal educational outcomes. These themes are the following: (1) exploration of innovative education technologies; (2) personalization teaching and learning; (3) time-saving; (4) professional development. (Al-Mughairi & Bhaskar, 2024, pp. 6-7). Teachers are quite aware of the fact that innovation in educational technologies involves exploring new teaching methods, while creating challenges for students, and adapting courses to leverage the capabilities of AI. The ability of machine learning to tailor course content, distribute tasks, and provide personalized feedback is another compelling reason to embrace AI's benefits in higher education. This ability to understand students' needs and address them properly is essential when personalizing tasks and assigning differentiated responsibilities. When young people engage in activities proper to their interests and skills, their emotional investment increases because they care about their work: "Furthermore, AI helps develop individualized learning plans, considering each student's learning style, interests, and objectives, which keeps students motivated and engaged, leading to better academic results." (Alqahtani et al., 2023, p. 1238)

Integrating AI into academic courses supports effective time management, fostering greater organization, efficiency, and investment in acquiring new knowledge, as well as developing both soft and hard skills. According to Al-Mughairi and Bhaskar (2024), saving time enhances the learning environment, encouraging students to get involved in more meaningful and relevant activities. Professional development depends on technical progress, on one hand, and the continuous enhancement of teachers' pedagogical skills, on the other. In the past, while teachers and trainers provided students or trainees with the required knowledge and expertise, they often lacked the time to be original, authentic, or to showcase their unique talents. This left little room for the holistic development that several young people might have hoped to achieve.

Concerns and Controversies of Using AI

Although AI tools have drawn attention in numerous positive ways, the article by Al-Mughairi and Bhaskar (2024) highlights several factors suggesting that machine-learning instruments are likely to fail to achieve success in the educational field. As the above-mentioned scholars noticed, the reasons for reconsider the role of ChatGPT are the following investigated themes: (1) reliability and accuracy concerns; (2) reduced human interaction; (3) privacy and data security; (4) lack of institutional support; (5) overreliance on ChatGPT (Mughairi & Bhaskar, 2024, pp. 7-8).

Teachers express concerns about the accuracy, honesty, and, sometimes, even the quality of the required answers. Most of the interviewees stated that they do not fully trust AI outputs and cannot overlook the risk of errors or misinformation. At this moment, people feel overwhelmed by AI, but a teacher's responsibility is too important to be clouded by confusion, disinformation, and disappointment. Such an attitude hinders students from receiving the best possible higher education. The relationship between mentor and mentee has its own distinct characteristics, especially between teachers at the beginning of their careers and those with accumulated expertise. A virtual assistant can never replace human interaction, emotions, or communication tools. Listening to advice, striving for similar teaching methods, and exchanging opinions all stem from real interaction, not from using rapid learning tactics. Moreover, failure and success drive progress in an educational institution, as teachers strive to overcome barriers and achieve their goals, which propel both themselves and their students towards evolution in their future careers.

Teachers highlight concerns about privacy, particularly the risk that ChatGPT might expose private data in undesirable contexts. At this point, machine learning could become a real danger, especially since it claims that information is objective and free from emotional involvement. The ethical aspects deserve further consideration, which explains the immediate efforts to establish legal policies and guidelines for using AI under strict supervision. The academia worried that the use of ChatGPT would lead to more plagiarism in scholarly writing even more (Singh, 2023).

Lack of institutional support arises from both financial and technical limitations, on the one hand, and from a cautious reaction by top management, who simultaneously faces numerous changes, on the other. Still, sometimes a reluctant attitude can be beneficial, as it encourages teachers to find new arguments, approach issues differently, gaining the trust of managers in their efforts. However, ChatGPT is not always embraced warmly due to ethical concerns and an obvious lack of control.

The fact that ChatGPT is sometimes granted significant power in terms of the speed at which it delivers information raises real concerns. Under time pressure, teachers do not always check the answers as thoroughly as they should. If any AI tool becomes more than just a tool—being seen as a second brain or an extension of the teacher's work—it could pose a real danger. The true risk lies in developing a dependency on AI tools without double-checking the outputs or, at the very least, investigating the provided data. The hallucination issue, which refers to generating non-existent or incorrect content, raised people's concerns on its liability (Alqahtani et al., 2023).

The Role of AI in Choosing Future Careers

In response to European Union regulations, Romania developed the 2021–2027 Strategy for the Digitalization of Romanian Education (SMART-Edu) in 2020. As part of this strategy, the European Commission explored the development of a European Digital Skills Certificate (EDSC) between 2022 and 2024. In this context, Romania is in the midst of a transition toward understanding the transformation of communication in education as a result of AI tools. However, even though Romania is a member of the European Union, it is important to note that it was only accepted into the Schengen Area in 2024. The country still operates with its national currency, not the Euro, and faces limited resources in the field of education. Equally important is the fact that most of the country's successful universities are public institutions, which means they rely on limited funding. This reality has been stressed by well-known scholars as well: "The use of AI in the context of education in developing countries is still not optimal due to the very wide geographical reach and the still limited supporting resources." (Nusivera et. al, 2025, p. 376)

AI can support program-specific goals by streamlining course design, creating curricula descriptions, outlining learning objectives, and developing assessment methodologies. Additionally, it addresses the challenges faced by stakeholders in adapting to emerging pedagogical approaches and the evolving job market. As Vitale, Bowyer and Bayerlein (2020) asserted that the evolution of technology has influenced pedagogical and academic standards, motivating curriculum designers to equip students with skills aligned with market expectations. AI tools can analyze labor market trends and predict future job opportunities, so teachers should frequently research this topic to better understand the implications for their own careers. One of the longstanding challenges faced by universities is the student dropout rate and graduation percentage, closely linked to student satisfaction with higher education. This sector has evolved alongside increasing concerns about future career prospects and a focus on specific factors that contribute to success beyond graduation. As Gorgone et al. (2003) stated universities should aim to integrate both academic and employability skills into courses, and propose a skillset framework that incorporates these elements throughout the curriculum (p. 63). The aforementioned scholars proposed a theoretical model focused on semantic-based curriculum planning together with the evaluation of students' comprehension of concepts and topics. This model's outcomes can assist students in better planning their professional careers, ultimately enhancing retention rates and employability (Gorgone et al., 2005).

In Romania, the phenomenon of university dropout has been observed since the 2010s, but the measurement rate was not calculated from the outset, as there was no intentional research focus on this issue at the time. Data were measured for the first time in the study *Dropout in Romanian Higher Education – Definition, Measurement, Interpretation*, recently published by UEFISCDI: the dropout rate is 47.96% for bachelor's degree students enrolled in 2015, 42% for master's degree students, and 70% for doctoral studies. Her eliu et. al. (2022) stated that there are relevant discrepancies regarding student dropout by study domain. The rates start from 4.6% in Military sciences, intelligence, public order and go to 64.1% for Philosophy and 59.2% for European studies and international relations. Consequently, recent articles have emphasized product-based learning through the alignment of competencies with relevant industries, while scholars underscore the importance of updating curricula to reflect emerging jobs and trends in the labor market. (Yudiono et al., 2021). Vocational schools and higher education institutions should collaborate with future employers to identify new competencies and skills developed through specific courses. Theoretical classes should be complemented by applied projects to meet the demands of contemporary industry. Education should respond to the needs of the labour market, and teachers should offer genuine support through effective communication and a deep understanding of students' needs.

Nowadays, generative AI (GenAI) connects employers with academia by highlighting the skills, competencies, and current needs that the labor market requires for efficiency and competitiveness. Drăghici and Iva cu made the difference between the demands of labor market characterized by industry 4.0 and the next one called 5.0:"The current requirements of the manufacturing industry refer to a series of business directions for automation, digitization, and sustainability. Automation and digitization define Industry 4.0 and prepare the industry for the next step, Industry 5.0." (2022, p. 2) At this stage, AI plays a key role in providing data and alternative solutions to protect the environment and ensure a sustainable future for people. Industry 5.0 is perceived as a revolution in the labor market, already making a significant impact on various businesses whose interests and demands have evolved. This shift in labor perception is widely recognized as part of Business Process Reengineering (BPR) and Business Intelligence (BI) processes, which are reshaping the frameworks of Business-to-Business (B2B) and Business-to-Consumer (B2C) models. (Patchek et al., 2022, p. 18) These new models and process transformations are driven by extensive interconnections, made possible through the collection of valuable data facilitated by AI-powered machine learning.

The coherence of implementing AI studies in university curricula to develop skills and dedicated expertise across various fields cannot be systematically achieved as long as the acceptance of this new human-machine learning partnership remains limited. Currently, progress has been made to ensure that all necessary knowledge is provided to support the educational goals of all stakeholders, fostering effective collaborative interactions between humans and machines. As Bigan (2022) highlighted, there are four categories of stakeholders closely linked to the integration of AI into educational activities, which aim to facilitate better career orientation. To be more specific, the following list aligns AI needs expressed by these actors with the labor market, due to their responsibilities:

- "Engineers, researchers, developers, advanced users, and maintenance teams members of practical implementations such as robotics operating in Industry 5.0 framework.
- Decision-makers either coming from the State policy Regulatory bodies or from the top management.
- Human Workers together with AI learning machines, processes, and systems increase the productivity and quality up to the Industry 5.0 level.
- General Public/Consumers requires personalized products." (Bigan, 2022, p. 258)

The first statement list relevant AI users in need of an Industry 5.0 to express their skills already acquired in schools and universities. Robotics represents one of the professions mostly appreciated by the Gen Z and maybe the next generations. Decision-makers stand for top management entities who establish which activities should be implemented via AI. The third category emphasizes the cooperation between human nature-workers and AI learning machines, which yields the efficiency. Last but not least consumers seek to be treated as unique personalities, thus requiring personalized products and even AI dialogues.

METHODOLOGY

Research Instruments

The research encompassed both quantitative and qualitative tools and followed an inductive approach. The concept of the inductive approach involves collecting qualitative data (in our case, interviews and the two open-ended questions from the questionnaire), identifying themes, and ultimately developing possible theories. The quantitative study conducted in Romania between May and July, 2024, consisted in applying a survey to students enrolled in higher education courses specialized in Communication, Design, Law even Maths programs, all of them at the University of Bucharest. This study respected the frame of the Research Ethics Commission from the University of Bucharest, following the guidelines and rules imposed by the EU General Data Protection Regulation (April 27, 2016/679). The qualitative approach relies on semi-structured interviews with six teachers from Romanian faculties specialized in Communication, Political Studies, Journalism, Public Relations studies from various universities, focusing on how they internalize the process of integrating AI in day-to-day academia. Thematic analysis is a qualitative research method aimed at identifying and interpreting various themes, which serve as codes within a specific corpus. The interviews were conducted in Bucharest between January 8th and 11th, 2025, with a duration ranging from a minimum of 30 minutes to a maximum of 45 minutes

According to Braun and Clarke (2006), thematic analysis is a "method for identifying, analysing, and reporting patterns (themes) within data. It minimally organises and describes your data set in (rich) detail" (p. 6). As authors state, a theme represents something significant within the data that addresses the research questions and serves as a key aspect of the analysis "some level of patterned response or meaning within the data set" (Braun & Clarke, 2006, p. 10).

The data were manually coded, following the steps described in Braun and Clarke's model (2006, p. 87): familiarization with the information obtained from the open-ended questions and semi-structured interviews, generation of the codes, searching and reviewing the codes. Using both qualitative and quantitative research methods as complementary approaches aims to explore how communication between students and teachers remains effective, especially as AI introduces new ways to achieve educational goals. Focusing solely on students' perspectives regarding the role of AI in their future lives, while overlooking their communication with classmates and teachers during their education, is not the best approach. Therefore, combining research methods represents the most effective approach to addressing the central question of communication in education: In what ways can AI enhance the efficiency of higher education? The word *adaptation* represents the link between students' activities and teachers' efforts to use technology as a means of communication to achieve high-quality training that meets the needs of the labor market.

Data Collection

We applied the questionnaire to students from different faculties because there is still no bachelor's or master's program dedicated to education through AI-driven communication. However, every faculty shows interest in preparing students for the labour market through the use of AI tools.

The research collected 250 questionnaires, of which 234 were validated. The questionnaire addresses the role of GenAI in preparing students for the labor market, its mandatory use during higher education, and the potential ethical risks associated with embracing this innovation. The data collection procedure was based on *Google Forms platform* and made it available via social media (Facebook, Reddit and even Instagram). The survey consisted of 17 questions, including socio-demographic ones such as age, gender, place of residence, and level of study. It also included questions about the context of using ChatGPT, the role of AI in contemporary society, its potential impact on their future careers, AI's involvement in teaching methods, and the advantages and disadvantages of using GenAI in various activities. The questionnaire featured two open-ended questions focusing on professional aspirations and the potential risks associated with using ChatGPT in future careers. Students were instructed to respond briefly, in a single sentence, to ensure their answers were specific and aligned with the purpose of the question. The remaining 15 questions were multiple-choice, with 2 of them designed using a Likert scale to allow respondents express their opinions.

After analyzing the survey data, it became clear that students expect a different approach from their teachers in academic communication—one that considers the integration of AI into the curriculum. Even though there are no bachelor's or master's programs specialized in AI education at the University of Bucharest, there are projects and initiatives led by professors from various faculties aimed at addressing these needs.The purpose of this research is to highlight how students' need to educate themselves in this area intersects with professors' ambition to enhance their teaching performance in this direction. This finding prompted the next step in the research: exploring teachers' perspectives on the matter. The age of the interviewees ranges from 30 to 50, with an effort made to ensure an equal distribution of gender. The interviews were conducted face-to-face and online (via Google Meet) and transcribed verbatim. The confidentiality of personal data was assured. The questions were designed taking into consideration the results of the questionnaire. They focused on the following topics: the contexts of using GenAI, the advantages and disadvantages of AI in teaching, specific activities suitable for AI, and changes in teaching methods, possible dangers of future career in academia. The teaching experience of the interviewees ranges from 10 to 18 years. They currently work at three universities with diverse specializations, including Political, Administrative and Communication Sciences, Communication Sciences, and Communication and Public Relations. This diversity is particularly valuable for the present research, as all respondents share a common academic background despite teaching subjects as varied as Mathematics, Law, Political Science, or Journalism—they have all taught at least one course related to offline and/or online communication. This shared focus justifies the relevance and motivation behind exploring this research theme. The list of courses further illustrates the diversity and depth of the academic expertise involved: Philosophy; Online and Offline Advertising; Public Relations; Lobbying; External Communication of the Company; Negotiation; Interpersonal Communication; Communication in Public Administration; Social Media Promotion Techniques; Institutional Branding; Media Planning and Implementation; Press and Current Affairs (PACT); Desktop Publishing; Online Journalism; Social Media Journalism; Ethics and Academic Integrity; Digital Journalism; Research Methods and Methodologies; Introduction to the Mass Media System; Digital Communication; Influencer Marketing and PR-Communication Campaigns; Marketing Strategies; Semiotics and Organizational Communication; Argumentative Techniques; Fashion Research Project; Politics; Crisis Communication; and Campaign Strategies in Advertising and Electoral Marketing.

Research Questions and Hypotheses

The main research questions this study addresses are as follows:

Q_1. -What is the main AI role in contemporary society ?
Q_2 - In what ways can the integration of AI into academic education impact students' future career paths?
Q_3. -What are students' and teachers' expectations regarding AI's role in higher education?
Q_4.- What are the risks associated with excessive use of GenAI?
Q_5. -To what extent can teachers use AI to enhance their activities?

The main hypotheses of this research emphasize the following aspects, bridging the relationship between higher education and AI innovation:

H_1 - The more teachers incorporate AI tools into their courses, the higher the level of student engagement.
H_2 - Students do not perceive AI as a threat to their future careers, but rather as an efficient tool for education.
H_3 - AI cannot always be regarded as a reliable method for academic work.

$H_{3.1}$ - Teachers are hesitant to use AI in their current activities due to a lack of control over information.
$H_{3.2}$ - Students place excessive trust in technology and often neglect verifying the accuracy of information.
H_4 - Teachers tend to associate AI not with a new approach to learning, but with specific fields of expertise, such as engineering, robotics, mathematics, medicine, and physics a.s.o.

RESULTS

The respondents of the self-administered questionnaire are specialized in fields such as public relations, journalism, advertising, and design, engineering, law at the bachelor's level. At the master's level, their areas of study are more diverse, including digital communication, advertising, and advertising and public relations campaigns. The Table 1 displays the socio-demographic characteristics of our respondents.

Table 1. Respondents' profile

Age		**Residence**		**Specialization**		**Do you have a job?**	
18-20	**54.1%**	**capital**	**89.2%**	**Advertising**	**43.8%**	**Yes**	**45.1%**
21-23	30%	Small city	5.2%	Emergent communication	16.3%	No	54.9%
24-26	6%	Big city	3.9%	Journalism	13.3%		
27-30	3%	Countryside	1.7%	Public relations	9.9%		
More than 30	6.9%			Law	6. 4%		
				Other specialization of communication	3%		
				Banking and economy	2.1%		
				Math and Computer sciences	1.7%		
				Other specializations	3.5%		

AI in Contemporary Society

One of the most intriguing perspectives shared by students highlights how AI is currently influencing society and how it is expected to transform interests, trends, jobs, and the overall flow of life in the future. Many respondents believe that work efficiency, success, and multitasking are closely tied to GenAI. They acknowledge that AI simplifies day-to-day responsibilities, provided that users understand its functionality and apply it within specific, controlled activities.

Figure 1. The role of AI in contemporary society

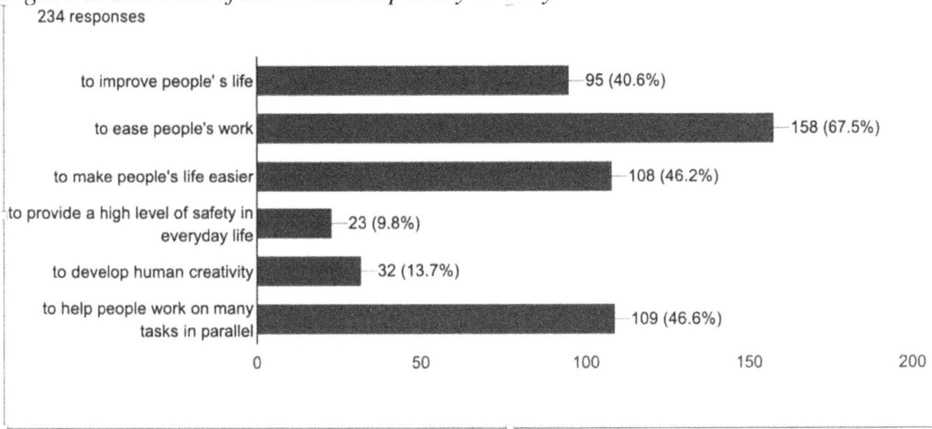

Respondents do not believe that creativity is inherently provided by AI tools, at least not on a broad scale. However, they acknowledge that research data, inspiration, innovative strategies, and technological resources can foster creativity. In other words, AI supports creativity by delivering data more quickly and facilitating the often challenging process of brainstorming. Frequently mentioned keywords such as "ease," "easy," "work," "help," "improve," and "develop" suggest that respondents view AI as a tool for collaboration rather than something capable of acting independently. The point is that the power of their own minds cannot be replaced, as AI tools primarily serve to facilitate better solutions and provide unexpected answers, particularly in addressing crisis situations more effectively. One of the interviewees persuasively highlighted that GenAI cannot surpass human power in terms of decision making and analyzing, stating, "This application is not ready to conduct its own research, as it is not developed at a neurological level." (Informant 6)

The Influence of AI Upon Work

Even though the purpose of this research does not primarily rely on a statistical approach, the use of the Likert scale has provided better organization of students' views regarding their emotional approach to work. The following table illustrates the extent to which GenAI is perceived as a threat to employees, directly linked to their generational cohort. Since the questionnaire was self-administered, the comparison between generations is based on Gen Z's rational perspective in contrast to Millennials' and Gen X's viewpoints.

Table 2. Viewpoints of different generations on work

Survey's statement	Strongly disagree	Disagree	Neither agree or disagree	Agree	Strongly agree
AI is a necessity for being successful at work.	29.18%	34.76%	21.04%	12.02%	3%
AI addresses to Generation Z and Milennials.	8.11%	26.95%	28.20%	26.06%	10.68%
AI will help me earn more money.	13.30%	22.31%	30.47%	24.46%	9.46%

Not surprisingly, respondents do not believe that AI can be predominantly used to guarantee success at work. However, they acknowledge that its area of influence is quite broad. This awareness of AI's potential underscores their acceptance of integrating machine-learning technologies into various aspects of life for varied purposes. 35.06% of students believe that AI is not exclusively tailored to Gen Z or Millennials, suggesting that it has the potential to appeal to other generations, interests, and activities. However, 28.20% of respondents remain undecided about associating AI with these technology-driven generations, who are often willing to invest in developing alternative areas of expertise. Students express significant doubts regarding the possibility of earning more money through the use of AI tools. This reflects their understanding that AI cannot replace their expertise, knowledge, skills, or abilities, as it remains a machine-learning tool whose benefits are dependent on human input and effort. They recognize that success is not guaranteed in this process of integrating AI into work and learning to enhance efficiency and income. The significant indecision among students (30.47%) reveals their fear of failure and a lack of trust in adapting to numerous changes simultaneously. Clearly, the next phase of this research should delve into the emotional attitudes towards AI, exploring fears, distrust, potential conflicts, and the challenges posed by rapid technological advancements.

Expectations Regarding AI in Education

This topic is equally significant for both key actors in the higher education process: teachers and students. Teachers design their courses by integrating AI facilities, aligning with their area of expertise and students' needs. Failing to do so risks a significant rise in student dropout rates, as a higher education system that cannot anticipate and address the demands of a rapidly evolving future becomes outdated and irrelevant to the labor market. Students are always inquisitive, always willing to try new technological experiences especially because they realize that individual efforts make a difference on the labor market in front of future employees.

Table 3. How academia meets students' needs

Survey's statement	Strongly disagree	Disagree	Neither agree or disagree	Agree	Strongly agree
The academic classes should use AI tools.	9.40%	17.96%	29.48%	27.35%	15.81%
Teachers should upgrade their methods because they could be replaced by AI.	14.97%	26.92%	25.21%	17.09%	15.81%
Students would be more interested in courses using AI tools.	6%	16.27%	28.63%	29.87%	19.23%
The distance between academia and future jobs increases without using AI tools.	5.55%	20.96%	35.04%	22. 22%	16.23%

Students expressed their agreement regarding the use of AI tools during classes in significant percentages (43.16%), with 27.35% agreeing and 15.81% strongly agreeing with the idea. The reasons for such strong support are quite diverse: curiosity, interest in technology, a sense of novelty, and the ability to solve tasks differently. In short, their behavior is often characterized as cutting-edge and thinking outside the box. It is interesting to note that respondents do not believe AI could fully replace a teacher's way of dealing with their subject. A significant percentage (25.21%) remains rather confused about the innovative methods teachers might implement. This confusion may stem from several factors: lack of understanding of AI tools, the relationship between academia and AI opportunities, AI's credibility, and, ultimately, the field of study. Most respondents study social sciences, communication, and law, and they tend to distrust AI-provided knowledge, often rejecting innovation and technology.

49. 10% of students agree or strongly agree that they would be more engaged in courses if teachers integrated AI tools into their lessons and academic activities. Even something as simple as a better presentation or a deeper analysis facilitated by machine learning reinforces their belief that AI is becoming an integral part of people's lives.

Regarding adaptation to the labor market, some students do not trust the idea of relying on AI as a prerequisite for success. Among the respondents, 5.55% disagree, while 20.96% strongly reject the notion of connecting the labor market with academia through extensive use of AI. However, 38.45% of the participants in this research support the view that AI plays a significant role in bridging the gap between higher education and future employment opportunities.

Interviewees' perspectives stand for relevant opinions, specially when it comes to the next question: "To what extent does the use of AI bring students closer to labor market?"

Through thematic analysis, interviewees reveal significant themes that are connected to the open-coded categories identified in the questionnaire. The subsequent table emphasizes the significant subjects that emerged from semi-structured interviews conducted with six teachers. These teachers are interested in a variety of knowledge areas and are preoccupied with GenAI. They are employed at three universities, a factor that is significant given the differences in organizational culture.

Table 4. Challenges of introducing AI tools in higher education

No	Themes	Open-coded category in questionnaire	No of comments made by respondents of the questionnaire	No of comments made by respondents of the interviews
1	Ethics and limits of application	Plagiarism " Being accused of poorly made task, lack of creativity and plagiarism." "All can use it in bad ways to copy others work. "	77	16 (counting all mentions related to the topic)
		Lack of communication	0	12
		Comfort "Getting too lazy and not checking the solutions that Chat GPT provides could lead to failure. "	14	8
		"a threat for reducing the thinking capabilities of anyone. "	43	16
		Inaccurate information	31	20
2	Institutional support	-new courses including AI	163	6
		-teachers' training	101	15
		-AI package premium paid	80	5
3	Coherence in education	-integrated higher education	165	25
4	Avoiding outdated information	-AI assistance during classes	158	14
		-AI use as a tool among other tools	77	20
5	Developing personality's characteristics	-creativity	27	5
		-organization	35	10
		-efficiency	53	24
		-new information, association	45	10
		-curiosity	56	4

The interviewees placed greater emphasis on this section of the discussion. The thematic analysis revealed several topics that are closely associated with students' opinions. As stated by Informant 4, training is essential for pedagogues to attain official authorization in employing AI instruments during instructional sessions, such as lectures and presentations, for the purpose of enhancing learning efficacy.

"We must take care how we make use of AI, there must be rules, I believe in future we should introduce a module, a course to teach us how to use AI and we should further teach the ethical way of this process."

Another interviewee inquired about the significance of both factors in higher education. Specifically, the interviewee sought to understand the extent to which full access to Open AI and other tools would be essential for developing critical thinking skills and the necessary competencies among students and teachers. The potential of unlimited access to GenAI tools is motivating both students and teachers to enhance their efficiency.

"It would be extremely interesting if both students and teachers had unlimited access to all AI paid tools to structure information and develop linguistic competencies. Using ChatGPT to comprehend the process of summarizing a book could be considered a method of self-teaching that fosters critical thinking and other skills. In my opinion, I don't believe they can replace a teacher, though." (Informant 6)

Another respondent is cautious and skeptical about the integration of AI tools in academic teaching because it is necessary to better investigate the credibility of the type of intelligence.

"On the other hand, there is no need to jump into the void. AI does not (at least at present) have unlimited capabilities. It is important, particularly in academia, to remain realistic and thoughtful. For some issues AI does not provide reliable support." (Informant 3)

Bridging Education With Labour Market

Table 5. Students' preparation for labour market during higher education

No	Themes	Open-coded category in questionnaire	No of comments made by respondents of the questionnaire	No of comments made by respondents of the interviews
1	Saving time	Updated information	22	5
		Rapidity of solving tasks	79	13
2.	Creativity	Creative and innovative tasks	41	12

continued on following page

Table 5. Continued

No	Themes	Open-coded category in questionnaire	No of comments made by respondents of the questionnaire	No of comments made by respondents of the interviews
3	Following tendencies	Interaction with industry	50	6
		Teacher's and industry example	163	14
4.	Updating curricula	New courses related to new jobs	114	10

In academia, technology is a priority for 123 students of our research study. This is because they want to be prepared for the new era of AI and the labour market. They think that academia must be strongly linked with new professional trends and demands. Teachers also know that they have to keep up to date with new tendencies, performances and standards required by employees. One of the people interviewed said:

> *"Teachers must always be in touch with the labour market. That is why they should always be updated with the latest discoveries. That's why I always invite many professionals in the field to ensure a fusion between the academic world and the professional one." (Informant 4)*

Another interviewee with a higher level of expertise believes that students should be prepared not only to embrace AI tools in their daily office work, but also to reject them when organizational culture dictates specific rules. In this context, students should learn to distinguish between AI's advantages and disadvantages in various circumstances, enabling them to solve tasks using different approaches.

> *"To the extent that practitioners in the relevant industry also use AI, essentially aligning with the expectations of those they will work with, according to the realities, shaping their field. For example, in the case of PR, there are agencies that use AI solutions. However, there are also cases where such tools are prohibited. I believe it is important for students to understand what these tools entail and how they are used, precisely to clarify their limitations and risks". (Informant 1)*

Discussing the extent to which AI can affect future professional life, almost all interviewees acknowledged that they are not afraid of being challenged, as transformations are a part of teachers' experiences. Moreover, they believe that ChatGPT's role has been to motivate them to improve their skills and technological knowledge. Only one informant expressed concerns about the limitations of technology and their ability to keep up with it.

> *"I wish I could keep up with these tendencies, though I'm not sure how far I could go/ this could take me. To be honest, I feel it as a threat to my career, but I do not necessarily realize how much of it is true, which level this threat will achieve in the future. The more advanced the technology, the more conservative*

we, Romanians, are. If I feel like this, if I am more aware then other older colleagues of mine from other specializations, then it is hard to say, we might as well close the university." (Informant 3)

There is no doubt that this was a subjective opinion, reflecting a lack of trust in the future due to the perceived difficulty in controlling innovation and technology. This perspective stands in contrast to the majority view, which sees AI as a motivating factor rather than a threat. However, it's important to note that teaching in contemporary society constantly involves controlling information, updating classes, and finding the balance between AI assistance and the human mind. Given these challenges, it is difficult to assert that there are no risks involved in training students for the labor market. This nuanced view acknowledges both the potential benefits of AI in education and the complexities it introduces to the teaching process and student preparation.

DISCUSSIONS AND CONCLUSIONS

According to the survey analysis, students' engagement levels increase when teachers incorporate AI tools into their courses, whether for conveying new information or providing feedback. This trend clearly reflects students' perceived necessity to be prepared for future professions. Consequently, teachers should pay attention to emerging trends and tendencies, leading to constant updates of their course syllabi and, occasionally, curricula.Interestingly, despite students' lifelong exposure to technology, they still require guidance and instruction in its effective use. As one interviewee astutely observed:

"I have noticed that most students, although natively digital, are naively digital." (Informant 4). This observation underscores an important distinction between mere familiarity with technology and the ability to use it critically and effectively in an academic or professional context. It suggests that while students may be comfortable with technology, they may lack the sophisticated understanding necessary to leverage it fully in their studies and future careers.

Given these findings, the second hypothesis is validated: young people are not afraid of losing their future jobs, considering that AI tools might consistently support their work. This aligns with the earlier observation that students see AI integration in their courses as necessary preparation for their future professions.

While students seem optimistic about AI's role in their future careers, teachers maintain a more reserved stance, recognizing both AI's potential and its current limitations in education.The observation about students being "naively digital" (Informant 4) gains additional significance in this context. It suggests that while students are enthusiastic about AI, they may not fully grasp its complexities and ethical implications. This further emphasizes the crucial role of teachers in guiding students to use AI tools critically and responsibly.

Regarding the last hypothesis, it was not validated, as teachers do not associate AI with particular fields of knowledge, such as engineering, robotics, mathematics, medicine, and physics. Instead, they comprehend that AI tools can enrich and diversify the academic approach beyond a specific area, as long as the idea consists of a new type of communication between the human brain and machine learning. This understanding suggests that teachers see AI's potential as a cross-disciplinary tool, capable of enhancing learning and communication across a wide range of subjects, rather than being limited to specific domains. This broader perspective aligns with the educators' cautious, but open-minded approach to integrating AI into their teaching practices.

REFERENCES

Abu Shawar, B., & Atwell, E. (2002). *A comparison between Alice and Elizabeth chatbot systems. Research Report 2002.19.* University of Leeds – School of Computing.

Abu Shawar, B. A., & Atwell, E. (2007). Chatbots: Are they really useful? *Journal for Language Technology and Computational Linguistics*, *22*(1), 29–49. DOI: 10.21248/jlcl.22.2007.88

Al-Mughairi, H. and Bhaskar, P. (2024), "Exploring the factors affecting the adoption AI techniques in higher education: insights from teachers' perspectives on ChatGPT", *Journal of Research in Innovative Teaching & Learning*, Vol. ahead-of-print No. ahead-of-print, 1-16. https://doi.org/DOI: 10.1108/JRIT-09-2023-0129

Alqahtani, T., Badreldin, H. A., Alrashed, M., Alshaya, A. I., & Alghamdi, S. S., bin Saleh, K., ... & Albekairy, A. M. (2023). The emergent role of artificial intelligence, natural learning processing, and large language models in higher education and research. *Research in Social & Administrative Pharmacy*, *19*(8), 1236–1242. DOI: 10.1016/j.sapharm.2023.05.016 PMID: 37321925

Azaiz, I., Deckarm, O., & Strickroth, S. (2023). AI-enhanced auto-correction of programming exercises: How effective is GPT-3.5? *International Journal Of Engineering Pedagogy*, *13*(8), 67–83. DOI: 10.3991/ijep.v13i8.45621

Batacharia, B., & Levy, D. A., R. C., Krotov, and Wilks, Y. (1999). CONVERSE: a conversational companion. In Wilks, Y., editor, *Machine conversations*, 205–215. Kluwer, Boston/ Dordrecht/ London.

Bigan, C. (2022). Trends in Teaching Artificial Intelligence for Industry 5.0. In Drăghici, A., & Iva cu, L. (Eds.), *Sustainability and Innovation in Manufacturing Enterprises, Advances in Sustainability Science and Technology* (pp. 257–275). Springer., DOI: 10.1007/978-981-16-7365-8_2

Braun, V., & Clarke, V. (2006). Using thematic analysis in psychology. *Qualitative Research in Psychology*, *3*(2), 77–101. DOI: 10.1191/1478088706qp063oa

Chan, C. K. Y., & Hu, W. (2023). Students' voices on generative AI: Perceptions, benefits, and challenges in higher education. *International Journal of Educational Technology in Higher Education*, *20*(43), 1–18. DOI: 10.1186/s41239-023-00411-8

Crompton, H., & Burke, D. (2023). Artificial intelligence in higher education: The state of the field. *International Journal of Educational Technology in Higher Education*, *20*(22), 1–22. DOI: 10.1186/s41239-023-00392-8

Drăghici, A., & Iva cu, L. (2022). Trends in Teaching Artificial Intelligence for Industry 5.0. In Drăghici, A., & Iva cu, L. (Eds.), *Sustainability and Innovation in Manufacturing Enterprises, Advances in Sustainability Science and Technology* (pp. 1–16). Springer., DOI: 10.1007/978-981-16-7365-8_2

Gibbs, G., Cameron, C., Kemenade, R., Teal, A., and Phillips, D. (2004). Using a chatbot conversation to enhance the learning of social theory. Published online: file:///Users/madamoraru/Downloads/Chatbots_are_they_really_useful.pdf

Glatthorn, A. A., Boschee, F., Whitehead, B. M., & Boschee, B. F. (2018). *Curriculum leadership: Strategies for development and implementation.* SAGE publications.

Gorgone, J., Davis, G. B., Valacich, J. S., Topi, H., Feinstein, D. L., & Longenecker, H. E. (2003). IS 2002 model curriculum and guidelines for undergraduate degree programs in information systems. *Communications of the Association for Information Systems, 11*(1), 1.

Gorgone, J., Gray, P., Stohr, E. A., Wigand, R. T., & Valacich, J. S. (2005). MSIS 2006 curriculum preview. *Communications of the Association for Information Systems, 15*(1), 30.

Herţeliu, C., Alexe-Coteţ, D., Hâj, C.M., & Pârvan, A.T. (2022). Defining and Measuring Dropout Phenomenon in Romanian Public Universities. InCuraj, A., Salmi, J., & Hâj, C.M. (eds) *Higher Education in Romania: Overcoming Challenges and Embracing Opportunities*. Springer, Cham. DOI: 10.1007/978-3-030-94496-4

Hu, K. (2023, February 2). ChatGPT sets record for fastest-growing user base—analyst note. Reuters. Retrieved from https://www.reuters.com/technology/chatgpt-sets-record-fastest-growing-user-base-analyst-note-2023-02-01/

Hutchens, J. (1996). How to pass the turing test by cheating. Research Report TR97-05, University of Western Australia – School of Electrical, Electronic and Computer Engineering, Perth.

Iku-Silan, A., Hwang, G.-J., & Chen, C. H. (2023). Decision-guided chatbots and cognitive styles in interdisciplinary learning. *Computers & Education, 201*. Advance online publication. DOI: 10.1016/j.compedu.2023.104812

Lee, H. (2023). Using ChatGPT as a learning tool in acupuncture education: Comparative study. *JMIR Medical Education, 9*, e47427. Advance online publication. DOI: 10.2196/47427 PMID: 37590034

Liang, J. C., Hwang, G. J., Chen, M. R. A., & Darmawansah, D. (2021). Roles and research foci of artifcial intelligence in language education: An integrated bibliographic analysis and systematic review approach. *Interactive Learning Environments*. Advance online publication. DOI: 10.1080/10494820.2021.1958348

Loyens, S. M. M., van Meerten, J. E., Schaap, L., & Wijnia, L. (2023). Situating higher-order, critical, and critical-analytic thinking in problem- and project-based learning environments: A systematic review. *Educational Psychology Review*, *35*(2), 39. Advance online publication. DOI: 10.1007/s10648-023-09757-x

Nusivera, E., Hikmat, A. & Ghani, A. A. R. (2025). Integration of Chat-GPT Usage in Language Learning Model to Improve Argumentation Skills, Complex Comprehension Skills, and Critical Thinking Skills. *International Journal of Learning, Teaching and Educational Research*, 24, No. 2, 375-390, February 2025. https://doi.org/. Received Dec 12, 2024; Revised Feb 3, 2025; Accepted Feb 19, 2025DOI: 10.26803/ijlter.24.2.19

Pérez, J., Daradoumis, T., & Puig, J. (2020). Rediscovering the use of chatbots in education: A Systematic literature review. *Computational Applications in Engineering Education,* 28, 1–https://www.semanticscholar.org/paper/ Rediscovering-the-use-of-chatbots-in-education%3A-A-P%C3%A9rez Daradoumis/6f07a03d6a96e943bee-b3cad641c700f124c5cf7

Popenici, S. A. D., & Kerr, S. (2017). Exploring the impact of artificial intelligence on teaching and learning in higher education. *Research and Practice in Technology Enhanced Learning*, *12*(22), 1–13. DOI: 10.1186/s41039-017-0062-8 PMID: 30595727

Singh, M. (2023). Maintaining the integrity of the SOUTH AFRICAN university: The impact of chatgpt on plagiarism and scholarly writing. *South African Journal of Higher Education*, *37*(5), 203–220. DOI: 10.20853/37-5-5941

Vitale, C., Bowyer, D., & Bayerlein, L. (2020). Developing and Presenting a Framework for Meeting Industry, Student and Educator Expectations in University Degrees. *E-Journal of Business Education & Scholarship of Teaching*, *14*(1), 57–65.

Weizenbaum, J. (1966). ELIZA – A computer program for the study of natural language communication between man and machine. *Communications of the ACM, 10*(8), 36–45. DOI: 10.1145/365153.365168

Yudiono, H., Maulana, S., Wijaya, M. B. R., Aprianto, R., & Karsan, K. (2021). Product-based learning model through the alignment of mechanical engineering competencies with industry. *Jurnal Pendidikan Teknologi dan Kejuruan, 27*(1), 74-80. DOI: 10.21831/jptk.v27i1.28832

Zawacki-Richter, O., Marín, V. I., Bond, M., & Gouverneur, F. (2019). Systematic review of research on artifcial intelligence applications in higher education—Where are the educators? *International Journal of Educational Technology in Higher Education, 16*(1), 1–27. DOI: 10.1186/s41239-019-0171-0

Chapter 7
Navigating AI in Learning: Communication, Ethics, and the Student Voice

Mayyer Ling
https://orcid.org/0000-0002-4632-6693
Universiti Brunei Darussalam, Brunei

ABSTRACT

This study explores the perception of Artificial Intelligence (AI) in an educational setting through the perspective of university students – focusing on students' attitudes towards AI and how they use or wish to utilise AI in their learning. Thirty-three undergraduates responded to an open-ended survey and a focus group. The survey results suggested that students generally favour using AI in university settings. However, the open-ended portion of the questionnaires indicated that there may still be uncertainty on how to use AI productively in an educational setting. The focus group findings were focused on the ethical concerns and implications of the use of AI in education. Participants also expressed their concerns over the possibility that AI will threaten humans in terms of creativity and novelty of ideas, which were seen as crucial learning values in the university by participants in the study. This study adds to the growing body of knowledge on AI literacy, particularly in providing human input, concerns, and objectives regarding the use of AI for learning.

INTRODUCTION

Artificial Intelligence (AI) is an emerging technology that has the potential to deliver value-added, innovative learning experiences for students. AI is seen to be a valuable tool in bridging the knowledge gap (Yuwono et al., 2024), particularly among teachers keen to enhance their subject matter expertise and provide the best

DOI: 10.4018/979-8-3373-6018-8.ch007

Copyright © 2026, IGI Global Scientific Publishing. Copying or distributing in print or electronic forms without written permission of IGI Global Scientific Publishing is prohibited.

pedagogical contribution to their students. In addition, with an understanding of the drawbacks and limitations of AI, students were found to be able to discern the different qualities of assistance they can obtain from the use of AI tools such as ChatGPT (van Niekerk et al., 2025). So, strides have indeed been made in investigating AI in education, but there is certainly more to be done.

In recent years, AI has sparked discussions in all sectors, particularly education, where issues such as fairness and bias (Ferrara, 2023) that resulted from the data sources fed into the algorithm design and training programmes, data security and privacy (Jezova, 2021) and humans losing their ability to produce novel ideas (Fügener et al., 2021) due to the lack of human interaction and increased dependence of AI. Despite the glaring concerns, students remain significant stakeholders in integrating AI into education (Sabraz Nawaz et al., 2024). In addition, AI remains extensively adopted in the education system – mainly by educational institutions for teaching and learning (Chen et al., 2020). Due to the aggressively ubiquitous nature of AI adoption in the educational setting, it is pertinent that we continue our quest to explore the relationship between AI and the stakeholders. To this end, this study explores university students' perception of AI in an educational setting, focusing on their attitudes towards AI and how they use or wish to utilise AI in their learning.

Therefore, the research question this study aims to answer reads: "How does AI facilitate communication in educational settings?". This research question will help to achieve two main aims. First, it will fill the gap in our knowledge of students' expectations in incorporating AI into their learning journey. Second, the study aims to improve our understanding of how students perceive the usefulness and limitations of AI in communication with instructors and peers.

LITERATURE REVIEW

Definition of AI

While there is a lack of consensus on the definition of AI, as it varies depending on the usage in particular settings, this paper will adopt a definition most suited for using AI in education. AI is thus defined as "machine-based systems that can, given a set of human-defined objectives, make predictions, recommendations, or decisions that influence real or virtual environments." (UNICEF, 2021). This definition is appropriate for this study for two reasons: (1) it highlights the importance of the human-defined objectives, and (2) it emphasises the influence of AI output on real or virtual environments. Students, being the focused stakeholders in this study, are assumed to have a defined objective in their use of AI, and the output of AI tools could very well impact their learning journey, providing assistance, guidelines, and feedback.

Previous studies have made strides in providing historical development of AI (Buchanan, 2005) and highlighting the various tools that could potentially enhance and enable personalised learning methods for students (Ch'ng, 2023; Baidoo-Anu et al., 2023; Kasneci et al., 2023). These studies shed light on the benefits of incorporating AI into students' learning. However, concerns were raised about the use of AI in educational settings. These issues include developing the appropriate competencies and literacies to manoeuvre AI productively and ethically (Kasneci et al., 2023). Previous studies have identified core literacies necessary for AI's critical interaction and evaluation (Long & Magerko, 2020) and the effectiveness of courses that aim to develop these literacies (Kong et al., 2021).

AI in Education

AI and teachers are also a productive focus of investigation for AI in educational settings. Previous findings have highlighted the various shifts in instructional designs brought about by AI (Ch'ng, 2023) and the usefulness of AI in performing routine and predictable tasks, such as creating rubrics for assessments and quizzes (Cooper, 2023). Similar to studies that focused on students' learning with the use of AI, concerns have also been raised for teachers along the same vein; teachers also need to be equipped with literacies and criticality in evaluating the usefulness and appropriateness of AI-generated assistance for their teaching contexts. The emphasis on literacy is apt in both contexts (i.e., teaching and learning) because it is impossible to fully utilise AI without honing the appropriate literacies (Olari & Romeike, 2021).

In a different yet related vein, other research has also focused on analysing and developing frameworks for the application of AI in the educational setting (Zhang & Cao, 2021) and evaluating the appropriateness of the adoption of AI as a platform for education (Thongprasit & Wannapiroon, 2022). AI in the educational setting is a force that we will need to embrace, and not oppose, to advance productively as we face the future of education in the digital age.

Institutional and Educator's Perspectives on AI

As part of this journey in embracing change and, dare I say, acceptance of AI as part of the future of education, HEIs have formal and significant roles to play in ensuring the readiness of the institution, educators and students in navigating the complex web of AI. Whether it is policy formation, infrastructure readiness or faculty support, institutional responses primarily shape the adoption practices of AI in higher education by setting the parameters within which educators and students can engage with AI. These parameters would influence how fast and wide the integration is into the curricula and administrative processes.

Universiti Brunei Darussalam, where this study took place, provided a policy and guidelines on using GenAI in 2023, which is available in the staff portal. In general, the university actively endorses the use of AI and made it clear in the policy document that UBD is committed to leveraging GenAI to achieve institutional academic goals. The document included comprehensive and practical advice on how to incorporate AI into the curricula and calls for curriculum redesign to allow the shift of focus onto higher-order thinking skills. Despite the generic tone of the document, it is clear that the university hinges on educators as the primary force driving the use of GenAI tools in the curriculum and is supportive of endeavours in this direction.

Universiti Brunei Darussalam is not alone in its endorsement. Many universities in the United States have also provided similar policies and guidelines for pedagogical and administrative purposes. McDonald et al. (2025) analysed policies from 116 R1 institutions. They found that 63% of these institutions encourage using GenAI, and 41% include detailed classroom usage guidance. In a complementary study, Wang et al. (2024) also found that most institutions from their 100 top universities sample were cautiously encouraging the use of AI, noting that no university completely bans the use of AI. They also deduced that many institutions do not have a one-size-fits-all policy, which gives educators the authority to decide what constitutes appropriate use of AI in the classroom. The infancy of using AI for instruction (Sebesta & Davis, 2023) also drives many higher education institutions to have policies that instead focus on maintaining academic integrity.

The professional autonomy given to educators in many universities, including Universiti Brunei Darussalam, can be empowering. The flexibility enables educators to tailor their and their students' use of AI to suit the subject matter, allowing for personalised teaching and learning experiences. Universiti Brunei Darussalam, similar to many other universities in McDonald et al. (2025) and Wang et al. (2024), encourages the use of AI to enhance educational practices as long as the integration is ethical and responsible. The resources in the form of classroom guidelines, sample activities, and assessment ideas are projected to help kick-start an educator's journey toward incorporating AI. However, while many institutions choose to acknowledge the increase in workload for educators should the inclusion of GenAI take place, the policy document from Universiti Brunei Darussalam does not explicitly address this issue. There is also a clear emphasis on curriculum redesign. Similar to other studies cited earlier, the framework proposed would benefit from more detailed strategies that support a wide range of evaluation methods to mitigate the misuse of AI in the educational setting. Despite the gap that suggests the need to examine the implications of the adoption of AI, particularly on educator's responsibility and institutional support, a large-scale study found that the incorporation of AI improves learner outcomes and offers potential cost-savings (Sebesta & Davis, 2023) – both are key priorities for many academic institutions, making the arduous endeavour one that is worthwhile.

AI in Education Assessment and Feedback

As institutions and educators find a balance in teaching and learning with AI, assessment and feedback become critical areas for re-evaluation. I have mentioned previously that the policy guidelines at Universiti Brunei Darussalam and other universities echo the need for curriculum redesign because traditional assessment methods are often product-based and reliant on written outputs. These two methods can easily be compromised with the use of AI. It is not entirely accurate to assume that all AI usage is unethical. However, it is a natural and timely response to viewing AI as a catalyst for innovation of assessment practices. Assessments can be designed to target higher-order thinking skills and be better aligned with digital tools and advances while at the same time preserving the authenticity of the work produced.

We must acknowledge that AI tools such as ChatGPT, while unable to be completely accurate, are certainly fluent and can produce well-structured texts. Educators and learners who wish to leverage AI's potential and strength, especially in language, could use this opportunity, which is completely ethical and acceptable. Assessments can be redesigned to include project-based tasks, process-based and reflective evaluations, and assignments that encourage critical thinking and creativity. The redesigned assessments would foster deeper learning (Gamage et al., 2023), creating valuable opportunities to harness essential skills such as analysis, ethical reasoning, metacognition and empathy – preparing learners for complex and real-world challenges.

Feedback practices have also been called under scrutiny. Usher (2025) compared feedback provided by GenAI, instructors and peers. AI provided detailed and structured comments – which is understandable and expected as ChatGPT, for example, is trained using a large volume of language training data. However, the feedback can be misaligned with the context or goal of the assignment. On the other hand, human feedback is generally more accurate and aligns with the assignment objectives, and it is personalised. The study highlighted the need to maintain human involvement – instructors and/or peers- in providing feedback and not relying solely on AI.

To redesign the curriculum, a growing body of literature aims to provide educators with principled frameworks. For example, the AAA framework (Against, Avoid, and Adopt) by Lye and Lim (2024) offers a values-based approach to assessment design. The framework encourages educators to critically challenge AI when the outcome aligns with the learning objectives, correctly identify and avoid assessments that can be easily compromised, and objectively adopt AI when it can bring added value and benefits to teaching and learning, especially in inculcating deep learning. In the policy guideline provided by Universiti Brunei Darussalam, the 4R model was introduced (Respond, Review, Readjust, Reflect) –adapted from Total Quality Management principles. The model emphasises educators' need to continuously reflect and adjust their teaching practices, assessment methods, and curriculum design to ensure maximum benefit from AI integration into educational settings.

AI as a Tool for Communication in Digital Learning

Part of the intended advancement is the change in how we communicate in the digital space. With AI, especially in the context of instructor-student and peer-to-peer communication, dynamics shift. Tools like ChatGPT enhance communication by improving text clarity assisting users in changing the tone and formality of the original texts. With the right prompts, users can also obtain suggestions on improving their vocabulary, perhaps by seeking ChatGPT's assistance in providing more appropriate synonyms and performing grammar checks. In this context, AI acts as a mediator in ensuring smooth collaboration and communication with instructors and peers as intended by the student.

Also, in relation to communication, there is a shift, particularly in student-instructor interaction, where there is more reliance on automated feedback from AI than strictly waiting for instructor feedback. Quillbot, for example, is an AI tool that allows writers to obtain feedback on grammar, spelling, punctuation, and other writing conventions. With automatic feedback, one can imagine saving more time and energy than when one needs to wait for instructors for feedback on their assignment, particularly in academic writing.

Student Perspectives on AI Research

Previous studies have generally reported positively on students' attitudes and perceptions of the use of AI in educational settings, especially for learning-support purposes (Pellas, 2023), automated feedback (Idroes et al., 2023), and research purposes (Pokrivcakova, 2023). Students also perceived that AI helps improve learning experiences and manage tasks (Al-Tkhayneh et al., 2023). These studies suggest a myriad of applications where students find AI helpful in assisting them and that students have been exploring AI tools for their learning, independently or guided.

Researchers have also investigated specific student profiles and their perceptions of AI integration. For example, AI is found to help provide support for international students (Wang et al., 2023) and learners with special needs (Vincent-Lancrin &

Vlies, 2020). Several factors are influential in generating such positive uptake on AI, including students' age, familiarity with electronic devices, interest in AI and technology-related experiences in general (Pellas, 2023; Kim & Lee, 2023).

Thus, we can deduce that students must be receptive to AI and be open to exploring and using AI in their education. However, the positive perception and attitudes toward AI incorporation into the educational setting do not necessarily mean that the education system is already implementing and incorporating AI appropriately in the education system (as highlighted in the earlier discussion on policies and guidelines imparted by institutions), nor does it affirm the alignment with students' expectations on how AI should be incorporated into their learning. Therefore, this study aims to shed light on this matter by focusing on how AI should be integrated into the educational setting based on students' perspectives.

METHODOLOGY

Research Design

This study employs a mixed-method approach; the qualitative approach involves a survey, and the quantitative approach includes a focus group discussion. Thematic analysis of the focus group discussion was employed to capture students' perceptions and other relevant and recurring themes with regard to the use of AI in educational settings.

Participants

A purposive sampling method was used to recruit participants to fulfil five criteria:

1. English proficiency of Grade C6 in English Language, or IELTS score of 6.0 and equivalent
2. Participants were L2 speakers of English
3. Participants were from the same major in the university (English Studies, which is a combination of English Language and Linguistics, English Literature and Professional Communication)
4. Participants were enrolled in level 3 and level 4 courses (more advanced level courses which require the application of theoretical knowledge)
5. Participants were female

Thirty-three undergraduates voluntarily took part in the survey. The criteria for purposive sampling was chosen to enable the selection of a small sample size for the study and control the influencing variables that may affect the survey results, such as language proficiency and academic major. Unique to this particular scale, where gender was found to be an influencing factor in reporting attitudes (Grassini, 2023), I have also ensured that the gender of all respondents was the same.

Data Collection

The survey employed is a measure of the general attitude of students towards AI. This measure is the AI attitude scale, *AIAS-4* (Grassini, 2023). The scale has high internal consistency, which assured the author that the four items were reliable indicators of attitude toward AI usage and integration. AIAS-4 is a self-reported instrument with two primary foci: (1) the perceived usefulness of AI and (2) the perceived impact of AI on society and humanity. These two focuses will help confirm the perception of students toward AI, which has been reported to be positive based on previous literature (Pellas, 2023; Pokrivcakova, 2023). However, it is still necessary to measure in the current study to not assume a uniform, positive perception toward AI for all students in different learning contexts.

In addition to the relevant scale foci, the self-reported component of the scale allows for internal reflection on the part of the participants in the study, which is of particular importance in this study. This reflection will help engage the participants to respond to the open-ended portion of the survey and provide more context to the Likert-scale responses.

After obtaining participants' consent, they were supplied a series of questions distributed via Qualtrics containing both the Likert scale and open-ended questions for the survey, as well as questions for the focus group.

Survey

The Likert portion of the survey was a 4-item scale where participants were required to select their responses between 1- Strongly Disagree (SD), 2- Disagree (D), 3 - Neutral (N), 4 - Agree (A), and Strongly Agree (SA). The 4-item scale asked the following questions:

1. I believe that AI will improve my life
2. I believe that AI will improve my work
3. I think I will use AI technology in the future
4. I believe AI technology is positive for humanity

There were open-ended questions embedded in the survey as well, which were prompted by Yes/No questions, as follows:

1. Have you used AI before? If yes, briefly describe when and how you used AI. If no, briefly explain why not.
2. Would you like to see AI being encouraged to be used in your studies? If yes, briefly describe why. If no, briefly explain why not.
3. How would you use AI to be used in your studies?
   - ☐ Translation
   - ☐ Language learning (e.g. vocabulary, grammar, etc.)
   - ☐ Writing (e.g. to write, to write in appropriate registers and styles, etc.)
   - ☐ Outsource assignments (e.g. AI to help with ideas and prompts)
   - ☐ Others (Briefly describe other usages): ____________________________ ____________
   - ☐ I would not like AI to be used in my studies
4. Do you have any other comments on using AI in educational settings or for educational purposes?

Focus Group

Students then formed groups of 3 to 4 people and participated in a focus group. They were audio-recorded, and in the recording, they all started the conversation by introducing themselves and their major or intended major in the university. The questions for the focus group were geared towards the issue of ethics, as this was one of the most prominent discussions on the use of AI in educational settings based on previous literature (Gonsalves, 2024):

1. What is your understanding of artificial intelligence (AI) and its applications?
2. Can you share any personal interactions with AI? Focus on your perception of its ethics and impact.
3. Are you concerned about AI's ethical implications in higher education? If so, please elaborate and suggest ways to mitigate these implications.
4. What steps can be taken to address the potential ethical biases and discrimination within AI algorithms?
5. How can we educate individuals about AI technology's potential risks and ethical implications?

Data Analysis

Data was analysed using descriptive statistics due to the small sample size, which will be presented in charts in the next section. Meanwhile, NVivo was used to perform thematic analysis with open coding for the focus group to identify themes transparently and rigorously. Transparency and rigour are vital in small samples, despite the results being non-generalisable to the larger population, as the responses may well be an issue that is recurring should the study be replicated in a large sample of respondents.

RESULTS

1. Survey

This section will first present the survey findings using Likert-scale and open-ended questions.

Likert-Scale

1. I believe that AI will improve my life.

Figure 1. Survey findings

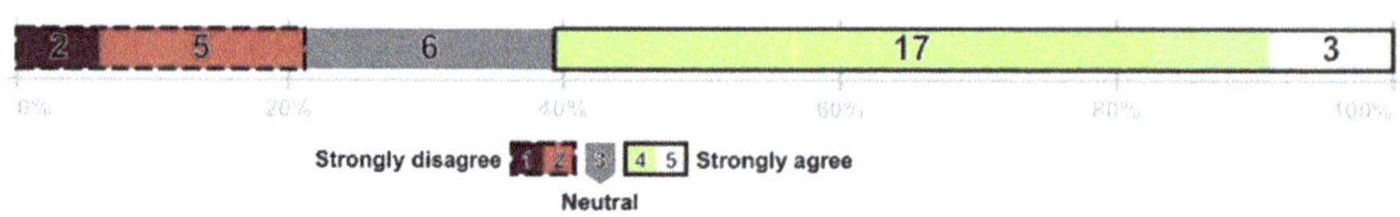

2. I believe that AI will improve my work.

Figure 2. Survey findings for AI improving work.

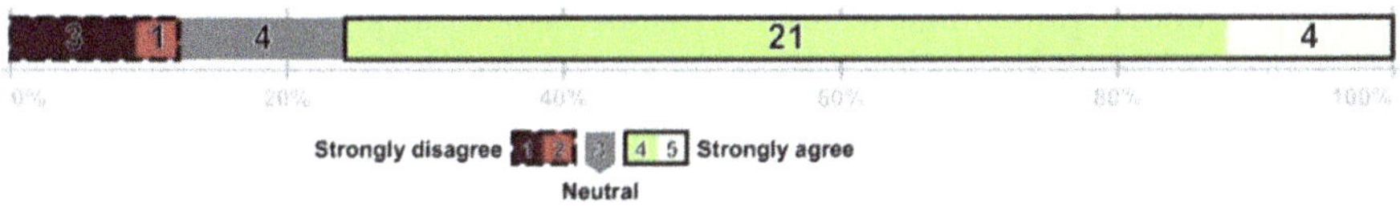

3. I think I will use AI technology in the future.

Figure 3. Use of AI in the future survey findings.

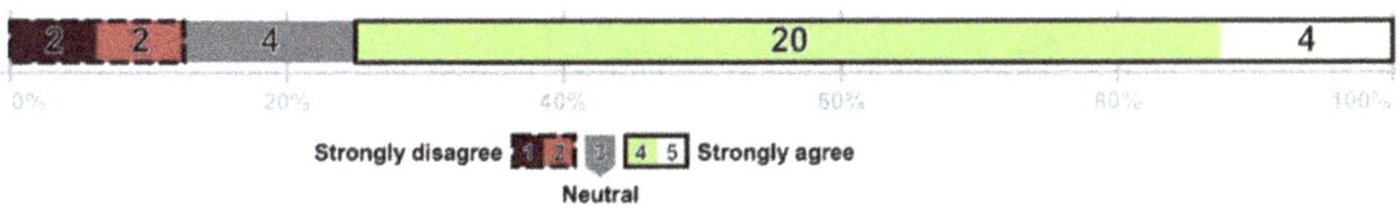

4. I think AI technology is positive for humanity.

Figure 4. Survey findings for AI being positive for humanity.

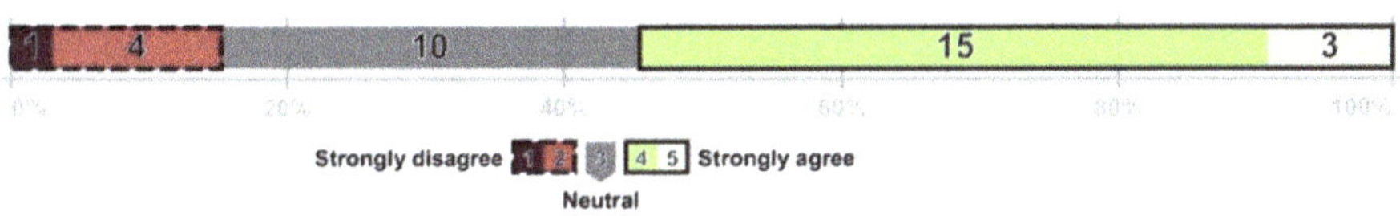

The Likert scale results, as expected based on previous studies (Pellas, 2023; Al-Tkhayneh et al., 2023), skewed towards the positive (indicated by *Agree* and *Strongly agree*) for the use of AI in the participants' lives, work and future. However, we have to be cautious in interpreting item 4; *I think AI technology is positive for humanity* as the value for positive (*Agree* and *Strongly agree*) when compared to the neutral and negative values (*Strongly disagree, Disagree* and *Neutral*), could fall under the margin of error.

Open-Ended Questions

The open-ended portion of the survey started with a question of whether the students have used AI before, and more than 80% (28 students) said they have, as indicated by the dark quadrant in Figure 5 below:

Figure 5. "Have you used AI before?" and "Would you like to see AI being encouraged to be used in your studies?"

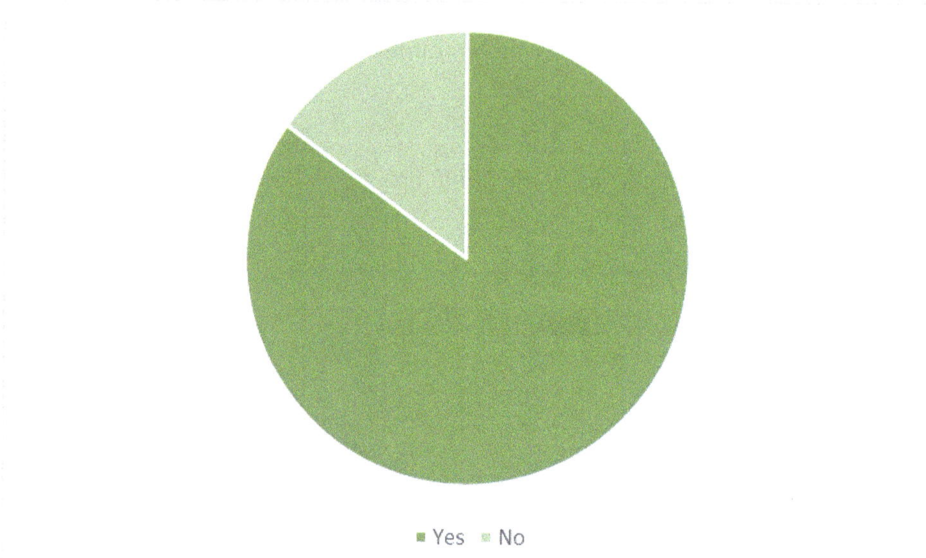

On whether they would like to see AI being encouraged to be used in their studies, 80% of the students (28 participants) responded positively to using AI in their educational setting. Upon closer investigation, the participants who have used AI before are the same individuals who think that AI should be encouraged in their educational settings.

Five themes emerged from the open-ended portion of the survey, where participants shared how they had previously used AI and how they wished AI would be used in their studies. These themes will be used as headings in the following subsection. All quotations used in the excerpts were copied verbatim from the survey, including grammatical inaccuracies and typographical errors, to ensure the authenticity of the data.

Essay and Presentation Structure

The participants use AI to provide headings and content breakdowns for their essays and presentations. In Excerpt 1, the participant shared the typical manner in which he/she sought assistance from AI.

Excerpt 1:

Mostly to structure my essays. I would type my prompt like: "I need to write a 1000 words essay with the title xxx. Could you help list down the headings I should include in the essay and how many words should I write for each section?"

Language Enhancement

Since the participants are all L2 speakers of English, they also used AI to assist in revising sentences for grammar and style and to perform spelling checks. This feature is not necessarily AI, as many word processors, such as Microsoft Word, also flag document language inaccuracies.

Excerpt 2:

Quillbot to help paraphrase sentences that I feel are not up to high educational standards. Rephrasing purposes (to correct grammar and styles/registers accordingly)

Research Assistance

As undergraduates, students will also need to constantly find relevant academic sources that they can use to complete their assignments and research. AI tools help locate these sources or point the participants in the right direction by brainstorming ideas on the given topic and questions.

Excerpt 3:

Yes, only for finding points for essays. For eg, i want to write an essay about a character named Emma, so i used AI to search for it. It gives me a few points as well as the sources tho theyre not as reliable

Overcoming Writer's Block

Participants also used AI to overcome writer's block, as seen in Excerpt 4. The participants may sometimes feel that they need assistance in elaborating on content or ideas, so AI is used to aid them in initiating the process of completing their assessments.

Excerpt 4:

I do use ChatGPT when I am in a mind block. And quillbot to help paraphrase sentences that I feel is not up to high educational standards.

Topic Understanding and Insights

Finally, participants who have used AI also shared that they use the tools to gain a better understanding and insights into the question or topic of their assessments, as seen in Excerpt 5.

Excerpt 5:

it is usually when i dont understand the question and need to be explained in a brief simple way just to give me some insight what do i know to include

Students generally use AI as an educational aid when completing their academic assignments. These aids range from providing structures for essays and presentations to refining language (e.g., accuracy, coherence, style) and gaining a deeper understanding of topics or questions. These assistances by AI generally are used either pre- or post-completion of academic tasks.

However, some participants also said that they had not used AI before and were firmly against the use of AI in their responses. Two themes emerged from the analysis of responses from participants who chose not to use AI, and these will be used as subheadings next.

Resistance to AI Dependency

Participants expressed concerns about AI dependency in their open-ended responses and emphasised the importance of maintaining autonomy in learning.

Excerpt 8:

I would like to stay ignorant about the idea of using AI. Even if it's for drawing, writing, or producing work. It's not efficient in helping me learn.

Preservation of Effort and Originality

The next theme concerns the individual's effort in learning and the originality of ideas. Because AI tools are derivative in extracting information from the data used to train the system, it was unsurprising that some participants were unenthusiastic about implementing AI in their educational settings.

Excerpt 7:

*My efforts in doing my assigned tasks became somewhat useless and under-appreciated because solving problems was somehow 'just one *AI* away'... There's no originality and kind of makes one think "Then, why did I even gain* *knowledge and build my skills when doing almost everything is by easily saying something like "Pakai ChatGPT saja"? [trans. "just use ChatGPT"]*

Some survey participants preferred independent thinking, emphasising the need to rely on one's brain and ideas to ensure that AI does not undermine human creativity. The reluctance of some participants to use AI in their educational setting is understandable as there is a risk of over-reliance on AI, which would adversely impact one's learning process, expressions of creativity and originality of ideas.

Finally, the survey also included a specific section on how participants would like AI to be used in their studies. The results of this section confirm the responses that were thematically grouped in the previous open-ended component of the survey, with participants sharing their range of uses of AI, from writing and language aids (i.e., correction of grammar and accuracy of style and registers) to outsourcing their assignments (i.e., asking AI to assist in creating an outline and suggesting directions for the participants' essays and presentations).

In addition, as seen in Figure 6, five participants selected the option *Others*. They explained that they used AI for "*asking questions when in doubt*" (2 responses), "*writing and language learning*" (2 responses" and "*all of the above*" (1 response).

Figure 6. "How would you like AI to be used in your studies?"

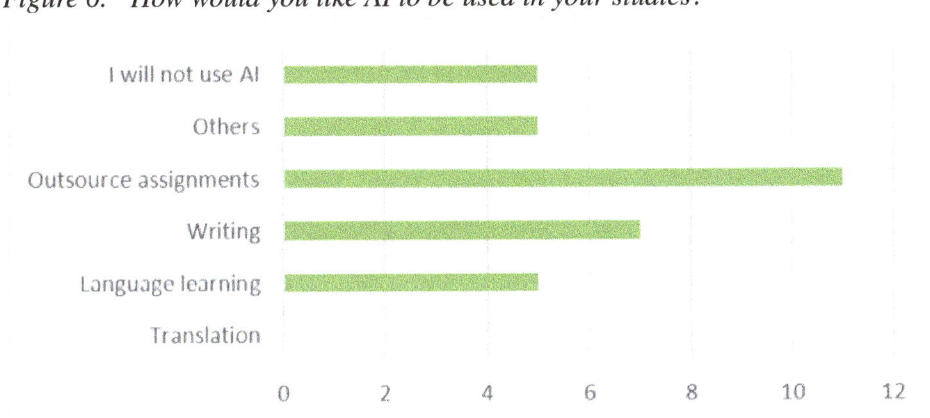

While there were participants who were reluctant to incorporate AI into their educational setting, the majority of the respondents were optimistic about the value of AI in their learning, which corroborates earlier research on the perception of learners in the use of AI (Pellas, 2023; Idroes et al., 2023; Pokrivcakova, 2023; Al-Tkhayneh, 2023).

2. Focus Group

In the focus group discussion, eight themes were found from the thematic analysis: Application of AI in Educational settings, Ethics and Plagiarism, AI and the Learning Process, Bias in AI Algorithms, Mitigating Ethical Issues, Social and Cultural Perceptions of AI, Data Privacy Concerns, and the Importance of Human Oversight.

Applications of AI in Educational Settings

In the focus group discussion, students admitted to using many AI tools in their studies, such as ChatGPT, Grammarly and Quillbot. As seen in Excerpts 8a and 8b, the usage included *topic understanding, insights, and language enhancement,* which was previously noted in the survey responses. The consistency in findings allows for the assumption that students are familiar with various AI tools and find them helpful as aids in improving the quality of their assignments and, to a certain extent, time management.

Excerpt 8a

I mainly use ChatGPT to summarise long texts for my literature modules when I don't have enough time to read everything.

Excerpt 8b

Grammarly and Quillbot help with paraphrasing and making my work more concise.

Ethics and Plagiarism

Students who took part in the study were aware of various issues related to ethics, which include dependency on AI (which aligned with the first part of the study, the survey) to complete tasks, plagiarism, which includes not citing sources properly and/or claiming ideas as one's own, and the lack of transparency for the sources of the outcomes generated by AI – in this case, ChatGPT was specified (see Excerpt 9). The volume of issues that fit this theme suggests that students recognise the drawbacks of using AI and the risks associated with over-dependency on AI and are also aware of the importance of personal effects and efforts in ensuring the ethical use of AI in educational settings.

Excerpt 9

You don't know where ChatGPT gets its information, and it's hard to cite it properly.

While concerns were raised about the use of AI, alongside opportunities and assistance, respondents also provided ample suggestions on mitigating ethical issues. The respondents wanted to be part of the solution and did not automatically dismiss the ubiquitous presence of AI and its increasing hold in technology and educational settings. For example, in Excerpt 10, the respondent was open to being schooled on the use of AI. The suggested workshops were responded to with agreements from the other respondents, who later discussed the contents of these sessions, including introducing educational modules on the proper use of AI, raising awareness of the biases and other issues with AI, and implementing stricter and transparent regulations on AI usage in the educational setting.

Excerpt 10

We need workshops or modules on how to use AI ethically and avoid plagiarism.

AI and the Learning Process

Students who participated in the study were enrolled in higher-level courses offered in their undergraduate study, levels 3 and 4. This means they are assumed to have a certain level of maturity, at least in their discipline (i.e. English Studies) and readiness to apply theoretical knowledge. With this assumption, we can also deduce that these students can perform specific tasks, such as critical thinking and independent learning and even have advanced knowledge in their specialisations.

In the case of AI usage in the learning process, some expressed concerns that the assumptions stated above may not be accurate (see Excerpt 11a) where the respondent has witnessed some colleagues copy from an AI tool, ChatGPT and neither evaluate nor make any alterations on the results generated.

Excerpt 11a

Some students just copy-paste from ChatGPT and don't think for themselves, which can make them lazy.

There were also responses from the focus group that suggested thoughtful use of AI. For instance, in Excerpt 11b, the respondent utilises AI to assist in completing assignments to meet the deadline satisfactorily. However, the respondent also integrated original thoughts into the results generated to refine the response to the assignment and limit dependence on AI usage. These excerpts (i.e. 11a and 11b) signify that regardless of the usefulness of AI in educational settings, there is still potential for misuse. It is up to the users themselves to be mindful of the potential drawbacks of using AI and explore opportunities to collaborate with AI instead of using it as a crutch that hampers one's ability to think for oneself.

Excerpt 11b

It helps me finish my essays on time, but I make sure to add my own thoughts so I understand the material.

Bias in AI Algorithms

Some respondents raised the issue of bias in AI algorithms and expressed concerns that these biases will affect the outcomes generated, leading to inaccuracies, misinformation and disinformation, and the amplification of echo chambers (see Excerpt 12a). In the context of education, the biases will also affect the reliability of systems such as AI detection (as mentioned in Excerpt 12b). The lack of reliability will lead to unfair academic evaluations, and as can be imagined, if the submissions of assignments are final, students may well be wrongly flagged for plagiarism and malpractice, and this accusation could affect their future.

Excerpt 12a

AI scrapes data from the internet, including biased or problematic information, which is hard to control.

Excerpt 12b

False positives in AI detectors unfairly flag students, creating stress and unfair outcomes.

Social and Cultural Perceptions of AI

It was an interesting observation made by some respondents who brought up how the social and cultural contexts also implicate AI in the educational setting, which could extend itself into the workplace setting. In particular, the respondents discussed creative fields such as creative writing and art, as seen in Excerpt 13.

There is, however, a misconception that should be highlighted when discussing the influence of AI in creative fields such as writing and art. AI is trained on existing data, and while the volume of data is vast, AI mimics patterns from these datasets and thus cannot produce novel ideas. Therefore, AI is impractical in assignments that include cultural nuances or niche genres. So, AI tools can be used to generate inspiration. However, they cannot replicate the depth and nuance of more specified cultural and societal contexts that embed the human experience and creativity.

Excerpt 13

AI art feels soulless compared to human-created art, and it risks taking jobs from artists.

Data Privacy Concerns

Respondents also expressed concerns over privacy breaches and data misuse when generating outcomes, such as texts and images (refer to Excerpt 14). This concern further confirms that the respondents are aware of issues surrounding not only AI usage but also AI training. Respondents understand that AI cannot draw ethical boundaries and recognise social and cultural sensitivities like humans.

Excerpt 14

AI systems might compromise privacy by using our data without consent.

Importance of Human Oversight

The final theme aptly encompasses the focus group discussion on the ethics of AI application in the educational setting, where the respondents unanimously agreed that human intervention is key in ensuring the ethical and practical use of AI, as seen in Excerpt 15. Other suggestions along the same vein include the need to maintain academic integrity by declaring the extent of AI usage, evaluating and validating outcomes generated by AI, and only using AI as a tool and not the final outcome in completing academic assignments.

Excerpt 15

You can't just trust AI's answers—you need to double-check with reliable sources.

The more significant finding in this study is students' perspective on AI's role in communication, particularly in the educational setting. We have seen from the survey that participants have used AI to assist in structuring and organising their essays and presentations, correcting the fluency and appropriateness of their language, researching and brainstorming content, overcoming writer's block and gaining more insights into a particular topic of interest or further explanation on relevant academic theories. We have explored the concerns expressed by participants who were more reluctant to incorporate AI into their educational settings. We have also further probed into ethical issues surrounding the use of AI from students' perspective in the focus group.

It would be in our best interest as educators to encourage the use of AI as an aid to empower students in pursuing personalised learning endeavours (Ch'ng, 2023; Baidoo-Anu et al., 2023; Kasneci et al., 2023; Wang et al., 2023; Vincent-Lancrin & Vlies, 2020) while providing the appropriate literacies (Kong et al., 2021; Long & Magerko, 2020) and raising awareness of the shortcomings of AI (Ferrara, 2023; Jezova, 2021; Fügener et al., 2021; Kasneci et al., 2023).

DISCUSSIONS

Building on the findings from both the survey and focus group revealed in the previous section and referring to the research question that drives this study, which reads, "How does AI facilitate communication in educational settings?", this discussion will reorganise the findings into themes that reflect students' perspective specifically on AI's role in communication in the educational setting. The three themes that emerged from the findings are AI in Communication, Challenges in AI as a Communication Tool and Ethics in Usage of AI in Communication.

Theme 1: AI in Communication

Two types of interactions prevail in the educational setting – instructor-student and peer-to-peer. In the findings, the most prominent type of interaction mentioned was instructor-student, where the respondents highlighted the completion of assignments, the need to understand materials for academic modules and improving the language they use so it will be at par with the expected academic standard. There was no mention of peer-to-peer interaction, such as discussions (either face-to-face or in online forums). The lack of peer-to-peer interaction represents a missed opportunity, as previous literature has already demonstrated that peer feedback tends to be aligned with the assignment objectives and is often more personalised and empathetic (Usher, 2025).

Several implications can be suggested here, one of which is that the learning environment is still instructor-centric in design. So, it could be that students view their instructors as their primary source of information for knowledge and feedback. Thus, they are the only ones who need to witness the clear, coherent, high-level academic language students use. This means that there is added pressure on teachers to be able to directly respond to students when support is required, on top of the responsibilities of curriculum redesign and being the primary driver of change in the adoption of AI in the educational setting.

Another implication is that the learning paradigm that the respondents are engaged in is individualised and product-focused. This is perhaps why we found excerpts that suggest learners are trying to understand academic materials themselves. Without the help of instructors or peers and other excerpts that emphasise writer's block, only AI tools were used as resolutions instead of discussions with peers. Learners are essentially demonstrating various levels of personalised, independent learning. The excerpts indicate that learning using AI as an added tool is not necessarily passive. Some excerpts highlighted the awareness of inaccuracies in results generated by AI, such as citations and references.

The third implication is the lost potential for peer learning. While we could suggest that not seeking assistance from peers is perhaps a cultural and contextual norm, the findings also suggest that the respondents may perceive that the contribution and, thus, communication with peers is not as valuable as their communication with AI and their instructors. Peer learning offers many benefits, such as shared perspectives, the opportunity to co-construct knowledge and even the provision of mutual support that cannot be accessed with AI and, sometimes, not even with instructors.

Therefore, while AI was seen to help assist respondents in being communicatively sound with instructors, they seem to have missed many opportunities from other sources of learning – their peers. However, many respondents also indicate that they seek assistance from AI mainly for language-related tasks. This is perhaps why peer interactions are less valuable than discussing and generating content/ideas.

Theme 2: Challenges in AI as Communication Tools

Following the first theme, there certainly are challenges in AI as a communication tool based on the survey findings and the focus group discussions. We have seen in Theme 1 that there is reduced human interaction as the respondents see instructors as their only source of information and knowledge and constantly use AI to ensure that they are communicatively sound academically to their instructors.

Another recurrent challenge in this study was the fear of over-reliance on AI. The data from the study suggested that respondents relied on AI to find information, correct language use, and improve their understanding of academic modules. Some also claimed to have witnessed unethical use of AI where colleagues merely use AI as a means to an end, the completion of assignments, without evaluation and validation of outcomes. This over-reliance may lead to lower interaction with peers, simultaneously reducing peer learning opportunities to nought and increasing the learning-in-silo where the only interaction and communication witnessed is increasingly instructor-student. The resistance to incorporating AI in academic settings was also supported by participants who seemed to think that using AI immediately discounts all facets of autonomy. Autonomy in learning includes engaging and evaluating the outcomes generated by AI making decisions that benefit their learning, such as choosing to reflect and compare outcomes generated by self and AI. While there may be users who do use AI unethically, blanketing all practices as unethical usage is unfair and, frankly, untrue, as indicated by how most participants choose to use AI.

Finally, miscommunication resulting from bias and inaccuracies in training data sets is also a challenge in using AI in communication. While AI helps correct language use, for example, grammar, tone and style, in tasks that require understanding cultural nuances or engagement with niche genres, suggestions from AI are less practical for users. Being mindful of these challenges and shortcomings will allow us to understand the limitations and the context in which AI tools will be helpful as a communication tool.

Theme 3: Ethics in the Usage of AI in Communication

While not all respondents use AI in their educational setting, most do, and the main tasks in which they use AI tools are to improve their language – clarity, style, tone, etc. The use of AI in such instances is supportive, suggesting that AI is used as an assistant and is certainly ethical in the educational setting. The findings suggest transparency and human oversight as essential factors in ensuring ethical usage, and this can be agreed upon. In addition, the data from which these language-improving assistants are trained is probably from reliable data sources such as language learning books and dictionaries – which are all objectively codified and do not contain sensitive information that may have been obtained without consent.

On the other hand, the data obtained also included concerns and reports of unethical usage of AI in communication, such as the issue of plagiarism and the use of unverified information in completing assignments. Some academic assignments, even at advanced level courses, contain lower level knowledge attainment, where students are expected to read and recall information from academic texts. AI tools can assist in completing such tasks, and unethical usage will include students presenting the summary and recall of information as their own. However, as seen from the findings, more ethical usage, even for tasks that AI can perform, will include verifying and evaluating information and including one's ideas and contribution to personalise the final submission of the academic module assignment. Previous literature has also recommended curriculum redesign to include process-focused assignments, promoting evaluation, and critical thinking – key components contributing to deep learning (Zhang & Chou, 2021; Lye & Lim, 2024).

On another note, the findings also suggest that the respondents were keen to learn more about AI and welcome the idea of AI inclusion as part of their academic journey. Several factors might contribute to such an attitude. First, it could be attributed to the perceived learner benefits where they can communicate less with their instructors on mundane tasks such as grammar, tone and style correction and focus on obtaining feedback for content information. Second, respondents are aware of the ubiquitous nature of AI and recognise the importance of integrating AI into their learning, as they will want to be skilled in AI usage in their future workplaces where proficiency in technology and AI is key. Third, having institutional support through actionable policy and guidelines (Wang et al., 2024; McDonald et al., 2025) means that AI tools are or can be supportive tools for learning and self-development instead of a threat to human existence. The support also means that AI tools are welcome, and students are encouraged to experiment and build familiarity with the tool as part of their learning journey. All in all, it is the responsibility of students to navigate the AI tools critically and use them ethically to achieve their communicative and academic goals.

CONCLUSION AND IMPLICATIONS

Many studies focus on AI adoption as misconduct (Gonsalves, 2024) and a potential threat to academic integrity. However, findings from this study suggest that AI is potentially more beneficial than a threat. I believe more institutions are aligning with this perspective, as reflected in formal policies and guidelines by Universiti Brunei Darussalam and other educational institutions (Wang et al., 2024; McDonald, 2025). While AI is understood to be disruptive to a certain extent, especially in tasks that are lower in knowledge attainment scale – like knowledge recall and reading of academic texts- higher order learning, academic contents that include cultural nuances or belong to niche genres still require human input. In this context, curriculum redesign could not be more timely. Such examples include applying knowledge in specific contexts and critical thinking in resolving problem-based assessments. Therefore, students, educators and institutions must continue experimenting with and adopting AI in the education system to further the educational agenda in the digital age.

Some limitations could influence the information in the study. For example, the instructions for assignments provided in the module, the L1s of respondents, and time spent on using AI indicate the level of familiarity – all not collected as part of the demographic information. This information could have been helpful as an informed background for the study.

There are several suggestions to improve future studies, two of which will be outlined next. First, including more demographic and background information on the courses and participants would have helped make sense of the findings. Second, this study only focused on a small sample of respondents from one discipline. It would be helpful for future studies to conduct a longitudinal study on AI's impact on communication and learning in the same and different fields and include educator and institutional perspectives to add to studies like the current one where students' perspective is focused.

It is an uphill battle to discourage the use of AI in communication due to the primary and apparent reason – that GenAI penetrates every aspect of technology. The main driving force for the surge of AI is to rid oneself of redundant and mundane tasks and to save time on routine actions. So, I am certain that going against AI is futile, and we should focus on a more productive streak of figuring out how students are using AI, how to mitigate unethical usage, and how to inculcate productive, ethical usage of AI. In addition, some AI tools, including Quillbot and Grammarly, are widely acknowledged as helpful tools, especially for ESL learners. So, where do we draw the line between allowable and non-allowable usage? Is it possible to remove AI altogether in the educational setting? The more critical and impactful question would be, is it worth our time to do so? Ultimately, our goal should be to ride the innovation of AI and use it to empower our learning, teaching and communication as both educators and learners.

Policy and Practical Implications

On that note, some implications for educational practices can be suggested. First, educators must find creative ways to balance AI-mediated communication with human interactions. This includes redesigning assessments with components less likely to be compromised by AI, such as process-based, evaluative assessments that promote critical engagement. Notably, the findings revealed the lack of peer-to-peer interactions, and what was overtly emphasised was instructor-student interactions. This imbalance of emphasis encourages and gives rise to instructor-led teaching and deteriorates the need and priority for peer learning, which is problematic. Educators must find activities that encourage dialogues between students without AI mediation, irrespective of how useful AI is perceived. Activities may include discussions that do not focus on the technical accuracies of language but instead on the quality of generated ideas.

The second implication is the importance of an institution-wide policy for using AI in educational settings. It is clear that the respondents are well-versed in how much assistance AI can provide in improving language quality, especially for ESL and EFL, and that these assistances are helpful. However, policies must include clear ethical boundaries on plagiarism (i.e. copy and paste of information) and over-reliance on AI (simultaneously reducing other interactions, especially peer-to-peer). As seen earlier, strides have been made to provide practical guidelines for adopting AI in educational settings; more can be done to support educators who are the primary drivers of change.

Finally, as was called for by the respondents in the study, incorporating AI literacy in the curricula cannot come at a more appropriate time and has never been more essential. These curricula could be a platform where students and academic instructors raise their concerns and reach a consensus on addressing the issues. It is also an important platform to make notable AI limitations such as critical thinking, display of emotion and empathy, and the ability to understand cultural nuances.

REFERENCES

Al-Tkhayneh, K. M., Alghazo, E. M., & Tahat, D. (2023). The advantages and disadvantages of using artificial intelligence in education. *Journal of Educational and Social Research, 13*(4), 105–117. DOI: 10.36941/jesr-2023-0094

Baidoo-Anu, D., & Owusu Ansah, L. (2023). Education in the era of Generative Artificial Intelligence (AI): Understanding the potential benefits of CHATGPT in promoting teaching and learning. SSRN *Electronic Journal*. https://doi.org/DOI: 10.2139/ssrn.4337484

Buchanan, B. G. (2005). A (Very) Brief History of Artificial Intelligence. *AI Magazine*, *26*(4), 53. DOI: 10.1609/aimag.v26i4.1848

Ch'ng, L. K. (2023). How AI makes its mark on instructional design. *Asian Journal of Distance Education*, *18*(2), 32–41. DOI: 10.5281/zenodo.8188576

Cooper, G. (2023). Examining Science Education in ChatGPT: An Exploratory Study of Generative Artificial Intelligence. *Journal of Science Education and Technology*, *32*, 444–452. DOI: 10.1007/s10956-023-10039-y

Ferrara, E. (2023). Fairness and bias in Artificial Intelligence: A brief survey of sources, impacts, and mitigation strategies. *Science*, *6*(1), 3. DOI: 10.3390/sci6010003

Fügener, A., Grahl, J., Gupta, A., & Ketter, W. (2021). Will humans-in-the-loop become Borgs? Merits and pitfalls of working with AI. *Management Information Systems Quarterly*, *45*(3), 1527–1556. DOI: 10.25300/misq/2021/16553

Gamage, K. A. A., Dehideniya, S. C. P., Xu, Z., & Tang, X. (2023). ChatGPT and higher education assessments: More opportunities than concerns? *Journal of Applied Learning and Teaching*, *6*(2), 358–369. DOI: 10.37074/jalt.2023.6.2.32

Gonsalves, C. (2024). Addressing student non-compliance in AI use declarations: Implications for academic integrity and assessment in higher education. *Assessment & Evaluation in Higher Education*, •••, 1–15. DOI: 10.1080/02602938.2024.2415654

Grassini, S. (2023). Development and validation of the AI Attitude Scale (AIAS-4): A brief measure of general attitude toward Artificial Intelligence. *Frontiers in Psychology*, *14*. Advance online publication. DOI: 10.3389/fpsyg.2023.1191628 PMID: 37554139

Idroes, G. M., Noviandy, T. R., Maulana, A., Irvanizam, I., Jalil, Z., Lensoni, L., Lala, A., Abas, A. H., Tallei, T. E., & Idroes, R. (2023). Student perspectives on the role of artificial intelligence in education: A survey-based analysis. *Journal of Educational Management and Learning*, *1*(1), 8–15. DOI: 10.60084/jeml.v1i1.58

Jezova, D. (2021). Artificial intelligence and privacy. *Human Rights - From Reality to the Virtual World*, 226–237. https://doi.org/DOI: 10.13166/wsge//xuxl1897

Kasneci, E., Sessler, K., Küchemann, S., Bannert, M., Dementieva, D., Fischer, F., Gasser, U., Groh, G., Günnemann, S., Hüllermeier, E., Krusche, S., Kutyniok, G., Michaeli, T., Nerdel, C., Pfeffer, J., Poquet, O., Sailer, M., Schmidt, A., Seidel, T., & Kasneci, G. (2023). ChatGPT for good? On opportunities and challenges of large language models for education. *Learning and Individual Differences*, *103*, 102274. DOI: 10.1016/j.lindif.2023.102274

Kim, S. W., & Lee, Y. (2023). Investigation into the influence of socio-cultural factors on attitudes toward artificial intelligence. *Education and Information Technologies*. Advance online publication. DOI: 10.1007/s10639-023-12172-y

Kong, S.-C., Man-Yin Cheung, W., & Zhang, G. (2021). Evaluation of an artificial intelligence literacy course for university students with diverse study backgrounds. *Computers and Education: Artificial Intelligence*, *2*, 100026. DOI: 10.1016/j.caeai.2021.100026

Long, D., & Magerko, B. (2020). What is AI literacy? Competencies and design considerations. *Proceedings of the 2020 CHI Conference on Human Factors in Computing Systems*, USA, 1-16. https://doi.org/DOI: 10.1145/3313831.3376727

Lye, C. Y., & Lim, L. (2024). Generative Artificial Intelligence in Tertiary Education: Assessment Redesign Principles and Considerations. *Education Sciences*, *14*(6), 569. DOI: 10.3390/educsci14060569

McDonald, N., Johri, A., Ali, A., & Collier, A. H. (2025). Generative artificial intelligence in higher education: Evidence from an analysis of institutional policies and guidelines. Computers in Human Behavior. *Artificial Humans*, *3*, 100121. DOI: 10.1016/j.chbah.2025.100121

Olari, V., & Romeike, R. (2021) Addressing AI and data literacy in teacher education: A review of existing educational frameworks. *The 16th Workshop in Primary and Secondary Computing Education*, USA, 1-2. https://doi.org/DOI: 10.1145/3481312.3481351

Pellas, N. (2023). The influence of sociodemographic factors on students' attitudes toward AI-generated video content creation. *Smart Learning Environment*, *10*(57). Advance online publication. DOI: 10.1186/s40561-023-00276-4

Pokrivcakova, S. (2023). Pre-service teachers' attitudes towards artificial intelligence and its integration into EFL teaching and learning. *Journal of Language and Cultural Education*, *11*(3), 100–114. DOI: 10.2478/jolace-2023-0031

Sabraz Nawaz, S., Fathima Sanjeetha, M. B., Al Murshidi, G., Mohamed Riyath, M. I., Mat Yamin, F. B., & Mohamed, R. (2024). Acceptance of ChatGPT by undergraduates in Sri Lanka: A hybrid approach of SEM-ANN. *Interactive Technology and Smart Education*. Advance online publication. DOI: 10.1108/itse-11-2023-0227

Sebesta, J., & Davis, V. L. (2023, June 30). *Supporting Instruction and Learning* through Artificial Intelligence: A Survey of Institutional Practices & Policies. WICHE Cooperative for Educational Technologies. wcet.wiche.edu/resources/wcet-report-supporting-instruction-learning-through-artificial-intelligence-a-survey-of-institutional-practices-policies/

Thongprasit, J., & Wannapiroon, P. (2022). Framework of artificial intelligence learning platform for education. *International Education Studies*, *15*(1), 76–86. DOI: 10.5539/ies.v15n1p76

UNICEF. (2021). *Policy guidance on AI for children.* Retrieved March 19, 2023, from https://www.unicef.org/globalinsight/media/1171/file/UNICEF-Global-Insight-policy-guidance-AI-childr

Usher, M. (2025). Generative AI vs. instructor vs. peer assessments: A comparison of grading and feedback in higher education. *Assessment & Evaluation in Higher Education*, •••, 1–16. DOI: 10.1080/02602938.2025.2487495

van Niekerk, J., Delport, P. M. J., & Sutherland, I. (2025). Addressing the use of generative AI in academic writing. *Computers and Education: Artificial Intelligence*, *8*, 1–11. DOI: 10.1016/j.caeai.2024.100342

Vincent-Lancrin, S., & van der Vlies, R. (2020, April 8). *Trustworthy artificial intelligence (AI) in education: Promises and challenges*. OECD Education Working Papers. https://doi.org/DOI: 10.1787/a6c90fa9-en

Wang, H., Dang, A., Wu, Z., & Mac, S. (2024). Generative AI in higher education: Seeing ChatGPT through universities' policies, resources, and guidelines. *Computers and Education: Artificial Intelligence*, *7*, 100326. DOI: 10.1016/j.caeai.2024.100326

Wang, T., Lund, B. D., Marengo, A., Pagano, A., Mannuru, N. R., Teel, Z. A., & Pange, J. (2023). Exploring the potential impact of artificial intelligence (AI) on international students in higher education: Generative AI, chatbots, analytics, and international student success. *Applied Sciences (Basel, Switzerland)*, *13*(11), 6716. DOI: 10.3390/app13116716

Yuwono, E. I., Tjondronegoro, D., Riverola, C., & Loy, J. (2024). Co-creation in action: Bridging the knowledge gap in artificial intelligence among innovation champions. *Computers and Education: Artificial Intelligence*, *7*, 1–16. DOI: 10.1016/j.caeai.2024.100272

Zhang, X., & Cao, Z. (2021). A framework of an intelligent education system for higher education based on deep learning. *International Journal of Emerging Technologies in Learning*, *16*(7), 233–248. DOI: 10.3991/ijet.v16i07.22123

Chapter 8
AI-Based Educational Training:
Mapping Portugal's Higher Education Landscape and Regulatory Framework

Sónia Pedro Sebastião
https://orcid.org/0000-0002-4341-8031
Universidade de Lisboa, Portugal

David Ferreia-Mendes Dias
https://orcid.org/0000-0001-8563-1853
Universidade de Lisboa, Portugal

ABSTRACT

This chapter presents a deductive empirical study examining how the Portuguese educational system adapts to the challenges of artificial intelligence (AI) integration. It focuses on AI-related offerings in higher education and the associated assessment regulations in Portugal for the 2024/2025 academic year. The study employs a two-stage content analysis: first, identifying advanced (master's) and specialised (postgraduate and minor) AI courses through a web search; second, analysing the assessment regulations of institutions offering AI education to understand measures implemented to mitigate academic misconduct in line with the ENAI Recommendations on the Ethical Use of AI in Education (Foltynek et al., 2023). The research highlights the lack of institutional strategies for AI governance and academic integrity, contributing insights that may benefit other higher education systems in Europe facing similar challenges, while also enhancing the literature on AI governance in educational contexts.

DOI: 10.4018/979-8-3373-6018-8.ch008

Copyright © 2026, IGI Global Scientific Publishing. Copying or distributing in print or electronic forms without written permission of IGI Global Scientific Publishing is prohibited.

INTRODUCTION

Technological innovation has transformed the nature and scope of education, prompting education systems worldwide to develop and adopt strategies and policies for integrating technology into learning objectives, teaching methods, and assessment models (Timotheou et al., 2023; Tuomi et al., 2018). This integration affects the quality of teaching and learning, particularly in terms of understanding, adapting, and designing educational systems that align with current technological trends. All stakeholders in this system must possess the skills to use technologies effectively, leverage their benefits, minimise risks, and ensure their responsible and ethical use.

AI-based tools represent the latest technological innovation fuelling the debate on adapting educational systems. Understanding AI and its fundamentals should be an essential element of education to develop successful global citizens (Southworth et al., 2023). AI tools in education, also known as Artificial Intelligence in Education (AIED), refer to computational systems that use machine learning algorithms, natural language processing, and other AI technologies to support and enhance teaching and learning processes (Adams & Chuah, 2022).

The transformation of the education system by AI is global in scope, attracting the attention of transnational institutions such as the OECD (2021), UNESCO (2021), and the Council of Europe (2022) due to its offering both opportunities and challenges. AI applications in education range from adaptive learning platforms and intelligent tutoring systems to predictive analytics tools, as well as teacher-support assistants (Holmes et al., 2019; Holmes & Tuomi, 2022; OECD, 2021; Tuomi et al., 2018). These technologies have the potential to personalise learning experiences, enhance feedback mechanisms, and expand access to quality education. However, it is still unclear how to scale pedagogical advantages on a broader scale (e.g., Southworth et al., 2023; Zawacki-Richter et al., 2019), and a constructive critical perspective on applying digital technologies in education is needed (Facer & Selwyn, 2021; Schiff, 2022).

The integration of AI in education also raises significant concerns. Privacy and data protection issues are paramount, given the vast amounts of sensitive student data processed by AI systems (Council of Europe, 2022). There are also risks of algorithmic bias, which could exacerbate educational inequalities, and concerns about over-reliance on AI at the expense of human interaction in education (UNESCO, 2021). The use of AI-based tools in education is prone to risks related to equity and accessibility issues, as it may affect human relationships and raise concerns about democratic values (Council of Europe, 2022).

AI-based tools can lead to "academic misconduct," which involves the unauthorised creation of academic work—either partially or entirely—using unapproved or undisclosed human or technological assistance for credit, advancement, or awards.

Although AIED can facilitate unauthorised content generation, it is not inherently unethical (Foltynek et al., 2023).

AI can potentially threaten academic integrity, but it also presents significant opportunities. AI enhances users' capabilities, which is why students and teachers need guidance on AI-based tools' benefits and limitations. This guidance ensures ethical use and helps maintain academic integrity. Moreover, as contemporary societies increasingly rely on automation, students will likely need AI-based tools in their future careers. Providing them with opportunities to develop these skills during their education is vital.

Policymakers and educational institutions must develop comprehensive strategies to address the challenges posed by AIED. This should involve investing in research on the ethical application of AI and providing teachers with training in AI literacy (Council of Europe, 2022; UNESCO, 2021). Additionally, it is crucial to educate students about AI—its definition, applications, risks, and how to integrate it effectively into their learning processes (Allen & Kendeou, 2024; Knox, 2020; Zhai et al., 2021). The acceptable standards for using AI can vary across academic disciplines, educational institutions, courses, types of assessments, cultures, regions, and countries.

While these challenges and opportunities are global, their implementation and impact vary significantly across different national contexts, since AI is a socially constructed assemblage (Lindgren, 2024). Portugal, like other countries, is adapting its educational system to the challenges of AI transformation. As part of the EU, it follows EU guidelines and has developed national strategies like INCoDe.2030 (2017) and the National Strategy for Artificial Intelligence (2019), highlighting the importance of AI literacy and digital skills in education. As noted by Schiff (2022), national AI policy strategies often emphasise the importance of education in preparing an AI-ready workforce and training more AI experts (often referred to as "education for AI"). This focus tends to overshadow the exploration of AI-based tools for teaching and learning ("AI for education") and the ethical implications surrounding their use.

Thus, there is still much to explore regarding the implementation of AI-based tools in higher education, particularly in areas like teaching methods, assessments, and academic integrity (e.g., Holmes & Porayska-Pomsta, 2023).

The response of Portugal's higher education system to AI challenges reflects global trends but is also influenced by its unique institutional framework, culture, and educational traditions. Understanding how Portuguese institutions adapt can provide insights for other nations with similar educational contexts and stages of AI integration.

This chapter has two main objectives. First, it characterises the offerings related to AI in master and postgraduate courses in Portugal for the 2024/2025 academic year through content analysis. Second, given that AI-based tools can affect academic integrity and raise ethical concerns, we examine the general assessment regulations of Portuguese higher education institutions (HEI) to identify the normative guidelines regarding AI use.

Our empirical study will use web research to collect data for two-stage content analysis. In the first stage, a search engine was used to identify advanced and specialised educational offerings related to AI, focusing on courses and subjects that included this term in their titles. In the second stage, we examined the assessment regulations of HEI that offer advanced AI education. We referred to the ENAI Recommendations on the Ethical Use of AI in Education (Foltynek et al., 2023) to identify potential risks and the measures institutions have implemented to reduce academic misconduct.

The chapter is structured into five key sections. First, it presents the main AI-based tools utilised in education, detailing their functions and following a review of their benefits and risks, emphasising ethical considerations and concerns regarding academic integrity. The third section outlines the methodological procedures used in the study. The fourth and fifth sections focus on the presentation and discussion of the results, respectively, concluding with the final thoughts and policy recommendations.

1. AI-BASED TOOLS IN EDUCATION

The concept of Artificial Intelligence (AI) is used to describe a "range of technologies and methods that include such as machine learning, natural language processing, data mining, neural networks, or an algorithm" (Zawacki-Richter et al., 2019, p. 3). The terminology around AI tools often overlaps. The expression "AI tools" generally refers to standalone applications or systems that directly implement AI algorithms. These are purpose-built systems where AI is the core functionality rather than a supporting feature (Russell & Norvig, 2022). The term "AI-based tools" is preferably used in this chapter, indicating systems that use AI as their foundational technology while integrating with other computational methods. These tools leverage AI algorithms as their core architecture but may incorporate additional non-AI components for complete functionality (Adams & Chuah, 2022).

AI has become a crucial tool in transforming the educational sector (Chen et al., 2020; Tuomi et al., 2018), attracting the attention of researchers all over the world (e.g., Knox, 2020; Sanusi et al., 2022).

With the evolution of technology and increased access to digital resources, both teachers and students utilise various AI-based tools to enhance teaching and learning processes (e.g., Cope & Kalantzis, 2019; Holmes & Tuomi, 2022; Zawacki-Richter et al., 2019). AI-based tools in education can perform several roles, including customising education, producing smart content, contributing to task automation, organising and supporting tutoring, and ensuring access to education for students with special needs (Yasmin & Mazhar, 2023). These tools can transform, create, or generate various types of content, including text, images, and programming code, employing different AI technologies, such as machine learning and neural networks, to enhance their capabilities (Foltynek et al., 2023).

Zhai et al. (2021) categorised the uses of AI-based tools in education into three layers: development, extraction, and application. The development layer involves using AI techniques to build a smart learning environment, focusing on algorithms such as classification, matching, recommendation, and deep learning for teaching and learning purposes. The extraction layer refers to applying these developed AI techniques, which are typically algorithm-based, to provide students with feedback, reasoning, and adaptive learning experiences. The application layer includes aspects such as affective computing, role-playing, immersive learning, and gamification.

By integrating these dimensions, it is possible to notice that AI techniques involve human factors as crucial variables for identifying and analysing personalised learner features. In such practices, human-computer interaction can enhance traits like creativity, responsibility, and critical thinking, which can influence learners' performance and perceptions.

From the teachers' perspective, AI can help personalise education by adapting content and teaching methods to meet the individual needs of students (Holmes et al., 2019; Timotheou et al., 2023). It can also automate administrative tasks such as grading assignments and tests, managing attendance, organising teaching materials, and summarising lessons (Luckin et al., 2016; Timotheou et al., 2023). Additionally, AI can analyse educational data to identify patterns in student performance and highlight areas that may require specific interventions. Furthermore, it can assist in creating educational content, including presentations, quizzes, and simulations (Chen et al., 2020; Timotheou et al., 2023). To do this, teachers need to be trained in how to integrate technology into their teaching models, have access to technologies in the classroom and receive clear indications from the educational institution about the policy for using AI-based tools.

Technical innovation and change are often viewed as progress, yet it is crucial to assess when these changes represent meaningful advancements in education. Technology significantly influences human development and cognition, though this impact is inherently complex (Holmes & Tuomi, 2022).

During the literature review, several studies were identified that provide systematic reviews of approaches to the use of AIED (e.g., Holmes & Tuomi, 2022; Laupichler et al., 2022; Timotheou et al., 2023; Wang et al., 2024; Zawacki-Richter et al., 2019; Zhai et al., 2022), including transnational reports (Council of Europe, 2022; OECD, 2021; UNESCO, 2021).

The authorised use of AI-based tools is generally acceptable for a variety of tasks (Foltynek et al., 2023). However, in an educational setting, using AI-based tools without proper declaration or authorisation to complete work for academic credit or progression - such as assignments, theses, or dissertations - may be seen as a form of academic misdemeanour. Additionally, it is becoming increasingly difficult to reliably differentiate between AI-generated content and content produced by humans.

The training of competencies in AI is highly relevant not only for future AI professionals but also for individuals who are not experts in the field. As these technologies become part of everyday life, everyone will need to interact with them regularly. As stated by Wong et al. (2020), AI concepts, applications, ethics, and safety are sub-elements of AI literacy. Consequently, when defining AI literacy definitions are based on setting goals for AI education (Yi, 2021). AI literacy encompasses the ability to grasp foundational knowledge and concepts underlying AI-driven technologies; however, it also extends beyond understanding, requiring individuals to critically evaluate, communicate effectively, and collaborate with AI in ways that achieve their goals (Allen & Kendeou, 2024; Ng et al., 2021).

The term “AI literate,” as defined by Laupichler et al. (2022), describes the ability to understand, use, monitor, and critically reflect on AI applications, even without the skill to develop AI models. AI literacy involves a set of competencies that allows individuals to critically evaluate AI technologies, communicate and collaborate effectively with AI, and use AI as a tool in their daily tasks (Laupichler et al., 2022). Given the widespread presence of technology, it is essential for the general population to possess AI literacy. In Yi’s (2021) words “AI literacy is the basic ability to become a subjective human in the AI era” (p. 360).

Realising the importance of AI training for non-specialists motivates our research objective 1 – *to characterise the offerings related to AI in master and postgraduate courses in Portugal for the 2024/2025 academic year* through content analysis. The focus is on advanced training to determine whether there is specific training available for young professionals and teachers to use AI-based tools effectively.

2. BENEFITS AND RISKS OF USING AI-BASED TOOLS

Using AI-based tools in educational settings provides numerous advantages due to their ability to adapt to changing environments. These tools can enhance student engagement during remote learning and offer additional study materials (Yasmin & Mazhar, 2023).

The implementation of AI-based tools in education can be categorised into three main dimensions: cognitive, efficiency, and ethical considerations. This framework allows for a comprehensive understanding of both the benefits and risks associated with integrating AI into educational contexts.

Considering the literature review, the benefits of employing AI-based tools in education can be organised into several categories, including accessibility, availability, creativity, digital skills, efficiency, feedback, multilingual support, and personalised learning, as explained in Table 1.

Table 1. Benefits of using AI-based tools in pedagogical and learning processes for teachers and students

Benefit	Explanation
Accessibility	Reformatting content for different needs (inclusivity), such as text-to-speech or automatic captioning (Hopcan et al., 2022).
Availability	Access to resources and support at any time with virtual assistants (Okonkwo & Ade-Ibijola, 2021).
Creativity	Generation of ideas, suggestion of different perspectives, approaches, and alternatives (Černý, 2023).
Digital Skills	Familiarity with emerging technologies and interaction with advanced systems (Hwang et al., 2020).
Efficiency	They can accelerate tasks such as automating processes, grading assessments, or organising teaching materials (Luckin et al., 2016).
Feedback	Automatic corrections, continuous learning, or automated assessments (Holmes et al., 2019).
Multilingual Support	Translation and language assistance (Johnson et al., 2017).
Personalised Learning	Adaptation to individual learning styles and paces, adjusting content based on performance (Kulik & Fletcher, 2016).

Authors' elaboration.

The literature review also highlights that AI-based technologies also bring several risks, namely concerning assessment, dependence, equity, ethical issues, integrity, misinformation, privacy, reduced human interaction, and deterioration of skills, as explained in Table 2.

Table 2. Risks of using AI-based tools in pedagogical and learning processes for teachers and students

Risk	Explanation
Assessment	Due to AI-based tools, verifying students' true skills and knowledge and teachers' pedagogical models becomes exponentially challenging (Dawson, 2021).
Dependence	Over-reliance on AI for teaching activities hinders analytical thinking and problem-solving (Selwyn, 2019).
Equity	Access to AI technologies is unequal for everyone, highlighting socio-economic inequalities (Holmes et al., 2019; Holmes & Porayska-Pomsta, 2023).
Ethical Concerns	Improper use of AI-based tools may contribute to dishonest and irresponsible academic practices (Greene et al., 2019).
Integrity	AI can reuse content produced, leading to plagiarism and complicating the assessment of genuine learning and academic integrity (Foltynek et al., 2020).
Misinformation	The presentation of inaccurate, incorrect, or biased information leads to the spread of false or partial content (Bender et al., 2021).
Privacy	Storage of personal data from teachers and students (Williamson & Piattoeva, 2019).
Reduced Human Interaction	Reduced interaction among peers and between teachers and students affects social and emotional development and collaborative learning (Knox, 2020).
Skills Deterioration	Decline in basic human skills, such as mental capacities or spelling (Carter et al., 2016).

Authors' elaboration.

The AIED implementation presents complex challenges that intersect with the previously discussed benefits and risks, requiring careful consideration across cognitive, efficiency, and ethical dimensions.

From a cognitive perspective, the adaptation of both teachers and students to AI technologies demands significant mental adjustment and pedagogical reconceptualisation. This adaptation process involves understanding how to effectively integrate AI-based tools while maintaining essential learning objectives. The challenge lies not only in technical proficiency but also in developing a balanced approach that leverages AI capabilities without compromising traditional learning methodologies. Furthermore, there exists a risk of developing unrealistic expectations about AI's capabilities, necessitating continuous professional development to understand its appropriate role in pedagogical contexts (Zhai et al., 2020).

Efficiency challenges manifest primarily through resource allocation and implementation concerns. The cost-effectiveness of AI implementation, particularly in large-scale educational settings, remains a significant consideration. Educational institutions must address technical infrastructure requirements, ongoing maintenance needs, and integration with existing educational systems. Customising AI-based tools to meet specific teaching goals and activities presents another layer of complexity, as generic AI solutions may not adequately address pedagogical needs.

These efficiency challenges directly impact the potential realisation of AI's benefits in educational settings (Holmes et al., 2019).

Ethical challenges emerge as particularly crucial in the implementation process. Ensuring equitable access across different socioeconomic contexts remains a fundamental concern, as disparities in resource availability could exacerbate existing educational inequalities. Additionally, institutions must maintain a delicate balance between embracing technological innovation and preserving essential human-centred teaching approaches. The development of appropriate governance frameworks and guidelines for responsible AI use in education becomes paramount, especially considering the privacy and integrity concerns previously discussed (Schiff, 2022; Williamson & Piattoeva, 2019).

Implementation challenges demonstrate the complexity of integrating AI in educational settings and highlight the need for thoughtful, systematic approaches that consider the interplay between cognitive, efficiency, and ethical dimensions. Success in addressing these challenges requires coordinated efforts from educational stakeholders, policymakers, and technology developers to ensure that AI implementation serves its intended educational purposes while minimising potential drawbacks.

Both teachers and students may find it difficult to adapt to these technologies. Their attitudes toward AI can vary widely - from complete resistance to overreliance. Resistance may arise from inadequate, irrelevant, or outdated professional development. Conversely, overreliance can occur when people develop unrealistic expectations about AI's capabilities (Zhai et al., 2021).

3. ETHICAL RECOMMENDATIONS FOR AIED AND ACADEMIC INTEGRITY

Ethical challenges are also significant, particularly concerning data privacy and academic integrity. According to reviews from Schiff (2022), Zawacki-Richter et al. (2019) and Zhai et al. (2020), previous research on AIED has not adequately addressed these ethical concerns. Addressing these challenges is crucial for successfully integrating AI into educational settings, especially since the use of AI-based tools may not always be in accordance with academic integrity.

AI ethical concerns are generally divided into two categories: data-centric and algorithm-centric. These include beneficence, non-maleficence, fairness, inclusivity, the absence of bias, reliability, autonomy, accountability, transparency, clear liability, explicability, and established privacy and data protection processes and security (Bhise et al., 2023; Schiff, 2022).

To help all education stakeholders understand how to use AI-based tools responsibly and in line with academic integrity practices and values, the European Network for Academic Integrity (ENAI) offers a set of recommendations aimed at supporting academics, researchers, and other educational stakeholders, including student organisations (Foltynek et al., 2023).

In addition to highlighting the necessity of equipping stakeholders with the skills and knowledge to ethically utilise AI-based tools, the recommendations stress the importance of creating educational policies that address both the opportunities and challenges presented by AIED.

AI-based tools can transform, produce, or generate various types of content, including text, images, art, music, and programming code. In the educational context, the widespread accessibility of AI could worsen existing threats to academic integrity. This includes issues such as essay and paper mills, data fabrication and falsification, and the unauthorised use of AI-based tools to complete assignments or final projects. These practices all constitute forms of academic misconduct (Foltynek et al., 2023).

Nevertheless, AI-based tools also present opportunities; therefore, students and teachers need to be guided on the limits and benefits of AI. These skills should be acquired in educational environments (Southworth et al., 2023).

The authorised and clear use of AI-based tools is generally acceptable. Services, sources, and tools suitable for this include proofreaders, proofreading tools, spelling checkers, and thesauruses. An ethical approach involves using a disclaimer, where authors specify how and for what purpose AI-based tools were utilised. An example can be found in the chapter by Rettig and Mickeleit (2023).

> *This article employed artificial intelligence in specific aspects, namely language clarity and checking. The paragraphs were drafted and then prompted into ChatGPT for grammatical adjustments and wording refinement, preserving the original phrasing wherever feasible. Additionally, RecapTalks was employed for the transcription and preliminary summarisation of the focus group discussion. Lastly, an AI-generated review of the literature was created by using ChatGPT to compile an initial summary and comparison. However, it is critical to note that the authors maintained full control over these areas to ensure authenticity and integrity. The guiding ideas and the central proposition, as well as the overall composition of the article, were performed manually by the authors, ensuring human oversight and expertise in the final output. (p. 69)*

It is important to note that AI-based tools cannot be listed as co-authors of content, as they cannot be held accountable nor do they have a commitment to integrity and truth (Hicks et al., 2024). Therefore, the results of AI creation can contain false, manipulated, biased content, which can have harmful effects on individuals and society. The outputs of AI are the result of its programming and training and it is important that users have AI literacy to prevent its misuse (Allen & Kendeou, 2024; Laupichler et al., 2022). If students do not have the opportunity to learn the ethical use of the tools, they will be more susceptible to bad practices and academic misconduct (Foltynek et al., 2023).

In the same vein, teachers need to be trained on how to use AI-based tools ethically. This includes developing appropriate learning outcomes, activities, and assessment strategies. Cope and Kalantzis (2019) and Swiecki et al. (2022) point out that traditional assessment methods have several problems, such as being expensive, providing limited insights into student performance, not catering to individual knowledge and skills, and often being outdated or inauthentic.

Although AI-based tools can help solve some of these issues, they can also bring new challenges for educational institutions. These challenges include ensuring the validity and reliability of assessments, dealing with technical and implementation difficulties, and addressing pedagogical and policy considerations.

Acknowledging the use of AI-based tools may be done in different ways, depending on the context, institutional regulations, and other requirements. That is why it is essential to understand how the institutions themselves are addressing the issue of teachers and students using AI-based tools in their assessment regulations. This leads us to our research objective 2 - *to identify the normative guidelines regarding AI use in the general assessment regulations of Portuguese higher education institutions.*

According to ENAI's recommendations (Foltynek et al., 2023), institutional regulations should clearly define default rules regarding the circumstances and manner in which students, teachers, researchers, and other educational stakeholders may utilise various AI-based tools. Additionally, there should be flexibility for specific guidelines at the course level. Furthermore, institutions should offer clear guidance on how users can properly acknowledge their use of AI-based tools in various outputs, including assignments, dissertations, theses, papers, articles, book chapters, computer programmes, graphics, artworks, and more. It is essential that these policies be effectively communicated to all relevant stakeholders.

4. METHOD

A deductive empirical study was developed to understand how the Portuguese educational system is adapting to the challenges of AI transformation, focusing on AI offerings in Portuguese higher education and assessment regulations.

This chapter has two research objectives (RO) that guide the presentation of results.

RO1. To characterise the offerings related to AI in master and postgraduate courses in Portugal for the 2024/2025 academic year.

RO2. To identify the normative guidelines regarding AI use in the general assessment regulations of Portuguese higher education institutions.

To achieve these objectives, web research was employed to gather data to conduct a two-stage content analysis. In the first stage, we used a web search engine to identify advanced (master) and specialised (postgraduate and minor) educational offerings related to Artificial Intelligence - whether in the course name, the name of curricular units or modules, or in the content of these units or modules provided by higher education institutions (HEI) in Portugal, for the 2024/2025 academic year.

The entire range of master's and postgraduate course offerings from HEI in Portugal was systematised in an Excel table, considering the public information made available on each institution's official websites between September 1st and 10th, 2024. The following categories were used to organise the information: type of institution, nature of the institution, type of course, name of the course, scientific field of the course, curricular unit/subject, and scientific field of the curricular unit/subject (Table 3).

Table 3. Categories and indicators of stage 1

Categories	Indicators
Type of institution	University, polytechnic institution
Nature of the institution	Public, private, hybrid
Type of course	Master, post-graduation, minor
Name of the course	Nominal
Scientific field of the course	Nominal
Curricular unit/subject	Nominal
Scientific field of the curricular unit/subject	Nominal

Authors' elaboration.

The second stage of the content analysis considers the assessment regulations of higher institutions' advanced offerings in AI education. We used the ENAI Recommendations on the Ethical Use of AI in Education (Foltynek et al., 2023) as a standard to identify the measures adopted by the institutions to minimise academic misconduct (Table 4).

Table 4. Coding for the Normative Guidelines analysis

Code	Explanation	Indicator
Public Information	The regulation is effectively communicated to all relevant stakeholders.	Yes No
Default rules	The regulation clearly defines default rules regarding the circumstances and manner in which students, teachers, researchers, and other educational stakeholders may utilise various AI-based tools.	Yes No Somehow
Disclaimer	The regulation explains how users can clearly and accurately acknowledge the use of AI-based tools in assignments.	Yes No
Flexibility	The regulation mentions the flexibility of adapting the use of AI-based tools according to the specifics of the course/module or the freedom of the teacher.	Yes No Somehow

Authors' Elaboration (explanation column based on Foltynek et al., 2023)

A preliminary review of the regulations governing HEI that offer advanced AI education indicates a significant gap, as there are no specific mentions of the use of AI-based tools or ethical considerations pertaining to AI. Consequently, we have decided to broaden our website search to include other publicly available documents that relate to AIED.

As part of our expansion, we included two position statements from understudied institutions: *Técnico Lisboa* and *Universidade Lusófona*. In November 2023, both institutions issued recommendations to their teaching staff on the use of AI-based tools for teaching and assessment.

5. RESULTS

In this section, we present the results of the content analysis, following the order of the research objectives. In the first sub-section, we identify the educational offer on AI in master's and postgraduate courses in Portugal for the academic year 2024-2025. Lastly, we present the results of the normative guidelines regarding AI use in the general assessment regulations of Portuguese higher education institutions, based on Foltynek et al. (2023) and using the coding presented in Table 4.

5.1 AI Offerings in Portuguese Higher Education

The entire range of master's and postgraduate course offerings from HEI in Portugal was analysed, whether in university or polytechnic settings, as advertised on the official websites of each institution between September 1st and 10th, 2024. Out of 101 institutions analysed, 26 HEI were found to offer master's or postgraduate programmes related to AI (13 in public institutions, 8 in private institutions, and 5 resulting from partnerships between public and private institutions).

The education offered by HEI consists primarily of master's courses (29), followed by postgraduate courses (28), and minors (4). When analysing the courses by scientific areas according to the school where they are taught, most of the courses are focused on Computer Engineering (20 master's degrees, 5 postgraduate courses, and 4 minors), followed by courses in schools within the scientific area of Communication Sciences (13 postgraduate courses and 3 master's degrees). Only two postgraduate courses were found in Education Science (Table 5).

Table 5. Types of courses with content related to AI in the 2024/2025 academic year

Course Area	Master's	Minor	Postgraduate	Subtotal
Computer Engineering	20	4	5	29
Communication Sciences	3	0	13	16
Management	4	0	4	8
Social Sciences	1	0	2	3
Education Sciences	0	0	2	2
Mathematics	1	0	1	2
Arts Science	0	0	1	1
Total	**29**	**4**	**28**	**61**

Authors' elaboration.

After analysing the syllabus of each curricular unit or module included in each study plan, a total of 1081, and classifying them by the scientific area of the majority of the content, 47% are dedicated to Computer Science, 15% are mainly related to Communication Sciences, and only 1% are in Education Sciences (Figure 1).

Figure 1. Distribution of curricular units/modules by the predominant scientific area in the presented curricula

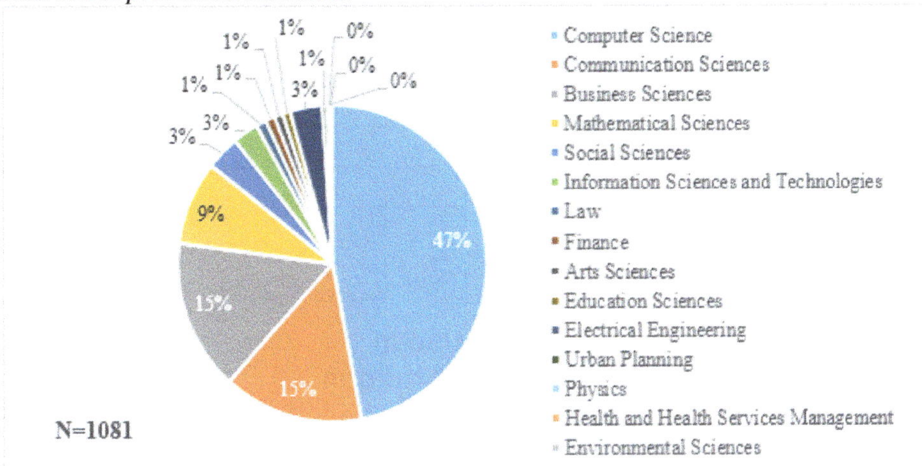

Authors' elaboration.

The two postgraduate courses identified in the field of Education Sciences are the postgraduate course in Digital and Network Education at the Open University and the postgraduate course in Artificial Intelligence and Emerging Technologies in Learning at ISLA Santarém.

An analysis of postgraduate programmes related to Artificial Intelligence for the 2024/2025 academic year reveals the distribution of modules based on their predominant scientific areas, according to the schools where they are offered. The findings indicate a significant emphasis on Communication Sciences (137), Computer Science (126) and Business Sciences (103), while Education Sciences has only 9 modules (see Table 6).

Table 6. Distribution of modules in postgraduate courses containing AI-related content for the 2024/2025 academic year

Predominant scientific area of the module's programme	No. of Modules
Communication Sciences	137
Computer Science	126
Business Sciences	103
Mathematical Sciences	28
Social Sciences	14
Law	12

continued on following page

Table 6. Continued

Predominant scientific area of the module's programme	No. of Modules
Finance	10
Arts Sciences	10
Education Sciences	9
Urban Planning	2
Health and Health Services Management	1

Authors' elaboration.

5.2 Normative Guidelines for AI Use in Portuguese Higher Education Institutions

After reviewing the educational offerings for master's degrees and postgraduate training related to AI, we examined the evaluation regulations for these programmes. As noted in section 5.1, we identified a total of 26 HEI that offer master's or postgraduate programmes focused on AI.

We reviewed the websites of 26 higher education institutions. It is important to note that *Universidade Nova de Lisboa* includes the *NOVA Information Management School*, the *Faculty of Social Sciences and Humanities*, and the *Faculty of Science and Technology*. *Universidade do Porto* comprises the *Faculty of Sciences*, the *Faculty of Economics*, and the *Faculty of Engineering*, while *Universidade de Lisboa* includes the *Lisbon School of Economics and Management* and *Técnico Lisboa*. Each of these universities is organised into autonomous faculties, each with its own evaluation regulations.

Our first observation concerns the availability of public information regarding the regulations for evaluating the courses offered. If these regulations are not accessible, it becomes impossible to assess their content and evaluate how AI-based tools are utilised in the assessment process.

Six evaluation regulations from the following institutions could not be publicly accessed: *NOVA Information Management School*, *Instituto Politécnico de Bragança*, *Instituto Politécnico de Portalegre*, *Universidade Católica de Lisboa*, *Universidade Fernando Pessoa*, and *Universidade Lusíada de Lisboa*.

In addition to the assessment regulations, we also refer to the disciplinary regulations whenever they are mentioned in the former. None of the regulations we analysed addresses AI in the context of pedagogy or assessment. Consequently, there are no established guidelines, disclaimers, or flexibility for adapting the use of AI-based tools to suit the specific needs of a course or module. Additionally, teachers are not given any individual discretion in this matter.

There are concerns regarding the integrity of assessments and degree work at certain institutions. As of June 14, 2023, the General Assessment Regulation from *ISLA Santarém*[1] does not specifically mention AI. However, it emphasises that computer-assisted teaching in non-face-to-face learning environments must be conducted in a way that ensures the authenticity of the elements used to assess each student's performance.

At the master's level, institutions commonly have ethical and legal requirements. Typically, students must submit a declaration of integrity or a sworn statement. In this document, students affirm that they have completed their work honestly, that the text submitted is entirely their own authorship, and that any contributions or texts from others are appropriately cited. Furthermore, students acknowledge that failure to adhere to these standards will be regarded as a disciplinary infraction.

Faced with the disappointing results, we looked further into the institutions' websites and identified two position statements: "On the use of AI in teaching methods and knowledge assessment" (Técnico Lisboa, November 2023) and "Universidade Lusófona - Academic Integrity and the Use of Artificial Intelligence Tools" (November 23, 2023).

The first document states that, where appropriate, teachers should use AI-based tools to enrich, simplify, and update the teaching process and the creation of teaching content. Students should also be encouraged to use these tools as learning assistants. The teacher's responsibility includes ensuring equity in access to these tools and promoting their use to enhance the quality of work and brainstorming, which can help trigger creativity. Good practices also involve making it clear that the use of AI-based tools is permitted and explicitly stating the conditions under which they can be used.

The document from *Universidade Lusófona* recognises that AI-based tools can assist both teachers and students in grasping the concept of skill acquisition. It emphasises that teachers should inform students about the permissibility of using AI in the teaching-learning process. Teachers need to clarify the model for using these tools and explain their functions, limitations, and appropriate ways to reference them, always considering the ethical implications these emerging technologies carry for learning.

Both documents highlight teachers' responsibility in selecting and implementing technology and educating students about the risks and benefits of AI. However, there is no evidence of guidelines or training provided by the institutions to enhance teachers' AI literacy.

6. DISCUSSION

As shown by the theoretical contributions presented earlier, several benefits of using AIED have been identified, particularly in the domains of accessibility, personalised learning, digital skills development, and improved efficiency in the educational process. AI-based tools, such as adaptive learning platforms, intelligent tutoring systems, and automated grading, are heralded as transformative for tailoring education to individual needs, allowing teachers to dedicate more time to instruction and mentorship (Holmes et al., 2019; Kulik & Fletcher, 2016).

The findings indicate that AI-related educational programmes in Portugal are predominantly offered in the fields of technology and business, with a notable concentration in master's and postgraduate programmes dedicated to technical and managerial domains. This suggests an alignment with preparing students for AI development and application; however, there is limited presence of AI education in pedagogical contexts and in non-technical disciplines (e.g., social sciences and humanities), where benefits such as personalised learning could be transformative. This discrepancy indicates that while technical skills are emphasised, broader applications in diverse learning environments remain underexplored (e.g., Facer & Selwyn, 2021; Laupichler et al., 2022; Schiff, 2022; Southworth et al., 2023; Zawacki-Richter, et al., 2019). Expanding AIED to include AI-based tools for pedagogic purposes and AI literacy could foster a more inclusive integration of personalised learning and greater accessibility to the benefits of this technology in educational settings (e.g., Allen & Kendeou, 2024; Ng et al., 2021; Timotheou et al., 2023; Tuomi et al., 2018).

The theoretical perspectives presented in sections 2 and 3 highlight the importance of ethical and equity concerns raised by AIED, particularly regarding data privacy, algorithmic biases, dependency on AI, and socio-economic disparities in access (Holmes et al., 2019; Holmes & Porayska-Pomsta, 2023; Schiff, 2022; UNESCO, 2021). Addressing these issues within AI education is crucial to equipping students with the skills to manage ethical challenges associated with AI systems, especially given the significant impact they can have in educational contexts. However, in the empirical findings, there is a lack of structured courses or modules explicitly dedicated to ethics and equity in AI use. The emphasis on computer science, communication sciences and business courses suggests that students may be well prepared to develop and use AI-based tools but may lack the necessary training to critically evaluate the ethical and social impacts of AI (Allen & Kendeou, 2024; Southworth et al., 2023). Without an integrated focus on ethics and equity, there is a risk of perpetuating biases and privacy risks, particularly in applications within educational settings, where equitable access and fairness in assessment are crucial (Holmes et al., 2019 and 2023; UNESCO, 2021). This gap highlights the need for

Portuguese educational institutions to incorporate ethics-centred modules into their AI programmes, promoting responsible use.

However, the Portuguese national strategies for AI, such as INCoDe.2030 (2017) and the National Strategy for Artificial Intelligence (Portugal INCoDe.2030, 2019) do not address ethical or legal training related to the use of AI-based tools. National strategies are as vague as assessment higher education guidelines.

The analysis of the normative guidelines for using AI, as outlined in the general assessment regulations of Portuguese higher education institutions, underscores the absence of institutional policies aimed at integrating AI-based tools into learning, teaching processes, and assessment. Our study includes evaluation regulations from institutions specialised in AI technologies, and it is reasonable to expect these types of institutions to have a greater awareness of the benefits and risks associated with AI in education, particularly concerning academic integrity issues (Greene et al., 2019).

In addition to the regulations, we found two position statements from the institutions analysed, indicating a need to neither prohibit the use of AI nor exclude it from evaluation elements (*Técnico Lisboa*). Furthermore, these statements emphasise delegating responsibility to teachers regarding the rules of use and disclaimers (*Técnico Lisboa* and *Universidade Lusófona*).

Considering Foltynek et al. (2023), our results show a lack of public accessibility of the assessment regulations of six institutions, which prevents potential students from gauging how they will be assessed in the courses offered by the institutions. In addition, there are regulations that have been in force for more than 10 years without revision. There is also a predominance of regulations that deal with assessment by exams, which runs counter to the possibility of pedagogical innovation and adaptation to new assessment models that are more in line with technological developments (e.g., Černý, 2023; Holmes et al., 2019; Hwang et al., 2020; Luckin et al., 2016).

Besides, traditional assessment methods are expensive, provide limited insights into student performance, and are often outdated or inauthentic (Cope & Kalantzis, 2019; Swiecki et al., 2022).

Moreover, the regulations do not provide default rules regarding the circumstances and the way in which different stakeholders in the education sector can use various AI-based tools. Also absent is the disclaimer i.e. the explanation of how users can clearly and accurately acknowledge the use of AI-based tools in assignments.

The results highlight a principle of flexibility in the use of AI-based tools, emphasising the importance of aligning these tools with the teacher's discretion. While AI can enhance educational experiences, it also brings risks concerning equity and accessibility (Holmes et al., 2019; Holmes & Porayska-Pomsta, 2023; UNESCO, 2021). Teachers' attitudes towards AI can differ significantly, ranging from outright resistance to excessive reliance on technology. Resistance often stems from a lack of relevant and up-to-date professional development, while overreliance may result from unrealistic expectations regarding AI's capabilities, potentially stifling critical thinking and problem-solving skills (Selwyn, 2019; UNESCO, 2021; Zhai et al., 2020). Furthermore, the integration of AIED can impact human relationships and raise concerns about upholding democratic values (Council of Europe, 2022; Holmes et al., 2019; UNESCO, 2021).

The increased accessibility of AI-based tools also raises concerns about academic misconduct, as previously highlighted, by enabling students to generate content, potentially compromising original thought and independent assessment (Foltynek et al., 2023).

Strong institutional policies embedded in regulations on AI use are essential to mitigate risks and prevent misuse, ensuring authentic and meaningful assessments. From the empirical work conducted, a lack of explicit guidelines and policies regulating AI use in academic contexts is noted. The absence of public frameworks responsible for defining acceptable AI use can lead to inconsistent practices across disciplines and increase the potential for academic misconduct. Clear guidance for students and faculty will also help define boundaries for AI assistance in coursework or research. Expanding AI-related courses to include domains of ethics, equity, and pedagogical application will enable responsible application in both social and professional contexts relevant to each programme and in academic contexts through an interdisciplinary approach that respects clear policies and direct usage guidelines.

CONCLUSION

Integrating technological innovation into educational systems influences the quality of teaching and learning. This integration is particularly important for understanding, adapting to, and designing systems that align with current technological trends. All stakeholders within the educational system must have the skills to effectively use technology, capitalise on its benefits, minimise risks, and ensure its responsible and ethical use.

Approaching AIED must go beyond AI-centred views on how to use the tools and the technology's features and outputs. It is paramount to consider the ecosystem of education, the ecology of technology, social interactions, cognition, and ethical values.

A successful digital transformation requires that educational institutions increase their digital capacity levels and establish the necessary culture, policies, and infrastructure, as well as the digital competence of teachers, students, and staff, to support the effective integration of technology in teaching and learning practices.

The current chapter emphasises the growing impact of AI-based tools in education within Portugal, specifically in technical fields such as computer science, communication sciences and business. It stresses the capacity for personalised teaching, optimisation of administrative tasks, and inclusion instruments in education as essential for teachers and students, as seen in the offered AI-based tools. However, there is a significant gap in the integration of ethics and interdisciplinary training, revealing a limitation to the technical spectrum without ethical considerations for the use of AI in educational contexts. Additionally, there is a lack of specific regulation on the use of AI in assessment processes, particularly through pedagogical regulations, to provide a unified perspective on this technology's use, aiming to prevent academic misconduct and reduce risks to academic integrity. A delegation of responsibilities is observed, especially among teachers, which may lead to inconsistent application of ethical norms. It is also necessary to consider teachers' possible lack of AI literacy and their predisposition to avoid technology.

The alignment between the theoretical benefits of AIED and the offerings in master's and postgraduate programmes in higher education in Portugal is evident, resulting in the development of students' technical skills. However, the gap in ethical training, regulatory guidance, and interdisciplinary application limit a balanced and inclusive integration of AI-based tools. A broader approach, including policy development, ethical training, and interdisciplinary programmes by Portuguese higher education institutions could significantly contribute to the technical, ethical, and social literacy required in professional and research domains, ensuring an innovative integration that respects democratic values and human rights within the context of AIED.

To address the existing gaps in institutional policies concerning AI in higher education, institutions must establish clear governance frameworks. These frameworks should outline acceptable uses of AI, disclosure obligations, and consequences for violations. Additionally, it is crucial to enhance transparency by making these policies easily accessible on institutional websites, which would help promote informed decision-making among students and faculty.

Support for faculty is crucial, necessitating robust development programmes that encompass technical training, pedagogical strategies, and ongoing updates on AI advancements. Meanwhile, student support systems should include clear ethical guidelines for AI use and training in AI literacy, ensuring accessibility for all levels of technical proficiency.

It is critical to set comprehensive guidelines for AI-assisted assessments, emphasising the need to declare AI use, verify submission authenticity, and maintain flexible yet consistent evaluation standards that respect academic integrity.

The successful implementation of these recommendations requires dedicated funding for infrastructure, investment in training, and educational resources to continuously monitor and assess the effects of AI integration in academia.

Considering AI's possible strategic value for education and its potential as an effective learning tool, establishing clear guidelines and oversight mechanisms for AI use in educational settings is essential to ensuring transparency, accountability, and alignment with human rights standards. As AI continues to evolve, ongoing stakeholder engagement and interdisciplinary research will be crucial to effectively managing its impact on education systems, balancing innovation with the protection of fundamental rights and democratic values.

The primary limitations of this study include a narrow focus on non-technical aspects, a lack of qualitative empirical data, and insufficient regulatory frameworks within the Portuguese context. There is a significant focus on master's and postgraduate programmes that include AI content, particularly in technical fields. However, this trend is coupled with a lack of courses dedicated to the humanities and social sciences. This absence hinders a comprehensive understanding of AI training in non-technical areas.

Furthermore, the study acknowledges a significant gap in qualitative data, particularly the absence of methodological approaches to gather direct feedback from teachers and students about their perceptions of AI usage in educational settings. The unclear and limited availability of regulations from higher education institutions adds to the difficulty in understanding established practices related to AI in developing and assessing educational content. Our data is restricted to public documents made available on educational institutions' websites. Although it is mandatory for higher education institutions in Portugal to publicise assessment regulations, compliance with this requirement is inconsistent. Additionally, focusing solely on regulations excludes internal practices and provisions that may affect the work of teachers and the assessment of students.

Finally, the study is confined to the Portuguese context, suggesting that a comparative analysis with international findings could either confirm the uniqueness of the observed trends or reveal similarities.

These limitations collectively highlight the imperative for a more extensive exploration of non-technical training, the incorporation of qualitative research methodologies, the establishment of clearer regulatory frameworks, and the necessity of adopting an international perspective on the integration of AI in education.

Furthermore, the chapter highlights the necessity of developing an ethical training model for AI use, which would emerge from a comprehensive investigation of training programmes that incorporate modules focused on ethics, privacy, and the responsible application of AI-based tools within educational contexts. Moreover, it calls for longitudinal evaluations of AI use in educational settings, specifically analysing the impact of AI-based tools on academic performance, the cultivation of critical thinking skills, and the ability to adapt to emerging technologies. Finally, the chapter points to the significance of gathering existing literature and analysing current practices to establish foundational standards for educational institutions concerning the use of AI by both teachers and students within a Western educational framework.

AI is one of the most widely adopted technologies in history. It has become ubiquitous and is now part of everyday life, serving as a common tool in education and learning.

A new civic skill must be developed to understand how AI can serve human purposes and what AI means in our lives. Support for this should be part of school curricula and easily available in society. AI users need basic knowledge about AI, its features and applications, and the ethical regulations needed for its safe use. AI will be a powerful tool in our future, with risks and benefits, requiring the conscientisation that human beings have the ultimate responsibility when developing and using AI.

DISCLAIMER

This chapter uses artificial intelligence to translate original Portuguese sentences into English using DeepL. Artificial intelligence was also employed in specific aspects, namely language clarity and checking using Grammarly Business (paid version). The authors double-checked all AI-assisted texts to correct selected wordings, grammatical adjustments, and paraphrases. The authors, safeguarding human oversight and expertise in the final output, performed the overall composition of the chapter manually.

REFERENCES

Adams, D., & Chuah, K.-M. (2022). Artificial intelligence-based tools in research writing: Current trends and future potentials. In Churi, P. P., Joshi, S., Elhoseny, M., & Omrane, A. (Eds.), *Artificial Intelligence in Higher Education: A practical approach* (pp. 169–184). CRD Press., DOI: 10.1201/9781003184157-9

Allen, L. K., & Kendeou, P. (2024). ED-AI Lit: An Interdisciplinary Framework for AI Literacy in Education. *Policy Insights from the Behavioral and Brain Sciences, 11*(1), 3–10. DOI: 10.1177/23727322231220339

Bender, E. M., Gebru, T., McMillan-Major, A., & Shmitchell, S. (2021). On the dangers of stochastic parrots: Can language models be too big? In *Proceedings of the 2021 ACM Conference on Fairness, Accountability, and Transparency* (pp. 610–623). DOI: 10.1145/3442188.3445922

Bhise, A., Munshi, A., Rodrigues, A., & Sawant, V. (2023). Overview of AI in Education. In Churi, P. P., Joshi, S., Elhoseny, M., & Omrane, A. (Eds.), *Artificial Intelligence in Higher Education: A practical approach* (pp. 31–62). CRD Press., DOI: 10.1201/9781003184157-2

Carter, S. P., Greenberg, K., & Walker, M. S. (2016). The impact of computer usage on academic performance: Evidence from a randomized trial at the United States Military Academy. *Economics of Education Review, 56*, 118–132. DOI: 10.1016/j.econedurev.2016.12.005

Černý, M. (2023). Artificial intelligence, creativity and education: finding a new perspective. *Journal of Applied Technical and Educational Sciences, 13*(3), ArtNo 353. DOI: 10.24368/jates353

Chen, L., Chen, P., & Lin, Z. (2020). Artificial intelligence in education: A review. *IEEE Access : Practical Innovations, Open Solutions*, *8*, 75264–75278. DOI: 10.1109/ACCESS.2020.2988510

Cope, B., & Kalantzis, M. (2019). Education 2.0: Artificial intelligence and the end of the test. *Beijing International Review of Education*, *1*(2-3), 528–543. DOI: 10.1163/25902539-00102009

Council of Europe. (2022). Artificial Intelligence and Education. A critical view through the lens of human rights, democracy and the rule of law. https://rm.coe.int/prems-092922-gbr-2517-ai-and-education-txt-16x24-web/1680a956e3

Dawson, P. (2021). *Defending Assessment Security in a Digital World: Preventing E-cheating and Supporting Academic Integrity in Higher Education*. Routledge., DOI: 10.4324/9780429324178

Facer, K., & Selwyn, N. (2021). *Digital technology and the futures of education – towards 'non-stupid' optimism*. UNESCO's Futures of Education report. https://unesdoc.unesco.org/ark:/48223/pf0000377071

Foltynek, T., Bjelobaba, S., Glendinning, I., Khan, Z. R., Santos, R., Pavletic, P., & Kravjar, J. (2023). ENAI Recommendations on the Ethical Use of Artificial Intelligence in Education. *International Journal for Educational Integrity*, *19*, 12. DOI: 10.1007/s40979-023-00133-4

Foltynek, T., Dlabolova, D., Anohina-Naumeca, A., & Linkeschova, D. (2020). Academic plagiarism detection: A systematic literature review. *Journal of Academic Ethics*, *18*(1), 1–31. DOI: 10.1145/3345317

Greene, D., Hoffmann, A. L., & Stark, L. (2019). Better, Nicer, Clearer, Fairer: A critical assessment of the movement for ethical artificial intelligence and machine learning. In *Proceedings of the 52nd Hawaii International Conference on System Sciences* (pp. 2122–2131). https://doi.org/DOI: 10.24251/HICSS.2019.258

Hicks, M. T., Humphries, J., & Slater, J. (2024). ChatGPT is bullshit. *Ethics and Information Technology*, *26*, 38. DOI: 10.1007/s10676-024-09775-5

Holmes, W., Bialik, M., & Fadel, C. (2019). *Artificial intelligence in education: Promises and implications for teaching and learning*. Center for Curriculum Redesign.

Holmes, W., & Porayska-Pomsta, K. (Eds.). (2023). *The Ethics of Artificial Intelligence in Education. Practices, Challenges, and Debates*. Routledge.

Holmes, W., & Tuomi, I. (2022). State of the art and practice in AI in education. *European Journal of Education*, *57*, 542–570. DOI: 10.1111/ejed.12533

Hopcan, S., Polat, E., Ozturk, M. E., & Ozturk, L. (2022). Artificial intelligence in special education: A systematic review. *Interactive Learning Environments, 31*, 7335–7353.

Hwang, G.-J., Xie, H., Wah, B. W., & Gašević, D. (2020). Vision, challenges, roles and research issues of artificial intelligence in education. *Computers & Education: Artificial Intelligence, 1*, 100001. DOI: 10.1016/j.caeai.2020.100001

Johnson, M., Schuster, M., Le, Q. V., Krikun, M., Wu, Y., Chen, Z., Thorat, N., Viégas, F., Wattenberg, M., Corrado, G., Hughes, M., & Dean, J. (2017). Google's multilingual neural machine translation system: Enabling zero-shot translation. *Transactions of the Association for Computational Linguistics, 5*, 339–351. DOI: 10.1162/tacl_a_00065

Knox, J. (2020). Artificial Intelligence and Education in China. *Learning, Media and Technology, 45*(3), 298–311. DOI: 10.1080/17439884.2020.1754236

Kulik, J. A., & Fletcher, J. D. (2016). Effectiveness of Intelligent Tutoring Systems: A Meta-Analytic Review. *Review of Educational Research, 86*(1), 42–78. DOI: 10.3102/0034654315581420

Laupichler, M. C., Aster, A., Schirch, J., & Raupach, T. (2022). Artificial intelligence literacy in higher and adult education: A scoping literature review. *Computers and Education: Artificial Intelligence, 3*, 100101. DOI: 10.1016/j.caeai.2022.100101

Lindgren, S. (2024). *Critical Theory of AI*. Polity Press.

Luckin, R., Holmes, W., Griffiths, M., & Forcier, L. B. (2016). *Intelligence Unleashed: An argument for AI in education*. Pearson Education.

Ng, D. T. K., Leung, J. K. L., Chu, S. K. W., & Qiao, M. S. (2021). Conceptualizing AI literacy: An exploratory review. *Computers and Education: Artificial Intelligence, 2*, 100041. DOI: 10.1016/j.caeai.2021.100041

OECD. (2021). *OECD digital education outlook 2021: Pushing the frontiers with artificial intelligence, blockchain and robots*. OECD Publishing., DOI: 10.1787/589b283f-

Okonkwo, C. W., & Ade-Ibijola, A. (2021). Chatbots applications in education: A systematic review. *Computers and Education: Artificial Intelligence, 2*, 100033. DOI: 10.1016/j.caeai.2021.100033

Portugal INCoDe. 2030 (2017). Iniciativa Nacional Competências Digitais e.2030, Portugal INCoDe.2030. https://www.incode2030.gov.pt/

Portugal INCoDe. 2030 (2019). Estratégia Nacional de Inteligência Artificial (National Strategy for Artificial Intelligence). https://www.incode2030.gov.pt/aip-2030/

Rettig, C., & Mickeleit, T. (2023). There is no shortcut to AI. Or is there? How German communications professionals are navigating the AI revolution: Insights from a focus group discussion of the members of AG CommTech. In Adi, A. (Ed.), *Artificial Intelligence in Public Relations and Communications: cases, reflections, and predictions* (pp. 63–72). Quadriga University of Applied Sciences.

Russell, S. J., & Norvig, P. (2022). *Artificial Intelligence: A Modern Approach* (4th ed.). Pearson.

Sanusi, I. T., Olaleye, S. A., Agbo, F. J., & Chiu, T. K. F. (2022). The role of learners' competencies in artificial intelligence education. *Computers and Education: Artificial Intelligence, 3,* 100098. Advance online publication. DOI: 10.1016/j.caeai.2022.100098

Schiff, D. (2022). Education for AI, not AI for Education: The Role of Education and Ethics in National AI Policy Strategies. *International Journal of Artificial Intelligence in Education, 32,* 527–563. DOI: 10.1007/s40593-021-00270-2

Selwyn, N. (2019). *Should robots replace teachers? AI and the Future of Education.* Polity Press.

Southworth, J., Migliaccio, K., Glover, J., Glover, J., Reed, D., McCarty, C., Brendemuhl, J., & Thomas, A. (2023). Developing a model for *AI Across the curriculum*: Transforming the higher education landscape via innovation in AI literacy. *Computers and Education: Artificial Intelligence, 4,* 100127. DOI: 10.1016/j.caeai.2023.100127

Swiecki, Z., Khosravi, H., Chen, G., Martinez-Maldonado, R., Lodge, J. M., Milligan, S., Selwyn, N., & Gasevic, D. (2022). Assessment in the age of artificial intelligence. *Computers and Education: Artificial Intelligence, 3,* 100075. DOI: 10.1016/j.caeai.2022.100075

Técnico Lisboa. (November 2023). Sobre a utilização de IA nos métodos de ensino e de avaliação de conhecimentos (On the use of AI in teaching methods and knowledge assessment) https://conselhopedagogico.tecnico.ulisboa.pt/files/sites/32/ferramentas-de-ai-no-ensino-v8-1.pdf

Timotheou, S., Miliou, O., Dimitriadis, Y., Sobrino, S. V., Giannoutsou, N., Cachia, R., Monés, A. M., & Ioannou, A. (2023). Impacts of digital technologies on education and factors influencing schools' digital capacity and transformation: A literature review. *Education and Information Technologies, 28,* 6695–6726. DOI: 10.1007/s10639-022-11431-8 PMID: 36465416

Tuomi, I., Cachia, R., & Villar-Onrubia, D. (2023). *On the Futures of Technology in Education: Emerging Trends and Policy Implications.* Joint Research Center. *Publications Office of the European Union., JRC134308.* Advance online publication. DOI: 10.2760/079734

Tuomi, I., Punie, Y., Vuorikari, R., & Cabrera, M. (2018). *The impact of Artificial Intelligence on learning, teaching, and education.* European Commission: Joint Research Centre. Publications Office of the European Union.

UNESCO. (2021). *AI and education: Guidance for policy-makers.* https://unesdoc.unesco.org/ark:/48223/pf0000376709

Wang, S., Wang, F., Zhu, Z., Wang, J., Tran, T., & Du, Z. (2024). Artificial intelligence in education: A systematic literature review. *Expert Systems with Applications, 252*(A), 124167. DOI: 10.1016/j.eswa.2024.124167

Williamson, B., & Piattoeva, N. (2019). Objectivity as standardization in data-scientific education policy, technology and governance. *Learning, Media and Technology, 44*(1), 64–76. DOI: 10.1080/17439884.2018.1556215

Wong, G., Ma, X., Dillenbourg, P., & Huan, J. (2020). Broadening artificial intelligence education in K-12: Where to start? *ACM Inroads, 11*(1), 20–29. DOI: 10.1145/3381884

Yasmin, H., & Mazhar, R. (2023). AI in Education. A few decades from now. In Churi, P. P., Joshi, S., Elhoseny, M., & Omrane, A. (Eds.), *Artificial Intelligence in Higher Education: A practical approach* (pp. 1–30). CRD Press. DOI: 10.1201/9781003184157-1

Yi, Y. (2021). Establishing the concept of AI literacy: Focusing on competence and purpose. *JAHR – European. Journal of Bioethics, 12*(2), 353–368. DOI: 10.21860/j.12.2.8

Zawacki-Richter, O., Marín, V. I., Bond, M., & Gouverneur, F. (2019). Systematic review of research on artificial intelligence applications in higher education - Where are the educators? *International Journal of Educational Technology in Higher Education, 16*(1), 39. DOI: 10.1186/s41239-019-0171-0

Zhai, X., Chu, X., Chai, C. S., Jong, M. S. Y., Istenic, A., Spector, M., & Chen, Y. (2021). A review of artificial intelligence (AI) in education from 2010 to 2020. *Complexity. Article ID, 8812542.* Advance online publication. DOI: 10.1155/2021/8812542

ADDITIONAL READING

Douali, L., Selmaoui, S., & Bouab, W. (2022). Artificial intelligence in education: Fears and faiths. *International Journal of Information and Education Technology (IJIET), 12*(7), 650–657. DOI: 10.18178/ijiet.2022.12.7.1666

International Journal of Artificial Intelligence in Education | https://link.springer.com/journal/40593

International Journal of Educational Technology in Higher Education | https://educationaltechnologyjournal.springeropen.com/

Miao, F., & Holmes, W. (2023). *Guidance for generative AI in education and research.* UNESCO. https://www.unesco.org/en/articles/guidance-generative-ai-education-and-research

Smeyers, P., & Smith, R. (2014). *Understanding Education and Educational Research.* Cambridge University Press. DOI: 10.1017/CBO9780511920714

Tahiru, F. (2021). AI in Education: A Systematic Literature Review. [JCIT]. *Journal of Cases on Information Technology, 23*(1), 1–20. DOI: 10.4018/JCIT.2021010101

Uskov, V. L., Bakken, J. P., Howlett, R. J., & Jain, L. C. (Eds.). (2018). *Smart Universities. Concepts, Systems, and Technologies*. Springer Cham. DOI: 10.1007/978-3-319-59454-5

KEY TERMS AND DEFINITIONS

Academic Integrity: Academic integrity refers to the expectation that educators, students, researchers, and all individuals within the academic community conduct themselves with honesty, trustworthiness, fairness, respect, responsibility, and a strong adherence to ethical principles.

Adaptive Learning Platforms: The ability of AI tools to adapt content and teaching methods to the individual needs of students, considering their performance, skills, and capabilities.

AI Literacy: A set of competencies enabling students and educators to understand, use, and monitor AI applications, even without thc ability to dcvclop AI models, as well as critically reflect on their use.

AI Tools in Education (AIED): generally refer to standalone applications or systems that utilise machine learning algorithms, natural language processing, and other AI technologies to support and enhance teaching and learning processes.

AI-based tools: indicate systems that use AI as their foundational technology while integrating with other computational methods. These tools leverage AI algorithms as their core architecture but may incorporate additional non-AI components for complete functionality.

Digital Competence: Digital Competence comprises a combination of knowledge, skills, and attitudes concerning the use of technology to undertake tasks, resolve problems, communicate, manage information, collaborate, and create and share content. It highlights the effective, appropriate, secure, critical, creative, independent, and ethical application of digital tools.

Digital skills: specifically refer to the abilities needed to navigate and utilise digital devices and platforms to successfully achieve these tasks.

Educational Stakeholders: Educational stakeholders are individuals and organisations that have a vested interest in the success of an educational system. This group includes students and teachers as its core, supported by parents and school administrators who directly influence daily learning activities. Surrounding this core group is a wider network that encompasses government bodies, local authorities, and community representatives, all of whom play a role in shaping educational outcomes. Their collective involvement ensures that the educational system remains responsive to societal needs while upholding academic standards and institutional effectiveness.

Educational System / Education System: The educational system typically encompasses the framework of various institutions and the opportunities available for gaining knowledge and skills within a nation. Education, in this context, refers to the process of acquiring knowledge, values, and competencies through formal instruction, training, and experiences.

ENDNOTES

1. ISLA Santarém is a private institution offering a Master's degree in Web Technologies and Systems Engineering and a postgraduate programme in Artificial Intelligence and Emerging Technologies in Learning.

Chapter 9
Is AI in Higher Education a Real Help for Students?
Phenomenological Experiences Among the University Students in Bangladesh

Aftab Hossain
https://orcid.org/0000-0003-4759-8372
Daffodil International University, Bangladesh & Universiti Sains Malaysia

Abu Nowfel Shazed
Daffodil International University, Bangladesh

Md. Meherabul Haque
Daffodil International University, Bangladesh

Alifennesa Alif
https://orcid.org/0009-0005-7223-744X
Daffodil International University, Bangladesh

Sakibul Alam
Daffodil International University, Bangladesh

ABSTRACT

Artificial intelligence has transformed higher education by improving academic efficiency and delivering personalized learning experiences; yet, it raises concerns about data security and algorithmic bias. This study explores how undergraduate and graduate students in journalism, media, and communication perceive AI-driven educational systems, focusing on data privacy, ethical challenges, and algorithmic

DOI: 10.4018/979-8-3373-6018-8.ch009

Copyright © 2026, IGI Global Scientific Publishing. Copying or distributing in print or electronic forms without written permission of IGI Global Scientific Publishing is prohibited.

inequalities. We gathered insights through semi-structured interviews with students of varying academic abilities, using a phenomenological approach, and thematic analysis. Findings reveal limited awareness of data management processes, fears of misuse, and concerns about AI biased feedback. The study emphasises the need for greater transparency, inclusive AI development, and educational initiatives to address these ethical issues. By amplifying student perspectives, it contributes to the conversation on ethical AI practices, offering actionable recommendations for policymakers, educators, and developers to promote trust, equity, and accountability in AI-integrated education.

INTRODUCTION

Artificial intelligence (AI) has become a new phenomenon in human society. Especially in the academic environment after the Covid-19 pandemic pushed more online education and digitization and changed the way students learn and interact with educational materials (Wang et al., 2024; Rafa, 2024; Adedoyin & Soykan, 2020). Since the inception of artificial intelligence-based chatbots like ChatGPT, Gemini, Dall-E, Siri and Alexa, AI has become an integral part of education (Nathani, 2025; De Simone et al., 2025). Later, on November 22, 2022, the release of the revolutionary chatbot ChatGPT further enhanced the power of AI in education ("Generative AI and the Future of Education," 2023). The impact of AI in higher education has been significant and continues to change the way students learn (Javaid et al., 2023).

As Holmes et al. (2021) mentioned, not only among teachers but students are the largest AI community in the world. It's been a tradition in the past couple of years to use AI in class. From classroom activities to science texts, AI is becoming an integral part of learning (Mageira et al., 2022; Kumar et al., 2023). Moreover, AI-based education was also seriously integrated into our education systems, and this was integrated into education, arguably in a positive way. AI has also changed the way teachers measure student performance and provide personalized feedback, leading to more effective learning outcomes. As AI technology evolves, it is expected to play an even more important role in education in the future (Hooda et al., 2022; *Personalized Education in the Artificial Intelligence Era: What to Expect Next*, 2021).

Background of AI in Education:

Artificial intelligence has been a necessity for decades. It was introduced into the education system in the early 1990s. Subsequently, AI's involvement in education increased during and after Covid-19. AI in education has transformed the traditional classroom environment by providing students with new tools and resources to enhance the learning experience. Furthermore, Abulibdeh et al. (2024) found in his study that, Artificial Intelligence (AI) plays a pertinent role in bridging the gap between students and teachers. Especially while distance learning or online learning during any problematic situation for in-person education. Besides, AI chatbots like ChatGPT, Gemini and DALL-E became widely accepted to provide personalized help to students and teachers. AI chatbots can answer academic and non-academic questions, provide reviews. They can even create creative content for academic support in tasks and assignments. Furthermore, AI technology has also enabled academic automation too. As it is allowing educators to focus more on personalized instructions and engage the students in dynamic ways (Watermeyer et al., 2023). The integration of AI into academia has shown a great potential in many ways. It led to improving and achieving learning outcomes as well as creating an interactive and personalized learning ecology (Lin, 2023).

With all the facilities of using AI, there is the other side of the coin too. Data security and algorithmic bias have been issues of concern among scholars worldwide (Kordzadeh & Ghasemaghaei, 2021; Baker & Hawn, 2021; Wu & Goldman School of Public Policy, University of California, Berkeley, 2023). It is important for educators and policymakers to address these ethical considerations and ensure that AI technology is used responsibly in educational settings (Makaryan, 2024). By implementing proper safeguards and regulations, the potential benefits of AI in education can be maximized while minimizing potential risks (World Economic Forum, 2025). As the students are young users of AI, while they use it for their academic purposes, they are little exposed to data security and algorithmic bias that AI systems are susceptible to. According to Yang and Beil (2024), the lack of knowledge about AI's data security and algorithmic bias may breach the line of security of digital life, and algorithmic bias may result in unfair treatment or discrimination. Therefore, it is crucial for policymakers to prioritize educating students about these issues and implementing measures to protect their privacy and ensure equitable access to AI technology in education. By fostering a culture of transparency and accountability surrounding AI use in schools, students can fully benefit from its potential while minimizing any negative consequences (Chan, 2023; World Economic Forum, 2025).

Although, according to recent studies, there is still a long way to go in terms of addressing these concerns, it is important for educators and policymakers to work together to create a safe and inclusive learning environment for all students (UNESCO Education Sector, 2021; Le et al., 2023). Additionally, as per Eden et al. (2024) and Fedele et al. (2024) ongoing research and development in AI ethics and data security will be essential in ensuring that the benefits of AI technology in education can be maximized while minimizing any potential risks. By promoting transparency and accountability, academic institutions can ensure that AI is used responsibly and ethically to enhance the learning experience for students. Collaboration between all stakeholders will be crucial in navigating the complex landscape of AI in education and ensuring that it is used to empower students rather than harm them (Alqodsi et al., 2024; Chan, 2023b).

Research Problem and Significance:

The incorporation of artificial intelligence (AI) in higher education has revolutionized the academic environment, providing customized learning experiences, automated analytics, and data-informed insights (Sajja et al., 2024). However, the potential risks of AI in education, such as data privacy concerns and algorithmic bias, must be carefully addressed to prevent negative consequences for students (Rane et al., 2023; Rahiman & Kodikal, 2023). Additionally, Chiu et al. (2022) and Zhai et al. (2021) recognises the ongoing research and evaluation of AI systems in education will be necessary to continually improve their effectiveness and impact on student learning outcomes.

Nonetheless, the dependence of AI systems on extensive student data raises significant problems. Data, both academic and personal, disclosed to AI tools may be susceptible to privacy violations, as hosts and service providers frequently obtain access to sensitive information, such as search history and confidential academic records (X. Wu et al., 2023; Okon et al., 2024). These concerns erode confidence and provoke ethical inquiries regarding the responsible application of AI in education. Furthermore, the potential for bias in AI algorithms, based on the data they are trained on, raises questions about fairness and equity in educational settings. It is crucial for developers and educators to address these issues to ensure that AI systems in education are used ethically and responsibly.

Moreover, Nazer et al. (2023) mentioned, AI algorithms are susceptible to biases, potentially leading to disparate treatment of young people. Biased feedback systems, course suggestions, and racial or cultural misrepresentations in data may intensify existing disparities (*Bias and Discrimination in AI: A Cross-Disciplinary Perspective*, 2021). These biases can undermine trust, sustain prejudice, and disseminate misinformation inside the educational process, ultimately jeopardizing the integrity of learning outcomes.

This study examines the viewpoints of communication undergraduate students about two primary issues: data security and algorithmic prejudice. It also seeks to illuminate the problems and ethical ramifications of AI in higher education by analyzing the perceptions and interactions of students with diverse academic capacities about AI tools (Akgun & Greenhow, 2021; Tzimas & Demetriadis, 2021).

In Bangladesh the usage of AI in higher education became very significant, especially during the COVID-19 pandemic (Roy et al., 2021). After that, AI and chatbots, especially ChatGPT, Gemini, Dall-E, and many more. AI platforms like ChatGPT and Gemini have changed digital resources for online education in Bangladesh, with students using them to clarify theoretical concepts and complete assignments. While some ethical concerns exist, these tools are seen as helpful for learning and research purposes by students and educators alike (Shohel et al., 2022). However, mostly students in higher education use AI for their academic assignments or tasks, but they can sometimes rely too heavily on AI and fail to fully engage with the material themselves (Raji et al., 2022; De Sio & Mecacci, 2021). In this case, they provide their personal and academic information to AI chatbots that may lead to unethical use, data security, and algorithmic bias. It is important for students to strike a balance between utilizing AI tools for assistance and actively engaging with the material to ensure a deeper understanding. This will help minimize the potential risks associated with over-reliance on AI technology and understanding of potential bias risks.

This study explores the ethical implications of AI in higher education, focusing on journalism and communication students' perspectives on data collection, storage, and utilization. It highlights the need for protecting student privacy and addressing algorithmic bias, which can lead to disparate treatment of students in feedback, grading, and course recommendations. The findings will help developers develop more fair AI algorithms and guide instructors in using these tools appropriately.

It also addresses a gap in literature by amplifying the voices of communication undergraduate students with diverse academic talents. It analyzes students' perceptions of the trade-offs between AI's advantages and risks, offering a grassroots perspective on ethical AI practices in education (Early, 2024; Corrêa et al., 2024; Ashok et al., 2021). The findings will help legislators, educational institutions, and AI developers create frameworks that handle data privacy and bias concerns. The study emphasizes the importance of student-centered design and encourages universities to engage students in the creation and oversight of AI technologies. It also examines algorithmic bias and data security, offering insights on promoting equity and restoring trust in educational technologies. The goal is to ensure technology functions as a means of inclusion rather than exclusion.

This study serves as a basis for future investigations into the ethical implications of AI in education, focusing on journalism and communication students and highlighting the intricacies of how AI systems influence specific fields and academic competencies (Center for News, Technology & Innovation, 2024; Wenger et al., 2024). The results may stimulate further research and guide educators and institutions globally. The study aims to reconcile the revolutionary potential of AI with its ethical obligations, ensuring AI technologies are deployed in ways that maintain trust, equity, and inclusivity in higher education.

This study addresses two concerns related to data security and algorithmic bias from the perspective of communication graduate students. How do students with different academic abilities perceive this information and how do they use AI? By examining these concerns, the chapter contributes to the ongoing debate on the use of ethical AI in higher education by raising these questions to investigate phenomenologically.

RQ 1: How do communication, journalism, media studies undergraduate and postgraduate students perceive the security of their data in AI-powered educational systems?
RQ 2: What concerns do communication students have about the potential misuse, leakage, or unauthorized sharing of their personal and academic data?
RQ 3: To what extent are communication students aware of algorithmic biases in AI systems, and how do these biases impact their trust and reliance on such tools?

DEVELOPMENTS OF ARTIFICIAL INTELLIGENCE (AI)

Artificial intelligence (AI) has advanced dramatically over the last few decades transforming industries and redefining human experiences which was first conceived in the mid-twentieth century has progressed at a rapid pace (Pasquinelli, M. 2023).

In its early phases, AI concentrated on symbolic thinking, logic-based systems and rule-based methods. The 1956 Dartmouth Conference laid the groundwork for AI research by picturing computers capable of doing activities that need human intellect. However, Kitsara (2022) stated that restrictions on computer power and data availability hindered development during the so-called "AI winters."

The turn of the twenty-first century produced transformational developments. Machine learning, a type of AI, has emerged as an important method. Dargan et al. (2020) mentioned that Unlike traditional programming, machine learning allows computers to learn and improve over time. This was exacerbated by the emergence of deep learning, which uses neural networks to simulate human brain operations. Speech recognition, picture categorization and natural language processing are now common applications as a result of these advancements.

AI's impact on sectors has been tremendous. AI-powered diagnostic tools, medication discovery and tailored treatment all aid the healthcare industry. In finance algorithms identify fraudulent behavior and optimize trading tactics. Autonomous cars driven by AI are revolutionizing transportation while smart assistants like Siri and Alexa have become commonplace in everyday life (Valavanidis, 2023).

Generative AI models such as OpenAI's GPT series and DALL·E can create human-like literature, art and music (Gupta, 2023). These models use large datasets and powerful architectures to produce material of unparalleled quality and coherence. However, AI's fast growth creates obstacles. Ethical considerations, such as algorithm bias, data privacy and the possibility of employment displacement require careful examination. Furthermore, Chesterman (2024) stated that the growth of generative AI creates issues of misrepresentation and intellectual property rights.

In the future, AI research will focus on topics such as general AI, quantum computing and edge AI. These developments promise to increase AI's efficiency and applicability fostering innovation while solving social challenges. With proper governance and ethical development, AI has the ability to solve some of humanity's most urgent problems paving the path for a smarter and more connected future (Oliver, 2022) .

AI AND CHATBOTS

Artificial intelligence (AI) has substantially accelerated the development and usage of chatbots, changing the way businesses communicate with consumers and people access information. Nguyen (2024) stated that AI-powered chatbots are supposed to replicate human conversations and give real-time automated help, such as answering questions, completing tasks and even participating in informal talk.

AI chatbots employ natural language processing (NLP) to comprehend, interpret and create human-like answers. Early chatbots such as ELIZA in the 1960s used programmed answers and basic keyword recognition. However, Casheekar et al., (2024) stated that current AI-powered chatbots use powerful machine learning algorithms and massive language models to provide more contextually aware and dynamic conversations. They can understand complicated questions, identify linguistic subtleties and deliver individualized solutions, making them significantly superior to their predecessors.

AI chatbots have a wide range of applications across sectors. In customer support, (Sinokki, S. 2024) mentioned that chatbots such as Zendesk and Intercom handle routine requests lowering wait times and increasing customer satisfaction. In the healthcare industry, chatbots like Ada and Woebot provide medical advice and mental health help. E-commerce sites utilize chatbots to promote items and aid with purchases whereas educational institutions use them for tutoring and administrative support (Rane et al. 2024).

Generative AI as demonstrated by models such as OpenAI's ChatGPT has further transformed chatbots. These models may produce complex, conversational and human-like replies making encounters more engaging and natural. As a result, organizations are increasingly using chatbots for creative jobs like content creation and more complex issue resolution (Ramaul et al., 2024).

Despite their benefits, AI chatbots present obstacles. Ensuring data privacy and security is crucial, particularly when dealing with sensitive information (Giordani, 2024). Additionally, biases in AI training data might result in incorrect or erroneous results. Maintaining a balance between automation and human intervention is an ongoing problem for ensuring quality and empathy in interactions (Izadi & Forouzanfar, 2024).

As AI advances, the future of chatbots seems bright. Chatbots are predicted to become more flexible and influential as emotion detection, voice-based interactions and multilingual capabilities advance. With ethical concerns and strong design, chatbots are set to become vital tools for improving user experiences and facilitating communication across sectors.

AI IN EDUCATION

Artificial intelligence (AI) is redefining education by providing novel tools and individualized learning experiences as well as disrupting traditional teaching techniques and increasing access to knowledge. From adaptive learning platforms to administrative automation, AI is changing the way students study and educators educate.

One of the most significant contributions of AI to education is individualized learning. Maghsudi et al., (2021) describes AI-powered services such as Khan Academy and Duolingo that customize information to individual learning styles and paces. These systems employ data analytics to detect strengths, weaknesses and learning gaps before delivering personalized lessons and activities. This tailored approach guarantees that students receive focused assistance, resulting in improved retention and academic success.

AI-powered virtual instructors and chatbots are also making a significant impact on education (Cruz, M et al 2024). ChatGPT and other similar tools help students by answering questions, clarifying topics and offering writing aid. These 24/7 learning tools ensure that students may get guidance at any time regardless of their location. Additionally, Lytvynova et al. (2024) said AI-powered tools are being utilized to teach programming, mathematics and languages in an interactive manner making learning more enjoyable.

In the classroom, AI helps instructors by automating administrative duties like grading, attendance monitoring and curriculum preparation. Platforms such as Turnitin use AI to identify plagiarism, while others help with essay evaluation by offering input on grammar, structure and content (Baron, P. 2024). By lowering administrative burdens, educators may devote more time to teaching and guiding students.

AI is also breaking down obstacles to education by increasing accessibility. Speech recognition and text-to-speech capabilities assist students with impairments, while real-time translation systems facilitate multilingual education. AI-powered solutions, such as Prodigy and Microsoft's Immersive Reader are intended to meet a wide range of learning demands while remaining inclusive (Tomei, L. A., et al 2024) .

However, Akgun & Greenhow (2022) stated that incorporating AI into teaching presents obstacles. Ensuring data privacy and ethical usage of AI is critical, especially when working with kids' information. There are also worries about over-reliance on AI which may diminish critical thinking and problem-solving abilities if not supplemented with traditional education techniques.

As AI advances, its potential in teaching is limitless. Future developments may include emotional intelligence in AI to better comprehend student emotions as well as completely immersive virtual classrooms. AI has the potential to democratize education by making it more customized, efficient and accessible to students all around the world (Ayeni et al., 2024) .

Usage of AI in Higher Education

Artificial intelligence (AI) is revolutionizing higher education by increasing learning outcomes, reducing administrative operations and expanding research capacity. AI is being used by institutions all around the world to provide customized, efficient and creative learning environments for both students and instructors (Sajja et al., 2024) .

Personalized learning is one of the most important uses of artificial intelligence in higher education. AI-powered systems analyze students' learning styles, strengths, and weaknesses to provide personalized course content, evaluations, and feedback. (Smyrnova-Trybulska, et al., 2022) stated that Adaptive learning systems such as Smart Sparrow and Coursera adjust lessons to each student's speed and needs resulting in more effective information acquisition.

AI is also transforming academic support with virtual tutors and chatbots. ChatGPT and Cognii are tools that help students grasp complicated topics, answer questions and write more effectively (Sandhu et al., 2024). These AI-powered assistants are available 24/7 allowing students to seek assistance outside of typical office hours. In addition, AI-based language processing technologies help foreign students learn languages and translate in real time.

Administrative operations in higher education are also being enhanced using AI (George & Wooden, 2023). Enrollment management, grading and student advising are all automated saving both time and resources. AI-powered systems evaluate student data to anticipate performance and retention rates allowing institutions to make early interventions and enhance results. (Alhammadi, 2023) said Chatbots are used to answer regular requests which reduces administrative effort and improves response times.

In research, AI speeds up data processing and discoveries. Researchers utilize AI algorithms to handle massive datasets, mimic trials and create insights in a variety of areas including medicine and engineering. AI-powered systems also help academic publication by automating peer review procedures and increasing research visibility with tailored suggestions (Youvan, 2024).

Despite its benefits, the use of AI in higher education presents obstacles. Concerns around data privacy, algorithmic bias and the ethical usage of AI must be addressed to enable fair and secure applications. Additionally, educators must strike a balance between AI-driven automation and human-centric teaching methodologies in order to encourage critical thinking and interpersonal skills.

Looking ahead, AI has enormous potential to influence the future of higher education (Katsamakas et al., 2024). Advances in emotional intelligence, augmented reality, and predictive analytics have the potential to improve learning settings, making education more accessible, inclusive and successful for a varied global student population.

AI Usage and Students

Artificial intelligence (AI) is quickly changing how students learn, study and engage with educational materials. From individualized learning experiences to automated assistance systems, artificial intelligence is transforming traditional education, making it more accessible, efficient and adaptable to individual requirements.

Personalized learning is one of the most often used AI applications for students. AI-powered programs such as Khan Academy and Duolingo customize lessons to each student's learning rate and style (Khan, 2025). These systems recognize strengths and weaknesses and provide tailored activities and feedback to improve comprehension and memory. This tailored method allows students to proceed at their own speed, addressing knowledge gaps more efficiently.

Students can also benefit from AI systems for academic help. Virtual tutors and chatbots such as ChatGPT offer real-time assistance with homework, essay writing and concept explanations. These resources are available 24 hours a day, seven days a week so students may get help whenever they need it. (Cortés Guerrero, 2024) stated that Grammarly and other language processing tools help students improve their writing quality whilst AI-powered calculators and problem-solving applications like Photomath aid with hard mathematical issues.

AI encourages inclusion among students with impairments by providing tools like text-to-speech, speech-to-text and real-time transcription. These technologies improve learning for those with hearing, vision or mobility disabilities enabling equal access to education.

AI also enables collaborative learning. Platforms employ artificial intelligence (AI) to encourage group conversations, assign tasks based on individual abilities and offer performance metrics (Ouyang, 2023) . These insights assist students in developing the necessary collaboration and problem-solving abilities for their future employment.

However, the employment of AI in education presents obstacles. Students may become increasingly reliant on AI technologies, thus compromising their critical thinking and problem-solving skills. Furthermore, (Boppiniti, 2023) stated that concerns like data privacy and algorithmic bias must be addressed in order to assure ethical and secure usage. AI also has the potential to expand the digital divide, since economic gaps prevent all pupils from having equal access to AI-powered technologies. Bridging this gap is critical to ensuring that AI serves all students equally. Looking ahead, AI has the ability to empower students even more by integrating emotional intelligence and powerful analytics into learning systems. AI, with ethical integration, has the potential to make education more accessible, engaging and supportive for students all across the world.

USAGE OF AI IN MEDIA

Artificial intelligence (AI) is disrupting the media sector by changing the way information is generated, disseminated and consumed. Prasad & Makesh, (2024) mentioned that AI is transforming journalism, entertainment, advertising and audience interaction by processing massive quantities of data and automating operations.

Lim, (2023) found that AI tools are used to create articles, scripts and multimedia content. News agencies such as the Associated Press and Reuters employ artificial intelligence to provide automated reporting on sports, financial news and weather predictions. OpenAI's DALL·E and ChatGPT are examples of generative AI models that create visually attractive visuals, movies and textual material while dramatically lowering production time. AI-powered editing software such as Adobe Sensei improves video and picture editing by automating color correction, noise reduction and scene recognition.

AI also plays an important role in content customization. Streaming services such as Netflix and Spotify employ AI algorithms to evaluate user preferences and offer personalized content, hence enhancing user engagement and pleasure. Similarly, news applications use AI to construct tailored news feeds ensuring that consumers see content that is relevant to their interests.

AI is helping journalists with investigative reporting by analyzing data and recognizing patterns. Natural language processing (NLP) tools aid in the analysis of large datasets in order to detect patterns, identify disinformation and verify facts. AI-powered transcription solutions such as Otter.ai help to simplify interviews and reporting by effectively converting speech to text. Haleem et al. (2022) referred, AI in advertising allows for more tailored ads by monitoring customer behavior and demographics. AI solutions optimize ad placements, generate dynamic ads and forecast market trends, resulting in increased engagement and return on investment.

AI-powered analytics are also improving audience engagement. Media firms use AI to track real-time viewing, clicks and shares, delivering insights on audience behavior. These insights assist to enhance content strategy and make better decisions. However, the use of AI in media presents ethical challenges, such as the proliferation of deepfakes and disinformation (Bontridder & Poullet, 2021; Shoaib et al., 2023). AI-generated material can blur the boundary between fact and fiction, demanding strict criteria to ensure authenticity and believability.

As AI technology advances, its function in the media sector will become increasingly important. By combining automation and ethical issues, AI has the potential to boost creativity, efficiency and audience engagement while tackling the problems of a fast-changing media landscape.

THEORETICAL FRAMEWORK

This study uses phenomenology as its primary theoretical framework to explore the lived experiences of undergraduate students with AI-driven educational systems (Larsen & Adu, 2021). Focusing on data security and algorithmic bias. Phenomenology, based on Husserl et al. (1980) and Heidegger's (1988) theories, is a qualitative research methodology that helps researchers understand how individuals perceive and interpret things in their daily lives. By utilizing phenomenology, this study aims to provide a deep understanding of how students interact with AI-driven educational systems and how these interactions shape their perceptions and behaviors (Kim et al., 2022). By focusing on data security and algorithmic bias, the research seeks to uncover the nuanced ways in which these factors impact the educational experiences of undergraduate students. It is particularly useful for understanding students' perceptions of AI systems' management of personal data and potential biases. It can also inform the development of more equitable and inclusive AI technologies in educational settings (Xia et al., 2022).

Phenomenology reveals students' comprehension and interpretation of data collection, storage, and use processes within AI-driven educational systems regarding data security (Harrell, n.d.; Abduljaber, n.d.). It also reveals students' emotional reactions to data privacy issues, including their faith in these systems and anxiety about potential exploitation of their personal and academic information (Lin & Chen, 2024). Students may experience vulnerability if they perceive their private data is shared without agreement or cautious optimism if they believe AI tools are crucial for academic efficiency while acknowledging the associated risks. Ultimately, the way students perceive and respond to data security in AI-driven educational systems can impact their overall trust in technology and their willingness to engage with digital learning platforms. It is important for educators and policymakers to address these concerns and ensure that students feel empowered and informed about how their data is being used.

As Abduljaber (n.d.) mentioned, phenomenology also examines students' awareness of possible disparities in AI-generated feedback, recommendations, or grading systems about algorithmic bias. This paradigm analyzes how students recognize and analyze biases in AI outputs, especially when they perceive specific groups being favored or marginalized due to systematic algorithmic tendencies(Zajko, 2022). This approach also examines the wider ramifications of these biases on students' belief in AI systems and their academic choices.

The study's objective is to encapsulate the essence of students' encounters with AI systems using phenomenology, providing profound insights into the issues they face and the ethical dilemmas they face. By examining both technical and procedural challenges, the study enhances a thorough and human-centered examination of AI's function in higher education.

METHODOLOGY

Research Design

This research adopts a phenomenological design to investigate the lived experiences of journalism, media studies, and communication students concerning AI systems in their education. Cresswell (2013) emphasised the importance of understanding how people perceive and interpret phenomena in their daily lives when he defined phenomenology. According to Sholokhova et al. (2022), this approach focuses on capturing the substance of participants' experiences, allowing the researcher to reveal profound, subjective insights into the phenomena being studied.

In this study, as following Antony and Ramnath (n.d.), phenomenology is essential as it facilitates a comprehensive analysis of how communication students perceive and engage with AI-driven educational platforms. The study specifically examines students' perceptions of data security, apprehensions over the exploitation of personal and academic data, and their understanding of algorithmic bias. The phenomenological approach facilitates a detailed examination of these matters, offering significant insights into the ethical and experiential aspects of AI utilisation in education.

Demographics and Sampling Methodology

The study population comprises students engaged in communication programs (journalism, media studies, and communication) at both undergraduate (1st to 4th year, Bachelor of Social Sciences) and postgraduate (Masters of Social Sciences, MSS) levels. The target group comprises a varied cohort actively utilising AI-driven technologies in their academic endeavours, including Learning Management Systems (LMS), automated feedback mechanisms, or AI-assisted research tools. Additionally, the study utilised a purposive sampling method to recruit 15 participants, ensuring a diverse array of opinions (J. W. Creswell & Poth, 2017; Mapp, 2008). The sampling was stratified to reflect three types of academic achievement:

High CGPA: Exceptional students with robust academic achievements.
Mid CGPA: Students exhibiting moderate academic achievement.
Low CGPA: Students exhibiting subpar academic achievement.

This stratification guarantees that the study encompasses a varied array of experiences, illustrating differences in academic proficiency and year of study (López, 2021; Williams & Martin, 2021). Students were selected according to their availability and readiness to engage in the study. The study offers a thorough knowledge of AI's impact on pupils by selecting participants from diverse academic levels and performance categories.

Data collection

Data were gathered via semi-structured, comprehensive interviews with the chosen 15 individuals (Adeoye-Olatunde & Olenik, 2021; Hossain et al., 2022). This strategy was selected to facilitate flexibility in examining individual experiences while preserving a consistent emphasis on essential research issues.

The semi-structured interview guide (SSIG) was created to address the fundamental domains, including Student Perceptions of Data Security in AI-Enhanced Educational Systems (Hossain et al., 2022). To apprehensions do they possess regarding possible data exploitation or privacy violations. Are students cognisant of the inherent biases in AI-generated comments or recommendations? To identify their perception of the influence of these biases on their academic experiences. The ways have students utilised AI tools in their academic endeavours and the obstacles or advantages they have experienced (Mahat-Shamir et al., 2019; Knott et al., 2022).

Selection Procedure

Interviews were done face to face with audio recording and interviewees taking short notes, facilitating flexibility and ensuring participant comfort (Knott et al., 2022). Each interview lasted roughly 20 to 30 minutes and was recorded (with consent) for transcription and analysis (Flick, 2021). The interviewer provided participants the opportunity to expand on their answers, prompting them to convey comprehensive, nuanced viewpoints.

Data Analysis

Computer-assisted qualitative data analysis software, NVivo, made it easier to analyse the interview data using a thematic analysis methodology (Hossain & Wahab, 2021). This strategy facilitated the systematic organisation and analysis of data, ensuring that major themes arose naturally from the participants' responses (Lochmiller, n.d.; Majumdar, 2021).

Phases of Thematic Analysis

Transcripts were examined often to achieve a comprehensive comprehension of the topic. Christou (2022) stated, preliminary notes and observations were documented to discern probable patterns. Key phrases, concepts, and insights were carefully categorised (Naeem et al., 2023). The codes indicated the research emphasis, including "trust in AI systems," "concerns regarding data misuse," and "awareness of bias."

Later, codes were categorised into sub-themes, which were subsequently integrated into overarching themes (Espedal et al., 2022). For instance, the sub-theme "Limited understanding of AI data handling" was categorised under the theme "Perception of Data Security."

Themes were evaluated to confirm their proper representation of the data. Themes that were overlapping or redundant were clarified. The themes were concluded to encapsulate the fundamental insights of the study, emphasising students' perspectives, apprehensions, and experiences with AI systems. This iterative procedure guaranteed that the study encompassed the depth and intricacy of students' experiences, yielding a thorough comprehension of the topic being examined (Espedal et al., 2022; Hossain & Wahab, 2021).

Ethical Considerations

The study complied with rigorous ethical standards to safeguard participants' rights and privacy. As guided by Stanier (2022), participants were thoroughly informed of the study's objectives and extent, the voluntary aspect of their involvement, and their entitlement to withdraw at any moment without repercussions. All participant data were anonymised to safeguard their identity. Pseudonyms were employed in transcripts and reports, and data were securely secured to avert unauthorised access (Ayton, 2023).

Participants were apprised of the use of their responses in the research and ensured that their candid feedback was esteemed and honoured.

The interviewer established a secure, non-judgemental atmosphere to promote candid and sincere communication. Participants were informed that they might omit any question or terminate the interview if they experienced discomfort.

RESULTS

The results of the analysed data found that students are well aware of the AI in their academic usage, but they have concerns regarding their data security as well (Van Manen, 2017). Also, in terms of trust issues, they trust their universities or renowned platforms like Google or their products while using AI, but they have limited trustworthiness regarding lesser-known or third-party applications of chatbots. However, in some of the participants, it was seen that although AI makes their life easier, they are concerned if they are risking their data privacy in return for their academic ease. It's a trade-off that some concerned students are still trying to navigate.

Furthermore, it was found that many of the respondents believe that algorithmic bias is happening in the AI chatbots as they have raised their concerns. They think that the bias in recommendations or initial answers may have bias and cultural aspects or visual representation of AI tools (Christou, 2022). The respondents urged for more transparency and accountability in the development and implementation of AI tools and technologies used by the students. Finally, it was seen among the responses that students found some misleading information by the AI chatbots while they were working. They also suggested using AI technologies or chatbots may help their academic work easier, but it should be used wisely for guidance for their academic help rather than unconditionally trusting AI chatbots.

During the analysis, four major themes emerged from the developed codes using data analysis computer-based software NVivo. To provide a thorough understanding of the data, the researchers derived various and dynamic themes from the codes as guided by Christou (2022). The four major themes were i) Perception of Data Security, ii) Concerns about Data Security, iii) Concerns about Algorithmic Bias, and iv) Behavioral Adaptations and Emotional Responses. The major themes are discussed in the following details. The emerged sub-themes are marked as bold and italic during the section.

PERCEPTION OF DATA SECURITY

The communication students of tertiary level were conscious about their data security. According to them, they have very little knowledge about where their data was stored and if the data is being shared with any other third party. As it has become a norm of the young people that they just hit the button 'I Agree" before using any website or application, it is a common norm to agree without reading the terms and conditions of the application agreement. As a final-year student, she raised her concern and explained that she has a ***limited awareness of data collection processes***. *"I know my data is being collected, but I'm not sure what kind of data or how it's stored."* – Participant 1. Additionally, Participant 5, a second year student said, *"I probably accepted the terms, but I didn't read what I was agreeing to.*

This lack of awareness and understanding of data collection processes is a growing concern among young people, especially as technology continues to advance and play a larger role in our daily lives. Participant 1's statement highlights the need for more education and transparency around data privacy and security while using artificial intelligence. It is important for individuals to be informed about how their data is being used and shared in order to protect their privacy and make informed decisions about the services they use.

Another student from the postgraduate section of the journalism and communication department mentioned he uses artificial intelligence often for his academic purposes and also official usage. While explaining the answers of the interviewer, the participant said while they use AI for their academic purposes, their educators sometimes encourage using AI technology or accept AI tools if they are used. But as the universities are accepting and encouraging AI tools and technologies, he thinks the authorities are not well aware of the situations regarding risks related to data safety, and his concern regarding ***cautious trust in institutions*** has become a part of his thoughts. As he thinks, *"I think universities mean well, but I'm not sure if they fully understand the risks involved."*

Another participant (participant 8) from the final year highlights the importance of educating institutions about the potential risks associated with AI technology, especially in regard to data safety. It is a serious issue for universities to practice in-depth understanding and addressing these risks to ensure the ***responsible use of AI tools in academic settings***. Because academic institutions encourage students to use chatbots and AI tools to become more effective and efficient, there may be trade-offs between efficiency and privacy risks. *"AI makes my work easier, but I always wonder if I'm paying for it with my data,"* participant eight mentioned. This sentiment shows the growing concern among the university students about the potential misuse of their personal data in exchange for convenience is rising. As universities continue to integrate AI technology into their academic programs, it is crucial for them to prioritize data privacy and security. By implementing strict guidelines and protocols for the ethical use of AI tools, universities can protect their students' sensitive information and promote responsible innovation in the education sector. It is essential for academic institutions to stay informed about the evolving risks associated with AI technology and take proactive measures to mitigate them.

CONCERNS ABOUT DATA MISUSE

According to a major number of participants, the misuse of the provided data by the AI tool and application service provider organisations may cause some serious issues in the future. For example, if a student shares that his/her healthcare AI tool improperly handles patient data, it could lead to breaches of privacy and compromised medical information. Additionally, misuse of financial data by AI applications could result in identity theft and financial fraud for users. Additionally, if they share their project data of their journalism information where the project requires confidentiality or a communication strategy, they are building with the help of AI, they may take the data and sell the strategy to professional organisations. Later, the professional organisations could use this information to manipulate public opinion or gain a competitive advantage, potentially leading to unethical practices in journalism.

This highlights the importance of implementing strict ethical guidelines and regulations when developing AI tools to protect sensitive information and prevent misuse. It is crucial for developers and organisations to prioritise ethical considerations and transparency in the use of AI technology to maintain trust and integrity in journalism. By establishing clear guidelines and regulations, potential risks of data misuse can be minimised, ensuring responsible use of AI tools in journalism practices. As per participant 2 (second year), the ***general distrust of data handling*** is a serious concern among the university students. As she mentioned, *"I worry that my data might be sold to other companies without me knowing."*

Another participant from the second year is in ***fear of data leaks and breaches*** of the information she provides to the AI tools. As per her concern, the participant 6 trusts the AI tool providers to some extent, but the safety of those servers is a concern to the participant. According to her, *"If someone hacks into the system, my personal and academic information could be at* risk.". This fear of data security and privacy is not irrelevant. There have been numerous cases of data breaches and leaks in recent years. Building trust with students and users from the service provider's side by being transparent about data handling practices and implementing strong security measures can help alleviate these concerns and ensure the safety of their information.

The providers of AI applications and tools alarmed another student from year 3, participant 6. As per his reservations, he is not comfortable with his data being used without his consent. The ***unauthorised use of data*** by the service providers makes him uncomfortable if the data he is providing is getting into the server in the name of system development by the authorities. As per his saying, *"I'm not comfortable with my data being used for things I didn't agree* to.".It is crucial for service providers to clearly communicate how data will be used and obtain permission from users before accessing their information. By prioritising user privacy and security, AI developers can build trust with their users and mitigate fears surrounding data misuse. Additionally, implementing strict data protection protocols and regularly updating security measures can help reassure individuals like participant 6 that their information is being handled responsibly.

Participant 11, a third-year Journalism and Communication student, shared her fear in terms of her provided data's ***long-term implications of data storage.*** As per her unknowingness of the shared data to the AI applications and tools, she is aware of the situation where, after her usage, the AI platforms may save her data to their storage, and in the long term, one day she may find the data somewhere else. *"Who ensures my data is deleted when I'm no longer using these platforms?"*

In addition, participant 13, a final-year student, raised a serious issue regarding the lawsuit and affordability from a developing nation. He worries that if the developers or providers of AI platforms discover a misuse of his data, it will be too late. Also, he cannot go against them legally. As he says, "Some *people can't afford legal help if their data is misused, so they're more vulnerable."* Participant 13's fear is the importance of data privacy regulations. Also, the need for accountability from AI platform developers. Additionally, government and stakeholder organisations must be helpful and aware of the situation.

AWARENESS OF ALGORITHMIC BIAS

Bias is not always a word that spreads negativity. When it goes along with us, bias could be a positive thing. While discussing algorithmic bias, some students were blessed, and the majority were uncertain about the algorithmic bias. Here, it is important to notice that the fresher or sophomore students are more agreeable to the AI solutions and are feeling amazed with the results, whereas seniors or postgrads are confused and negative about the algorithmic bias of chatbots and AI-generated content. From politics to education, leadership to followers, and gender diversity to colour, the biases of AI technologies are not unknown. Critical reviewers have drawn this issue public several times. The developers are working on the problem, but it needs to be solved gradually.

Some possible solutions are there to implement more training data to help reduce bias in AI algorithms. By integrating a wider range of perspectives and experiences, developers can create more inclusive and fair AI systems that accurately represent diverse populations. For example, by including input from individuals from different cultural backgrounds and demographic groups, AI algorithms can be trained to make more unbiased decisions in areas such as hiring practices or content recommendations.AI systems can become more inclusive and accurate in their decision-making processes. Additionally, transparency in the development and deployment of AI technologies is crucial in order to address bias and ensure accountability. It is essential for developers to continually assess and address bias in AI systems to ensure fair and ethical outcomes for all users.

According to participant 10, a first-year undergraduate student, *"When I use AI tools, they often struggle with examples from my culture or language."*. The statement reflects the ***cultural and linguistic bias*** of the feedback by the artificial intelligence tools and applications. Other students have also noticed the bias in visual representation, which is not just limited to cultural and textual form. As we have mentioned previously, the senior students are more uncomfortable regarding the AI algorithmic bias, and a postgraduate student (participant 15) of the Department of Journalism, Media, and Communication of Daffodil International University stated, *"AI tools often show white males in leadership roles and minorities in service positions."*. Additionally, there have been trust issues by the students on AI's algorithmic biases. ***Algorithmic bias on trust*** was raised by my participant 14, a postgraduate student, mentioning, *"If AI can't be fair in small tasks, how can I trust it for grading or recommendations?"*

According to participant 12, a first-year undergraduate student thinks AI provides a generic answer even in complex[REMOVED NUMPAGES FIELD] issues. As per his thinking, the ***oversimplification of complex concepts*** is providing general solutions for everyone in academic issues. The students seemed alert about the potential consequences of AI bias on their academic performance and opportunities for growth. There is a clear disparity between the expectations of students and the actual capabilities of AI in providing personalised and unbiased solutions. *"The explanations feel generic and don't really capture the complexity of the topic."*

Participant four, a final-year student, found some socio political disparities while using artificial intelligence for his academic purpose. He found ***bias in politically sensitive topics*** or sociopolitical issues is not always contextual. According to his statement, *"AI seemed to favour one perspective over another on topics like climate change."*. The outcomes of AI technology are biased in the mostly western world. Cases in the global south are not solving the problems as needed. Additionally, there are some ***limitations in understanding individual cases*** with artificial intelligence. This raises concerns about the potential impact of AI on decision-making processes in diverse regions and the need for further research to address these disparities. Participant four's findings highlight the importance of ensuring that AI technologies are developed and utilised in a way that is fair and unbiased across different socio political contexts. *"The AI tool doesn't understand the specific instructions of my professor."* – participant 8, a final-year student, revealed.

BEHAVIOURAL ADAPTATIONS AND EMOTIONAL RESPONSES

The gradual increasing usage of AI tools and applications in higher education has profoundly influenced how students approach. Their educational tasks and interactions with technology are regular actions they needed in the current academic sphere. While these tools promise efficiency and personalised support, they also challenge students to adapt their behaviour and manage their emotional responses to AI-generated outputs.

Understanding these adaptations and emotional reactions is critical for evaluating the broader impact of AI on student learning experiences. As they have trust issues, sometimes they face incorrect information while working on data, which leads them to frustration. Participant one, a final-year undergraduate student, mentioned her trust issues with AI-powered information, so she suggested ***trusting but verifying the information*** provided by the tools and applications.

Students frequently cross-checked AI outputs with other sources or their own knowledge to ensure accuracy. She mentioned, *"I don't take AI results at face value—I always double-check."*

Additionally, issues with inaccurate information may lead to misinformation, which is another challenge while working with AI chatbots. Despite the fact that AI platforms warn that data and information may not be current or that there is a chance that it may be inaccurate, students frequently assume that the information they receive from these platforms is accurate. It may not be the responsibility of AI tools and applications, but it can lead to the misinformation that is affecting the academic environment on many occasions. In these situations, the students get confused, and ***frustration with inaccuracies*** increases among the students. It also creates a gap between the learners and trainers when they check the learners examination scripts with misinformation. Incorrect or irrelevant AI responses led to frustration, and students find a lack of confidence in the tools. A second-year undergraduate student (participant 6) raised this issue while collecting data from the participant. *"I tried using AI for my assignment, but the suggestions were way off."*

While AI tools were seen as helpful for academic purposes too, the students avoided over-reliance. They are using them mainly for brainstorming or efficiency. Our participant 11, a third-year undergraduate student, expressed, *"AI gives me ideas, but I prefer to refine them myself."*. This indicates that in the era of artificial intelligence, the students are mainly using AI platforms for brainstorming rather than total dependency. They are showing their encouragement of using AI platforms for their academic purposes, but the ***cautious usage tendency*** is in their mind as well.

DISCUSSION

This chapter of the study in-depth analyses the results on journalism, media, and communication students' perceptions of AI systems in higher education. Situating the findings within established literature and overarching pedagogical frameworks. This part critically examines the results, emphasising the complexity of incorporating AI into academic settings, while acknowledging its revolutionary potential and inherent challenges.

The findings indicate an ignorance among journalism and communication tertiary students about the methods on how the AI platforms gather, retain, and analyse their personal and academic data. This corresponds with research indicating that end-users, especially students, frequently disregard the terms and conditions of digital platforms, resulting in cursory involvement with significant privacy concerns (Nguyen, 2023). Students exhibited conditional faith in institutions and established platforms, yet displayed cynicism towards third-party resources included into educational systems.

These findings highlight a substantial deficiency in digital literacy, especially regarding data privacy and security inside school settings. Brand awareness seems to hold greater significance for students' trust than a comprehensive comprehension of data protection protocols. This misguided trust prompts apprehensions over the ethical obligations of institutions and developers in safeguarding data security and informing end-users. The findings indicate that although institutions emphasise technological adoption, they frequently neglect the essential requirement for transparency in data management processes (Toufaily et al., 2021).

This study reveals the disparity of power between AI platforms, chatbots, tools and unawareness of the students about them (Stöhr et al., 2024). As data is controlled by AI developers, leaving little room for student. Educational institutions should prioritise the implementation of transparent data policies that explicitly convey data management practices to students. Integrating data literacy into courses to empower students to critically assess AI systems. Implementing supervising systems, including independent audits, to guarantee adherence to ethical data standards.

Participants showed their concerns over the misuse, leakage, and unauthorised personal data dissemination. These concerns by the students illustrate widespread social anxieties over the ethical issues in education. Students specifically emphasised the possibility for enduring repercussions, including identity theft and the unauthorised commercialisation of their data. Marginalised students and other vulnerable groups were recognised as being disproportionately impacted by these hazards, hence intensifying existing disparities.

The apprehension around data exploitation highlights the ethical challenges associated with the marketing of education via AI. Related to the findings of Curran (2023) these findings correspond with critiques of surveillance capitalism, which contend that data-driven platforms exploit users' personal information for profit. This commercialisation prompts enquiries over the institutions' responsibilities as stewards of student data in higher education. Systemic disparities reflected and exacerbated by AI technologies are also apparent in their disproportionate effects on marginalised populations.

These apprehensions align with Foucault's notion of biopolitics, wherein individuals are monitored and regulated via technological mechanisms (Lorenzini, 2020). The findings indicate that AI systems may, instead of equalising opportunities, perpetuate hierarchical arrangements that favour specific groups over others. Addressing these systemic challenges necessitates a reevaluation of the design and use of AI systems within educational settings. To address these issues, schools must implement equity-centered AI policies that emphasise the needs of at-risk students and restrict the commercialisation of educational data by establishing stringent separations between academic and corporate interests. Furthermore, improving transparency by offering students explicit opt-in options for data utilisation.

The results indicate differing degrees of awareness of algorithmic bias among students. Some participants acknowledged biases in feedback, grading, and course recommendations, while others were less aware of these concerns. Biases were especially observed in culturally sensitive or politically heated circumstances, with students recognising a Western-centric bias in AI-generated outputs. These findings correspond with established criticisms of AI systems trained on homogeneous datasets that do not represent varied viewpoints (West, 2023).

Algorithmic bias is a substantial obstacle to the fair implementation of AI in education (Baker & Hawn, 2021). The results indicate that AI systems frequently reinforce existing societal disparities instead of alleviating them. The Western-centric orientation of numerous AI systems exemplifies a colonial heritage in knowledge generation, wherein dominant cultures and languages are favoured over others. This trend not only marginalises non-Western pupils but also diminishes the legitimacy and equity of AI technologies.

The results correspond with Critical Race Theory, emphasising the integration of systemic prejudices across socio cultural frameworks, including technology. The reproduction of biases in AI systems highlights the necessity for a decolonial methodology in AI development that intentionally aims to confront and remove these frameworks. Broaden training datasets to encompass a variety of cultural and linguistic contexts, perform regular fairness audits to detect and correct biases in AI systems, and involve students from diverse backgrounds in the development and testing phases of AI tools to promote inclusivity.

Students exhibited pragmatic methodologies towards AI, defined by a "trust but verify" principle, exasperation with mistakes, and a judicious dependence on AI tools. Students acknowledged the efficacy of AI in facilitating ideation and streamlining activities, although they expressed reservations over its limitations, especially in intricate or nuanced academic situations.

These behavioral changes among the students shows a lack of understanding of AI technologies. The "trust but verify" understanding displays that students are not just consumers but active participants. They critically analyses the AI outcomes. Sometimes they may be politically, socio-politically or situationally incorrect. Nonetheless, the frustration shown by students defies the constraints of existing AI systems. Especially their inadequacy in managing context-specific outcome proficiently. This indicates that although AI can enhance human judgement, it cannot supplant it.

The results correspond with the principle of technological determinism, which asserts that technology influences, but does not control, human behaviour. Students' prudent interaction with AI tools reflects a reluctance to become overly dependent, indicating a measured approach that prioritises critical thinking and human autonomy (Hallström, 2020).

CONCLUSION

This study offers significant findings to the academic context while its limitations encompass a limited sample size. Depending on self-reported data, and a concentration on journalism, media and communication students, subsequent in-dept studies may rectify these constraints. By extending the sample to encompass students from other academic disciplines. Additionally, a quantitative survey study from the findings of this study may provide some more leading data.

Executing longitudinal investigations to investigate the enduring effects of AI in education. Examining the convergence of artificial intelligence and broader societal elements, including socioeconomic position and cultural diversity.

Finally, this study showcases the dynamic characteristics of AI in higher education, presenting both advantages and obstacles. This research undergoes the imperative for ethical and inclusive AI practices. By critically analysing students' point of views of data security, apprehensions regarding data exploitation, awareness of algorithmic bias, and behavioural responses. Going forward, cooperation among students, educators, and developers will be crucial to guarantee that AI systems function as instruments of empowerment rather than catalysts of unfairness.

REFERENCES

Abduljaber, M. F. (n.d.). *Perceived influence of artificial intelligence on Educational Leadership's Decision-Making, teaching, and learning Outcomes: A Transcendental phenomenological Study*. Scholars Crossing. Retrieved January 19, 2025, from https://digitalcommons.liberty.edu/doctoral/5714/

Abulibdeh, A., Zaidan, E., & Abulibdeh, R. (2024). Navigating the confluence of artificial intelligence and education for sustainable development in the era of industry 4.0: Challenges, opportunities, and ethical dimensions. *Journal of Cleaner Production*, *437*, 140527. DOI: 10.1016/j.jclepro.2023.140527

Adedoyin, O. B., & Soykan, E. (2020). Covid-19 pandemic and online learning: The challenges and opportunities. *Interactive Learning Environments*, *31*(2), 863–875. DOI: 10.1080/10494820.2020.1813180

Adeoye-Olatunde, O. A., & Olenik, N. L. (2021). Research and scholarly methods: Semi-structured interviews. *JACCP JOURNAL OF THE AMERICAN COLLEGE OF CLINICAL PHARMACY*, *4*(10), 1358–1367. DOI: 10.1002/jac5.1441

Akgun, S., & Greenhow, C. (2021). Artificial intelligence in education: Addressing ethical challenges in K-12 settings. *AI and Ethics*, *2*(3), 431–440. DOI: 10.1007/s43681-021-00096-7 PMID: 34790956

Alhammadi, M. (2023). Optimising Customer Service Delivery and Response Time through AI-Enhanced Chatbots in Facilities Management-A Mixed-Methods Research. *American Journal of Smart Technology and Solutions*, *2*(2), 43–54.

Alqodsi, E. M., Jadalhaq, I. M., Maknouzi, M. E. H. E., & Abdulhay, I. E. A. (2024). Navigating the legal landscape. In *Advances in educational technologies and instructional design book series* (pp. 212–230). https://doi.org/DOI: 10.4018/979-8-3693-0880-6.ch015

Antony, S., & Ramnath, R. (n.d.). *A phenomenological exploration of students' perceptions of AI chatbots in higher education.* Retrieved January 20, 2025, from https://eric.ed.gov/?id=EJ1403709

Ashok, M., Madan, R., Joha, A., & Sivarajah, U. (2021). Ethical framework for Artificial Intelligence and Digital technologies. *International Journal of Information Management*, *62*, 102433. DOI: 10.1016/j.ijinfomgt.2021.102433

Ayeni, O. O., Al Hamad, N. M., Chisom, O. N., Osawaru, B., & Adewusi, O. E. (2024). AI in education: A review of personalized learning and educational technology. *GSC Advanced Research and Reviews*, *18*(2), 261–271.

Ayton, D. (2023, March 21). *Chapter 6: Phenomenology*. Pressbooks. https://oercollective.caul.edu.au/qualitative-research/chapter/__unknown__-6/

Baker, R. S., & Hawn, A. (2021). Algorithmic bias in education. *International Journal of Artificial Intelligence in Education, 32*(4), 1052–1092. DOI: 10.1007/s40593-021-00285-9

Baron, P. (2024). Are AI detection and plagiarism similarity scores worthwhile in the age of ChatGPT and other Generative AI? *Scholarship of Teaching and Learning in the South, 8*(2), 151–179.

Bontridder, N., & Poullet, Y. (2021). The role of artificial intelligence in disinformation. *Data & Policy, 3*. Advance online publication. DOI: 10.1017/dap.2021.20

Boppiniti, S. T. (2023). Data Ethics in AI: Addressing Challenges in Machine Learning and Data Governance for Responsible Data Science. International Scientific Journal for Research, 5(5).

Casheekar, A., Lahiri, A., Rath, K., Prabhakar, K. S., & Srinivasan, K. (2024). A contemporary review on chatbots, AI-powered virtual conversational agents, ChatGPT: Applications, open challenges and future research directions. *Computer Science Review, 52*, 100632.

Center for News. Technology & Innovation. (2024, October 11). *Artificial Intelligence in Journalism - Center for News, Technology & Innovation*. https://innovating.news/article/ai-in-journalism

Chan, C. K. Y. (2023a). A comprehensive AI policy education framework for university teaching and learning. *International Journal of Educational Technology in Higher Education, 20*(1). Advance online publication. DOI: 10.1186/s41239-023-00408-3

Chan, C. K. Y. (2023b). A comprehensive AI policy education framework for university tcaching and lcarning. *Intcrnational Journal of Educational Technology in Higher Education, 20*(1). Advance online publication. DOI: 10.1186/s41239-023-00408-3

Chesterman, S. (2024). Good models borrow, great models steal: Intellectual property rights and generative AI. *Policy and Society*, puae006.

Chiu, T. K., Xia, Q., Zhou, X., Chai, C. S., & Cheng, M. (2022). Systematic literature review on opportunities, challenges, and future research recommendations of artificial intelligence in education. *Computers and Education Artificial Intelligence, 4*, 100118. DOI: 10.1016/j.caeai.2022.100118

Christou, P. A. (2022). How to use thematic analysis in qualitative research. *Journal of Qualitative Research in Tourism, 3*(2), 79–95. DOI: 10.4337/jqrt.2023.0006

Corrêa, N. K., Santos, J. W., Galvão, C., Pasetti, M., Schiavon, D., Naqvi, F., Hossain, R., & De Oliveira, N. (2024). Crossing the principle–practice gap in AI ethics with ethical problem-solving. *AI and Ethics*. Advance online publication. DOI: 10.1007/s43681-024-00469-8

Cortés Guerrero, S. (2024). AI for educational board games.

Creswell, J. W., & Poth, C. N. (2017). *Qualitative inquiry and research design: Choosing Among Five Approaches*. Sage Publications, Incorporated.

Cruz, M., Sousa, M. E., Costa, J., & Mascarenhas, D. (2024). AI-POWERED RECONFIGURATION OF TEACHER TRAINING: A CASE STUDY IN HIGHER EDUCATION. In ICERI2024 Proceedings (pp. 8212-8222). IATED.

Curran, D. (2023). Surveillance capitalism and systemic digital risk: The imperative to collect and connect and the risks of interconnectedness. *Big Data & Society*, *10*(1). Advance online publication. DOI: 10.1177/20539517231177621

Dargan, S., Kumar, M., Ayyagari, M. R., & Kumar, G. (2020). A survey of deep learning and its applications: A new paradigm to machine learning. *Archives of Computational Methods in Engineering*, *27*, 1071–1092.

De Simone, M. E., Tiberti, F., Mosuro, W., Manolio, F., Barron, M., & Dikoru, E. (2025, January 8). From chalkboards to chatbots: Transforming learning in Nigeria, one prompt at a time. *World Bank Blogs*. https://blogs.worldbank.org/en/education/From-chalkboards-to-chatbots-Transforming-learning-in-Nigeria

De Sio, F. S., & Mecacci, G. (2021). Four Responsibility Gaps with Artificial Intelligence: Why they Matter and How to Address them. *Philosophy & Technology*, *34*(4), 1057–1084. DOI: 10.1007/s13347-021-00450-x

Early, C. (2024). Sustainability profession scrambles to fill "extreme gap" in digital skills to harness power of AI. *Reuters*. Retrieved January 16, 2025, from https://www.reuters.com/sustainability/society-equity/sustainability-profession-scrambles-fill-extreme-gap-digital-skills-harness-2024-11-28/

Eden, N. C. A., Chisom, N. O. N., & Adeniyi, N. I. S. (2024). Integrating AI in education: Opportunities, challenges, and ethical considerations. *Magna Scientia Advanced Research and Reviews, 10*(2), 006–013. https://doi.org/DOI: 10.30574/msarr.2024.10.2.0039

Espedal, G., Jelstad Løvaas, B., Sirris, S., & Wæraas, A. (2022). *Researching Values: Methodological approaches for understanding values work in organisations and leadership* (Gry Espedal, Beate Jelstad Løvaas, Stephen Sirris, & Arild Wæraas, Eds.). https://library.oapen.org/bitstream/handle/20.500.12657/53343/978-3-030-90769-3.pdf#page=198

Fedele, A., Punzi, C., & Tramacere, S. (2024). The ALTAI checklist as a tool to assess ethical and legal implications for a trustworthy AI development in education. *Computer Law & Security Review*, *53*, 105986. DOI: 10.1016/j.clsr.2024.105986

Flick, U. (2021). Doing interview research: The Essential How To Guide. *Sage (Atlanta, Ga.).*

Generative AI and the future of education. (2023). In *UNESCO eBooks*. https://doi.org/DOI: 10.54675/hoxg8740

George, B., & Wooden, O. (2023). Managing the strategic transformation of higher education through artificial intelligence. *Administrative Sciences*, *13*(9), 196.

Giordani, J. (2024). Mitigating chatbots AI data privacy Violations in the banking sector: A Qualitative Grounded Theory study. *Deleted Journal*, *2*(4), 14–65. DOI: 10.59324/ejaset.2024.2(4).02

Gupta, K. D. (2023). A review of generative AI from historical perspectives. *Authorea Preprints*.

Haleem, A., Javaid, M., Qadri, M. A., Singh, R. P., & Suman, R. (2022). Artificial intelligence (AI) applications for marketing: A literature-based study. *International Journal of Intelligent Networks*, *3*, 119–132. DOI: 10.1016/j.ijin.2022.08.005

Hallström, J. (2020). Embodying the past, designing the future: Technological determinism reconsidered in technology education. *International Journal of Technology and Design Education*, *32*(1), 17–31. DOI: 10.1007/s10798-020-09600-2

Harrell, M. V. (n.d.). *Data Literacy in the Age of Artificial Intelligence: A Hermeneutic Phenomenological study*. Scholars Crossing. https://digitalcommons.liberty.edu/doctoral/6433/

Heidegger, M. (1988). *The Basic Problems of Phenomenology* (revised Edition). Indiana University Press.

Holmes, W., Porayska-Pomsta, K., Holstein, K., Sutherland, E., Baker, T., Shum, S. B., Santos, O. C., Rodrigo, M. T., Cukurova, M., Bittencourt, I. I., & Koedinger, K. R. (2021). Ethics of AI in Education: Towards a Community-Wide framework. *International Journal of Artificial Intelligence in Education*, *32*(3), 504–526. DOI: 10.1007/s40593-021-00239-1

Hooda, M., Rana, C., Dahiya, O., Rizwan, A., & Hossain, M. S. (2022). Artificial intelligence for assessment and feedback to enhance student success in higher education. *Mathematical Problems in Engineering*, *2022*, 1–19. DOI: 10.1155/2022/5215722

Hossain, A., Wahab, J. A., Islam, M. R., Khan, M. S. R., & Mahmud, A. (2022). Cyberbullying perception and experience among the university students in Bangladesh. In *Advances in human and social aspects of technology book series* (pp. 248–269). https://doi.org/DOI: 10.4018/978-1-7998-9187-1.ch012

Husserl, E., Klein, T. E., & Pohl, W. E. (1980). Phenomenology and the foundations of the sciences. In *M. Nijhoff, Distributors for the U.S. and Canada, Kluwer Boston eBooks*. https://ci.nii.ac.jp/ncid/BA07953382

Izadi, S., & Forouzanfar, M. (2024). Error Correction and Adaptation in Conversational AI: A Review of Techniques and Applications in Chatbots. *AI*, *5*(2), 803–841.

Javaid, M., Haleem, A., Singh, R. P., Khan, S., & Khan, I. H. (2023). Unlocking the opportunities through ChatGPT Tool towards ameliorating the education system. *BenchCouncil Transactions on Benchmarks Standards and Evaluations*, *3*(2), 100115. DOI: 10.1016/j.tbench.2023.100115

Katsamakas, E., Pavlov, O. V., & Saklad, R. (2024). Artificial intelligence and the transformation of higher education institutions: A systems approach. *Sustainability*, *16*(14), 6118.

Khan, S. M. (2025). AI-Powered Tools for Teaching English as a Second Language (ESL) in TNE. In Bridging Global Divides for Transnational Higher Education in the AI Era (pp. 121-140). IGI Global Scientific Publishing.

Kim, J., Lee, H., & Cho, Y. H. (2022). Learning design to support student-AI collaboration: Perspectives of leading teachers for AI in education. *Education and Information Technologies*, *27*(5), 6069–6104. DOI: 10.1007/s10639-021-10831-6

Kitsara, I. (2022). Artificial intelligence and the digital divide: From an innovation perspective. In *Platforms and artificial intelligence: The next generation of competences* (pp. 245–265). Springer International Publishing.

Knott, E., Rao, A. H., Summers, K., & Teeger, C. (2022). Interviews in the social sciences. *Nature Reviews. Methods Primers*, *2*(1). Advance online publication. DOI: 10.1038/s43586-022-00150-6

Kordzadeh, N., & Ghasemaghaei, M. (2021). Algorithmic bias: Review, synthesis, and future research directions. *European Journal of Information Systems*, *31*(3), 388–409. DOI: 10.1080/0960085x.2021.1927212

Kumar, A., Singh, D., & Vohra, R. (2023). Improving learning abilities using AI-Based education systems. In *Advances in educational technologies and instructional design book series* (pp. 137–155). https://doi.org/DOI: 10.4018/979-8-3693-0378-8.ch006

Larsen, H. G., & Adu, P. (2021). The theoretical framework in phenomenological research. In *Routledge eBooks*. https://doi.org/DOI: 10.4324/9781003084259

Le, T. T., Sharma, P., Bora, B. J., Tran, V. D., Truong, T. H., Le, H. C., & Nguyen, P. Q. P. (2023). Fueling the future: A comprehensive review of hydrogen energy systems and their challenges. *International Journal of Hydrogen Energy*, *54*, 791–816. DOI: 10.1016/j.ijhydene.2023.08.044

Lim, J. (2023). How news organizations and journalists understand artificial intelligence: application of news language database to AI-related news stories. In *Research Handbook on Artificial Intelligence and Communication* (pp. 108–124). Edward Elgar Publishing.

Lin, H., & Chen, Q. (2024). Artificial intelligence (AI) -integrated educational applications and college students' creativity and academic emotions: Students and teachers' perceptions and attitudes. *BMC Psychology*, *12*(1). Advance online publication. DOI: 10.1186/s40359-024-01979-0 PMID: 39285268

Lin, Z. (2023). Why and how to embrace AI such as ChatGPT in your academic life. *Royal Society Open Science*, *10*(8). Advance online publication. DOI: 10.1098/rsos.230658 PMID: 37621662

Lochmiller, C. R. (n.d.). *The Qualitative report The Qualitative Report*. https://www.semanticscholar.org/paper/The-Qualitative-Report-The-Qualitative-Report-Lochmiller/271f61ca8c699d5f41436fd70b8da1bd321a0ad9?p2df

López, D. G. (2021). A phenomenological approach to the study of social distance. *Human Studies*, *44*(2), 171–200. DOI: 10.1007/s10746-021-09582-7 PMID: 33967362

Lorenzini, D. (2020). Biopolitics in the time of coronavirus. *Critical Inquiry*, *47*(S2), S40–S45. DOI: 10.1086/711432

Lytvynova, S. H., Rashevska, N. V., & Proskura, S. L. (2024). The use of artificial intelligence in teaching students programming languages. In Proceedings of the IX International Workshop on Professional Retraining and Life-Long Learning using ICT: Person-oriented Approach (3L-Person 2024) co-located with 19th International Conference on ICT in Education, Research, and Industrial Applications (No. 3781, pp. 10-29). CEUR Workshop Proceedings

Mageira, K., Pittou, D., Papasalouros, A., Kotis, K., Zangogianni, P., & Daradoumis, A. (2022). Educational AI chatbots for content and language integrated learning. *Applied Sciences (Basel, Switzerland)*, *12*(7), 3239. DOI: 10.3390/app12073239

Maghsudi, S., Lan, A., Xu, J., & Van Der Schaar, M. (2021). Personalized education in the Artificial intelligence era: What to expect next. *IEEE Signal Processing Magazine*, *38*(3), 37–50. DOI: 10.1109/msp.2021.3055032

Mahat-Shamir, M., Neimeyer, R. A., & Pitcho-Prelorentzos, S. (2019). Designing in-depth semi-structured interviews for revealing meaning reconstruction after loss. *Death Studies*, *45*(2), 83–90. DOI: 10.1080/07481187.2019.1617388 PMID: 31116652

Majumdar, A. (2021). Thematic analysis in qualitative research. In *IGI Global eBooks* (pp. 604–622). https://doi.org/DOI: 10.4018/978-1-6684-3881-7.ch031

Makaryan, M. (2024, August 6). Policymakers should capitalize on positive public opinion to promote beneficial AI use. *Center for Data Innovation*. https://datainnovation.org/2024/08/policymakers-should-capitalize-on-positive-public-opinion-to-promote-beneficial-ai-use/

Mapp, T. (2008). Understanding phenomenology: The lived experience. *British Journal of Midwifery*, *16*(5), 308–311. DOI: 10.12968/bjom.2008.16.5.29192

Naeem, M., Ozuem, W., Howell, K., & Ranfagni, S. (2023). A Step-by-Step process of thematic analysis to develop a conceptual model in qualitative research. *International Journal of Qualitative Methods*, *22*. Advance online publication. DOI: 10.1177/16094069231205789

Nathani, Y. (2025, January 16). AI in education: The quiet revolution India needs. *Times of India Voices*. https://timesofindia.indiatimes.com/blogs/voices/ai-in-education-the-quiet-revolution-india-needs/

Nazer, L. H., Zatarah, R., Waldrip, S., Ke, J. X. C., Moukheiber, M., Khanna, A. K., Hicklen, R. S., Moukheiber, L., Moukheiber, D., Ma, H., & Mathur, P. (2023). Bias in artificial intelligence algorithms and recommendations for mitigation. *PLOS Digital Health*, *2*(6), e0000278. DOI: 10.1371/journal.pdig.0000278 PMID: 37347721

Nguyen, G. T. B. S. (2024). *An exploration of Faculty and Students' Self-Reported Awareness and use of Blackboard Ally for online course accessibility* (By R. M. Aye Ed. D., A. Catterson Ph. D., & C. McDuffie Ph. D.). https://www.bakeru.edu/images/pdf/SOE/EdD_Theses/Nguyen_Gaileen.pdf

Nguyen, M. (2024). Artificial Intelligence Chatbots in Telecommunications: Transforming Customer Service in the Digital Age.

Okon, S. U., Olateju, O., Ogungbemi, O. S., Joseph, S. A., Olisa, A. O., & Olaniyi, O. O. (2024). Incorporating Privacy by Design Principles in the Modification of AI Systems in Preventing Breaches across Multiple Environments, Including Public Cloud, Private Cloud, and On-prem. SSRN *Electronic Journal*. https://doi.org/DOI: 10.2139/ssrn.4945564

Oliver, N. (2022). Artificial intelligence for social good-the way forward. Science, Research and Innovation Performance of the EU 2022 Report, 604-707.

Ouyang, F., Wu, M., Zheng, L., Zhang, L., & Jiao, P. (2023). Integration of artificial intelligence performance prediction and learning analytics to improve student learning in online engineering course. *International Journal of Educational Technology in Higher Education*, *20*(1), 4. PMID: 36683653

Pasquinelli, M. (2023). *The eye of the master: A social history of artificial intelligence*. Verso Books.

Personalized education in the Artificial intelligence era: What to expect next. (2021, May 1). IEEE Journals & Magazine | IEEE Xplore. https://ieeexplore.ieee.org/abstract/document/9418572

Prasad, R., & Makesh, D. (2024). *Impact of AI on Media & Entertainment Industry. Media & Journalism Transformations-Emerging Trends and Paradigm Shifts*. Emerald Publications.

Rafa, A. T. (2024, February 18). Paving way for a more inclusive Bangladesh. *The Daily Star*. https://www.thedailystar.net/anniversary-supplement-2024/innovate-educate-elevate/news/paving-the-way-more-inclusive-bangladesh-3545126

Rahiman, H. U., & Kodikal, R. (2023). Revolutionizing education: Artificial intelligence empowered learning in higher education. *Cogent Education*, *11*(1). Advance online publication. DOI: 10.1080/2331186x.2023.2293431

Raji, I. D., Kumar, I. E., Horowitz, A., & Selbst, A. (2022). The fallacy of AI functionality. *2022 ACM Conference on Fairness, Accountability, and Transparency*, 959–972. https://doi.org/DOI: 10.1145/3531146.3533158

Ramaul, L., Ritala, P., & Ruokonen, M. (2024). Creational and conversational AI affordances: How the new breed of chatbots are revolutionizing the knowledge industries. *Business Horizons.*

Rane, N., Choudhary, S., & Rane, J. (2023). Education 4.0 and 5.0: Integrating Artificial Intelligence (AI) for personalized and adaptive learning. SSRN *Electronic Journal.* https://doi.org/DOI: 10.2139/ssrn.4638365

Rane, N., Choudhary, S., & Rane, J. (2024). Artificial intelligence, natural language processing, and machine learning to enhance e-service quality on e-commerce platforms. Available at *SSRN* 4847952.

Roy, G., Babu, R., Kalam, M. A., Yasmin, N., Zafar, T., & Nath, S. R. (2021). Response, readiness and challenges of online teaching amid COVID-19 pandemic: The case of higher education in Bangladesh. *The Educational and Developmental Psychologist, 40*(1), 40–50. DOI: 10.1080/20590776.2021.1997066

Sajja, R., Sermet, Y., Cikmaz, M., Cwiertny, D., & Demir, I. (2024). Artificial Intelligence-Enabled Intelligent Assistant for Personalized and Adaptive Learning in Higher Education. *Information (Basel), 15*(10), 596. DOI: 10.3390/info15100596

Sajja, R., Sermet, Y., Cikmaz, M., Cwiertny, D., & Demir, I. (2024). Artificial intelligence-enabled intelligent assistant for personalized and adaptive learning in higher education. *Information (Basel), 15*(10), 596.

Sandhu, R., Channi, H. K., Ghai, D., Cheema, G. S., & Kaur, M. (2024). An Introduction to Generative AI Tools for Education 2030. Integrating Generative AI in Education to Achieve Sustainable Development Goals, 1-28.

Shoaib, M. R., Wang, Z., Ahvanooey, M. T., & Zhao, J. (2023). Deepfakes, Misinformation, and Disinformation in the Era of Frontier AI, Generative AI, and Large AI Models. In *Unmasking DeepFake Visual Content with Generative AI.* https://doi.org/DOI: 10.1109/icca59364.2023.10401723

Shohel, M. M. C., Roy, G., Ashrafuzzaman, M., & Babu, R. (2022). Teaching and Learning in Higher Education in Bangladesh during the COVID-19 Pandemic: Learning from the Challenges. *Education Sciences, 12*(12), 857. DOI: 10.3390/educsci12120857

Sholokhova, S., Bizzari, V., & Fuchs, T. (2022). Exploring phenomenological interviews: Questions, lessons learned and perspectives. *Phenomenology and the Cognitive Sciences, 21*(1), 1–7. DOI: 10.1007/s11097-021-09799-y

Sinokki, S. (2024). A Day in the Life of a Technical Support Specialist.

Smyrnova-Trybulska, E., Morze, N., & Varchenko-Trotsenko, L. (2022). Adaptive learning in university students' opinions: Cross-border research. *Education and Information Technologies*, *27*(5), 6787–6818. PMID: 35095326

Stanier, J. (2022). An introduction to engaged phenomenology. *JBSP : the Journal of the British Society for Phenomenology. British Society for Phenomenology*, *53*(3), 226–242. DOI: 10.1080/00071773.2022.2081533 PMID: 35813180

Stöhr, C., Ou, A. W., & Malmström, H. (2024). Perceptions and usage of AI chatbots among students in higher education across genders, academic levels and fields of study. *Computers and Education Artificial Intelligence*, *7*, 100259. DOI: 10.1016/j.caeai.2024.100259

Tomei, L. A., Maine, J., Moussa, K., Holler, M. B., Hobbs, B., & Austin, S. (2024). The top 12 technologies for teaching and learning in the post-pandemic era. In *Exploring technology-infused education in the post-pandemic era* (pp. 1–95). IGI Global.

Toufaily, E., Zalan, T., & Dhaou, S. B. (2021). A framework of blockchain technology adoption: An investigation of challenges and expected value. *Information & Management*, *58*(3), 103444. DOI: 10.1016/j.im.2021.103444

Tzimas, D., & Demetriadis, S. (2021). Ethical issues in learning analytics: A review of the field. *Educational Technology Research and Development*, *69*(2), 1101–1133. DOI: 10.1007/s11423-021-09977-4

UNESCO Education Sector. (2021). *AI and education: guidance for policymakers*. UNESCO. https://books.google.com.bd/books?hl=en&lr=&id=yyE7EAAAQBAJ&oi=fnd&pg=PA3&dq=there+is+still+a+long+way+to+go+in+terms+of+addressing+these+concerns,+it+is+important+for+educators+and+policymakers+to+work+together&ots=cBj9D3zrK5&sig=FbdHaZLejkpn-IA1G8G7AoBupVk&redir_esc=y#v=onepage&q&f=false

Valavanidis, A. (2023). Artificial Intelligence (AI) Applications. Department of Chemistry, National and Kapodistrian University of Athens, University Campus Zografou, 15784.

Van Manen, M. (2017). Phenomenology in its original sense. *Qualitative Health Research*, *27*(6), 810–825. DOI: 10.1177/1049732317699381 PMID: 28682720

Wang, C., Chen, X., Yu, T., Liu, Y., & Jing, Y. (2024). Education reform and change driven by digital technology: A bibliometric study from a global perspective. *Humanities & Social Sciences Communications*, *11*(1). Advance online publication. DOI: 10.1057/s41599-024-02717-y

Watermeyer, R., Phipps, L., Lanclos, D., & Knight, C. (2023). Generative AI and the automating of academia. *Postdigital Science and Education*, *6*(2), 446–466. DOI: 10.1007/s42438-023-00440-6

Wenger, D., Hossain, M. S., & Senseman, J. R. (2024). *AI and the Impact on Journalism Education*. Journalism & Mass Communication Educator., DOI: 10.1177/10776958241296497

Williams, B. M., & Martin, G. (2021). Exploring the rhetoric of social class among first-generation, low-income college students in US higher education. *Higher Education Research & Development*, *41*(6), 2094–2107. DOI: 10.1080/07294360.2021.1967885

Wu, X., Duan, R., & Ni, J. (2023). Unveiling security, privacy, and ethical concerns of ChatGPT. *Journal of Information and Intelligence*, *2*(2), 102–115. DOI: 10.1016/j.jiixd.2023.10.007

Wu, Y. & Goldman School of Public Policy, University of California, Berkeley. (2023). Data Governance and Human Rights: An algorithm Discrimination Literature review and Bibliometric analysis. *Journal of Humanities, Arts and Social Science*. https://doi.org/DOI: 10.26855/jhass.2023.01.018

Xia, Q., Chiu, T. K., Lee, M., Sanusi, I. T., Dai, Y., & Chai, C. S. (2022). A self-determination theory (SDT) design approach for inclusive and diverse artificial intelligence (AI) education. *Computers & Education*, *189*, 104582. DOI: 10.1016/j.compedu.2022.104582

Yang, E., & Beil, C. (2024). Ensuring data privacy in AI/ML implementation. *New Directions for Higher Education*, *2024*(207), 63–78. DOI: 10.1002/he.20509

Youvan, D. (2024, January). The role of AI in revolutionizing academic publishing and knowledge dissemination.

Zajko, M. (2022). Artificial intelligence, algorithms, and social inequality: Sociological contributions to contemporary debates. *Sociology Compass*, *16*(3). Advance online publication. DOI: 10.1111/soc4.12962

Zhai, X., Chu, X., Chai, C. S., Jong, M. S. Y., Istenic, A., Spector, M., Liu, J., Yuan, J., & Li, Y. (2021). A Review of Artificial Intelligence (AI) in Education from 2010 to 2020. *Complexity*, *2021*(1). https://doi.org/DOI: 10.1155/2021/8812542

KEY TERMS AND DEFINITIONS

AI (Artificial Intelligence): A branch of computer science that enables machines to simulate human intelligence, including tasks like problem-solving, learning, and decision-making.

Chatbots: AI-powered virtual assistants designed to simulate human conversation, often used in customer service, educational support, and other interactive systems.

Data Misuse: The unethical or unauthorized use of data, often resulting in breaches of privacy, exploitation, or harm to individuals or organizations.

Data Security: The practice of protecting digital data from unauthorized access, breaches, and corruption to ensure confidentiality, integrity, and availability.

Higher Education: Post-secondary education provided by universities, colleges, and other institutions, focusing on academic and professional training.

Phenomenology: A qualitative research approach focused on understanding individuals' lived experiences and the meanings they attach to specific phenomena.

Thematic Analysis: A qualitative data analysis method that identifies, organizes, and interprets patterns or themes within a dataset.

UGC (User-Generated Content/University Grants Commission): Refers to any form of content, such as text, images, or videos, created and shared by users on digital platforms.

University Grants Commission (Bangladesh): The apex body responsible for overseeing, regulating, and funding higher education institutions in Bangladesh.

Chapter 10

Artificial Intelligence and Student Fear, Resistancem and Creativity in the Classroom:

The Public Relations Teaching Perspective

Elizabeth Bridgen
https://orcid.org/0000-0002-4296-9755
Buckinghamshire New University, UK

Sarah Williams
Buckinghamshire New University, UK

ABSTRACT

This chapter explores the use of AI for teaching and learning among students studying public relations. In particular, it focuses on the reception by students taking a module (course) designed for first year students at a university in the UK. The module has run for a number of years but for the 2023/4 academic year students were allowed to use generative AI tools for their assessed work, which took the form of a public relations plan and a creative portfolio. Taking a reflective case study approach, this chapter explores the student experience of this module, focusing in particular on the themes of student fear and resistance to using AI in the classroom.

DOI: 10.4018/979-8-3373-6018-8.ch010

Copyright © 2026, IGI Global Scientific Publishing. Copying or distributing in print or electronic forms without written permission of IGI Global Scientific Publishing is prohibited.

INTRODUCTION

This chapter takes a reflective case study approach and focuses on a specific use of generative artificial intelligence (AI) in public relations teaching among first-year students studying public relations at an English university.

In the case under investigation, students were actively encouraged to use generative AI for their end-of-year assessment and this chapter discusses the experiences of the lecturer and students in the context of current research in this area. AI - and the way it is used in public relations and communications workplaces - is an area where familiarity with both practice and ethical/governance issues is essential (Gregory, 2023) and this familiarity can start within a teaching setting (Yang, 2023). Thus, encouraging public relations students to use AI in a controlled setting could help them become informed practitioners of the future.

This research aimed to explore and understand student reaction to the use of AI in assessment. It asked the following research questions:

1. To what extent did students engage with AI tools (1) in a classroom setting and (2) in their assignments?
2. How did students react to being permitted to use AI in their university work?

LITERATURE REVIEW

This brief literature review examines recent literature on generative artificial intelligence (AI) encompassing research and practice-based writings from the broad fields of AI, pedagogy, and public relations. It focuses largely on publications since 2022 to reflect the rapid developments in these fields and also explores ethical and regulatory issues. It should be noted that no literature review covering AI developments can ever be complete but the authors' aim is to signpost some of the current debates and research.

Pedagogical Foundations

Understanding AI's role in education requires clarity about what constitutes AI. Holmes and Tuomi (2022) highlight UNICEF's definition as particularly useful for educational contexts:

AI refers to machine-based systems that can, given a set of human-defined objectives, make predictions, recommendations, or decisions that influence real or virtual environments. AI systems interact with us and act on our environment, either directly or indirectly. Often, they appear to operate autonomously, and can adapt their behaviour by learning about the context." (UNICEF, 2021, p. 16, as cited in Holmes & Tuomi, 2022, p. 546).

There is a growing concern that universities which fail to discuss AI with students risk it becoming a covert activity (e.g. Foltynek, 2023). Sharples (2022) suggests engaging students and instructors in shaping and harnessing AI tools to support learning rather than stopping the students from using them - and that this approach may better prepare students for their future workplace. As such, the extent to which students are permitted to use generative AI in the classroom is a rapidly-developing pedagogic area. While fears about generative AI being used for poor academic practice by students (e.g. Oravec, 2023) are often justified, there is also acknowledgement that students need the opportunity to experiment with, use, and learn about AI in the classroom (Yang, 2024).

While pedagogical discussions originally focused on concerns about academic integrity and plagiarism, the discourse has evolved to encompass the broader implications for pedagogy, equity, and professional preparation. Students can and will use AI in their work and consequently they need to understand both the use, and ethics, of AI and how it can impact on organisations, individuals and institutions in their educational, personal and professional lives.

Holmes & Tuomi (2022, p. 542) note that this paradigm shift in education has also attracted heavy financial investment and "high-profile policy statements about the need to promote and regulate this emerging technology" but this is a developing situation and essentially there is no clear view (even within subjects) of what should or can be taught. This may, however, be inevitable due to the "differences between academic disciplines, education institutions, courses, types of assessment, cultures, regions, and countries as to what is considered acceptable use of AI and what is not" (Foltynek et al, 2023, online).

Consequently, the introduction of generative AI has prompted significant discussion about academic integrity. Susnjak (2022) investigated the challenges of detecting AI-generated content and the implications for plagiarism policies. Similarly, Stokel-Walker (2022) examined ethical concerns surrounding student use of AI in academic work and concluded that education should focus on improving students' creativity and critical thinking rather than on general skills (which could be automated in the workplace of the future).

It is worth noting that when Rahimi, Jones and Bailey (2024) reviewed two decades of literature on student contract cheating conducted they summarised that eight to nine per cent of awarded degrees could be unsafe. This suggests that one of the much-discussed causal problems of AI (poor academic practice) is not a new phenomenon and students struggling with aspects of their studies may have always looked outside their institutions for help.

Meanwhile Rudolph et al. (2023) argued that concerns about AI in academia may be overstated and that AI has many valuable pedagogical features, noting that while ChatGPT may cause anxiety among educators "it may prove most useful to teachers when it comes to facilitating more innovative teaching and learning" (2023 p. 249). Likewise, Gedera and Griffiths (2012) believe that AI has the potential to transform education positively, but that nuanced human judgement and intervention when using AI is equally important.

It appears that recent literature suggests a shift from viewing AI solely as a threat to academic integrity toward considering how it might enhance assessment practices. This aligns with Pratschke's (2024) advocacy for 'assessment as learning' rather than 'assessment of learning,' suggesting a more nuanced approach to evaluating student work in an AI-enabled environment.

Pratschke (2024) presented a compelling framework for understanding this shift in thinking, advocating for a process-oriented approach to learning that emphasised collaboration and co-creation between students and AI technologies rather than a 'top down' approach. This perspective moved beyond viewing AI merely as a tool, instead considering it as a potential partner in the learning process. To this end, a literature review by Deng et al. (2024) noted that ChatGPT improved student performance, especially in languages and humanities, and simplified tasks for students thus enhancing their focus on learning. Their review also noted that there were methodological concerns around recent research in their field, especially concerning sample size and metrics.

The impact of generative AI on student teaching and learning has prompted a fundamental reconsideration of pedagogical approaches. However, multiple perspectives and opinions exist and navigation of these is not straightforward. For instance, Gao et al. (2023) and Yang (2024) have documented the varied faculty perspectives on AI integration. Gao et al. highlight the need for comprehensive professional development programmes and Yang (2024) reinforces these findings, emphasising the importance of supporting academics as they adapt to AI-enhanced teaching environments. Going further, Zhai et al. (2023) proposed frameworks for responsibly integrating AI tools into curricula, emphasizing the importance of digital literacy and critical thinking skills among both academics and students.

Schiff (2021) reviewed the national AI policies of more than 30 countries and found that "the use of AI in education (AIED) is largely absent from policy conversations, while the instrumental value of education in supporting an AI-ready workforce and training more AI experts is overwhelmingly prioritized" (p. 527). Meanwhile, Holmes and Tuomi (2022) identified several key ethical considerations in AI education, for instance *implementation* - which includes the right to human dignity in teaching and assessment, autonomy for students and protection from excessive profiling, access to AI-enhanced educational opportunities (although this can be difficult as Azıonya & Nhedzı (2021) have demonstrated) and transparency in AI decision-making processes.

It can be seen that there are a multitude of approaches and perspectives in AIED although the European Network for Academic Integrity has attempted to introduce a series of recommendations to support educators (Foltynek, 2023) which include clarity about where and how AI is used in teaching and assessment and the need for AI education for both students and teachers.

Zhai et al. (2023) have also contributed to the development of frameworks for responsible AI integration in higher education curricula and their work emphasises the importance of developing students' digital literacy and critical thinking skills alongside technical competencies. Their review of literature suggests several key areas for future research and development including building equitable access policies for AI educational tools, the creation of comprehensive frameworks for AI literacy in higher education and exploration of discipline-specific applications and implications of generative AI.

Recent developments have seen AI systems designed to augment rather than replace teacher capabilities. Rudolph et al (2023) argue that AI-powered applications may prove most useful in facilitating innovative teaching and learning approaches while Holmes and Tuomi (2022) emphasize the importance of seeing AI as supporting rather than replacing teachers, particularly in professional development contexts.

One of the most common applications of AI in education is that of Intelligent Tutoring Systems (ITS), which provide step-by-step tutorials through structured subjects like mathematics (Holmes & Tuomi, 2022). These systems capture thousands of data points about student interactions to personalise learning pathways. However, as Zeb et al (2024) point out, while such systems can provide tailored material, they risk exacerbating digital divides between students with and without access to such technology, something which writers such as Celik (2023) have also noted. Celik observed that "the digital divide might be a significant antecedent of AI literacy among people" (2023 p.2) adding that it was essential to explore the relationship between AI literacy and the digital divide.

Holmes and Tuomi (2022) further suggest that the future of AI in education likely lies in hybrid approaches combining knowledge-based and data-driven systems with human cognition. They emphasise the need for developing ethical frameworks specifically for educational AI, a focus on supporting rather than replacing lecturers and addressing equity concerns in AI tool development and deployment.

Equity and Diversity Considerations

Any critical examination of generative AI in education must consider its implications for educational equity. As mentioned above, Zeb et al. (2024) highlight disparity between students with ready access to advanced AI tools, and those without such privileges, something which is seen frequently in a higher education context (e.g. Azıonya & Nhedzı (2021).

The implementation of AI in education raises significant equity concerns. Bogen and Rieke's (2018) findings about AI bias in recruiting systems remain relevant to educational contexts while Holmes and Tuomi (2022) warn about potential 'AIED colonialism' where Global North companies export AI tools to Global South contexts without adequate consideration of local needs and circumstances.

The issue of AI bias also remains a significant concern in educational contexts. Bogen and Rieke (2018) identified anti-Black bias in AI-supported recruiting systems, attributing this partly to lack of diversity among AI developers. This is frequently raised as a concern, although Albusays et al (2021) noted that there is still a lack of research into the long-term implications of this lack of diversity among development team and that furthermore there are few studies which fully consider intersectionality.

While much research on diversity among software developers predates recent developments in generative AI it raises important considerations about potential bias in AI systems that remain relevant to current educational applications; lecturers need to ensure that students are aware of the risks inherent in using such systems. For instance, Palea and Buciuman (2024) observe that, since AI algorithms can sometimes perpetuate biases, students must be taught to critically assess the outputs generated by such tools.

Disciplinary Applications in Public Relations and Communications

Public relations and education writers agree (e.g. Lund, 2022, Gregory 2023) that students need more help understanding the use and implications of AI. How far this should go down the route of training is debatable. For instance, does the industry want 'oven ready' graduates (as reported by Yaxley, 2017) or informed, reflective, critical thinkers who are willing to learn? Or do they want both? Notwithstanding these debates, there is broad agreement that public relations graduates and practitioners should have the following basic knowledge:

What is AI?
What are its uses?
What are the threats and opportunities that AI poses?

What are the tool sets and their characteristics?
What are the ethical issues?
What are the implications for the practice and the organisation? (Gregory, 2023)

Gregory goes on to divide this foundation knowledge into 'use' and 'governance' where higher-level knowledge and skills explore the risks and opportunities posed by AI at a strategic level on one hand and an operational one on the other. However, Bruce Smith (2024) reports that 85% of practitioners had never received any kind of training in using generative AI tools, adding, "Perhaps unsurprisingly then, 66% of respondents told us they thought training would be useful" (online).

Rudolph et al (2023) believe that students should "use AI as a set of tools as a way to improve writing skills and generate new ideas, rather than simply copying and pasting text" (p.366) adding that wide and voracious reading, the improving of critical thinking, learning how to use key tools and learning how to write and debug code would all help students navigate a future with AI. To add these competencies to a public relations curriculum would not be without its problems, not least due to the non-technical background of many public relations practitioners and educators.

This view is supported by Ho who adds:

if public relations educators can make good use of the deep learning of artificial intelligence machine learning, master the teaching goals, further use big data analysis, update teaching content and market information, and provide teaching content that meets the needs and practices of enterprises, it will definitely improve public relations teaching (2022, online)

and it appears that the public relations industry agrees. Bruce-Smith (2024) notes that research shows that 80% of content writers (a public relations role) in the UK are already using generative AI tools like ChatGPT either frequently or occasionally and public relations practitioners also use AI for creative tasks, workflow, content creation, research, and to resolve daily problems and issues.

Thus, students on practice-based courses require familiarity with AI to be able to navigate both current and future education and workplace challenges. According to Yang (2024) it no longer appropriate to tell public relations and communication students that they cannot use generative AI for professional or practice-based learning when they will be using it in their future careers. These students may, in the future, work in roles where as well as using AI in their practice-based work they will also potentially be dealing with the wider implications of poor use of AI, issues of data security, or issues surrounding malicious use of AI which affects client reputation (as discussed by Palea and Buciuman, 2024).

The potential of AI in specific disciplines is an expanding topic and recent studies have explored various applications and implications of generative AI in university teaching settings. For instance, Lateef et al. (2023) examined AI applications in medical education, particularly focusing on its capacity to create realistic patient scenarios and provide adaptive learning experiences. Meanwhile Jussupow et al (2022) explored the reasons for resistance to AI among both established and student medics, something which is explored in our discussion below. They found that the more experienced physicians believed they had unique skills which AI systems could not substitute to the point of seeing AI as a threat to their professional identify.

McAlister. et al. (2024) followed a similar theme, looking at fear, uncertainty, and risk-aversion in the use of AI technologies in marketing education and scholarship, while Yang (2023) took a more positive view and observed that advertising students had a strong interest in "thinking about how generative AI could impact the development of advertising and their jobs in the future and how consumer privacy and data bias can cause more societal programs" (online).

In public relations and communications education Swiatek and Galloway (2022) pointed to the need for public relations scholars to become interpreters of AI-related issues and emphasised the growing importance of AI literacy among public relations practitioners and educators.

Similarly, Palea and Buciuman (2024) noted that one of the primary challenges in teaching public relations in the age of AI "is the need to bridge the gap between traditional public relations practices and the new skills required to navigate an AI-driven industry" (p.11). They noted that many public relations educators come from a creative or business background rather than a technical one. Consequently, they argue, digital literacy can be lacking among teaching staff which means that training and knowledge development should be encouraged. To this end, Palea and Buciuman (2024) observe that one of the most effective ways to teach AI in public relations is through hands-on experience.

Writers such as Ho (2021), Yang (2023), Palea and Buciuman (2024) and Yang (2024) stress that students and lecturers need to develop a thorough understanding of how AI works, including its limitations and ethical considerations. Ho (2021) was clear that "the diversity of public relations education makes it necessary to keep pace with the pulse of the technological age" (online). The article argues that educators and scholars need to develop their skills; longer-term, the author argues, this can only benefit the practice of public relations.

The literature review reveals the rapid evolution in thinking about generative AI in higher education which has moved from initial concerns about academic integrity towards more nuanced consideration of pedagogy, equity, and professional preparation. Issues of fear and resistance have also been explored. Pratschke's (2024) vision of a symbiotic relationship between educators, students, and AI technologies provides a useful framework for future developments in this field.

The literature also points to a complex landscape where AI's potential benefits must be carefully weighed against ethical, practical, and pedagogical concerns. As Holmes and Tuomi (2022, p. 562) note, "[t]echnical innovation and change is often assumed to mean progress but, in education, we also need to ask when change equals welcomed development."

METHODOLOGY

This section outlines the study's methodological approach to analysing educational interventions where AI (artificial intelligence) is used in a classroom setting. The capture and analysis of the complex dynamics of teaching interventions in ways that generate meaningful insights for future practice remains a fundamental challenge in educational research and while traditional research methods often focus on measuring specific outcomes it is important to acknowledges the importance of understanding the full context and process behind educational change.

The Reflective Case Study Approach

This study's methodological framework draws on established traditions of case study research while incorporating elements of reflective practice and action research (e.g. Cohen et al, 2017). This integration allows us to examine not only what changes were made and their outcomes, but also the decision-making processes, implementation challenges, and contextual factors that shaped the development of the intervention.

Central to this methodology is the systematic collection and analysis of multiple data sources, some of which were anecdotal or historical in their collection. These ranged from quantitative metrics of student performance and engagement (such as grades and submission rates), qualitative feedback from participants (often collected informally in conversation), emails and WhatsApp between teaching staff, observational data, and interrogation of the virtual learning environment site where student scripts were kept and marked. They also included reflection, which sometimes revealed unexpected barriers to student learning – for instance, the learning space assigned to the students was a room with no external light and with slow computers which proved problematic throughout the term.

The theoretical underpinning of reflective case studies in educational research draws from both Schön's (1983) foundational work on reflective practice and Stake's (1995) instrumental case study methodology. Schön's concept of reflection-in-action and reflection-on-action provides the framework for examining how educators analyse and learn from their teaching experiences, while Stake's approach offers systematic methods for documenting and analysing specific instances of educational practice. While documentation of this particular case was not systematic, the collation of multiple data points – such as emails, WhatsApp messages between staff, and student work – gave rise to valuable observations. This echoes Yin's (2018) emphasis on using multiple sources of evidence, which aligns particularly well with educational contexts where both quantitative and qualitative data can illuminate intervention outcomes (e.g. Campbell et al, 2023). It was not the aim of this study to align student outcomes with digital literacy but rather to use multiple sources of data to consider some of the challenges and implications of introducing AI into the classroom.

Mezirow's (1991) theory of transformative learning adds another crucial theoretical layer, explaining how critical reflection can lead to fundamental changes in teaching practice – something which is key to this chapter - while Kolb's (1984) experiential learning cycle provides a structure for understanding how reflection contributes to professional development and improved practice. It is hoped that the reflection that comes from this research can be helped to design future modules which integrate AI and public relations practice, especially in terms of the assessment as well as helping lecturers understand how students respond to technology.

It is important to note that this module was not designed as a research project. The realisation that this module's teaching and learning would make a good subject of academic study was only made as the module progressed. While contemporaneous notes are, consequently, incomplete, recollections were noted during and after the module so as not to diminish or become altered over the passage of time. The value and complexity of recollection in educational settings presents both methodological opportunities and challenges. Clifford and Marcus (1986) highlight how field notes serve as both interpretive acts and records of observation, while Hammersley and Atkinson (2007) emphasise the importance of systematic documentation alongside reflexive awareness which the author teaching the module attempted to put into action.

While there is undoubtedly value in personal reflections on critical incidents and interventions (or even the mundane), there is also the potential for memory to become "tainted", as addressed by Van Maanen (1988) who explores how retrospective interpretation can reshape initial observations. However, as Walford (2008) argues, the embedded nature of teacher-researchers also provides unique advantages through their sustained immersion in the classroom culture. This immersive position allows for what Delamont (2016) describes as a deep understanding of the contextual nuances and implicit practices that might be missed by external observers. The trust that was built between lecturer and students allowed students to discuss their issues and fears with the lecturers and allowed lecturers to build a relationship with the students during the term. The key lies in what Woods (1996) terms "critical events" in educational ethnography - ensuring significant moments are documented promptly while acknowledging how immediate experiences interweave with reflective interpretation.

While the method chosen allows for informed insights to emerge it is also important to acknowledge some of the limitations of using reflections as an aspect of case study data. The inherent subjectivity of reflective accounts presents a significant challenge, as the practitioner-researcher's dual role can introduce bias in both data collection and interpretation. In addition, data collection can be interrupted by events – for instance, one student required significant assistance throughout the module and more time was spent with that student at the expense of helping (or gaining feedback from) the other students.

Ball's (1990) work on researcher positionality highlights how personal investment in educational outcomes can influence perceptions of intervention success. The temporal nature of reflection also poses methodological challenges. Post-event rationalisation can inadvertently reshape the narrative of events, and a researcher's worldview can potentially emphasise some aspects while minimising others. There are also practical limitations regarding data capture, particularly when the practitioner must balance their teaching responsibilities with systematic documentation which is certainly true in the subject under discussion where recollection of conversations took place after the teaching and sometimes academic pressures got in the way of systematic documentation. The power dynamics inherent in teacher-student relationships may also impact the candour of student feedback, requiring careful consideration of ethical implications and data collection methods that mitigate these concerns. Further issues also impacted on data collection such as student attendance (which declined over the term, as is standard in UK academic institutions). Details of the students – and even the university where the study took place – have been anonymised and key details omitted to protect student identity.

Even with these caveats, the reflections on the teaching and learning within this module are still valuable, especially considering the nascent state of research into AI and education.

The University Setting

The students' second-term studies in their first year included a compulsory module which focused on digital public relations planning and skills. The competencies taught and assessed by the module historically included fundamental public relations skills such as researching, planning, and implementing a digital communications campaign, something which was novel to many of the students. Since these skills needed to be taught and developed to a foundational professional standard, an experiential learning method had been adopted within the module where students developed their practical work in class through their experience of working with a client. This teaching method, module structure and learning outcomes (see Figure 1: Module Learning Outcomes) had remained unchanged for several years due to the difficulty (and inadvisability) of changing module outcomes for one-off activities within a public university setting. However, for the 2023/2024 intake, student use of AI was both encouraged and incorporated into the module within the existing module framework.

Figure 1. Module Learning Outcomes Figures and tables Bridgen Williams.docx

This module aims to explore digital public relations practice and examine its growing use and influence. In particular, the module will help you to:

Devise memorable and sharable social and digital content which supports client objectives
Understand the role of narrative and storytelling in digital PR practice
Develop knowledge of digital PR tools and be able to use them effectively
Understand how to measure and monitor online activity and how to act on these results
Understand how individuals, communities and influencers behave online and how organisations and individuals can understand this behaviour to meet organisational or personal objectives

The study took place in what is referred to in the UK as a 'post-1992' university, a nomenclature synonymous with new university or modern university that was given university status through the Further and Higher Education Act 1992. Students at these universities may have lower post-16 exam results than those at traditional universities and there may be a higher proportion of students from lower income families, with a disability, or who attended state (rather than a private) school. These universities also tend to teach have a higher proportion of vocational degrees.

While all students in the group were digitally literate, the willingness to engage with technology was sometimes negatively affected by disability and personal beliefs or lifestyle. While the university had ample provision for students in digital poverty, the digital divide observed by Celik (2023) may also have been a factor in student engagement with AI.

The Module Under Investigation

Around 60 students took the module. These students were split across three timetabled classes (once a week for two hours) with a weekly hour-long lecture that brought all students together. However, this chapter focusses on the activities and views of one class, although drawing generalised data from all three. The class under investigation was taught by one of the authors, the other two by a non-academic member of teaching staff.

While Yang (2024) emphasised the importance of supporting academics as they adapt to AI-enhanced teaching environments the university had given little formal guidance to academics in terms of AI use and governance beyond a developing academic misconduct policy. In the case of this module, the two lecturers met before the start of term to discuss the teaching and assignment and one of the authors carried out checks to ensure that the second lecturer had the knowledge to teach the subjects (as well as providing them with additional reading and information). In this sense, the lecturers were unsupported and unguided and while they kept programme colleagues informed of the activities in the module, there was no guidance from university leadership.

Classes were held weekly over a period of 12 weeks. In weekly hour-long lectures students were instructed in the use of generative AI programmes, industry developments, and the practical and ethical issues surrounding their use, while in their practical classes they had the opportunity to experiment with AI tools. Later in the term students were encouraged to work on their assignments in the classroom with tutor support.

In the class which was the main focus of this study, only one student demonstrated vocal resistance to AI tools from the start of the term and did not change their focus during the 12 weeks of teaching. This student said they did not use social media and was also unwilling to use class computers – this provided a further challenge for the lecturer.

As this was a first-year module any grades did not count towards a final degree result (although students must pass their first year to progress to their second year) so some experimentation was appropriate. The teaching team were aware that this assignment provided an excellent opportunity for students to learn about good academic practice and importantly it started a conversation about AI and assessment early in their university career.

The Assessment

This module's assessment required students to create industry-standard material for a client who was recruited by the university specifically for the module. Students had to produce two interlocking elements for their final assessment – a public relations plan (a standard document created at the start of many public relations campaigns) and secondly, examples of creative work which related to concepts and ideas proposed in the public relations plan. The creative work could include examples of Instagram posts and reels, suggested email and WhatsApp message texts to journalists/influencers, press releases on specific subjects, TikTok videos, and Facebook posts adapted for relevant pages, etc.

The students worked with an overseas client who communicated with the students via Microsoft Teams and email. The client's product was a podcast and other social media assets aimed at several highly specific demographics and the students' public relations plan aimed to explore how they would engage and educate these audiences. Teaching was highly focused and specific and took place in computer labs where students were given advice and coaching on using generative AI for professional work. This included the appropriate programs to use, how to write effective prompts, how to use AI for research, and an understanding of privacy issues (such as how to avoid misusing client data when interrogating AI programs). As Foltynek et al (2023) observe, students "will likely use AI tools in their professional life. Therefore, they should be given opportunities to learn these skills during their education" (online).

Students were guided towards specific AI tools, the selection based on lecturer familiarity and the acceptance of tools in the PR community (e.g. Nero, 2024). Large language AI tools ChatGPT and Claude.ai were recommended to students but students also made their own choices, in particular, AI image creation tools. Students were encouraged to consider what happened to personal and commercial information after they inputted it into commercial AI tools and to avoid sharing any information which was not already publicly available. As Zhai et al. (2023) recommends, AI ethics, critical thinking skills, and broader issues were discussed in lectures and this learning was regularly brought into classroom discussions.

The content of each part of the assignment was explained to students in a colloquial format (see Figure 2: Assignment Content and Figure 3: Assignment Q&A) so that the students (some of whom came from non-academic backgrounds and others who had had breaks from study) were not intimidated by the assignment instructions. The instructions demonstrated to students how and where they could use AI and were accompanied by screengrabs explaining how they could evidence their use of AI in a visual form. The use of clear language is seen as vital by writers such as Rudolph et al (2023) to ensure that students have a clear understanding of the assessment and do not feel the need to cheat. Using non-academic language was supported by Fudge et al (2022) who noted that when writing student instructions the importance of "adjust[ing] the wording of some phrases ensuring consistency with the official policy but demonstrating our respectful guidance for students' learning" (p. 11).

Figure 2. Assignment content

We'll show you some ways that you can be transparent when using AI – but if you're not sure, speak to your tutor

The approach is the same in both parts of your assignment

Appendix – not in your word count but very important

Make it super clear what you have done and refer to an appendix

Don't put your prompts etc. in the bod text – try to keep the flow

Make it super clear what you have done and refer to an appendix

Don't put your prompts etc. in the body text – try to keep the flow

The lecturer also supplied a Q&A for students (Figure 3)

Figure 3. Assignment Q&A

Q: Do I have to use AI? I'd rather be creative

A: It is ENTIRELY up to you. Using (or not using) AI will not affect your grade

Q: What happens if what AI gives me is rubbish, so I refine my prompts a few times and eventually get some good stuff. Do I have to admit this?

A: Yes – admit it in your narrative in the appendix but you don't have to screenshot all your prompt iterations

Q: Do I still have to submit through Turnitin?

A: Yes, because it's good practice and I'm interested to see what we get!

Q: Basically ... my whole assignment is generated by AI is that OK?

A: Well – yes but you need to be TOTALLY TRANSPARENT about this

The module had tight parameters to reduce (and ensure student understanding of the nature of) plagiarism and so that students understood that what was allowed in this module was not necessarily permissible in others. Effectively the module was turned into a 'walled garden' because the university had not yet developed a robust policy on professional AI use in assessments. As Foltynek et al (2023) observes, acknowledgement of AI use is crucial although "acknowledgement may be done in different ways, according to the context, the institutional policies or other requirements [and] [w]hen possible, the input given to the AI tool should be specified" (online). To avoid poor academic practice in the final assignments and to ensure that lecturers understood the origin of each piece of work students were required to include PDFs of their prompts, and responses to prompts, in their assignment submission to show how they had used and developed the AI responses. To this end, the students could show their completion of module learning outcomes and demonstrated how they got there – whether they used AI tools or not.

RESULTS AND FINDINGS

Key Themes

Several themes became apparent from interrogating tutor notes and observations from the lecturer's discussions with students who were studying the module, and staff involved in the teaching.

The themes revealed through the research were (1) resistance to artificial intelligence (AI) and (2) fear of AI. These are discussed below in relationship to pedological, behavioural, communications and public relations literature. This is to allow us to build an understanding of student motivations and concerns in the classroom, particularly relating and public relations and communications students, but as has been shown by Jussupow et al (2022) these concerns may be mirrored in other occupations and occupational studies.

Theme 1: Resistance to AI

As discussed above, the students were new to the subject of public relations and while they were part of what is known as 'Generation Z' (most were aged 18-19), and should have familiarity with computer software, there was often nervousness when using the university PCs for work. Some would rather work on their home devices and were unhappy saving work to 'the cloud' or didn't think that they could do their best work on the university's PCs. This proved to be an unexpected but important barrier to teaching and learning. While students were willing to experiment on the university PCs, they were less inclined to work on their assessed work (where they would have received tutor support in class) preferring to carry out this work at home. This resistance, interestingly, went beyond AI and towards a resistance of the unfamiliar, especially in regard to technology and teaching areas. Research by Siddiquah and Salim (2017) suggested that this may simply be the result of slow computers and the poor working condition of the class computers – something which may have been causal in the case under investigation.

There is little research where students are encouraged to reflect on their use of AI or understand their opinions on technology. Lund (2024) explored the links between age, gender identity, ethnicity, geographic location, educational attainment, residence, and the levels of anxiety and fear associated with AI but used a quantitative approach. Yang (2023) reported student opinions about AI use in the classroom but first-hand reflections from the students are largely absent. As Jussupow et al (2022) observed: “While multiple studies investigated attitudes towards AI, they did not consider how resistance attitudes towards AI are formed” (p. 2).

Rudolph et al (2023) note (possibly controversially) that “[s]tudents are often digital natives who use technology more effortlessly and intuitively than their teachers” (2023, p. 256). However, the findings of this study only partially uphold this as not all the students were willing or natural users of technology in the classroom and even the able students expressed doubts around the value AI could add to their work.

The research notes and observations revealed that students firmly wanted their own work to be recognised and often did not want any AI assistance or were suspicious of how it could augment their work. This resistance to using AI was visible and clearly articulated in class by the students – while some were happy to use AI to develop logos and graphics (which is not taught on their degree programme but would add a professional ‘look’ to their portfolio) they did not want to use it for researching their PR plan, for their written work or for the creative work that was part of their module and their degree (such as developing Facebook and Instagram posts and writing creative communications copy). This chimes with the findings of Jussupow (2022) who observed that the implementation of AI was perceived as leading to a loss of status and prestige.

The students worked with a client whose promotional output was highly visual – however, students did not feel the client’s branding and imagery reflected the brand personality and that it was not appropriate for their target audience (professionals in specific occupations aged 18-45). Some students went through endless iterations with AI image generators to create a new client logo and graphics. This moved the students into areas of graphic design, and it appeared that students were happier using AI in an area where they were not meant to be expert. It appears that their resistance was partially linked to areas where they were meant to excel, which ties in with Jussupow et al’s (2022) work with physicians; those who were expert (or thought they were) were less likely to rely on AI. This is an under-explored theme in academic literature but Habib’s (2024) research suggested that students felt that using AI was the ‘easy way out’ - what they wanted to do was think on their own.

Furthermore, many students reported that the AI written work they received when they practiced in class was unsatisfactory – it was often very U.S.-focused or repetitive. -Smith (2024) reported on research into the perceived lack of quality of AI outputs, noting:

> *Writers consistently reported being underwhelmed with the style and authorial tone of voice that these tools provide. [...] AI text tools are described as producing writing that is ‘slightly shallow and repetitive’ (Peter, head of communications), ‘very bland’ (George, senior consultant), ‘very salesy’ (Fay, managing director)*

or as a survey participant put it 'just plain dross' (survey respondent, content writer. (online)

As a side note to this, the lecturer showed students the results of a lecture which had been written by an AI program (Claude.ai) on AI ethics. While the structure and headings of the lecture was useable, the content was very generalised and it lacked academic rigour.

The phenomena of students wanting their work to be seen as their own (or not wanting to acknowledge assistance) went further with a resistance by students to acknowledge the existence of AI in their submitted work. Few students followed the model set by the lecturer of taking screenshots of prompts and responses and showing where they had augmented AI suggestions. As a result, it became difficult to understand whether work submitted was generated by generative AI programs or whether the students had used images and templates found on the internet to create their own work. This then led us into the problem identified by many of the writers on AI in education, such as Rudolph et al. (2023), Susnjak (2022), and Zeb, et al (2024), of whether we could we tell if a piece of work was AI generated. The answer was that it was and is difficult and becoming more so over time, as generative AI systems increase in sophistication. The written AI content produced by students tended to be short pieces for their portfolios such as social media posts where it was difficult to pick up on the tell-tale signs of AI use (such as differing styles between paragraphs, an Americanised writing style, or hallucinated references). The only time work could be clearly identified as AI content is when it was so far removed from the assignment brief that the student could not possibly have created it themselves (although it should be asked – was this simply because the student failed to understand the brief?). Sometimes students had clearly used material pulled from online (such as social media templates and images) but this is not the same as using AI.

Pratschke's (2024) argued that AI should push students to be more creative (which was only partly demonstrated by this study) while Yang (2023 went further, noting: "Specifically, students showed strong interest in thinking about how generative AI could impact the development of advertising and their jobs in the future and how consumer privacy and data bias can cause more societal programs" (2023, online).

Yang argues that creativity is becoming more important than ever with the advent of AI. Creativity – not just in activity but in understanding the implications of AI– is where practitioners can demonstrate their value in the workplace so potentially the suspicions and resistance demonstrated by the students were part of their journey to being a critical thinker on AI.

The similarity between medical students' resistance to AI and public relations students' apprehension is particularly noteworthy. Just as medical professionals feared being reduced to "a mere voice of the AI system" (Jussupow, 2023, p.11), public relations students expressed concern about AI diminishing the uniqueness and authenticity of their creative work and in this sense saw AI tools as a threat in the same way as medical practitioners.

This connects with other research on AI resistance in education. For instance, Mollick and Mollick (2023) found that students' concerns about AI often centred on questions of authenticity and creative ownership. Similarly, Oravec (2023) noted that students' resistance to AI tools often stemmed from a desire to protect what they saw as uniquely human capabilities. Resistance to using AI isn't simply about fear of technology, but about threats to professional recognition and status. For public relations students, their expertise in writing is often central to their identity and future professional aspirations so when AI appears to encroach on this domain, it creates what Jussupow et al. (2022) would recognise as an identity threat - challenging not just what they do, but who they understand themselves to be.

As the students were in their first year of a three-year degree programme, discussions about 'the future of work' tended not to be productive, countering Yang's (2023) findings relating to advertising students. Only one student in the class had experience of working in public relations but she was not a regular attendee at workshops so it was difficult to understand whether her views differed from the students whose understanding was not well formed.

The class discussions suggests that addressing student resistance to AI in public relations requires more than just demonstrating AI's capabilities or limitations, it needs to engage with deeper questions of creative identity, professional recognition, and the relationship between human and artificial creativity and potentially can only take place once students have developed a fuller understanding of the nature of public relations work. It also needs to address issues relating to the learning and teaching environment, which may not be the place where students feel they can do their best work.

Theme 2: Fear of AI

Throughout the course of human history, there has consistently existed a prevalent fear of emerging technologies (Albikawi and Abuadas, 2025). Gregory (2023) writes that the reluctance to adopt AI tools may be due to "fear that technology could replace jobs and lack of confidence in using tools like ChatGPT which are error prone" adding that "[t]he biggest challenge appears to be keeping up with changes and the avalanche of new tools" (online).

Gregory (2023) summarised the 'threats of AI, as seen by PR [public relations] professionals as follows (see Table 1: Threats of AI (Gregory, 2023)):

Table 1. Threats of AI (Gregory, 2023)

Misinformation, authenticity
Privacy, trust implications
Understanding correct usage of tools
Ethics, safety (input client's information)
Need for intervention, controlled environment
Generic content/ quality
Out of date information
Copyright, plagiarism
Lack of understanding how technology works
Tools can crash because of simultaneous use

Although Gregory's research was carried out among public relations practitioners, not public relations students, it was felt that the fears expressed by students augmented Gregory's research findings. Some students joked that their distrust of AI was due to a fear of "machines taking over the world" but that led to a conversation in class about manners and whether it mattered that we said "please" and "thank you" when dealing with AI tools – the consensus was that it did matter as the machines were 'learning' from the cues of everyone who used them.

There was concern among some (but not all) students about how the data and information they inputted into generative AI programmes would be used. Some were not at all bothered, on the grounds that much of their personal information was already known and used by social media companies while others were more circumspect. Students needed to be reminded regularly about the importance of treating client material appropriately when using AI tools.

Lund et al. (2024) explored the relationship between social, gender, ethnic and age-related groups and their fears of AI, observing that targeted education was the potentially the best way to ensure equality of use and access (and understanding). In particular, Lund noted that an urban-rural divide existed for AI anxiety. This is interesting as the university cohort under investigation was socially and culturally diverse and around half the class came from small towns and rural areas and while we did not explore links between diverse characteristics and fear of AI it would be useful for further studies. However, the high-performing students (based on outcome at the end of the module) anecdotally seemed more willing to experiment with AI programs. There also appeared to be more curiosity and willingness to 'play' with AI tools among some of the students from urban backgrounds, but again this requires further investigation.

Bruce Smith suggested that "concerns about transparency and the potential for Gen AI to replace human roles linger" (online) which corresponds with Jussupow (2023) who expressed fear of AI as a 'threat to identity.' Jussupow noted that physicians responded to this with a form of protection response where AI or its suggestions were rejected, meanwhile, some decided to focus their career on soft skills instead of analytical decision-making skills which would rather be performed by an AI. This finding was partially mirrored by the students who eschewed the use of AI on tasks where they felt that the AI product was inferior (such as creative writing) but were willing to use it when they thought that AI could help with their lack of ability (such as design and photography). In particular, a fear of AI was noted where students had unfettered access to generative AT tools – many preferred tools designed for highly-specific tasks such as digital image creation, or tools designed for a highly specific use (e.g. a grammar-checking tool). On reflection it appeared that rather than a 'sandbox' approach to use of AI did not encourage student use and a more prescriptive way of teaching may have been preferred.

Fear of and resistance to AI in education are intertwined and may have similar causes. The implications of each, however, are less certain but both would benefit from further study, especially in creative subjects where the use of AI is more nuanced. It would also be useful to not just link the diverse characteristics of today's learners to any fear of AI but also to explore the area holistically, addressing areas such as assessment instruction and design and classroom environment.

CONCLUSION

This research aimed to explore and understand student reaction to the use of AI in assessment thought two research questions:

1. To what extent did students engage with AI tools (1) in a classroom setting and (2) in their assignments?
2. How did students react to being permitted to use AI in their university work?

The reflective case study approach identified two primary themes arising from students' engagement and with AI technology in the classroom and in their final submission which centred around a fear of, and resistance to, using AI for university work.

In particular, the study revealed several key insights: Students, despite being 'digital natives,' displayed unexpected resistance to using AI for core academic work, particularly in areas where they felt they should excel naturally (like writing and creative communications). Interestingly, they were more comfortable using AI for supplementary skills outside their core curriculum, such as graphic design. The classroom experience also seemed to affect student confidence in using technology.

Writing this chapter has allowed a degree of reflection on the design and teaching of this module and drawing on Mezirow's (1991) view of transformative learning and it is clear that while the experience was valuable for both lecturers and students; critical reflection suggests considerable changes would need to be designed into the module in the future to take account of student resistance to AI and the fear and anxiety that using the tools produced. It was clear that students required a more rigid framework in which to experiment and perhaps rather than making AI optional, making its use mandatory in certain parts of the assignment to encourage experimentation and use (and declaration of use).

Kolb's (1984) noted how reflection contributed to professional development and improved practice. Certainly, both members of staff learned much from the module process both in terms of its use and its governance. The learning could sometimes be basic (e.g. which tool was best for writing press releases? Which tool was best for writing social media posts?) but was nonetheless necessary. It is hoped that the reflection that comes from this research can be helped to design future modules which integrate AI and teaching public relations practice. Certainly, at the time of writing, the pedagogical frameworks within which AI teaching would take place, as recommended by Zhai et al. (2023), were lacking and potentially could be developed by professional bodies. Any such developments would not just include the teaching of practice skills but also follow any national policy framework for teaching governance and ethics, as suggested by Schiff (2021).

Furthermore, this reflection generated an awareness that resistance and distrust of AI needs to be explored early in the module when it is taught to a new cohort and the issue of the learning space needs to be addressed as well. Furthermore, an appreciation of students' digital literacy and AI knowledge needs to be understood at the start of term so that teaching can be pitched accordingly - potentially with personalised pathways introduced. Ultimately, the impact of this intervention will only be fully understood as the students continue through their degree programme studies and demonstrate their familiarity – or otherwise – with the use and governance of AI.

In summary, the students that used AI for their studies were getting a first glimpse of the public relations industry's relationship with generative AI and its issues but largely from a creative perspective. If they are to truly understand and use AI in the future, research suggests that they also need the technical skills which would not just help their operational use of the technologies but also reduce their fear and resistance to using AI. However, resistance isn't merely about technological adoption but also about protecting professional identity and creative authenticity. This indicates that successful AI integration in education requires addressing not just technical competency but also deeper questions about professional identity and the relationship between human and artificial creativity.

Future research would benefit from exploring these themes across diverse student populations and creative disciplines, particularly examining how different demographic characteristics might influence AI adoption and resistance.

REFERENCES

Albikawi, Z., & Abuadas, M. (2025). A Novel Scale to Measure Nursing Students' Fear of Artificial Intelligence: Development and Validation. *The Open Nursing Journal*, •••, 19.

Albusays, K., Bjorn, P., Dabbish, L., Ford, D., Murphy-Hill, E., Serebrenik, A., & Storey, M. A. (2021). The diversity crisis in software development. *IEEE Software*, *38*(2), 19–25.

Azıonya, C. M., & Nhedzı, A. (2021). The digital divide and higher education challenge with emergency online learning: Analysis of tweets in the wake of the COVID-19 lockdown. *Turkish Online Journal of Distance Education*, *22*(4), 164–182.

Ball, S. J. (1990). Self-doubt and soft data: Social and technical trajectories in ethnographic fieldwork. *International Journal of Qualitative Studies in Education : QSE*, *3*(2), 157–171.

Bogen, M., & Rieke, A. (2018). Help wanted: An examination of hiring algorithms, equity, and bias. *Upturn.* https://www.upturn.org/static/reports/2018/hiring-algorithms/files/Upturn%20--%20Help%20Wanted%20-%20An%20Exploration%20of%20Hiring%20Algorithms,%20Equity%20and%20Bias.pdf

Bruce Smith, A. (2024). LinkedIn post (no title). https://www.linkedin.com/posts/andrewbrucesmith_cheatgpt-generative-text-ai-use-in-uk-pr-activity-7260591234862170114-ecuL

Campbell, L., Highton, M., & McAndrew, E. (2023). Supporting open education practice: Reflective case studies from the University of Edinburgh. *Edutec. Revista Electrónica de Tecnología Educativa*, (85), 9–28.

Celik, I. (2023). Exploring the determinants of artificial intelligence (Ai) literacy: Digital divide, computational thinking, cognitive absorption. *Telematics and Informatics*, *83*, 102026.

Clifford, J., & Marcus, G. E. (1986). *Writing culture: The poetics and politics of ethnography*. University of California Press.

Cohen, L., Manion, L., & Morrison, K. (2017). Action research. In *Cohen, L., Manion, L., & Morrison, K. (2017) Research methods in education* (pp. 440–456). Routledge.

Delamont, S. (2016). *Fieldwork in educational settings: Methods, pitfalls and perspectives* (3rd ed.). Routledge.

Deng, R., Jiang, M., Yu, X., Lu, Y., & Liu, S. (2024). Does ChatGPT enhance student learning? A systematic review and meta-analysis of experimental studies. *Computers & Education*, •••, 105224.

Foltynek, T., Bjelobaba, S., Glendinning, I., Khan, Z. R., Santos, R., Pavletic, P., & Kravjar, J. (2023). ENAI Recommendations on the Ethical Use of Artificial Intelligence in Education. *International Journal for Educational Integrity*, *19*, 12.

Fudge, A., Ulpen, T., Bilic, S., Picard, M., & Carter, C. (2022). Does an educative approach work? A reflective case study of how two Australian higher education Enabling programs support students and staff uphold a responsible culture of academic integrity. *International Journal for Educational Integrity*, *18*(1), 5.

Gao, Y., Shum, S. B., Chen, M., & Alzahrani, S. (2023). Artificial Intelligence in Education: A Review of Learning Analytics and Educational Data Mining Studies. *Journal of Educational Technology & Society*, *26*(1), 31–46.

Gregory, A. (2023). *Humans Not Needed.* Chartered Institute of Public Relations.

Habib, S. (2024). Beyond the AI hype: Real effects on student creativity explored in new research. *PsyPost*. https://www.psypost.org/beyond-the-ai-hype-real-effects-on-student-creativity-explored-in-new-research/

Hammersley, M., & Atkinson, P. (2007). *Ethnography: Principles in practice* (3rd ed.). Routledge.

Ho, C. H. (2021). A preliminary study of artificial intelligence deep learning amid teaching of public relations course. In *2021 2nd International Conference on Education, Knowledge and Information Management,* (pp. 539-542).

Holmes, W., & Tuomi, I. (2022). State of the art and practice in AI in education. *European Journal of Education*, *57*, 542–570.

Jussupow, E., Spohrer, K., & Heinzl, A. (2022). Identity threats as a reason for resistance to artificial intelligence: Survey study with medical students and professionals. *JMIR Formative Research*, *6*(3). PMID: 35319465

Kolb, D. A. (1984). *Experiential learning: Experience as the source of learning and development*. Prentice Hall.

Lateef, F., Stehman, C. R., & Plitt, M. (2023). Artificial intelligence: Emerging roles in medical education. *Education and Information Technologies*, *28*(1), 741–756.

Lund, B. D., Mannuru, N. R., & Agbaji, D. (2024). AI anxiety and fear: A look at perspectives of information science students and professionals towards artificial intelligence. *Journal of Information Science*, •••, 01655515241282001.

McAlister, A. R., Alhabash, S., & Yang, J. (2024). Artificial intelligence and ChatGPT: Exploring Current and potential future roles in marketing education. *Journal of Marketing Communications, 30*(2), 166–187.

Mezirow, J. (1991). *Transformative dimensions of adult learning*. Jossey-Bass.

Mollick, E. R., & Mollick, L. (2023). Assisting, Augmenting, and Evaluating Creativity with Generative AI. https://ssrn.com/abstract=4375796

Nero, V. (2024). We Tested 20+ AI PR Tools, So You Don't Have To. https://www.buzzstream.com/blog/pr-ai-tools/

Oravec, J. A. (2023). Artificial intelligence implications for academic cheating: Expanding the dimensions of responsible human-AI collaboration with ChatGPT. *Journal of Interactive Learning Research, 34*(2), 213–237.

Palea, A., & Buciuman, C. (2024). The Impact of Artificial Intelligence (AI) on Teaching Public Relations (PR). *Emerging Technologies, Challenges and Opportunities in Education and Research,* 11.

Pratschke, B. M. (2024). *Generative AI and Education: Digital Pedagogies, Teaching Innovation and Learning Design*. Springer.

Rahimi, R., Jones, J., & Bailey, C. (2024). Exploring contract cheating in further education: Student engagement and academic integrity challenges. *Ethics and Education, 19*(1), 38–58.

Rudolph, J., Tan, S., & Tan, S. (2023). ChatGPT: Bullshit spewer or the end of traditional assessments in higher education? *Journal of Applied Learning and Teaching*, *6*(1), 342–363.

Schiff, D. (2021). Education for AI, not AI for Education: The Role of Education and Ethics in National AI Policy Strategies. *International Journal of Artificial Intelligence in Education, 32*, 527–563.

Schön, D. A. (1983). *The reflective practitioner: How professionals think in action*. Basic Books.

Sharples, M. (2022). New AI tools that can write student essays require educators to rethink teaching and assessment. London School of Economics Blog. https://blogs.lse.ac.uk/impactofsocialsciences/2022/05/17/new-aitools-that-can-write-student-essays-require-educators-torethink-teaching-and-assessment/

Siddiquah, A., & Salim, Z. (2017). The ICT facilities, skills, usage, and the problems faced by the students of higher education. *Eurasia Journal of Mathematics, Science and Technology Education, 13*(8), 4987–4994.

Stake, R. E. (1995). *The art of case study research.* Sage Publications.

Stokel-Walker, C. (2022). AI text generators could help write student essays. *Nature, 611*(7935), 227–228. PMID: 36344616

Susnjak, T. (2022). ChatGPT: The end of online exam integrity? *arXiv preprint* arXiv:2212.09292.

Swiatek, L., & Galloway, C. (2022). Artificial intelligence and public relations: Growing opportunities, questions, and concerns. In *The Routledge Companion to Public Relations* (pp. 352–362). Routledge.

Van Maanen, J. (1988). *Tales of the field: On writing ethnography.* University of Chicago Press.

Walford, G. (2008). *How to do educational ethnography.* Tufnell Press.

Woods, P. (1996). *Researching the art of teaching: Ethnography for educational use.* Routledge.

Yang, A. (2024). Preparing Public Relations' Practitioners for the AI Era: Advancing Pedagogical Principles in Public Relations' Artificial Intelligence Education. *Journalism & Mass Communication Educator*, 10776958241277682.

Yang, J. (2023). Preparing for the New Era of Artificial Intelligence: My Experience of Teaching "Artificial Intelligence in Advertising". *Journal of Advertising Education, 27*(2), 101–116.

Yaxley, H. (2017). *Career strategies in public relations: constructing an original tapestry paradigm* (Doctoral dissertation). Bournemouth University.

Yin, R. K. (2018). *Case study research and applications: Design and methods* (6th ed.). Sage Publications.

Zeb, A., Ullah, R., & Karim, R. (2024). Exploring the role of ChatGPT in higher education: Opportunities, challenges and ethical considerations. *The International Journal of Information and Learning Technology, 41*(1), 99–111.

Zhai, X., Chu, X., Chai, C. S., Jong, M. S. Y., Istenic, A., Spector, M., & Li, Y. (2021). A Review of Artificial Intelligence (AI) in Education from 2010 to 2020. *Complexity, 2021*(1), 8812542.

Chapter 11
Does Human Still Have a Place in the Age of AI:
Positive Versus Negative Valence of ChatGPT

Arij Jmour
https://orcid.org/0000-0002-2327-5643
Faculty of Economics and Managment of Sfax, Tunisia

ABSTRACT

This study examines the users' perspective on the opportunities, challenges and implications related to artificial intelligence technologies such as ChatGPT in the context of scientific writing. To achieve the research objective, the study adopts an inductive exploratory study, carried out through a qualitative approach and based on 15 in-depth interviews with researchers analyzed using QDA-miner software. The respondents perceive ChatGPT as a useful tool that simplifies activities and reduces time and human errors. However, risks associated with the use of this tool have been identified, such as the reliability of the information provided, superficiality, redundancy, misinformation, the need for more confidentiality for the personal data requested and the risk of human extinction.o the authors' knowledge, this is the first study to examine a holistic perspective containing both the benefits and challenges of the AI ChatGPT tool in the context of research publication from the researchers' perspective.

DOI: 10.4018/979-8-3373-6018-8.ch011

Copyright © 2026, IGI Global Scientific Publishing. Copying or distributing in print or electronic forms without written permission of IGI Global Scientific Publishing is prohibited.

INTRODUCTION

On November 30, 2022, OpenAI unveiled a chatbot named "Chat Generative Pre-trained Transformer (ChatGPT)," quickly attracting the attention of artificial intelligence researchers and scholars (OpenAI, 2022; Hao, 2022; Zhai, 2022; Jin and Kruppa, 2023; Kumar, 2023; Pasca and Arcese, 2023). The release of ChatGPT also sparked widespread public interest, with people around the world eager to learn about the innovation and evaluate its capabilities. Designed to generate detailed textual responses and articulate answers to any query (Kumar, 2023), ChatGPT has attracted attention for its application in several fields. This OpenAI tool (ChatGPT), a popular artificial intelligence extended language model, has recently attracted attention for its potential applications and implications in various fields, including academic writing (Thorp, 2023; Bom, 2023; Water et al., 2023). Indeed, many AI-based tools like ChatGPT are used by researchers during their academic writing (Herwanto et al., 2024). Recently, the integration of artificial intelligence in academic writing has become very popular (Herwanto et al. 2024).

Therefore, to determine the benefits of digital transformation in scientific writing, it is important to study researchers' attitudes toward AI tools like ChatGPT in scientific writing. As confirmed by Stahl and Eke (2024), we use ChatGPT as the best-known example of a large-scale interactive language model due to its prevalence in discourse. ChatGPT has the ability to create well-written student essays, summarize research papers, answer questions well enough to pass medical exams, and generate useful computer codes. It has even created research summaries that scientists have had difficulty distinguishing from those written by a human (Dis EAM et al., 2023; Dergaa et al., 2023). Dwivedi et al. (2023) have stated the ability of ChatGPT to improve productivity. Similarly, Zhai (2022) have suggested that ChatGPT is capable of helping researchers write a coherent, (partially) accurate, informative, and systematic paper. However, there are concerns about its reliability and the potential risks associated with its use (Mondal and Mondal, 2023). This technology has the potential to produce spam, ransomware, and other harmful outcomes, which is very worrisome for our societies (Dis EAM et al., 2023; Dergaa et al., 2023). The emergence of ChatGPT has posed many challenges, such as the violation of academic integrity and honesty (Adeshola and Adepoju, 2023). Researchers are concerned that AI is emerging as the next disruptive innovation (Zhai et al., 2021). Given the potential of ChatGPT to disrupt various fields, there is an urgent need for the research community to engage in a comprehensive debate on the potential uses, threats, and limitations of these tools (Van Dis et al., 2023; Dergaa et al., 2023). According to Karan and Bakina (2024), ChatGPT has become a topic of debate. The sentiments, opinions, and feedback on its use in education are mixed.

Several studies have examined the use of AI, highlighting its benefits, challenges, and ethical considerations in different contexts such as education, healthcare, law, etc. (Sallam, 2023; Tlili et al., 2023; Pasca and Arcese, 2023). However, when we look at the studies on the use of ChatGPT in scientific writing, we find that the number of academic studies is low. A few researches have questioned the issue while being limited to purely conceptual research or case studies. Alharbi and Al-shargabi (2023) stated that their study was limited in nature to conceptual research and thus could be extended to quantitative or qualitative research methodology for better observation and evaluation. According to Brunetti et al. (2024), no empirical research has so far examined the continued development of digitalization in favor of the research publication process. They reported that the importance of this topic and the lack of studies on the subject imply that it requires further research.

According to Karan and Bakina (2024), future researchers can explore the influence of individuals' academic discipline on the acceptance or rejection of this fast-growing OpenAI tool in education. According to Stahl and Eke (2024), future studies are needed to better understand the detailed empirical impacts of ChatGPT. As recommended by Karan and Bakina (2024) and Stahl and Eke (2024) in their future directions, this paper has a dual objective. On the one hand, this research aims to build a comprehensive pedagogical framework on the use of OpenAI by focusing on its advantages and mitigating possible challenges. On the other hand, it attempts to conduct an empirical study to determine the use of ChatGPT. Therefore, the objectives of this paper were to provide an overview of ChatGPT and, its emergence, limitations, and associated practical implications; and to examine the prospects and consequences of using these tools in academic writing. Due to this increasing use of AI, there is an urgent need to understand researchers' attitudes towards this technology. This understanding is essential for educators, policy makers as well as AI developers due to the ongoing debate on whether the use of ChatGPT in academic writing is beneficial or detrimental. It is about increasing the potential benefits and reducing the potential harms, so it is necessary to know how researchers feel when using ChatGPT in their academic writing Herwanto et al. (2024).

The remainder of this article is structured as follows. After presenting the theoretical background in terms of the research publication process, ChatGPT and expectations, the research method is described and the results are proposed and discussed. Implications, limitations and future research avenues then conclude the study.

LITERATURE REVIEW

1. Process of Scientific Writing

According to Brunetti et al. (2023), as an integral part of academic life, researchers are encouraged to write and publish (Gilmore et al., 2006), and in particular, to publish in top-tier journals (Shchemeleva, 2021), i.e. journals that have a high impact factor or H-index, or three and four stars as major criteria for research output (Kuteeva and McGrath, 2014) and, consequently, to be included in the most prestigious international bibliographic databases (Gralka et al., 2019; Shchemeleva, 2021). The pressure to publish in top-tier journals for non-English speakers adds to the anxiety about writing in English rather than the local language and the need to accommodate non-English contexts (Curry & Lillis, 2014; Plo & Peres-Llantada, 2015). This can lead to such anxiety that acute academic writing is described as "a minefield, a roller coaster, or at least an obstacle course" (Leki, 2003, p. 136). In the early 1900s, writing an academic paper was similar to writing an essay or unstructured prose text. After World War II, specialization in different fields, especially scientific ones, gave rise to more standardized papers, which now have to follow the so-called IMRAD structure, i.e. Introduction, Materials and Methods, Results, and Discussion (Wu, 2011). Nowadays, writing an academic article is not like writing an essay (e.g. West, 1992); such an activity requires a lot of time (Aguinis and Vaschetto, 2011), commitment and various aspects of research expertise (Neuhauser et al., 2000) throughout the publication process (Caniato et al., 2018; Adams, 2014). Some studies (i.e. Troutt, 1998) have highlighted the importance of quality improvement principles in reference to the process of writing scientific articles, including offering advice to doctoral students who wish to publish their research in peer-reviewed academic journals (Paltridge and Starfield, 2016). The research publication process follows a complex and structured model (Levitt et al., 2018) that integrates several typical steps (Bordens and Abbott, 2002; Hair et al., 2007), from planning the scope and content to the final production of the manuscript (Perry et al., 2003). During this process, each author develops an individual approach to planning, preparing, writing, and submitting articles to an academic journal (Gilmore et al., 2006).

2. Technology Acceptance Theory "TAM"

The Technology Acceptance Model (TAM) developed by Davis in 1989 provides insights into how users adopt new technologies. According to TAM, two factors shape researchers' propensity to use technologies during education: perceived usefulness and ease of use. Perceived usefulness refers to the extent to which researchers believe that technology will improve their research, while perceived ease of use concerns the ease of using the technology. Both perceived usefulness and ease of use positively influence researchers' attitudes and intentions toward technology. According to TAM, researchers' technological attitudes and intentions depend on their perceptions of the usefulness and ease of use of a technology. Researchers who adequately account for these factors through TAM are likely to improve their academic writing.

3. ChatGPT

ChatGPT, a general-purpose conversational chatbot in the Generative Pre-Training Transformer (GPT) family of models, launched on November 30, 2022 by OpenAI (OpenAI, 2022; Hao, 2022; Zhai, 2022; Jin and Kruppa, 2023; Kumar, 2023), is an advanced language model that uses deep learning techniques to generate human-like responses to natural language inputs. It is currently one of the largest publicly available language models (Dave et al., 2023). ChatGPT is an interactive system that uses deep learning techniques to produce human-like responses to natural language inputs (Radford et al., 2018; Stahl and Eke, 2024). ChatGPT produces answers to questions as people do and uses combinations that give answers as if they were experts on that topic. Technically, ChatGPT is based on OpenAI's Generative Pre-trained Transformer (GPT) language models (specifically GPT-3 and GPT-4), a large-scale neural network-based language generation model trained on a wide range of internet-based texts (Stahl and Eke, 2024). It was trained using reinforcement learning from human feedback (Stahl and Eke, 2024). We refer to ChatGPT as a "technology" as defined by the Encyclopaedia Britannica (2023) as "the application of scientific knowledge to the practical purposes of human life" (Stahl and Eke, 2024). Artificial intelligence (AI), which is considered a multidisciplinary approach to computer science and linguistics (Yağar, 2023, p. 1228; Tanyildizi and Yildiz, 2024), has achieved positive results in tasks such as comprehension, response, coding, summarization, and inference (Zhang and Li, 2021; Tanyildizi and Yildiz, 2024). According to Pasca and Arcese (2023), chatGPT is a tool that can produce narratives, generate computer code, automatically complete images, translate between languages, and perform calculations. It also uses existing language models in web pages, books, articles, and social media conversations (Uc¬Cetina et al., 2022; Tanyildizi and Yildiz, 2024).

ChatGPT is on the verge of being adopted worldwide as the latest technology in development. This situation is a result of the widespread use of technology, particularly software development (Metz, 2022; Reed, 2022; Tanyildizi and Yildiz, 2024). However, these developments also give rise to various debates. There are concerns that artificial intelligence will change the roles that humans have traditionally had to play by doing the work that humans do (Else, 2023; Stokel¬Walker, 2023; Tanyildizi and Yildiz, 2024). According to OpenAI, the organization that developed it, the dialogue format used by ChatGPT allows it to answer follow-up questions, admit errors, question incorrect premises, and reject inappropriate requests (OpenAI, 2022; Stahl and Eke, 2024). Unlike search engines, ChatGPT does not search the web for information about current events and its knowledge is limited to things learned before 2021 (Pasca and Arcese, 2023). The artificial intelligence behind these difficulties provides both positive and negative feedback by answering many problems in actions such as text creation, writing, and speaking.

ChatGPT is thus one of the most transformative AI tools and is undergoing increasing development. It also presents challenges and opportunities for institutions and organizations, societies, and individuals (Dwivedi, et al. 2023).

According to Zhai (2022), chatGPT is expected to impact all aspects of society. However, the potential impacts of this NLP tool on scientific writing remain unknown. Such an impact may be enormous because ChatGPT's capability may lead to changes in educational learning objectives, learning activities, and assessment practices.

METHODOLOGY

In keeping with the exploratory nature of this study, we follow a qualitative approach (Creswell and Creswell, 2018) through in-depth interviews with 15 individuals to explore their perceptions regarding the increasing diffusion and use of ChatGPT. Interviews were conducted with researchers from different specialties to investigate their perceptions of this AI tool, study its impact on the scientific writing process, and examine researchers' expectations regarding the future use of these AI tools. Previous literature has considered this collection method as suitable for conducting exploratory research. Indeed, interviews offer the researcher the opportunity to obtain a wide range of ideas and impressions regarding the topic by understanding individuals' perceptions and attitudes toward a phenomenon (Krueger and Casey, 2000). In addition, interviews offer participants the freedom and flexibility to communicate their ideas and beliefs in their own words and use storytelling to converse in a relaxed manner (Creswell and Creswell, 2018). The qualitative approach is appropriate for exploring a new phenomenon and providing useful information for theory development and future research. With this methodology, it is possible to study individual beliefs, thoughts and experiences about the use of AI, especially ChatGPT (Bluhm et al., 2011). Qualitative methods explore how individuals interpret a specific problem (McCusker and Gunaydin, 2015). For this reason, the inductive approach guided the qualitative method (Eisenhardt, 1989; Venkatesh et al., 2016; Saldaña, 2021).

Based on the research objective, this study chose the following two criteria: (1) being a researcher, (2) being a user of ChatGPT.

The interview path is presented in Appendix 1. The first theme analyzed is the concept of AI, especially the ChatGPT tool, which represents the starting point of the investigation in order to highlight the advantages and disadvantages of this tool. Subsequently, respondents were presented with practical applications of AI in different contexts to analyze their opinions. After this general discussion about AI, the interviewers began the core of the survey, which consists of investigating the perceptions of the use of ChatGPT in scientific writing. For this theme, respondents were asked to identify the advantages and disadvantages, to evaluate the quality of the service provided and, in particular, to explore how ChatGPT can contribute to improving scientific writing. Finally, the interviews ended by asking respondents in which sector ChatGPT can be more useful and how it can help them if it can improve the quality of its service offered. The link between this tool and the education sector was analyzed in detail. The interviews were conducted in August 2024 and the participants were selected using a snowball approach (Guido, 1999; Lucia-Palacios et al., 2016). The final sample consisted of 40% males and 60% females aged 28–63 years. In line with data saturation principles for grounded theory interview research (Francis et al., 2010), data collection continued for 15 interviews until data saturation was reached. Consistent with this approach, additional data collection is based on the non-emergence of new themes and the researcher's sense of what they are hearing (Saunders et al., 2018). Marshall et al. (2013) recommend a range of 15–30 for qualitative interviews. The interviews were recorded and transcribed, and then two researchers performed a text analysis and coding activity using a text analysis software "QDA-miner" to eliminate bias and subjective interpretations (Barrattet et al., 2011; Di Pietro et al., 2018). Similar concepts were coded and grouped into categories, and key themes were identified.

Qualitative data analysis was conducted using QDA Miner software. This tool supports a range of qualitative research methodologies and is particularly effective for coding, annotating, retrieving, and analyzing collections of documents and images (Lewis and Maas, 2007; Beltran et al., 2024). The software has been used successfully by other researchers to systematically review government documents, facilitating the extraction of relevant topics (Arts, 2012; Saheb and Saheb, 2023; Beltran et al., 2024).

RESULTS

Researchers find themselves at a crossroads between the opportunities and challenges of ChatGPT. The following Figure 1 illustrates well the advantages and disadvantages following the use of this AI tool by researchers. Indeed, the theme of reformulation and the theme of guarantee are strongly linked (see Figure 1). This can be explained by the fact that ChatGPT helps researchers with reformulation but researchers are aware that care must be taken when using it. As shown in Figure 1, ChatGPT generates ideas and summarizes information quickly but it is unreliable and may increase plagiarism. It seems that ChatGPT generates errors and misinformation despite producing a language that resembles human writing. It has been admitted that ChatGPT automates the tasks of a researcher like the analysis of a large mass of data but it always remains superficial, it cannot reach the scientific criticism carried out by a researcher. Therefore, the intervention of the researcher always remains essential. Thus, as admitted by the interviewees, ChatGPT cannot ignore the role of the researcher: "writing a scientific article requires in-depth reflection, critical analyses, and precise structuring that only a researcher can really provide" (interviewee 1, male, 28 years old, doctoral student). "Synthesize your own readings" (interviewee 4, woman, 63 years old, retired teacher). "The researcher must remain in control of his work and his research project" (interviewee 5, man, 37 years old, teacher).

Figure 1. Benefits and disadvantages of using ChatGPT in scientific writing

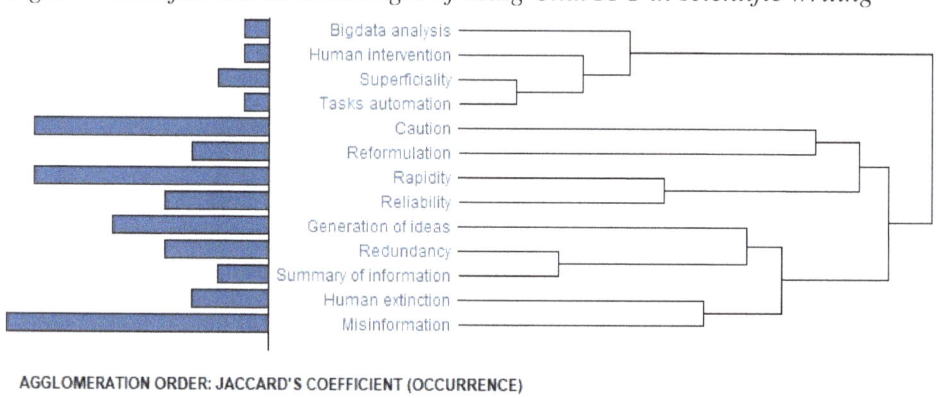

The identified themes are described, interpreted, and illustrated with examples of verbatim quotes below.

1. Usefulness. This theme emerged from participants' reflections on the usefulness of ChatGPT in helping researchers in writing, structuring their thoughts, and facilitating tasks. This usefulness lies mainly in helping with reformulation. Some participants stated: "to write and rephrase sentences," "help with reformulation." Also, interviewees suggested that ChatGPT provides a synthesized overview of a large amount of information. As interviewee #1 commented: "to summarize information," "I think ChatGPT would be useful for summaries." In her results, McInnis-Dominguez (2023) found that 4 out of 21 students found the AI tool useful for generating ideas. Moreover, it has been confirmed that ChatGPT can quickly identify relevant studies, summarize key findings, and even discover links across fields (Abbasi et al., 2016; Namous and Bouigha, 2024).

Figure 2. Sub-themes of ChatGPT utility

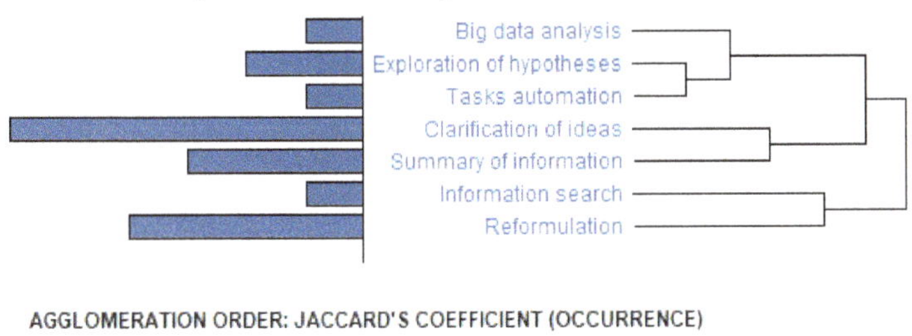

2. Speed. Speed is an important factor in the use of ChatGPT. The word speed was stated in 80% of the cases in the corpus. Previous researchers (i.e., Lee and Lee, 2020; Jmour, 2020) have demonstrated that all these technologies have significantly enabled agility, adaptability, and flexibility. According to Abbes and Hallem (2016), speed reflects the ability of the technology to limit the time and effort provided by the consumer. Also, it provides a sense of physical and psychological comfort. This was clearly stated in the interviewees' comments: "ChatGPT can be very useful, especially to speed up the search for information or to generate ideas quickly." "The main advantage is saving time... helps to explore hypotheses quickly." "to speed up the search." Therefore, as shown by Karan and Bakina (2024), ChatGPT provides rapid answers.
3. Reliability. The majority of respondents postulated the unreliability of ChatGPT. They reported that this type of chatbot is not yet reliable enough to produce comprehensive scientific content. This is illustrated in the following statements:

"the unreliability of the information", "lack of reliable references". In addition, they compared this AI tool with the traditional writing method: "Traditional methods remain more reliable" "currently it is not a 100% reliable source". According to a study conducted by McInnis-Dominguez (2023), 2 out of 21 students expressed concerns about its reliability and accuracy, which dissuaded them from using it. The results of Garg et al. (2024) suggested that AI models such as ChatGPT and Bard are not yet reliable for academic writing tasks. It seems too early to depend on AI for such tasks.

4. Human intervention. For many respondents, the emergence of different AI tools cannot ignore human intervention. It is just a writing aid, or even a starting point. McInnis-Dominguez (2023), students chose to use it as a starting point for generating ideas, which could be further developed and validated by traditional academic methods. McCook (2017) and Brunetti et al. (2022) mentioned that digital tools can only generate a first draft that needs to be revised by the researcher: "But there will always have to be a balance between the use of AI and human intervention." According to Al-harbi and Al-shargabi (2023), ChatGPT fails to reach the level of accuracy of human-generated information. According to Namous and Bouigha (2024), it is essential to maintain a balance, using AI as a tool to augment human expertise and not replace it.
5. Human extinction. Although not all participants expressed human extinction, most of them seemed to share the belief that ChatGPT can destroy human effort: "among the disadvantages of ChatGPT is to write in place of the author." According to Namous and Bouigha (2024), ChatGPT can produce language that resembles human writing. Similarly, McInnis-Dominguez (2023) posited that ChatGPT provides information while offering the temptation to simply copy and use it as if it were expressing personally generated ideas.
6. Interaction with ChatGPT. Interviews suggest that interaction improves research results on ChatGPT: "Interaction improves my research results." According to Al-harbi and Al-shargabi (2023), the results of the responses change depending on the context of the conversation.
7. Learning. Some respondents report that they use ChatGPT to get ideas on a topic: "to clarify ideas." "it is a source of inspiration," "I think the integration of ChatGPT has improved my learning experience." These results are consistent with previous studies (i.e., McInnis-Dominguez, 2023) confirming that ChatGPT could encourage them to explore new avenues for their topics. According to Dai et al. (2023), ChatGPT is an important lever to improve the learning experience. These responses support the argument of Kshetri (2023a,b) and Karan and Bakina (2024) on the use of ChatGPT as a data source.

8. Caution. According to Karan and Bakina (2024) 38.3% of people do not trust the content of ChatGPT. Consistent with Karan and Bakina (2024), the majority of interviewees confirmed the use of ChatGPT during their scientific writing but with great caution: "with verification", "but with caution, because it lacks exact references and verifiable results", "get help from AI by being careful about the results obtained".
9. Misinformation. Although the participants considered that the use of ChatGPT for scientific writing is useful, they also found it problematic to identify credible information. They were fully aware that this AI tool sometimes provided poor quality and inaccurate information. As mentioned by Peres et al., (2023) and Pasca and Arcese (2023), the accuracy of the information generated by ChatGPT has been identified as a significant risk. Given the importance of this tool, it has shown its tendency to share information without verifying the relevance of the information or the credibility of the resource. Alternatively, some of the information comes from sources that are not always reliable, such as forums, personal blogs or non-academic content that often contains errors. As interviewee #4 commented: "presenting an erroneous synthesis of existing references". This consideration is consistent with recent research (i.e., Namous and Bouigha, 2024) that suggests that ChatGPT can lead to biased results that distort the underlying phenomenon. Furthermore, Karan and Bakina (2024) indicated that the generated content is problematic due to many errors. Thus, chatbots should not be considered as authors due to their inability to provide accurate information (Al-harbi and Al-shargabi, 2023). This is evident in the following two statements for example: "ChatGPT can generate errors or biased content", "sometimes incorrect results". In addition, the interviewees postulated that ChatGPT can even provide false references.
10. Content Redundancy/Similarity. The interviewees announced that AI generally generates very similar content for all users. As a result, they feared that scientific writings could quickly fall into similarity, which would degrade the diversity of the scientific landscape. "I have the impression that the use of ChatGPT has encouraged plagiarism or academic dishonesty". This is in line with the statements of Namous and Bouigha (2024) stating that ChatGPT could lead to the creation of content identical to previously published material.
11. Superficial/no criticism. The interviews showed that ChatGPT is superficial and lacks criticism. This tool is content to gather a large amount of information: "you have to synthesize your readings yourself". This result diverges from the results of McInnis-Dominguez (2023) who found that students consider ChatGPT as a springboard for critical thinking.

12. Comparison with traditional writing. We noted that respondents are still attached to traditional writing methods: "Traditional methods are essential for in-depth analysis, but AI can make some tasks much faster". Interviewees insisted on the balance between the two methods: "the two are complementary", "AI can be a powerful complement".

CONCLUSION AND RECOMMENDATIONS

This exploratory study was the first to reveal, in a scientific writing context, the advantages and disadvantages of using ChatGPT following an empirical study. Thus, it fills the gap in the use of ChatGPT in a scientific writing context. It provides an answer to the mixed opinions regarding the use of this AI tool. The results of the study showed that the use of ChatGPT will be very beneficial to provide better learning while paying attention to misinformation for a better use of this technology.

First of all, as has been admitted by the majority of researchers (i.e., Dai et al., 2023), our study shows that ChatGPT advances knowledge. According to Pasca and Arcese (2023), ChatGPT allows learning about new topics. Moreover, many researchers use this tool in particular for reformulation, they consider them as a starting point for research. In addition, researchers can use ChatGPT to help them synthesize large documents and save time or reformulate complex passages. Pasca and Arcese (2023) confirmed the speed of writing texts using this AI tool. However, this tool can give false information. For this reason, it would be used with caution as mentioned by Karan and Bakina (2024). Which can negatively affect their emotions.

The rapid evolution of writing needs has sparked a growing interest from research professors in adopting emerging technologies, such as ChatGPT. This study provides useful implications for research professors, seeking to exploit the potential of this AI tool to improve their scientific writing.

First, as academic researchers, it is imperative to use ChatGPT with a critical eye, understanding that while this tool offers unique opportunities, its integration into the writing of scientific papers requires careful and methodical reflection. The study highlighted that scientific researchers are not ready to rely entirely on this new AI tool because they are looking for human interaction, more reliability and more accuracy. According to Morgan (2023), ChatGPT should not be considered as a substitute for human expertise, effort in the writing process and critical thinking.

Secondly, as found by Pasca and Arcese (2023), all respondents agree that the use of AI tools will not replace the work done by humans. It therefore appears that AI can be a supporting tool rather than a substitute (Pasca and Arcese, 2023).

Regarding the second objective of this research such as, examining the expectations of researchers regarding the future improvement of ChatGPT performance, this study highlights a common opinion regarding the positive development of these tools, as researchers have expressed expectations particularly regarding the improvement of the features and functionalities of this AI tool.

In conclusion, in line with the findings of Brunetti et al. (2022) and Al-harbi and Al-shargabi (2023), ChatGPT cannot be considered scientific or suitable for academic research. It still requires some improvements as stated by McInnis-Dominguez (2023).

Our findings also have important implications for marketing publication. Combining researchers' human skill with technology will make the most of scientific learning. By using this AI tool, researchers can bring innovative ideas and thus improve scientific research worldwide.

As a future avenue of research, the study used a qualitative approach to support the theory and serve as a starting point for further research. Future studies should therefore continue the investigation by implementing quantitative techniques to test the consumer behavior model.

REFERENCES

Abbes, I., & Hallem, Y. (2016). Co-création et technologie mobile au sein d'un espace marchand: quelles valeurs pour le consommateur? une application dans le secteur de la restauration. *Revue Française du Marketing*, (256).

Adeshola, I., & Adepoju, A. P. (2023). The opportunities and challenges of ChatGPT in education. *Interactive Learning Environments*, 1–14. DOI: 10.1080/10494820.2023.2253858

Al-harbi, N. K., & Al-shargabi, A. A. (2023). An Exploratory Analysis of using Chatbots in Academia. *International Journal of Advanced Computer Science and Applications*, *14*(12).

Beltran, M. A., Ruiz Mondragon, M. I., & Han, S. H. (2024, June). Comparative analysis of generative ai risks in the public sector. In *Proceedings of the 25th Annual International Conference on Digital Government Research* (pp. 610-617).

Bluhm, D. J., Harman, W., Lee, T. W., & Mitchell, T. R. (2011). Qualitative research in management: A decade of progress. *Journal of Management Studies*, *48*(8), 1866–1891.

Brunetti, F., Bonfanti, A., Chiarini, A., & Vannucci, V. (2023). Digitalization and academic research: Knowing of and using digital services and software to develop scientific papers. *The TQM Journal*, *35*(5), 1135–1155.

Dai, W., Lin, J., Jin, H., Li, T., Tsai, Y. S., Gašević, D., & Chen, G. (2023). Can large language models provide feedback to students? A case study on ChatGPT. *IEEE International Conference on Advanced Learning Technologies (ICALT)* (pp. 323-325).

Dave, T., Athaluri, S. A., & Singh, S. (2023). ChatGPT in medicine: An overview of its applications, advantages, limitations, future prospects, and ethical considerations. *Frontiers in Artificial Intelligence*, *6*, 1169595. PMID: 37215063

Davis, F. D. (1989). Perceived usefulness, perceived ease of use, and user acceptance of information technology. *Management Information Systems Quarterly*, 319–340.

Dergaa, I., Chamari, K., Zmijewski, P., & Saad, H. B. (2023). From human writing to artificial intelligence generated text: Examining the prospects and potential threats of ChatGPT in academic writing. *Biology of Sport*, *40*(2), 615. PMID: 37077800

Dwivedi, Y. K., Kshetri, N., Hughes, L., Slade, E. L., Jeyaraj, A., Kar, A. K., ... & Wright, R. (2023). Opinion Paper:"So what if ChatGPT wrote it?" Multidisciplinary perspectives on opportunities, challenges and implications of generative conversational AI for research, practice and policy.

Eisenhardt, K. M. (1989). Building theories from case study research. *Academy of Management Review*, *14*(4), 532–550.

Else, H. (2023). "Abstracts Written by Chatgpt Fool Scientists", 423-423 Nature, 613 (7944). https://doi.org/.DOI: 10.1038/d41586-023-00056-7

Francis, J. J., Johnston, M., Robertson, C., Glidewell, L., Entwistle, V., Eccles, M. P., & Grimshaw, J. M. (2010). What is an adequate sample size? Operationalising data saturation for theory-based interview studies. *Psychology & Health*, *25*(10), 1229–1245. PMID: 20204937

Garg, S., Ahmad, A., & Madsen, D. Ø. (2024). Academic writing in the age of AI: Comparing the reliability of ChatGPT and Bard with Scopus and Web of Science. *Journal of Innovation & Knowledge*, *9*(4), 100563.

Herwanto, W. H., Setiawan, S., & Munir, A. (2024). What Lies Beneath English Major Students' Attitudes towards ChatGPT for Academic Writing: A TAM Perspective? *Equilibrium: Jurnal Pendidikan*, *12*(2), 152–159.

Jin, B., & Kruppa, M. (2023). Cheating with ChatGPT: can an AI chatbot pass AP lit? *The Wall Street Journal.*

Jin, M. K. B., & Kruppa, M. (2023). ChatGPT creator is talking to investors about selling shares at $29 billion valuation. *The Wall Street Journal.*

Jmour, A. (2020). «Man-machine» interaction: the determinants of the untact service's use. In *Digital Economy. Emerging Technologies and Business Innovation: 5th International Conference on Digital Economy, ICDEc 2020, Bucharest, Romania, June 11–13* [Springer International Publishing.]. *Proceedings*, *5*, 105–114.

Karan, K., & Bakina, W. (2024). Generative artificial intelligence (ai) in education: A cross-national survey on university teachers'perceptions on the use of chatgpt.

Krueger, R. A., & Casey, M. A. (2000). *Focus Groups: A Practical Guide for Applied Research* (3rd ed.). Sage Publications.

Kshetri, N. (2023a). Regulatory technology and supervisory technology: Current status, facilitators and barriers. *IEEE Computer*, *56*(1), 64–75.

Kshetri, N. (2023b). (forthcoming). ChatGPT in developing economies. *IEEE IT Professional*, *25*(2).

Kumar, A. H. (2023). Analysis of ChatGPT tool to assess the potential of its utility for academic writing in biomedical domain. *Biology, Engineering. Medicine and Science Reports*, *9*(1), 24–30.

Lee, S. M., & Lee, D. (2020). "Untact": A new customer service strategy in the digital age. *Service Business*, *14*(1), 1–22.

Levitt, H. M., Bamberg, M., Creswell, J. W., Frost, D. M., Josselson, R., & Suárez-Orozco, C. (2018). Journal article reporting standards for qualitative primary, qualitative meta-analytic, and mixed methods research in psychology: The APA Publications and Communications Board task force report. *The American Psychologist*, *73*(1), 26. PMID: 29345485

Lewis, R. B., & Maas, S. M. (2007). QDA Miner 2.0: Mixed-model qualitative data analysis software. *Field Methods*, *19*(1), 87–108.

Lucia-Palacios, L., Pérez-López, R., & Polo-Redondo, Y. (2016). Cognitive, affective and behavioural responses in mall experience: A qualitative approach. *International Journal of Retail & Distribution Management*, *44*(1), 4–21.

Marshall, B., Cardon, P., Poddar, A., & Fontenot, R. (2013). Does sample size matter in qualitative research?: A review of qualitative interviews in IS research. *Journal of Computer Information Systems*, *54*(1), 11–22.

McCook, A. (2017). *Newly released AI software writes papers for you—What could go wrong*. Retraction Watch.

McCusker, K., & Gunaydin, S. (2015). Research using qualitative, quantitative or mixed methods and choice based on the research. *Perfusion*, *30*(7), 537–542. PMID: 25378417

McInnis-Domínguez, M. (2023). An AI Solution: Using ChatGPT to Counter Plagiarism and Boost Enrollments in Hispanic Literature Courses. *Middle Atlantic Review of Latin American Studies, 7*(2).

Metz, A. (2022). "6 Exciting Ways to Use Chatgpt – From Coding to Poetry". TechRadar. htt ps://www.techradar.com/features/6- exciting- ways- to- use- chatgpt -from-coding-to -poetry.

Mondal, H., & Mondal, S. (2023). ChatGPT in academic writing: Maximizing its benefits and minimizing the risks. *Indian Journal of Ophthalmology*, *71*(12), 3600–3606. PMID: 37991290

Morgan, D. L. (2023). Exploring the use of artificial intelligence for qualitative data analysis: The case of ChatGPT. *International Journal of Qualitative Methods*, *22*, 1–10. DOI: 10.1177/16094069231211248

Namous, A., & Bouigha, K. (2024). *Teachers' and Students' Perception about the Effects of Using ChatGPT, Grammarly, and Quillbot on Students' Writing Skills* (Doctoral dissertation, university center of abdalhafid boussouf-MILA).

Pasca, M. G., & Arcese, G. (2023). ChatGPT between opportunities and challenges: an empirical study in Italy. *The TQM Journal*, (ahead-of-print).

Saldaña, J. (2021). Coding techniques for quantitative and mixed data. *The Routledge reviewer's guide to mixed methods analysis*, pp.151-160.

Sallam, M. (2023). The utility of ChatGPT as an example of large language models in healthcare education, research and practice: Systematic review on the future perspectives and potential limitations. *MedRxiv*.

Saunders, B., Sim, J., Kingstone, T., Baker, S., Waterfield, J., Bartlam, B., & Jinks, C. (2018). Saturation in qualitative research: Exploring its conceptualization and operationalization. *Quality & Quantity*, *52*, 1893–1907. PMID: 29937585

Stahl, B. C., & Eke, D. (2024). The ethics of ChatGPT–Exploring the ethical issues of an emerging technology. *International Journal of Information Management*, *74*, 102700.

Tanyildizi, N. I., & Yıldız, I. (2024). The Use of Artificial Intelligence in Health Communication: A Research on ChatGPT. In *Machine Learning and Generative AI in Smart Healthcare* (pp. 117–138). IGI Global.

Thorp, H. H. (2023). ChatGPT is fun, but not an author. *Science*, *379*(6630), 313–313. PMID: 36701446

Tlili, A., Shehata, B., Adarkwah, M. A., Bozkurt, A., Hickey, D. T., Huang, R., & Agyemang, B. (2023). What if the devil is my guardian angel: ChatGPT as a case study of using chatbots in education. *Smart Learning Environments*, *10*(1), 15. DOI: 10.1186/s40561-023-00237-x

Van Dis, E. A. M., Bollen, J., Zuidema, W., van Rooij, R., & Bockting, C. L. (2023). ChatGPT: Five priorities for research. *Nature*, *614*(7947), 224–226. PMID: 36737653

Venkatesh, V., Brown, S. A., & Sullivan, Y. W. (2016). Guidelines for conducting mixed-methods research: An extension and illustration. *Journal of the Association for Information Systems*, *17*(7), 2.

Zhai, X. (2022). ChatGPT user experience: Implications for education. *Available at SSRN* 4312418.

Zhai, X., Chu, X., Chai, C. S., Jong, M. S. Y., Istenic, A., Spector, M., Liu, J.-B., Yuan, J., & Li, Y. (2021). A Review of Artificial Intelligence (AI) in Education from 2010 to 2020. *Complexity*, 1–18.

Zhang, M., & Li, J. (2021). A commentary of GPT-3 in MIT Technology Review 2021. *Fundamental Research (Beijing)*, *1*(6), 831–833. DOI: 10.1016/j.fmre.2021.11.011

Chapter 12
Lost in Automation:
How Generative AI Puts Communication Students' Skills at Risk

Ioana Iancu
https://orcid.org/0000-0001-8374-853X
Babe -Bolyai University, Romania

ABSTRACT

The integration of generative AI into creative fields is transforming education and professional environments. However, this shift raises concerns about the potential loss or dilution of human skills in favor of faster AI-driven solutions. This study explores how communication students specializing in advertising and public relations perceive and use generative AI in their higher education context, as well as the skills they believe are at risk due to AI integration. Based on semi-structured interviews, the findings reveal that while AI enhances soft skills like creativity and critical thinking, these abilities are paradoxically at risk of diminishing in importance. Among hard skills, writing and content creation are heavily impacted, with AI improving but simultaneously devaluing their relevance. Respondents emphasize the need for ethical AI use, highlighting the importance of transparency and guidance. They call on educators to address these challenges, promoting responsible and balanced use of AI in academia.

DOI: 10.4018/979-8-3373-6018-8.ch012

Copyright © 2026, IGI Global Scientific Publishing. Copying or distributing in print or electronic forms without written permission of IGI Global Scientific Publishing is prohibited.

INTRODUCTION

The current state of Artificial Intelligence (AI) represents a disruptive moment in history, fundamentally reshaping industries, revolutionizing how people approach problem-solving, and challenging traditional ways of thinking about technology and human potential especially in knowledge domains, such as creative work or education (Woodruff et al., 2024). AI is defined as computer systems that mimic human intelligence and capabilities, as image recognition, speech recognition, and decision-making (Dornis, 2020; Townsend & Hunt, 2019). The development of AI focuses on closely replicating the functions of the human brain (Woinaroschy, 2020). Generative AI, a highly promising unsupervised machine learning (Fui-Hoon Nah et al., 2023), is trained on extensive datasets of text, images, audio, and video, allowing it to become progressively more adept at generating new content in response to specific input or prompts (Orchard & Tasiemski, 2023). Generative AI leverages natural language processing and advanced statistical models, trained on vast datasets, to identify patterns and generate novel content in response to given inputs, called prompts (Orchard & Tasiemski, 2023).

The release of generative AI, as ChatGPT, has elicited both excitement and apprehension in the field of education. While some see it as a chance to innovate teaching and learning methods, others are concerned about its potential impact on traditional essay-based assessments. While AI can enhance co-creation, it also raises concerns about reducing human agency in the creative process. McMurtrie (2022) suggests that tools like ChatGPT may become as essential to writing as calculators and computers are to math and science. However, worries persist that students might exploit ChatGPT to generate assignments quickly, bypassing plagiarism detection systems, and compromising academic integrity, authenticity, copyright, or ethical considerations (Cotton et al., 2023; Fui-Hoon Nah et al., 2023; Gragnaniello et al., 2022; Murray, 2023; Ooi et al., 2023; Pavlik, 2023; Rudolph et al., 2023; Zhuo et al., 2023).

The widespread integration of AI into creative fields, both in educational settings and professional environments, is inevitable (Hong et al., 2020). A growing range of content, including advertisements, short videos, and narratives, is being generated by AI algorithms customized to users' preferences (Fui-Hoon Nah et al., 2023). AI is transforming creative industries by facilitating content creation, generating text and video content, and revolutionizing art (Fui-Hoon Nah et al., 2023; Wong et al., 2022). Generative AI tools (e.g., ChatGPT, Jasper, DALL-E, Imagen, Midjourney etc.) can now handle tasks like copywriting or content creation, visual content creation or design, video and audio content creation, campaign optimization and strategy development, social media management and monitoring, idea generation, or data analysis and audience insights highlighting.

Since these tools become more widely used, there is the risk that certain human skills (e.g., idea conceptualization, crafting narratives, visual design, brainstorming etc.) can be lost or diluted in favor of quicker AI-driven solutions. Consequently, alongside the disruption of creative industries, concerns about the need for reskilling have come to the forefront (Dwivedi et al., 2023). Therefore, understanding how AI impacts human skills (Giordano et al., 2024) and examining which skills may be lost is crucial to comprehending the evolution of creative industries, including communication education and the broader industry.

This paper aims to explore how students in communication domain perceive and use generative AI in their educational environment and creative requirements and which skills they believe are already, or will potentially be, diminished or lost because of AI integration in their field of expertise. With generative AI still in a relatively nascent stage but rapidly growing in capability, this is a critical moment to investigate this topic.

A series of semi-structured interviews are conducted with communication students specializing in advertising and/or public relations. Thus, the study assesses only perceptions and attitudes of how AI negatively impacts their skills, rather than measuring the actual competencies affected by AI. The interview guide includes questions exploring the understanding and use of generative AI, its acceptance, and its perceived impact on skills, particularly in academic contexts. Topics such as appropriate use of AI, guilt, or ethical considerations are also addressed. The collected data are analyzed using Atlas.ti software, applying thematic content analysis for interpretation.

Despite the growing concern over how AI is perceived and its impact on professional fields, driven by the recent surge in public awareness of generative AI, there remains limited research on the subject, with few domain-specific studies available (Woodruff et al., 2024). Furthermore, most existing studies on students' perceptions of AI tend to focus on general attitudes toward this technology, emotional responses to using a new and challenging tool, or the dynamics between teachers and students within the educational process.

Therefore, to the best of our knowledge, this research represents one of the first attempts to specifically examine communication students' perceptions of AI, with a particular focus on the potential loss of skills in their creative work while meeting the demands of academic coursework. Typically, the assignments given to students in the field of communication within an academic setting focus on areas such as research and analysis, strategic and campaign development, content creation and copywriting, media planning, graphic design, as well as event planning (Anderson, 2019). Therefore, the key competencies associated with these tasks include critical, strategic, and creative thinking, data analysis, writing, design, editing, public speaking, and organizational abilities (Bernhard & Russmann, 2023; Lowry & Xie, 2008; Meganck et al., 2020).

The relevance of this study is three-fold. First, the study is a timely exploration of a rapidly evolving creative field. Since communication, advertising, and public relations are fast-developing domains, the way emerging adults studying in these disciplines perceive technology provides valuable insights on the way AI will shape the industry's future. Second, having AI taking over tasks traditionally done by humans, understanding which skills students believe are being lost, diminished, or transformed is critical for educational institutions. Thus, the development of curriculum can be adapted and can strengthen skills that AI cannot replicate (e.g., critical thinking, creativity, ethical judgement etc.). Finally, the findings can help educators and employers understand how well-prepared students feel for a job market that integrates AI. This knowledge could guide strategies for teaching new skills, adjusting training programs, and preparing students for evolving job roles in these domains.

Strongly related to the relevance, the novelty of the study lies mainly in highlighting the downsides of generative AI. Most research on AI emphasizes the advantages it brings, such as automation and efficiency. However, this paper innovatively addresses a potential downside, namely skill diminish or loss. It investigates which abilities students learning in a creative domain believe may become obsolete or underdeveloped due to AI, a less explored area that can have significant implications for the future of education and professional training. In addition, while much research has focused on professionals' use of AI in the workplace, there is limited research on how students, emerging adults found in the formative stages of their careers, perceive AI in their educational settings. This paper uniquely captures the views of future industry leaders and provides insights into how they are adapting to AI integration early in their professions.

Essential Skills In The Communication Field

With the rapid advancement of generative AI across various domains, it is crucial to examine its impact on the communication field, as advertising and public relations. In this context, the development of students' skills shaped by AI must be explored, emphasizing their relevance to future professional growth and the inevitable integration of AI into educational environments (Luttrell et al., 2020). Educational institutions must adapt to the evolving advertising and public relations labor market shaped by the AI era (Kovacs & Zarandne, 2022), recognizing and addressing the skills students develop as a result of AI's influence. AI also has the potential to significantly enhance student learning (Luttrell et al., 2020). However, it is equally important for students to develop a sense of responsibility and critically engage with the ethical issues associated with AI (Galloway & Swiatek, 2018; Luttrell & Ward, 2018).

Literature underscores the importance of both hard and soft skills in the communication field. Hard skills refer to measurable abilities, such as digital, language, and profession-specific expertise, while soft skills pertain to personality traits, social attitudes, and behaviors, including communication, integrity, professionalism, work ethics, responsibility, and teamwork (Cimatti, 2016; Fazekas, 2020; Robles, 2012). Both hard skills, like writing, and soft abilities, like time management, collaboration, or creativity, are essential (Brunner et al., 2018; DiStaso et al., 2009). However, a content analysis of 5,548 digital marketing job advertisements highlights the growing emphasis on soft skills in recent decades (Kovacs & Zarandne, 2022). Employers increasingly prefer well-rounded candidates with proficiency in English, communication, presentation, internet marketing, software knowledge, teamwork, and attention to detail.

Specific studies have further detailed these skill requirements. Meganck et al. (2020), analyzing 1,000 job advertisements for entry-level public relations roles, identified key attributes in demand, including communication skills (writing, verbal communication, editing, and interpersonal abilities), creative thinking, graphic design proficiency, media relations expertise, organizational capabilities, research skills, and strategic thinking. Similarly, Doyle (2019) emphasizes technical offline and online expertise, communication, written presentation, time management, and creative problem-solving as essential for marketing roles. Expanding on this, Rios et al. (2020), in an analysis of 120,000 job advertisements, highlight content and textual analysis, critical thinking, and problem-solving as additional critical skills.

Research on professional development in communication fields further corroborates these findings. Krishna et al. (2020) identified writing and creativity as critical skills for public relations practitioners at all professional levels. Research and measurement skills were particularly valued among early-career professionals. However, contrary to the focus on teamwork and leadership in academic soft skill training, employers prioritize independent work and the ability to produce high-quality results under pressure and tight deadlines (Bee & Hie, 2015).

Studies focusing on advertising also highlight the importance of information literacy and soft skills. Gilbert (2017), through a content analysis of job requirements in advertising agencies, found that evaluation (e.g., data management), collaboration, information use (e.g., creating reports and marketing plans), and technology proficiency are vital for early-career roles. Windels et al. (2013), in a quasi-ethnographic study of six advertising agencies, identified critical thinking, persuasion, interpersonal communication, and presentation as the most essential soft skills for success in advertising.

AI Challenges In Communication Skills For Creative Industries And Education

There is growing interest in examining the impact of generative AI on creative industries and related educational fields as its applications continue to evolve. In creative industries, AI development brings forth both novel working capabilities and new human-computer interaction skills (Chuang & Graham, 2018; Giordano et al., 2024; Van Roy et al., 2018). AI systems have the potential to support users in creative endeavors such as writing, problem-solving, and innovation (Garbuio & Lin, 2021; Haefner et al., 2021; Kim & Kim, 2021). Beyond ChatGPT's text generation capabilities, tools like DALL-E and MidJourney demonstrate the transformative power of AI in creating visual content (Oppenlaender, 2022). These advancements highlight the growing impact of generative AI on creative skills, which were considered irreplaceable by machines just a few years ago (Giordano et al., 2024).

New skills, called prompt engineering, are needed to fully benefit from generative AI outcomes (Orchard & Tasiemski, 2023). In a comprehensive study analyzing 616,073 tweets about ChatGPT, Giordano et al. (2024) quantitatively examine its impact on human skills by identifying the specific tasks users requested the AI to perform. The results emphasize that the proposed skill set for effectively using ChatGPT includes: defining task goals by setting clear and measurable objectives; mastering prompt language to communicate efficiently with AI models through well-structured and clear requests; understanding the principles of generative AI, including its capabilities and limitations, to set realistic expectations; and measuring performance by evaluating the AI's output against predefined metrics to assess its effectiveness and accuracy (Giordano et al., 2024).

By focusing on a range of different professions, AbuMusab (2023) explores the disruptive influence of generative AI technologies, such as ChatGPT and Midjourney. These AI systems are now capable of performing tasks once believed to be uniquely human, like essay writing and art creation. As a result, a new skill known as "prompt engineering" has emerged, where people design strategic prompts to generate specific outputs from AI models. The article emphasizes the existential threat that AI poses to jobs traditionally viewed as secure, including those of artists, writers, and academics. Likewise, other creative professions, such as media content creation and news curation, have been significantly impacted by the rise of AI (Orchard & Tasiemski, 2023).

Another study involving 758 consultants revealed that generative AI, specifically OpenAI's GPT-4, significantly boosts performance in creative tasks like product innovation but hinders performance in complex problem-solving tasks. Considering the dual nature of generative AI in creating and destroying value within an organization, AI is perceived as restraining creative abilities over time (Candelon et al.,

2023). Likewise, investigating the impact of generative AI on academic researchers, Giray (2024) identifies three main issues. First, generative AI accelerates the content creation process, leading specialists to prioritize quantity over quality. Second, experts may develop overconfidence by engaging with AI-generated content, believing they possess expertise without truly understanding the material. This cognitive bias can hinder learning and growth, as individuals may not seek further education or feedback. Finaly, reliance on generative AI for tasks like brainstorming, outlining, and editing can weaken the ability to develop rigorous skills that can lead to intellectual laziness and a decline in critical thinking and creative abilities (Giray, 2024).

Likewise creative industries, the related educational sector is not immune to AI influence. AI use in higher education is characterized as an intelligent, sophisticated, and personalized tutoring system designed to handle complex tasks, deliver feedback, and engage in human-like interactions (Popenici & Kerr, 2017). AI tools are designed to perform a variety of tasks, including text generation, rewriting, answering questions, summarizing, and brainstorming (Ouyang et al., 2022). In educational settings, these tools can be utilized to draft essays or create storylines, in creating Power Point Presentations, or in collaborative projects (Riapina, 2024; Qadir, 2022). However, AI tools like ChatGPT, which can produce content with minimal input while exhibiting critical thinking abilities, present a potential challenge to the integrity of education (Susnjak, 2022). This raises concerns about the authenticity of student-generated work and its implications for academic honesty, cheating, plagiarism, or misleading information (Fütterer et al., 2023; Rospigliosi, 2023; Susnjak, 2022; Tlili et al., 2023).

In their study on ChatGPT and its implications for higher education assessments and learning, Rudolph et al. (2023) outline the strengths and limitations of this AI tool as identified in the literature. Among its key strengths are its advanced language understanding, human-like conversational abilities, adaptability to domain-specific requirements, speed, cost-efficiency, and well-structured responses. However, ChatGPT also exhibits limitations, such as challenges in comprehending context, specific language nuances, and emotions. Additionally, it faces constraints in knowledge and creativity, as it is reliant on the data used for its training (Rudolph et al., 2023).

Another study examining the potential impact of generative AI, specifically ChatGPT, on business education, drawing from academic and professional perspectives, reveals that this tool fosters pedagogical innovation and enriches experiential learning within the teaching, learning, and assessment processes (Kumar et al., 2024). Literature also shows that ChatGPT enhances personalized learning, provides continuous feedback, supports evaluations, fosters creative thinking, simplifies complex content, and assists with copyediting, translation, and language editing, benefiting students with language challenges (Kumar et al., 2024; Michel-Villarreal et al., 2023). However, concerns about plagiarism and a decline in interpersonal skills have been identified as significant drawbacks (Kumar et al., 2024).

The existing studies on students' perceptions of AI are still limited, yet technology's growing potential is increasingly influencing both their academic experiences and future professional pursuits (Ka Yuk Chan & Tsi, 2024). Obenza et al. (2023), in their survey of students' opinions on ChatGPT's utility and usability, found that students generally hold a positive attitude toward the AI tool, with only limited concerns regarding the associated risks. Similarly, Ka Yuk Chan and Tsi (2024) demonstrate that students generally hold a positive attitude toward the integration of generative AI technologies in the educational process and feel comfortable using them as supportive tools. ală et al. (2024) found that both undergraduate and master's students in business and tourism demonstrated a high level of awareness about generative AI and expressed a growing desire to explore this technology further.

Despite being impressed by AI's potential and recognizing its benefits, students tend to overlook its negative impacts and appear unaware of the associated ethical risks (Chiu, 2024). Chan (2024) focuses on the negative implications of AI in secondary education, particularly examining the concept of "AI guilt." This term refers to the discomfort experienced when using AI tools for tasks traditionally performed by humans, such as homework. Through a qualitative analysis, the study highlights key aspects of AI guilt, including perceived laziness and authenticity, fear of judgment, and concerns related to identity and self-efficacy (Chan, 2024). Similarly, Wang et al. (2022) found that although learning self-efficacy and motivations positively impacted university students' intentions to learn about AI, anxieties related to AI, particularly learning-related anxieties, negatively affected both intrinsic and extrinsic motivation.

METHOD

Sample

The study sample consists of $N = 13$ Romanian students specialized in advertising and/or public relations (Table 1), including four men and nine women. All participants are pursuing a master's degree. The sample was selected using a convenience sampling method. Data collection was concluded once saturation was reached, meaning that no new themes or insights emerged from additional responses, indicating sufficient depth and comprehensiveness of the data (Guest et al., 2020; Hennink & Kaiser, 2022). Given the limited sample in terms of specialization, future research should aim to include a broader range of communication specializations (e.g., media studies, journalism, digital marketing, design etc.) and academic degrees to address the limitation of representativeness.

Table 1. The sample description and the assigned codes

Respondent's code	Age	Sex	Education degree	Year of study	Specialization
R1	23	M	Master	2	Advertising
R2	25	F	Master	2	PR & Advertising
R3	23	F	Master	2	PR & Advertising
R4	29	F	Master	2	Advertising
R5	25	M	Master	2	PR & Advertising
R6	25	F	Master	2	PR & Advertising
R7	22	F	Master	1	PR & Advertising
R8	22	M	Master	1	PR & Advertising
R9	22	F	Master	1	PR & Advertising
R10	22	M	Master	2	Advertising
R11	23	F	Master	2	PR & Advertising
R12	23	F	Master	2	PR & Advertising
R13	24	F	Master	2	Advertising

Procedure

The interviews were conducted between November and December 2024, with data gathered in written format to accommodate the respondents' availability (Hunt & McHale, 2007; Lee & Hollister, 2020). The interviews were conducted in Romanian, and the quotations were later translated into English. Data analysis was performed using Atlas.ti version 23 software. Participants were fully informed about the study's purpose, their right to withdraw at any time, and the measures implemented to maintain the confidentiality of their information. Verbal informed consent was obtained from all participants. One potential limitation of this study is the possibility of researcher bias, as the data collection was conducted through interviews administered by a professor. The power dynamics inherent in this relationship may have influenced students' answers, leading them to provide socially desirable responses due to concerns about judgment or evaluation. Future research could mitigate this limitation by employing anonymous surveys, third-party interviewers, or mixed methods to enhance the authenticity of responses.

Instrument Description

The interview guide comprised fourteen open-ended questions along with sections to gather socio-demographic information. It was developed based on insights from literature and addressed topics such as: the general understanding and use of generative AI and its role in academic projects, the acceptance of AI technology in academic contexts, the perceived impact of generative AI on academic skill development, the appropriateness, feelings of guilt and ethical concerns associated with using generative AI for academic tasks.

To explore the general understanding and use of generative AI and its role in class projects, respondents were initially asked to describe this technology in their own words. They were then prompted to identify the AI tools they commonly use and the purposes for which they use them. Focusing specifically on the academic context, respondents were interviewed about their potential use of generative AI for academic projects or tasks (Ka Yuk Chan & Tsi, 2024; Obenza et al., 2023).

The Technology Acceptance Model (Davis, 1989) was employed to gain a deeper understanding of how generative AI is accepted, particularly in the context of academic tasks. This involved examining the perceived ease of use and perceived usefulness of AI tools. Furthermore, attention was given to respondents' intentions to use generative AI in future education projects and the underlying reasons for their decisions.

A significant emphasis was placed on understanding respondents' perceptions of the impact of generative AI on their skills. They were encouraged to discuss the skills they feel are enhanced using generative AI in academic context. Simultaneously, they were asked to identify which skills they believe might become less essential due to the widespread use of AI, particularly in academic projects and tasks. To adopt a comparative perspective between AI-augmented skills and personal skills, respondents were asked to reflect on whether there were projects where they relied more heavily on AI than on their own abilities. In connection with this, they were invited to elaborate on and provide examples of skills they felt were diminishing because of using AI tools in academic projects. Similarly, respondents were asked to predict which skills communication students might potentially lose in the future as a result of advancements in AI technology. Both soft and hard skills are considered (Brunner et al., 2018; DiStaso et al., 2009; Cimatti, 2016; Fazekas, 2020; Ouyang et al., 2022; Robles, 2012).

Lastly, the study explored feelings related to the appropriate use of AI, as well as associated guilt and ethical concerns. Respondents were asked about their views on the boundaries between appropriate and inappropriate use of AI tools in academic settings. Moreover, communication students were invited to share instances where they experienced guilt while using AI tools for academic projects (Chan, 2024).

They were also asked to elaborate on situations where using AI for academic work felt like crossing an ethical boundary, such as issues related to cheating, ownership, or intellectual property (Cotton et al., 2023; Fui-Hoon Nah et al. 2023; Fütterer et al., 2023; Rospigliosi, 2023; Zhuo et al., 2023).

Data Analysis

The data interpretation process includes coding, organizing, and forming thematic categories, supported by key respondent quotes (Dawson, 2007). A hybrid approach is applied in the coding process (Table 2), combining both deductive and inductive methods. Some codes are drawn from existing literature (deductive approach), as emphasized within the Instrument description section above, while others emerge during the analysis, based on the respondents' answers (inductive approach) (Fereday & Muir-Cochrane, 2006).

Table 2. The coding book

Categories	Sub-categories	Codes
Generative AI understanding	Personal associations	
	Computational expertise	Content generation, Data analysis
	Interactive skills	Input dependent, Prompt dependent
	Productivity-optimized skills	Time efficiency
	Limitations of AI	Inaccurate information, Lack of copyright, lack of reasoning
Generative AI use	Tools used	ChatGPT, Perplexity, Grammarly, PhotoshopAI, DALL-E, ChatPDF
	Reasons to use in general	
	Content creation and enhancement	Ideas/content generation, Structuring ideas, Ideas explanation
	Language processing	Rephrase, Summarize, Translate, Correction
	Analytical and informational tasks	Data analysis, Search information
	Editing	Photo editing, Adding emojis on social media posts
	Reasons to use in the academic context	
	Content creation and enhancement	Brainstorming, Combination of ideas, Ideas development, Content generation, Explain concepts

continued on following page

Table 2. Continued

Categories	Sub-categories	Codes
	Language processing	Rephrase, Summarize, Translate, Correction
	Information gathering	Information about new topics, Literature review
	Content structuring	Create the structure of a content,
Generative AI acceptance in the academic context	Ease of use	
	Easy	Prompt dependent, Human creativity dependent, Intuitive
	Hard	For generating images, Complex explanations needed, The need to check the outputs
	Usefulness	
	Content creation and enhancement	Ideas generation, New perspectives, Ideas explanation
	Language processing	Rephrase, Correction, Summarize
	Information gathering	Search for information
	Productivity	Time efficiency
	Intention to use	
	Yes	Idea generation, Ideas structuring, Guidance Rephrase, Correction, Summarize, Double-check Time efficiency
	No	Lack of work ownership, Lack of self-effort, Lack of coherent ideas, Environmentally unfriendly
Generative AI's impact on skills in the academic context	Skills improved by AI	
	Soft skills	
	Critical and creative thinking abilities	Creativity, Critical thinking, Understanding information
	Time management	Time efficiency
	Hard skills	
	Content creation and enhancement	Writing, Content generation, Learning expression
	Analytical and informational skills	Skimming, Data gathering, Organizing information
	Language processing skills	Simplifying language

continued on following page

Table 2. Continued

Categories	Sub-categories	Codes
	Editing skills	Design
	Skills becoming less essential	
	Soft skills	
	Critical and creative thinking abilities	Creativity, Critical thinking
	Hard skills	
	Content creation and enhancement	Writing, Content generation
	Analytical and informational skills	Data analysis, Skimming, Organizing information
	AI skills favored over personal abilities	
	Soft skills	
	Time management	Time efficiency
	Hard skills	
	Content creation and enhancement	Content generation, Ideas improvement
	Analytical and informational skills	Data gathering, Planning
	Language processing skills	Correcting, Rephrasing, Summarizing information
	Skills diminished/lost	
	Soft skills	
	Critical and creative thinking abilities	Creativity, Critical thinking
	Personal and emotional attributes	Patience
	Hard skills	
	Content creation and enhancement	Writing, Ideas development
	Analytical and informational skills	Research, Planning, Organizing information
	Language processing skills	Rephrasing, Summarizing information
	Skills at risk in the future	
	Soft skills	
	Critical and creative thinking abilities	Creativity, Critical thinking, Reasoning, Strategic thinking, Content understanding
	Personal and emotional attributes	Patience, Authenticity, Determination, Confidence, Motivation to imagine

continued on following page

Table 2. Continued

Categories	Sub-categories	Codes
	Interpersonal and social skills	Teamwork, Communication
	Hard skills	
	Content creation and enhancement	Writing
	Analytical and informational skills	Research
	Editing skills	Design, Photo and video editing
Appropriate use of generative AI, guilt and ethical concerns in the academic context	Appropriate use of AI tools in academic settings	
	Language processing skills	Correcting, Translating, Organizing
	Analytical and informational skills	Verify information, Find information, Brainstorm
	General supportive functions	Inspiration, Guidance
	Inappropriate use of AI tools in academic settings	
		Creative tasks, Replace critical thinking, Plagiarism
	Feelings of guilt	
	Content creation and enhancement	Content generation
	Analytical and informational skills	Data organizing, Literature review
	Language processing skills	Rephrasing
	Editing skills	Design
	Ethical concerns	
	Yes	Crossing ethical boundaries
	No	Not crossing ethical boundaries

RESULTS

Generative AI Understanding And Use In The Academic Context

To assess the general understanding of generative AI, respondents were asked to define it in their own words. The answers varied widely, though certain patterns emerged. The most common association, mentioned by ten respondents, was computational expertise, particularly in content generation. Within this context, data analysis capabilities were also noted. Notably, interactive AI skills were emphasized, with respondents highlighting the importance of input dependency and the role of prompts as key features. Additionally, while only mentioned once, time efficiency was recognized as a critical factor for optimizing tasks. Finally, some respondents pointed out limitations of generative AI, including its potential for inaccurate information, lack of copyright considerations, and absence of reasoning.

> *"Generative AI is a form of AI that can generate content in different forms – text, image, video, audio, on the data that it has been trained on. As I see it, it is a model that gathers and analyzes a lot of data and information, and it generates a response depending on the users' prompt." (R5)*

> *"Generative artificial intelligence is a tool that simplifies the process of research and idea generation, allowing the user to save time when working on a project." (R1)*

> *"Generative AI is a large language model that is trained on huge data set (a good part of the information is copyrighted and taken without permission), it cannot reason and it only outputs things based on the data set it was trained with." (R8)*

The next question sought to identify the most used generative AI applications and the reasons behind their use. ChatGPT emerged as the most frequently used tool. However, other tools like Perplexity, Grammarly, DALL-E, ChatPDF, and PhotoshopAI were mentioned, albeit infrequently (Figure 1). The reasons for using generative AI tools can be categorized into four main subgroups: content creation and enhancement, language processing, analytical and informational tasks, and media editing. Among these, content generation was the most frequently cited reason, mentioned by eleven respondents, followed by searching for information and data analysis.

Figure 1. The generative AI tools used and the reasons behind their use

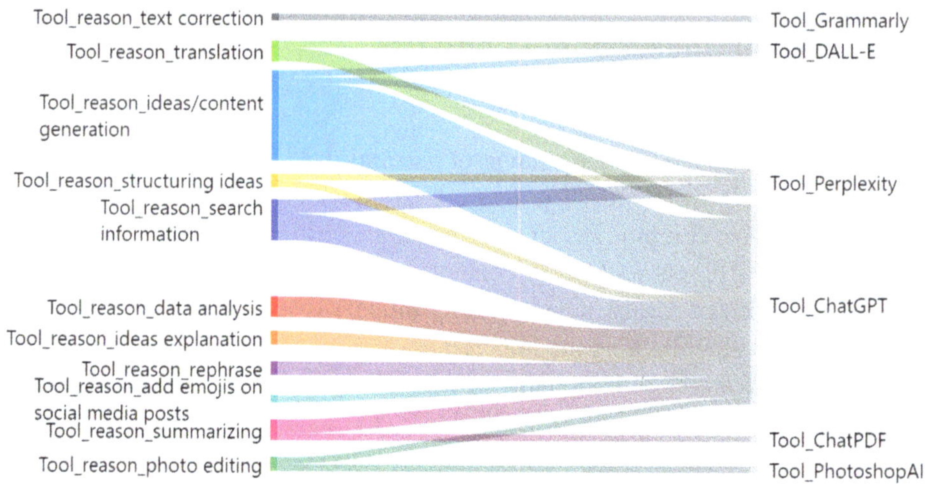

(figure generated in Atlas.ti software)

"I tend to turn to ChatGPT whenever I am in need of new ideas or I have ideas that are in need of some fine-tuning. I use it to rephrase sentences and paragraphs whenever I am writing, and I feel like I am repeating words and expressions, and I am in need of new word combinations that are more appropriate for the context. [...] It is also handy when complicated concepts and research papers need to be explained, ChatGPT can break it down in understandable chunks that are easier to digest and incorporate into my work later on." (R2)

"Mostly ChatGPT - for everything - personal use - how to cook risotto, or more professional tasks - code debugging, social media copy generator, summarizer, strategy - brainstorming generator, translate tool, technical info synthesizer, message personalization for lead generation." (R6)

"I use ChatGPT as a versatile tool for various activities, from writing messages and emails to summarizing articles. This helps me extract the essence of a text and quickly determine its relevance to my studies. I also use it to gain a general perspective on complex topics, develop marketing strategies, and analyze the emotions conveyed by Instagram accounts I follow to create similar content." (R10)

"I primarily rely on ChatGPT and DALL-E, which I use extensively to translate diverse content for work. Additionally, due to the high volume of tasks and the lack of information about certain products we promote, I use ChatGPT to generate content ideas for work purposes." (R13)

To focus on the academic environment, respondents were asked whether they use AI applications for school projects and how they incorporate generative AI into their work. One respondent has never used generative AI for school projects (R3).

Most interviewees reported using AI tools primarily for idea generation, utilizing them to develop ideas, generate content, brainstorm, and combine various concepts. Similarly, significant importance is placed on AI-assisted language processing, with frequent use of functions such as rephrasing, summarizing, correcting, and translating. Additionally, in terms of information gathering and structuring, AI tools are used to provide insights into new concepts and to suggest appropriate content structures.

"I use ChatGPT for school projects and tasks, primarily for written ones, whenever I am in need of some inspiration or guidance. I usually run my ideas by ChatGPT and ask it to develop them or give me more ideas so that I can combine them and come up with something better than what I initially had in mind. Recently, I used the aforementioned tool to help me decide on a dissertation topic, combine three topics and come up with some new research directions that were not explored previously and to provide me with some guidance when it comes to the overall structure of the paper. I also utilized it to explain complex concepts that I came across in research articles, and I struggled to wrap my head around them. I used it to rephrase sentences and paragraphs and to correct them in cases when I was not sure about them or I was running out of expressions and synonyms" (R2)

"Yes, I use it for brainstorming in general. I ask it for new ideas or for something that can inspire me, but I do not take exact information from it." (R11)

To gain a clearer and more profound understanding of how students use generative AI tools in their academic projects, a map is being created based on their responses (Figure 2).

Figure 2. Reasons for using generative AI in academic context

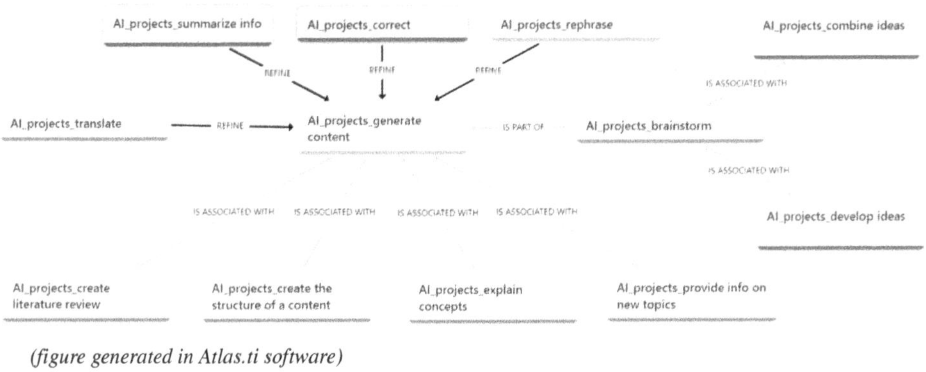

(figure generated in Atlas.ti software)

At the core of the diagram lies content generation, which serves as the foundation for several related tasks. Generative AI is widely utilized to produce content, which is then refined through processes such as summarizing information, correcting text, rephrasing, and translating. These tasks highlight the role of generative AI in improving and tailoring academic outputs to meet specific requirements, ensuring that the generated content is accurate, coherent, and well-structured. Another significant area of application is brainstorming and idea development. The diagram shows that brainstorming activities are closely linked with combining ideas and developing ideas. Generative AI is perceived as playing a crucial role in facilitating creativity and organization during the ideation phase of academic projects. Students rely on these tools to generate new perspectives, merge diverse concepts, and develop structured ideas for their work. Beyond content creation and brainstorming, generative AI is also used for content structuring and contextual understanding. This includes tasks such as creating literature reviews, structuring content, explaining concepts, and providing information on new topics. Generative AI is perceived not only as a tool for generating content but also as a support mechanism for organizing and presenting complex information.

Generative AI Acceptance In The Academic Context

Technology Acceptance Model (Davis, 1989) is one of the most widely used theoretical frameworks for explaining technology acceptance. The main variables are ease of use, usefulness, and intentional behavior.

Regarding ***ease of use***, most respondents state that using tools like ChatGPT is not particularly challenging (Figure 3). However, they acknowledge certain issues related to this. While generative AI tools are intuitive and serve as excellent starting points for inspiration and fostering personal creativity, the quality of the outputs heavily depends on the inputs or prompts used, as eleven respondents emphasized. As a result, using prompts can range from being straightforward to quite complex. Challenges arise when detailed or complex explanations are required to ensure the application fully understands the request. Similarly, generating images, which are inherently more complex, presents similar difficulties. In terms of outputs, respondents emphasize the need to verify the accuracy of AI-generated results, which can make the process of using generative AI tools more demanding. This additional step of checking and refining the results adds to the overall complexity of using such tools effectively.

Figure 3. Perceptions on generative AI's ease of use

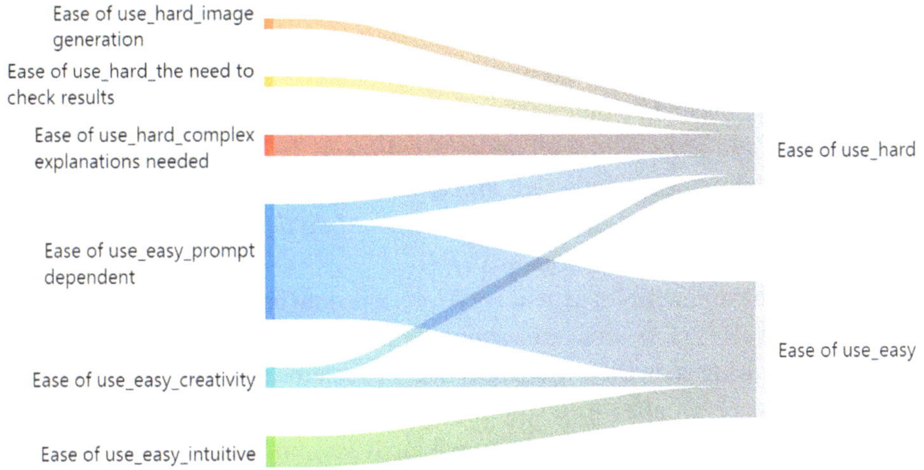

(figure generated in Atlas.ti software)

"Using generative AI applications is not inherently complicated, but it is important to apply our own creativity to enhance the results and achieve high-quality outcomes." (R1)

"ChatGPT is very easy to use – the only thing that might be harder, depending on the situation, is giving it a very good prompt." (R3)

"It can be quite challenging to explain to artificial intelligence what you want to do, what structure you want, and which methods to use. Ultimately, you need to think about how to structure and design the study yourself, as AI contributes minimally by helping more with organizing and formulating ideas or suggestions than with constructing a fully developed and well-founded methodological framework." (R10)

"[…] When it comes to harder tasks or more creative ones, you need to give it a lot more indications and it takes a lot to re-generate the thing you asked for." (R12)

Generative AI is widely regarded as a ***useful*** tool for academic projects and tasks. Among its most frequently mentioned capabilities are language processing functions such as correcting, rephrasing, and summarizing. Additionally, it is recognized for its usefulness in information searching, idea development, concept understanding, and providing new perspectives. However, the standout benefit of generative AI is its ability to save time, making it a key aspect of its perceived usefulness. The responses highlight a balanced perspective on the role of generative AI in academic projects, emphasizing its value in enhancing efficiency while maintaining the importance of personal effort. Respondents recognize the significant time-saving benefits of AI tools, particularly in information gathering and task completion, with one noting that AI can make work "*10x faster*" (R6). However, they stress that these tools should be used as aids rather than replacements for student effort, ensuring that critical thinking and active engagement in the learning process are preserved. This cautious yet optimistic view reflects an understanding of AI's potential to transform traditional workflows while upholding the integrity of academic work.

> *"I believe these tools help with university projects because they save a lot of time in the information-gathering process. I don't agree with using them as a replacement for my own effort as a student, but I do think they are useful tools that can aid in completing projects." (R4)*

In addition to the benefits of generative AI, certain drawbacks are also recognized. One respondent (R8) raises concerns about the long-term impact of relying on AI, suggesting that using such tools to solve creative problems may diminish a person's creative capacity, even after they stop using them. Moreover, it is perceived that AI cannot produce original information, making it essential to combine AI outputs with personal input to ensure originality and depth.

> *"In a way I think it is useful because it can help you with brainstorming, but as downside it cannot give original information, so I don't think it is okay to only use ChatGPT without your own personal input." (R11)*

Closely tied to the perceived usefulness of generative AI, the expressed ***intention to use*** it for future academic tasks remains uncertain. AI is widely recognized by respondents as a tool for guidance, idea generation and structuring, summarizing, and rephrasing, with its primary appeal being time efficiency. However, concerns have been raised about its limitations, including the generation of incoherent ideas, reduced personal effort, diminished sense of work ownership, and even potential environmental impacts. These challenges underscore the importance of students taking responsibility for their own learning process, exercising maturity in how they integrate AI into their academic work, and ensuring that they maintain critical engagement and personal input in their projects.

> *"Honestly, at the moment, I prefer to rely on my own knowledge and gather information directly from credible sources (research articles). That's why I've started to avoid using AI until it becomes sufficiently advanced to provide coherent ideas for university projects." (R1)*

> *"Honestly, after using it for my theoretical review, I feel fake and want to take all the sources and re-read it. Probably I will still ask ChatGPT to summarize the information, but not to fill my paper with numbers or facts I didn't validate in multiple sources." (R6)*

Generative AI's Impact On Skills In The Academic Context

Within the context of generative AI use and acceptance in the academic environment, the subsequent interview questions focused on the impact of this technology on various skills. Specifically, the discussion explored skills enhanced by AI, those deemed less essential, the prioritization of AI-related skills over personal abilities, skills that have already declined or been lost, and those at risk of diminishing in the future. Table 3 provides a summary of the investigation, showcasing both the soft and hard skills highlighted by the respondents, along with the evolution of these mentions across different discussion points. Additionally, the table includes the number of respondents who referenced each skill, offering a quantitative perspective on the trends and priorities identified throughout the discussion.

Table 3. A summary of the skills impacted by AI in the academic environment

	Skills	Skills improved by AI	Skills becoming less essential	AI skills favored over personal abilities	Skills diminished/ lost	Skills at risk in the future
SOFT SKILLS	Critical and creative thinking abilities					
	Creativity	2	4		4	6
	Critical thinking	2	4		1	2
	Understanding information	1				1
	Reasoning					3
	Strategic thinking					1
	Personal and emotional attributes					
	Patience				2	2
	Authenticity					2
	Determination					1
	Confidence					1
	Motivation to imagine					1
	Interpersonal and social skills					
	Teamwork					1
	Communication					2
	Time management					
	Time efficiency	2		3		

continued on following page

Table 3. Continued

	Skills	Skills improved by AI	Skills becoming less essential	AI skills favored over personal abilities	Skills diminished/ lost	Skills at risk in the future
HARD SKILLS	Content creation and enhancement					
	Writing	2	5		3	6
	Content generation	1	1	2		
	Ideas improvement/ development			1	2	
	Learning expression	2				
	Analytical and informational skills					
	Skimming	1	3			
	Data gathering	2		1		
	Organizing information	2	1		3	
	Data analysis		3			
	Planning			1	1	
	Research				1	2
	Language processing skills					
	Simplifying language	4				
	Correcting			1		
	Rephrasing			2	1	
	Summarizing information			2	1	
	Editing skills					
	Design	1				1
	Photo / video editing					2

Note: The numbers in the table represent the count of interviewees who mentioned each specific skill.

The respondents believe that the primary soft ***skills enhanced*** by using AI are creativity and critical thinking. Additionally, they consider that, among hard skills, AI use helps students in simplifying language, as well as writing, data gathering, and organizing information.

"I think that my explaining skills improved as most of the times I needed to give AI a lot of examples and indications to what I wanted. Also, I think that my writing skills improved as I needed to be more creative and find the perfect way for me as AI couldn't give me the most pleasing solutions." (R12)

However, some students believe that AI does not actually improve their skills. Instead, they see AI as a tool that only enables them to complete certain tasks more efficiently but in a less creative manner.

"I don't feel that my skills have been significantly improved. I think these are more like tools that help me spend less time on a particular task, but at the same time, I feel they limit me." (R13)

AI is making many ***skills less essential*** in the academic environment due to its ability to handle tasks traditionally performed manually. In soft skills, creativity and critical thinking are perceived as less necessary anymore, as AI often provides ready-made solutions and ideas. This raises concerns about over-reliance on AI, potentially leading to a reduction in students' active engagement in developing these abilities. Hard skills like writing, skimming, and data analysis are becoming less essential as well, as AI automates much of the labor involved. Interestingly, some respondents highlight a nuanced perspective on the role of skills in an AI-driven context. They argue that no skills will become less necessary because human abilities remain essential for evaluating and refining AI-generated outputs. While AI can assist in tasks, such as generating ideas or content that require skills like strategic thinking, the responsibility to assess, interpret, and ensure the quality of those outputs still lies with humans. This implies that relying on AI without maintaining or improving one's own skills could undermine human agency, critical thinking, and self-reliance.

"I wouldn't say any skills will become less necessary, as you need them to be able to understand if what AI generates is appropriate and is in line with what you wanted it to generate. If you have underdeveloped skills, you might end up relying more on AI than on yourself, which I think is the wrong direction. Definitely, in my opinion, skills do not become less necessary, but are somewhat even more needed. You might use it to generate something that involves the skill of strategic thinking, but you still need the skill to decide for yourself if what it generated is good or bad, or if it needs improvement from your input." (R5)

Although five respondents stated that they have never prioritized AI over their own skills, the data indicates a growing emphasis on ***AI-related skills over personal abilities***. For example, in areas such as content generation, AI is heavily relied upon, with students favoring its efficiency over traditional, manual processes. Similarly, language processing skills like rephrasing and summarizing are now frequently handled by AI, shifting the focus from personal skill development to mastering how to use AI effectively. AI is primarily used for tasks like organizing references, summarizing articles, correcting language in general or grammar, and transforming bullet points into paragraphs.

"For a project management group project [...], my colleagues and I heavily relied on AI tools for information purposes; this does not mean we placed information from the AI app in a Word document. We rephrased it to make it sound like ours." (R2)

"For projects requiring the reading of a large amount of specialized literature, I used artificial intelligence to summarize articles. These summaries helped me draft the literature review section. Initially, I felt a bit guilty for using this method due to the limited time for submitting the paper. However, after evaluating the final quality, I realized that the work included significant human contribution, and the result was high-quality. Ultimately, this realization helped me overcome the feeling of guilt." (R10)

While these applications enhance productivity, they raise ethical concerns, especially in academic settings. Respondents strive to maintain a significant human contribution in their work, reflecting a strong awareness of ethical boundaries and the societal perception of AI use. They emphasize authenticity by rephrasing or complementing AI-generated content, showing a commitment to ethical and professional standards. However, AI use often triggers emotions like guilt, anxiety, and self-doubt, especially when relying on it for academic tasks, even when the ideas remain their own. Many also worry about skill erosion or cognitive decline with frequent AI reliance. While AI is valued for efficiency in repetitive tasks, respondents are cautious about overusing it for intellectual or creative efforts, with some intentionally limiting its use to preserve their skills and sense of accomplishment.

"As I studied in Italian, even if I learned the language well, I always use it to correct my texts. On one side, I feel good about myself having correct grammar, but I always doubt myself, I am insecure. [...] Then, I always felt like I was incoherent, or I could not express ideas in simple terms when writing. I always use the AI to simplify my texts or to tell me how coherent the message is I want to convey in an email. Then I am lazy, I write bullet points and it transforms it into paragraphs. I feel like I am losing some brain connections if I continue doing that." (R6)

When asked about ***skills that are diminishing or at risk of being lost*** in the academic environment, responses varied. Some students believe that skills cannot be lost, arguing that "*artificial intelligence has not yet reached its full potential*" (R1). Conversely, others identified specific skills as already declining or at risk. Soft skills, such as creativity and patience, are being affected as students increasingly rely on AI to generate ideas and solve problems, reducing opportunities to develop these attributes. Hard skills, including writing, idea development, and information organization, are also becoming less utilized as AI tools handle these tasks. This trend highlights the potential long-term impact of AI on personal and academic growth. Some respondents acknowledge that repetitive use of AI can lead to the loss of certain abilities. To counter this, they strive to limit its use, reserving it primarily for "*repetitive, boring, or time-consuming tasks*" (R5).

> *"I feel that since the advent of artificial intelligence, I'm gradually losing some of my ability to generate content and ideas independently. My creativity seems to have declined, especially when trying to come up with ideas better than those offered by AI. Sometimes, this competition leaves me feeling overwhelmed. To keep up with the changes, I've also started using AI, but I feel this has somewhat altered my creative process. That said, I understand that producing many ideas in a short amount of time is incredibly energy-consuming, and without this energy, creativity cannot thrive. In essence, it's a double-edged sword." (R10)*

When discussing the ***skills at risk in the future*** of being lost in the academic environment, the focus shifts significantly. Beyond writing, research, and editing skills, soft skills take on greater importance. New abilities, not previously mentioned in the interviews, emerge in the discussion. Creativity stands out as the most essential skill, alongside creative thinking, reasoning, patience, authenticity, determination, confidence, motivation, communication, or teamwork, all of which are seen as vulnerable to decline if students overly rely on AI-generated outputs. This highlights the need for thoughtful integration of AI to preserve these critical skill sets.

> *"I believe that the ability to generate creative ideas, draft an original PR text, or write a unique copy in a personal and engaging style risks being affected by the increasingly frequent use of artificial intelligence. As AI becomes a standard resource, there is a risk that all styles will become increasingly similar, leading to a loss of diversity and uniqueness that make texts and ideas truly special. Originality could become a rarity, diminishing the richness and authenticity of the creative process." (R10)*

One of the respondents (R5) reflects a deep concern about the potential negative impact of unregulated AI use in education. The respondent identifies several critical skills at risk, including creativity, critical thinking, patience, teamwork, and strategic thinking, which they believe could deteriorate if students rely too heavily on AI without proper guidance. He expresses a worst-case scenario where students might become entirely dependent on AI, losing the ability to perform basic academic tasks independently. He emphasizes the crucial role of educators in addressing the responsible use of AI to prevent such outcomes. They highlight a gap in current discussions about AI use in education, urging professors to actively engage with the topic. The response suggests a need for structured conversations and education about AI to ensure that students use it as a tool for enhancement rather than replacement of essential skills.

"Ultimately, they could (in a worst-case scenario) depend on it fully, not being able to do school related tasks and projects without it. […] I think professors need to address AI […] I don't know if they realize this, as we haven't spoken that much about the use of AI, but I hope me writing this will get to at least some professors, to emphasize the fact that we need to talk about it." (R5)

While AI improves efficiency and enhances certain skills, it risks diminishing the necessity and development of others, particularly foundational personal and cognitive abilities. This analysis underscores the importance of using AI as a tool to complement, rather than replace, personal effort and skill-building in academic environments.

Appropriate Use Of Generative AI, Guilt, and Ethical Concerns In The Academic Context

The respondents were asked to define the boundaries between appropriate and inappropriate uses of generative AI in academic tasks. Seven interviewees believe it is appropriate to use AI as a tool for guidance. Others find it acceptable to use AI for tasks such as language processing, brainstorming, or verifying information. However, using AI for plagiarism or as a substitute for critical thinking is widely regarded as inappropriate.

When asked about the feelings of guilt associated with using generative AI for academic purposes, the responses reveal mixed feelings emphasizing transparency, efficiency, and ethical boundaries. Four respondents stated that they did not experience guilt regarding AI use, primarily because they used it responsibly and ethically. However, in most cases, guilt arises from using AI to generate content or rephrase existing material. Many respondents expressed guilt when relying on AI, driven by uncertainty about how teachers perceive its use or the fear that it might undermine the authenticity of their work. For instance, some respondents noted feeling uneasy but emphasized that transparency is key, citing and acknowledging AI use to maintain honesty. They emphasized that AI should complement, not replace, personal contributions, suggesting that human input should always dominate ("*51% at least*", R5) .

"I do sometimes feel guilty when receiving credit for something that AI helped with, that's why I think it's essential to be transparent, and to admit that you used it. Doing that does not make your work less valuable, but it makes you honest, a value which I highly regard. If a teacher/colleague applauds your work, it means you did a good job, with or without AI, as you used it in an appropriate way for your campaign/task/project. If the project lacks originality, is basic, and it's clearly AI generated, there is the problem. So, as I see it, you have to apply AI to your work, not it being your work." (R5)

For other respondents, however, the issue went beyond transparency, as they expressed regret over using unverifiable AI-generated content. These reflections underscore the need for balance, transparency, and accountability in the integration of AI tools into academic work.

"I was in a rush to meet a deadline for my paper and just copied numbers from stats generated by the AI and I was not able to verify the information as I didn't get the access to those stats. The paper was not submitted yet, but it's sort of fake/unverified. I promised myself that's better to delay the paper than using evidence I am not 100% confident about." (R6)

Efficiency and practicality also played a significant role in respondents' decisions to use AI. Some respondents admitted relying on AI for creating visuals and literature analysis, despite having the skills to perform these tasks manually, justifying the choice as a time-saving measure.

"Honestly, I feel guilty almost every time I use it for school because it feels wrong getting this kind of help and I feel bad if something is not done 100% by me, but at the same time it makes my life easier as I have less free time than I did when AI tools didn't exist. " (R12)

When asked about situations where using AI for academic projects might have crossed an ethical boundary, the responses were nearly evenly split. Seven respondents stated they were unaware of such cases, while six acknowledged knowing such examples. Overall, the responses reflect varied perspectives on the ethical use of generative AI in academic tasks, emphasizing themes of transparency, adherence to ethical standards, and concerns about over-reliance. Some respondents stress their commitment to academic integrity and credit education on ethical standards for guiding their actions. Transparency is seen as essential, with some respondents highlighting the need to openly acknowledge AI's role in tasks and cautioning against misrepresenting AI-generated work as solely personal effort. Concerns about unethical practices include using AI for tasks requiring critical thought or even minor tasks like paraphrasing or organizing references, which some view as cheating. Broader ethical implications are raised related to how AI systems exploit artists' works without credit or compensation. The respondents stress the importance of balancing ethical AI use with transparency and honesty while recognizing the need for clear guidelines and ongoing discussions about AI's role in academia and beyond.

"Using it in any way, even for a simple task like arranging some references in alphabetical order or paraphrasing something feels like cheating." (R12)

"Even though it's very easy to cross this line, we as students have been educated about ethical standards. I'm not sure if we avoid crossing it out of fear or from a genuine desire to be proud of our results, but these reasons can combine to guide us toward not overusing artificial intelligence." (R13)

DISCUSSIONS AND CONCLUSION

This paper seeks to explore how students specializing in communication science perceive generative AI and identify the skills that may be at risk of diminishing or being lost due to the use of these tools. The main inquiries focus on the actual use of generative AI, its acceptance in terms of ease of use, usefulness, and intended use. Additionally, they address its impact on skills, the appropriateness of AI use, feelings of guilt, and ethical concerns associated with these tools. The discussion is entirely framed within the context of the academic environment. The study focuses solely on perceptions of AI's negative impact on skills, rather than evaluating the actual competencies influenced by AI, which could serve as a direction for future research. Furthermore, it is essential to acknowledge that, while all respondents are enrolled in the same degree and receive similar academic tasks, they may vary in terms of prior academic experiences, specific subdomain interests, and professional backgrounds, factors that cannot be fully controlled.

The data reveals that ChatGPT is the most commonly used generative AI tool. In general, AI tools are primarily employed for content generation, language processing, data analysis, and media editing, with content creation being the most common use. In academic settings, most respondents use AI for idea generation, language tasks (e.g., rephrasing and summarizing), and information structuring.

The respondents find tools like ChatGPT generally easy to use, though challenges exist. While intuitive and helpful for inspiration and creativity, the quality of outputs heavily depends on the quality of prompts. These findings align with the assertions made by AbuMusab (2023) and Orchard & Tasiemski (2023). Crafting effective prompts can range from simple to complex, particularly when detailed or nuanced inputs are required. Tasks like generating images or verifying the accuracy of AI outputs add complexity, as refining results often requires additional effort. Despite these challenges, generative AI is widely recognized as a useful tool, especially for tasks like language processing, idea generation, and information gathering, with time-saving being its standout benefit. As in the case of Ka Yuk Chan and Tsi's (2024) study, respondents emphasize that AI should serve as an aid rather than replace personal effort, preserving critical thinking and engagement in the learning process. However, drawbacks are acknowledged, including concerns about the long-term impact on creativity (e.g., diminishing creative capacity after AI reliance) and the inability of AI to produce entirely original work. Combining AI outputs with personal input is seen as essential to maintain depth and originality. Additionally, limitations such as generating incoherent ideas, reducing ownership of work, and potential environmental impacts are noted. While respondents appreciate AI's efficiency and guidance, they stress the importance of maintaining responsibility, maturity, and active participation in their learning process to ensure the integrity of academic work.

Soft skills, as creative and critical thinking abilities are significantly impacted by AI. These findings align with the perspectives of Candelon et al. (2023), Krishna et al. (2020), or Susnjak, (2022). Paradoxically these skills are both improved by AI and simultaneously at risk of diminishing in importance. On the one hand, AI improves critical and creative thinking by acting as an assistant or catalyst. For instance, AI can provide data-driven insights, generate innovative ideas, identify patterns humans might overlook, or simplify complex problems. On the other hand, these skills are at risk of diminishing because as AI becomes more capable, it increasingly takes over functions that once relied heavily on human cognition. AI's ability to produce creative content, solve problems, or offer strategic recommendations reduces the need for humans to engage in those processes actively. Among the soft skills, creativity is most vulnerable, indicating that AI advancements might eventually dominate or replace this human ability. Similarly, reasoning and strategic thinking are not directly improved by AI but are already showing signs of being diminished or at risk, suggesting a growing challenge for humans to retain these cognitive strengths. Personal and emotional attributes are, for the moment, perceived as less influenced by AI improvement. However, patience shows signs of being diminished and at risk, reflecting how AI might increasingly manage tasks requiring long-term focus or endurance. Emotional traits like authenticity, determination, confidence, and motivation remain untouched for now but could face indirect challenges in a world where AI dominates cognitive and functional skills. Within interpersonal and social skills, AI is perceived as having a lesser impact. Skills like teamwork and communication are not directly enhanced by AI but remain critical for human interaction. Communication is already at risk, hinting at AI's ability to replace certain forms of communicative functions or streamlined collaboration processes.

Regarding hard skills, content creation and enhancement sees significant disruption. AI improves skills like writing, content generation, and learning expression, but it simultaneously diminishes their relevance and risk. Writing, for instance, is heavily impacted, as emphasized by AbuMusab (2023), Krishna et al. (2020) or McMurtrie (2022). This reflects how AI tools like generative models are rapidly overtaking traditional human content creation roles. Ideas improvement and content generation are also influenced but perceived as slightly less at risk in the future than writing. In analytical and informational skills, AI improves skills such as skimming, data gathering, and organizing information, suggesting its ability to process and categorize data more efficiently. However, these skills also face a decline in importance. Data analysis remains highly influenced by AI, reflecting the dominance of AI-driven analytical tools in managing and interpreting complex data. Planning and research are perceived at similar risks. Language processing skills, such as simplifying language, are significantly perceived as being enhanced by AI. Other skills like correcting, rephrasing, and summarizing information are preferred to be AI-based. Lastly, editing skills, including design and photo/video editing, face clear risks. While AI is not perceived as currently improving these skills directly, they are highly at risk in the future, reflecting AI's growing ability to automate complex creative processes.

Overall, the data reveals clear duality. While AI is seen as enhancing certain skills, many of these same skills are also viewed as already diminishing or at risk in the future. Notably, both soft and hard skills are currently perceived as equally vulnerable, but future projections place a stronger emphasis on soft skills, with some of them emerging in discussions only when considering future scenarios. Additionally, writing, as a hard skill, stands out as a significant skill at risk.

Respondents highlight the ethical use of generative AI in academia, deeming it appropriate for tasks like guidance, language processing, and brainstorming, while viewing plagiarism and replacing critical thinking as inappropriate. These findings reinforce the notion that plagiarism and cheating (e.g., as copying text word-for-word without citation, rewriting someone else's ideas without proper credit, data fabrication etc.) pose significant concerns, potentially disrupting educational norms and compromising academic integrity (Cotton et al., 2023; Fui-Hoon Nah et al., 2023; Fütterer et al., 2023; Rospigliosi, 2023; Rudolph et al., 2023; Susnjak, 2022; Tlili et al., 2023; Zhuo et al., 2023). Transparency is emphasized as essential, with some respondents feeling guilty about using AI for content creation or rephrasing, especially when its role is not acknowledged. Experiencing guilt over AI use can lead to emotional distress, anxiety, and avoidance behaviors, potentially hindering students' engagement with beneficial educational tools and limiting their digital literacy development. In the long term, unresolved guilt may contribute to mental health challenges and skill gaps, impacting both academic performance and career readiness in an AI-driven world (Chan, 2024; Kalam et al., 2024).

Efficiency is a key benefit (Bee & Hie, 2015), with AI used for time-saving tasks like visuals and literature analysis. Broader concerns include the exploitation of artists' works by AI and the need for clear guidelines to balance AI's advantages with maintaining personal effort and integrity in academic work. These findings contradict studies suggesting that students often overlook AI's negative impacts and remain unaware of its ethical risks (Chiu, 2024).

Importantly and somehow unexpectedly, the respondents highlight the importance of educators in promoting responsible AI use, addressing a gap in current discussions. They call for structured conversations and education about AI to ensure students use it to enhance, rather than replace, essential skills. These findings somewhat contradict the concerns raised by Giray (2024), which suggest that AI use prioritizes quantity over quality and discourages individuals from seeking further education or feedback.

Scientific and Managerial Implications

Regarding the scientific implications, the study highlights the dual role of generative AI in both enhancing and diminishing essential skills. The vulnerability of specific soft and hard skills, particularly creativity and writing, is emphasized in the data. Thus, findings contribute to understanding the changes in how students think and learn due to AI, providing a foundation for further research on AI's long-term effects on skill development and human cognition, especially in the academic context. Moreover, they underscore the need for academic and technological studies to explore methods for preserving these skills while integrating AI tools effectively. The study also identifies the ethical challenges associated with AI use, including transparency and intellectual honesty, highlighting the necessity for developing robust academic guidelines and frameworks to ensure integrity in education and research.

From the perspective of managerial implications, educational institutions must prioritize incorporating AI literacy into their curricula to ensure students can use AI responsibly and effectively. Structured discussions on ethical use, transparency, and balancing AI assistance with personal effort are essential components of this approach. Additionally, managers and educators should design strategies that actively engage students in activities requiring creativity, critical thinking, and emotional resilience to prevent these skills from being overshadowed by AI capabilities. Clear policies on acceptable AI use in academic work are also necessary to define ethical boundaries and promote transparency. These policies can help prevent issues such as plagiarism and over-reliance on AI. Educators play a critical role in shaping students' responsible use of AI. Training programs should be implemented to equip teachers and academic staff with the skills to integrate AI into their teaching practices effectively. These programs should also focus on promoting the retention and development of essential human skills. Finally, institutions should establish monitoring systems to assess the impact of AI on learning outcomes and provide feedback loops for both students and educators.

Limits and Research Perspectives

The study is subject to the following limitations. The interviews were conducted exclusively online in written format, potentially constraining the depth and richness of responses due to the absence of face-to-face interaction. Additionally, the findings are limited by a relatively small number of respondents, which may affect the generalizability of the results. The sample consisted solely of master's students selected through convenience sampling. The inclusion of undergraduate students and respondents from a wider range of domains could have provided broader and more diverse insights. Furthermore, the study may be influenced by social desirability bias, as it was conducted by a professor with students as respondents, which could have impacted their willingness to candidly discuss their use of AI for academic work and projects. Regarding the coding process, many of the categories partially overlap, with only subtle differences in meaning (e.g., writing, content generation, or ideas development). However, the decision was made to keep these categories separate, as they were originally stated by the respondents, to preserve and accurately reflect their intended nuances.

Future research should focus on expanding the sample size to ensure broader representation and reliability of findings, while also including a more diverse range of participants within the communication field, beyond advertising and public relations, to capture varied perspectives. Comparative analyses across different specializations can provide deeper insights into how generative AI impacts skills differently in distinct areas of study. Similarly, comparing students' perceptions of AI across different countries could provide additional insights into the topic. Longitudinal studies are needed to assess the long-term effects of AI on skill development and potential cognitive shifts over time. Experimental settings could be employed to explore causality and test interventions for effective AI integration into education with specific impact on skills use. Future studies should also investigate more in-depth the precise impact of AI on certain potentially underrated skills in creative industries, as interpersonal and social skills. Additionally, research should develop and apply robust measurement tools to evaluate AI literacy and ethical considerations, offering actionable insights for educational strategies and policy frameworks. Future research could explore the implementation and impact of AI literacy courses designed to enhance students' ability to critically evaluate AI-generated content. Furthermore, studies could investigate the effectiveness of hybrid assignment models, where students engage in both AI-assisted work and traditional methods, enabling comparative analysis of learning outcomes and skill development.

ACKNOWLEDGEMENT

I would like to sincerely thank all the student interviewees for their valuable contributions and honest responses to this research.

REFERENCES

AbuMusab, S. (2023). Generative AI and human labor: Who is replaceable? *AI & Society*. Advance online publication. DOI: 10.1007/s00146-023-01773-3

Anderson, L. N. (2019). Teaching the introductory public relations course: Pedagogical recommendations. *Journal of Communication Pedagogy*, *2*, 58–62. DOI: 10.31446/JCP.2019.13

Bee, O., & Hie, T. (2015). Employers' Emphasis on Technical Skills and Soft Skills in Job Advertisements. *Melta Journals. English Teaching*, *44*(1), 1-12.

Bernhard, J., & Russmann, U. (2023). Digitalization in public relations—Changing competences: A longitudinal analysis of skills required in PR job ads. *Public Relations Review*, *49*(1), 102283. DOI: 10.1016/j.pubrev.2022.102283

Brunner, B., Zarkin, K., & Yates, B. (2018). What do employers want? What should faculty teach? A content analysis of entry-level employment ads in public relations. *Journal of Public Relations Education*. Retrieved from https://aejmc.us/jpre/2018/08/17/what-do-employers-want-what-should-faculty-teach-a-content-analysis-of-entry-level-employment-ads-in-public-relations/

Candelon, F., Krayer, L., Rajendran, S., & Zuluaga Martínez, D. (2023). *How People Can Create—and Destroy—Value with Generative AI*. Boston Consulting Group, Henderson Institute.

Chan, C. K. Y. (2024). Exploring the factors of "AI guilt" among students – Are you guilty of using AI in your homework? *arXiv*. https://arxiv.org/abs/2407.10777

Chiu, T. K. F. (2024). Future research recommendations for transforming higher education with generative AI. *Computers and Education: Artificial Intelligence*, *6*, 100197. Advance online publication. DOI: 10.1016/j.caeai.2023.100197

Chuang, S., & Graham, C. M. (2018). Embracing the sobering reality of technological influences on jobs, employment and human resource development: A systematic literature review. *European Journal of Training and Development*, *42*(7/8), 400–416. DOI: 10.1108/EJTD-03-2018-0030

Cimatti, B. (2016). Definition, development, assessment of soft skills and their role for the quality of organizations and enterprises. *International Journal of Qualitative Research, 10*(1), 97–130.

Cotton, D. R., Cotton, P. A., & Shipway, J. R. (2023). Chatting and cheating: Ensuring academic integrity in the era of ChatGPT. *Innovations in Education and Teaching International, 61*(2), 228–239. DOI: 10.1080/14703297.2023.2190148

Davis, F. (1989). Perceived Usefulness, Perceived Ease of Use, and User Acceptance of Information Technology. *Management Information Systems Quarterly, 13*(3), 319–340.

Dawson, C. (2007). *A practical guide to research methods*. How To Books Ltd.

DiStaso, M. W., Stacks, D. W., & Botan, C. H. (2009). State of public relations education in the United States: 2006 report on a national study of executives and academics. *Public Relations Review, 35*, 254–269. DOI: 10.1016/jpubrev.2009.03.006

Dornis, T. (2020). Artificial Creativity: Emergent Works and the Void in Current Copyright Doctrine. *Yale Journal of Law & Technology, XXII*(1). Advance online publication. DOI: 10.2139/ssrn.3451480

Doyle, A. (2019. March 8). What Are Soft Skills? Retrieved from https://www.thebalancecareers.com/whatare-soft-skillsEuropea

Dwivedi, Y. K., Kshetri, N., Hughes, L., Slade, E. L., Jeyaraj, A., Kar, A. K., Baabdullah, A. M., Koohang, A., Raghavan, V., Ahuja, M., Albanna, H., Albashrawi, M. A., Al-Busaidi, A. S., Balakrishnan, J., Barlette, Y., Basu, S., Bose, I., Brooks, L., Buhalis, D., & Wright, R. (2023). Opinion paper: "So what if ChatGPT wrote it?" Multidisciplinary perspectives on opportunities, challenges and implications of generative conversational AI for research, practice and policy. *International Journal of Information Management, 71*, 1–63. DOI: 10.1016/j.ijinfomgt.2023.102642

Fazekas, K. (2020). Impact of technological development on skills expected in the labour market. Köz-Gazdaság -. *Review of Economic Theory and Policy, 14*(4). https://retp.eu/index.php/retp/article/view/221

Fereday, J., & Muir-Cochrane, E. (2006). Demonstrating rigor using thematic analysis: A hybrid approach of inductive and deductive coding and theme development. *International Journal of Qualitative Methods, 5*(1), 80–92.

Fui-Hoon Nah, F., Zheng, R., Cai, J., Siau, K., & Chen, L. (2023). Generative AI and ChatGPT: Applications, challenges, and AI-human collaboration. *Journal of Information Technology Case and Application Research, 25*(3), 277–304. DOI: 10.1080/15228053.2023.2233814

Fütterer, T., Fischer, C., Alekseeva, A., Chen, X., Tate, T., Warschauer, M., & Gerjets P. (2023). ChatGPT in education: global reactions to AI innovations. *Scientific Reports, 15, 13*(1),15310. DOI: 10.1038/s41598-023-42227-6

Galloway, C., & Swiatek, L. (2018). Public relations and artificial intelligence: It's not (just) about robots. *Public Relations Review*, *44*(5), 734–740. https://www.doi.org/10.1016/j.pubrev.2018.10.008

Garbuio, M., & Lin, N. (2021). Innovative idea generation in problem finding: Abductive reasoning, cognitive impediments, and the promise of artificial intelligence. *Journal of Product Innovation Management*, *38*(6), 701–725. DOI: 10.1111/jpim.12602

Gilbert, S. (2017). Information literacy skills in the workplace: Examining early career advertising professionals. *Journal of Business & Finance Librarianship*, *22*(2), 111–134. DOI: 10.1080/08963568.2016.1258938

Giordano, V., Spada, I., Chiarello, F., & Fantoni, G. (2024). The impact of ChatGPT on human skills: A quantitative study on twitter data. *Technological Forecasting and Social Change*, *203*, 123389. DOI: 10.1016/j.techfore.2024.123389

Giray, L. (2024). Negative effects of Generative AI on researchers: Publishing addiction, Dunning-Kruger effect and skill erosion. *Journal of Applied Learning & Teaching*, *7*(2), 1–8. DOI: 10.37074/jalt.2024.7.2.38

Gragnaniello, D., Marra, F., & Verdoliva, L. (2022). Detection of AI-Generated synthetic faces. In Rathgeb, C., Tolosana, R., Vera-Rodriguez, R., & Busch, C. (Eds.), *Handbook of digital face manipulation and detection: From deepfakes to morphing attacks* (pp. 191–212). Springer International Publishing.

Guest, G., Namey, E., & Chen, M. (2020). A simple method to assess and report thematic saturation in qualitative research. *PLoS One, 15*(5), e0232076. DOI: 10.1371/journal.pone.0232076

Haefner, N., Wincent, J., Parida, V., & Gassmann, O. (2021). Artificial intelligence and innovation management: A review, framework, and research agenda. *Technological Forecasting and Social Change*, *162*, 120392. DOI: 10.1016/j.techfore.2020.120392

Hennink, M., & Kaiser, B. (2022). Sample sizes for saturation in qualitative research: A systematic review of empirical tests. *Social Science & Medicine*, *292*, 114523. DOI: 10.1016/j.socscimed.2021.114523 PMID: 34785096

Hong, J.-W., Peng, Q., & Willims, D. (2020). Are you ready for artificial Mozart and Skrillex? An experiment testing expectancy violation theory and AI music. *New Media & Society*, *23*(7), 1920–1935. DOI: 10.1177/1461444820925798

Hunt, N., & McHale, S. (2007). A practical guide to the e-mail interview. *Qualitative Health Research, 17*(10), 1415–1421. DOI: 10.1177/1049732307308761 PMID: 18000080

Ka Yuk Chan, C., & Tsi, L. (2024). Will generative AI replace teachers in higher education? A study of teacher and student perceptions. *Studies in Educational Evaluation, 83*, 101395. DOI: 10.1016/j.stueduc.2024.101395

Kalam, K. T., Rahman, J. M., Islam, M. R., & Dewan, S. M. R. (2024). ChatGPT and mental health: Friends or foes? *Health Science Reports, 7*(2), e1912. DOI: 10.1002/hsr2.1912 PMID: 38361805

Kim, D., & Kim, S. (2021). A model for user acceptance of robot journalism: Influence of positive disconfirmation and uncertainty avoidance. *Technological Forecasting and Social Change, 163*, 120448. DOI: 10.1016/j.techfore.2020.120448

Kovacs, I., & Zarandne, K. V. (2022). Digital Marketing Employability Skills in Job Advertisements - Must-Have Soft Skills for Entry-Level Workers: A Content Analysis. *Economia e Sociologia, 15*(1), 178–192. DOI: 10.14254/2071789X.2022/15-1/11

Krishna, A., Wright, D., & Kotcher, R. (2020). Curriculum Rebuilding in Public Relations: Understanding what Early Career, Mid-Career, and Senior PR/Communications Professionals Expect from PR Graduates. *Journal of Public Relations Education, 6*(1), 33–57.

Kumar, S., Rao, P., Singhania, S., Verma, S., & Kheterpal, M. (2024). Will artificial intelligence drive the advancements in higher education? A tri-phased exploration. *Technological Forecasting and Social Change, 201*, 123258. DOI: 10.1016/j.techfore.2024.123258

Lee, J., & Hollister, J. M. (2020). Internet-mediated research in the age of social distancing: Methodological reflections and recommendations from two online research projects. *Journal of Korean Library and Information Science Society, 51*(2), 319–353. DOI: 10.16981/kliss.51.2.202006.319

Lowry, D. T., & Xie, L. (2008). Employers' Perspectives on Skills Needed for Entry-Level Advertising and Marketing Jobs: A New Computerized Approach. *Journal of Advertising Education, 12*(2), 17–24. DOI: 10.1177/109804820801200206

Luttrell, R., Wallace, A., McCollough, C., & Lee, J. (2020). The Digital Divide: Addressing Artificial Intelligence in Communication Education. *Journalism & Mass Communication Educator, 75*(4), 470–482. DOI: 10.1177/1077695820925286

Luttrell, R., & Ward, J. (2018). Looking in to see out: An introspective approach to teaching ethics in PR. *Journal of Public Relations Education*, *4*(2), 123–127. https://aejmc.us/jpre/2018/08/17/looking-in-to-see-out-an-introspective-approach-to-teaching-ethics-in-pr/

McMurtrie, B. (2022, December 13). AI and the future of undergraduate writing. *The Chronicle of Higher Education*. https://www.chronicle.com/article/ai-and-the-future-of-undergraduate-writing

Meganck, S., Smith, J., & Guidry, J. (2020). The skills required for entry-level public relations: An analysis of skills required in 1,000 PR job ads. *Public Relations Review*, *46*(5), 101973. DOI: 10.1016/j.pubrev.2020.101973 PMID: 32952274

Michel-Villarreal, R., Vilalta-Perdomo, E., Salinas-Navarro, D. E., Thierry-Aguilera, R., & Gerardou, F. S. (2023). Challenges and Opportunities of Generative AI for Higher Education as Explained by ChatGPT. *Education Sciences*, *13*(9), 856. DOI: 10.3390/educsci13090856

Murray, M. D. (2023). Generative and AI authored artworks and copyright law. *Hastings Communications & Entertainment Law Journal*, *45*(1), 27–44. DOI: 10.2139/ssrn.4152484

Obenza, B. N., Salvahan, A., Rios, A. N., Solo, A., Alburo, R. A., & Gabila, R. J. (2023). University students' perception and use of ChatGPT: Generative artificial intelligence (AI) in higher education. *International Journal of Human-Computer Studies*, *5*(12), 76–107. DOI: 10.31149/ijhcs.v5i12.5033

Ooi, K. B., Tan, G. W. H., Al-Emran, M., Al-Sharafi, M. A., Capatina, A., Chakraborty, A., & Wong, L. W. (2023). The Potential of Generative Artificial Intelligence Across Disciplines: Perspectives and Future Directions. *Journal of Computer Information Systems*, *65*(1), 1–32. DOI: 10.1080/08874417.2023.2261010

Oppenlaender, J. (2022). The creativity of text-to-image generation. *Proceedings of the 25th International Academic Mindtrek Conference*, 192–202. DOI: 10.1145/3569219.3569352

Orchard, T., & Tasiemski, L. (2023). The rise of Generative AI and possible effects on the economy. *Economics and Business Review*, *9*(2), 9–26. DOI: 10.18559/ebr.2023.2.732

Ouyang, L., Wu, J., Jiang, X., Almeida, D., Wainwright, C. L., Mishkin, P., & Lowe, R. (2022). Training Language Models to Follow Instructions with Human Feedback. *arXiv*, 2203.02155. /arXiv.2203.02155DOI: 10.48550

Pavlik, J. V. (2023). Collaborating with ChatGPT: Considering the implications of generative artificial intelligence for journalism and media education. *Journalism & Mass Communication Educator*, *78*(1), 84–93. DOI: 10.1177/10776958221149577

Popenici, S. A. D., & Kerr, S. (2017). Exploring the impact of artificial intelligence on teaching and learning in higher education. *RPTEL*, *12*, 22. DOI: 10.1186/s41039-017-0062-8 PMID: 30595727

Qadir, J. 2023. Engineering Education in the Era of ChatGPT: Promise and Pitfalls of Generative AI for Education. *IEEE Global Engineering Education Conference (EDUCON)*, Kuwait, 1-9. DOI: 10.1109/EDUCON54358.2023.10125121

Riapina, N. (2024). Teaching AI-Enabled Business Communication in Higher Education: A Practical Framework. *Business and Professional Communication Quarterly*, *87*(3), 511–521. DOI: 10.1177/23294906231199249

Rios, J. A., Ling, G., Pugh, R., Becker, D., & Bacall, A. (2020). Identifying critical 21stcentury skills for workplace success: A content analysis of job advertisements. *Educational Researcher*, *49*(2), 80–89. DOI: 10.3102/0013189X19890600

Robles, M. M. (2012). Executive Perceptions of the Top 10 Soft Skills Needed in Today's Workplace. *Business Communication Quarterly*, *75*(4), 453–465.

Rospigliosi, P. (2023). Artificial intelligence in teaching and learning: What questions should we ask of ChatGPT? *Interactive Learning Environments*, *31*(1), 1–3. DOI: 10.1080/10494820.2023.2180191

Rudolph, J., Tan, S., & Tan, S. (2023). ChatGPT: Bullshit spewer or the end of traditional assessments in higher education? *Journal of Applied Learning and Teaching*, *6*(1). Advance online publication. DOI: 10.37074/jalt.2023.6.1.9

Susnjak, T. (2022). ChatGPT: The End of Online Exam Integrity? *arXiv, 2212.09292*. DOI: 10.48550/arXiv.2212.09292

ală, M. L., Müller, C. N., Năstase, I. A., State, O., & Georghe, G. (2024). Exploring university students' perceptions of generative artificial intelligence in education. *Amfiteatru Economic Journal*, *26*(65), 71–88. DOI: 10.24818/EA/2024/ 65/71

Tlili, A., Shehata, B., Adarkwah, M. A., Bozkurt, A., Hickey, D., Huang, R., & Agyemang, B. (2023). What if the devil is my guardian angel: ChatGPT as a case study of using chatbots in education. *Smart Learning Environments*, *10*, 15. DOI: 10.1186/s40561-023-00237-x

Townsend, D., & Hunt, R. (2019). Entrepreneurial action, creativity, & judgment in the age of artificial intelligence. *Journal of Business Venturing Insights*, *11*, e00126. DOI: 10.1016/j.jbvi.2019.e00126

Van Roy, V., Vertesy, D., & Vivarelli, M. (2018). Technology and employment: Mass unemployment or job creation? Empirical evidence from European patenting firms. *Research Policy*, *47*(9), 1762–1776. DOI: 10.1016/j.respol.2018.06.008

Wang, Y.-M., Wei, C.-L., Lin, H.-H., Wang, S.-C., & Wang, Y.-S. (2022). What drives students' AI learning behavior: A perspective of AI anxiety. *Interactive Learning Environments*, *32*(6), 2584–2600. DOI: 10.1080/10494820.2022.2153147

Windels, K., Mallia, K. L., & Broyles, S. J. (2013). Soft Skills: The Difference between Leading and Leaving the Advertising Industry? *Journal of Advertising Education*, *17*(2), 17–27. DOI: 10.1177/109804821301700204

Woinaroschy, A. (2020). Personal considerations about creativity and artificial intelligence. *Journal of Engineering Sciences and Innovation*, *5*(1), 63–68. DOI: 10.56958/jesi.2020.5.1.7

Wong, Y., Fan, S., Guo, Y., Xu, Z., Stephen, K., Sheoran, R., & Kankanhalli, M. (2022). Compute to tell the tale: Goal-driven narrative generation. In *Proceedings of the 30th ACM International Conference on Multimedia* (pp. 6875–6882), Lisboa, Portugal.

Woodruff, A., Shelby, R., Gage Kelley, P., Rousso-Schindler, S., Smith-Loud, J., & Wilcox, L. (2024). How Knowledge Workers Think Generative AI Will (Not) Transform Their Industries. In *Proceedings of the CHI Conference on Human Factors in Computing Systems (CHI '24),* May 11–16, 2024, Honolulu, HI, USA. ACM, New York, NY, USA. DOI: 10.1145/3613904.3642700

Zhuo, T. Y., Huang, Y., Chen, C., & Xing, Z. (2023). Exploring AI ethics of ChatGPT: A diagnostic analysis. *arXiv,* 2301.12867. /arXiv.2301.12867DOI: 10.48550

Chapter 13
Emerging Artificial Intelligence Trends in Education

Sarita Peddi
https://orcid.org/0009-0002-6964-3357
SR University, India

Geetha Manoharan
https://orcid.org/0000-0002-8644-8871
SR University, India

ABSTRACT

Digital technologies have created dynamic, cutting-edge learning settings that emphasise communication and cooperation. Communication is crucial to improve education in digital contexts, as discussed in this chapter. First, we analyse how internet platforms and technologies alter traditional teaching and learning paradigms. This chapter explores AI's growing importance in education, identifying key ideas and current AI application directions. Recently, AI technology has made significant advances. AI-powered chatbots let students and teachers communicate, and adaptive learning systems personalise instruction. These innovations boost learner engagement and assistance and reveal communications that might inform pedagogy. The chapter explains how AI and communication tactics create effective digital learning experiences. AI can make education more accessible, interactive, and personalised, preparing students for a digital future.

DOI: 10.4018/979-8-3373-6018-8.ch013

Copyright © 2026, IGI Global Scientific Publishing. Copying or distributing in print or electronic forms without written permission of IGI Global Scientific Publishing is prohibited.

1. INTRODUCTION

1.1 Context of Education in the Digital Age

As technology advances, education has evolved into interactive, modern digital learning environments (Bates, 2015) that emphasize effective communication and collaboration. This chapter is devoted to the critical role of communication in enhancing an educational experience in these digital settings. Let's start with discussing specific digital context in education-that is, the formative role of the online (Kiran, Manoharan, Durai, Ashtikar, & Kunchala, 2024) platforms and tools in question, which shape traditional paradigms of teaching and learning. Education has changed dramatically over time, especially with technology, in that there are digital learning environments that utilize technology to enhance both teaching and learning. Digital learning environments (Bates, 2015) range from encompass platforms and tools such as Learning Management Systems, Massive Open Online Courses and virtual classrooms. Such environments promote a more flexible and accessible approach to teaching and learning, meaning learners can reach content and instructors independently of geographical barriers (Bates, 2015).

Communicative aspects are very central to creating effective, or rather learning-prone environments within these settings. The implementation of the best strategies for good communication will prove very important in providing a feeling of community with other learners-a factor not frequently found in traditional teaching schemes. Evidence shows that effective communication can positively impact student engagement, motivation, and satisfaction, leading to better academic outcomes (Garrison, 2016a). Beyond that, the asynchronous nature of most digital learning environments requires clear and unambiguous communication to avoid miscomprehensions and ensure the learner is able to operate in course materials easily (Swan, 2021).

However, with the increased adoption of digital learning (Bates, 2015) environments in higher education institutions, the effective use of communication becomes more critical. Instructors need to become flexible in communication by adapting to students varied digital literacy levels. This flexibility is essential in making education more accessible for a diverse set of learners, tailored to the needs of each learner (Shaun, De Baker, & Inventado, 2014). Moreover, recent collaboration learning tools, such as discussion forums, and group projects, raise the issue of constant effective communication (Manoharan, Rao, Ashtikar, Razak, Durai, & Kukreja, 2024) among peers, this may change drastically the learning process.

1.2 The Role of Artificial Intelligence in Education

Artificial Intelligence refers to the process of simulating human intelligence by machines, especially computer systems. Such processes comprise learning, reasoning, and self-correction, and enable AI in the performance of tasks that are carried out under usual human intelligence (Manoharan & Ashtikar, 2024a). AI has become a transformative force in education, offering innovative solutions that improve teaching and learning experiences.

Current trends in AI applications in education are diverse and impactful. Among those is the adoption of AI-based analytics to deliver personalized learning (Singh et al., 2024) experiences. Adaptive learning technologies analyze data about student performances to provide more customized education content according to individual learners needs, thereby promoting a more personalized journey through learning. For example, DreamBox and Knewton are some of the platforms which use AI-based algorithms to alter math problems according to a student's previous answer so that their minds keep on challenging the learners.

Another relevant trend is the implementation of AI chatbots and virtual assistants in academic learning (Singh et al., 2024) environments. Such tools are likely to improve student-instructor interaction by quickly answering repetitive inquiries and addressing other administration issues. It saves time for educators (Razak et al., 2023) and improves support towards students, especially with massive online courses that offer less individual attention.

For instance, AI is being used to analyze communication patterns in digital learning environments to help instructors understand how students interact and engage with the material and with each other. For instance, AI can recognize the students who may be struggling based on their communication frequency or content engagement so that instructors can reach out proactively.

To summarize, AI is progressively more crucial in education because it fosters and personalizes improvement in the overall learning experience while enhancing communication. Educative practices, which had for long been evolved theoretically, are likely to be transformed into more accessible, efficient, and engaging learning processes for all students by these technological interactions.

2. THEORETICAL FOUNDATIONS OF COMMUNICATION IN EDUCATION

2.1 Communication Theories Relevant to Education

Constructivist Theory

Indeed, as technology advances, education turns into interactive, modern digital learning environments nowadays that stress effective communication (Manoharan, Rao, Ashtikar, Razak, Durai, & Kukreja, 2024) and collaboration. This chapter is dedicated to the critical role of communication in enhancing an educational experience in these digital settings. Let's discuss a specific type of digital context in education-that is, the formative role of the online platforms and tools in question, which shape traditional paradigms of teaching (Winchester & Winchester, 2012) and learning.

Education has been dramatically changed overtime, especially with technology, in that there are digital learning environments that use technology to enhance the teaching and learning process. Digital learning environments vary from and include platforms and tools like the Learning Management Systems, Massive Open Online Courses and virtual classrooms. Such environments promote a flexible, learner-centered teaching method that is more accessible, meaning learners can reach content and instructors independently of geographical barriers (Bates, 2015).

This merging of technology into constructivist approaches has led to innovative pedagogical practice. For instance, the interactive scenarios of game-based learning environments promote collaborating and communicating, and learners build knowledge collectively while sharpening their critical thinking abilities. In short, constructivist theory stresses the communicative approach (Russell & Norvig, 2016) to create an interactive yet collaborative learning environment that matches modern learners' needs.

Socio-Cultural Theory

In socio-cultural theory, which is primarily linked with Vygotsky, social interaction and cultural context play a vital role in learning (Wertsch, 1988). This theory emphasizes the use of language as a tool in saying and thinking. Effective communication, in this case, connects learners to their different backgrounds and opens them up to thinking from other people's perspectives (Fosnot, 2013).

Socio-cultural theory can be very relevant in the digital learning environment. Forums and social media are only two examples of some of the collaborative tools which allow learners to communicate and share knowledge across various contexts.

This type of interaction has been proven to improve learner's critical thinking and cultural awareness so that they can negotiate meanings and construct knowledge together (Wertsch, 1988). The socio-cultural theory also highlights the Zone of Proximal Development as applied to the difference between the learner's independent operation and what such learners are able to accomplish with support from others, who are in a better position and have more knowledge. Effective communication during the said process leads to feedback and support from peers and instructors, thereby enhancing learning outcomes.

Recent studies have called for more inclusive (Onwuegbuzie & Abrams, 2021) communication practices that respect the cultural diversity in digital learning environments. Educators can make the learning environment more vibrant through teaching and encouraging students to share their experiences and viewpoints. Generally, socio-cultural theory takes the idea that communication is essential not only in knowledge construction but also in creating a community (Garrison, 2016b) or sense of belonging in learning communities.

2.2 The Importance of Communication in Learning

Impact on Student Engagement

Effective communication (Manoharan, Rao, Ashtikar, Razak, Durai, & Kukreja, 2024) plays a crucial role in enhancing student's engagement within the education sector. Students are more likely to become active participants of their learning when connected to their fellow students and instructors through clearly open communication channels. Strong instructor presence, immediate feedback, and change in communication method have often been said to make for good engagement and satisfaction among students according to a number of studies.

Maintaining engagement (Deka, 2021) in the digital learning environment is a bit challenging, but embracing good communication strategies, like posting regular announcements, interesting polls, and personalized messages, can help act as a bridge between both students and educators (Razak et al., 2023) who will create a feeling of community. In addition, multimedia elements within communication have also been shown to capture the attention of students and further explain issues or concepts using videos or info graphics.

Significantly, communication has contributed to fostering collaborative learning experiences. As students have discussions and engage in group work, they not only learn from each other but also acquire very important critical social skills essential to mastering the new workforce of the 21st century (Sawyer, 2022). Thus, the impact of communication on a student's engagement is multifaceted and constitutes emotional bonding, active involvement, and collaborative learning.

Limitations of Traditional Communication Methods

Although lectures and face-to-face interactions have been part of the education system for a long time, they do not come without limitations. Mainly, these methods incline towards one-way information (Ziemba & Wątróbski, 2024) flow, where instructors transfer their knowledge to the students while the latter simply receive it. This doesn't encourage a sense of engagement among the students and, thus, diminishes the potential for meaningful dialogue.

Moreover, in diverse classrooms, the old ways of communication may not help cater to the different needs of students. For example, some learners may feel hard pressed when taught in large lecture settings, as they often lack opportunities for inquiry and expression of thoughts. This generally results in alienation and disengagement, especially for less confident communicators.

The new opportunities emerging from digital learning environments help to step past the identified limitations. Asynchronous communication tools, such as discussion boards, provide students with an opportunity to reflect on their thoughts and contribute to conversations at their own pace, thereby allowing for a potentially richer exchange of ideas and a more inclusive (Onwuegbuzie & Abrams, 2021) learning environment. Nevertheless, educators must remain vigilant about ensuring that digital communication is purposeful and engaged to combat potential isolation or confusion in online learning (Joyner, Fuller, Holzweiss, Henderson, & Young, 2014) contexts.

Conclusion In education, good communication has to come first. Theoretical underpinning include constructivist and socio-cultural (Vlasenko, Zhyliak, Voloshchuk, Humeniuk, & Storozhuk, 2023) theories that promote innovative goal-oriented communication approaches which engage, collaborate, and include people. As with education always changing, in the implementation of digital technologies in the learning process, effective and considerate communication will be instrumental in supporting diversified learners and improving their general experience.

3. DIGITAL LEARNING ENVIRONMENTS: CHARACTERISTICS AND TOOLS

3.1 Overview of Digital Learning Environments

Definition and Types

DLEs stands for digital learning environments. DLEs refer to online platforms and technologies invented to further facilitate the learning process. Through DLEs, learners can engage with educational content, collaborate with their peers, and instructors, and access materials from any corner of the world. Based on how the DLEs are constructed and operated, there exist three general kinds: LMS, MOOC, and virtual classrooms.

1. Learning Management Systems (LMS):

LMS refers to the software applications that manage, record, and track educational courses or training programs (Kim, 2017). An LMS will give instructors a structured framework in which to upload course materials, track assignments, and monitor their students' progress. Some of the popular ones include Moodle, Canvas, and Blackboard. Such tools facilitate means for grading and communication between teachers and students.

2. Massive Open Online Courses (MOOCs):

They are open courses where one receives free access to educational (Bernacki, Greene, & Lobczowski, 2021) resources. MOOCs are known for their scalability and diversity in content; they are offered by virtually all universities and institutes of education. Coursera, edX, and Future Learn exemplify MOOCs; learners can often enter completely into programs free or pay a fee. MOOCs often incorporate various multimedia resources (Durga et al., 2024), quizzes, and discussion forums to enhance learning.

3. Virtual Classrooms:

Virtual classrooms are replicas of a traditional classroom but using online (Deka, 2021) technology to model the usual traditional teaching environment. These platforms facilitate real-time interaction and collaboration (Bond et al., 2024) among instructors with students. The channels most used for virtual lectures, group projects, and discussion are Zoom, Microsoft Teams, and Google Meet. Virtual classrooms, in particular, often carry other features such as the ability to share screens, breakout rooms, and interactive polling, which heighten participant engagement.

Features that Facilitate Learning

Digital learning environments incorporate several key features that enhance the learning experience:

- **Interactivity and Accessibility:**

Effective DLEs can promote active participation through participative features such as quizzes, simulations, and gamification for learning. There is evidence that interactivity does not only enhance engagement (Deka, 2021) but also has better memory retention outcomes. DLEs afford the learners opportunities to access educational material regardless of place and time, hence breaking geographical barriers to education; this feature is very essential in promoting life-long learning and accommodating the needs of different learners.

- **Multimodal Resources and Collaboration:**

A digital learning environment typically contains numerous kinds of contents like videos, readings, podcasts, and interactive simulations. It addresses multiple kinds of learning styles and preferences, hence enhancing understanding and participation. Most DLEs provide tools that facilitate co-operative learning among students, including discussion forums, group projects, and peer review. Co-operative learning promotes critical thinking and social skills, which are essential for competing in the modern workplace.

- **Personalization and Analytics and Assessment:**

DLEs frequently contain adaptive learning technology. Such systems utilize learner data to provide individualized feedback or recommendations and even create learning paths that are specific to each learner's needs (Bernacki, Greene, & Lobczowski, 2021). Most DLEs have analytics that monitor the learner's progress and engagement. Such data can enable teachers to check for understanding, identify struggling students, and make changes in teaching strategies.

The essence is that digital learning environments represent an important transformation in education, in which technology allows for flexible, enjoyable, and personalized learning. Understanding the types of DLEs and the characteristics that make learning happen may help teachers create better digital learning strategies.

3.2 Communication Tools in Digital Learning

In the context of digital learning, effective communication is paramount for fostering engagement, collaboration, and knowledge sharing. Communication tools can be categorized into synchronous and asynchronous options, each offering unique advantages for educational purposes.

Synchronous Tools

Synchronous communication tools enable real-time interaction among participants to get into immediate feedback and very dynamic discussions. These tools are particularly useful for live learning scenarios where the intention is almost to recreate some kind of traditional classroom interaction.

1. Video Conferencing Tools:

Zoom, Microsoft Teams, and Google Meet are virtual classroom environments where instructors can conduct live lectures, facilitate discussions, and manage group activities. These tools support functions like screen sharing, breakout rooms for small group work, and chat functions for Q&A. Video conferencing may significantly improve the engagement of students in the class when it is integrated with interactive features.

2. Live Polling and Quizzes:

Mentimeter and Kahoot! Are tools that allow instructors to perform instant polls and quizzes during lectures, thus creating lively participation. These tools can gauge student understanding immediately and can create active learning where the student is able to interact with the information (Ziemba & Wątróbski, 2024) dynamically.

3. Virtual Whiteboards:

The Miro or Jamboard allows for real-time collaboration among students and teachers. Participants can brainstorm or share ideas visually as they visualize concepts, so learning is enhanced. Such an application will help a lot, especially during courses that need many complex problems or group projects to be accomplished.

Asynchronous Tools

The asynchronous tools provide flexibility because the learner is allowed to engage with content and interact with discussions in a flexible manner. That flexibility is there because of accommodative schedules as well as learning paces.

1. Discussion Forums:

Structured online discussions on discussion boards like Canvas and Piazza allow for asking questions, sharing insights, and engaging with peers over time (Kiran, Manoharan, Durai, Ashtikar, & Kunchala, 2024). Research shows that asynchronous discussions promote deeper understanding of information as they encourage students to reflect on their contributions before responding. This interaction fosters critical thinking and supports peer learning.

2. Emails and Messaging Apps:

Traditional email is still used as a core tool to communicate with students. This allows instructors to illustrate assignments and send feedback to students. Beyond that, messaging software such as Slack and Microsoft Teams also provide chat features where instructors can quickly respond with informal conversations or rapid questions. These tools can also make student-staff interactions more engaging.

3. Collaborative Platforms:

Tools that enable the same document, presentation, or project to be worked on by people at the same time are Google Docs, Microsoft Office 365, or Notion. The methods with which students can work simultaneously, give each other feedback, and view changes enhance collaborative learning. Few studies indicate that peer-to-peer feedback is promoted, and group productivity is enhanced with the use of collaborative tools.

Comparison of Synchronous and Asynchronous Tools

The roles of synchronous and asynchronous communication tools in digital learning environments are very important. Synchronous tools enable active engagement and real-time interaction, hence suitable for discussions and instant feedback. Conversely, asynchronous tools allow the learners to process information at their own pace, engage deeper with course materials, and reflect on their contributions (Cohen, Manion, & Morrison, 2002).

In a nutshell, an effective tool for communication in the digital environment of learning is a recipe for developing sound engagement and collaboration while making learning more engaging. Flexibility, therefore, requires cooperation by educators in using both synchronous and asynchronous tools to create an interactive and flexible, inclusive (Onwuegbuzie & Abrams, 2021) learning atmosphere that meets the needs of the learner.

4. THE INTERSECTION OF AI AND EDUCATIONAL COMMUNICATION

The communication landscape between teachers and students has evolved as a result of the integration of AI in education. It makes people learn, improve feedback, and communication channels that promote it. The discussion continues in this paper by outlining how the reshaping of communication takes place in education through various AI technologies and methods.

4.1 AI Technologies Reshaping Communication in Education

Chatbots and Virtual Assistants

One of the key tools arising in educational communication is the chatbot and virtual assistant, which delivers on-demand assistance to students and teachers. The kinds of conversational possibilities, question-and-answer, and resources (Durga et al., 2024) from AI-driven tools indeed increase the accessibility of information significantly.

1. 24/7 Availability:

One of the most significant benefits of using Chatbots is that they provide their users with round-the-clock help. Every student can obtain support at any time, which may be crucial for students studying in other time zones or through the dead of night. For example, using tools from such leaders as IBM Watson Assistant and Google Dialog flow, institutions may offer Chatbots who are able to answer the most common questions about course content, deadlines, and administrative processes. This availability reduces the burden on faculty and administrative staff while ensuring that students receive timely support.

2. Scalability:

AI Chatbots can respond to a volume of questions at one time, thus being well suited for large institutions of learning. For instance, at peak registration times or exam periods, Chatbots can attend to thousands of inquiries without lowering the quality of the response. This way, all students' questions are attended to, and therefore, the overall learning environment is more supportive.

3. Enhanced Engagement:

A chatbot can create engagement opportunities with interactive learning experiences. For example, it can take students through quizzes, give immediate feedback, and even provide resources based on each one's learning path. It has been proven that interactive Chatbots boost the motivation and engagement (Deka, 2021) of students to achieve better scores in academics.

4. Language Support:

AI Chatbots can also support multilingual communication, breaking down language barriers for international students. By offering responses in multiple languages, these tools ensure that all students can access information (Ziemba & Wątróbski, 2024) and support, fostering an inclusive (Manoharan, Ashtikar, Rao, & Nivedha, 2024) educational environment.

AI-Driven Analytics for Communication

AI-driven analytics basically help to enhance educational institution communication strategies. It analyses data, coming from various sources, to provide insight that may inform decision-making and make the communication more effective.

1. Predictive Analytics:

AI will allow the analysis of student data in predicting their academic performance and thereby identify those at risk. Examining the patterns of attendance, assignment submission, and engagement levels will allow educators (Razak et al., 2023) to tailor their communication strategy according to the individual needs of students. If for instance, there is a drop in participation of the student, the educator can proactively contact him or her with support or available resources to enhance retention (Shaun, De Baker, & Inventado, 2014).

2. Sentiment Analysis:

Such AI tools can analyze student feedback and communication to gauge sentiment. AI can identify trends in student satisfaction and engagement by processing large volumes of text data from surveys, discussion forums, and social media. This information helps educators adjust their communication strategies and course offerings based on student preferences and concerns.

3. Customized Communication:

AI-based analytics enable a personalized communication strategy because messages can be tailored to a specific student's learning pattern and preference by educators (Razak et al., 2023). Relevance is enhanced, thus increasing the chances that the material will reach the students.

4. Data-Driven Insights:

Institutions can use AI analytics to measure how effective their communication strategies have been. With key metrics like open rates on email, speed of response, and level of engagement, educators can tweak their approaches to achieve maximal impact. This data-driven approach (Russell & Norvig, 2016) ensures that communication efforts are aligned with student needs and institutional goals.

4.2 Enhancing Communication with AI

Beyond tools and analytics, AI has an application in educational communication, which fundamentally improves the learning experience through personalization and real-time feedback mechanisms.

Personalization of Learning Experiences

AI technologies enable the personalization of learning experiences, allowing educators to tailor content and communication to meet the diverse needs of students.

1. Adaptive Learning Systems:

Some adaptive learning platforms, powered by AI, change the content delivery based on student performance. An example of this is DreamBox and Knewton. They study how students interact with their systems and the learning outcomes and deliver content based on the needs of individual students. It supports communication with students' needs and how well they are moving ahead in the system.

2. Personalized Communication:

AI can enable personalized communication in the sense that it analyzes the data of students to ascertain the appropriate techniques and times when one can reach out. For example, AI systems can identify the times that are most active for students online and provide guidance on the optimal times for sending reminders or announcements (Kiran, Manoharan, Durai, Ashtikar, & Kunchala, 2024). This targeted approach thereby increases chances for engagement by students and thereby ensures timely delivery of information.

3. Tailored Resources and Recommendations:

AI can suggest resources (Durga et al., 2024) for a student based on personal preferences and performance. For example, when a student performs poorly in a given area, AI systems can suggest additional resources or learning methods. This personalized support facilitates the learning process and contributes to positive engagement with the curriculum.

4. Culturally Responsive Communication:

Analyzing the demographic data using AI can inform culturally responsive communication strategies. Educators know and understand the diversity of backgrounds of students; they will develop ways to communicate and content to communicate that resonate differently from varying cultural perspectives (Fosnot, 2013). This further enhances inclusivity, meaning everyone feels valued (Hammond, 2000) and understood.

Real-Time Feedback Mechanisms

AI technologies enable real-time feedback mechanisms that enhance communication and support student learning.

1. Instant Feedback on Assignments:

Another good example is tools like Turnitin and Gradescope, which provide instant feedback on assignments. This information helps inform the students about their strengths as well as weaknesses. So, this instant loop of feedback spurs continuous learning and keeps them active in their coursework. Studies have indeed shown that timely feedback is necessary for uplifting student performance and motivation (Ryan, 2017).

2. Interactive Assessment Tools:

AI review tools offer instant quizzes and reviews, which alter their direction as a result of the response given by students. For example, a platform like Socrative or Quizzes offers teachers the opportunity to develop interactive quizzes that give learners instant feedback. This immediate feedback reinforces learning and creates a feel-good factor and motivates further interest.

3. Continuous Monitoring of Progress:

AI systems can continuously monitor student progress and engagement levels, providing educators with valuable insights into individual and group performance. By identifying trends and patterns in real-time, educators can adjust their communication strategies and interventions to better support student needs.

4. Encouraging Peers Feedback:

A mechanism of peer feedback needs to be incorporated where all the students provide input about each other's work. Using such tools of AI that can analyze peer review ensures that feedback given by the educator is constructive and appropriate. This collaborative approach enhances communication between students and encourages community (Garrison, 2016b) building in the learning environment.

The interface of AI and educational communication is a significant step forward in the interaction of teachers with their learners. Educational institutions can formulate more effective and engaging strategies for communicating, taking advantage of chatbots, AI-driven analytics, and personalization in learning experience and opportunities. As AI technologies advance, it is undeniable that they will even more significantly shape the future of education by greatly improving the overall experience of learning for all stakeholders.

5. EFFECTS OF COMMUNICATION ON LEARNING OUTCOMES IN AI-ENHANCED ENVIRONMENTS

The advent of AI-enhanced digital learning environments has revolutionized the delivery and experience of education. Communication forms a critical component of these contexts as it informs how students engage with content, relate with peers and instructors, and ultimately attain learning outcomes. This section addresses the role played by communication in influencing learning outcomes by outlining the positive impact of effective communication (Manoharan, Rao, Ashtikar, Razak, Durai, & Kukreja, 2024), as well as the challenges (Lai & Cheong, 2022) related to communication at fault in digital learning environments.

5.1 Positive Impacts of Effective Communication

Improved Student Engagement and Collaboration

Effective communication is the very backbone of any engagement and collaboration (Çeken & Taşkın, 2022) in AI-enhanced learning environments. The AI tools shall thus create dynamic interactions that encourage students to be actively engaged in their learning processes.

1. Enabling Active Learning

Clear, timely, and interesting communication enhances the activeness of students in learning. Interactive tools supported by AI, such as forums for discussions and collaborative platforms, increase the engagement of students. For example, an investigation carried out concluded that students who used AI-integrated platforms were highly active, hence leading to high retention and a better understanding of their courses.

2. Technology in Improved Collaboration

AI-facilitated portals have integrated collaborative features that enable learners to collaborate on projects irrespective of geographical location. Google Workspace and Microsoft Teams are other tools that have facilitated the ability for real-time contributions, encouraging learner community (Garrison, 2016a) to stipulate that communication within a collaborative environment enhances peer-to-peer relationships and achieves an enabling environment to learn.

3. Feedback and Peer Learning:

Instant feedback through available communication channels is one of the main reasons for the engagement of students. AI tools can thus provide instant responses allowing students to change their learning strategies within a very short period. For instance, Peergrade allows students to give and receive structured peer feedback. And such interactive feedback mechanisms boost engagement, as well as enhance collaborative skills, allowing students to learn from each other.

4. Building Relationships with Instructors:

Open and honest communication between students and teachers enhances the learning environment. AI tools can facilitate office hours, offer insights into student progress, and enable personalized communication. When students feel comfortable communicating with their instructors, they are likely to ask questions and participate in discussions, thereby improving their academic success.

Enhanced Learning Outcomes and Academic Performance

Effective communication in AI-enhanced environments not only fosters engagement but also significantly impacts learning outcomes and academic performance.

1. Improved Academic Performance:

Several studies have proved that effective communication is directly proportional to better academic performance. For instance, in a study conducted, it was found that the students who expressed themselves comfortably with their teacher and peers had a better academic performance as compared to those students who did not express themselves much in class. This indicates that comprehensive strategies for communication will also bring about academic success.

2. Personalized Learning Experiences:

AI technologies allow for personified response, delivering learning insights adjusted to a learner's pace and learning style. Automated grading facilities allow one to provide personified recommendations on improvement. Such personalized communication improves motivation (Zarzycki, Morrison, Bei, & Seddon, 2023) and efficacy among students, resulting in improved academic performance.

3. Increased Retention Rates:

More retention rates are associated with effective communication in educational programs. Organizations that value (Hammond, 2000) communication using AI platforms tend to show lower dropout rates. In a case, it is indicated that students engaging more actively within AI-supported frameworks of communication were likely to continue studies since they felt supported and are connected to the educational community (Swan, 2021).

4. Motivation and Attitude toward Learning:

There is, therefore a direct influence of the quality of communication on student's feelings about their educational process. Positive communication experiences often increase student's motivation (Ryan, 2017) and attitudes regarding commitment to learning. Favorable communication environments develop the growth mindset that is fundamental for success in learning and lifelong learning.

5.2 Challenges and Miscommunication in Digital Learning

Despite the paramount benefits brought about by effective communication within AI-enhanced environments, challenges (Lai & Cheong, 2022) persist that may disable learning results. Hence, a miscommunication would result in confusion, frustration, and disengagement from the learner and instructor.

Issues of Clarity and Interpretation

1. Interpretation of Digital Communication:

The lack of nonverbal communications in digital, which also includes emails, text messages, and other forms, can cause significant miscommunication. Constructive or supportive feedback meant for the students may be interpreted as critical and unhelpful when delivered through text-based apps. Students rarely interpret feedback received digitally, which affects engagement and performance.

2. Overload of Information:

The digital learning environment presents students with an overabundance of information, which often hinders them in communicating appropriately. Students get overwhelmed by various notices and messages that come at once, which may make it challenging for them to decipher and prioritize the information effectively. Information (Wu, 2024b) overload can be a distraction to learning, which diminishes learners' ability to focus and engage with course material.

3. Cultural Differences:

As most learning conditions become increasingly globalized, the variances in communication styles across different cultures lead to misunderstandings. Students from different backgrounds may perceive messages differentially because of their cultural contexts. For instance, direct communication may be valued by some but construed as rude by others (Shaun, De Baker, & Inventado, 2014). Such differences must, therefore, be recognized and managed in order to improve effective communication (Manoharan & Ashtikar, 2024b) among all participants.

Solutions for Overcoming Communication Barriers

1. Implementing Clear Communication Guidelines:

Improved clarity in communication can be achieved through clear expectations regarding protocols of communication. For example, setting expectations for response times, the desired frequency of feedback, and preferred channels of communication can contribute to a reduction in misunderstandings. Educating students on best practices in digital communication can also pave the way for more effective interactions.

2. Utilizing Multimedia Communication:

Multimedia elements, such as videos, infographics, and voice messages, may be added to make communication clearer and more effective. The visual and auditory tools help to explain detailed information (Wu, 2024a) better than in words, minimizing the room for misunderstanding them. The multiformat engagement addresses the various styles of learning, thus making the communication (Onwuegbuzie & Abrams, 2021).

3. AI Tools for Enhanced Clarity:

AI technologies can be used to resolve ambiguity in a more contextual manner by providing recommendation suggestions. For example, intelligent feedback systems may propose or solicit comments to help clarify messages and responses so that students understand all aspects. Chatbots can also facilitate intermediaries, explaining and guiding when there is an unclear meaning communicated.

4. Encouraging Open Dialogue:

Creating open avenues of communication between students and instructors can facilitate the alleviation of confusions as they arise. Routine check-ins, feedback sessions, and discussion boards can be used as avenues to address confusions and establish rapport. According to a research, education environments that cultivate open communication promote a trustworthy community, therefore, academic experiences are improved.

5. Training and Professional Development:

There is a need to invest in professional development programs for educators about effective communication (Manoharan & Ashtikar, 2024b) in the digital environment. Professional development (Bradford, 2024) may equip instructors with tools that will help them navigate the communication challenge and engage students better.

In the learning contexts of AI enhancement (Papakostas, Troussas, & Sgouropoulou, 2024), effective communication has a dramatic impact on student's attentiveness and collaborative learning, which reflects on academic performance. The difficult challenges include ineffective communication (Manoharan & Ashtikar, 2024b) and unclear messages; however, these can be overcome if students apply appropriate communication skills. This way, educational organizations can take all the benefits of AI technology and make learning more inclusive (Manoharan, Ashtikar, Rao, & Nivedha, 2024), engaging, and effective for all kinds of students.

6. CASE STUDIES: SUCCESSFUL IMPLEMENTATION OF AI IN EDUCATIONAL COMMUNICATION

Artificial Intelligence (AI) (Ahmad, Shokeen, & Raj, 2025) in the educational communication context now opens new possibilities to create fresh teaching and learning experiences within different levels of education. This section will discuss excellent examples of AI tools used in K-12 education and higher education (Purushottamashtikar & Manoharan, 2024), demonstrating how these technologies enrich communication and further enhance engagement for better educational outcomes.

6.1 K-12 Education Examples

Case Study 1: Chatbots in Primary Education

One of the impressive examples of AI in K-12 education is Chatbots at the primary level. Such a system can be referred to as a virtual assistant that answers student questions, offers homework help, and learns interactively. According to Kaur and Singh's research paper titled "EduBot: A Case Study of Chatbot Implementation in a Primary School in India," that was conducted in 2023, students' engagement and satisfaction were significantly enhanced through the interaction with the chatbot. The EduBot was able to respond to the kinds of questions that students ask, such as homework, schedules, and policies, in a real-time basis, freeing up educators to teach and not to address administrative queries.

The study has also showed that students liked the informal style of chatbots, which they found more relatable than the traditional way of the teacher-student formal approach (Russell & Norvig, 2016). This case is such an example of how AI-driven communication tools can enhance learning by providing immediate feedback, catering to student needs, and creating a more interactive learning environment.

Case Study 2: AI-Enhanced Learning Management Systems in Secondary Education

Another critical implementation is the AI-based Learning Management (Kim, 2017) Systems (LMS) in a secondary school. The AI-based LMS called "ClassAI" in a United States secondary school changed the landscape of class delivery and communication, asserted that ClassAI was tailored to detect student performance and learning behavior, thereby content and communication could be appropriately adapted by teachers.

It was using predictive analytics (Cerezo, Lara, Azevedo, & Romero, 2024) to flag students who were likely to fall behind, thereby allowing interventions at the right point in time. The teachers said that it helped them have more individualized communication with each child, they could start a focused conversation for that child given the data-driven insights into that child's progress. With ClassAI improving communication between teachers and students, there was subsequent improvement in student performance alongside a better aggregate perception of the learning process.

Case Study 3: Voice Assistants for Special Needs Education

The use of voice assistants, including Amazon's Alexa, has also been well established in K-12 education-even for students with special needs. For example, Smith et al. (2024) conducted a study about using Alexa in a classroom setting for a group of students who had autism spectrum disorder (ASD). The researchers concluded that the voice assistant allowed for more independence as students could finish learning through verbal prompts, interactive games, and reminders to complete their daily tasks.

Teachers ascribed reduced anxiety in students with a willingness to engage in class activities, because of the reduced number of anxious moments associated with communication through voice assistants. Furthermore, automation of reminders and instructions significantly decreased distractions within lessons, with improved learning settings. This case shows how AI technologies can improve communication and provide support for students with varying needs. Such successful implementations of AI tools are quite promising for K-12 education to transform communication and learning experiences. Chatbots, AI-enhanced LMS platforms, and voice assistants have all positively influenced aspects such as student engagement, personalized learning, and providing support to students with special needs, making education more accessible and effective.

6.2 Higher Education Examples

Case Study 1: AI-Powered Academic Advising Systems

AI-assisted academic advising has changed students and their institutions' communication. At Georgia State University, for example, the AI-driven "Pounce" advising system was designed to enhance student retention and graduation. In fact, report that Pounce analyzed data on every student to provide recommendations, schedule advising sessions, and keep students reminded of deadlines.

The study showed that Pounce indeed increased student engagement by 12 percent and reduced advising workload for human advisors so that they could focus better on more complex student issues. This case study underlines the effectiveness of using AI to streamline the process of communication while enabling proactive academic advising.

Case Study 2: AI-Driven Feedback Tools for Writing Enhancement

Another great example of success in higher education (Purushottamashtikar & Manoharan, 2024) is using AI-driven feedback tools to enhance writing. Universities have adopted the Grammarly tool to assist students in improving their writing skills. It is highlighted the impact made by it in a large university composition course where the students used Grammarly for real-time feedback on grammar, style, and readability.

The results, therefore, showed a marked improvement in the writing quality produced by the students utilizing the tool immediately. This was because of the immediate feedback and assistance offered by the tool. Moreover, the tool helped to enhance the student-instructor interaction because students were able to get specific areas on which they needed improvement before presenting their work. This depicts how AI can improve communication on writing assignments for better success.

Case Study 3: Virtual Reality (VR) Simulations for Remote Learning

The COVID-19 pandemic (Deka, 2021) had a furthering effect on the implementation of AI-powered virtual reality (VR) (Baceviciute et al., 2022) simulations in higher education. A Stanford University case study discussed how AI-powered VR improved learning for remote engineering courses. The students could cooperate in real-time in these complex problem-solving VR environments despite the distance between them.

Interweaving AI helped ensure smooth, responsive interactions within the VR environment, thus improving the general communication experience. The students were satisfied and engaged with their learning resources more than in any other form of online learning (Joyner, Fuller, Holzweiss, Henderson, & Young, 2014), and thus a better learning outcome resulted.This example illustrates how AI and immersive technology may be used to change communication methods in distance learning environments.

Examples of ways AI is applied in higher education (Bond et al., 2024) showcase how technology can advance communication and learning. For instance, advising systems that get the students involved beforehand, writing improvement tools that allow feedback, to mention but a few. Simulations with VR (Baceviciute et al., 2022) further demonstrate the role of immersive technologies in changing the education landscape, with a room for real-time collaboration (Çeken & Taşkın, 2022) and communication.

The fact that AI tools have been implemented successfully within educational communication in K-12 and higher education (Purushottamashtikar & Manoharan, 2024) actually demonstrates the potential of such technologies to transform. From chatbots and learning management (Kim, 2017) systems in primary and secondary education to academic advising systems and advanced mechanisms for feedback within universities, AI is changing how educators and students communicate. As these technologies develop further, more enhancing educational communication, raising engagement, and leading toward better learning outcomes are promised.

7. FUTURE TRENDS IN AI AND EDUCATION COMMUNICATION

Rapid technology change covers rapid integration into educational communication. Emergence of AI has opened the door to new opportunities, but it also poses new challenges (Lai & Cheong, 2022) to educators, learners, and institutions. In this section, emerging technologies and innovations in AI are viewed as ones that shape future education landscapes, indicating changes in education and communication practices.

7.1 Emerging Technologies and Innovations

Adaptive Learning Technologies

Perhaps one of the biggest trends of AI in education is adaptive learning technology that employs AI algorithms for evaluating students' learning behaviors, learning styles, and performance in a real-time process. For example, in the context of Smart Sparrow, personalization can shape the learning experience, making adjustments in content and pacing for individual student needs; this again goes on to impact both engagement and effectiveness in students and allow learning paths to be personalized toward diverse learning styles.

Adaptive learning systems allow for immediate feedback that helps learners eradicate any misconceptions and move forward confidently with material. Adaptive learning can therefore continue to assess how well the learners are progressing and thus apply focused interventions that will definitely not leave anyone behind. In so doing, the ability also ensures better learning outcomes through an inclusive environment.

Predictive Analytics

Predictive analytics also becomes popular as educators and institutions look to enhance the retention and success rates of students. Such a technology entails data analysis for predicting outcomes in terms of performances and behavior trends of students. For example, the research work of Alavi and Mahan (2024) indicates that the use of predictive analytics at universities can predict which students are at risk early in their studies. Data analyzed based on several sources-from GPA to attendance and usage of learning management systems-allows educators to proactively reach out to students needing extra academic support.

The implications to communication are profound. From reactive measures to communication strategies, institutions can move forward with supporting and guiding students in accordance with the individual need of every student. Shifting from a reactive approach to a proactive one helps build a supportive educational community and enhances experiences generally within the system.

Intelligent Tutoring Systems

ITS is another technological (Rukmini, Sreenivasulu, Raghu, Nagatulasi, & Manoharan, 2024) frontier of AI that changes the education landscape. ITS provides one-on-one tutoring with the use of AI as an interface tool. According to Zawacki-Richter, the ITS-ones include Carnegie Learning and Knewton, which offer personal learning and continued assessment of student performance. The system changes the difficulty of the tasks offered as well as giving hints or explanations as seen fit for the level of the learner's understanding.

ITS integration supports personalized learning and bridges instructional support gaps at an arena where there would be the lack of human resources. The technology supports transforming educational communication to facilitate more dialogical interaction between the student and the learning material. Students receive activation through this as it subjects the learner to an element of self-directed learning.

7.2 Anticipated Changes in Educational Communication

Future Pedagogical Strategies

Further, as AI continues to intrude into education, pedagogical strategies will be increasingly technological (Rukmini, Sreenivasulu, Raghu, Nagatulasi, & Manoharan, 2024) to enhance communication and learning. A possibility in this direction is the establishment of blended learning models which integrate traditional face-to-face instruction with online components (Deka, 2021). Creating a community of inquiry in blended learning environments through AI tools facilitates communication between students and instructors (Garrison, 2016a).

Moreover, pedagogies will be significantly portrayed in the context of collaborative learning, where AI powered platforms for students will offer them the possibility to effortlessly work together, even remotely. For instance, such tools as Microsoft Teams or Google Classroom are constantly updated with AI-based features that promote collaboration (Çeken & Taşkın, 2022) and dialogue, such as smart scheduling of group projects .

Evolving Roles of Teachers and Learners

With these innovations, the roles of teachers and learners are expected to change dramatically. Teachers would become facilitators, coaches, rather than the traditional dispense providers of knowledge. Using AI tools offering customized instruction and feedback, teachers are able to focus their time on higher-order support, such as the development of critical thinking and problem-solving among their students (Shaun, De Baker, & Inventado, 2014).

On the learner's side, they will tend to take more autonomy and self-management themselves. With AI-powered platforms creating pathways specific to their needs, learners will grow more accountable for mastering the teaching processes; hence, they will rely more on exploratory and project-based learning approaches. This makes it a total change from the previous teacher-student relationship involving one-way communication in favor of collaboration and co-creation of knowledge.

Emerging AI technology and innovations will fundamentally reshape the future of educational communication. According to scholars who preface the book, "adaptive learning, predictive analytics, and intelligent tutoring systems" will form a foundation that transforms the communication strategies of educators and learners. As pedagogies are changing to be blended with technology, teacher and student roles will change in a way that underlines collaboration and active engagement in the process of teaching and learning.

8. CONCLUSION

In this respect, Artificial Intelligence (AI) (Ahmad, Shokeen, & Raj, 2025) integration into education is transforming the different dimensions of communications strategy, reshaping pedagogical practices, and defining roles both for instructors and learners. The trends become more significant over time and should therefore be viewed up close, specifically as to whether they influence the educational communication and learning results.

8.1 Summary of Key Findings

This investigation of AI (Manoharan, Ashtikar, & Nivedha, 2024) trends and their implications on educational communication reveals a number of significant developments. First, adaptive learning technologies have proven quite promising in tailoring educational experiences. These systems use algorithms to tailor learning to the style and pace of individual learners, helping increase student engagement and comprehension. This does help tailor immediate feedback, enabling students to drive their own learning, which is very important to promote an inclusive (Vlasenko, Zhyliak, Voloshchuk, Humeniuk, & Storozhuk, 2023) learning environment.

Predictive analytics (Cerezo, Lara, Azevedo, & Romero, 2024) empowers educators further to identify the pattern or potential risk of students at very early stages of their career. In this way, an institution can follow suitable interventions in time, which would then have facilitated even better retention and overall academic outcome. Using predictive analytics, institutions can shift from reactive support to proactive communication strategies that not only attend to students' instant needs but also foster a supportive learning culture.

ITS has also become significant in shaping the face of education by providing one-on-one tutoring via AI. The systems adapt the difficulty level of lessons in real-time, based on student performance, and thereby provide an individualized instructional approach (Russell & Norvig, 2016) that accompanies traditional teaching methods. The shift from teacher-centered toward a more student-centered learning model further underlines how learning environments are becoming increasingly interactive and engaged with the emergence of more AI-based instructions.

Anticipated shifts in pedagogical practice reflect changes in the teacher and learner. Teachers are being called to serve as a facilitator or a guide by moving learners into self-directed learning experiences. This shift aligns and stressed the community of inquiry must be fostered by teachers allowing for multiple perspectives and critical thinking to find a sense of cooperative work among students (Garrison, 2016a). With more autonomy, it is now expected that learners will interact more deeply with content as they collaborate and use AI tools to improve their outcomes of learning.

Trend convergence-all point to a revolutionary shift in the manner in which communication occurs in educational settings. Most importantly, the technologies aimed at enhancing collaboration and feedback are changing educational practices permanently; consequently, there is a need to change the instructor's approach to instruction and student contact.

8.2 Recommendations

The transformative potential of AI in education offers multiple future avenues for research. Of utmost importance is the longitudinal impact of adaptive learning technologies on student outcomes across different demographics and learning environments. Future studies could focus on how personalized learning paths influence motivation (Zarzycki, Morrison, Bei, & Seddon, 2023), engagement, and academic achievement among diverse student populations. Research on the variables shows that deep understanding of these variables might lead to standardized best practices that embrace equity in educational settings. Yet another promising area of research is the ethics of AI in educational arenas. With institutions necessarily growing dependent on predictive analytics (Cerezo, Lara, Azevedo, & Romero, 2024) and data-driven decision-making, ethical concerns about data privacy, algorithmic bias, and AI tool transparency become prevalent. Responsible use of AI in education, protecting student data, and practicing equity and inclusion must be developed as frameworks for future research (Shaun, De Baker, & Inventado, 2014).

Perhaps, it is equally important to consider the professional development needs of educators adapting to environments with AI enhancements (Papakostas, Troussas, & Sgouropoulou, 2024). Research could investigate how to prepare teachers to best integrate AI tools effectively into their instructional practice. Education programs should be designed so that educators are informed on using AI to enhance communication, collaboration, and student engagement. This is in agreement with the report of Johnson (2024) that indicated that focused professional development can highly contribute to increased educators (Purushottamashtikar & Manoharan, 2024) confidence and competence when using new technologies.

Another area that deserves more emphasis is the empirical study of the effects of AI on the role of the learner. It is important to consider how AI tools affect students' self-directed learning and collaboration skills to understand the dynamic changes in the teacher-student relationship. As students take more initiative in their educational processes, it would be important for educators (Razak et al., 2023) to know how students experience and perceive AI tools to develop effective strategies in educational settings.

The future of AI in education promises to be dynamic and transformative. Continued research will need to be conducted on the optimization of these technologies into advanced learning and communication methodologies, ensuring that the benefits of AI in education are achieved while mitigating associated challenges.

REFERENCES

Ahmad, W., Shokeen, R., & Raj, R. (2025). Artificial Intelligence: Solutions in Special Education. In *Transforming Special Education through Artificial Intelligence* (pp. 459-520). IGI Global.

Baceviciute, S., Cordoba, A. L., Wismer, P., Jensen, T. V., Klausen, M., & Makransky, G. (2022). Investigating the value of immersive virtual reality tools for organizational training: An applied international study in the biotech industry. *Journal of Computer Assisted Learning*, *38*(2), 470–487.

Bates, A. W. (2015). *Teaching in a digital age: Guidelines for designing teaching and learning*. BCcampus.

Bernacki, M. L., Greene, M. J., & Lobczowski, N. G. (2021). A systematic review of research on personalized learning: Personalized by whom, to what, how, and for what purpose (s)? *Educational Psychology Review*, *33*(4), 1675–1715.

Bond, M., Khosravi, H., De Laat, M., Bergdahl, N., Negrea, V., Oxley, E., & Siemens, G. (2024). A Meta systematic review of artificial intelligence in higher education: A call for increased ethics, collaboration, and rigour. *International Journal of Educational Technology in Higher Education*, *21*(1), 4.

Bradford, A. (2024). *Implementation of Developmental Feedback as a Performance Strategy in Small Businesses* (Doctoral dissertation, Walden University).

Çeken, B., & Taşkın, N. (2022). Multimedia learning principles in different learning environments: A systematic review. *Smart Learning Environments*, *9*(1), 19.

Cerezo, R., Lara, J. A., Azevedo, R., & Romero, C. (2024). Reviewing the differences between learning analytics and educational data mining: Towards educational data science. *Computers in Human Behavior*, *154*, 108155.

Cohen, L., Manion, L., & Morrison, K. (2002). *Research methods in education*. routledge.

Deka, P. K. (2021). Factors influencing student engagement in online learning during the COVID-19 pandemic period in India. *Journal of Management in Practice*, *6*(1).

Durga, S., Gupta, P., Kharb, L., Ranjit, P. S., Dornadula, V. H. R., Modak, K. C., & Manoharan, G. (2024). 9Leveraging Distributed Systems for Improved Educational Planning and Resource Allocation. *Meta Heuristic Algorithms for Advanced Distributed Systems*, 141-159.

Fosnot, C. T. (2013). *Constructivism: Theory, perspectives, and practice*. Teachers College Press.

Garrison, D. R. (2016). E-learning in the 21st century: A community of inquiry framework for research and practice.

Garrison, D. R. (2016). E-learning in the 21st century: A community of inquiry framework for research and practice.

Hammond, M. (2000). Communication within on-line forums: The opportunities, the constraints and the value of a communicative approach. *Computers & Education*, *35*(4), 251–262.

Joyner, S. A., Fuller, M. B., Holzweiss, P. C., Henderson, S., & Young, R. (2014). The importance of student-instructor connections in graduate level online courses. *Journal of Online Learning and Teaching*, *10*(3), 436–445.

Kim, D. (2017). The impact of learning management systems on academic performance: Virtual Competency and student Involvement. *Journal of Higher Education Theory and Practice*, *17*(2), 23–35.

Kiran, G. R., Manoharan, G., Durai, S., Ashtikar, S. P., & Kunchala, R. (2024). Higher Education in India and the Influence of Online Certification Programs. In *Evaluating Global Accreditation Standards for Higher Education* (pp. 149–163). IGI Global.

Lai, J. W., & Cheong, K. H. (2022). Educational opportunities and challenges in augmented reality: Featuring implementations in physics education. *IEEE Access : Practical Innovations, Open Solutions*, *10*, 43143–43158.

Manoharan, G., & Ashtikar, S. P. (2024). A Theoretical Framework for Emotional Intelligence in Academic Leadership in Higher Education. In *Building Organizational Resilience with Neuroleadership* (pp. 96–112). IGI Global.

Manoharan, G., & Ashtikar, S. P. (2024). Nexus between Leadership and Effective Communication: Implications for Educational Institutions. In *Neuroleadership Development and Effective Communication in Modern Business* (pp. 274–291). IGI Global.

Manoharan, G., Ashtikar, S. P., & Nivedha, M. (2024). Integrating Artificial Intelligence in Library Management: An Emerging Trend. *AI-Assisted Library Reconstruction*, 144-157.

Manoharan, G., Ashtikar, S. P., Rao, C. G., & Nivedha, M. (2024). A Pedagogical Landscape: Narrative Study on Emerging Artificial Intelligence Trends in Education. In *Inclusive Educational Practices and Technologies for Promoting Sustainability* (pp. 22–41). IGI Global.

Manoharan, G., Rao, B. S., Ashtikar, S. P., Razak, A., Durai, S., & Kukreja, J. (2024). A Study of Influence of Leadership with Effective Communication in Educational Institutions. In *Neuroleadership Development and Effective Communication in Modern Business* (pp. 214–227). IGI Global.

Onwuegbuzie, A. J., & Abrams, S. S. (2021). Nonverbal communication analysis as mixed analysis. In *The Routledge reviewer's guide to mixed methods analysis* (pp. 239–258). Routledge.

Papakostas, C., Troussas, C., & Sgouropoulou, C. (2024). Review of the Literature on AI-Enhanced Augmented Reality in Education. *Special Topics in Artificial Intelligence and Augmented Reality: The Case of Spatial Intelligence Enhancement*, 13-50.

Purushottamashtikar, S., & Manoharan, G. (2024, June). Emotional intelligence on higher education educators: A systematic literature review. In *AIP Conference Proceedings* (Vol. 2971, No. 1). AIP Publishing.

Razak, A., Nayak, M. P., Manoharan, G., Durai, S., Rajesh, G. A., Rao, C. B., & Ashtikar, S. P. (2023). Reigniting the power of artificial intelligence in education sector for the educators and students competence. In *Artificial Intelligence and Machine Learning in Smart City Planning* (pp. 103–116). Elsevier.

Rukmini, S., Sreenivasulu, Y., Raghu, T., Nagatulasi, K., & Manoharan, G. (2024, June). English language teaching in technological and management studies in India: An edu-techno approach. In *AIP Conference Proceedings* (Vol. 2971, No. 1). AIP Publishing.

Russell, S. J., & Norvig, P. (2016). *Artificial intelligence: a modern approach.* Pearson.

Ryan, R. M. (2017). *Self-determination theory: Basic psychological needs in motivation, development, and wellness.* Guilford Press.

Sawyer, R. K. (2022). 33 The Learning Sciences in the 2020s: Implications for Schools and Beyond.

Shaun, R., De Baker, J., & Inventado, P. S. (2014). *Educational Data Mining and Learning Analytics.*

Singh, D., Makkar, S., Manoharan, G., Durai, S., Purushottamashtikar, S., & Alexrajesh, G. (2024, June). The impact of information technology enabler and organizational learning on performance: A systematic literature review. In *AIP Conference Proceedings* (Vol. 2971, No. 1). AIP Publishing.

Swan, K. (2021). The Community of Inquiry Framework, Online and Blended Learning, and the i2Flex Classroom Model. In *Handbook of Research on K-12 Blended and Virtual Learning Through the i^{2}Flex Classroom Model* (pp. 1-17). IGI Global.

Vlasenko, Y., Zhyliak, N., Voloshchuk, M., Humeniuk, I., & Storozhuk, N. (2023). Socio-psychological and socio-cultural features of communication in an inclusive educational space and in the conditions of multiculturalism. *Iaroslava Levchenko, Anton Kholodov*, 104.

Wertsch, J. V. (1988). *Vygotsky and the social formation of mind.* Harvard university press.

Winchester, M. K., & Winchester, T. M. (2012). If you build it will they come? Exploring the student perspective of weekly student evaluations of teaching. *Assessment & Evaluation in Higher Education, 37*(6), 671–682.

Wu, X. Y. (2024). Exploring the effects of digital technology on deep learning: A meta-analysis. *Education and Information Technologies, 29*(1), 425–458.

Wu, X. Y. (2024). Exploring the effects of digital technology on deep learning: A meta-analysis. *Education and Information Technologies, 29*(1), 425–458.

Zarzycki, M., Morrison, V., Bei, E., & Seddon, D. (2023). Cultural and societal motivations for being informal caregivers: A qualitative systematic review and meta-synthesis. *Health Psychology Review, 17*(2), 247–276. PMID: 35081864

Ziemba, E., & Wątróbski, J. (Eds.). (2024). *Adoption of Emerging Information and Communication Technology for Sustainability*. CRC Press.

Chapter 14
"It's a Social Practice, and Schools Cannot Ignore It": Exploring the Usage of GenAI in Media and Communication Higher Education

Camelia Cusnir
https://orcid.org/0000-0002-6055-6006
University of Bucharest, Romania

Romina Surugiu
https://orcid.org/0000-0003-2731-2058
University of Bucharest, Romania

ABSTRACT

This research explores digital transformation within the educational sector, with a specific focus on how Generative Artificial Intelligence (GenAI) is reshaping the educational landscape. The purpose of this case study is to assess the perceptions of students and educators within the field Media and Communication, focusing on potential benefits and risks associated with GenAI usage. A special attention was given to ethical considerations arising from utilizing these new tools in higher education. We used a survey performed on Media and Communication students and a focus group with faculty members specialized on Media, Communication and Digital Pedagogy at the University of Bucharest (our case study). We identified two different approaches to GenAI: enthusiasm among students and cautiousness among educators. Students have largely adopted GenAI tools in academic tasks

DOI: 10.4018/979-8-3373-6018-8.ch014

Copyright © 2026, IGI Global Scientific Publishing. Copying or distributing in print or electronic forms without written permission of IGI Global Scientific Publishing is prohibited.

while for educators the effective integration of AI into educational practices is still at the beginning. Both students and teachers are in favour of regulating the use of AI in universities.

INTRODUCTION

The launch of ChatGPT-3 by OpenAI in late November 2022 opened the debate regarding the implications of artificial intelligence usage across intellectual domains. Generative AI (GenAI), in particular, is prompting higher education institutions to reconsider traditional pedagogical practices, assessment methods and curricula. While recent advancements in GenAI have offered substantial learning opportunities, they also may present risks. Therefore, these tools could challenge the existing paradigm of learning, teaching, and evaluation in higher education. Our research attempts to determine how higher education has reacted to this new technology, in the specific Romanian context (our case study), assessing both the reaction of teachers and students to GenAI emergence.

The UNESCO report *Guidance for generative AI in education and research* (2023) emphasizes that the introduction of GenAI applications in the educational process should be done following a critical perspective. "Researchers, teachers and learners should take a critical view of the value orientations, cultural standards and social customs embedded in GenAI training models", argues the report (UNESCO, 2023, p. 14). One disadvantage noted by the UNESCO report is that the speed of development of tools or applications exceeds the possibility of national legislative systems to regulate the use of GenAI. The report underlines that the algorithms used by GenAI are not transparent or publicly explained: "the GenAI systems operate as black boxes and (...) it is consequently difficult, if not impossible, to know why particular content has been created" (UNESCO, 2023, p. 15).

The UNESCO report mentions that generative artificial intelligence can produce offensive or unethical material, can "hallucinate" and spread deepfakes. Moreover, a very important observation is that these programs do not really understand the world we live in, although they create this impression by using natural language. "The output of a text GenAI can look impressively human-like, as if it understood the text that is generated. However, GenAI does not understand anything. Instead, these tools string words together in ways that are common on the Internet. The text that is generated may also be incorrect. Researchers, teachers, and learners need to be aware that a GPT does not understand the text it generates; that it can, and often does, generate incorrect statements; and that they therefore need to take a critical approach to everything that it does generates" (UNESCO, 2023, p. 17).

The challenges brought by the already widespread use of GenAI lead to the need of exploring the intersection of technology and education, taking into account the disruption of norms, practices and frameworks in different educational fields.

THEORETICAL FRAMEWORK

In a literature review about the challenges and opportunities associated with the use of generative artificial intelligence (GenAI), with a focus on ChatGPT, Wach et al. (2023, p.7) identified threats related to GenAI in seven main areas: no regulation of the GenAI market and urgent need for regulation; poor quality, lack of quality control, disinformation, deepfake content, algorithmic bias; automation spurred job losses; personal data violation, social surveillance, and privacy violation; social manipulation, weakening ethics and goodwill; widening socio-economic inequalities, and AI technostress.

The literature on this topic in education presents conflicting perspectives. On one hand, AI has become an increasingly important part of the teaching process, often enhancing learning experiences for both educators and students (Boissière & Bruillard, 2021). On the other hand, there are growing concerns regarding the possible replacement of educators' roles by AI and about the ethical implications that may accompany its usage (Zawacki-Richter et al., 2019). Previous research has explored GenAI's influence on higher education practices, drawing from diffusion theory (Miller, 2024) and examining the disruptive impact of such technologies on professional roles (Dianova & Schutz, 2023). Further studies have investigated institutional responses within universities to these emerging challenges (Moorhouse & Kohnke, 2024; Luo, 2024). Moorhouse and Kohnke (2024) analyzed the codes of ethics of the top 50 universities, while Luo (2024) conducted a critical analysis of the codes of ethics from the world's top 20 universities to identify existing regulations on the use of generative AI. Moorhouse and Kohnke (2024) found that fewer than half of the universities analyzed had already considered policies regarding the use of generative AI by students. The codes of ethics reviewed by the mentioned authors suggest using GenAI to assess how well the assignments could be solved by it, or even integrating GenAI into the evaluation process, which would require educators to acquire the necessary skills, i.e. training in GenAI.

Central to the ongoing discourse is GenAI's impact on evaluation processes in higher education (Farazouli et al., 2024; Luo, 2024). Concerns regarding authorship and originality have emerged, with educators increasingly questioning the origin of student-submitted work in the digital age. The existing literature (Walczak & Cellary, 2023; Chan & Hu, 2023; Smolansky et al., 2023; Chan, 2023; Lopezosa et al., 2023) shows a high level of GenAI adoption among students, who generally maintain positive attitudes toward AI-powered tools. Conversely, educators are calling for stricter regulations surrounding GenAI use, advocating for disclosure when students incorporate GenAI in their work (Rajabi et al., 2023; Barrett & Pack, 2023). Another challenge is related to the loss of critical thinking, and consequently the openness to disinformation among students (Fernández-Alameda, 2024). Some researchers view GenAI integration in teaching optimistically: Laato et al. (2023) argue that tools like ChatGPT and Google's Bard constitute valuable knowledge resources, encouraging students to utilize them for academic purposes. Pesovski et al. (2024) further suggest that GenAI offers potential for personalized learning approaches. Yim and Wegerif (2024) bring into consideration the technical challenges and stakeholder acceptance, and the school infrastructure and budget constraints. Hamerman et al. (2025) found that students were more likely to use generative AI (GenAI) when they perceived it as beneficial to their learning outcomes and when its use aligned with prevailing social norms. Conversely, the perception of GenAI as a form of academic dishonesty significantly decreased its adoption. The authors recommended that educational institutions develop clear policies delineating appropriate uses of GenAI, while also encouraging and training faculty to integrate it effectively into course assignments.

The study of the impact of AI on Romanian education remains limited (Cusnir et al., 2024, Grădinaru et al., 2024, Tugui et al., 2022, Fotea et al., 2019). Grădinaru et al. (2024) investigate the academic and professional competence needed by Romanian students to succeed in data science, an increasingly relevant field shaped by the evolution of artificial intelligence. The authors highlight the role of machine learning techniques (e.g., principal component analysis, K-means clustering, logistic regression) in understanding the professional landscape, academic training, and career opportunities for data science specialists.

In a study focusing on human interaction with artificial intelligence, Tugui et al. (2022) underline that the Romanian experts in society and technology accept the roles humans might adopt in the interaction with the artificial intelligence, such as: integrator, master, or limited participant.

A study of 288 Romanian young people (Fotea et al., 2019) highlights significant gaps in formal education on AI, with most respondents perceiving their knowledge of the subject as low to medium and the majority never having taken an AI-related course. Despite this, participants in this study expressed strong confidence in AI's ability to support their career aspirations, largely influenced by information sourced from social media and the Internet. However, trust in AI's integration into educational settings, such as AI-based teaching, was notably low. While respondents generally viewed AI positively in personal interactions, concerns about its impact on privacy and data security emerged as a prominent negative perception, signaling awareness of its potential ethical and societal challenges (Fotea et al., 2019). We believe that this research conducted before the ChatGPT-3 sudden emergence has already pointed out several trends among Generation Z usage of technology that we will be able to verify in the present research.

Our case study aims to examine the use of generative AI within higher education among students and faculty in Media and Communication in Romania (University of Bucharest, our case study) focusing on how these two groups perceive its impact on academic practices. Specifically, we intend to ascertain whether GenAI is perceived as beneficial or not, and to underline the ethical issues raised for both groups.

Our main research objectives are:

> RO1: To explore the use of generative AI (GenAI) in higher education among students and faculty in the field of Media and Communication at the University of Bucharest.
> RO2: To analyze the perceptions of students and educators regarding the impact of generative AI on academic and pedagogical practices.
> RO3: To compare and contrast the ethical concerns and perspectives of students and faculty regarding generative AI in higher education.

The field of Media and Communication Sciences offers a particularly relevant context for this inquiry, as its associated professional sectors already widely employ GenAI in journalism (Broussard et al., 2019), communication (Cusnir & Nicola, 2024; Cusnir et al., 2024; Galloway & Swiatek, 2018), and advertising (Vakrats & Wang, 2020). This reality underscores the necessity of adapting academic practices to address evolving professional needs.

METHODOLOGY

In pursuit of the research objectives, we conducted:

- A quantitative survey, utilizing a questionnaire targeted to Media and Communication students at the University of Bucharest.
- A qualitative survey, consisting of a focus group with faculty members specialized on Media, Communication and Digital Pedagogy at the University of Bucharest.

Drawing from the case study methodology (Yin, 2009), we employed a mixed-methods approach, integrating both quantitative and qualitative tools. The survey (n =145) was conducted to examine students' usage of and their perceptions toward GenAI tools. This was complemented by a focus group with faculty members, which explored the GenAI usage among educators, their perceptions related to GenAI tools as well as their reflections on the survey findings. This combined approach aimed to provide a comprehensive understanding of the utilization and perceptions of GenAI among students and faculty in the field of Media and Communication.

Quantitative methods emphasize the use of objective measurements and statistical or other numerical techniques to analyze data. Such data are typically collected through instruments such as polls, questionnaires, surveys, or by applying computational methods to process existing statistical datasets. According to Babbie (2020, p. 287), survey research advantages are its cost-effectiveness, its capacity to collect substantial amounts of data, and its ability to sample large populations. Additionally, the standardization of data collection is a notable strength, ensuring consistency and facilitating comparisons across respondents.

The questionnaire was distributed to 145 Media and Communication students - representing approx. 10% of the 1420 student body at the Faculty of Journalism and Communication Studies of University of Bucharest (according to Facultatea de Jurnalism si Stiintele Comunicarii, 2023, pp. 18-25) who completed it online (via Google Forms) between March 26 and May 17, 2024. The questionnaire was self-administered online and was filled in exclusively by students in Media and Communication from the University of Bucharest (we included a filter question in order to exclude anyone that would not fit in this category).

The questionnaire included a series of questions on socio-demographic characteristics; questions on the use of GenAI-based tools in general and ChatGPT in particular (type of activities, type of content, at teacher's request or not); another series of questions concerned the perceived advantages and disadvantages of GenAI-based tools and the degree of satisfaction with the results obtained with GenAI tools; finally, a fourth series of questions concerned ethical issues, regulation and the future of GenAI in both education and the Media and Communication professions. 14 questions were closed ("Yes", "No", "I do not know"), and 10 questions offered several options, and the respondents could choose multiple answers.

The survey sample comprised a majority identifying as female (77.2%, n=112). Male participants constituted 22.1% (n=32) of the sample, while 0.7% (n=1) identified as "Other" (see Table 1a).

Table 1a. Demographic characteristics of the corpus of students - Gender

Gender	**Frequency**	**%**
Female	112	77,2%
Male	32	22,1%
Other	1	0,7%
Total	**145**	**100%**

The age distribution (see Table 1b) of the survey sample revealed that the majority of participants (73.2%, n=106) were between 18 and 21 years old. Students aged 22 to 25 comprised 19.3% (n=28) of the sample, while those aged 26 and older accounted for 7.5% (n=11).

Table 1b. Demographic characteristics of the corpus of students - Age

Age	**Frequency**	%
18-21	106	73,2%
22-25	28	19,3%
+26	11	7,5%
Total	**145**	**100%**

The survey sample predominantly consisted of undergraduate (BA) students (see Table 1c), who made up 86.9% (n=126) of the respondents. Graduate (Master's) students accounted for 13.1% (n=19). This demographic distribution reflects to a great extent the gender, age and level of study composition of the student cohort in Media and Communication at the University of Bucharest, as described in the institution's annual reports (Facultatea de Jurnalism si Stiintele Comunicarii, 2023, pp. 18-25).

Table 1c. Demographic characteristics of the corpus of students - Level of study

Level of study	**Frequency**	%
BA	126	86,9%
Master	19	13,1%
Total	**145**	**100%**

Taking into account the explorative characteristics of this case study, which aimed at observing the perceptions of students, and the limited quantity of data (n=145), the dataset was summarized and described by the use of descriptive statistics (frequency).

The focus group method, also known as group interviewing, is a core qualitative research approach (Babbie, 2020, p. 316). It is particularly effective for examining complex social phenomena through dynamic and interactive discussions among participants. According to Babbie (2020), participants in a focus group are "selected on the basis of relevance to the topic under study" (p. 317), ensuring that the discussion benefits from diverse yet contextually relevant perspectives. This method complements field research, which, as Babbie notes, is "especially appropriate for topics and processes that are not easily quantifiable, that change over time, or that are best studied in natural settings" (2020, p. 323).

The focus group followed a discussion guide, with participants' written consent to recording. The focus group included six faculty members, five from Media and Communication Sciences (two of whom are also communication professionals) and one from Education Sciences (see Table 2). The session took place on May 13, 2024. We used purposive sampling with a balanced gender distribution and varied professional experience levels across participants.

The focus group discussion guide began with an icebreaker activity in the form of a projective test, inviting participants to share their primary word associations with AI and to reflect on any prior professional discussions regarding GenAI. Subsequent questions focused on several key areas: the use of GenAI in pedagogical activities, perceptions of GenAI applications within the university context, ethical considerations and regulations surrounding GenAI use in academia, and the anticipated impact of AI on education and related professions.

Table 2. List of the focus group participants (teachers)

	Specialization	**Gender**	**Title**	**Teaching Experience (years)**
Participant 1	Education Sciences	Female	Associate Professor, PhD	20-25
Participant 2	Media & Communication Studies	Female	Senior Lecturer, PhD	15-20
Participant 3	Media &Communication Studies	Female	Senior Lecturer, PhD	5-10
Participant 4	Media &Communication Studies	Male	Teaching Assistant IT manager	15-20
Participant 5	Media &Communication Studies	Male	PhD student, Teaching Assistant Advertising Digital Copywriter	1-5
Participant 6	Media &Communication Studies	Female	Assistant Professor, PhD	1-5

Both the focus groups and the survey were conducted with the approval of the Ethics Committee of the University of Bucharest, in full compliance with its guidelines. The focus group was recorded and transcribed verbatim, resulting in 22 standard pages of text. The findings were analysed using the model of thematic analysis, as described by Braun and Clarke (2006). The manual coding was performed by the two researchers together in order to ensure the consistency of the usage of codes (see Table 3).

Table 3. Main themes

No	Themes	Open-coded category	Number of comments (n= 103)
1	GenAI tools as opportunities	1.1 Opportunities for learning - documenting, structuring information, time-saving 1.2 Opportunity for pedagogical innovation 1.3 Already used in communication industry and in society	44 (42,71% of all)
2	GenAI tools as threats	2.1. Students using GenAI without fully and critically understanding how it works 2.2 Educators are unable to fully assess the impact of GenAI in education for the time being 2.3 GenAI hallucinates 2.4. Concerns related to the evaluation of students	32 (31,06% of all)
3	Ethical considerations related to the GenAI tools	3.1. Plagiarism 3.2 Usage in academic work without any mention 3.3 Academic misconduct 3.4 The need for regulations	27 (26,21% of all)

The most prominent theme, "GenAI tools as opportunities" (n=44; 42.71%), highlights participants' recognition of GenAI's potential to support learning through improved information structuring, time efficiency, and pedagogical innovation, as well as its relevance in professional contexts. The second theme, "GenAI tools as threats" (n=32; 31.06%), captures concerns about students' uncritical use of GenAI, educators' limited understanding of its impact, the issue of hallucinated content, and challenges in assessment. Finally, "Ethical considerations" (n=27; 26.21%) focus on plagiarism, undisclosed use of GenAI in academic work, academic misconduct, and the growing need for institutional regulation. The relatively balanced distribution suggests a nuanced perspective, with both enthusiasm and caution shaping the discourse around GenAI in education. These data will be interpreted in the Findings chapter, in relation to each research objective.

FINDINGS

Students' and Teachers' Use of GenAI Tools

Our findings reveal a predominant reliance on AI tools among students, with 86.9% of respondents (126 out of 145) indicating generative AI usage in their studies. Key areas of AI usage include "gathering information for understanding course content" (80,2%), "completing assignments" (66,7%), and "creating presentations or graphic projects" (38,1%). Other activities for which Romanian students use GenAI tools are: "drafting application documents" (26.2%), "writing exam answers with the teacher's consent" (11.9%) or even "without the teacher's consent" (6.3%), and for "communicating with teachers or administration" (4%). AI tools also are used for non-academic tasks like creating social media content or projects, students using them beyond academic tasks.

AI's impact appears most significant in text-based content creation, used by approximately 94,4% of students admitting the use of GenAI tools, followed by image generation (49,2%) and, to a smaller extent, video or audio production (less than 5%). This substantial use of AI for textual tasks underscores the importance of AI literacy in university guidelines, with ethical considerations becoming increasingly essential.

In addition to student-driven AI use, 46.8% of the respondents noted professors suggesting or even integrating AI tools, with ChatGPT (86,4%) being most commonly cited. Other tools mentioned include Gemini, MidJourney, Bard, or DALL-E.

Only two teachers participating in the focus group have already used AI in teaching, such as for "preparing guidelines for assessments" or "integrating it into a practical assignment requiring multiple solutions, one of which involved AI" (P2). P2 explained that she intends to deepen the use of GenAI in teaching because the exercise allowed students to see the advantages, but also the limitations of using such a tool. "I used ChatGPT by prompting it to define a concept I knew very well. It gave me a very common descriptive summary. I could name this brief user experience a documentation at the most", explained P3, arguing she is not satisfied with this experience. "But I am open to including it in the future in my teaching work", concluded P3.

The focus group participants are cautious about integrating AI into their courses. Some reject it outright: "Technology support is often criticized for potentially causing cognitive decline in learning. I would exclude using it professionally" (P1); "I haven't used it in my teaching because I haven't yet seen its usefulness" (P4); "To really use artificial intelligence to its fullest standard, you need a lot of knowledge" (P5); "I don't necessarily want to encourage them to use AI tools, because I"m interested in how they think, not how to use some texts" (P6).

The widespread use of GenAI-based tools by Media and Communication students can be seen as consistent with what is already happening in the professions for which they are training. However, this is not the case for teachers who seem rather overwhelmed by the developments taking place in their respective industries.

Students' and Teachers' Perception on GenAI Tools

While 84% of Romanian students using ChatGPT report satisfaction with GenAI-generated content, 66.2% do not view these results as better than their own work. This illustrates the following perspective: AI is considered beneficial for efficiency ("time-saving") and creativity but it is often seen as supplemental rather than a replacement for personal effort. 67.6% of Romanian students who use GenAI tools consider their use for academic tasks to be "clearly positive" or "rather positive", while only 23.5% consider it "clearly negative" or "rather positive".

The majority (62,8%) of those interviewed consider that the use of GenAI tools in doing assignment works and projects brings them advantages in assessment (higher grades). Interestingly, only 36.5% of the students report disclosing GenAI usage in assignments, aligning with high rates of guilt (nearly half - 43,7%) associated with AI use for academic work. These responses suggest a complicated relationship with AI, where its benefits, such as time-saving (78.6%) and simplification of tasks (68%), are downplayed by ethical concerns and doubts related to the transparency of algorithms used by the companies. The most common reasons for abstaining from GenAI use include concerns about ethics, reliability, fear of penalties, and difficulty of access to different GenAI tools or lack of knowledge in using them. This question was only answered by students who stated that they do not use GenAI tools (19 out of 145).

Teachers participating in focus groups view AI as an opportunity for pedagogical innovation: "It's an innovative approach; trained professors can use it as a complementary resource to extract its innovative potential" (P1); "For professors, it's an opportunity to approach teaching innovatively" (P4); "For the teacher, I would associate GenAI with the word 'architecture' because things are evolving so fast that we need to adapt the teaching of and the curriculum" (P5). Similar to students, some participants see AI as a time-saver: "It can provide structure, synthesize documents and concepts that would otherwise be time-consuming" (P6). However, they express doubts about AI's ability to meet academic standards: "It can serve as a documentation resource, but of low quality" (P3).

If, when talking about integrating GenAI in teaching activities, professors use words like "innovation", "structure", "architecture", when it comes to AI use by students, most interviewees associate student AI use with risks: "The risks are higher when students use AI, but they can be mitigated with digital self-education" (P1); "There are just 'cutting corners' [tools] because I don't think students use it thoughtfully for academic work" (P3). Faculty reacted critically to the survey results, highlighting that students often view AI as a shortcut: "They see it as a benefit, like 'Thanks, AI, now we don't have to think…" (P6).

Only a few participants in the focus group associate it with positive outcomes in learning: "It can provide structure for unfamiliar topics" (P5); "It can inspire creativity, pushing them [students] out of their bubble" (P6). However, some faculty members expressed empathy toward students' use of AI, comparing ChatGPT to an "advanced Google". One respondent suggested examining the profile of those who use AI: "Is it the underprepared student that searches for basic knowledge or the smart student that seeks inspiration?" (P1).

One of the participants in the focus group concluded that "teachers will always be more reluctant (to change), young people will always be eager to embrace the new, and the gap is there (...) The point is how do we do it because it's a social practice already and the school should not ignore these things" (P6); "I'm not surprised by the high percentage of GenAI use because young people are very keen to test new things, especially in this area and especially if it helps them to cut corners" (P4).

AI Ethics and Regulation: Students and Teachers Perspectives

35.9% of surveyed students consider GenAI use in university as unethical. When asked about specific ethical concerns, students chose "lack of transparency" (68.5%), "impact on developing critical thinking" (59,4%), "using ideas not generated exclusively by a human", (41.3%) "issues with the reliability of provided information" (33.6%), "potential algorithmic alteration of content" (28%), "impact on equal access to tools" (23.8%), and "lack of instruments to identify AI-generated projects" (18.2%). These responses show students' awareness of ethical challenges, which universities should address through policies, especially as a large majority (64.8%) underlined that AI use should be regulated, either through university ethical codes or national legislation.

A vast majority of respondents (91.7%) foresees the increase of AI use in academia, with more than 50% (67.6%) seeing AI as essential to future careers, suggesting the need for AI integration in Media and Communication courses in order to reflect the reality of day-to-day practice.

Several teachers in the focus group disapprove of student AI use and call for strict regulation. While some advocate for its integration in Media and Communication education, others favor more restrictions and remark the lack of regulations: "We should specify fields and contexts where GenAI has been used. How can we evaluate a project created with or without AI?" (P6); "I support stricter regulations, as this content is not self-generated… It could be useful in practical activities, but not in thesis writing" (P4). The need for training is also mentioned: "Students must be taught to use these tools in a responsible and controlled manner" (P1). Some of the participants underlined the need to distinguish between using GenAI to generate academic texts to be presented as homework and using the same tool as a more advanced search engine. They noted that there are currently no limits drawn on this use in university regulations. "We should identify real situations, create a typology of usages, practical assignments and so on. There should also be a critical discussion about this use and its limits", emphasized P2.

The majority of the teachers participating in the focus group are calling for the clear exclusion of the use of GenAI "in assessment contexts that have social stakes" (P1), as well as the mandatory introduction of a disclaimer for the situations in which it has been used: “I would make it mandatory to take responsibility for its use and that there be some limits on its use” (P3).

Faculty expressed concern about the most appropriate approach to the fact that in the Media and Communication professional field GenAI tools are already in use: “But what do we want from an educational point of view? Do we want students to know how to use them [AI tools] or do we want to teach them to think?” (R6). More nuanced positions were also expressed on a more permissive regulation of use: “I’m for a more permissive view, because it’s out there, it’s already present in the profession, at jobs” (R2).

When talking about the prospects of GenAI in education, the teachers participating in the focus group use the word “opportunity”, conditioned by certain situations: the existence of prior training for teachers (P2, P6), the existence of research to prove its effectiveness (P1), the proof that it is a technology that eases our repetitive work without exploiting us (P3). One participant prefers to use the word “threat” instead of opportunity when talking about the future of GenAI in education: “I would say that until there are some rules, guidelines in which to use them, it’s a threat rather than an opportunity. The opportunity is there, but it is somewhat overwhelmed by the threat of short-circuiting the process of learning and assimilating all the information and skills” (P4). Other participants (P2, P5) emphasized the fact that GenAI is already used in the profession (in Advertising or graphic design, for example) for repetitive activities and, in this context, it’s a clear opportunity. “The profession seems to move faster than us”, concluded P2.

DISCUSSION

The findings from the quantitative survey and focus group discussions address the research objective (RO1) by providing a comparative perspective on the use of GenAI among students and faculty in the field of Media and Communication at the University of Bucharest. The data indicate the widespread GenAI adoption among students, with tools like ChatGPT being frequently employed for academic activities such as research, assignment completion, and project creation, including graphic design. In contrast, only a small number of faculty members reported using AI in their teaching practices. Most expressed caution or outright rejection of integrating AI into their courses. This apprehension was underscored by the language used when referring to GenAI, which was often accompanied by caveats, reflecting a hesitant stance. The absence of institutional discussions or formal regulations regarding GenAI exacerbates this cautious attitude among faculty, further distancing their perspectives from the obvious enthusiasm and frequent use observed among students. These findings highlight a significant gap between students’ adoption of

GenAI and faculty readiness to engage with these technologies, underlining the need for institutional dialogue and policy development to bridge this divide.

The findings address the second research objective (RO2) by revealing the perceptions of GenAI among students and faculty regarding its impact on academic and pedagogical practices. The students' usage of GenAI tools is accompanied by a high level of satisfaction with GenAI-derived outcomes. However, a notable paradox arises: despite their satisfaction, a majority of surveyed students do not perceive AI-generated projects as superior to those created exclusively by human intelligence. When referring to GenAI, students have contradictory positions. On the one hand, they are enthusiastic about using GenAI tools, emphasizing its qualities and advantages. On the other hand, students are aware of the gray area in which the use of GenAI in higher education is. They confess that, in most cases, they do not report using GenAI in the realization of projects, but they are also distrustful of the IA product. They also seem to be aware of the ethical issues raised by the use of GenAI in academia. These findings suggest that while students recognize AI's time-saving and supportive capabilities, they also acknowledge limitations in quality and a need for ethical guidelines and regulatory oversight in academic environments.

In contrast, faculty members adopt a more cautious stance, demonstrating skepticism about the widespread use of GenAI in academic contexts. Although they acknowledge its potential to innovate pedagogy, many are reluctant to integrate these tools into their teaching. Faculty criticism centers on concerns that GenAI use among students encourages shortcuts, risks academic misconduct such as plagiarism, and undermines the development of critical thinking skills. These findings highlight a clear divergence in perceptions between students and faculty, underscoring the need for open dialogue, clear ethical frameworks, and new policy development to address the challenges and opportunities posed by GenAI in higher education.

Our results confirm the high level of adoption of GenAI among students and the positive attitudes shown by them observed in previous studies (Walczak & Cellary, 2023; Chan & Hu, 2023; Smolansky et al., 2023; Chan, 2023; Lopezosa et al., 2023). In addition, our research shows a critical perspective shown by students towards the quality of the results provided by GenAI, as well as an awareness of the ethical issues raised by its usage. Also, our findings contrast the enthusiasm of the students and the cautious pragmatism of the teachers.

Regarding the third research objective (RO3), the findings highlight both shared and divergent ethical concerns and perspectives of students and faculty regarding GenAI in higher education. Teachers acknowledge the need for regulation, signaling a consensus on the importance of institutional oversight in managing GenAI use, confirming previous studies which mentioned the need for regulation mentioned by educators (Rajabi et al., 2023; Barrett & Pack, 2023). A significant number of Romanian students mentioned the need for GenAI regulation, identifying core ethical concerns such as lack of transparency, potential impacts on critical thinking development, and uncritical adoption of AI-generated ideas by users. Faculty member respondents favour strict regulation, mentioning challenges in verifying authorship and concerns about the validity of evaluations (e.g., competitive assessments and thesis defences). The Romanian education case fits in the situation described by Moorhouse and Kohnke (2024) who found that half of the top 50 universities in the world did not regulate the use of GenAI.

CONCLUSIONS

Our study explored how the Generative Artificial Intelligence (GenAI) has started to reshape educational practice among teachers and students from Media and Communication higher education. Our aim was to assess students' and faculty members' perceptions, focusing on potential benefits and risks associated with GenAI.

We identified two different approaches to GenAI: enthusiasm among students and cautiousness among educators. Students have largely adopted GenAI tools in academic tasks and they manifest a high level of satisfaction with GenAI-derived outcomes, even if they are aware that GenAI projects are not superior to their own work.

Educators believe that AI could offer an opportunity for pedagogical innovation, the effective integration of AI into educational practices is still at the beginning. Teachers have been critical of the high rate of AI use among students, arguing that tools based on generative artificial intelligence are used as "shortcuts" to avoid learning and that they can lead to academic plagiarism. It could also lead to the usage of information produced by AI without critical reflection. Both students and teachers are rather in favour of regulating the use of AI in universities. Students consider that the main ethical issues raised by AI relate to the lack of transparency, the negative impact on the development of one's own critical thinking or the danger of using "ready-made" ideas. Teachers argue for the regulation of the use of GenAI, mentioning the difficulty of correctly identifying the real authors of the assessed works or the fact that it could harm assessments that have an academic stake. They share a pragmatic perspective acknowledging the spread of GenAI in the media and the communication industry, but also at the societal level. As one focus group participant put it: "It's a social practice, and schools cannot ignore it" (P 6).

Drawing from the results of a case study research, our paper contributes to filling a gap regarding the use and perception of the use of GenAI tools in specific educational fields. In our case, data must be understood in the particular context of a higher education system, where there are no national regulations on the use of GenAI by students and teachers.

Nevertheless, the results of our research may be considered as an important resource for higher education in Media and Communication at several levels. First of all, these results need to be shared among teachers and students so that both groups can better accommodate new competence in the usage of technology in education. Secondly, the positions expressed in this study by both categories (teachers and students) can be a source of inspiration for the possible integration of GenAI in the teaching of Media and Communication subjects, where appropriate. Finally, these data should be used at institutional level for the regulation of GenAI at several levels: in the teaching and assessment methods of each subject, in the University's ethical codes, in the regulations on teaching and student work. The findings also indicate the need for training and education in the area of GenAI for students and teachers, such as: critical thinking (based on reliable information), ethical judgement (with a focus on biases in AI and misuse of GenAI), adaptability, and openness (to new technologies). They point to a clear indication related to reflecting on the present-day information ecosystem, with its advantages and potential biases. Students underlined the problematic data governance of GenAI tools, while teachers expressed deep concerns related to assessment methods in the GenAI world. All these recommendations should be considered for setting institutional policies in higher education.

LIMITATIONS

This study's findings are limited to the case study and its specific socio-cultural and institutional context. The generalizability of the results is thus constrained by its focus on a specific educational field: Media and Communication. Moreover, public discourse in Romania is notably influenced by ongoing discussions about academic integrity, particularly concerns related to plagiarism (ercan & Voicu, 2022). Public figures have been accused of plagiarizing in their doctoral theses. As a consequence, additional measures have been taken at all universities to check the originality of theses, but also of other student work in general. Compulsory courses on academic ethics have also been introduced at all levels of study (bachelor, master, doctorate). The issue of originality of any intellectual output is very topical in the context of the use of GenAI tools and both student and teacher responses showed that they take this reality into account. This distinctive backdrop may have influenced participant responses and stakeholder attitudes, potentially limiting the broader applicability of the conclusions.

We are aware that the data collected in this study is likely to be overtaken by the time the book is published by the speed at which things are moving, in terms of teachers' attitudes towards integrating AI into their work, but also on the evolution and refinement of AI tools and society's reaction to their use.

A methodological limitation of our study is the limited number of students who participated in the survey and their belonging to a specific institution. Also, the educators participating in the focus group were part of one university. The quantitative approach for students may have limited the exploration of subtle perspectives, as surveys or structured data collection tools may not fully capture the complexity of their experiences or attitudes. Conversely, the qualitative approach used for teachers provided rich, in-depth insights but cannot be easily generalized due to the smaller sample size. However, the use of a qualitative method after the implementation of a quantitative one in order to interpret the first results obtained is a common practice and we consider it to be one of the strengths of our case study, allowing an interpretation of the students' positioning from the teachers' perspective.

ACKNOWLEDGEMENTS

The research was supported by Agence Universitaire Francophone (AUF), within the framework of the project "L'impact de l'IA sur les pratiques professionnelles dans l'enseignement universitaire de communication et médias (IACOM)"/"The Impact of AI on the Professional Practices in Higher Education in Communication and Media (IACOM)", jointly organized by the University of Bucharest and Université Lumière Lyon 2, Institut de la Communication between 2023 and 2024, and financed in the call "AUF-ECO 2023 - Soutien aux Équipes de Recherche SER-ECO".

The authors would like to show their gratitude to Associate Professor Dana Popescu-Jourdy, Université Lumière Lyon 2, Institut de la Communication, who contributed to this research, by evaluating the research design and by providing interesting and useful remarks and suggestions for the Discussion part.

REFERENCES

Babbie, E. (2020). *The practice of social research* (15th ed.). Cengage Learning.

Barrett, A., & Pack, A. (2023). Not quite eye to AI: Student and teacher perspectives on the use of generative artificial intelligence in the writing process. *International Journal of Educational Technology in Higher Education, 20*(1), 59. DOI: 10.1186/s41239-023-00427-0

Boissière, J., & Bruillard, É. (2021). *L'école digitale. Une éducation à apprendre et à vivre*. Armand Colin.

Braun, V., & Clarke, V. (2006). Using thematic analysis in psychology. *Qualitative Research in Psychology, 3*(2), 77–101. DOI: 10.1191/1478088706qp063oa

Chan, C. K. Y. (2023). A comprehensive AI policy education framework for university teaching and learning. *International Journal of Educational Technology in Higher Education, 20*(1), 38. DOI: 10.1186/s41239-023-00408-3

Chan, C. K. Y., & Hu, W. (2023). Students' voices on generative AI: Perceptions, benefits, and challenges in higher education. *International Journal of Educational Technology in Higher Education, 20*(1), 43. DOI: 10.1186/s41239-023-00411-8

Cusnir, C., & Nicola, A. (2024). Using generative Artificial Intelligence tools in Public Relations: Ethical concerns and the impact on the profession in the Romanian context. *Communicatio Socialis, 37*(4), 309–323. DOI: 10.15581/003.37.4.309-323

Cusnir, C., Popescu-Jourdy, D., & Surugiu, R. (2024). Inteligen a artificială generativă i învă ământul superior. Studiu de caz asupra domeniului tiin e ale comunicării. In Momoc, A., & Surugiu, R. (Eds.), *Media i Inteligen a Artificială* (pp. 43–55). Tritonic Books.

Dianova, V. G., & Schultz, M. D. (2023). Discussing ChatGPT's implications for industry and higher education: The case for transdisciplinarity and digital humanities. *Industry and Higher Education, XXXVII*(5), 593–600. DOI: 10.1177/09504222231199989

Facultatea de Jurnalism si Stiintele Comunicarii. (2023). Anexe Raport autoevaluare FJSC – 2022-2023. https://drive.google.com/file/d/1tokZtcZ0DX5_TrvfXiPEtdWPes8OEW3y/view

Farazouli, A., Cerrato-Pargman, T., Bolander-Laksov, K., & McGrath, C. (2024). Hello GPT! Goodbye home examination? An exploratory study of AI chatbots impact on university teachers' assessment practices. *Assessment & Evaluation in Higher Education, 49*(3), 363–375. DOI: 10.1080/02602938.2023.2241676

Fernández-Alameda, C. (2024). *IA generativa en el aula. 10 ideas para trabajar el pensamiento critico.* Amazon Kindle Publishing.

Fotea, S., Fotea, I., & undrea, E. (2019). Artificial intelligence in education: Romanian students' attitudes toward artificial intelligence and its impact on their career development. In *ICERI2019 Proceedings, (pp. 9330–9338).* IATED.

Galloway, C., & Swiatek, L. (2018). Public relations and artificial intelligence: It's not (just) about robots. *Public Relations Review, 44*(5), 734–740. DOI: 10.1016/j.pubrev.2018.10.008

Grădinaru, G. I., Dinu, V., Rotaru, C.-L., & Toma, A. (2024). The development of educational competence for Romanian students in the context of the evolution of data science and artificial intelligence. *Amfiteatru Economic, 26*(65), 14–32. DOI: 10.24818/EA/2024/65/14

Hamerman, E. J., Aggarwal, A., & Martins, C. (2025). An investigation of generative AI in the classroom and its implications for university policy. *Quality Assurance in Education, 33*(2), 253–266. DOI: 10.1108/QAE-08-2024-0149

Laato, S., Morschheuser, B., Hamari, J., & Björne, J. (2023). AI-assisted learning with ChatGPT and large language models: Implications for higher education. *2023 IEEE International Conference on Advanced Learning Technologies (ICALT)*, 226–230. IEEE. https://doi.org/DOI: 10.1109/ICALT58122.2023.00072

Lopezosa, C., Codina, L., Pont-Sorribes, C., & Vallez, M. (2023). Use of generative artificial intelligence in the training of journalists: Challenges, uses, and training proposal. *Profesional de la información/Information Professional, 32*(4). https://doi.org/DOI: 10.3145/epi.2023.jul.08

Luo, J. (2024). A critical review of GenAI policies in higher education assessment: A call to reconsider the "originality" of students' work. *Assessment & Evaluation in Higher Education*, •••, 1–14. DOI: 10.1080/02602938.2024.2309963

Miller, R. E. (2024). Pandora's can of worms: A year of generative AI in higher education. *Portal (Baltimore, Md.)*, *24*(1), 21–34. DOI: 10.1353/pla.2024.a916988

Moorhouse, B. L., & Kohnke, L. (2024). The effects of generative AI on initial language teacher education: The perceptions of teacher educators. *System*, *122*, 103290. DOI: 10.1016/j.system.2024.103290

Pesovski, I., Santos, R., Henriques, R., & Trajkovik, V. (2024). Generative AI for customizable learning experiences. *Sustainability*, *16*(7), 3034. DOI: 10.3390/su16073034

Rajabi, P., Taghipour, P., Cukierman, D., & Doleck, T. (2023). Exploring ChatGPT's impact on post-secondary education: A qualitative study. *Proceedings of the 25th Western Canadian Conference on Computing Education*, 1–6. https://doi.org/DOI: 10.1145/3593342.3593360

ercan, E., & Voicu, B. (2022). Patterns of Academic Integrity Definitions among BA Romanian Students'. The Impact of Rising Enrolments. *Revista de Cercetare si Interventie Sociala*, *78*, 87–106.

Smolansky, A., Cram, A., Raduescu, C., Zeivotos, S., Huber, E., & Kizilcec, R. F. (2023). Educator and student perspectives on the impact of generative AI on assessments in higher education. *Proceedings of the Tenth ACM Conference on Learning @ Scale*, 378–382. https://doi.org/DOI: 10.1145/3573051.3596191

Tugui, A., Jeflea, F-V., Opariuc, C., Filipeanu, D., Agheorghiesei, D-T. (2022). Societal Transformations in Romanian Society: Humanity's Interaction with Artificial Intelligence towards the Technological Singularity. *Transformations in Business & Economics, 21* (2A /56A), 435-461.

UNESCO. (2023). *Guidance for generative AI in education and research.* https://unesdoc.unesco.org/ark:/48223/pf0000386693

Vakrats, D., & Wang, X. (2020). Artificial intelligence in advertising creativity. *Journal of Advertising*, *50*(1), 39–51. DOI: 10.1080/00913367.2020.1843090

Wach, K., Duong, C. D., Ejdys, J., Kazlauskaitė, R., Korzynski, P., Mazurek, G., & Ziemba, E. (2023). The dark side of generative artificial intelligence: A critical analysis of controversies and risks of ChatGPT. *Entrepreneurial Business and Economics Review, 11*(2). Advance online publication. DOI: 10.15678/EBER.2023.110201

Walczak, K., & Cellary, W. (2023). Challenges for higher education in the era of widespread access to generative AI. *Economics and Business Review*, *9*(2), 71–100. DOI: 10.18559/ebr.2023.2.743

Yim, I. H. Y., & Wegerif, R. (2024). Teachers' perceptions, attitudes, and acceptance of artificial intelligence (AI) educational learning tools: An exploratory study on AI literacy for young students. *Future in Educational Research, 2*, 313–345. DOI: 10.1002/fer3.65

Yin, R. K. (2009). *Case Study Research. Design and Methods* (4th ed.). Sage.

Zawacki-Richter, O., Marin, V. I., Bond, M., & Gouverneur, F. (2019). Systematic review of research on artificial intelligence applications in higher education – Where are the educators? *International Journal of Educational Technology in Higher Education, 16*(1), 1–27. DOI: 10.1186/s41239-019-0171-0

Chapter 15
Use cases of Internet of Things and Machine Learning in Education

T. Narayanaswamy
https://orcid.org/0000-0002-3781-3297
REVA University, India

A. Shivasharana
REVA University, India

A. Thamotharan
REVA University, India

B. Harani
REVA University, India

A. Shubha
REVA University, India

ABSTRACT

Education in the 21st century has moved beyond traditional classrooms, powered by technologies like the Internet of Things (IoT). IoT connects devices globally, enabling students and teachers to share resources and communicate anytime, fostering seamless interaction and expanding learning networks. Digital natives, familiar with smartphones and apps, benefit from IoT tools like smartboards, which offer interactive displays, cloud-based lessons, and multi-touch functionality. Beyond classrooms, IoT applications include video creation, automated payments, and smart school buses, enhancing overall efficiency. Parents also gain real-time insights

DOI: 10.4018/979-8-3373-6018-8.ch015

Copyright © 2026, IGI Global Scientific Publishing. Copying or distributing in print or electronic forms without written permission of IGI Global Scientific Publishing is prohibited.

into their children's academic performance. This integration of IoT and Machine Learning redefines education, making it more efficient, interactive, and accessible for all stakeholders while shaping its future. This chapter delves into global IoT and Machine Learning use cases, showcasing their advantages for students, educators, and parents, and how they shape the future of education.

INTRODUCTION

After the COVID-19 pandemic, educational institutions across the globe started to explore new modes of teaching -learning which involves the use of both offline and online. This in turn created the need for integrating the offline infrastructure with online infrastructure using technology to meet the diverse needs of students (Imran et al., 2023).In this line, IoT technologies which comprise of interconnected smart devices are enhancing educational experiences by enabling smart classrooms, wearable learning tools and efficient remote learning environments. Smart classrooms use automation for lighting, temperature control, and attendance monitoring while wearable devices support health monitoring and personalized instruction. IoT also enhances campus security through smart surveillance and facial recognition systems and improves resource management by monitoring energy usage and tracking educational assets in real-time (Matellio Inc., 2023). IoT enables the learner to access learning infrastructure anywhere anytime with the support of devices connected through the internet. On the other hand, machine learning (ML) algorithms are used to analyze education-related data and generates valuable insights to enhance the learning experience of the learners. These insights are generated from the recommendation engines of online Learning platforms, adaptive learning applications and data analytics software for student performance tracking (Ahramovich, 2023).

1. INTERNET OF THINGS AND EDUCATION

IoT is a technology that connects objects /things of an organisation each other and also with the outside environment through Internet. The major objective of this is to make certain routine monotonous tasks easy and comfortable by automatically connecting various objects with the help of internet.

Any object can be converted into IoT/smart device suppose it can be linked to the internet and at the same time, made to transmit the information. IoT system being a smart technology eases processing and analysis of information collected. The necessary conclusions are made so as to achieve the objective /goal /target. There are variety IoT devices which ranges from monitoring the school bus/smart bus (while school kids are travelling) to connecting to a device that can be controlled via a mobile phone from wherever an individual is. Covid-19 Pandemic created opportunities in schools and higher educational institutions to get connected to teachers anywhere anytime online through various internet meeting platforms/app such as google meet, zoom and WebEx. This in turn really makes teaching-learning more flexible. Apart from classroom sessions, assistance for learning happens through the devices which are connected through internet. A survey conducted during the year 2021 by Agilie Consultancy at Ukraine reveals regarding school education reveals that 70% of the students felt boredom at schools all the time, 80% of them felt constant stress. This clearly shows teaching-learning should go beyond physical classroom sessions so as to engage students for majority of the time. Many of the teaching-learning related problems (which are solvable using IoT) faced by schools and Higher education institutions are listed below (Builtin 2020).

- Current traditional classroom teaching does not impart new skills demanded by the industry.
- Outdated assessment tests/ methodology puts the students into emotional stress and anxiety thus failing to get through the assessment.
- Teachers are not provided with adequate training programs to adopt innovative ways of teaching-learning.

1.1 Benefits of IoT in Education

Internet of Things (IoT) has positively impacted the way the educational institutions operate as physical environments are linked to smart devices and interconnects many infrastructures. One can imagine IoT applications that include interactive digital boards, video management, real-time updating of information about students' progression and attendance by teachers to parents, smart school buses for ensuring safe on-boarding of school kids and many more applications.

For teachers, IoT helps in automatically recording **class attendance** of students, effective delivery of academic sessions using technology. **IoT sensors** installed within the premise of educational institutions helps to track and monitor students' activities and presence across different locations of the campus such as cafeteria and library. IoT enabled classrooms makes it easier for teachers to communicate with students from remote locations, collect feedback pertaining to subjects being taught and also render necessary support to specially-abled learners (Educba 2020). **Noise sensors** will help teachers to communicate quickly to neighbouring class students and accordingly advise them to reduce the noise level. Other scenarios include noise detection and warning of the same to the students immediately during examinations by means of IoT embedded LCD screens (Builtin 2020)

IoT facilitates to pool large amounts of data by using embedded sensors and smart devices. The data thus collected can be used to **take necessary actions** for the betterment of students and teachers. Also, students can also gain access to educational live content through multiple channels such as apps, television, computers and many more especially when they are on sick leave. When it comes to **learning material,** 3D graphical textbooks which includes video content, read aloud options and storing key points/notes by converting voice in a digital notebook can be made available to students' community (Educba 2020). Some of the major benefits of incorporating IoT in education are discussed in the following section.

1.1.1 Smart Teaching Plans and Web Based Discussions

The students can attend the live class room sessions through the internet and the same can be recorded for future reference and revision. Remote connectivity helps the educators to promote an interaction of students with other subject expert available in different locations of the globe thus creating a relevant and elaborate lesson plan (Education World 2021).

Web based discussions enables the students to engage with other students and teachers across the globe. Web based discussions have become an active part of the large study groups where in students are able to engage with other students and teachers from all across the globe. This in turn improves the access to additional information and suitable learning material for the students' community. Suppose the students fail to attend the classes offline due to some reasons, students can learn by accessing the recorded lectures and discussions, then take a test and receive feedback from the teacher through web platform after test.

SMART, a tech company is the first company to introduce interactive whiteboard during the year 1991. This in turn really paved the way for enhancing the interaction between the students and teachers who can connect to real time subject information on various websites, access published reports and multimedia items within no time. Apps such as ClassDojo enables the parents to have a look at the school work done by their wards. This app is by used currently by 95% of all middle schools in 180 countries including the united states because of its versatility to translate into 35 languages.

1.1.2 Energy Saving and Cost Control

IoT enabled classrooms facilitate to identify the devices such as projector, AC, electricity bulbs which are still not switched off even after the classroom sessions are over. Thereafter switching off is done just by clicking from mobile device not only from within the campus but also from wherever the supervisors are at that point of time. Pre-scheduling of operating times of these devices are also possible with the help of IoT devices. Thus, IoT enabled devices in the classroom enables schools to save energy and trim electricity bills (Gilman et al., 2020).

Internet of Things finds it uses in a wide variety of sectors out of which education has expanded its boundaries in terms of instructional approaches and learning opportunities.

IoT enables school education to have better connected classrooms with the help of devices linked through internet. These devices open the door for students to access various learning resources and also teachers can monitor the learning efficiency of students on a real time basis. Apart from learning aspects, IoT also enhances the security features in schools by means of using climate control devices, smart cameras, smart lighting systems and many more to list out (Builtin 2020).

This clearly indicates that IoT is not just a technology, it's the new way of sharing information & knowledge, communicating and creating learning communities thus bringing about the culture of being professional in schools. As a result of this, all educational leaders are able to deliver the above key responsibilities in an effective and efficient manner.

1.1.3 Personalized Learning (PL)

It refers to a method of education that focuses on customising learning instruction to each student based on the needs, preferences and pace by deploying technology and data-driven insights (Shemshack & Spector, 2020).

Personalized learning is in existence since the dawn of teaching-learning in the form of one-to-one mentoring and apprenticeship. As educational technologies started to emerge in the previous century, personalized learning gained much importance and made possible in the form of smart/intelligent tutoring systems. In this century, big data and learning analytics are the two major pillars that transform personalized learning once again. Integrating emerging technologies such as IoT with analytics has opened the doors for significant improvement in personalised learning opportunities. IoT helps to track the learning pattern for each of the learner/student and accordingly customise learning materials and assessments to simplify the learning process and significantly. The data generated from in-class and eLearning activities (such as Learning Management Systems (LMS)) provides a comprehensive picture of learner's journey and the insights generated through analytics would help identify individual learning styles (Eyal, 2012).

1.1.4 Assistive Technology for Disabled Students

A new branch of IoT solutions, known as Assistive Technology has emerged in the domain of education. This technology comprises of specialized tools and software that facilitate students with disabilities in navigating their learning environments in a user-friendly manner. Some of the alternative devices for computer navigation includes voice-activated tablet controls, real-time voice-to-text translation, and customized tools for students with autism and dyslexia. One such device, the C-Pen, combines optical character recognition with a built-in camera to capture printed text. It can translate and pronounce words using nine dictionaries, helping international students and those with learning difficulties grasp new concepts more efficiently. (Parcel Pending, 2024).

1.1.5 Smart Library Systems

The concept of a IoT based smart library system is to enable library operations with minimal human intervention. The proposed system of (Jayawardena et al., 2021) was to automate important tasks such as issuing, returning, and reserving books, collecting late return fines, detecting theft and managing inventory through IoT technologies such as RFID and Raspberry Pi. A primary focus is shelf management, where each book is assigned a unique key and identified using RFID for organized arrangement. The study conducted by (Bakar & Zakaria, 2023) revealed that IoT supported library professionals are able to improve service efficiency, offer context-based library services, by ensuring the provision of tracking facilities. This helped deliver effective utilisation and quicker access to library resources and hence the management of library systems. However, barriers to the successful adoption of IoT applications in university libraries included security and privacy concerns, insufficient technical infrastructure, limited technological skills, and the absence of clear policies and strategic planning.

1.2 Challenges/ Risks/Limitations Associated with IoT

The challenges associated with IoT are discussed in this section as follows,

1.2.1 Security risks associated with IoT

The Internet of Things (IoT) faces several security challenges such as issues related to RFID tag security, cybersecurity, wireless security, network transmission security and privacy protection (Daud, Khan, & Saleem, 2017). Some of the major risks associated with IoT are given in the figure 1.

Figure 1. List of IoT security challenges

Source: https://www.sprintzeal.com/blog/iot-security-challenges

IoT devices face inadequate **physical security** and becomes vulnerable to unauthorized access. Devices deployed in remote or unattended locations for extended periods are especially susceptible, as there are high chances for attackers to physically tamper them. Devices which don't have sufficient physical safeguards are easy targets for exploitation. For example, attackers can introduce malware into IoT systems through infected USB flash drives and tamper IoT devices Ensuring the physical security of IoT devices is primarily the responsibility of manufacturers. However, designing secure and tamper-resistant transmitters and sensors, particularly for low-cost IoT devices, presents a significant challenge (Sprintzeal, n.d., Aqeel et al., 2022). Next comes the **visibility risk.** Gaining full visibility of all devices connected to a network is a daunting task for IT teams, as many devices would often be missing from official inventory records. Items such as coffee machines, ventilation units and air conditioning systems are frequently overlooked and not prioritized for tracking. Without a clear view of all connected devices, security teams will be unable to prevent breaches to a greater extent . The absence of visibility makes it challenging for the IT department to maintain an accurate list of assets that require protection and monitoring. Next, **Ransomware** is a kind of security threat encrypts and restricts access to critical files by hackers who demand a payment in exchange for the decryption key. IoT devices with poor security measures are particularly susceptible to such attacks. Although incidents of ransomware targeting IoT devices are rare, the growing importance and dependence on IoT devices, smart education systems and other smart equipment could become prime targets in the future as their value and criticality to users continue to rise(Sprintzeal, n.d., Sahu & Mazumdar, 2024). IoT also raises some concerns about **privacy and cybersecurity** such as, lack of user awareness, the misconfiguration of secure protocols, improper device updates or the mismanagement of active device monitoring. For example, the details of students can be hacked by cyber attacker and reveal it, trade it, or leverage it to blackmail the owner (Tawalbeh et al., 2020). A **botnet** refers to a network of machines which are infected with malware. Attackers use these compromised devices to flood a target with thousands of requests per second, aiming to devastate and disable it. Unlike traditional computers, IoT devices typically will not receive regular security updates and this makes them particularly vulnerable to malware attacks. Consequently, they can be quickly hijacked and incorporated into botnets, which are then exploited to launch large-scale traffic attacks against targeted systems.

1.2.2 Cost of Implementation And Maintenance of IoT Devices

A considerable number of resources must be dedicated to getting the most out of IoT technology. This includes costly hardware and software expenditures and adequate Wi-Fi coverage across all campuses. Institutions need to be able to equip every student with devices like laptops or tablets, which may be pricey in bulk quantities.

Additionally, identification systems must be set up, and everything needs regular maintenance. This is no easy task; requiring plenty of tech knowledge, schools would also have to hire experienced professionals trained in data management solutions. This could add up to an exponential cost for which most institutional budgets are unprepared (Edly, n.d., Abbasy et al,2017).

1.2.3 Organisational Factors

Though the industrialized nations such as the United States, the United Kingdom, Japan, and China are leading in the forefront in terms of successfully implementing IoT, developing countries, specifically Saudi Arabia, Malaysia, Pakistan, and Bangladesh, lags behind. Ali et al(2023) made a study to analyse study centers in Saudi Arabia to identify the factors catalysing/hindering the adoption with special reference to e-learning sector of Higher educational institutions. The data were collected from 384 respondents in Saudi Arabian HEIs. Financial obstacles, interactive capability, self-efficacy, training programs, data safeguarding measures were found to be major factors influencing the adoption of IoT. When it comes to training faculty of higher education institutions, attitude, acceptance and digital competence are most fundamentals parameters to be taken care(Romero-Rodríguez et al., 2020)

In terms of Training faculty on IoT in the domain of education, acceptance, positive attitude and digital competence are the major aspects in order to ensure adoption (Romero-Rodríguez et al., 2020). Therefore, the need to train faculty becomes a challenging task if the faculty does not show interest/curiosity in adopting IoT for educational purpose (Kiryakova et al., 2017).

2. MACHINE LEARNING AND EDUCATION

Machine learning algorithms are designed in such a way that it identifies patterns/behaviour/sentiment/trends in data and accordingly make predictions or decisions based on those patterns. The concept has evolved significantly over a period of time and is applied across various domains, including healthcare, finance, education, and the list extends to all other sectors. According to Mitchell (1997), machine learning is defined as "a field of study that gives computers the ability to learn without being explicitly programmed". Machine learning in education can be used to study the learning patterns of students/learners and accordingly provide e-learning resources/teacher support to fulfil the outcome of learning.

Ahramovich (2023) stated that Machine learning(ML) is reshaping education by providing new tools that allow educational institutions to monitor and enhance student performance and also the engagement. Through personalized learning strategies powered by ML, education is becoming more interactive, inclusive and accessible. According to Machine learning technologies boost students' academic performance. According to McKinfsey & Company (2022), 71% of students stated that machine learning-powered teaching assistants as positive innovations in their educational process. According to Global Market Insights (2023), the AI in education market would reach $30 billion by 2032, with machine learning accounting for a share of 20% of the market revenue in 2022.

Machine learning in education, provides a range of learning and training tools powered by self-improving deep learning algorithms. These algorithms can process great volumes of data, detect recurring patterns, key metrics and relationships among variables and thus facilitates better insights on major trends and scenarios in the education sector. First one is

Ahramovich (2023) has defined two major functions of machine learning with respect to education namely analytical and operational functions. In terms of **Analytical functions**,

Machine learning algorithms are used for analysing the educational data and generate insights to improve the learning process. Recommendation systems on eLearning platforms, adaptive learning applications and tracking of student performance through data analytics tools. Al-Alawi et al (2023) applied supervised machine learning algorithms to identify the factors that hamper the academic performance of college students during probation (especially those who were academically not performing well in terms of minimum passing requirement). Authors have used Knowledge Discovery in Databases (KDD) methodology with a sample 6514 college students for a period of 11 years ranging from 2009 to 2019 (details of respondents were provided by a major public university in Oman). The authors had used Information Gain algorithm to select the most important features and applied ensemble methods to compute and compare the accuracy with algorithms that are more robust in terms of prediction accuracy. The study revealed the identified major factors driving student academic achievement as study/program duration in the university and their past performance during secondary school education. The study also found that academic specialization, estimated graduation year, cohort and gender significantly contributed for predicting whether a student was in promotion/ probation. In terms of **Operational functions,** Fields like natural language processing (NLP) and computer vision depend on machine learning to identify/recognize linguistic and visual patterns, enabling systems to mimic human abilities such as communication and visual recognition. These capabilities form the foundation of interactive technologies such as virtual tutors, educational robots and real-time translation software.

2.1 Use Case of IoT in Education

2.1.1 Use Case of Promethean ActivWalls at Palmer High School

Palmer High School is located in Seattle, Washington and it has adopted Promethean's ActivWalls (an advanced interactive display technology) for enhancing its English tutoring programs. This technology has features such as a dry-erase surface, natural writing capability, cloud-based lesson delivery software and customized teacher training (Builtin, 2020). The school implemented ActivWalls to create more engaging and student-centered English language instruction environments. After the implementation of ActivWalls, Palmer High School observed many positive outcomes. Academic performance improved, with a reported 18% increase in English test scores among students engaged with the technology-enhanced tutoring (Promethean, 2021). Teachers reported increased student participation and engagement, particularly among those who had previously struggled in traditional classroom settings. The technology allowed for personalized instruction, helping students visualize literary concepts and collaborate more effectively during group activities. Moreover, administrative efficiency saw notable improvement. Digital lesson delivery and centralized storage of instructional content led to a 12% reduction in the use of printed materials and related administrative costs over the academic year (District EdTech Report, 2022). Teachers also spent less time preparing and duplicating physical learning materials, allowing them to focus more on student interaction. Despite the benefits, the school faced several challenges during the implementation phase. First, there was a learning curve for both students and teachers in adapting to the digital interface and new teaching dynamics. Initial teacher training, though comprehensive, required supplementary sessions, as educators requested additional support in integrating the technology with their curriculum.

Additionally, technical issues such as connectivity lags and syncing problems between the cloud-based lesson delivery platform and school servers disrupted some early lessons. The school also had to address infrastructure limitations, including insufficient high-speed internet in some classrooms, which temporarily hindered full-scale deployment.

To overcome these challenges, Palmer High School increased its investment in IT support and organized peer-led workshops to foster collaborative learning among staff. Over time, these strategies helped ensure a smoother integration process and maximized the benefits of the ActivWall system.

Figure 2. Implementation and Impact of Promethean ActivWalls at Palmer High School

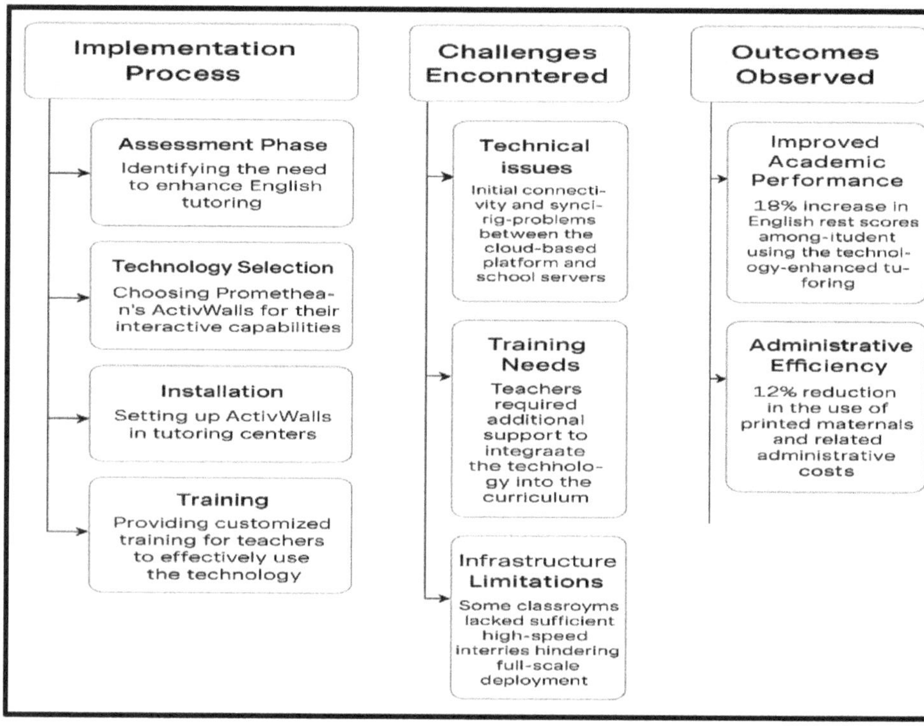

Source: Author's own work

2.1.2 Digital Highlighter

Scanmarker (also known as portable digital highlighter) is used to scan any text content from any documents such as books and papers and transfer the scanned content to a computer, tablet or phone in the form of editable text. This text can also be translated into not less than 40 other languages. This technology is not only useful in scanning but also reading and listening simultaneously. This helps the learners to quickly grasp the key points during examinations. Scanmarker is used by many schools in Kansas City of Missouri.

2.1.3 Teaching-Learning and e-Learning

SweetRush a tech-based start-up is into providing education solutions using e-learning platforms and mobile apps. It provides customised education/training programs in the form of animations, competitive games which enhances learner's participation and retention. For example, it created IoT for simulating call-centre environment of financial services. This really helps the call-centre staff members to get trained on new skills in the domain of financial services without physical classroom training and role plays. The company is situated at San Francisco, California (Alcatel 2020).

Blackboard, a firm which provides educational technology services offers virtual classroom, digital platform for personalised learning, and also website access (by both students and parents) to updated information about grades, attendance, news and events. These technologies are provided to schools and higher education institutions. *LocoRobo* of Philadelphia, Pennsylvania is engaged in providing robots for teaching coding languages such as JavaScript, C, MATLAB and Python. This company introduced a small robot (which works based on Artificial Intelligence) named as My Loopy which enables children to learn coding skills. This robot is equipped with sensors which can respond to light, sound and other changes in the surroundings. Kaltura of New York offers video management tools that enable students and teachers to create, edit and deliver high-quality video at any point in time irrespective of whether they are inside or outside the classroom. Digital mode of teaching-learning not only requires responses to student queries but also providing timely feedback. This becomes possible by employing artificial intelligence and machine learning algorithms which can create a chatbot to act as virtual assistants. Ashok Goel was working as a professor at Georgia Tech in USA(Nagarro 2021). When he was teaching Artificial Intelligence through online mode during the year 2015, a ***bot*** named as Jill Watson was (a self-directed computer program that works on the internet which can interact with systems/users) assisting him in his teaching process. This bot was actually answering most of the questions raised by the students. It became possible by recording chats that were generated during a period of one year and feeding them to AI program which could respond to frequently raised queries with an accuracy of 97%. Nagarro, a digital product engineering firm designed an Edu Bot called as Hermoine that can provide feedback to the students on their subsequent assignments, quizzes attended by getting connected to learning management system. One of the most important applications of AI being the voice assistance that s been completely and successfully employed by teachers in student learning process like Alexa (product of amazon), Corotana (product of Microsoft), Siri (product of Apple). These applications allow the students to converse effectively with the educational materials without the support of educators (Analytics Steps 2021). These can be applied anywhere. Voice assistant facilities provided by educational institutions bring out the answers for commonly raised queries by students on campus related needs, course/subject areas, handbooks. This reduces the need for internal support services and also the cost of printing college handbooks is avoided.

2.1.4 Attendance Tracking And Access To Facilities At Educational Institutes

Magic card of Weymouth, U.K is into making smart cards used by students. The smart cards are linked through IoT to access control system. Then these cards can be presented to readers for physical access to facilities, marking attendance, monitor the status of e-learning courses, monitor the use of printers, internet. Also used for accessing vending machines, photocopying machines and data such as emergency contacts (KDnuggets 2018).

2.1.5 Smart Buses

McLean of Virginia is into making wi-fi systems for smart buses. This system helps drivers to regularly monitor the behaviour of students inside the bus while travelling to school. These Wi-Fi enabled buses have an internet facility which enables the students to turn-in homework. The parents can also monitor on-board safety of their wards/child on a real-time basis when they are travelling to schools. Figure 3 depicts the working system of IoT based bus tracking system.

Figure 3. The working system of IoT based bus tracking system.

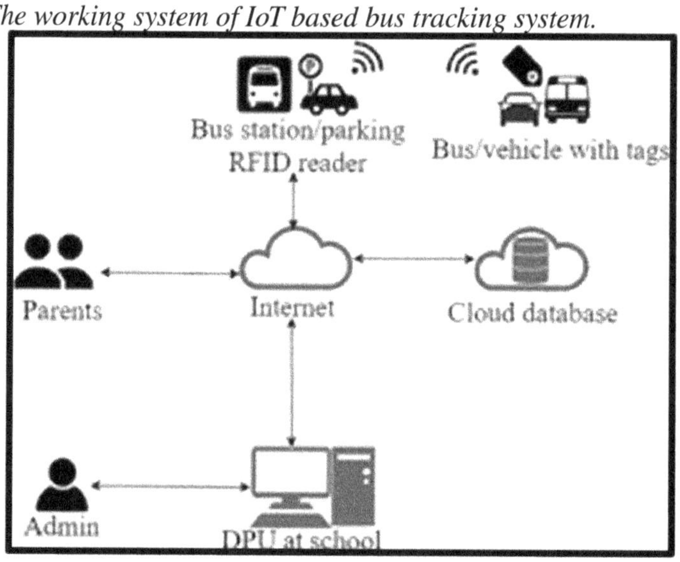

Source: Al-Alawi et al., (2023).

An **IoT-based bus tracking system** works by combining IoT devices, GPS technology/RFID, cloud servers and mobile/web applications to monitor and manage buses in a real time basis. Each bus is equipped with a GPS module and a microcontroller that continuously collects location data such as latitude, longitude, and speed. This data is then transmitted through an IoT communication module such as GSM, 4G, or Wi-Fi to a cloud server. On the server side, the information is stored, processed, and organized using advanced algorithms that compute real-time positions, estimated times of arrival and traffic conditions. Passengers are given live access through mobile apps/web portals, where they could view the real-time location of buses, get Estimated Time for Arrival for upcoming stops, and receive notifications whenever there are delays or route changes. For fleet managers, the system offers an administrative interface to track operations, monitor the bus performance and hence ensure safety. Additional features include geofencing, emergency alerts and predictive maintenance can also be integrated in order to enhance security and efficiency. Overall, the IoT-based bus tracking system improves the commuting experience, operational transparency and fleet management.

2.1.6 Digital Examinations, Evaluation Systems and Administration

Companies such as Mercer-Mettl and LittleMore Innovation labs are into providing online examination products/solutions. The solution includes remote proctoring systems using Artificial intelligence, recording during proctored exams and digital evaluation systems (LittleMore Innovations 2021). Mercer-Mettl's robust AI system was trained with higher than 2.8 million proctored exam assessments which could identify more than 18 type of diversions of students/candidates with an accuracy of 95%. As of now, the company has conducted higher than 20 million online examinations/tests successfully over the past few years delivering mistake free results. Teachers spend huge time in performing clerical / paper work and other variety of tasks apart from teaching activities. Non-teaching tasks include evaluation of internal assessment tests, preparing and managing classroom study materials, interacting with and responding to queries raised by parents, managing field visits, etc. AI helps the teachers to handle these routine non-teaching tasks and facilitate personalised response to students. This not only reduces the times spent non-teaching tasks but also removes monotony in the work and solves the problem of logistics (anytime anywhere the queries raised by parents and the students can be handled).

3. USE CASES OF MACHINE LEARNING IN EDUCATION

3.1 Adaptive Learning

With the help of machine learning (ML), adaptive learning platforms such as MobyMax, SchooLinks, Carnegie Learning's LiveLab, and Kidaptive had transformed the educational landscape by ensuring personalized learning experiences in real time. **MobyMax** uses Machine Learning algorithms to check gaps in student knowledge and automatically adjust the difficulty of tasks assigned, ensuring that each student receives instruction customised to their needs (MobyMax, 2024). Schools using MobyMax reported that students master skills at three times the usual rate and experience significant improvements in standardized test scores. However, challenges still remain in terms of information overload for teachers who must interpret vast amounts of real-time data and a reduction in peer interaction, which can impact student motivation.

Similarly, **SchooLinks** make use of ML to guide K-12 students in college and facilitate career planning by analyzing academic and personal data to recommend suitable career paths, colleges(higher educational institutions) and scholarships (SchooLinks, 2024). The platform is really helpful in increasing student engagement and more informed decision-making regarding future careers. Nevertheless, challenges persist, particularly with respect to algorithmic bias, where career suggestions may unintentionally reflect historical inequities, and privacy concerns surrounding sensitive student data.

Carnegie Learning's LiveLab uses a different approach by using real-time ML monitoring to track student engagement and performance during classroom sessions (Carnegie Learning, 2024). The system provides immediate alerts to teachers about students who are struggling or disengaged during class sessions and enables proactive interventions before issues escalate. This real-time feedback loop has been shown to enhance student focus and improve classroom dynamics. Yet, teachers sometimes struggle with trust issues, preferring their own judgment over ML recommendations, and may find the system's alerts unclear without sufficient explanation.

For early childhood education, **Kidaptive** uses ML to develop dynamic learner profiles, recommending activities and content based on a child's developmental patterns (Kidaptive, 2024). This allows early identification of learning delays and provides parents with actionable insights to support their children's education. While Kidaptive enhances early intervention and parental engagement, challenges include difficulties in interpreting ML-generated recommendations and the high costs associated with scaling such individualized solutions across entire education systems.

Despite their immense potential, ML-based adaptive learning platforms share common challenges: biases in algorithmic predictions, concerns over data privacy and security, the need for significant teacher training, and the risk of over-reliance on automated systems at the expense of human judgment. As these technologies continue to evolve, addressing these challenges will be crucial to ensuring equitable, effective, and sustainable educational improvements (Al-Alawi et al., 2023).

3.2 Inclusive Learning

Machine learning and other artificial intelligence-driven technologies is highly useful in ensuring the achievement of learning outcome by customising the learning resources and facilities depending on diverse social backgrounds, learning styles, and personalities. Additionally, AI/ML facilities also take care of learners with disabilities pertaining to learning, speaking, hearing/other physical/mental state. However, all deserve equal opportunities to study (Ahramovich., 2023). In terms of Personalized Learning, AI algorithms customise educational content to individual student needs, enhancing engagement and comprehension (Gibson, 2024). In terms of Early Detection of Learning Disabilities, ML models can identify signs of learning difficulties/challenges, facilitating timely support and interventions (Fitas, 2025). In terms of Enhanced Communication, AI-powered tools assist in overcoming language barriers and support communication for students with speech or hearing impairments (Artificial Intelligence +, 2024). AI can automate administrative tasks, allowing teachers to focus more on individualized instruction (Artificial Intelligence +, 2024).

ML-driven inclusive education eliminates partialities and enhances accessibility for a wider audience from diverse background/diverse disabilities without compromising education quality. Assistive technologies (AT) and learning systems for disabled /older people enables them access to online education and help overcome learning barriers. Assistive learning technologies are discussed in Table 1, Table 2, Table 3 and Table 4 below,

Table 1. **Input Technologies***(Jensen, 2023).*

Technology	Application
Braille Keyboards	Enable tangible input for visually impaired users
Eye, Head, and Foot Control Systems	Allow users with limited mobility to interact with devices using alternative control methods
Sip-and-Puff Mouth-Controlled Joysticks	Facilitate computer navigation through inhaling and exhaling actions
Mouse Emulation Devices	Provide alternative means to control cursor movement

continued on following page

Table 1. Continued

Technology	Application
Single-Switch Entry Devices	Simplify input for users with motor impairments
Speech Input/Dictation Software	Convert spoken words into text, aiding users with physical disabilities

Table 2. **Output Technologies***(Jensen, 2023).*

Technology	Application
Refreshable Braille Displays	Translate on-screen text into Braille characters .
Screen Magnification Software	Enlarge content for users with low vision .
Screen Readers	Convert text to speech or Braille output .
Text Input Improvement Software	
Abbreviation Expansion	Automatically expands short codes into full words or phrases .
Efficient Text Entry Interfaces	Optimize typing for users with mobility challenges .
Spelling and Grammar Check Software	Assist users with learning disabilities .
Word Prediction	Suggests words to expedite typing .

Table 3. **Assistive Listening Systems***(Jensen, 2023).*

Technology	Application
Audio Induction Loops	Transmit sound directly to hearing aids.
FM Microphone and Receiver Systems	Enhance sound clarity in noisy environments.
Infrared (IR) Listening Systems	Use light waves to transmit audio signals.

Table 4. **Assistive Technologies for the Visually Impaired(Jensen, 2023).**

Technology	Application
Braille Embossers	Produce hard copy Braille documents.
Closed-Circuit Television (CCTV)	Magnify printed materials for easier reading.
Scanners with Optical Character Recognition (OCR)	Convert printed text into digital format.
Tactile Diagrams	Provide raised representations of images and graphs.

Table 5. **Assistive Technologies for the Hearing Impaired***(Jensen, 2023)*

Technology	Application
Sign Language-Text Conversion Software	Translates sign language into written text
Subtitles (Closed Captions)	Display spoken dialogue as text on screens

3.3 Reducing Drop-Out Rates

In the traditional method of identifying dropout students, teachers learn the exact reasons only at the end of the academic session, making it difficult for educational institutions to provide timely support to retain the students(Brasca et al., 2022). This is due to multiple risk factors on aspects such as academic, financial, mental health and other relevant issues and the difficulty lies in detecting specific reason(s). As a result, students with decent grades and attendance but face ongoing struggles such late submission of assignments or financial difficulties, may go unnoticed, limiting the effectiveness of such interventions. A machine-learning model helps in overcoming the challenges of identifying at-risk (likely to dropout) students by analysing a ten-year data to reveal subtle risk factors which includes such as changes in payment methods or late assignment submissions. This allows universities to intervene early and improve retention rate of students who are more likely to drop out of the program. Institutions can extend the use of analytics across the entire student journey, starting from prospective to former students(alumni). For example, advanced analytics can identify high schools or areas to target for recruitment(admissions) and suggest tailored interventions for enrolled students to improve satisfaction. Over time, as the model improves, institutions can offer personalized support, including post-graduation skills development and alumni engagement.

Brasca et al., (2022) of McKinsey and Company had applied advanced machine learning algorithm to increase the enrolment of a private nonprofit university in order to increase the enrolment. Based on the insights from machine learning model, important actions were taken. The machine-learning model indentified the top 10% of prospective leads which accounted for 90% of applications, maximizing marketing ROI. A second model predicted the list of applicants who were most likely to enrol for various programs, helping the university focus on the top 40% and segment them into five categories for targeted yield efforts. By identifying "look-alike" markets with strong potential, the university expanded its applicant pool by 15–20%. This data-driven strategy became a success story, achieving higher enrolment without major increases in investment (Rastrollo-Guerrero et al.,2020).

Hussain and Khan (2023)'s study focused on forecasting student grades/marks using supervised machine learning (ML) techniques in order to improve education quality and also to support sustainability goals. The dataset was sourced from BISE Peshawar which includes seven regions, is pre-processed to improve data quality. A regression model was built to predict student marks, while a decision tree (DT) classifier was used to forecast grades based on 30 key attributes/features. The analysis demonstrated that ML approaches are effective for academic performance prediction, offering better insights for improving educational planning, administration and teaching quality across educational institutions. some of the commonly used methods in machine learning are Recommender Systems, Machine Learning, Collaborative Filtering, Artificial Neural Networks among others.

3.4 Task Automation

Brasca et al., (2022) of McKinsey and Company reported that educators dedicate about 50% of their working time for preparation, evaluation and other clerical activities. As a result, time constraints cause a significant challenge to the adoption of personalized learning. However, machine learning (ML) software can automate many of these tasks such as grading assessments. For example, Century Tech, a UK-based company, provides ML-driven solutions for students/learners and educators by using leveraging big data analytics and cognitive neuroscience in order to enhance student outcomes and lessen teachers' workloads by automating repetitive tasks such as creating learning resources, grading, and distributing assignments.

3.5 Quicker Translation Of Languages

Amazon Translate was continuously improving to produce more accurate translations. Since its launch, Amazon had constantly met customer demands by adding more sought-after languages (Amazon Web Services, n.d.). The service was said to go beyond simple word-level translations by understanding the context of the words it translated. As the service leverages the power of machine learning, it could be up to 1,000 times more cost-effective than traditional/human translation methods. This efficiency allows organizations to allocate their resources toward enhancing customer experiences instead of spending time on repetitive and manual translation tasks. Furthermore, Amazon Translate could be easily integrated into applications to process content in various formats, fitting diverse business needs. Privacy and security were emphasized as strict access control measures, core aspects of the service with built-in content encryption and robust policies ensuring that sensitive information remained secure and confidential.

CONCLUSION

This chapter highlighted the use of internet-of-things in different domains of education such as administration, attendance monitoring, non-teaching routine tasks, examination, teaching-learning. Use cases with reference to different countries in these domains have been discussed. These cases underlined the effectiveness of internet of things in dealing with various issues in education. There are a very few studies conducted on implementation/use case of Internet of Things and Machine learning in the discipline of education. In-depth research is required to get clarity in terms of resources required, costs incurred and the realised benefits of Internet of Things. Thus, there is lot scope to carry out research on how IoT can be implemented in different levels of school and higher education by various Government and private educational institutions.

REFERENCES

Abbasy, M. B., & Quesada, E. V. (2017). Predictable influence of IoT (Internet of Things) in the higher education. *International Journal of Information and Education Technology (IJIET)*, *7*(12), 914–920. DOI: 10.18178/ijiet.2017.7.12.995

Ahramovich, A. (2023, June 23). Machine learning in education: 10 use cases, examples, and benefits. *Itransition*. https://www.itransition.com/machine-learning/education

Al-Alawi, L., Al Shaqsi, J., Tarhini, A., & Al-Busaidi, A. S. (2023). Using machine learning to predict factors affecting academic performance: The case of college students on academic probation. *Education and Information Technologies*, *28*(10), 1–26. DOI: 10.1007/s10639-023-11700-0 PMID: 37361752

Alcatel. (2020). The Internet of Things in Education. https://www.al-enterprise.com/-/media/assets/internet/documents/iot-for-education-solutionbrief-en.pdf

Ali, J., Madni, S. H. H., Jahangeer, M. S. I., & Danish, M. A. A. (2023). IoT Adoption Model for E-Learning in Higher Education Institutes: A Case Study in Saudi Arabia. *Sustainability*, *15*, 9748. DOI: 10.3390/su15129748

Analytics Steps. (2021). 6 Applications of AI in Education Sector. https://www.analyticssteps.com/blogs/4-major-applications-artificial-intelligence-education-sector

. Bakar, A., & Zakaria, N. H. (2023). Factors influencing the adoption of Internet of Things (IoT) in university libraries: A systematic literature review (SLR). *The Electronic Library*, ahead-of-print(ahead-of-print). https://doi.org/DOI: 10.1108/EL-07-2023-0174

Builtin. (2020). How education technology is changing the classroom. *Builtin*. https://builtin.com/edtech

Builtin. (2020). The Connected Classroom: 9 Examples of IoT in Education. https://builtin.com/internet-things/iot-education-examples

Carnegie Learning. (2024). LiveLab: Real-time classroom monitoring with machine learning. https://www.carnegielearning.com/

Daud, M., Khan, Q., & Saleem, Y. (2017). A study of key technologies for IoT and associated security challenges. *2017 International Symposium on Wireless Systems and Networks (ISWSN)*, 1–6. https://doi.org/DOI: 10.1109/ISWSN.2017.8250042

Edly. (n.d.). IoT in education: Main solutions IoT brings to education. Retrieved April 27, 2025, from https://edly.io/blog/iot-in-education-main-solutions-iot-brings-to-education/

Education World. (2021). IoT and its impact on education. https://www.educationworld.in/iot-and-its-impact-on-education/

Educba. (2020). IoT in Education. https://www.educba.com/iot-in-education/

Eyal, L. (2012). Digital assessment literacy — The core role of the teacher in a digital environment. *Journal of Educational Technology & Society*, *15*(2), 37–49.

Fitas, R. (2025). Inclusive Education with AI: Supporting Special Needs and Tackling Language Barriers. *arXiv*. https://arxiv.org/abs/2504.14120

Gibson, R. (2024). The Impact of AI in Advancing Accessibility for Learners with Disabilities. *EDUCAUSE Review*. https://er.educause.edu/articles/2024/9/the-impact-of-ai-in-advancing-accessibility-for-learners-with-disabilitiesEDUCAUSE Review

Gilman, E., Tamminen, S., Yasmin, R., & Ristimella, E. (2020). Internet of Things for smart spaces: A university campus case study. *Sensors (Basel)*, *20*(13), 3716. DOI: 10.3390/s20133716 PMID: 32630833

Global Market Insights. (2023). AI in education market size, growth trends 2024–2032. https://www.gminsights.com/industry-analysis/ai-in-education-market

Hussain, S., & Khan, M. Q. (2023). Student-performulator: Predicting students' academic performance at secondary and intermediate level using machine learning. *Annals of Data Science*, *10*(3), 637–655. DOI: 10.1007/s40745-021-00341-0 PMID: 38624826

Imran, R., Fatima, A., Salem, I. E., & Allil, K. (2023). Teaching and learning delivery modes in higher education: Looking back to move forward post-COVID-19 era. *International Journal of Management Education*, *21*(2), 100805. DOI: 10.1016/j.ijme.2023.100805

Jayawardena, C., Reyal, S., Kekirideniya, K. R., Wijayawardhana, G. H. T., Rupasinghe, D. G. I. U., & Lakranda, S. Y. R. M. (2021). Artificial intelligence based smart library management system. *2021 6th IEEE International Conference on Recent Advances and Innovations in Engineering (ICRAIE)* (pp. 1–6). https://doi.org/DOI: 10.1109/ICRAIE52900.2021.9703998

KDnuggets. (2018). Role of IoT in Education. https://www.kdnuggets.com/2018/04/role-iot-education.html

Kidaptive. (2024). Adaptive learning for early childhood education. https://theindexproject.org/award/nominees/1838

Leapfrog. (2019). Evolution of AI. https://www.lftechnology.com/blog/ai/ai-evolution/

LittleMore Innovations. (2021). 3 million paperless digital exams. https://www.littlemoreinnovation.com/lm-exam/

Matellio Inc. (2023, October 13). A guide to IoT use cases in education: Unlocking the future of learning. *Matellio*. https://www.matellio.com/blog/iot-use-cases-in-education/

McKinsey & Company. (2022, August 19). Machine learning meets higher learning. https://www.mckinsey.com/featured-insights/sustainable-inclusive-growth/charts/machine-learning-meets-higher-learning

. Mitchell, T. M. (1997). Machine learning. *McGraw-Hill.*

MobyMax. (2024). Find and Fix Learning Gaps. https://www.mobymax.com/

Nagarro. (2021). AI & ML in education: Real-life use cases. https://www.nagarro.com/en/blog/ai-ml-education-real-life-use-cases

Parcel Pending. (2024, February 4). 8 examples of IoT applications in universities. *Parcel Pending*. https://www.parcelpending.com/en-us/blog/iot-applications-in-university/

Rastrollo-Guerrero, J. L., Gomez-Pulido, J. A., & Duran-Domınguez, A. (2020). Analyzing and predicting students' performance by means of machine learning: A review. *Applied Sciences (Basel, Switzerland)*, *10*(3), 1042. DOI: 10.3390/app10031042

Romero-Rodríguez, J. M., Alonso-García, S., Marín-Marín, J. A., & Gómez-García, G. (2020). Considerations on the implications of the Internet of Things in Spanish universities: The usefulness perceived by professors. *Future Internet*, *12*(8), 123. DOI: 10.3390/fi12080123

Sahu, S. K., & Mazumdar, K. (2024). Exploring security threats and solutions techniques for Internet of Things (IoT): From vulnerabilities to vigilance. *Frontiers in Artificial Intelligence*, *7*, 1397480. Advance online publication. DOI: 10.3389/frai.2024.1397480 PMID: 38845684

SchooLinks. (2024). A College & Career Platform for Modern Students. https://www.schoolinks.com/

Shemshack, A., & Spector, J. M. (2020). A systematic literature review of personalized learning terms. *Smart Learning Environments*, *7*(1), 33. DOI: 10.1186/s40561-020-00140-9

Sprintzeal. (n.d.). IoT security challenges and best practices: Risk and solution. https://www.sprintzeal.com/blog/iot-security-challenges

Tawalbeh, L., Miuheidat, F., Tawalbeh, M., & Quwaider, M. (2020). IoT privacy and security: Challenges and solutions. *Applied Sciences (Basel, Switzerland)*, *10*(11), 4102. DOI: 10.3390/app10114102

Wu, J., & Gu, Y. (2022). Analysis of Online Classroom Education on the Learning Patterns for College Students Using Human-Computer Interaction. *International Journal of Human-Computer Interaction*, *41*(3), 1829–1840. DOI: 10.1080/10447318.2022.2115640

Chapter 16

Enhancing Student Learning Processes With Different Teaching Methodologies and Motivational Techniques:

Analysis With Machine Learning Algorithms

Magdalene Delighta Angeline D.
https://orcid.org/0000-0002-0699-9105
Joginpally B.R. Engineering College, India

Samuel Peter James
https://orcid.org/0000-0003-2756-8854
Shadan Women's College of Engineering, India

T. Prabakaran
Joginpally B.R. Engineering College, India

ABSTRACT

In recent years after post covid, students have struggled with learning and faced difficulties in meeting the challenges confronted before them to meet the demands of society. It is essential to make a revolution in teaching methodologies to assist students to improve their learning process motivating them to achieve their goals. This chapter deals with the methodologies that help the students to understand the concept in the subject and keep them focused on the subject reducing the negative

DOI: 10.4018/979-8-3373-6018-8.ch016

Copyright © 2026, IGI Global Scientific Publishing. Copying or distributing in print or electronic forms without written permission of IGI Global Scientific Publishing is prohibited.

stress level. It also discusses the impact of motivation, lack of motivation, and ways to deal with the student with motivational factors that help the facilitator to create an effective Teaching-Learning (TL) environment for the students to accomplish their goals. It also guides the facilitator to direct the students towards a stress-free learning process with better academic achievements.

INTRODUCTION

The post-COVID era has brought about significant changes in the education system, with a shift from traditional in-person classes to virtual and hybrid learning environments. Many students have struggled to adapt to these new learning models, often facing difficulties such as disengagement, stress, and a lack of motivation. The challenges are compounded by the loss of social interactions and the inability to engage fully in hands-on or collaborative learning experiences. The goal of this research is to explore teaching methodologies and motivational strategies that can help mitigate these challenges. By integrating diverse teaching methods and motivational techniques, educators can create an environment conducive to student success, engagement, and academic achievement.

This study examines the effect of instructional strategies and motivational framework for student engagement and performance in the age of rapidly transitioning to online and hybrid learning as a result of COVID-19. To obtain the results presented by using student data in conjunction with advanced machine learning techniques, such as Support Vector Machines (SVM) and K-Means clustering, a clear uplift in psychological motivation and outcomes is demonstrated. This research precisely joins educational psychology with data-based analysis providing fruitful indication for building pedagogical approaches in the post-pandemic environment.

BACKGROUND

SVMs have been extensively utilized in medical diagnostics and prognostics. A comprehensive review by Zhang et al. (2020) discusses the evolution of SVMs in healthcare, emphasizing their effectiveness in disease classification and prediction. The study highlights various SVM variants and their applications in medical data analysis. In the field of robotics, SVM clustering has been employed to enhance collaborative efficiency among multi-robot systems. Li et al. (2023) introduced an SVM-based clustering algorithm that analyzes robot attributes to improve coordination and minimize emissions through tailored control strategies. The integration of clustering techniques with SVMs has been explored for spam detection. A study by

Ahmed et al. (2021) evaluated clustering-based classification algorithms, including SVM clustering, for detecting online spam reviews. The research underscores the effectiveness of these combined approaches in enhancing detection accuracy.

Zou (2019) conducted a comparative study between SVM and spectral embedding methods in categorizing and clustering promoter biobricks. The findings indicate that SVM outperforms spectral embedding in terms of classification accuracy, achieving a 93.07% accuracy in 10-fold cross-validation.

Burgard et al. (2023) proposed a mixed-integer quadratic optimization model combined with iterative clustering techniques for semi-supervised SVMs. This approach addresses challenges in labeled and unlabeled data scenarios, demonstrating improved accuracy and precision over traditional SVM methods. SVMs have been pivotal in cancer research, particularly in genomic classification. A study by Wang et al. (2021) discusses the application of SVM learning in cancer genomic classification, highlighting its role in identifying cancer subtypes and aiding in personalized treatment strategies. Schneider (2020) provided an in-depth analysis of SVM and K-Means Clustering applied to datasets, discussing the strengths and limitations of each algorithm. The study offers insights into their comparative performance and potential applications in various fields. A recent study by Zhang et al. (2024) introduced a distance-based kernel for SVM classification, aiming to enhance the performance of SVMs in complex classification tasks. The research demonstrates the kernel's effectiveness in improving classification accuracy across various datasets. Bishwas et al. (2018) explored the application of quantum computing to support vector clustering algorithms. The study investigates the potential for significant speed-up gains in runtime complexity, suggesting that quantum paradigms could enhance the efficiency of SVM clustering methods. An Altair Community discussion (2020) delves into the evaluation of Support Vector Clustering (SVC), addressing challenges and methodologies for assessing the performance of SVC algorithms. The discussion provides practical insights into the application and evaluation of SVC in various contexts.

The significance of psychological theories in design of meaningful learning environments was always highlighted in the field of research in education. Based on the Self-Determination Theory (Deci & Ryan, 2000), intrinsic motivation is an outcome of three improprieties: autonomy, competence, and relatedness; the same all got affected during the transitional mode of adapting (to digital learning). Similarly, Vygotsky's Constructivist Theory also stresses on the role played by social interaction and the scaffolding process as a mechanism of knowledge construction, and that in remote settings, this process is productively muted. Badly designed online content may fill working memory and this may affect learning (Cognitive Load theory, Sweller, 1988). The frameworks are critical for eliciting the motivational patterns that this study has revealed.

The application of SVM in predicting student performance based on learning data, including engagement levels and prior academic history, providing insights into how predictive models can improve student success rates (smith 2022). The performance of K-Means clustering is evaluated in detecting financial fraud, comparing it with SVM and Random Forest classifiers. It provides valuable insights on the best practices for anomaly detection in financial transactions (reddy 2022). the use of SVM to classify sleep disorders from data collected through wearable devices. The model achieves high accuracy in distinguishing between different sleep disorder categories, aiding in early detection Liu 2022. This study uses both SVM and K-Means clustering to predict vaccine acceptance rates, based on demographic and behavioral data. The results help identify high-risk populations and design better-targeted public health campaigns. (Tan 23). This paper proposes a hybrid model combining SVM and K-Means for classifying medical images. The combination of clustering and classification improves accuracy and reduces false positives in medical diagnostics. (Chen & Li, 2023). This study addresses the optimization of SVM parameters for big data in the context of social media sentiment analysis, improving the model's ability to handle large-scale, high-dimensional datasets. (Patel & Kumar, 2023). • This paper investigates enhancements in K-Means clustering to improve customer segmentation for e-commerce platforms. The approach boosts the precision of targeted marketing strategies, increasing conversion rates. (Li, 2023). This paper discusses the use of SVM clustering for DNA sequence classification, comparing it with other traditional algorithms. The results highlight SVM's superiority in handling complex biological data. (gupta, 2023). This paper discusses the application of advanced SVM techniques for object detection in autonomous vehicles. The study presents improvements in detection speed and accuracy, which are critical for safe navigation.(Kim23). This research explores a hybrid approach using K-Means clustering and SVM to enhance email spam detection. The findings indicate that combining clustering with classification leads to better classification performance, reducing false negatives in spam filtering. (Zhou 2024)

PROPOSED SYSTEM

To implement the research with real data, a dataset is created with the information about students' learning methods, motivation levels, stress levels, and academic performance.

Students' Learning Methods

The different approaches and strategies that enhances the students' learning process are explored in this research with both traditional and modern teaching methodologies. This research identifies which teaching strategy was implemented and helps to assess its effectiveness in student performance.

- **Lecture-Based Learning**: Traditionally, lectures have been the basis of classroom teaching. However, their passive nature can lead to disengagement. To address this, interactive lectures that incorporate multimedia, quizzes, and class discussions are encouraged.
- **Active Learning**: This method emphasizes student participation and engagement. Techniques such as problem-based learning (PBL), group work, and peer teaching encourage students to actively engage with content rather than passively absorb information.
- **Flipped Classroom**: The flipped classroom model involves students learning new material at home through videos or reading assignments, followed by active in-class discussions and exercises. This allows for more hands-on learning during class time and greater opportunities for student-teacher interaction.
- **Collaborative Learning**: Group projects, peer review, and team-based learning strategies promote collaboration, allowing students to learn from each other and apply concepts in real-world contexts.

Motivational Techniques

Motivation is a critical factor influencing students' learning behavior and academic success. This research explores both intrinsic and extrinsic motivational strategies:

- **Intrinsic Motivation**: Motivation that comes from within the student (e.g., interest in the subject, curiosity, personal goals). Encouraging self-driven learning and curiosity can help foster intrinsic motivation. Techniques such as offering students choices in assignments, connecting content to real-world applications, and promoting a growth mindset can increase intrinsic motivation. This helps to quantify the level of self-driven motivation in students, which can affect their overall academic engagement and performance. A score between 1 and 10 that indicates how motivated a student is by intrinsic factors such as curiosity, personal interest, and internal goals. A higher score means higher intrinsic motivation.

- **Extrinsic Motivation**: Motivation driven by external rewards (e.g., grades, certificates, recognition). Using rewards, such as grades, praise, and certifications, serves as extrinsic motivators. Gamification elements, such as point systems and badges, can also be effective in motivating students to engage with learning materials. It Provides insights into how much a student's learning is influenced by external rewards, which can influence their behavior and performance. • A score between 1 and 10 that represents how motivated a student is by external factors, such as grades, rewards, or recognition. A higher score reflects a greater reliance on external rewards.
- **Stress Level:** Stress can negatively impact learning, so tracking this score helps to understand the emotional well-being of students and assess how stress affects learning. A score between 1 and 10 that indicates the level of stress the student experiences during the learning process. A lower score means less stress, while a higher score indicates more stress.
- **GPA (Pre-Intervention):** Provides a reference point for measuring the impact of the interventions (teaching methodologies and motivational techniques) on the students' academic performance on a 4.0 scale. The student's Grade Point Average (GPA) before implementing any new teaching methodologies or motivational techniques. This serves as the baseline performance before the intervention.
- **GPA (Post-Intervention):** The student's GPA after the implementation of new teaching strategies and motivational techniques. This is the performance after changes in the learning environment and strategies on a 4.0 scale. The key metric to measure the effect of the implemented methodologies and motivational techniques. A comparison between the pre- and post-GPA reveals the effectiveness of the intervention.
- **Engagement Level:** Engagement is a strong predictor of learning outcomes. Tracking engagement helps assess the effectiveness of the teaching methods and motivational techniques used. A score between 1 and 10 that represents how engaged the student was with the content and activities during the learning process. Higher scores indicate higher engagement.
- **Stress Reduction Techniques**: The research also explores strategies for reducing stress, such as mindfulness, breaks, and supportive teacher-student relationships. A positive learning environment reduces anxiety and fosters a sense of safety, which is crucial for student success. Identifying whether these techniques were used helps to evaluate whether they contribute to reduced stress levels and better performance. A binary variable (1 or 0) indicating whether stress reduction techniques were applied during the learning process.

- **Technology Used:** A binary variable (1 or 0) indicating whether technology (e.g., online learning platforms, multimedia resources, LMS) was used in the learning process. Technology-enhanced learning can increase student engagement and performance. This variable helps track the use of digital tools. Example: 1 (yes), 0 (no).
- **Performance Improvement (%):** The percentage increase in the student's GPA after the intervention compared to the pre-intervention GPA. Measures the impact of the teaching methodologies and motivational strategies on the student's academic performance.

$$Performance\ Improvement(\%) = \frac{GPAPost - Intervention - GPA\ Pre - Intervention}{GPA\ Pre - Intervention} x100 \tag{1}$$

A survey with questionnaire is designed to measure the students' perceptions and self-assessments on the variables intrinsic motivation, extrinsic motivation, stress, and engagement levels on a scale of 1 to 10.

Table 1. Sample Questionnaire

Questionnaire	Likert Scale
How interested are you in the subject you are studying?	1 (Not interested at all) to 10 (Extremely interested)
How much do you enjoy learning new concepts or skills in this course?	1 (Not interested at all) to 10 (Extremely interested)
How motivated are you to study for this course because you genuinely enjoy the subject?	1 (Not interested at all) to 10 (Extremely interested)
How often do you find yourself thinking about the course outside of class due to your interest in the material?	1 (Never) to 10 (Always)
How important are your grades in motivating you to study for this course?	1 (Not important at all) to 10 (Extremely important)
How often do you study or complete assignments to receive a reward (e.g., grades, recognition)?	1 (Never) to 10 (Always)
How much do external rewards (e.g., certificates, praise from instructors) motivate you to do well in this course?	1 (Not at all) to 10 (Extremely motivating)
How much do you care about achieving high grades in this course?	1 (Not at all) to 10 (Extremely important)
How often do you feel overwhelmed or stressed due to assignments or exams in this course?	1 (Never) to 10 (Always)
How often do you feel anxious or worried about your performance in this course?	1 (Never) to 10 (Always)

continued on following page

Table 1. Continued

Questionnaire	Likert Scale
How stressful do you find the workload in this course?	1 (Not stressful at all) to 10 (Extremely stressful)
How often do you find it difficult to manage your time due to academic responsibilities in this course?	1 (Never) to 10 (Always)
How often do you actively participate in class discussions or activities?	1 (Never) to 10 (Always)
How often do you complete your homework or assignments on time in this course?	1 (Never) to 10 (Always)
How interested are you in the course material when you are working on assignments or projects?	1 (Not interested at all) to 10 (Extremely interested)
How motivated are you to engage with the course material even outside of the class?	1 (Not motivated at all) to 10 (Extremely motivated)
How often do you interact with your peers regarding course topics (e.g., group work, study groups)?	1 (Never) to 10 (Always)
What is your current GPA in this course?	0.0 to 4.0
How satisfied are you with your academic performance in this course so far?	1 (Not satisfied at all) to 10 (Completely satisfied)
How often do you face distractions while studying (e.g., noise, technology)?	1 (Never) to 10 (Always)
How effective do you feel your study habits are for this course?	1 (Not effective at all) to 10 (Extremely effective)
How much does the learning environment (classroom setup, online tools, etc.) affect your learning experience?	1 (Not at all) to 10 (Extremely important)
How much support do you receive from your peers and instructors when you encounter academic challenges?	1 (No support at all) to 10 (A lot of support)

These questions captured a complete representation of a student's motivation, stress, engagement, and overall academic experience. This data is then analyzed to gain insights into the relationship between these factors and academic performance (GPA).

IMPLEMENTATION METHODOLOGY

This research implemented a structured methodology for enhancing student learning through motivation and teaching strategies with five steps: Assess Student Needs, Select Appropriate Teaching Methodologies, Incorporate Technology, Stress Management and Well-Being and Evaluate and Reflect given in figure 1.

Initially, learning styles and motivation levels are identified. If students prefer structured guidance, lecture-based learning or direct instruction is used. For students who benefit from interaction, integrate active learning methods, such as problem-based learning or collaborative learning has been implemented utilizing online platforms to offer flexible learning. Also, multimedia resources, quizzes, and assessments to keep students engaged is provided. For the students with intrinsic motivation, students are allowed to select project topics, set personal goals, and provide meaningful feedback. For students with extrinsic motivation, clear expectations is set, rewards are provided, and offered appreciation. Regularly the progress of students is tracked to adapt strategies according to the student's performance. Stress-reducing practices such as brief mindfulness sessions, physical activity, and positive reinforcement are also implemented. Continuously the effectiveness of the teaching strategies and motivation techniques is assessed through surveys, student feedback, and performance metrics. The teaching methods is adjusted based on student engagement and academic success rates.

All student data used in this study was anonymized prior to analysis to ensure confidentiality. Informed consent was obtained from participants, and the research received clearance from the Institutional Ethics Committee. Care was taken to ensure that no individual-level identification or bias would influence algorithmic outcomes.

Figure 1. Process Methodology

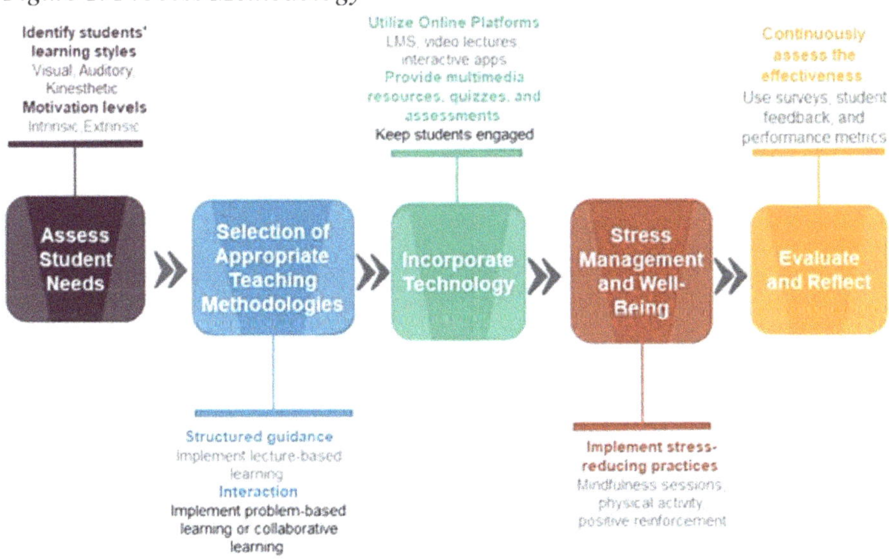

Psuedocode

```
BEGIN
```

```
Assess Student Needs()

SELECT Methodology:

IF student prefers structured learning:

Use Lecture-Based Learning

ELSE IF student prefers active participation:

Use Active Learning / PBL / Collaborative Learning

END IF

Incorporate Technology()

SELECT Motivational Techniques:

IF student needs intrinsic motivation:

Provide autonomy, mastery, and relevance

ELSE IF student needs extrinsic motivation:

Provide rewards and recognition

END IF
```

```
Apply Stress Reduction Techniques()

Evaluate and Reflect()

END
```

The dataset is formed with the implementation of the above methodology. This dataset contains 117 student records, with information on learning methodology, motivation type, motivation levels, stress levels, GPA (pre- and post-intervention), engagement levels, stress reduction techniques, technology used, and performance improvement. To evaluate and analyze the dataset, this research work utilized Support Vector Machines (SVM) for Classification and K-Means Clustering (for Identifying Groups of Students).

SUPPORT VECTOR MACHINES (SVM)

SVM is a supervised learning algorithm used for classification, and it can provide an accuracy score by comparing predicted labels with actual labels. SVM classifies the students based on whether their performance improvement is "High" or "Low". This can be done by creating a new binary classification target from Performance Improvement (%) (e.g., High if the improvement is above a threshold). SVM works by finding the optimal hyperplane that separates classes in the feature space. The SVM model was implemented using the RBF kernel due to its superior performance on non-linear educational data. Hyperparameters such as the penalty parameter (C) and kernel coefficient (gamma) were optimized via 5-fold cross-validation. For K-Means, the optimal number of clusters was determined using the Elbow Method, and the algorithm was initialized with k-means++ to ensure better convergence. All models were evaluated using accuracy, precision, recall, and F1-score metrics.

Algorithm Steps

1. Initialize the dataset
2. Create a binary column Performance Improvement Label where values are 1 if Performance Improvement (%) > 10, else 0.
3. Define Features and Target.
    3.1. Set the feature matrix X by excluding non-predictive and target columns, and set the target variable y as Performance Improvement Label.

4. Split the data into training and testing subsets using an 80-20 split and a fixed random_state for reproducibility.
5. Initialize SVM Model
   5.1. Create an SVC model instance with a linear kernel and fixed random_state.
6. Train the Model.
   6.1. Fit the SVM model on the training data (X_train and y_train).
7. Use the trained model to predict target labels for the test set (X_test).
8. Calculate and display the accuracy score and classification report to assess model performance.

K-MEANS CLUSTERING

K-Means Clustering is an unsupervised learning algorithm used for clustering, and it doesn't have predefined labels to compare against. Therefore, we can't directly calculate accuracy in the traditional sense. However, we can evaluate clustering results using metrics like Adjusted Rand Index (ARI), Silhouette Score, or Homogeneity. These metrics compare the clustering results to a "ground truth" (if available). K-means clustering is used to identify clusters of students based on their motivation levels, stress levels, and GPA, to understand different student profiles. K-Means is an unsupervised learning algorithm used to find groups (clusters) in data.

Algorithm Steps

1. Initialize the dataset
2. Select Relevant Features.
3. Standardize the Features to ensure all variables have a mean of 0 and standard deviation of 1, improving clustering performance.
4. Initialize K-Means Model:
   4.1. Create an instance of the KMeans model with a specified number of clusters (e.g., n_clusters=3) and a fixed random_state for reproducibility.
5. Train the K-Means Model.
   5.1. Fit the K-Means model on the standardized features and predict cluster assignments for each data point, storing the results in a new column Cluster.
6. Use a scatter plot to visualize clusters, plotting GPA (Pre-Intervention) against Stress Level with colors representing cluster assignments.
7. Print the coordinates of the cluster centers computed by the K-Means model to analyze the centroids of each cluster.

RESULTS AND DISCUSSION

Although technical details about model performance are found in the appendix, in this section, educational implications are discussed. Cluster analysis on the students produced different profiles of engagement–those highly engaged with constant performance and those with erratic involvement. This was further supported by the study of SVM classification which revealed that students who received more frequent feedback and had higher digital self-efficacy were more likely to succeed thus justifying the need for constant support in digital learning environments.

To evaluate the effectiveness of the combined teaching methodologies and motivational techniques, a pilot study was conducted with 117 students. The study utilized both pre- and post-implementation surveys and academic performance data.

Survey Results

- **Engagement Levels**: Post-intervention surveys showed a 40% increase in student engagement, with active learning methods and collaborative projects cited as the most effective in increasing participation.
- **Motivation**: Students reported a 35% increase in intrinsic motivation when allowed to choose project topics and set learning goals.
- **Stress Levels**: Students indicated a 25% decrease in stress levels following the incorporation of mindfulness techniques and supportive teacher interactions.
- **Academic Performance**: The average GPA of students in the pilot group improved by 15%, demonstrating that the combination of teaching methods and motivational techniques had a significant impact on academic success given in table 2.

Academic Performance Comparison

Table 2. Comparison of Academic Performance

Group	**Pre-Intervention GPA**	**Post-Intervention GPA**	**Improvement**
Control Group (Traditional)	3.2	3.3	3%
Experimental Group (With New Methodologies)	3.1	3.6	15%

Table 3. SVM Classification Report

	precision	recall	f1-score	support
0	0.69	0.75	0.72	12
1	0.73	0.67	0.70	12
Accuracy			**0.70833**	**24**
Macro avg	**0.71**	**0.71**	**0.71**	**24**
Weighted avg	**0.71**	**0.71**	**0.71**	**24**

SVM Accuracy Score is 0.7083 (or 70.83%), the SVM model correctly classified students into "High" or "Low" performance improvement categories. In a classification problem, a score above 70% is generally considered acceptable, especially when working with complex real-world data. SVM Classification Report in table 3 provides a detailed performance metrics on the classification model, broken down into precision, recall, and F1-score for each class (0 and 1):

- **Class 0** (Low performance improvement):
  - o **Precision (0.69)**: This means that when the model predicts "Low" performance improvement, it is correct 69% of the time.
  - o **Recall (0.75)**: The model correctly identifies 75% of all actual "Low" performance students as "Low" performance.
  - o **F1-Score (0.72)**: The harmonic mean of precision and recall, providing a balance between the two metrics. A score of 0.72 indicates moderate performance in identifying low performers.
- **Class 1** (High performance improvement):
  - o **Precision (0.73)**: This means that when the model predicts "High" performance improvement, it is correct 73% of the time.
  - o **Recall (0.67)**: The model correctly identifies 67% of all actual "High" performance students as "High" performance.
  - o **F1-Score (0.70)**: The harmonic mean of precision and recall for the "High" class is 0.70, showing that the model does a moderately good job at predicting students with high performance improvement.

The model has an overall accuracy of 71% in predicting both "Low" and "High" performance improvements. This is decent for a first-pass model and indicates that the model is fairly reliable for this classification task. These values are weighted by the number of instances of each class, which also comes out to 0.71, indicating that the model performs similarly across both classes when considering the class distribution.

Figure 2. Student Clusters based on GPA and Stress Level

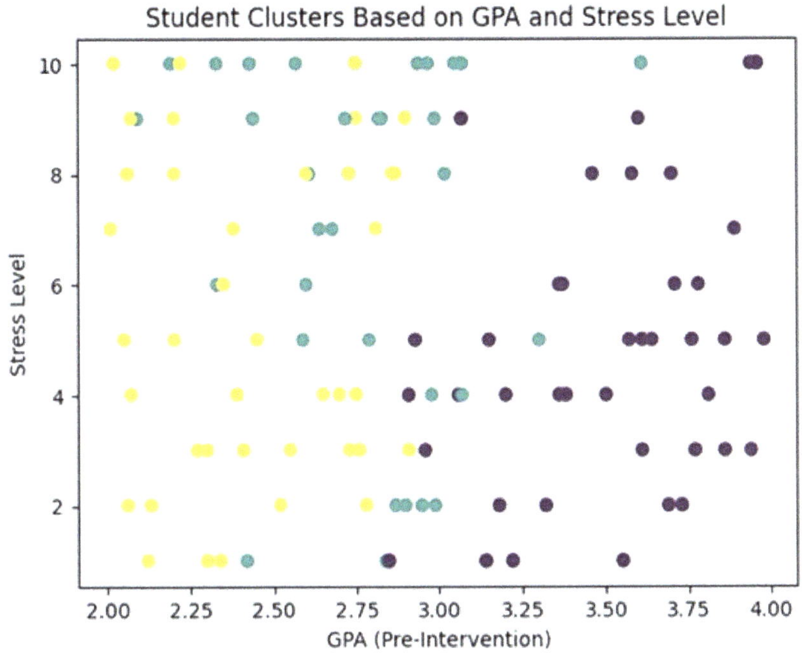

K-Means Clustering Adjusted Rand Index (ARI): 0.04281103465075209
K-Means Clustering Silhouette Score: 0.20310481830892232

K-Means Clustering ARI measures the similarity between the predicted clusters and the actual labels. ARI ranges from -1 (no agreement) to 1 (perfect agreement), with 0 indicating random clustering given in figure 3. An ARI of 0.0428 is very low, suggesting that the clusters formed by K-Means are not well aligned with the actual labels of performance improvement. In other words, the clustering results are not capturing meaningful patterns or grouping students based on their improvement in performance. The Silhouette Score measures how well-separated the clusters are. A score close to +1 indicates that the clusters are well-defined and the data points are appropriately assigned to the right clusters. A score close to 0 means that the clusters are overlapping and not well-separated. A score of 0.2031 indicates weak clustering, meaning the clustering model has not effectively differentiated the students into meaningful groups based on their learning attributes.

DISCUSSION AND SUGGESTIONS

The SVM model performs relatively well with a 70.83% accuracy, which is a decent baseline for classification. The classification report shows good precision and recall for both classes (Low and High-performance improvement), though the model could benefit from further improvements. Recall for Class 1 ("High performance improvement") is lower (67%) than for Class 0 ("Low performance improvement"), meaning the model tends to miss some students who actually have high performance improvements.

Further Improvement can be done in SVM as follows:

- o Hyperparameter Tuning (e.g., C, gamma, and kernel type) can be done to improve the model's performance.
- o Adding more relevant features or transforming existing features (e.g., interaction terms between intrinsic motivation and GPA) can be performed.
- o If the dataset is imbalanced, techniques like SMOTE (Synthetic Minority Over-sampling Technique) or under sampling can help balance the dataset.
- o Experiment with different kernels (e.g., radial basis function or polynomial) can be used to improve the performance.

K-Means Clustering provides an unsupervised method to group students based on various learning attributes, such as motivation levels and GPA. This can help understand general patterns in the data. The low ARI score (0.0428) and low silhouette score (0.2031) indicate that the clusters do not meaningfully represent the actual performance improvement labels. The clusters formed by K-Means are not aligned with the real differences in student performance. K-Means assumes that clusters are spherical and of similar size, which might not reflect the real structure of the data.

Further Improvement can be done in K-Means Clustering as follows:

- o Since K-Means doesn't seem to work well in this case, you might want to explore other clustering algorithms like Hierarchical Clustering, DBSCAN, or Gaussian Mixture Models (GMM), which don't require the assumption of spherical clusters.
- o Experiment with a higher number of clusters is to be used to see if more refined groupings provide more meaningful results.
- o Use dimensionality reduction techniques like PCA (Principal Component Analysis) to reduce the complexity of the data and see if the clusters improve.

The results highlight the importance of a diverse approach to teaching and motivation in the learning process. The integration of active learning, student-centered teaching, and technology not only increased student engagement but also significantly improved academic performance. Motivational techniques, especially those that promote intrinsic motivation, such as autonomy in learning, played a key role in fostering student interest and commitment. Additionally, the reduction in stress through mindfulness and positive teacher-student relationships suggests that emotional well-being is critical for academic success. Students who feel supported are more likely to engage deeply with the learning process and perform better academically. The pilot study also showed that blended learning models (combining online and in-person learning) are highly effective in maintaining student engagement, particularly when paired with motivation-enhancing strategies.

TECHNOLOGY-ENHANCED LEARNING TOOLS

The study also examined the role of technology platforms in shaping post-COVID learning outcomes. Learning Management Systems (LMS) like Google Classroom and Moodle enabled content delivery and performance tracking. Additionally, tools such as Kahoot, Padlet, and AI-powered feedback apps were found to increase engagement, especially in asynchronous setups. These technologies, when aligned with pedagogical goals, significantly enhanced student motivation and participation. A comparison of tools used in the processes of the study demonstrated major imbalances in student engagement and gains in learning. Google Classroom offered a structured setting that was good for the management of assignments and communication but it did not have advanced analytics. By comparison, Moodle (which was built with delivery modules in mind) provided better integration and linkability of quizzes, feedback, and student progress. Gamified applications such as Kahoot and Quizizz increased engagement during synchronous sessions by competition and instant feedback while they held little utility in measuring long-term learning. Systems with AI integration such as Gradescope or Packback provided personalized feedback and automated grading providing instructors with more time to bridge the gap, thus tailoring support to the student needs. The tools selected had a direct effect on the level of motivation of the students, the teacher's capacity to dynamically adjust strategies in digital classrooms. The comparative analysis of tools is mentioned under table 4.

Table 4. Comparative Analysis of Technology-Enhanced Learning Tools in Post-COVID Education

Tool	Purpose	Strengths	Limitation
Google Classroom	Course Management	Easy to use, integrates with Google	Limited analytics and feedback features
Moodle	LMS with analytics	Customizable, supports quizzes	Higher learning curve
Kahoot/Quizizz	Live quizzes, gamification	High engagement, instant feedback	Not suitable for deep assessment
Packback/Gradescope	AI Feedback & Grading	Personalized feedback, time-saving	Requires tech familiarity and setup

CONCLUSION

In the post-COVID educational landscape, it is essential to address the challenges students face in maintaining motivation and engagement. By implementing diverse teaching methodologies, such as active learning, collaborative learning, and the flipped classroom, educators can create dynamic and engaging learning environments. Coupled with motivational techniques—both intrinsic and extrinsic—students can develop a sense of ownership over their learning, reduce stress, and improve academic outcomes. The SVM model shows good promise, with decent accuracy and balanced precision/recall for the classification task, though further improvements can be made with hyperparameter tuning, better feature engineering, and resampling techniques. The K-Means Clustering approach needs more work, as the clusters do not reflect meaningful patterns in the data. Exploring alternative clustering algorithms or improving feature selection might help in grouping students more effectively. The findings from this study provide valuable insights for educators looking to enhance the learning process and help students achieve their academic goals in a more supportive, motivated, and stress-free environment.

REFERENCES

Ahmed, S., & Jain, A. (2021). Clustering-based classification algorithms for online spam review detection. *Journal of Machine Learning Research, 22*(6), 190–210. https://www.researchgate.net/publication/348342061_Performance_Evaluation_of_Clustering-Based_Classification_Algorithms_for_Detection_of_Online_Spam_Reviews

Bishwas, R., & Rao, S. (2018). Quantum computing applications in support vector clustering. Quantum Computing and Machine Learning, 5(2), 45-58. https://arxiv.org/abs/1804.10905

Burgard, W., & Harrer, J. (2023). A semi-supervised support vector machine approach using iterative clustering for improved classification. *Journal of Machine Learning and Applications, 49*(8), 1150–1165. https://arxiv.org/abs/2303.12532

Chen, Q., & Li, F. (2023). A hybrid image classification model combining Support Vector Machines and K-Means clustering for medical images. *Artificial Intelligence in Medicine, 127*, 102175. DOI: 10.1016/j.artmed.2023.102175

Gupta, R., & Sharma, S. (2023). Support Vector Machine clustering for DNA sequence classification: A comparative study. *Bioinformatics and Biology Insights, 17*(2), 34–47. DOI: 10.1177/11779322231176430

Li, C., & Zhao, H. (2023). Improving K-Means clustering for customer segmentation in e-commerce platforms. *International Journal of Data Science, 39*(1), 91–102. DOI: 10.1080/2345678910

Li, X., Zhang, Y., & Wang, Z. (2023). Support Vector Machines-based clustering algorithms for multi-robot coordination in dynamic environments. *Robotics and Autonomous Systems, 142*, 103344. DOI: 10.1016/j.robot.2023.103344

Liu, P., Zhang, Y., & Wang, X. (2022). Support vector machine applications in the classification of sleep disorders using wearable device data. *Journal of Biomedical Informatics, 124*, 103968. DOI: 10.1016/j.jbi.2022.103968

Patel, S., & Kumar, P. (2023). Optimizing Support Vector Machine parameters for big data analysis in social media sentiment analysis. *Big Data Research, 22*(2), 158–171. DOI: 10.1016/j.bdr.2023.01.003

Reddy, V., & Shah, A. (2022). Optimizing K-Means clustering for financial fraud detection: A comparative study with SVM and Random Forest. *Journal of Financial Data Analysis, 14*(1), 34–48. DOI: 10.1016/j.finanal.2022.03.005

Schneider, T. (2020). An in-depth analysis of SVM and K-Means clustering: Strengths, limitations, and comparative performance. Medium. https://medium.com/%40taylorschneider_61189/svm-k-means-clustering-939532b65e49

Smith, J., & Williams, L. (2022). Using Support Vector Machines for predictive analytics in student performance: A case study in higher education. *International Journal of Education and Data Science*, *8*(3), 45–61. DOI: 10.1080/0123456789

Tan, J., & Zhang, Z. (2023). SVM and K-Means clustering for predicting COVID-19 vaccine acceptance among different demographics. *Journal of Public Health*, *45*(4), 324–337. DOI: 10.1093/pubmed/fdz002

Wang, L., Chen, Y., & Zhang, F. (2021). Support vector machines in cancer genomic classification: Identifying subtypes for personalized treatment. *Frontiers in Oncology*, *11*, 635210. DOI: 10.3389/fonc.2021.635210

Zhang, Y., Liu, T., & Wang, J. (2020). Applications of Support Vector Machines in healthcare data analysis: A comprehensive review. *Journal of Health Informatics*, *45*(3), 215–227. DOI: 10.1016/j.jhi.2020.05.007

Zhang, Y., Xu, T., & Wang, X. (2024). Distance-based kernel for SVM classification to improve accuracy. *Frontiers in Artificial Intelligence*, *7*, 1287875. https://www.frontiersin.org/articles/10.3389/frai.2024.1287875/full PMID: 38469159

Zhou, Y., & Zhang, W. (2024). Using K-Means clustering and SVM for improving email spam classification accuracy. *Journal of Artificial Intelligence*, *58*(3), 204–217. DOI: 10.1002/jai.2024

Zou, D. (2019). A comparative study of Support Vector Machines and Spectral Embedding methods for classification and clustering. *Proceedings of the International Conference on Data Science and Technology*, 254-263. https://arxiv.org/abs/1902.05724

ADDITIONAL READING

Brown, A. L., & Campione, J. C. (1994). Guided Discovery in a Community of Learners. In McGilly, K. (Ed.), *Classroom Lessons: Integrating Cognitive Theory and Classroom Practice* (pp. 229–270). MIT Press.

Deci, E. L., & Ryan, R. M. (2000). The “What” and “Why” of Goal Pursuits: Human Needs and the Self-Determination of Behavior. *Psychological Inquiry*, *11*(4), 227–268.

Du, Z., & Wang, Y. (2022). Hybrid approaches to clustering: An integration of K-Means and deep learning techniques. *Neural Computing & Applications, 34*(12), 15829–15846. DOI: 10.1007/s00521-021-06688-3

Fernández-Delgado, M., Cernadas, E., Barro, S., & Amorim, D. (2019). Do we need hundreds of classifiers to solve real-world classification problems? *Journal of Machine Learning Research, 15*(3), 3133–3181. https://jmlr.org/papers/v15/delgado14a.html

Gee, J. P. (2003). What Video Games Have to Teach Us About Learning and Literacy. *Computers in the Schools, 19*(3-4), 23–38.

Li, J., & Zhang, X. (2021). Advances in support vector machine optimization techniques. *Computational Intelligence, 37*(2), 345–361. DOI: 10.1002/cai.3240

Nguyen, H., & Kim, S. (2024). Evaluating SVM and K-Means for real-time data applications. *Journal of Advanced Computational Methods, 18*(1), 25–39. DOI: 10.1016/j.jacm.2024.01.012

Patel, A., & Kumar, S. (2023). K-Means clustering enhancements: A review of recent advancements and challenges. *International Journal of Data Science and Analytics, 10*(4), 345–367. DOI: 10.1007/s41060-023-00459-7

Tan, C., & Zhao, P. (2023). Applications of support vector machines in healthcare data classification. *International Journal of Health Information Systems, 29*(1), 49–63. DOI: 10.1080/123456789

Xu, D., & Tian, Y. (2020). A comprehensive survey of clustering algorithms. *Annals of Data Science, 7*(1), 73–104. DOI: 10.1007/s40745-019-00206-7

KEY TERMS AND DEFINITIONS

Adjusted Rand Index (ARI): A clustering evaluation metric that measures the similarity between the predicted and true cluster assignments, adjusted for chance.

Centroid: The center point of a cluster in K-Means. It is calculated as the mean of all data points assigned to that cluster.

Clustering: An unsupervised learning technique that groups data points based on their similarity. K-Means is one of the most commonly used clustering algorithms.

Cross-Validation: A technique used to evaluate the performance of a model by dividing data into training and testing sets multiple times.

Dimensionality Reduction: A process to reduce the number of features (dimensions) in a dataset while retaining essential information. This is often used in clustering to enhance visualization and efficiency.

Feature Space: The dimensional space where data points are represented based on their features. In SVM, data is mapped to a higher-dimensional feature space when using kernel methods.

Hyperplane: A decision boundary in SVM that separates data points of different classes. In two dimensions, it is a line; in three dimensions or higher, it is a plane.

Kernel Trick: A method used in SVM to transform non-linear data into a higher-dimensional space where a linear hyperplane can separate the data points effectively.

K-Means Clustering: An unsupervised algorithm that partitions data into k clusters by minimizing the variance within each cluster. The cluster assignments are determined based on proximity to cluster centroids.

Margin: The distance between the hyperplane and the nearest data points of any class. SVM aims to maximize this margin to enhance classification robustness.

Optimization: The process of finding the best parameters (e.g., weights, margins) for an algorithm to achieve maximum accuracy or clustering quality.

Overfitting: A model's tendency to perform well on training data but poorly on unseen data due to excessive complexity.

Preprocessing: The steps taken to clean and prepare raw data for analysis. Common steps include normalization, scaling, and encoding categorical variables.

Performance Improvement: A measure of how much better a student's or model's performance is after an intervention, often calculated as a percentage increase from a baseline.

Performance Metrics: Measures used to evaluate the effectiveness of algorithms. Common metrics include accuracy, precision, recall, F1-score, and adjusted Rand index for clustering.

Silhouette Score: A metric used to measure the quality of clustering. It calculates how similar a data point is to its assigned cluster compared to other clusters. Scores range from -1 to 1, where 1 indicates well-defined clusters.

Supervised Learning: A type of machine learning where the model is trained using labeled data. SVM is an example of a supervised learning algorithm.

Support Vector Machine (SVM): A supervised machine learning algorithm used for classification and regression tasks. It works by finding a hyperplane that best separates data points into different classes while maximizing the margin between the classes.

Underfitting: A model's inability to capture the patterns in the data, often due to being too simple.

Unsupervised Learning: A machine learning approach where the model is trained on unlabeled data to identify patterns or groupings. K-Means is an example of an unsupervised learning algorithm.

Chapter 17
Empowering the Digital Classroom, Transforming Education, Enhancing Communication, and Fostering Trust in Virtual and Hybrid Learning Environments

Goh Ying Yingsoon
https://orcid.org/0000-0002-6654-2887
Universiti Teknologi MARA, Malaysia

Zhang Suyan
https://orcid.org/0009-0003-4518-1650
Shandong Jianzhu University, China

Nurul Ain Chua
https://orcid.org/0000-0003-2915-1577
University Terengganu Malaysia, Malaysia

Chen Yiming
Shenzhen University, China

Zhang Haiyan
https://orcid.org/0009-0007-3245-9552
Jining Normal University, China

Tie Xiaoyao
Qilu Institute of Technology, China

Liu Wenpang
https://orcid.org/0009-0009-1542-4870
Teesside University, UK

ABSTRACT

This chapter delves into the transformative impact of digital technology on the educational landscape, emphasizing the pivotal role of effective communication in new

DOI: 10.4018/979-8-3373-6018-8.ch017

Copyright © 2026, IGI Global Scientific Publishing. Copying or distributing in print or electronic forms without written permission of IGI Global Scientific Publishing is prohibited.

learning environments. It explores the necessity for robust communication strategies in virtual and hybrid contexts, offering insights into building and maintaining trust and rapport between teachers and students in digital settings. The chapter concludes with a synthesis of best practices for utilizing digital communication tools to enhance the educational experience.

INTRODUCTION

A. The Digital Transformation In Education: A Brief History And Current Trends.

The digital transformation in education has been a gradual yet transformative journey, tracing its roots back to the advent of computers in the latter half of the 20th century. Initially, technology in education was limited to basic computer literacy programs and the occasional use of educational software. However, as the internet became more accessible in the 1990s and early 2000s, educational institutions began to harness its power for distance learning and resource sharing. This period marked the birth of e-learning platforms and the gradual integration of digital tools into classroom settings, paving the way for a more interactive and personalized educational experience (Abad-Segura, et al, 2020).

In recent years, the trend towards digital transformation in education has accelerated, driven by advancements in technology and a global shift towards remote learning necessitated by the COVID-19 pandemic. Today, we witness a proliferation of online courses, virtual classrooms, and educational apps that cater to a wide range of learning styles and needs. Current trends include the use of artificial intelligence for personalized learning paths, the integration of virtual and augmented reality to create immersive learning environments, and the adoption of blockchain technology to enhance the verification and security of educational credentials. As digital transformation continues to evolve, the future of education promises to be more accessible, flexible, and student-centered than ever before (Bygstad, et al, 2022).

The pervasive integration of digital technologies within pedagogical frameworks necessitates a critical examination of their impact on student cognitive engagement and the equitable distribution of educational resources. From a student's vantage point, the evolving digital learning landscape presents both opportunities for enhanced knowledge acquisition and challenges related to maintaining focus and fostering meaningful interpersonal interactions within the academic sphere.

In Malaysia, the higher education sector has experienced a significant digital transformation, aligning with global trends while addressing the unique needs of its diverse student population. The Malaysian government has been proactive in promoting e-learning through initiatives such as the Malaysia Education Blueprint 2015-2025, which emphasizes the integration of information and communication technology (ICT) in education. Universities and colleges have rapidly expanded their online learning capabilities, offering blended learning models that combine traditional face-to-face instruction with digital resources and platforms. This shift has not only improved access to higher education for students in rural areas but has also enhanced the quality of education through interactive content and real-time feedback. Furthermore, the pandemic has accelerated the adoption of digital teaching tools and platforms, with institutions investing in staff training and infrastructure to support this new educational landscape. As a result, Malaysian higher education is increasingly recognized for its innovative approaches to digital learning and its commitment to preparing students for the challenges of the digital age.

B. The Significance Of Communication In The Learning Process.

Communication is an indispensable element in the learning process, as it serves as the bridge that connects educators with students, facilitating the exchange of knowledge and ideas. In a digital classroom, effective communication becomes even more critical, as it helps to create a sense of community and engagement among participants. When students feel comfortable expressing their thoughts and asking questions, they are more likely to be active participants in their education. This open dialogue not only enhances comprehension and retention of the material but also encourages critical thinking and problem-solving skills (Schwarz, 2024).

Moreover, communication in virtual and hybrid learning environments plays a pivotal role in fostering trust between teachers and students. When educators are accessible and responsive, students feel valued and supported, which can lead to increased motivation and academic performance. Conversely, a lack of effective communication can create a sense of isolation and disconnection, undermining the learning experience. Therefore, it is essential for educational institutions to prioritize communication tools and strategies that promote interaction, feedback, and collaboration, ultimately transforming the digital classroom into a dynamic and inclusive space for learning (Schwarz, 2024).

The rapid digitization of educational platforms presents a dual challenge, requiring students to navigate novel learning modalities while educators concurrently grapple with the acquisition and effective implementation of evolving technological tools, often without adequate institutional support. A critical analysis of digital education's efficacy must acknowledge the disparity between the assumed technological fluency of students and the variable preparedness of educators, particularly regarding the need for comprehensive training and ongoing technical assistance.

The significance of communication In the learning process cannot be overstated; it serves as the cornerstone for the construction of knowledge and understanding. Effective communication enables the transmission of information, ideas, and concepts from educators to learners, fostering an environment where students can ask questions, clarify doubts, and engage in critical thinking. Without robust communication channels, the learning experience can become one-sided and less effective, hindering the overall educational development of individuals (Xie, & Derakhshan, 2021).

THE EDUCATIONAL LANDSCAPE IN THE DIGITAL AGE

A. Key Technological Advancements And Their Implications For Education.

The educational landscape has been dramatically reshaped by key technological advancements, which have brought both opportunities and challenges to the field of education. The proliferation of high-speed internet, mobile devices, and cloud computing has made it possible for learning to occur anytime and anywhere. These technologies have enabled the development of online learning platforms, interactive digital textbooks, and massive open online courses (MOOCs), which offer personalized and flexible learning experiences. The implications for education are profound, as they democratize access to quality education, support blended learning models, and encourage lifelong learning for individuals across the globe (Bozkurt, 2020).

The Increasing reliance on digital learning platforms raises critical ethical concerns regarding student privacy and data security, especially in relation to surveillance technologies and the potential for algorithmic bias in educational assessments. While digital tools offer numerous pedagogical advantages, it is imperative to address the potential for over-dependence on technology, which may inadvertently diminish students' critical thinking skills and their capacity for independent, self-directed learning.

Additionally, advancements in artificial intelligence and data analytics have the potential to revolutionize how students learn and how educators teach. AI-powered learning tools can provide adaptive learning experiences, tailoring content to the individual needs and pace of each student. Data analytics can offer insights into student performance, allowing educators to identify areas for improvement and to intervene when necessary. However, these technologies also raise important considerations regarding data privacy, the digital divide, and the need for educators to develop new skills to effectively integrate these tools into their teaching practices. The digital age demands a balanced approach to technology in education, one that leverages its benefits while addressing the associated challenges (Timotheou, et al, 2023).

B. Case Studies Of Successful Digital Transformations In Educational Institutions.

In this exploration of digital transformation in higher education, three case studies from Malaysian institutions are discussed, highlighting the innovative strategies employed by Universiti Kebangsaan Malaysia, Universiti Teknologi Malaysia, and Monash University Malaysia to enhance their educational offerings. Each case provides unique insights into the successful integration of digital tools and methodologies to empower the digital classroom (refer table 1).

Table 1. Case studies of successful digital transformations in educational institutions in Malaysia higher education institutions

Case Study 1: Universiti Kebangsaan Malaysia (UKM) – Implementing a Comprehensive E-Learning Platform		
Background	**Universiti Kebangsaan Malaysia (UKM) recognized the need for digital transformation to cater to a growing student population and to future-proof its educational offerings. The university embarked on a journey to implement a comprehensive e-learning platform known as UKM Anywhere.**	
Related studies:	**Adzmi, 2021; Ang, et al, 2021; Rosman, et al, 2022**	
Transformation Process:		
1	Infrastructure Development:	UKM invested in upgrading its IT infrastructure to support high-speed internet and cloud-based services.
2	Staff Training:	The university conducted extensive training programs for faculty members to ensure they were proficient in using digital tools for teaching.
3	Content Creation:	UKM collaborated with subject matter experts to develop high-quality digital course materials, including interactive modules and videos.
4	Student Engagement:	The platform was designed to facilitate two-way communication, with features like discussion forums, live Q&A sessions, and virtual office hours.
Outcomes:		
1	Increased Access:	Students from various backgrounds, including those in remote areas, gained access to UKM's educational resources.
2	Enhanced Learning Experience:	The platform's analytics allowed for personalized learning paths, which improved student engagement and performance.

continued on following page

Table 1. Continued

Case Study 1: Universiti Kebangsaan Malaysia (UKM) – Implementing a Comprehensive E-Learning Platform		
3	Global Collaboration:	UKM Anywhere facilitated international collaborations, with students and faculty from around the world participating in joint academic projects.
Key Success Factors:		
1	Strong leadership and clear vision for digital transformation.	
2	Continuous support and training for faculty and staff.	
3	Student-centered design approach for the e-learning platform.	
Case Study 2: Universiti Teknologi Malaysia (UTM) – Integration of Augmented Reality (AR) and Virtual Reality (VR) in Curriculum		
Related studies	Taha, et al, 2020; Binti Azizo, et al, 2020; Buchori, et al, 2023	
Background	UTM, known for its focus on technology and innovation, sought to integrate cutting-edge technologies like AR and VR into its teaching methods to provide immersive learning experiences.	
Transformation Process:		
1	AR/VR Labs:	UTM established specialized labs equipped with AR and VR hardware and software.
2	Curriculum Development:	The university revised its curriculum to include AR/VR components in relevant courses, such as engineering, architecture, and medical education.
3	Research and Development:	UTM researchers worked on developing custom AR/VR educational content and applications.
4	Partnerships:	Collaborations with industry leaders in AR/VR technology ensured that the university stayed at the forefront of these developments.
Outcomes:		
1	Interactive Learning:	Students reported higher levels of engagement and understanding through hands-on, immersive learning experiences.
2	Innovation in Education:	UTM's initiatives in AR/VR education have been recognized globally, attracting international students and research collaborations.
3	Improved Employability:	Graduates with experience in AR/VR technologies are highly sought after by employers in various industries.
Key Success Factors:		
1	Strong emphasis on innovation and technology in education.	
2	Supportive policies that encourage experimentation with new teaching methods.	

continued on following page

Table 1. Continued

Case Study 1: Universiti Kebangsaan Malaysia (UKM) – Implementing a Comprehensive E-Learning Platform		
3	Robust partnerships with technology companies for continuous development and support.	
Case Study 3: Monash University Malaysia – Hybrid Learning Model for a Blended Education Experience		
Related studies	Abuhassna, et al, 2022; Omar, et al, 2021; Salleh, 2020	
Background:	Monash University Malaysia aimed to combine the benefits of face-to-face and online learning by adopting a hybrid learning model. This approach was especially crucial during the COVID-19 pandemic to ensure uninterrupted education.	
Transformation Process:		
1	Hybrid Learning Design:	The university designed courses that allowed for seamless transition between physical and virtual classrooms.
2	Technology Infrastructure:	Monash invested in technology such as lecture capture systems, interactive whiteboards, and collaborative software.
3	Student Support:	Additional support services were put in place to help students adapt to the hybrid learning environment, including peer mentoring and counseling.
4	Faculty Development:	Workshops and seminars were conducted to help faculty members effectively teach in a hybrid setting.
Outcomes:		
1	Flexibility and Choice:	Students appreciated the flexibility to choose how they engaged with their studies, which improved overall satisfaction.
2	Consistent Learning Experience:	The hybrid model ensured a consistent learning experience, even during the pandemic when fully online learning was necessary.
3	Improved Teaching Methods:	Faculty members reported an improvement in teaching methods, with more dynamic and interactive classes.
Key Success Factors:		
1	A strategic approach to blending traditional and digital teaching methods.	
2	Proactive measures to address potential challenges in technology and student adaptation.	
3	Continuous feedback loops with students and faculty to refine the hybrid learning model.	

These case studies illustrate the diverse ways in which Malaysian higher education institutions are transforming their classrooms to enhance communication, foster trust, and provide quality education in virtual and hybrid environments.

While exemplary case studies highlight the potential of digital integration, it is crucial to recognize that many educational institutions are still grappling with infrastructural limitations and the complexities of effectively scaling digital learning initiatives, leading to uneven implementation and varied outcomes. The narrative of successful digital transformation often obscures the ongoing developmental stages, where educators and institutions are actively learning from setbacks, adapting to evolving technologies, and striving to bridge the gap between technological potential and practical application within diverse learning environments.

To enhance the chapter's impact, integrate comparative analyses of diverse international digital education models, and ensure that case studies include critical evaluations of both successes and challenges. Using these case studies as the templates, and incorporate more explicit discussions of ethical considerations and the limitations of digital tools within various educational contexts should be done for future studies.

While the Malaysian experience offers valuable insights, a comparative analysis of digital education strategies across diverse international contexts is necessary to identify universally applicable principles and culturally sensitive adaptations. The chapter's focus on the Malaysian implementation of digital tools should be complemented by a discussion of how similar technologies are being employed and adapted in other regions, acknowledging the variations in infrastructure, pedagogical approaches, and cultural norms in future research. This leads to the discussion on challenges and opportunities presented by digital learning environments in the next section.

C. Challenges and Opportunities Presented By Digital Learning Environments.

The advent of digital learning environments has revolutionized the educational landscape, offering a blend of challenges and opportunities that are reshaping how we teach and learn. From interactive platforms to mobile applications, these environments provide a dynamic space for knowledge exchange. However, they also present unique obstacles that educators and learners must navigate (Adedoyin, & Soykan, 2023; Ferri, et al, 2020; Maatuk, et al, 2022).This chapter explores the multifaceted nature of digital learning environments, highlighting both the hurdles and prospects they afford (refer table 2).

Table 2. Challenges and opportunities presented by digital learning environments

Challenges:		
Number	**Challenge**	**Elaboration**
1	Access and Equity	One of the primary challenges of digital learning environments is the digital divide. Not all students have equal access to the necessary technology and internet connectivity, which can exacerbate existing educational inequalities. Ensuring that every learner has the resources to participate fully in digital education is a significant hurdle.
2	Digital Literacy	Students and educators must possess a certain level of digital literacy to effectively navigate digital learning environments. The lack of such skills can hinder engagement and learning outcomes. Providing adequate training and support to enhance digital literacy is essential.
3	Pedagogical Shift	Teachers often need to adapt their pedagogical approaches to fit the digital space. This shift can be challenging, requiring a reevaluation of teaching methods and a willingness to experiment with new tools and techniques.
4	Student Engagement and Motivation	Maintaining student engagement in an online setting can be difficult. The absence of face-to-face interaction can lead to feelings of isolation and decreased motivation. Strategies to foster active participation and intrinsic motivation are crucial.
5	Assessment and Authentication	Ensuring the integrity of assessments in digital learning environments is a concern. Authenticating student identities and preventing academic dishonesty pose challenges that require innovative solutions.
Opportunities:		
1	Personalized Learning	Digital learning environments offer the potential for personalized education. Adaptive learning technologies can tailor content to individual student needs, allowing for a more customized learning experience.
2	Collaboration and Global Connectivity	These environments break down geographical barriers, enabling collaboration with peers and experts from around the world. This global connectivity fosters a broader perspective and enhances learning through diverse interactions.
3	Access to Resources	Digital learning provides unparalleled access to a wealth of educational resources. Students can explore a vast array of materials, from e-books to interactive simulations, enriching their learning experience.
4	Flexibility and Convenience	The flexibility of digital learning environments allows students to learn at their own pace and on their own schedule. This can be particularly beneficial for non-traditional students, working professionals, and those with other commitments.
5	Continuous Improvement and Innovation	Digital platforms facilitate the collection of data on student performance and engagement, which can be used to continuously improve teaching methods and curriculum design. This data-driven approach supports innovation in education.

Digital learning environments present a complex interplay of challenges and opportunities. While issues such as access and digital literacy must be addressed to ensure inclusivity and effectiveness, the potential for personalized, collaborative, and flexible learning is immense. By embracing these digital spaces and thoughtfully mitigating their challenges, we can harness their power to enhance educational experiences and outcomes for all learners.

THE NECESSITY OF EFFECTIVE COMMUNICATION IN NEW LEARNING ENVIRONMENTS

A. Understanding the Communication Dynamics In Virtual And Hybrid Settings.

Having explored the multifaceted challenges and opportunities of digital learning environments, it is now imperative to examine the foundational role of effective communication within these evolving pedagogical landscapes. In the rapidly evolving landscape of virtual and hybrid learning environments, effective communication is not just an asset but a necessity. The shift from traditional, face-to-face interactions to digital platforms requires a nuanced understanding of communication dynamics. In these settings, the non-verbal cues that are so integral to in-person communication—such as body language, facial expressions, and tone of voice—can be lost or misinterpreted, leading to misunderstandings and a breakdown in the flow of ideas. Educators must adapt their communication styles to compensate for these limitations, using clear and concise language, visual aids, and interactive tools to ensure that their messages are received and understood as intended (Kahlow, et al, 2020).

Moreover, the asynchronous nature of virtual communication presents its own set of challenges. Students and teachers may not be interacting in real-time, which can lead to delays in feedback and a less dynamic exchange of thoughts. This necessitates a structured approach to communication, where expectations for response times and the format of communication are clearly established. Additionally, the diversity of communication channels—such as discussion forums, chat boxes, emails, and video conferencing—demands that all participants are proficient in navigating these platforms to maintain an effective dialogue. Understanding these dynamics is crucial for fostering an inclusive and productive learning environment where every voice is heard and valued (Reed, & Allen, 2022).

B. The Impact Of Communication On Student Engagement And Learning Outcomes.

Building upon the foundational understanding of communication dynamics in virtual and hybrid settings, we must now analyze the profound impact of these interactions on student engagement and ultimately, their learning outcomes. The impact of communication on student engagement and learning outcomes is profound and multifaceted. Effective communication is a cornerstone of student engagement, as it creates a sense of connection and community within the learning environment. When students feel that their voices are heard and valued, they are more likely to participate actively in class discussions, ask questions, and seek help when needed. This heightened engagement can lead to increased motivation and a deeper investment in the learning process. Consequently, students who are effectively communicated with are more likely to achieve higher levels of academic success, as they are better equipped to understand and retain the material being taught (Kahu, et al, 2024).

Moreover, the quality of communication directly influences learning outcomes. Clear, timely, and constructive feedback is essential for students to understand their strengths and areas for improvement. When educators communicate learning objectives and expectations clearly, students are better able to align their efforts with these goals, leading to more focused and productive study habits. Inadequate or ambiguous communication, on the other hand, can result in confusion, frustration, and a lack of direction, which can negatively impact academic performance. Therefore, by prioritizing effective communication, educators can create a learning environment that not only fosters engagement but also optimizes the potential for students to achieve their educational objectives (Xu, et al, 2020).

C. Barriers to Effective Communication And Strategies To Overcome Them.

Barriers to effective communication in digital learning environments can be multifaceted, posing significant challenges to the educational process. Technical issues such as poor internet connectivity, software glitches, and audio/video quality can disrupt the flow of communication and lead to misunderstandings. Additionally, the lack of non-verbal cues in virtual settings can make it difficult for students to interpret the tone and intention behind the message, potentially leading to miscommunication. Cultural and language differences can also act as barriers, especially in diverse classrooms, where varying communication styles and language proficiency levels can impede understanding. Furthermore, the digital divide, where not all students have equal access to technology and internet resources, can exacerbate these communication barriers, leading to inequalities in educational experiences (Brauer, & de Hei, 2021).

To overcome these barriers, a proactive and multifaceted approach is required. Educators can implement strategies such as providing clear guidelines for technology use, offering troubleshooting support, and ensuring that all students have access to necessary resources. Utilizing multiple modes of communication, such as text, audio, and video, can help compensate for the lack of non-verbal cues. Encouraging an inclusive classroom culture that values diverse communication styles and promoting language support programs can also facilitate better understanding among students. Regular check-ins and opportunities for feedback can help identify and address communication issues early on. By being adaptable and creative in their communication strategies, educators can help ensure that all students are able to engage fully and effectively in the digital learning environment (Morrison-Smith, & Ruiz, 2020).

Moreover, the psychological impact of learning through a screen must be considered, as it can lead to feelings of isolation and disconnection, further complicating the communication process. Additionally, the ever-evolving nature of digital tools and platforms requires continuous professional development for educators to effectively manage and leverage these tools for communication purposes (Børte, et al, 2023).

BUILDING TRUST AND RAPPORT IN VIRTUAL AND HYBRID SETTINGS

A. The Role Of Trust In The Teacher-Student Relationship.

The foundation of a successful teacher-student relationship is built on trust, a crucial element that becomes even more critical in virtual and hybrid settings. Trust enables students to feel safe and supported, which is essential for their emotional well-being and academic growth. When students trust their teachers, they are more likely to participate actively in class discussions, ask questions, and seek help when needed. This trust also encourages open and honest communication, allowing teachers to provide constructive feedback that students are more likely to accept and act upon. In essence, trust acts as a bridge that facilitates the transfer of knowledge and the development of a positive learning environment (Glazier, 2021).

In the absence of face-to-face interactions, building trust in virtual and hybrid settings requires intentional effort. Teachers must demonstrate consistency, reliability, and empathy in their interactions with students. By being approachable and showing genuine interest in their students' well-being and progress, educators can foster an atmosphere of trust. This can be achieved through regular one-on-one check-ins, personalized feedback, and creating a classroom culture that values respect and understanding. When trust is established, it not only enhances the teacher-student relationship but also contributes to a more cohesive and effective learning community (Baker, 2023).

In the pursuit of establishing trust in virtual and hybrid learning environments, educators must navigate a host of relevant issues that can impact their efforts. One such issue is the potential for miscommunication due to the lack of non-verbal cues, which can lead to misunderstandings and strain the trust-building process. Additionally, the digital fatigue experienced by both teachers and students can diminish the quality of interactions, making it harder to establish a meaningful connection. Furthermore, the challenge of maintaining student engagement in an online setting can erode trust if students feel disconnected from the learning process. Addressing these issues requires a multifaceted approach, including the use of multimedia tools to enhance communication, structured breaks to combat fatigue, and dynamic teaching methods to keep students engaged and invested in their education (Bellibaş, & Gümüş, 2023).

B. Techniques For Establishing And Nurturing Trust Online.

Given the critical role of trust in the teacher-student relationship, particularly within digital spaces, we must now examine specific techniques for establishing and nurturing this trust online. Establishing and nurturing trust online requires a blend of digital communication skills and a deep understanding of the nuances of virtual interactions (Brogan, & Smith, 2020; Kanaris, & Mujtaba, 2023). Here are several techniques that can help educators build trust in online environments (refer table 3).

Table 3. Techniques for establishing and nurturing trust online

Number	Technique	Elaboration
1	Consistent Communication	Maintain regular and predictable communication with students. This includes timely responses to emails, announcements about course updates, and clear instructions for assignments and activities.
2	Personalized Interaction	Use students' names in discussions and feedback. Personalize messages when possible to show that you are addressing their individual needs and concerns.
3	Active Listening	Pay close attention to students' questions and concerns. In written communication, this means reading and understanding their messages thoroughly before responding. In video calls, it means giving them your full attention and acknowledging their points.
4	Show Vulnerability	Share personal anecdotes or challenges related to the subject matter to create a sense of relatability and authenticity. This humanizes the teacher and builds a connection.
5	Be Transparent	Clearly explain your teaching methods, grading criteria, and any changes to the course structure. Transparency builds credibility and trust.
6	Provide Constructive Feedback	Offer detailed and constructive feedback that helps students improve. This shows that you are invested in their learning and growth.
7	Celebrate Successes	Acknowledge and celebrate students' achievements, both big and small. This can be done through shoutouts in class or through private messages.

continued on following page

Table 3. Continued

Number	Technique	Elaboration
8	Create a Supportive Community	Encourage peer support and collaboration. Use discussion forums and group projects to foster a sense of community where trust can grow among classmates.
9	Be Available	Offer virtual office hours and make yourself available for one-on-one consultations. This accessibility demonstrates your commitment to student success.
10	Respect Privacy	Protect students' privacy by maintaining confidentiality in all communications and by using secure platforms for all course activities.
11	Use Visual Cues	In video calls, use facial expressions, gestures, and body language to convey warmth and engagement, much as you would in a face-to-face setting.
12	Encourage Feedback	Regularly solicit feedback from students about the course and their learning experience. Show that you value their input and are willing to make adjustments based on their needs.

By implementing these techniques, educators can create an online learning environment where trust is not only established but also continually nurtured, leading to a more effective and engaging educational experience for all participants. In fostering an online learning environment centered on trust, educators must also address relevant issues that can either hinder or facilitate this goal. Among these are the digital divide, which can limit access to resources and communication for some students, potentially marginalizing them and weakening the trust bond. Additionally, the lack of face-to-face interaction can make it challenging to build rapport, necessitating the adoption of innovative strategies to simulate personal connections. Privacy concerns are also paramount, as trust can be eroded if students feel their data is not secure. Moreover, cultural and linguistic diversity in online classrooms calls for inclusive practices that respect and value each student's unique background, thereby strengthening trust and engagement. Educators must be proactive in identifying and mitigating these issues to ensure a cohesive and supportive online learning community (Bellibaş, & Gümüş, 2023).

C. Strategies For Creating A Supportive And Inclusive Digital Classroom Community.

With a foundation of trust established, we can now explore strategies for creating a supportive and inclusive digital classroom community, fostering a sense of belonging and collaborative learning. Creating a supportive and inclusive digital classroom community is essential for fostering a positive learning environment that caters to all students (Evans-Amalu, & Claravall, 2021; Lowenthal, et al, 2020). Here are several strategies to achieve this goal (refer table 4).

Table 4. Strategies for creating a supportive and inclusive digital classroom community

Number	Strategy	Elaboration
1	Set Clear Expectations and Norms	Establish clear guidelines for online behavior and communication from the start. Discuss and agree upon classroom norms that promote respect, inclusivity, and active participation.
2	Introduce Icebreakers and Community-Building Activities	Use icebreakers to help students get to know each other. Regular community-building activities can strengthen the sense of belonging among classmates.
3	Encourage Student Voice and Choice	Give students opportunities to contribute to the course content and structure. This can be through choice in assignments, topic selections, or project-based learning.
4	Use Inclusive Language	Be mindful of the language used in all communications. Use terms that are inclusive of all genders, cultures, abilities, and backgrounds.
5	Celebrate Diversity	Acknowledge and celebrate the diverse backgrounds and experiences of students. Incorporate a variety of perspectives into the curriculum to reflect this diversity.
6	Provide Multiple Means of Engagement	Offer various ways for students to engage with the material, such as discussions, group work, multimedia projects, and self-paced modules.
7	Ensure Accessibility	Make sure all course materials are accessible to students with disabilities. Use tools that accommodate different learning styles and needs.
8	Foster Peer Support	Encourage peer mentoring and study groups. Create platforms where students can support each other academically and socially.
9	Monitor and Moderate Online Discussions	Actively monitor online forums and discussions to ensure they remain respectful and on-topic. Step in to mediate if necessary.
10	Address Bullying and Harassment Promptly	Have a clear policy for dealing with any form of bullying or harassment. Address incidents swiftly and decisively to maintain a safe space for all.
11	Regular Check-Ins	Schedule regular one-on-one or small group check-ins to gauge how students are feeling about the course and their peers.
12	Personalize Feedback	Offer personalized feedback that addresses each student's strengths and areas for improvement. This shows that you are attentive to their individual progress.
13	Create Opportunities for Collaboration	Design group projects and collaborative assignments that require students to work together, fostering a sense of teamwork and shared purpose.
14	Reflect and Adapt	Regularly reflect on the classroom community's dynamics and be willing to adapt your strategies to better meet the needs of your students.

By implementing these strategies, educators can cultivate a digital classroom community where every student feels valued, supported, and motivated to participate fully in their education. In fostering a digital classroom community, educators must be mindful of the challenges that can hinder the creation of an inclusive and participatory environment. One relevant issue is the potential for social isolation, where the lack of face-to-face interaction can lead to feelings of disconnection among students. Additionally, issues of digital literacy become paramount, as not all students possess the same level of proficiency with technology, which can create inequalities in participation and engagement. Moreover, the need for ongoing professional development for educators is critical to ensure that they are equipped to manage and facilitate digital classrooms effectively. Addressing these issues requires a multifaceted approach, including the provision of technical support, the development of digital literacy skills for all students, and the integration of strategies that promote social interaction and community building within the digital space (Ovcharuk, et al, 2020).

BEST PRACTICES FOR USING DIGITAL COMMUNICATION TOOLS

A. Selecting the Right Tools For Different Educational Purposes.

Having explored strategies for fostering a supportive digital classroom community, we can now transition to discussing best practices for utilizing digital communication tools, beginning with selecting the right tools for diverse educational purposes. Selecting the right tools for different educational purposes involves matching the functionalities of digital communication platforms with the specific goals of your lessons. For instance, video conferencing tools like Zoom or Microsoft Teams are ideal for live discussions and interactive lectures, while learning management systems (LMS) such as Canvas or Moodle are effective for organizing course content, assignments, and assessments. Additionally, collaborative platforms like Google Workspace or Microsoft 365 can facilitate group work and project-based learning, ensuring that the chosen tools align with the diverse activities and objectives of your teaching curriculum (Ovcharuk, et al, 2020; Haleem, et al, 2022).

Choosing the appropriate digital communication tools is essential for achieving educational objectives effectively (Ovcharuk, et al, 2020; Haleem, et al, 2022). Here are some best practices for selecting the right tools for various educational purposes (refer table 5).

Table 5. Selecting the right tools for different educational purposes

Number	Practice	Elaboration
1	Identify Learning Objectives	Begin by clearly defining the learning objectives of your course or lesson. This will guide your choice of tools that best support these goals.
2	Assess Student Needs	Consider the technological proficiency and access of your students. Select tools that are user-friendly and compatible with the devices and internet connections your students are likely to use.
3	Functionality and Features	Look for tools that offer the specific functionalities you need. For example, if you require real-time collaboration, choose tools with live editing and chat features.
4	Integration	Choose tools that integrate seamlessly with your existing learning management system (LMS) or classroom setup. This facilitates a smoother workflow and reduces the learning curve for both students and educators.
5	Scalability	Select tools that can grow with your class size and complexity of the tasks. Ensure they can handle the load without significant performance issues.
6	Accessibility	Ensure the tools you choose are accessible to all students, including those with disabilities. Compliance with accessibility standards is crucial for an inclusive learning environment.
7	Privacy and Security	Prioritize tools that have robust privacy and security measures to protect student data and comply with educational regulations.
8	Cost-Effectiveness	Consider the cost implications of the tools, especially if they require subscriptions or have tiered pricing based on usage. Look for free or low-cost alternatives that still meet your needs.
9	Training and Support	Choose tools that offer adequate training resources and support for both educators and students. This can be critical for successful implementation.
10	Feedback Mechanisms	Tools that allow for easy feedback and assessment can enhance the learning experience. Look for features like quizzes, polls, and grading systems.
11	Flexibility	Select tools that offer flexibility in how they can be used. This allows for adaptability as your teaching methods evolve or as new educational trends emerge.
12	Community and Reviews	Research the tool's user community and read reviews from other educators. This can provide insights into the tool's effectiveness and any potential issues.

By adhering to these best practices, educators can select digital communication tools that not only align with their educational goals but also enhance the overall learning experience for their students.

Indeed, by adhering to best practices, educators can make informed decisions regarding digital communication tools. However, it is crucial to address relevant issues that may arise in this process. One such issue is the digital divide, where not all students have equal access to the necessary technology or internet connectivity, potentially marginalizing those from disadvantaged backgrounds. Additionally, privacy and security concerns must be considered to protect students' personal information and ensure a safe online learning environment. Furthermore, the over-reliance on digital tools may lead to a lack of social interaction and non-cognitive skill development, which are essential aspects of a well-rounded education. Educators must navigate these challenges to create an inclusive and effective digital learning ecosystem (Alenezi, 2023).

B. Integrating Digital Communication Tools Into Teaching Methodologies.

Following the selection of appropriate tools, we must then delve into the effective integration of these digital communication tools into diverse teaching methodologies. Integrating digital communication tools into teaching methodologies is a transformative process that can significantly enhance the educational experience. By incorporating these tools, educators can create dynamic and interactive lessons that cater to a variety of learning styles. For instance, video conferencing platforms can be used to host virtual lectures and discussions, allowing for real-time interaction and immediate feedback. Additionally, collaborative documents and shared online workspaces enable students to engage in group projects and peer reviews, fostering a sense of community and teamwork even in remote settings (Al-Rahmi, et al, 2020).

To ensure a smooth integration, educators must align the use of digital tools with their teaching objectives. This involves mapping out how each tool will facilitate specific learning outcomes, such as enhancing critical thinking or improving communication skills. By thoughtfully blending these digital tools with traditional teaching methods, educators can create a blended learning environment that leverages the strengths of both digital and in-person instruction, ultimately leading to a more enriching and effective educational journey for students (Valverde-Berrocoso, et al, 2021).

Despite the numerous benefits of integrating digital communication tools into teaching methodologies, there are potential issues that educators may encounter. One such issue is the digital literacy gap among both students and educators. Not all individuals possess the same level of proficiency with digital tools, which can lead to inequalities in participation and learning outcomes. Teachers who are not fully comfortable with technology may struggle to implement these tools effectively, while students who lack digital skills may find it challenging to keep up with their peers. Another issue is the potential for distraction; the multifunctionality of digital devices can lead to off-task behavior, which can disrupt the learning process. Additionally, there are concerns about data privacy and security, particularly when using third-party platforms that may not adhere to strict educational standards. These issues underscore the need for comprehensive training for educators, ongoing support for students, and careful consideration of the digital tools chosen to ensure that they align with educational goals while mitigating potential risks (Valverde-Berrocoso, et al, 2021).

C. Ensuring Accessibility And Equity In The Use Of Digital Communication Tools.

With effective integration of digital communication tools into teaching methodologies established, it is crucial to address the paramount concern of ensuring accessibility and equity in their utilization. Ensuring accessibility and equity in the use of digital communication tools is a paramount concern in modern education. To achieve this, educators must prioritize the inclusion of all students, regardless of their physical abilities, socioeconomic status, or access to technology. This involves selecting tools that are compliant with accessibility standards, such as those that offer screen reader compatibility, closed captioning, and adjustable settings for users with different needs. By doing so, educators ensure that students with disabilities can fully participate in digital learning activities, thus promoting a fair and just learning environment (Aguilar, 2020).

Moreover, addressing the digital divide is crucial for equity. Educators should be aware of the varying levels of access to technology and internet connectivity among their students. Strategies to bridge this gap might include providing loaner devices, ensuring free or low-cost internet access, and offering alternative methods of content delivery for those with limited resources. By taking these steps, educators can help level the playing field, ensuring that all students have an equal opportunity to benefit from the use of digital communication tools in their education (Pittman, et al, 2021).

One significant issue that may arise in ensuring accessibility and equity in digital communication tools is the potential for over-reliance on a one-size-fits-all approach. While educators may strive to implement universally accessible tools, the diverse and often nuanced needs of students can be overlooked. For instance, a standard accessibility feature might not cater to the specific requirements of students with rare disabilities or those from culturally and linguistically diverse backgrounds. This can inadvertently create new barriers to participation and engagement, highlighting the need for personalized solutions and ongoing dialogue with students to understand their individual challenges and adapt accordingly. Without this tailored approach, well-intentioned efforts to promote equity may fall short, leaving some students without the necessary support to fully engage in digital learning environments (Radanliev, et al, 2024).

THE EFFECTS OF EDUCATION COMMUNICATION IN DIGITAL LEARNING ENVIRONMENTS

A. Evaluating the Impact Of Communication On Digital Learning Success.

Having addressed the importance of accessibility and equity in digital communication tools, we now turn our attention to evaluating the direct impact of communication on overall digital learning success. The effects of education communication in digital learning environments are profound, shaping the success of both instructors and students. Effective communication is the cornerstone of digital education, facilitating the transfer of knowledge, the clarification of concepts, and the establishment of a productive learning community. When evaluating its impact, one must consider metrics such as student engagement, participation rates, and academic performance. For example, studies often show that clear, consistent, and timely communication from educators leads to higher levels of student motivation and lower dropout rates in online courses (Al-Fraihat, et al, 2020).

Moreover, the quality of communication in digital learning environments can significantly influence student outcomes. When instructors use a variety of communication channels and strategies to cater to different learning styles, they can enhance comprehension and retention of material. Feedback mechanisms, such as online forums and email, also play a critical role in assessing the effectiveness of communication. By examining these factors, educators can identify areas for improvement and implement strategies that ensure communication effectively supports the learning process, ultimately contributing to the overall success of the digital learning experience (El-Sabagh, 2021).

Despite the recognized importance of communication in digital learning environments, a significant issue remains: the inconsistent application and assessment of communication strategies by educators. Many instructors may not be adequately trained in digital communication techniques, leading to a mismatch between their communication efforts and the diverse needs of their students. This discrepancy can result in miscommunication, feelings of isolation among students, and a lack of personalized support, which are particularly problematic in asynchronous online learning settings where real-time interaction is limited. Consequently, the effectiveness of digital education is often compromised, highlighting the urgent need for professional development and standardized guidelines for communication in digital learning contexts (Kaufmann, & Vallade, 2022)

B. The future of Communication In Education: Emerging Trends And Predictions.

Building upon the evaluation of communication's impact on digital learning success, we can now explore the future of communication in education, examining emerging trends and making informed predictions. As technology continues to advance at an unprecedented pace, the future of communication in education is poised to undergo significant transformations (Chen, et al, 2020; Dimitriadou, & Lanitis, 2023; Frolova, et al, 2020; Huang, et al, 2023; Luan, et al, 2020). Here are some emerging trends and predictions that are likely to shape the landscape of educational communication in the coming years (refer table 6).

AI-driven communication tools are poised to revolutionize personalized learning, as evidenced by educational studies such as the one conducted by_flow, which demonstrated that AI tutors can significantly improve student outcomes by adjusting to their unique learning styles and pace. Similarly, research from the Stanford Center for Opportunity Policy in Education highlighted the potential of adaptive learning platforms to provide immediate and customized feedback, exemplified by programs that analyze student responses to quizzes and suggest personalized study materials accordingly. These studies underscore the transformative power of AI in tailoring educational experiences to meet the diverse needs of learners (Chen, et al, 2020).

The potential of augmented and virtual reality In educational communication has been explored in various studies, such as the one published in the Journal of Educational Psychology, which found that VR simulations significantly enhanced students' understanding and retention of complex scientific concepts by allowing them to interact with 3D models. Additionally, a study by the University of Maryland's Augmented Reality Learning Environments (ARLE) Lab demonstrated that AR applications can improve spatial reasoning skills and increase motivation among elementary students by overlaying educational content onto their physical surroundings. These examples illustrate how AR and VR technologies are making learning more interactive and effective in educational settings (Dimitriadou, & Lanitis, 2023).

The application of blockchain technology In the realm of academic credentials has been investigated in several educational studies. For instance, a research paper from the Stanford Center for Professional Development examined the implementation of blockchain-based records for storing academic achievements and found that this approach not only streamlined the verification process but also increased the security and immutability of educational credentials. Similarly, a study conducted by the MIT Media Lab's Digital Certificates project demonstrated the potential of blockchain to create a decentralized and tamper-proof system for issuing and validating degrees, thereby enhancing trust and transparency in the communication between educational institutions and employers (Frolova, et al, 2020).

The Impact of cloud-based collaborative learning platforms on educational experiences has been examined in several studies. For example, a study published in the "International Journal of Computer-Supported Collaborative Learning" analyzed the effectiveness of such platforms in promoting cross-cultural collaboration and found that they significantly enhanced students' ability to work in diverse teams. Similarly, research conducted by the Harvard Graduate School of Education explored the use of cloud-based tools for project-based learning and concluded that these platforms facilitate deeper engagement and improved learning outcomes by enabling real-time collaboration and resource sharing among students and educators worldwide (Huang, et al, 2023).

The role of data analytics In optimizing learning outcomes has been a focal point of several educational studies. For instance, a study in the "Journal of Educational Data Mining" examined the correlation between student communication patterns in online forums and academic success, revealing that certain types of interactions were predictive of course performance. Additionally, research from the University of Kentucky's Center for the Advanced Study of Technology Leadership in Education (CASTLE) analyzed the impact of real-time analytics on student engagement, demonstrating that educators who utilized data-driven insights to tailor their teaching strategies were able to significantly improve learning outcomes for their students (Luan, et al, 2020).

The Integration of voice-activated learning assistants in educational platforms has been the subject of innovative research. A study by the "Journal of Interactive Learning Research" investigated the efficacy of voice-activated intelligent tutoring systems and found that students who used these assistants showed improved comprehension and retention of material. Similarly, research conducted at the University of California, Berkeley, explored the use of voice recognition technology to support language learning, revealing that interactive voice-based exercises enhanced students' language proficiency and confidence. These studies highlight the potential of voice-activated learning assistants to facilitate a more personalized and interactive learning experience (Terzopoulos, & Satratzemi, 2020).

The growing trend of mobile learning has been substantiated by various educational studies. A research article in the "International Journal of Mobile and Blended Learning" demonstrated that m-learning initiatives increased participation rates among students who had limited access to traditional educational resources. Another study from the "Journal of Computer Assisted Learning" focused on the use of mobile apps for language learning and found that the flexibility and convenience of mobile platforms significantly enhanced student motivation and learning outcomes. These examples underscore the potential of m-learning to make education more accessible and engaging for a broader audience (Criollo-C, et al, 2021).

The development of AI with emotional Intelligence capabilities has been explored in the realm of education through pioneering studies. Research published in the "Journal of Educational Psychology" investigated the effects of an AI tutoring system that could detect and respond to students' emotions, finding that it improved student motivation and academic performance. Similarly, a study in the "IEEE Transactions on Affective Computing" examined the integration of emotional intelligence in educational chatbots and concluded that these bots were able to provide more personalized and supportive interactions, which in turn enhanced the learning experience for students. These studies suggest that AI with emotional intelligence can play a crucial role in creating more empathetic and effective educational environments (Velagaleti, et al, 2024). (refer Table 6).

Table 6. The Future of Communication in Education: Emerging Trends and Predictions

Number	Trend	Elaboration
1	Artificial Intelligence and Personalized Learning	AI-driven communication tools are expected to become more prevalent, offering personalized learning experiences. These tools can adapt to individual student needs, providing tailored feedback and resources in real-time, thus enhancing the learning process.
2	Augmented and Virtual Reality	The integration of AR and VR into educational communication is likely to become more widespread. These technologies can create immersive learning environments that simulate real-world scenarios, making abstract concepts more tangible and engaging for students.
3	Blockchain for Academic Credentials	Blockchain technology may be used to securely store and verify educational credentials, making the process of communication between educational institutions and potential employers more efficient and trustworthy.
4	Collaborative Learning Platforms	The rise of cloud-based platforms will enable more collaborative learning experiences, where students and educators from different parts of the world can work together seamlessly, fostering a global educational community.
5	Data Analytics and Learning Outcomes	The use of data analytics will continue to grow, allowing educators to track and predict student performance based on communication patterns and engagement data. This will enable proactive interventions to improve learning outcomes.
6	Voice-Activated Learning Assistants	Voice recognition technology will likely be integrated into learning platforms, providing students with voice-activated learning assistants that can answer questions, explain concepts, and guide students through their studies.
7	Mobile Learning	With the ubiquity of smartphones, mobile learning (m-learning) will become more prominent, allowing students to access educational content and communicate with educators on the go, thus breaking down barriers to education.
8	Emotional Intelligence in AI	Future communication tools may incorporate emotional intelligence to better understand and respond to the emotional states of students, providing more supportive and empathetic learning environments.

These trends and predictions suggest that the future of communication in education will be characterized by increased personalization, interactivity, and global connectivity, all aimed at creating more effective and inclusive learning experiences for students around the world. Educators and institutions that embrace these changes will be well-positioned to prepare students for the challenges of an ever-evolving digital landscape.

CONCLUSION

A. Summarizing the Chapter's Key Findings And Insights.

This chapter highlights the transformative effects of digital technology on education, underscoring the critical importance of effective communication in the digital learning environment. Key findings reveal that robust communication strategies are essential for virtual and hybrid learning contexts, where the absence of face-to-face interaction can challenge the establishment of trust and rapport. The chapter provides valuable insights into how educators can foster these crucial elements through various digital communication methods, thereby creating a more engaging and supportive educational experience.

In synthesizing best practices, the chapter concludes that the strategic use of digital communication tools can significantly enhance the educational journey. It emphasizes the need for educators to be adept at leveraging these tools to promote student engagement, facilitate knowledge transfer, and ensure that all learners, regardless of their circumstances, can participate fully in the digital classroom. The insights offered aim to guide educators in navigating the complexities of digital communication to ultimately improve learning outcomes and the overall quality of education.

B. Final Thoughts On The Importance Of Communication In The Evolving Digital Education Ecosystem.

As we reflect on the evolving digital education ecosystem, the importance of communication cannot be overstated. It is the linchpin that holds the entire system together, enabling the seamless exchange of knowledge, ideas, and feedback. In this dynamic environment, communication is not just about conveying information; it is about building a community of learners, fostering a sense of belonging, and empowering students to take ownership of their education. The digital realm, with its array of tools and platforms, offers unparalleled opportunities for interaction and collaboration, but it also presents challenges that can only be addressed through intentional and thoughtful communication practices (De Souza Rodrigues, et al, 2021).

While the Malaysian educational system navigates its unique digital transformation, the challenges encountered—such as equitable access and effective teacher training—mirror broader international debates concerning the integration of technology into diverse pedagogical frameworks. A comparative analysis of digital education initiatives reveals that while the specific implementation strategies vary across nations, the fundamental ethical considerations, including data privacy and the prevention of digital divides, remain universally relevant, underscoring the need for collaborative, global dialogues.

The Importance of communication in the digital education ecosystem is pivotal, as it not only facilitates the flow of knowledge and ideas but also cultivates a supportive and interactive learning community, which is essential for student engagement and educational success in the modern, technology-driven educational landscape (Xie, & Derakhshan, 2021).

While digital platforms offer expanded access to educational resources, a critical evaluation must acknowledge the potential for digital distraction and the erosion of essential face-to-face interaction, which are crucial for social and emotional learning. The uncritical adoption of digital tools can inadvertently exacerbate existing inequalities, as disparities in access to reliable internet and technological literacy may create a new form of educational divide.

In conclusion, as the digital education ecosystem continues to evolve, the role of communication will only grow in significance. It is the bridge that connects educators and students, the catalyst that drives engagement and learning, and the foundation upon which trust and understanding are built. For educators, embracing the power of communication in digital spaces is not just an option—it is a necessity. By doing so, we can ensure that the digital transformation of education enriches the learning experience for all, paving the way for a future where education is more accessible, equitable, and effective than ever before (Nativi, et al, 2021).

REFERENCES

Abad-Segura, E., González-Zamar, M. D., Infante-Moro, J. C., & Ruipérez García, G. (2020). Sustainable management of digital transformation in higher education: Global research trends. *Sustainability*, *12*(5), 2107.

Abuhassna, H., Awae, F., Al Zitawi, D. U. D., Bayoumi, K., & Alsharif, A. H. (2022). Hybrid learning for practical-based courses in higher education organizations: A bibliometric analysis. *International Journal of Academic Research in Progressive Education and Development*, *11*(1).

Adedoyin, O. B., & Soykan, E. (2023). Covid-19 pandemic and online learning: The challenges and opportunities. *Interactive Learning Environments*, *31*(2), 863–875.

Adzmi, M. (2021). E-Learning and the Importance of Implementation of Policies and Regulations: A Case Study of Multimedia University8. Malaysian Society 5.0: Selected Contemporary Socio-legal Issues, 221.

Aguilar, S. J. (2020). Guidelines and tools for promoting digital equity. *Information and Learning Science*, *121*(5/6), 285–299.

Al-Fraihat, D., Joy, M., & Sinclair, J. (2020). Evaluating E-learning systems success: An empirical study. *Computers in Human Behavior*, *102*, 67–86.

Al-Rahmi, W. M., Alzahrani, A. I., Yahaya, N., Alalwan, N., & Kamin, Y. B. (2020). Digital communication: Information and communication technology (ICT) usage for education sustainability. *Sustainability*, *12*(12), 5052.

Alenezi, M. (2023). Digital learning and digital institution in higher education. *Education Sciences*, *13*(1), 88.

Ang, W., Jedi, A., & Lohgheswary, N. (2021). Factors affecting the acceptance of open learning as e-learning platform by technical course students. *Journal of Engineering Science and Technology*, *16*(2), 903–918.

Baker, N. M. (2023). *Virtual K-8 Teaching: A Handbook for Building Productive Teacher-Student Relationships*. Rowman & Littlefield.

Bellibaş, M. Ş., & Gümüş, S. (2023). The effect of learning-centred leadership and teacher trust on teacher professional learning: Evidence from a centralised education system. *Professional Development in Education*, *49*(5), 925–937.

Binti Azizo, A. S. bin Mohamed, F., Siang, C. V., & Isham, M. I. M. (2020, December). Virtual reality 360 UTM campus tour with voice commands. In 2020 6th International Conference on Interactive Digital Media (ICIDM) (pp. 1-6). IEEE.

Børte, K., Nesje, K., & Lillejord, S. (2023). Barriers to student active learning in higher education. *Teaching in Higher Education*, *28*(3), 597–615.

Bozkurt, A. (2020). Educational technology research patterns in the realm of the digital knowledge age. *Journal of Interactive Media in Education, (1)*. Can be accessed at https://jime.open.ac.uk/articles/10.5334/jime.570

Brauer, H., & de Hei, M. (2021). Overcoming Barriers of Study Delay by Implementing a Warm Bounded Learning Community. *Higher Education Studies*, *11*(1), 94–104.

Brogan, C., & Smith, J. (2020). *Trust agents: Using the web to build influence, improve reputation, and earn trust*. John Wiley & Sons.

Buchori, A., Pramasdyasari, A. S., Senowarsito, S., Osman, S., & Fadila, N. (2023). Virtual Lab Geometry Development as Online Learning Media Alternatives at Universitas PGRI Semarang and Universiti Teknologi Malaysia. TEM Journal, 12(1).

Bygstad, B., Øvrelid, E., Ludvigsen, S., & Dæhlen, M. (2022). From dual digitalization to digital learning space: Exploring the digital transformation of higher education. *Computers & Education*, *182*, 104463.

Chen, X., Zou, D., Cheng, G., & Xie, H. (2020). Detecting latent topics and trends in educational technologies over four decades using structural topic modeling: A retrospective of all volumes of Computers & Education. *Computers & Education*, *151*, 103855.

Criollo-C, S., Guerrero-Arias, A., Jaramillo-Alcázar, Á., & Luján-Mora, S. (2021). Mobile learning technologies for education: Benefits and pending issues. *Applied Sciences (Basel, Switzerland)*, *11*(9), 4111.

De Souza Rodrigues, M. A., Chimenti, P., & Nogueira, A. R. R. (2021). An exploration of eLearning adoption in the educational ecosystem. *Education and Information Technologies*, *26*(1), 585–615.

Dimitriadou, E., & Lanitis, A. (2023). A critical evaluation, challenges, and future perspectives of using artificial intelligence and emerging technologies in smart classrooms. *Smart Learning Environments*, *10*(1), 12. PMID: 40478141

El-Sabagh, H. A. (2021). Adaptive e-learning environment based on learning styles and its impact on development students' engagement. *International Journal of Educational Technology in Higher Education*, *18*(1), 53.

Evans-Amalu, K., & Claravall, E. B. (2021). Inclusive online teaching and digital learning: Lessons learned in the time of pandemic and beyond. *Journal of Curriculum Studies Research*, *3*(1), i–iii.

Ferri, F., Grifoni, P., & Guzzo, T. (2020). Online learning and emergency remote teaching: Opportunities and challenges in emergency situations. *Societies (Basel, Switzerland), 10*(4), 86.

Frolova, E. V., Rogach, O. V., & Ryabova, T. M. (2020). Digitalization of education in modern scientific discourse: new trends and risks analysis. European journal of contemporary education, 9(2), 313-336.

Glazier, R. A. (2021). *Connecting in the online classroom: Building rapport between teachers and students*. JHU Press.

Haleem, A., Javaid, M., Qadri, M. A., & Suman, R. (2022). Understanding the role of digital technologies in education: A review. Sustainable operations and computers, 3, 275-285.

Huang, X., Zou, D., Cheng, G., Chen, X., & Xie, H. (2023). Trends, research issues and applications of artificial intelligence in language education. *Journal of Educational Technology & Society, 26*(1), 112–131.

Kahlow, J. K. J., Klecka, H. K. H., & Ruppel, E. R. E. (2020). What the differences in conflict between online and face-to-face work groups mean for hybrid groups: A state-of-the-art review. *Review of Communication Research, 8*, 51–77.

Kahu, E. R., Thomas, H. G., & Heinrich, E. (2024). 'A sense of community and camaraderie': Increasing student engagement by supplementing an LMS with a Learning Commons Communication Tool. *Active Learning in Higher Education, 25*(2), 303–316.

Kanaris, M. E., & Mujtaba, B. G. (2023). Trust shaping the social relationship of diverse learners in the online education environment. Environment and Social Psychology, 9(2).

Kaufmann, R., & Vallade, J. I. (2022). Exploring connections in the online learning environment: Student perceptions of rapport, climate, and loneliness. *Interactive Learning Environments, 30*(10), 1794–1808.

Lowenthal, P. R., Humphrey, M., Conley, Q., Dunlap, J. C., Greear, K., Lowenthal, A., & Giacumo, L. A. (2020). Creating accessible and inclusive online learning: Moving beyond compliance and broadening the discussion. *Quarterly Review of Distance Education, 21*(2).

Luan, H., Geczy, P., Lai, H., Gobert, J., Yang, S. J., Ogata, H., & Tsai, C. C. (2020). Challenges and future directions of big data and artificial intelligence in education. *Frontiers in Psychology, 11*, 580820. PMID: 33192896

Maatuk, A. M., Elberkawi, E. K., Aljawarneh, S., Rashaideh, H., & Alharbi, H. (2022). The COVID-19 pandemic and E-learning: Challenges and opportunities from the perspective of students and instructors. *Journal of Computing in Higher Education, 34*(1), 21–38. PMID: 33967563

Morrison-Smith, S., & Ruiz, J. (2020). Challenges and barriers in virtual teams: A literature review. *SN Applied Sciences, 2*(6), 1–33.

Nativi, S., Mazzetti, P., & Craglia, M. (2021). Digital ecosystems for developing digital twins of the earth: The destination earth case. *Remote Sensing, 13*(11), 2119.

Omar, R., Kaliappen, N., Khamis, K. A., & Sulisw
oro, D. (2021). Blended learning approach in graduate studies: A bibliometric analysis from 1997-2021. *International Journal of Information and Education Technology (IJIET), 11*(11), 546–552.

Ovcharuk, O., Ivaniuk, I., Soroko, N., Gritsenchuk, O., & Kravchyna, O. (2020). The use of digital learning tools in the teachers' professional activities to ensure sustainable development and democratization of education in European countries. *Information Technologies and Learning Tools, 75*(1), 163–176. DOI: 10.33407/itlt.v75i1.3533

Pittman, J., Severino, L., DeCarlo-Tecce, M. J., & Kiosoglous, C. (2021). An action research case study: Digital equity and educational inclusion during an emergent COVID-19 divide. *Journal for Multicultural Education, 15*(1), 68–84.

Radanliev, P., De Roure, D., Novitzky, P., & Sluganovic, I. (2024). Accessibility and inclusiveness of new information and communication technologies for disabled users and content creators in the Metaverse. *Disability and Rehabilitation. Assistive Technology, 19*(5), 1849–1863. PMID: 37585705

Reed, K. M., & Allen, J. A. (2022). *Suddenly hybrid: Managing the modern meeting.* John Wiley & Sons.

Rosman, M. R. M., Alias, N. R., Arshad, I. H., Hamid, H. A., & Idris, Z. (2022). Assessing Students' Perceived Engagement and Perceived Performance for E-Learning in East Coast Malaysia: A Partial Least Square Structural Equation Modeling Approach. *IEEE Engineering Management Review, 51*(1), 63–75.

Salleh, M. (2020). Teacher Learning Outcomes on Post COVID-19: A Review Based on Malaysia and other Asian Countries Perspective. *International Journal of Academic Research in Business & Social Sciences, 10*(11), 164–173. DOI: 10.6007/IJARBSS/v10-i11/8276

Schwarz, A. (2024). Instructional Risk and Crisis Communication at Higher Education Institutions during COVID-19: Insights from Practitioners in the Global South and North. *Journal of International Crisis and Risk Communication Research*, *7*(1), 1–47.

Taha, J. A. B. A., Hanid, M. F. B. A., & Said, M. N. H. M., bin Hassan, R., & Yik, L. H. (2020). Effectiveness of using augmented reality application in the subject of educational technology for undergraduate students. *Journal of Critical Reviews*, *7*(15), 1845–1850. DOI: 10.31838/jcr.07.15.337

Terzopoulos, G., & Satratzemi, M. (2020). Voice assistants and smart speakers in everyday life and in education. *Informatics in Education*, *19*(3), 473–490.

Timotheou, S., Miliou, O., Dimitriadis, Y., Sobrino, S. V., Giannoutsou, N., Cachia, R., & Ioannou, A. (2023). Impacts of digital technologies on education and factors influencing schools' digital capacity and transformation: A literature review. *Education and Information Technologies*, *28*(6), 6695–6726. PMID: 36465416

Valverde-Berrocoso, J., Fernández-Sánchez, M. R., Revuelta Dominguez, F. I., & Sosa-Díaz, M. J. (2021). The educational integration of digital technologies preCovid-19: Lessons for teacher education. *PLoS One*, *16*(8), e0256283. PMID: 34411161

Velagaleti, S. B., Choukaier, D., Nuthakki, R., Lamba, V., Sharma, V., & Rahul, S. (2024). Empathetic Algorithms: The Role of AI in Understanding and Enhancing Human Emotional Intelligence. *Journal of Electrical Systems*, *20*(3s), 2051–2060.

Xie, F., & Derakhshan, A. (2021). A conceptual review of positive teacher interpersonal communication behaviors in the instructional context. *Frontiers in Psychology*, *12*, 708490. PMID: 34335424

Xu, B., Chen, N. S., & Chen, G. (2020). Effects of teacher role on student engagement in WeChat-Based online discussion learning. *Computers & Education*, *157*, 103956.

ADDITIONAL READING

Almusaed, A., Almssad, A., Yitmen, I., & Homod, R. Z. (2023). Enhancing student engagement: Harnessing "AIED"'s power in hybrid education—A review analysis. *Education Sciences*, *13*(7), 632.

Bøjer, B. H., & Brøns, M. G. (2022). How co-design can contribute to the ongoing development of hybrid learning spaces by empowering the users. In *Hybrid learning spaces* (pp. 45–60). Springer International Publishing.

Joseph, S., Tahir, A., Bibi, F., Hamid, K., Iqbal, M. W., Ruk, S. A., & Ahmad, S. Z. (2024). A Review Analysis on Using" AIED" to Improve Student Engagement in Hybrid Education. [BBE]. *Bulletin of Business and Economics*, *13*(2), 424–435.

Manciaracina, A. (2022). *Designing hybrid learning environments and processes: Interactive communication tools for active learning*. Springer Nature.

Mondragon-Estrada, E., Kirschning, I., Nolazco-Flores, J. A., & Camacho-Zuñiga, C. (2023, August). Fostering digital transformation in education: Technology enhanced learning from professors' experiences in emergency remote teaching. []. Frontiers Media SA.]. *Frontiers in Education*, *8*, 1250461.

Pavlidou, I., Dragicevic, N., & Tsui, E. (2021). A multi-dimensional hybrid learning environment for business education: A knowledge dynamics perspective. *Sustainability*, *13*(7), 3889.

KEY TERMS AND DEFINITIONS

Communication Enhancement: The improvement of the ways in which information is shared and understood between educators and students, often through the use of digital tools and platforms, to facilitate more effective and efficient teaching and learning.

Digital Classroom: An educational environment that leverages digital technologies, such as computers, tablets, and online platforms, to facilitate teaching and learning activities, allowing for interactive, personalized, and often remote education experiences.

Fostering Trust: The process of building and maintaining a sense of reliability and confidence among all participants in a virtual or hybrid learning environment, which is crucial for creating a supportive and effective educational community.

Hybrid Learning: An educational model that combines traditional face-to-face classroom methods with online digital media, offering a flexible approach that allows for a blend of in-person and remote learning experiences.

Transforming Education: The process of fundamentally changing the traditional methods and structures of educational systems to better adapt to the needs of modern learners, often through the integration of technology, innovative teaching methods, and new educational philosophics.

Virtual Learning: A form of learning that takes place entirely online, without the need for physical presence in a traditional classroom setting, typically involving interactive software and digital communication tools.

Compilation of References

Abad-Segura, E., González-Zamar, M. D., Infante-Moro, J. C., & Ruipérez García, G. (2020). Sustainable management of digital transformation in higher education: Global research trends. *Sustainability*, *12*(5), 2107.

Abbasy, M. B., & Quesada, E. V. (2017). Predictable influence of IoT (Internet of Things) in the higher education. *International Journal of Information and Education Technology (IJIET)*, *7*(12), 914–920. DOI: 10.18178/ijiet.2017.7.12.995

Abbes, I., & Hallem, Y. (2016). Co-création et technologie mobile au sein d'un espace marchand: quelles valeurs pour le consommateur? une application dans le secteur de la restauration. *Revue Française du Marketing*, (256).

Abduljaber, M. F. (n.d.). *Perceived influence of artificial intelligence on Educational Leadership's Decision-Making, teaching, and learning Outcomes: A Transcendental phenomenological Study*. Scholars Crossing. Retrieved January 19, 2025, from https://digitalcommons.liberty.edu/doctoral/5714/

Abu Shawar, B. A., & Atwell, E. (2007). Chatbots: Are they really useful? *Journal for Language Technology and Computational Linguistics*, *22*(1), 29–49. DOI: 10.21248/jlcl.22.2007.88

Abu Shawar, B., & Atwell, E. (2002). *A comparison between Alice and Elizabeth chatbot systems. Research Report 2002.19*. University of Leeds – School of Computing.

Abuhassna, H., Awae, F., Al Zitawi, D. U. D., Bayoumi, K., & Alsharif, A. H. (2022). Hybrid learning for practical-based courses in higher education organizations: A bibliometric analysis. *International Journal of Academic Research in Progressive Education and Development*, *11*(1).

Abulibdeh, A., Zaidan, E., & Abulibdeh, R. (2024). Navigating the confluence of artificial intelligence and education for sustainable development in the era of industry 4.0: Challenges, opportunities, and ethical dimensions. *Journal of Cleaner Production*, *437*, 140527. DOI: 10.1016/j.jclepro.2023.140527

AbuMusab, S. (2023). Generative AI and human labor: Who is replaceable? *AI & Society*. Advance online publication. DOI: 10.1007/s00146-023-01773-3

Acemoglu, D., Laibson, D. I., & List, J. A. (2014). Equalizing superstars: The internet and the democratization of education. *The American Economic Review*, *104*(5), 523–527. DOI: 10.1257/aer.104.5.523

Adams, D., & Chuah, K.-M. (2022). Artificial intelligence-based tools in research writing: Current trends and future potentials. In Churi, P. P., Joshi, S., Elhoseny, M., & Omrane, A. (Eds.), *Artificial Intelligence in Higher Education: A practical approach* (pp. 169–184). CRD Press., DOI: 10.1201/9781003184157-9

Adedoyin, O. B., & Soykan, E. (2020). Covid-19 pandemic and online learning: The challenges and opportunities. *Interactive Learning Environments*, *31*(2), 863–875. DOI: 10.1080/10494820.2020.1813180

Adeoye-Olatunde, O. A., & Olenik, N. L. (2021). Research and scholarly methods: Semi-structured interviews. *JACCP JOURNAL OF THE AMERICAN COLLEGE OF CLINICAL PHARMACY*, *4*(10), 1358–1367. DOI: 10.1002/jac5.1441

Adeshola, I., & Adepoju, A. P. (2023). The opportunities and challenges of ChatGPT in education. *Interactive Learning Environments*, •••, 1–14. DOI: 10.1080/10494820.2023.2253858

Adzmi, M. (2021). E-Learning and the Importance of Implementation of Policies and Regulations: A Case Study of Multimedia University8. Malaysian Society 5.0: Selected Contemporary Socio-legal Issues, 221.

Aguilar, S. J. (2020). Guidelines and tools for promoting digital equity. *Information and Learning Science*, *121*(5/6), 285–299.

Ahmad, W., Shokeen, R., & Raj, R. (2025). Artificial Intelligence: Solutions in Special Education. In *Transforming Special Education through Artificial Intelligence* (pp. 459-520). IGI Global.

Ahmed, N., & Wahed, M. (2020). The De-democratization of AI: Deep Learning and the Compute Divide in Artificial Intelligence Research. ArXiv (Cornell University). https://doi.org//arxiv.2010.15581DOI: 10.48550

Ahmed, N., Saha, A. K., Al Noman, M. A., Jim, J. R., Mridha, M. F., & Kabir, M. M. (2024). Deep learning-based natural language processing in human–agent interaction: Applications, advancements and challenges. *Natural Language Processing Journal*, *9*(100112), 100112. DOI: 10.1016/j.nlp.2024.100112

Ahmed, S., & Jain, A. (2021). Clustering-based classification algorithms for online spam review detection. *Journal of Machine Learning Research, 22*(6), 190–210. https://www.researchgate.net/publication/348342061_Performance_Evaluation_of_Clustering-Based_Classification_Algorithms_for_Detection_of_Online_Spam_Reviews

Ahramovich, A. (2023, June 23). Machine learning in education: 10 use cases, examples, and benefits. *Itransition*. https://www.itransition.com/machine-learning/education

Akgun, S., & Greenhow, C. (2021). Artificial intelligence in education: Addressing ethical challenges in K-12 settings. *AI and Ethics, 2*(3), 431–440. DOI: 10.1007/s43681-021-00096-7 PMID: 34790956

Al-Alawi, L., Al Shaqsi, J., Tarhini, A., & Al-Busaidi, A. S. (2023). Using machine learning to predict factors affecting academic performance: The case of college students on academic probation. *Education and Information Technologies, 28*(10), 1–26. DOI: 10.1007/s10639-023-11700-0 PMID: 37361752

Albikawi, Z., & Abuadas, M. (2025). A Novel Scale to Measure Nursing Students' Fear of Artificial Intelligence: Development and Validation. *The Open Nursing Journal*, •••, 19.

Albusays, K., Bjorn, P., Dabbish, L., Ford, D., Murphy-Hill, E., Serebrenik, A., & Storey, M. A. (2021). The diversity crisis in software development. *IEEE Software, 38*(2), 19–25.

Alcatel. (2020). The Internet of Things in Education. https://www.al-enterprise.com/-/media/assets/internet/documents/iot-for-education-solutionbrief-en.pdf

Alenezi, M. (2023). Digital learning and digital institution in higher education. *Education Sciences, 13*(1), 88.

Al-Fraihat, D., Joy, M., & Sinclair, J. (2020). Evaluating E-learning systems success: An empirical study. *Computers in Human Behavior, 102*, 67–86.

Alhammadi, M. (2023). Optimising Customer Service Delivery and Response Time through AI-Enhanced Chatbots in Facilities Management-A Mixed-Methods Research. *American Journal of Smart Technology and Solutions, 2*(2), 43–54.

Al-harbi, N. K., & Al-shargabi, A. A. (2023). An Exploratory Analysis of using Chatbots in Academia. *International Journal of Advanced Computer Science and Applications, 14*(12).

Alias, N. F., & Razak, R. A. (2025). Revolutionizing learning in the digital age: A systematic literature review of microlearning strategies. *Interactive Learning Environments, 33*(1), 1–21. DOI: 10.1080/10494820.2024.2331638

Ali, J., Madni, S. H. H., Jahangeer, M. S. I., & Danish, M. A. A. (2023). IoT Adoption Model for E-Learning in Higher Education Institutes: A Case Study in Saudi Arabia. *Sustainability, 15*, 9748. DOI: 10.3390/su15129748

Allam, H., Khan, Z., Letsholo, K., Pandya, B., Shah, K., & Ahamed, J. (2023). A Proposed AI Method for Tracking College Students' Academic Progress. In *2023 9th International Conference on Information Technology Trends (ITT)* (pp. 215–219). IEEE.

Allen, L. K., & Kendeou, P. (2024). ED-AI Lit: An Interdisciplinary Framework for AI Literacy in Education. *Policy Insights from the Behavioral and Brain Sciences, 11*(1), 3–10. DOI: 10.1177/23727322231220339

Al-Mughairi, H. and Bhaskar, P. (2024), "Exploring the factors affecting the adoption AI techniques in higher education: insights from teachers' perspectives on ChatGPT", *Journal of Research in Innovative Teaching & Learning*, Vol. ahead-of-print No. ahead-of-print, 1-16. https://doi.org/DOI: 10.1108/JRIT-09-2023-0129

Alqahtani, T., Badreldin, H. A., Alrashed, M., Alshaya, A. I., & Alghamdi, S. S., bin Saleh, K., ... & Albekairy, A. M. (2023). The emergent role of artificial intelligence, natural learning processing, and large language models in higher education and research. *Research in Social & Administrative Pharmacy, 19*(8), 1236–1242. DOI: 10.1016/j.sapharm.2023.05.016 PMID: 37321925

Alqodsi, E. M., Jadalhaq, I. M., Maknouzi, M. E. H. E., & Abdulhay, I. E. A. (2024). Navigating the legal landscape. In *Advances in educational technologies and instructional design book series* (pp. 212–230). https://doi.org/DOI: 10.4018/979-8-3693-0880-6.ch015

Al-Rahmi, W. M., Alzahrani, A. I., Yahaya, N., Alalwan, N., & Kamin, Y. B. (2020). Digital communication: Information and communication technology (ICT) usage for education sustainability. *Sustainability, 12*(12), 5052.

Al-Rahmi, W. M., Alzahrani, A. I., Yahaya, N., Alalwan, N., & Kamin, Y. B. (2020). Digital Communication: Information and Communication Technology (ICT) Usage for Education Sustainability. *Sustainability, 12*(12), 5052. DOI: 10.3390/su12125052

Al-Tkhayneh, K. M., Alghazo, E. M., & Tahat, D. (2023). The advantages and disadvantages of using artificial intelligence in education. *Journal of Educational and Social Research, 13*(4), 105–117. DOI: 10.36941/jesr-2023-0094

Amaral, L. A., & Meurers, D. (2011). On using intelligent computer-assisted language learning in real-life foreign language teaching and learning. *ReCALL, 23*(1), 4–24. DOI: 10.1017/S0958344010000261

Analytics Steps. (2021). 6 Applications of AI in Education Sector. https://www.analyticssteps.com/blogs/4-major-applications-artificial-intelligence-education-sector

Anand, M. O., Krishnaswamy, J., Kumar, A., & Bali, A. (2010). Sustaining biodiversity conservation in human-modified landscapes in the Western Ghats: Remnant forests matter. *Biological Conservation, 143*(10), 2363–2374. DOI: 10.1016/j.biocon.2010.01.013

Anderson, M. (2015). Renaissance Language and Memory Forms. In M. Anderson, *The Renaissance Extended Mind* (pp. 116–144). Palgrave Macmillan UK. https://doi.org/DOI: 10.1057/9781137412850_4

Anderson, L. N. (2019). Teaching the introductory public relations course: Pedagogical recommendations. *Journal of Communication Pedagogy, 2*, 58–62. DOI: 10.31446/JCP.2019.13

Anderson, L. W., & Krathwohl, D. R. (Eds.). (2001). *A taxonomy for learning, teaching, and assessing: A revision of Bloom's taxonomy of educational objectives*. Pearson Education.

Ang, W., Jedi, A., & Lohgheswary, N. (2021). Factors affecting the acceptance of open learning as e-learning platform by technical course students. *Journal of Engineering Science and Technology, 16*(2), 903–918.

Antony, S., & Ramnath, R. (n.d.). *A phenomenological exploration of students' perceptions of AI chatbots in higher education.* Retrieved January 20, 2025, from https://eric.ed.gov/?id=EJ1403709

Arter, J. A., & Spandel, V. (1992). *Creating a framework for classroom assessment: Guidelines for teachers*. ERIC Clearinghouse on Assessment and Evaluation.

Ashalatha, K., & Narasimhulu, K. (2024). Enhancing concrete durability: Structural health monitoring of polypropylene fiber-reinforced concrete with accelerometer sensors. *E3S Web of Conferences, 591*, 09003.

Ashok, M., Madan, R., Joha, A., & Sivarajah, U. (2021). Ethical framework for Artificial Intelligence and Digital technologies. *International Journal of Information Management, 62*, 102433. DOI: 10.1016/j.ijinfomgt.2021.102433

Athinarayanan, S., Navaz, K., & Joel, M. R. (2024, January). Analysing various algorithms applied to Alzheimer's disease dataset to help the future generation. In *2024 International Conference on Intelligent and Innovative Technologies in Computing, Electrical and Electronics (IITCEE)* (pp. 1–5). IEEE.

Attanasi, G., Chessa, M., Gil-Gallen, S., & Llerena, P. (2021). A survey on experimental elicitation of creativity in economics. *Revue d'Economie Industrielle, 174*, 273–324. DOI: 10.4000/rei.10448

Ayeni, O. O., Al Hamad, N. M., Chisom, O. N., Osawaru, B., & Adewusi, O. E. (2024). AI in education: A review of personalized learning and educational technology. *GSC Advanced Research and Reviews, 18*(2), 261–271.

Ayton, D. (2023, March 21). *Chapter 6: Phenomenology*. Pressbooks. https://oercollective.caul.edu.au/qualitative-research/chapter/__unknown__-6/

Azaiz, I., Deckarm, O., & Strickroth, S. (2023). AI-enhanced auto-correction of programming exercises: How effective is GPT-3.5? *International Journal Of Engineering Pedagogy, 13*(8), 67–83. DOI: 10.3991/ijep.v13i8.45621

Azıonya, C. M., & Nhedzı, A. (2021). The digital divide and higher education challenge with emergency online learning: Analysis of tweets in the wake of the COVID-19 lockdown. *Turkish Online Journal of Distance Education, 22*(4), 164–182.

Babbie, E. (2020). *The practice of social research* (15th ed.). Cengage Learning.

Baceviciute, S., Cordoba, A. L., Wismer, P., Jensen, T. V., Klausen, M., & Makransky, G. (2022). Investigating the value of immersive virtual reality tools for organizational training: An applied international study in the biotech industry. *Journal of Computer Assisted Learning, 38*(2), 470–487.

Baïdoo-anu, D., & OWUSU ANSAH, L. (2023). Education in the Era of Generative Artificial Intelligence (AI): Understanding the Potential Benefits of ChatGPT in Promoting Teaching and Learning. Journal of AI, 7(1), 52-62. https://doi.org/DOI: 10.61969/jai.1337500

Baidoo-Anu, D., & Owusu Ansah, L. (2023). Education in the era of Generative Artificial Intelligence (AI): Understanding the potential benefits of CHATGPT in promoting teaching and learning. SSRN *Electronic Journal*. https://doi.org/DOI: 10.2139/ssrn.4337484

Bai, X. (2024). THE ROLE AND CHALLENGES OF ARTIFICIAL INTELLIGENCE IN INFORMATION TECHNOLOGY EDUCATION. *Pacific International Journal, 7*(1), 86–92. DOI: 10.55014/pij.v7i1.524

Baker, R. S., & Siemens, G. (2014). *Educational data mining and learning analytics.* In R. K. M. K. L. E. A. G. S. (Ed.), *Handbook of learning analytics* (pp. 61-72). Society for Learning Analytics Research.

Baker, N. M. (2023). *Virtual K-8 Teaching: A Handbook for Building Productive Teacher-Student Relationships*. Rowman & Littlefield.

Baker, R. S.. (2020). *Artificial Intelligence in education: Promise and implications for teaching and learning*. Taylor & Francis.

Baker, R. S., & Hawn, A. (2021). Algorithmic bias in education. *International Journal of Artificial Intelligence in Education, 32*(4), 1052–1092. DOI: 10.1007/s40593-021-00285-9

Ball, S. J. (1990). Self-doubt and soft data: Social and technical trajectories in ethnographic fieldwork. *International Journal of Qualitative Studies in Education : QSE, 3*(2), 157–171.

Barnes, E., & Hutson, J. (2024). Navigating the ethical terrain of AI in higher education: Strategies for mitigating bias and promoting fairness. *Forum for Education Studies, 2*(2), 1229. DOI: 10.59400/fes.v2i2.1229

Baron, P. (2024). Are AI detection and plagiarism similarity scores worthwhile in the age of ChatGPT and other Generative AI? *Scholarship of Teaching and Learning in the South, 8*(2), 151–179.

Barrett, A., & Pack, A. (2023). Not quite eye to AI: Student and teacher perspectives on the use of generative artificial intelligence in the writing process. *International Journal of Educational Technology in Higher Education, 20*(1), 59. DOI: 10.1186/s41239-023-00427-0

Barrows, H. S., & Tamblyn, R. M. (1980). *Problem-based learning: An approach to medical education*. Springer Publishing Company.

Batacharia, B., & Levy, D. A., R. C., Krotov, and Wilks, Y. (1999). CONVERSE: a conversational companion. In Wilks, Y., editor, *Machine conversations*, 205–215. Kluwer, Boston/ Dordrecht/ London.

Bates, A. W. (2015). *Teaching in a digital age: Guidelines for designing teaching and learning*. BCcampus.

Bee, O., & Hie, T. (2015). Employers' Emphasis on Technical Skills and Soft Skills in Job Advertisements. *Melta Journals. English Teaching, 44*(1), 1-12.

Bellibaş, M. Ş., & Gümüş, S. (2023). The effect of learning-centred leadership and teacher trust on teacher professional learning: Evidence from a centralised education system. *Professional Development in Education, 49*(5), 925–937.

Beltran, M. A., Ruiz Mondragon, M. I., & Han, S. H. (2024, June). Comparative analysis of generative ai risks in the public sector. In *Proceedings of the 25th Annual International Conference on Digital Government Research* (pp. 610-617).

Bender, E. M., Gebru, T., McMillan-Major, A., & Shmitchell, S. (2021). On the dangers of stochastic parrots: Can language models be too big? In *Proceedings of the 2021 ACM Conference on Fairness, Accountability, and Transparency* (pp. 610–623). DOI: 10.1145/3442188.3445922

Benson, P., & Lor, W. (1999). Conceptions of language and language learning. *System, 27*(4), 459–472. DOI: 10.1016/S0346-251X(99)00045-7

Bernacki, M. L., Greene, M. J., & Lobczowski, N. G. (2021). A systematic review of research on personalized learning: Personalized by whom, to what, how, and for what purpose (s)? *Educational Psychology Review, 33*(4), 1675–1715.

Bernhard, J., & Russmann, U. (2023). Digitalization in public relations—Changing competences: A longitudinal analysis of skills required in PR job ads. *Public Relations Review, 49*(1), 102283. DOI: 10.1016/j.pubrev.2022.102283

Bian, J., Al Arafat, A., Xiong, H., Li, J., Li, L., Chen, H., Wang, J., Dou, D., & Guo, Z. (2022). Machine learning in real-time internet of things (iot) systems: A survey. *IEEE Internet of Things Journal, 9*(11), 8364–8386.

Bielaczyc, K., & Collins, A. (1999). Design research: An emerging paradigm for transforming the practice of teaching. *Yearbook of the National Society for the Study of Education, 98*(1), 44–62.

Bigan, C. (2022). Trends in Teaching Artificial Intelligence for Industry 5.0. In Drăghici, A., & Iva cu, L. (Eds.), *Sustainability and Innovation in Manufacturing Enterprises, Advances in Sustainability Science and Technology* (pp. 257–275). Springer., DOI: 10.1007/978-981-16-7365-8_2

Binti Azizo, A. S. bin Mohamed, F., Siang, C. V., & Isham, M. I. M. (2020, December). Virtual reality 360 UTM campus tour with voice commands. In 2020 6th International Conference on Interactive Digital Media (ICIDM) (pp. 1-6). IEEE.

Bishwas, R., & Rao, S. (2018). Quantum computing applications in support vector clustering. Quantum Computing and Machine Learning, 5(2), 45-58. https://arxiv.org/abs/1804.10905

Black, P., & Wiliam, D. (1998). Assessment and classroom learning. *Assessment in Education: Principles, Policy & Practice*, *5*(1), 7–74. DOI: 10.1080/0969595980050102

Bluhm, D. J., Harman, W., Lee, T. W., & Mitchell, T. R. (2011). Qualitative research in management: A decade of progress. *Journal of Management Studies*, *48*(8), 1866–1891.

Blumenfeld, P. C., Soloway, E., Marx, R. W., Krajcik, J. S., Guzdial, M., & Palincsar, A. S. (1991). Motivating project-based learning: Sustaining the doing, supporting the learning. *Educational Psychologist*, *26*(3-4), 369–398. DOI: 10.1080/00461520.1991.9653137

Bogen, M., & Rieke, A. (2018). Help wanted: An examination of hiring algorithms, equity, and bias. *Upturn.* https://www.upturn.org/static/reports/2018/hiring-algorithms/files/Upturn%20--%20Help%20Wanted%20-%20An%20Exploration%20of%20Hiring%20Algorithms,%20Equity%20and%20Bias.pdf

Boissière, J., & Bruillard, É. (2021). *L'école digitale. Une éducation à apprendre et à vivre*. Armand Colin.

Bond, M., Khosravi, H., De Laat, M., Bergdahl, N., Negrea, V., Oxley, E., & Siemens, G. (2024). A Meta systematic review of artificial intelligence in higher education: A call for increased ethics, collaboration, and rigour. *International Journal of Educational Technology in Higher Education*, *21*(1), 4.

Bontridder, N., & Poullet, Y. (2021). The role of artificial intelligence in disinformation. *Data & Policy*, *3*. Advance online publication. DOI: 10.1017/dap.2021.20

Boothe, D., & Caspary, M. (2018). Critical Issues and Practices for Hybrid and Online Teaching and Learning: Building Improved Models for 21st Century English Language Learning. *Cognitive Science – New Media – Education, 2*(1), 99. https://doi.org/DOI: 10.12775/CSNME.2017.006

Boppiniti, S. T. (2023). Data Ethics in AI: Addressing Challenges in Machine Learning and Data Governance for Responsible Data Science. International Scientific Journal for Research, 5(5).

Børte, K., Nesje, K., & Lillejord, S. (2023). Barriers to student active learning in higher education. *Teaching in Higher Education*, *28*(3), 597–615.

Boud, D., & Falchikov, N. (2006). *Rethinking assessment in higher education: Learning for the longer term*. Routledge.

Boud, D., Keogh, R., & Walker, D. (Eds.). (1985). *Reflection: Turning experience into learning*. Kogan Page.

Bozkurt, A. (2020). Educational technology research patterns in the realm of the digital knowledge age. *Journal of Interactive Media in Education, (1).* Can be accessed at https://jime.open.ac.uk/articles/10.5334/jime.570

Bradford, A. (2024). *Implementation of Developmental Feedback as a Performance Strategy in Small Businesses* (Doctoral dissertation, Walden University).

Bradley, V. M. (2021). Learning management system (LMS) use with online instruction. *International Journal of Technology in Education*, *4*(1), 68–92.

Bransford, J. D., Brown, A. L., & Cocking, R. R. (2000). *How people learn: Brain, mind, experience, and school.* National Academy Press.

Brauer, H., & de Hei, M. (2021). Overcoming Barriers of Study Delay by Implementing a Warm Bounded Learning Community. *Higher Education Studies*, *11*(1), 94–104.

Braun, V., & Clarke, V. (2006). Using thematic analysis in psychology. *Qualitative Research in Psychology*, *3*(2), 77–101. DOI: 10.1191/1478088706qp063oa

Brogan, C., & Smith, J. (2020). *Trust agents: Using the web to build influence, improve reputation, and earn trust.* John Wiley & Sons.

Bruce Smith, A. (2024). LinkedIn post (no title). https://www.linkedin.com/posts/andrewbrucesmith_cheatgpt-generative-text-ai-use-in-uk-pr-activity-7260591234862170114-ecuL

Brunetti, F., Bonfanti, A., Chiarini, A., & Vannucci, V. (2023). Digitalization and academic research: Knowing of and using digital services and software to develop scientific papers. *The TQM Journal*, *35*(5), 1135–1155.

Brunner, B., Zarkin, K., & Yates, B. (2018). What do employers want? What should faculty teach? A content analysis of entry-level employment ads in public relations. *Journal of Public Relations Education*. Retrieved from https://aejmc.us/jpre/2018/08/17/what-do-employers-want-what-should-faculty-teach-a-content-analysis-of-entry-level-employment-ads-in-public-relations/

Brynjolfsson, E., & McAfee, A. (2014). *The second machine age: Work, progress, and prosperity in a time of brilliant technologies.* W.W. Norton & Company.

Buchanan, B. G. (2005). A (Very) Brief History of Artificial Intelligence. *AI Magazine*, *26*(4), 53. DOI: 10.1609/aimag.v26i4.1848

Buchori, A., Pramasdyasari, A. S., Senowarsito, S., Osman, S., & Fadila, N. (2023). Virtual Lab Geometry Development as Online Learning Media Alternatives at Universitas PGRI Semarang and Universiti Teknologi Malaysia. TEM Journal, 12(1).

Builtin. (2020). How education technology is changing the classroom. *Builtin.* https://builtin.com/edtech

Builtin. (2020). The Connected Classroom: 9 Examples of IoT in Education. https://builtin.com/internet-things/iot-education-examples

Burgard, W., & Harrer, J. (2023). A semi-supervised support vector machine approach using iterative clustering for improved classification. *Journal of Machine Learning and Applications*, *49*(8), 1150–1165. https://arxiv.org/abs/2303.12532

Bygstad, B., Øvrelid, E., Ludvigsen, S., & Dæhlen, M. (2022). From dual digitalization to digital learning space: Exploring the digital transformation of higher education. *Computers & Education*, *182*, 104463.

Byron, K., & Khazanchi, S. (2012). Rewards and creative performance: A meta-analytic test of theoretically derived hypotheses. *Psychological Bulletin*, *138*(4), 809–830. DOI: 10.1037/a0027652

Campbell, L., Highton, M., & McAndrew, E. (2023). Supporting open education practice: Reflective case studies from the University of Edinburgh. *Edutec. Revista Electrónica de Tecnología Educativa*, (85), 9–28.

Candelon, F., Krayer, L., Rajendran, S., & Zuluaga Martínez, D. (2023). *How People Can Create—and Destroy—Value with Generative AI*. Boston Consulting Group, Henderson Institute.

Carnegie Learning. (2024). LiveLab: Real-time classroom monitoring with machine learning. https://www.carnegielearning.com/

Carson, B. (2017). *Learning in the Age of Immediacy: 5 Factors for How We Connect, Communicate, and Get Work Done*. Association for Talent Development.

Carter, S. P., Greenberg, K., & Walker, M. S. (2016). The impact of computer usage on academic performance: Evidence from a randomized trial at the United States Military Academy. *Economics of Education Review*, *56*, 118–132. DOI: 10.1016/j.econedurev.2016.12.005

Casheekar, A., Lahiri, A., Rath, K., Prabhakar, K. S., & Srinivasan, K. (2024). A contemporary review on chatbots, AI-powered virtual conversational agents, ChatGPT: Applications, open challenges and future research directions. *Computer Science Review*, *52*, 100632.

Cazzaniga, M. (2024). *Gen-AI: Artificial Intelligence and the Future of Work*. International Monetary Fund., DOI: 10.5089/9798400262548.006

Çeken, B., & Taşkın, N. (2022). Multimedia learning principles in different learning environments: A systematic review. *Smart Learning Environments*, *9*(1), 19.

Celik, I. (2023). Exploring the determinants of artificial intelligence (Ai) literacy: Digital divide, computational thinking, cognitive absorption. *Telematics and Informatics*, *83*, 102026.

Cengage. (2024). Exploring AI in higher education. Cengage. https://cengage.widen.net/s/wmnqhdkqwx/genai-report-2024?j=2122864&sfmc_sub=926794796&l=6504_HTML&u=44990356&mid=515011284&jb=225&utm_source=marketing&utm_medium=email&mid=515011284&utm_campaign=Gen-AI-report&utm_content=Gen-AI-report&segment=Faculty&region=HED_EMEA

Center for News. Technology & Innovation. (2024, October 11). *Artificial Intelligence in Journalism - Center for News, Technology & Innovation*. https://innovating.news/article/ai-in-journalism

Cerezo, R., Lara, J. A., Azevedo, R., & Romero, C. (2024). Reviewing the differences between learning analytics and educational data mining: Towards educational data science. *Computers in Human Behavior*, *154*, 108155.

Černý, M. (2023). Artificial intelligence, creativity and education: finding a new perspective. *Journal of Applied Technical and Educational Sciences, 13*(3), ArtNo 353. DOI: 10.24368/jates353

Ch'ng, L. K. (2023). How AI makes its mark on instructional design. *Asian Journal of Distance Education*, *18*(2), 32–41. DOI: 10.5281/zenodo.8188576

Chadha, A. (2024). Transforming Higher Education for the Digital Age: Examining Emerging Technologies and Pedagogical Innovations. *Journal of Interdisciplinary Studies in Education, 13*(1), 53–70. DOI: 10.32674/em2qsn46

Chan, C. K. Y. (2023a). A comprehensive AI policy education framework for university teaching and learning. *International Journal of Educational Technology in Higher Education*, *20*(1). Advance online publication. DOI: 10.1186/s41239-023-00408-3

Chan, C. K. Y. (2024). Exploring the factors of "AI guilt" among students – Are you guilty of using AI in your homework? *arXiv*. https://arxiv.org/abs/2407.10777

Chan, C. K. Y., & Hu, W. (2023). Students' voices on generative AI: Perceptions, benefits, and challenges in higher education. *International Journal of Educational Technology in Higher Education*, *20*(43), 1–18. DOI: 10.1186/s41239-023-00411-8

Charness, G., & Grieco, D. (2019). Creativity and Incentives. *Journal of the European Economic Association*, *17*(2), 454–496. DOI: 10.1093/jeea/jvx055

Chen, J., Zhang, M., Xu, B., Sun, J., & Mujumdar, A. S. (2020). Artificial intelligence assisted technologies for controlling the drying of fruits and vegetables using physical fields: A review. *Trends in Food Science & Technology*, *105*, 251–260. DOI: 10.1016/j.tifs.2020.08.015

Chen, L., Chen, P., & Lin, Z. (2020). Artificial intelligence in education: A review. *IEEE Access : Practical Innovations, Open Solutions*, *8*, 75264–75278. DOI: 10.1109/ACCESS.2020.2988510

Chen, Q., & Li, F. (2023). A hybrid image classification model combining Support Vector Machines and K-Means clustering for medical images. *Artificial Intelligence in Medicine*, *127*, 102175. DOI: 10.1016/j.artmed.2023.102175

Chen, X., Zou, D., Cheng, G., & Xie, H. (2020). Detecting latent topics and trends in educational technologies over four decades using structural topic modeling: A retrospective of all volumes of Computers & Education. *Computers & Education*, *151*, 103855.

Chen, X., Zou, D., Cheng, G., & Xie, H. (2021). Artificial intelligence-assisted personalized language learning: Systematic review and co-citation analysis. *2021 International Conference on Advanced Learning Technologies (ICALT)*, 241–245. https://doi.org/DOI: 10.1109/ICALT52272.2021.00079

Chesterman, S. (2024). Good models borrow, great models steal: Intellectual property rights and generative AI. *Policy and Society*, puae006.

Chiu, T. K. F. (2024). Future research recommendations for transforming higher education with generative AI. *Computers and Education: Artificial Intelligence*, *6*, 100197. Advance online publication. DOI: 10.1016/j.caeai.2023.100197

Chiu, T. K., Xia, Q., Zhou, X., Chai, C. S., & Cheng, M. (2022). Systematic literature review on opportunities, challenges, and future research recommendations of artificial intelligence in education. *Computers and Education Artificial Intelligence*, *4*, 100118. DOI: 10.1016/j.caeai.2022.100118

Choi, J. H., & Schwarcz, D. B. (2023). AI Assistance in Legal Analysis: An Empirical Study. SSRN Electronic Journal. https://doi.org/DOI: 10.2139/ssrn.4539836

Christou, P. A. (2022). How to use thematic analysis in qualitative research. *Journal of Qualitative Research in Tourism*, *3*(2), 79–95. DOI: 10.4337/jqrt.2023.0006

Chuang, S., & Graham, C. M. (2018). Embracing the sobering reality of technological influences on jobs, employment and human resource development: A systematic literature review. *European Journal of Training and Development*, *42*(7/8), 400–416. DOI: 10.1108/EJTD-03-2018-0030

Cimatti, B. (2016). Definition, development, assessment of soft skills and their role for the quality of organizations and enterprises. *International Journal of Qualitative Research, 10*(1), 97–130.

Clifford, J., & Marcus, G. E. (1986). *Writing culture: The poetics and politics of ethnography*. University of California Press.

Cohen, L., Manion, L., & Morrison, K. (2002). *Research methods in education*. routledge.

Cohen, L., Manion, L., & Morrison, K. (2017). Action research. In *Cohen, L., Manion, L., & Morrison, K. (2017) Research methods in education* (pp. 440–456). Routledge.

Collins, C., Dennehy, D., Conboy, K., & Mikalef, P. (2021). Artificial intelligence in information systems research: A systematic literature review and research agenda. *International Journal of Information Management, 60*(102383), 102383. DOI: 10.1016/j.ijinfomgt.2021.102383

Cooper, G. (2023). Examining Science Education in ChatGPT: An Exploratory Study of Generative Artificial Intelligence. *Journal of Science Education and Technology, 32*, 444–452. DOI: 10.1007/s10956-023-10039-y

Cope, B., & Kalantzis, M. (2019). Education 2.0: Artificial intelligence and the end of the test. *Beijing International Review of Education, 1*(2-3), 528–543. DOI: 10.1163/25902539-00102009

Corrêa, N. K., Santos, J. W., Galvão, C., Pasetti, M., Schiavon, D., Naqvi, F., Hossain, R., & De Oliveira, N. (2024). Crossing the principle–practice gap in AI ethics with ethical problem-solving. *AI and Ethics*. Advance online publication. DOI: 10.1007/s43681-024-00469-8

Corsten, D., & Skousen, B. (2023). 'Get AI Answer?' – Exploring the Effects of Embedding ChatGPT in Exams to Improve Student Learning Outcomes. SSRN Electronic Journal. https://doi.org/DOI: 10.2139/ssrn.4409035

Cortés Guerrero, S. (2024). AI for educational board games.

Cotterall, S. (1999). Key variables in language learning: What do learners believe about them? *System, 27*(4), 493–513. DOI: 10.1016/S0346-251X(99)00047-0

Cotton, D. R., Cotton, P. A., & Shipway, J. R. (2023). Chatting and cheating: Ensuring academic integrity in the era of ChatGPT. *Innovations in Education and Teaching International, 61*(2), 228–239. DOI: 10.1080/14703297.2023.2190148

Council of Europe. (2022). Artificial Intelligence and Education. A critical view through the lens of human rights, democracy and the rule of law. https://rm.coe.int/prems-092922-gbr-2517-ai-and-education-txt-16x24-web/1680a956e3

Creswell, J. W., & Poth, C. N. (2017). *Qualitative inquiry and research design: Choosing Among Five Approaches*. Sage Publications, Incorporated.

Criollo-C, S., Guerrero-Arias, A., Jaramillo-Alcázar, Á., & Luján-Mora, S. (2021). Mobile learning technologies for education: Benefits and pending issues. *Applied Sciences (Basel, Switzerland)*, *11*(9), 4111.

Crompton, H., & Burke, D. (2023). Artificial intelligence in higher education: The state of the field. *International Journal of Educational Technology in Higher Education*, *20*(22), 1–22. DOI: 10.1186/s41239-023-00392-8

Cruz, M., Sousa, M. E., Costa, J., & Mascarenhas, D. (2024). AI-POWERED RE-CONFIGURATION OF TEACHER TRAINING: A CASE STUDY IN HIGHER EDUCATION. In ICERI2024 Proceedings (pp. 8212-8222). IATED.

Cui, R., Li, M., & Zhang, S. (2022). AI and procurement. *Manufacturing & Service Operations Management*, *24*(2), 691–706. DOI: 10.1287/msom.2021.0989

Curran, D. (2023). Surveillance capitalism and systemic digital risk: The imperative to collect and connect and the risks of interconnectedness. *Big Data & Society*, *10*(1). Advance online publication. DOI: 10.1177/20539517231177621

Cusnir, C., & Nicola, A. (2024). Using generative Artificial Intelligence tools in Public Relations: Ethical concerns and the impact on the profession in the Romanian context. *Communicatio Socialis*, *37*(4), 309–323. DOI: 10.15581/003.37.4.309-323

Cusnir, C., Popescu-Jourdy, D., & Surugiu, R. (2024). Inteligen a artificială generativă i învă ământul superior. Studiu de caz asupra domeniului tiin e ale comunicării. In Momoc, A., & Surugiu, R. (Eds.), *Media i Inteligen a Artificială* (pp. 43–55). Tritonic Books.

CZSO. (2023). Evropský srovnávací program. Český statistický úřad. Retrieved January 11, 2024, from https://www.czso.cz/csu/czso/evropsky_srovnavaci_program

Dai, W., Lin, J., Jin, H., Li, T., Tsai, Y. S., Gašević, D., & Chen, G. (2023). Can large language models provide feedback to students? A case study on ChatGPT. *IEEE International Conference on Advanced Learning Technologies (ICALT)* (pp. 323-325).

Dakakni, D., & Safa, N. (2023). Artificial intelligence in the L2 classroom: Implications and challenges on ethics and equity in higher education: A 21st century Pandora's box. Computers and education. *Artificial Intelligence*, *5*, 100179. DOI: 10.1016/j.caeai.2023.100179

Dargan, S., Kumar, M., Ayyagari, M. R., & Kumar, G. (2020). A survey of deep learning and its applications: A new paradigm to machine learning. *Archives of Computational Methods in Engineering*, *27*, 1071–1092.

Darling-Hammond, L.. (2017). *Using assessment to improve learning in schools.* Harvard Education Press.

Daud, M., Khan, Q., & Saleem, Y. (2017). A study of key technologies for IoT and associated security challenges. *2017 International Symposium on Wireless Systems and Networks (ISWSN)*, 1–6. https://doi.org/DOI: 10.1109/ISWSN.2017.8250042

Dave, T., Athaluri, S. A., & Singh, S. (2023). ChatGPT in medicine: An overview of its applications, advantages, limitations, future prospects, and ethical considerations. *Frontiers in Artificial Intelligence*, *6*, 1169595. PMID: 37215063

Davies, A., & Elder, C. (Eds.). (2004). *The Handbook of Applied Linguistics* (1st ed.). Wiley., DOI: 10.1002/9780470757000

Davis, F. (1989). Perceived Usefulness, Perceived Ease of Use, and User Acceptance of Information Technology. *Management Information Systems Quarterly*, *13*(3), 319–340.

Davis, F. D. (1989). Perceived usefulness, perceived ease of use, and user acceptance of information technology. *Management Information Systems Quarterly*, •••, 319–340.

Dawson, C. (2007). *A practical guide to research methods.* How To Books Ltd.

Dawson, P. (2021). *Defending Assessment Security in a Digital World: Preventing E-cheating and Supporting Academic Integrity in Higher Education.* Routledge., DOI: 10.4324/9780429324178

De Simone, M. E., Tiberti, F., Mosuro, W., Manolio, F., Barron, M., & Dikoru, E. (2025, January 8). From chalkboards to chatbots: Transforming learning in Nigeria, one prompt at a time. *World Bank Blogs.* https://blogs.worldbank.org/en/education/From-chalkboards-to-chatbots-Transforming-learning-in-Nigeria

De Sio, F. S., & Mecacci, G. (2021). Four Responsibility Gaps with Artificial Intelligence: Why they Matter and How to Address them. *Philosophy & Technology*, *34*(4), 1057–1084. DOI: 10.1007/s13347-021-00450-x

De Souza Rodrigues, M. A., Chimenti, P., & Nogueira, A. R. R. (2021). An exploration of eLearning adoption in the educational ecosystem. *Education and Information Technologies, 26*(1), 585–615.

Deka, P. K. (2021). Factors influencing student engagement in online learning during the COVID-19 pandemic period in India. *Journal of Management in Practice, 6*(1).

Delamont, S. (2016). *Fieldwork in educational settings: Methods, pitfalls and perspectives* (3rd ed.). Routledge.

Deng, R., Jiang, M., Yu, X., Lu, Y., & Liu, S. (2024). Does ChatGPT enhance student learning? A systematic review and meta-analysis of experimental studies. *Computers & Education, •••*, 105224.

Dergaa, I., Chamari, K., Zmijewski, P., & Saad, H. B. (2023). From human writing to artificial intelligence generated text: Examining the prospects and potential threats of ChatGPT in academic writing. *Biology of Sport, 40*(2), 615. PMID: 37077800

Dewey, J. (1933). *How we think*. D.C. Heath & Co.

Dewey, J. (1938). *Experience and education*. Kappa Delta Pi.

Dianova, V. G., & Schultz, M. D. (2023). Discussing ChatGPT's implications for industry and higher education: The case for transdisciplinarity and digital humanities. *Industry and Higher Education, XXXVII*(5), 593–600. DOI: 10.1177/09504222231199989

Dimitriadou, E., & Lanitis, A. (2023). A critical evaluation, challenges, and future perspectives of using artificial intelligence and emerging technologies in smart classrooms. *Smart Learning Environments, 10*(1), 12. PMID: 40478141

DiStaso, M. W., Stacks, D. W., & Botan, C. H. (2009). State of public relations education in the United States: 2006 report on a national study of executives and academics. *Public Relations Review, 35*, 254–269. DOI: 10.1016/jpubrev.2009.03.006

Dolle, N., Wilhelm, C., & Rössle, M. (2019, October). Applying modern text processing technologies to implement a self-learning marketplace by using cloud services as an example. In *International Conference on Reliability and Statistics in Transportation and Communication* (pp. 450-459). Cham: Springer International Publishing.

Dornis, T. (2020). Artificial Creativity: Emergent Works and the Void in Current Copyright Doctrine. *Yale Journal of Law & Technology, XXII*(1). Advance online publication. DOI: 10.2139/ssrn.3451480

Doyle, A. (2019. March 8). What Are Soft Skills? Retrieved from https://www .thebalancecareers.com/whatare-soft-skillsEuropea

Durga, S., Gupta, P., Kharb, L., Ranjit, P. S., Dornadula, V. H. R., Modak, K. C., & Manoharan, G. (2024). 9Leveraging Distributed Systems for Improved Educational Planning and Resource Allocation. *Meta Heuristic Algorithms for Advanced Distributed Systems*, 141-159.

Dwivedi, Y. K., Kshetri, N., Hughes, L., Slade, E. L., Jeyaraj, A., Kar, A. K., ... & Wright, R. (2023). Opinion Paper: "So what if ChatGPT wrote it?" Multidisciplinary perspectives on opportunities, challenges and implications of generative conversational AI for research, practice and policy.

Dwivedi, Y. K., Kshetri, N., Hughes, L., Slade, E. L., Jeyaraj, A., Kar, A. K., Baabdullah, A. M., Koohang, A., Raghavan, V., Ahuja, M., Albanna, H., Albashrawi, M. A., Al-Busaidi, A. S., Balakrishnan, J., Barlette, Y., Basu, S., Bose, I., Brooks, L., Buhalis, D., & Wright, R. (2023). Opinion paper: "So what if ChatGPT wrote it?" Multidisciplinary perspectives on opportunities, challenges and implications of generative conversational AI for research, practice and policy. *International Journal of Information Management*, *71*, 1–63. DOI: 10.1016/j.ijinfomgt.2023.102642

Early, C. (2024). Sustainability profession scrambles to fill "extreme gap" in digital skills to harness power of AI. *Reuters*. Retrieved January 16, 2025, from https://www.reuters.com/sustainability/society-equity/sustainability-profession-scrambles-fill-extreme-gap-digital-skills-harness-2024-11-28/

Eden, N. C. A., Chisom, N. O. N., & Adeniyi, N. I. S. (2024). Integrating AI in education: Opportunities, challenges, and ethical considerations. *Magna Scientia Advanced Research and Reviews, 10*(2), 006–013. https://doi.org/DOI: 10.30574/msarr.2024.10.2.0039

Edly. (n.d.). IoT in education: Main solutions IoT brings to education. Retrieved April 27, 2025, from https://edly.io/blog/iot-in-education-main-solutions-iot-brings-to-education/

Education World. (2021). IoT and its impact on education. https://www.educationworld.in/iot-and-its-impact-on-education/

Educba. (2020). IoT in Education. https://www.educba.com/iot-in-education/

Eisenhardt, K. M. (1989). Building theories from case study research. *Academy of Management Review*, *14*(4), 532–550.

Elley, W. B., & Mangubhai, F. (1983). The Impact of Reading on Second Language Learning. *Reading Research Quarterly*, *19*(1), 53. DOI: 10.2307/747337

El-Sabagh, H. A. (2021). Adaptive e-learning environment based on learning styles and its impact on development students' engagement. *International Journal of Educational Technology in Higher Education*, *18*(1), 53.

Else, H. (2023). "Abstracts Written by Chatgpt Fool Scientists", 423-423 Nature, 613 (7944). https://doi.org/.DOI: 10.1038/d41586-023-00056-7

Espedal, G., Jelstad Løvaas, B., Sirris, S., & Wæraas, A. (2022). *Researching Values: Methodological approaches for understanding values work in organisations and leadership* (Gry Espedal, Beate Jelstad Løvaas, Stephen Sirris, & Arild Wæraas, Eds.). https://library.oapen.org/bitstream/handle/20.500.12657/53343/978-3-030-90769-3.pdf#page=198

Eurostat. (n.d.). Individuals' level of digital skills. European Commission. Retrieved December 19, 2024, from https://ec.europa.eu/eurostat/databrowser/view/ISOC_SK_DSKL_I21/default/table

Evans-Amalu, K., & Claravall, E. B. (2021). Inclusive online teaching and digital learning: Lessons learned in the time of pandemic and beyond. *Journal of Curriculum Studies Research*, *3*(1), i–iii.

Eyal, L. (2012). Digital assessment literacy — The core role of the teacher in a digital environment. *Journal of Educational Technology & Society*, *15*(2), 37–49.

Facer, K., & Selwyn, N. (2021). *Digital technology and the futures of education – towards 'non-stupid' optimism.* UNESCO's Futures of Education report. https://unesdoc.unesco.org/ark:/48223/pf0000377071

Facultatea de Jurnalism si Stiintele Comunicarii. (2023). Anexe Raport autoevaluare FJSC – 2022-2023. https://drive.google.com/file/d/1tokZtcZ0DX5_TrvfXiPEtdWPes8OEW3y/view

Farazouli, A., Cerrato-Pargman, T., Bolander-Laksov, K., & McGrath, C. (2024). Hello GPT! Goodbye home examination? An exploratory study of AI chatbots impact on university teachers' assessment practices. *Assessment & Evaluation in Higher Education*, *49*(3), 363–375. DOI: 10.1080/02602938.2023.2241676

Fazekas, K. (2020). Impact of technological development on skills expected in the labour market. Köz-Gazdaság -. *Review of Economic Theory and Policy*, *14*(4). https://retp.eu/index.php/retp/article/view/221

Fedele, A., Punzi, C., & Tramacere, S. (2024). The ALTAI checklist as a tool to assess ethical and legal implications for a trustworthy AI development in education. *Computer Law & Security Review*, *53*, 105986. DOI: 10.1016/j.clsr.2024.105986

Fereday, J., & Muir-Cochrane, E. (2006). Demonstrating rigor using thematic analysis: A hybrid approach of inductive and deductive coding and theme development. *International Journal of Qualitative Methods*, *5*(1), 80–92.

Fernández-Alameda, C. (2024). *IA generativa en el aula. 10 ideas para trabajar el pensamiento critico*. Amazon Kindle Publishing.

Ferrara, E. (2023). Fairness and bias in Artificial Intelligence: A brief survey of sources, impacts, and mitigation strategies. *Science*, *6*(1), 3. DOI: 10.3390/sci6010003

Ferrara, E. (2023). Should ChatGPT be biased? Challenges and risks of bias in large language models. *First Monday*, *28*(11), 1. DOI: 10.5210/fm.v28i11.13346

Ferri, F., Grifoni, P., & Guzzo, T. (2020). Online learning and emergency remote teaching: Opportunities and challenges in emergency situations. *Societies (Basel, Switzerland)*, *10*(4), 86.

Firat, M. (2023). What ChatGPT means for universities: Perceptions of scholars and students. *Journal of Applied Learning & Teaching*, *6*(1), 57–63. DOI: 10.37074/jalt.2023.6.1.22

Fitas, R. (2025). Inclusive Education with AI: Supporting Special Needs and Tackling Language Barriers. *arXiv*. https://arxiv.org/abs/2504.14120

Flavell, J. H. (1979). Metacognition and cognitive monitoring: A new area of cognitive-developmental inquiry. *The American Psychologist*, *34*(10), 906–911. DOI: 10.1037/0003-066X.34.10.906

Flick, U. (2021). Doing interview research: The Essential How To Guide. *Sage (Atlanta, Ga.)*.

Foltynek, T., Bjelobaba, S., Glendinning, I., Khan, Z. R., Santos, R., Pavletic, P., & Kravjar, J. (2023). ENAI Recommendations on the Ethical Use of Artificial Intelligence in Education. *International Journal for Educational Integrity*, *19*, 12. DOI: 10.1007/s40979-023-00133-4

Foltynek, T., Dlabolova, D., Anohina-Naumeca, A., & Linkeschova, D. (2020). Academic plagiarism detection: A systematic literature review. *Journal of Academic Ethics*, *18*(1), 1–31. DOI: 10.1145/3345317

Fosnot, C. T. (2013). *Constructivism: Theory, perspectives, and practice*. Teachers College Press.

Fotea, S., Fotea, I., & undrea, E. (2019). Artificial intelligence in education: Romanian students' attitudes toward artificial intelligence and its impact on their career development. In *ICERI2019 Proceedings, (pp. 9330–9338)*. IATED.

Francis, J. J., Johnston, M., Robertson, C., Glidewell, L., Entwistle, V., Eccles, M. P., & Grimshaw, J. M. (2010). What is an adequate sample size? Operationalising data saturation for theory-based interview studies. *Psychology & Health, 25*(10), 1229–1245. PMID: 20204937

Franková, E. (2011). *Kreativita a inovace v organizaci* (1st ed.). Grada.

Frolova, E. V., Rogach, O. V., & Ryabova, T. M. (2020). Digitalization of education in modern scientific discourse: new trends and risks analysis. European journal of contemporary education, 9(2), 313-336.

Fudge, A., Ulpen, T., Bilic, S., Picard, M., & Carter, C. (2022). Does an educative approach work? A reflective case study of how two Australian higher education Enabling programs support students and staff uphold a responsible culture of academic integrity. *International Journal for Educational Integrity, 18*(1), 5.

Fügener, A., Grahl, J., Gupta, A., & Ketter, W. (2021). Will humans-in-the-loop become Borgs? Merits and pitfalls of working with AI. *Management Information Systems Quarterly, 45*(3), 1527–1556. DOI: 10.25300/misq/2021/16553

Fui-Hoon Nah, F., Zheng, R., Cai, J., Siau, K., & Chen, L. (2023). Generative AI and ChatGPT: Applications, challenges, and AI-human collaboration. *Journal of Information Technology Case and Application Research, 25*(3), 277–304. DOI: 10.1080/15228053.2023.2233814

Fütterer, T., Fischer, C., Alekseeva, A., Chen, X., Tate, T., Warschauer, M., & Gerjets P. (2023). ChatGPT in education: global reactions to AI innovations. *Scientific Reports, 15, 13*(1),15310. DOI: 10.1038/s41598-023-42227-6

Galloway, C., & Swiatek, L. (2018). Public relations and artificial intelligence: It's not (just) about robots. *Public Relations Review, 44*(5), 734–740. https://www.doi.org/10.1016/j.pubrev.2018.10.008

Gamage, K. A. A., Dehideniya, S. C. P., Xu, Z., & Tang, X. (2023). ChatGPT and higher education assessments: More opportunities than concerns? *Journal of Applied Learning and Teaching, 6*(2), 358–369. DOI: 10.37074/jalt.2023.6.2.32

Gao, Y., Shum, S. B., Chen, M., & Alzahrani, S. (2023). Artificial Intelligence in Education: A Review of Learning Analytics and Educational Data Mining Studies. *Journal of Educational Technology & Society, 26*(1), 31–46.

Garbuio, M., & Lin, N. (2021). Innovative idea generation in problem finding: Abductive reasoning, cognitive impediments, and the promise of artificial intelligence. *Journal of Product Innovation Management, 38*(6), 701–725. DOI: 10.1111/jpim.12602

Garg, S., Ahmad, A., & Madsen, D. Ø. (2024). Academic writing in the age of AI: Comparing the reliability of ChatGPT and Bard with Scopus and Web of Science. *Journal of Innovation & Knowledge*, *9*(4), 100563.

Garrett, N. (2009). Computer-Assisted Language Learning Trends and Issues Revisited: Integrating Innovation. *Modern Language Journal*, *93*(s1), 719–740. DOI: 10.1111/j.1540-4781.2009.00969.x

Garrison, D. R. (2016). E-learning in the 21st century: A community of inquiry framework for research and practice.

Generative AI and the future of education. (2023). In *UNESCO eBooks*. https://doi.org/DOI: 10.54675/hoxg8740

George, B., & Wooden, O. (2023). Managing the strategic transformation of higher education through artificial intelligence. *Administrative Sciences*, *13*(9), 196.

Gezici, G., Lipani, A., Saygin, Y., & Yilmaz, E. (2021). Evaluation metrics for measuring bias in search engine results. *Information Retrieval Journal*, *24*, 85–113.

Gibbs, G., Cameron, C., Kemenade, R., Teal, A., and Phillips, D. (2004). Using a chatbot conversation to enhance the learning of social theory. Published online: file:///Users/madamoraru/Downloads/Chatbots_are_they_really_useful.pdf

Gibson, R. (2024). The Impact of AI in Advancing Accessibility for Learners with Disabilities. *EDUCAUSE Review*. https://er.educause.edu/articles/2024/9/the-impact-of-ai-in-advancing-accessibility-for-learners-with-disabilitiesEDUCAUSE Review

Gilbert, S. (2017). Information literacy skills in the workplace: Examining early career advertising professionals. *Journal of Business & Finance Librarianship*, *22*(2), 111–134. DOI: 10.1080/08963568.2016.1258938

Gilman, E., Tamminen, S., Yasmin, R., & Ristimella, E. (2020). Internet of Things for smart spaces: A university campus case study. *Sensors (Basel)*, *20*(13), 3716. DOI: 10.3390/s20133716 PMID: 32630833

Giordani, J. (2024). Mitigating chatbots AI data privacy Violations in the banking sector: A Qualitative Grounded Theory study. *Deleted Journal*, *2*(4), 14–65. DOI: 10.59324/ejaset.2024.2(4).02

Giordano, V., Spada, I., Chiarello, F., & Fantoni, G. (2024). The impact of ChatGPT on human skills: A quantitative study on twitter data. *Technological Forecasting and Social Change*, *203*, 123389. DOI: 10.1016/j.techfore.2024.123389

Giray, L. (2024). Negative effects of Generative AI on researchers: Publishing addiction, Dunning-Kruger effect and skill erosion. *Journal of Applied Learning & Teaching*, *7*(2), 1–8. DOI: 10.37074/jalt.2024.7.2.38

Glatthorn, A. A., Boschee, F., Whitehead, B. M., & Boschee, B. F. (2018). *Curriculum leadership: Strategies for development and implementation*. SAGE publications.

Glazier, R. A. (2021). *Connecting in the online classroom: Building rapport between teachers and students*. JHU Press.

Glesne, C. (2016). *Becoming qualitative researchers: An introduction* (5th ed.). Pearson.

Global Market Insights. (2023). AI in education market size, growth trends 2024–2032. https://www.gminsights.com/industry-analysis/ai-in-education-market

Gonsalves, C. (2024). Addressing student non-compliance in AI use declarations: Implications for academic integrity and assessment in higher education. *Assessment & Evaluation in Higher Education*, •••, 1–15. DOI: 10.1080/02602938.2024.2415654

Gorgone, J., Davis, G. B., Valacich, J. S., Topi, H., Feinstein, D. L., & Longenecker, H. E. (2003). IS 2002 model curriculum and guidelines for undergraduate degree programs in information systems. *Communications of the Association for Information Systems*, *11*(1), 1.

Gorgone, J., Gray, P., Stohr, E. A., Wigand, R. T., & Valacich, J. S. (2005). MSIS 2006 curriculum preview. *Communications of the Association for Information Systems*, *15*(1), 30.

Goyal, I. (2023). AI Renaissance, artificial intelligence, information overload, human-computer interaction, decision-making. *Review of Artificial Intelligence in Education*, *4*(00), e012. DOI: 10.37497/rev.artif.intell.educ.v4i00.12

Grădinaru, G. I., Dinu, V., Rotaru, C.-L., & Toma, A. (2024). The development of educational competence for Romanian students in the context of the evolution of data science and artificial intelligence. *Amfiteatru Economic*, *26*(65), 14–32. DOI: 10.24818/EA/2024/65/14

Graf, S., Chang, T.-W., Kersebaum, A., Rath, T., & Kurcz, J. (2014). Investigating the Effectiveness of an Advanced Adaptive Mechanism for Considering Learning Styles in Learning Management Systems. *2014 IEEE 14th International Conference on Advanced Learning Technologies*, 112–116. https://doi.org/DOI: 10.1109/ICALT.2014.41

Gragnaniello, D., Marra, F., & Verdoliva, L. (2022). Detection of AI-Generated synthetic faces. In Rathgeb, C., Tolosana, R., Vera-Rodriguez, R., & Busch, C. (Eds.), *Handbook of digital face manipulation and detection: From deepfakes to morphing attacks* (pp. 191–212). Springer International Publishing.

Grassini, S. (2023). Development and validation of the AI Attitude Scale (AIAS-4): A brief measure of general attitude toward Artificial Intelligence. *Frontiers in Psychology, 14*. Advance online publication. DOI: 10.3389/fpsyg.2023.1191628 PMID: 37554139

Greene, D., Hoffmann, A. L., & Stark, L. (2019). Better, Nicer, Clearer, Fairer: A critical assessment of the movement for ethical artificial intelligence and machine learning. In *Proceedings of the 52nd Hawaii International Conference on System Sciences* (pp. 2122–2131). https://doi.org/DOI: 10.24251/HICSS.2019.258

Gregory, A. (2023). *Humans Not Needed.* Chartered Institute of Public Relations.

Guest, G., Namey, E., & Chen, M. (2020). A simple method to assess and report thematic saturation in qualitative research. *PLoS One, 15*(5), e0232076. DOI: 10.1371/journal.pone.0232076

Gupta, K. D. (2023). A review of generative AI from historical perspectives. *Authorea Preprints.*

Gupta, R., & Sharma, S. (2023). Support Vector Machine clustering for DNA sequence classification: A comparative study. *Bioinformatics and Biology Insights, 17*(2), 34–47. DOI: 10.1177/11779322231176430

Habib, S. (2024). Beyond the AI hype: Real effects on student creativity explored in new research. *PsyPost.* https://www.psypost.org/beyond-the-ai-hype-real-effects-on-student-creativity-explored-in-new-research/

Haefner, N., Wincent, J., Parida, V., & Gassmann, O. (2021). Artificial intelligence and innovation management: A review, framework, and research agenda. *Technological Forecasting and Social Change, 162*, 120392. DOI: 10.1016/j.techfore.2020.120392

Haleem, A., Javaid, M., Qadri, M. A., & Suman, R. (2022). Understanding the role of digital technologies in education: A review. Sustainable operations and computers, 3, 275-285.

Haleem, A., Javaid, M., Qadri, M. A., Singh, R. P., & Suman, R. (2022). Artificial intelligence (AI) applications for marketing: A literature-based study. *International Journal of Intelligent Networks, 3*, 119–132. DOI: 10.1016/j.ijin.2022.08.005

Hallström, J. (2020). Embodying the past, designing the future: Technological determinism reconsidered in technology education. *International Journal of Technology and Design Education, 32*(1), 17–31. DOI: 10.1007/s10798-020-09600-2

Halper, F. (2017). *Advanced analytics: Moving toward AI, machine learning, and natural language processing*

Hamerman, E. J., Aggarwal, A., & Martins, C. (2025). An investigation of generative AI in the classroom and its implications for university policy. *Quality Assurance in Education, 33*(2), 253–266. DOI: 10.1108/QAE-08-2024-0149

Hammersley, M., & Atkinson, P. (2007). *Ethnography: Principles in practice* (3rd ed.). Routledge.

Hammond, M. (2000). Communication within on-line forums: The opportunities, the constraints and the value of a communicative approach. *Computers & Education, 35*(4), 251–262.

Harrell, M. V. (n.d.). *Data Literacy in the Age of Artificial Intelligence: A Hermeneutic Phenomenological study*. Scholars Crossing. https://digitalcommons.liberty.edu/doctoral/6433/

Harvard Graduate School of Education. (2020). *The art of asking questions: How inquiry-driven education promotes critical thinking*. Harvard University Press.

Heidegger, M. (1988). *The Basic Problems of Phenomenology* (revised Edition). Indiana University Press.

Hennink, M., & Kaiser, B. (2022). Sample sizes for saturation in qualitative research: A systematic review of empirical tests. *Social Science & Medicine, 292*, 114523. DOI: 10.1016/j.socscimed.2021.114523 PMID: 34785096

Herţeliu, C., Alexe-Coteţ, D., Hâj, C.M., & Pârvan, A.T. (2022). Defining and Measuring Dropout Phenomenon in Romanian Public Universities. InCuraj, A., Salmi, J., & Hâj, C.M. (eds) *Higher Education in Romania: Overcoming Challenges and Embracing Opportunities*. Springer, Cham. DOI: 10.1007/978-3-030-94496-4

Herwanto, W. H., Setiawan, S., & Munir, A. (2024). What Lies Beneath English Major Students' Attitudes towards ChatGPT for Academic Writing: A TAM Perspective? *Equilibrium: Jurnal Pendidikan, 12*(2), 152–159.

Hicks, M. T., Humphries, J., & Slater, J. (2024). ChatGPT is bullshit. *Ethics and Information Technology, 26*, 38. DOI: 10.1007/s10676-024-09775-5

Higgins, J. (1983). Computer assisted language learning. *Language Teaching, 16*(2), 102–114. DOI: 10.1017/S0261444800009988

Ho, C. H. (2021). A preliminary study of artificial intelligence deep learning amid teaching of public relations course. In *2021 2nd International Conference on Education, Knowledge and Information Management,* (pp. 539-542).

Hoffreumon, C., Forman, C., & van Zeebroeck, N. (2024). Make or buy your artificial intelligence? Complementarities in technology sourcing. *Journal of Economics & Management Strategy*. Advance online publication. DOI: 10.1111/jems.12586

Holmes, W., Bialik, M., & Fadel, C. (2019). *Artificial intelligence in education: Promises and implications for teaching and learning*. Center for Curriculum Redesign.

Holmes, W., & Porayska-Pomsta, K. (Eds.). (2023). *The Ethics of Artificial Intelligence in Education. Practices, Challenges, and Debates*. Routledge.

Holmes, W., Porayska-Pomsta, K., Holstein, K., Sutherland, E., Baker, T., Shum, S. B., Santos, O. C., Rodrigo, M. T., Cukurova, M., Bittencourt, I. I., & Koedinger, K. R. (2021). Ethics of AI in Education: Towards a Community-Wide framework. *International Journal of Artificial Intelligence in Education*, *32*(3), 504–526. DOI: 10.1007/s40593-021-00239-1

Holmes, W., & Tuomi, I. (2022). State of the art and practice in AI in education. *European Journal of Education*, *57*, 542–570. DOI: 10.1111/ejed.12533

Hong, J.-W., Peng, Q., & Willims, D. (2020). Are you ready for artificial Mozart and Skrillex? An experiment testing expectancy violation theory and AI music. *New Media & Society*, *23*(7), 1920–1935. DOI: 10.1177/1461444820925798

Hooda, M., Rana, C., Dahiya, O., Rizwan, A., & Hossain, M. S. (2022). Artificial intelligence for assessment and feedback to enhance student success in higher education. *Mathematical Problems in Engineering*, *2022*, 1–19. DOI: 10.1155/2022/5215722

Hopcan, S., Polat, E., Ozturk, M. E., & Ozturk, L. (2022). Artificial intelligence in special education: A systematic review. *Interactive Learning Environments*, *31*, 7335–7353.

Hossain, A., Wahab, J. A., Islam, M. R., Khan, M. S. R., & Mahmud, A. (2022). Cyberbullying perception and experience among the university students in Bangladesh. In *Advances in human and social aspects of technology book series* (pp. 248–269). https://doi.org/DOI: 10.4018/978-1-7998-9187-1.ch012

Hu, K. (2023, February 2). ChatGPT sets record for fastest-growing user base—analyst note. Reuters. Retrieved from https://www.reuters.com/technology/chatgpt-sets-record-fastest-growing-user-base-analyst-note-2023-02-01/

Huang, X., Zou, D., Cheng, G., Chen, X., & Xie, H. (2023). Trends, research issues and applications of artificial intelligence in language education. *Journal of Educational Technology & Society*, *26*(1), 112–131.

Hunt, N., & McHale, S. (2007). A practical guide to the e-mail interview. *Qualitative Health Research*, *17*(10), 1415–1421. DOI: 10.1177/1049732307308761 PMID: 18000080

Hussain, S., & Khan, M. Q. (2023). Student-performulator: Predicting students' academic performance at secondary and intermediate level using machine learning. *Annals of Data Science*, *10*(3), 637–655. DOI: 10.1007/s40745-021-00341-0 PMID: 38624826

Husserl, E., Klein, T. E., & Pohl, W. E. (1980). Phenomenology and the foundations of the sciences. In *M. Nijhoff, Distributors for the U.S. and Canada, Kluwer Boston eBooks*. https://ci.nii.ac.jp/ncid/BA07953382

Hutchens, J. (1996). How to pass the turing test by cheating. Research Report TR97-05, University of Western Australia – School of Electrical, Electronic and Computer Engineering, Perth.

Hwang, G.-J., Xie, H., Wah, B. W., & Gašević, D. (2020). Vision, challenges, roles and research issues of artificial intelligence in education. *Computers & Education: Artificial Intelligence*, *1*, 100001. DOI: 10.1016/j.caeai.2020.100001

Idroes, G. M., Noviandy, T. R., Maulana, A., Irvanizam, I., Jalil, Z., Lensoni, L., Lala, A., Abas, A. H., Tallei, T. E., & Idroes, R. (2023). Student perspectives on the role of artificial intelligence in education: A survey-based analysis. *Journal of Educational Management and Learning*, *1*(1), 8–15. DOI: 10.60084/jeml.v1i1.58

Iku-Silan, A., Hwang, G.-J., & Chen, C. H. (2023). Decision-guided chatbots and cognitive styles in interdisciplinary learning. *Computers & Education*, *201*. Advance online publication. DOI: 10.1016/j.compedu.2023.104812

Imran, R., Fatima, A., Salem, I. E., & Allil, K. (2023). Teaching and learning delivery modes in higher education: Looking back to move forward post-COVID-19 era. *International Journal of Management Education*, *21*(2), 100805. DOI: 10.1016/j.ijme.2023.100805

Izadi, S., & Forouzanfar, M. (2024). Error Correction and Adaptation in Conversational AI: A Review of Techniques and Applications in Chatbots. *AI*, *5*(2), 803–841.

Javaid, M., Haleem, A., Singh, R. P., Khan, S., & Khan, I. H. (2023). Unlocking the opportunities through ChatGPT Tool towards ameliorating the education system. *BenchCouncil Transactions on Benchmarks Standards and Evaluations, 3*(2), 100115. DOI: 10.1016/j.tbench.2023.100115

Jayawardena, C., Reyal, S., Kekirideniya, K. R., Wijayawardhana, G. H. T., Rupasinghe, D. G. I. U., & Lakranda, S. Y. R. M. (2021). Artificial intelligence based smart library management system. *2021 6th IEEE International Conference on Recent Advances and Innovations in Engineering (ICRAIE)* (pp. 1–6). https://doi.org/DOI: 10.1109/ICRAIE52900.2021.9703998

Jezova, D. (2021). Artificial intelligence and privacy. *Human Rights - From Reality to the Virtual World*, 226–237. https://doi.org/DOI: 10.13166/wsge//xuxl1897

Jia, F., Sun, D., Ma, Q., & Looi, C.-K. (2022). Developing an AI-Based Learning System for L2 Learners' Authentic and Ubiquitous Learning in English Language. *Sustainability, 14*(23), 15527. DOI: 10.3390/su142315527

Jin, B., & Kruppa, M. (2023). Cheating with ChatGPT: can an AI chatbot pass AP lit? *The Wall Street Journal.*

Jin, M. K. B., & Kruppa, M. (2023). ChatGPT creator is talking to investors about selling shares at $29 billion valuation. *The Wall Street Journal.*

Jin, D., Wang, L., Zhang, H., Zheng, Y., Ding, W., Xia, F., & Pan, S. (2023). A survey on fairness-aware recommender systems. *Information Fusion, 100*, 101906.

Jmour, A. (2020). «Man-machine» interaction: the determinants of the untact service's use. In *Digital Economy. Emerging Technologies and Business Innovation: 5th International Conference on Digital Economy, ICDEc 2020, Bucharest, Romania, June 11–13* [Springer International Publishing.]. *Proceedings, 5*, 105–114.

Joel, M. R., Ebenezer, V., Jeyaraj, K. A., Navaneethakrishnan, M., Arunadevi, R., & Jenifa, D. R. (2023, February). Decoding and analysing consumer feedback for companies and goods using machine learning. In *2023 Third International Conference on Artificial Intelligence and Smart Energy (ICAIS)* (pp. 1085–1091). IEEE.

Joel, M. R., Rajakumari, K., Priya, S. A., & Navaneethakrishnan, M. (2024). Big data classification using SpinalNet-Fuzzy-ResNeXt based on spark architecture with data mining approach. *Data & Knowledge Engineering, 154*, 102364.

Johnson, M., Schuster, M., Le, Q. V., Krikun, M., Wu, Y., Chen, Z., Thorat, N., Viégas, F., Wattenberg, M., Corrado, G., Hughes, M., & Dean, J. (2017). Google's multilingual neural machine translation system: Enabling zero-shot translation. *Transactions of the Association for Computational Linguistics*, *5*, 339–351. DOI: 10.1162/tacl_a_00065

Jonassen, D. H. (2003). *Learning to solve problems: A handbook for designing problem-solving learning environments*. Educational Technology Publications.

Jones, L., Smith, S. L., & Durham, C. (2022). Teachers as digital composers: Designing digital jumpstarts to scaffold for emerging bilingual learners. *Computers & Education*, *189*, 104592. DOI: 10.1016/j.compedu.2022.104592

Joyner, S. A., Fuller, M. B., Holzweiss, P. C., Henderson, S., & Young, R. (2014). The importance of student-instructor connections in graduate level online courses. *Journal of Online Learning and Teaching*, *10*(3), 436–445.

Jussupow, E., Spohrer, K., & Heinzl, A. (2022). Identity threats as a reason for resistance to artificial intelligence: Survey study with medical students and professionals. *JMIR Formative Research*, *6*(3). PMID: 35319465

Ka Yuk Chan, C., & Tsi, L. (2024). Will generative AI replace teachers in higher education? A study of teacher and student perceptions. *Studies in Educational Evaluation*, *83*, 101395. DOI: 10.1016/j.stueduc.2024.101395

Kahlow, J. K. J., Klecka, H. K. H., & Ruppel, E. R. E. (2020). What the differences in conflict between online and face-to-face work groups mean for hybrid groups: A state-of-the-art review. *Review of Communication Research*, *8*, 51–77.

Kahu, E. R., Thomas, H. G., & Heinrich, E. (2024). 'A sense of community and camaraderie': Increasing student engagement by supplementing an LMS with a Learning Commons Communication Tool. *Active Learning in Higher Education*, *25*(2), 303–316.

Kalam, K. T., Rahman, J. M., Islam, M. R., & Dewan, S. M. R. (2024). ChatGPT and mental health: Friends or foes? *Health Science Reports*, *7*(2), e1912. DOI: 10.1002/hsr2.1912 PMID: 38361805

Kamalov, F., Santandreu Calonge, D., & Gurrib, I. (2023). New Era of Artificial Intelligence in Education: Towards a Sustainable Multifaceted Revolution. *Sustainability*, *15*(16), 12451. DOI: 10.3390/su151612451

Kanaris, M. E., & Mujtaba, B. G. (2023). Trust shaping the social relationship of diverse learners in the online education environment. Environment and Social Psychology, 9(2).

Kanglang, L. (2021). Artificial Intelligence (AI) and Translation Teaching: A Critical Perspective on the Transformation of Education. *International Journal of Educational Sciences, 33*(1–3). Advance online publication. DOI: 10.31901/24566322.2021/33.1-3.1159

Kannan, J., & Munday, P. (2018). New Trends in Second Language Learning and Teaching through the lens of ICT, Networked Learning, and Artificial Intelligence. *Círculo de Lingüística Aplicada a la Comunicación, 76*, 13–30. DOI: 10.5209/CLAC.62495

Karan, K., & Bakina, W. (2024). Generative artificial intelligence (ai) in education: A cross-national survey on university teachers' perceptions on the use of chatgpt.

Karlsson, F. (2020). The opportunities of applying artificial intelligence in strategic sourcing.

Kasneci, E., Sessler, K., Küchemann, S., Bannert, M., Dementieva, D., Fischer, F., Gasser, U., Groh, G., Günnemann, S., Hüllermeier, E., Krusche, S., Kutyniok, G., Michaeli, T., Nerdel, C., Pfeffer, J., Poquet, O., Sailer, M., Schmidt, A., Seidel, T., & Kasneci, G. (2023). ChatGPT for good? On opportunities and challenges of large language models for education. *Learning and Individual Differences, 103*, 102274. DOI: 10.1016/j.lindif.2023.102274

Katsamakas, E., Pavlov, O. V., & Saklad, R. (2024). Artificial intelligence and the transformation of higher education institutions: A systems approach. *Sustainability, 16*(14), 6118.

Kaufmann, R., & Vallade, J. I. (2022). Exploring connections in the online learning environment: Student perceptions of rapport, climate, and loneliness. *Interactive Learning Environments, 30*(10), 1794–1808.

KDnuggets. (2018). Role of IoT in Education. https://www.kdnuggets.com/2018/04/role-iot-education.html

Khan, S. M. (2025). AI-Powered Tools for Teaching English as a Second Language (ESL) in TNE. In Bridging Global Divides for Transnational Higher Education in the AI Era (pp. 121-140). IGI Global Scientific Publishing.

Kidaptive. (2024). Adaptive learning for early childhood education. https://theindexproject.org/award/nominees/1838

Kim, D. (2017). The impact of learning management systems on academic performance: Virtual Competency and student Involvement. *Journal of Higher Education Theory and Practice, 17*(2), 23–35.

Kim, D., & Kim, S. (2021). A model for user acceptance of robot journalism: Influence of positive disconfirmation and uncertainty avoidance. *Technological Forecasting and Social Change*, *163*, 120448. DOI: 10.1016/j.techfore.2020.120448

Kim, J., Lee, H., & Cho, Y. H. (2022). Learning design to support student-AI collaboration: Perspectives of leading teachers for AI in education. *Education and Information Technologies*, *27*(5), 6069–6104. DOI: 10.1007/s10639-021-10831-6

Kim, S. W., & Lee, Y. (2023). Investigation into the influence of socio-cultural factors on attitudes toward artificial intelligence. *Education and Information Technologies*. Advance online publication. DOI: 10.1007/s10639-023-12172-y

Kiran, G. R., Manoharan, G., Durai, S., Ashtikar, S. P., & Kunchala, R. (2024). Higher Education in India and the Influence of Online Certification Programs. In *Evaluating Global Accreditation Standards for Higher Education* (pp. 149–163). IGI Global.

Kitsara, I. (2022). Artificial intelligence and the digital divide: From an innovation perspective. In *Platforms and artificial intelligence: The next generation of competences* (pp. 245–265). Springer International Publishing.

Knott, E., Rao, A. H., Summers, K., & Teeger, C. (2022). Interviews in the social sciences. *Nature Reviews. Methods Primers*, *2*(1). Advance online publication. DOI: 10.1038/s43586-022-00150-6

Knowles, M. S. (1980). *The modern practice of adult education: From pedagogy to andragogy* (2nd ed.). Cambridge Books.

Knox, J. (2020). Artificial Intelligence and Education in China. *Learning, Media and Technology*, *45*(3), 298–311. DOI: 10.1080/17439884.2020.1754236

Kolb, D. A. (1984). *Experiential learning: Experience as the source of learning and development*. Prentice Hall.

Kong, S.-C., Man-Yin Cheung, W., & Zhang, G. (2021). Evaluation of an artificial intelligence literacy course for university students with diverse study backgrounds. *Computers and Education: Artificial Intelligence*, *2*, 100026. DOI: 10.1016/j.caeai.2021.100026

Kordzadeh, N., & Ghasemaghaei, M. (2021). Algorithmic bias: Review, synthesis, and future research directions. *European Journal of Information Systems*, *31*(3), 388–409. DOI: 10.1080/0960085x.2021.1927212

Kovacs, I., & Zarandne, K. V. (2022). Digital Marketing Employability Skills in Job Advertisements - Must-Have Soft Skills for Entry-Level Workers: A Content Analysis. *Economia e Sociologia*, *15*(1), 178–192. DOI: 10.14254/2071789X.2022/15-1/11

Krishna, A., Wright, D., & Kotcher, R. (2020). Curriculum Rebuilding in Public Relations: Understanding what Early Career, Mid-Career, and Senior PR/Communications Professionals Expect from PR Graduates. *Journal of Public Relations Education*, *6*(1), 33–57.

Krueger, R. A., & Casey, M. A. (2000). *Focus Groups: A Practical Guide for Applied Research* (3rd ed.). Sage Publications.

Kshetri, N. (2023a). Regulatory technology and supervisory technology: Current status, facilitators and barriers. *IEEE Computer*, *56*(1), 64–75.

Kshetri, N. (2023b). (forthcoming). ChatGPT in developing economies. *IEEE IT Professional*, *25*(2).

Kuddus, K. (2022). Artificial Intelligence in Language Learning: Practices and Prospects. In Mire, A., Malik, S., & Tyagi, A. K. (Eds.), *Advanced Analytics and Deep Learning Models* (1st ed., pp. 1–17). Wiley., DOI: 10.1002/9781119792437.ch1

Kulik, J. A., & Fletcher, J. D. (2016). Effectiveness of Intelligent Tutoring Systems: A Meta-Analytic Review. *Review of Educational Research*, *86*(1), 42–78. DOI: 10.3102/0034654315581420

Kumar, A., Singh, D., & Vohra, R. (2023). Improving learning abilities using AI-Based education systems. In *Advances in educational technologies and instructional design book series* (pp. 137–155). https://doi.org/DOI: 10.4018/979-8-3693-0378-8.ch006

Kumar, A. H. (2023). Analysis of ChatGPT tool to assess the potential of its utility for academic writing in biomedical domain. *Biology, Engineering. Medicine and Science Reports*, *9*(1), 24–30.

Kumar, S. (2024). The Role of Digital Marketing on Customer Engagement in the Hospitality Industry. In Bansal, R., Ngah, A. H., Chakir, A., & Pruthi, N. (Eds.), (pp. 177–191). Advances in Business Information Systems and Analytics. IGI Global., DOI: 10.4018/979-8-3693-0815-8.ch010

Kumar, S., Dhiraj, A., Shah, M. A., & Rani, D. (2023). Application of Metaverse in the Hospitality Industry. In *Influencer Marketing Applications Within the Metaverse* (pp. 178–194). IGI Global.

Kumar, S., Rao, P., Singhania, S., Verma, S., & Kheterpal, M. (2024). Will artificial intelligence drive the advancements in higher education? A tri-phased exploration. *Technological Forecasting and Social Change*, *201*, 123258. DOI: 10.1016/j.techfore.2024.123258

Kun, H. (2020). Performance incentives, divergent thinking training, and creative problem solving. *Journal of Management Accounting Research*, *32*(1), 159–176. DOI: 10.2308/jmar-52479

Laato, S., Morschheuser, B., Hamari, J., & Björne, J. (2023). AI-assisted learning with ChatGPT and large language models: Implications for higher education. *2023 IEEE International Conference on Advanced Learning Technologies (ICALT)*, 226–230. IEEE. https://doi.org/DOI: 10.1109/ICALT58122.2023.00072

Lagemann, E. C. (2000). *An elusive science: The troubling history of education research*. University of Chicago Press.

Lai, C. (2019). Technology and Learner Autonomy: An Argument in Favor of the Nexus of Formal and Informal Language Learning. *Annual Review of Applied Linguistics*, *39*, 52–58. DOI: 10.1017/S0267190519000035

Lai, J. W., & Cheong, K. H. (2022). Educational opportunities and challenges in augmented reality: Featuring implementations in physics education. *IEEE Access : Practical Innovations, Open Solutions*, *10*, 43143–43158.

Lai, K., & Pratt, K. (2004). Information and communication technology (ICT) in secondary schools: The role of the computer coordinator. *British Journal of Educational Technology*, *35*(4), 461–475. DOI: 10.1111/j.0007-1013.2004.00404.x

Larsen, H. G., & Adu, P. (2021). The theoretical framework in phenomenological research. In *Routledge eBooks*. https://doi.org/DOI: 10.4324/9781003084259

Lateef, F., Stehman, C. R., & Plitt, M. (2023). Artificial intelligence: Emerging roles in medical education. *Education and Information Technologies*, *28*(1), 741–756.

Laupichler, M. C., Aster, A., Schirch, J., & Raupach, T. (2022). Artificial intelligence literacy in higher and adult education: A scoping literature review. *Computers and Education: Artificial Intelligence*, *3*, 100101. DOI: 10.1016/j.caeai.2022.100101

Leapfrog. (2019). Evolution of AI. https://www.lftechnology.com/blog/ai/ai-evolution/

Lee, H. (2023). Using ChatGPT as a learning tool in acupuncture education: Comparative study. *JMIR Medical Education*, *9*, e47427. Advance online publication. DOI: 10.2196/47427 PMID: 37590034

Lee, J., & Hollister, J. M. (2020). Internet-mediated research in the age of social distancing: Methodological reflections and recommendations from two online research projects. *Journal of Korean Library and Information Science Society, 51*(2), 319–353. DOI: 10.16981/kliss.51.2.202006.319

Lee, S. M., & Lee, D. (2020). "Untact": A new customer service strategy in the digital age. *Service Business, 14*(1), 1–22.

Legowo, B., Nurhasanah, F., Saddhono, K., Budiastuti, V. I., Sutomo, A. D., & Murwaningsih, T. (2024). *Enhancing Educational Outcomes Through Exploring the Optimized Options Artificial Intelligence and Deep Learning*. IEEE., DOI: 10.1109/ICACITE60783.2024.10616772

Le, T. T., Sharma, P., Bora, B. J., Tran, V. D., Truong, T. H., Le, H. C., & Nguyen, P. Q. P. (2023). Fueling the future: A comprehensive review of hydrogen energy systems and their challenges. *International Journal of Hydrogen Energy, 54*, 791–816. DOI: 10.1016/j.ijhydene.2023.08.044

Levitt, H. M., Bamberg, M., Creswell, J. W., Frost, D. M., Josselson, R., & Suárez-Orozco, C. (2018). Journal article reporting standards for qualitative primary, qualitative meta-analytic, and mixed methods research in psychology: The APA Publications and Communications Board task force report. *The American Psychologist, 73*(1), 26. PMID: 29345485

Levy, M. (2009). Technologies in Use for Second Language Learning. *Modern Language Journal, 93*(s1), 769–782. DOI: 10.1111/j.1540-4781.2009.00972.x

Lewis, R. B., & Maas, S. M. (2007). QDA Miner 2.0: Mixed-model qualitative data analysis software. *Field Methods, 19*(1), 87–108.

Liang, J.-C., Hwang, G.-J., Chen, M.-R. A., & Darmawansah, D. (2023). Roles and research foci of artificial intelligence in language education: An integrated bibliographic analysis and systematic review approach. *Interactive Learning Environments, 31*(7), 4270–4296. DOI: 10.1080/10494820.2021.1958348

Li, C., & Zhao, H. (2023). Improving K-Means clustering for customer segmentation in e-commerce platforms. *International Journal of Data Science, 39*(1), 91–102. DOI: 10.1080/2345678910

Lim, J. (2023). How news organizations and journalists understand artificial intelligence: application of news language database to AI-related news stories. In *Research Handbook on Artificial Intelligence and Communication* (pp. 108–124). Edward Elgar Publishing.

Lin, C. C., Huang, A. Y., & Lu, O. H. (2023). Artificial intelligence in intelligent tutoring systems toward sustainable education: A systematic review. *Smart Learning Environments*, *10*(1), 41.

Lindgren, S. (2024). *Critical Theory of AI*. Polity Press.

Ling, Y., Simsek, Z., Lubatkin, M. H., & Veiga, J. F. (2008). Transformational Leadership's Role in Promoting Corporate Entrepreneurship: Examining the CEO-TMT Interface. *Academy of Management Journal*, *51*(3), 557–576. DOI: 10.5465/amj.2008.32626023

Lin, H., & Chen, Q. (2024). Artificial intelligence (AI) -integrated educational applications and college students' creativity and academic emotions: Students and teachers' perceptions and attitudes. *BMC Psychology*, *12*(1). Advance online publication. DOI: 10.1186/s40359-024-01979-0 PMID: 39285268

Lin, Z. (2023). Why and how to embrace AI such as ChatGPT in your academic life. *Royal Society Open Science*, *10*(8). Advance online publication. DOI: 10.1098/rsos.230658 PMID: 37621662

LittleMore Innovations. (2021). 3 million paperless digital exams. https://www.littlemoreinnovation.com/lm-exam/

Liu, P.-L., & Chen, C.-J. (2015). Learning English through actions: A study of mobile-assisted language learning. *Interactive Learning Environments*, *23*(2), 158–171. DOI: 10.1080/10494820.2014.959976

Liu, P., Zhang, Y., & Wang, X. (2022). Support vector machine applications in the classification of sleep disorders using wearable device data. *Journal of Biomedical Informatics*, *124*, 103968. DOI: 10.1016/j.jbi.2022.103968

Li, X., Zhang, Y., & Wang, Z. (2023). Support Vector Machines-based clustering algorithms for multi-robot coordination in dynamic cnvironmcnts. *Robotics and Autonomous Systems*, *142*, 103344. DOI: 10.1016/j.robot.2023.103344

Li, Y., & Zhao, Z. (2024). The Role of Education in the Era of AI: Challenges Along with Opportunities. Journal of Humanities. *Arts and Social Science*, *8*(4), 1034–1039. DOI: 10.26855/jhass.2024.04.039

Lochmiller, C. R. (n.d.). *The Qualitative report The Qualitative Report*. https://www.semanticscholar.org/paper/The-Qualitative-Report-The-Qualitative-Report-Lochmiller/271f61ca8c699d5f41436fd70b8da1bd321a0ad9?p2df

Long, D., & Magerko, B. (2020). What is AI literacy? Competencies and design considerations. *Proceedings of the 2020 CHI Conference on Human Factors in Computing Systems*, USA, 1-16. https://doi.org/DOI: 10.1145/3313831.3376727

López, D. G. (2021). A phenomenological approach to the study of social distance. *Human Studies*, *44*(2), 171–200. DOI: 10.1007/s10746-021-09582-7 PMID: 33967362

Lopezosa, C., Codina, L., Pont-Sorribes, C., & Vallez, M. (2023). Use of generative artificial intelligence in the training of journalists: Challenges, uses, and training proposal. *Profesional de la información/Information Professional, 32*(4). https://doi.org/DOI: 10.3145/epi.2023.jul.08

Lorenzini, D. (2020). Biopolitics in the time of coronavirus. *Critical Inquiry*, *47*(S2), S40–S45. DOI: 10.1086/711432

Lowenthal, P. R., Humphrey, M., Conley, Q., Dunlap, J. C., Greear, K., Lowenthal, A., & Giacumo, L. A. (2020). Creating accessible and inclusive online learning: Moving beyond compliance and broadening the discussion. *Quarterly Review of Distance Education*, *21*(2).

Lowry, D. T., & Xie, L. (2008). Employers' Perspectives on Skills Needed for Entry-Level Advertising and Marketing Jobs: A New Computerized Approach. *Journal of Advertising Education*, *12*(2), 17–24. DOI: 10.1177/109804820801200206

Loyens, S. M. M., van Meerten, J. E., Schaap, L., & Wijnia, L. (2023). Situating higher-order, critical, and critical-analytic thinking in problem- and project-based learning environments: A systematic review. *Educational Psychology Review*, *35*(2), 39. Advance online publication. DOI: 10.1007/s10648-023-09757-x

Luan, H., Geczy, P., Lai, H., Gobert, J., Yang, S. J., Ogata, H., & Tsai, C. C. (2020). Challenges and future directions of big data and artificial intelligence in education. *Frontiers in Psychology*, *11*, 580820. PMID: 33192896

Lucia-Palacios, L., Pérez-López, R., & Polo-Redondo, Y. (2016). Cognitive, affective and behavioural responses in mall experience: A qualitative approach. *International Journal of Retail & Distribution Management*, *44*(1), 4–21.

Luckin, R., Holmes, W., Griffiths, M., & Forcier, L. B. (2016). *Intelligence Unleashed: An argument for AI in education*. Pearson Education.

Lund, B. D., Mannuru, N. R., & Agbaji, D. (2024). AI anxiety and fear: A look at perspectives of information science students and professionals towards artificial intelligence. *Journal of Information Science*, •••, 01655515241282001.

Luo, J. (2024). A critical review of GenAI policies in higher education assessment: A call to reconsider the "originality" of students' work. *Assessment & Evaluation in Higher Education*, *49*(5), 651–664. DOI: 10.1080/02602938.2024.2309963

Luttrell, R., Wallace, A., McCollough, C., & Lee, J. (2020). The Digital Divide: Addressing Artificial Intelligence in Communication Education. *Journalism & Mass Communication Educator*, *75*(4), 470–482. DOI: 10.1177/1077695820925286

Luttrell, R., & Ward, J. (2018). Looking in to see out: An introspective approach to teaching ethics in PR. *Journal of Public Relations Education*, *4*(2), 123–127. https://aejmc.us/jpre/2018/08/17/looking-in-to-see-out-an-introspective-approach-to-teaching-ethics-in-pr/

Luukkonen, T., Persson, O., & Sivertsen, G. (1992). Understanding Patterns of International Scientific Collaboration. *Science, Technology & Human Values*, *17*(1), 101–126. DOI: 10.1177/016224399201700106

Lu, X. (2018). Natural Language Processing and Intelligent Computer-Assisted Language Learning (ICALL). In Liontas, J. I. (Ed.), *The TESOL Encyclopedia of English Language Teaching* (1st ed., pp. 1–6). Wiley., DOI: 10.1002/9781118784235.eelt0422

Lye, C. Y., & Lim, L. (2024). Generative Artificial Intelligence in Tertiary Education: Assessment Redesign Principles and Considerations. *Education Sciences*, *14*(6), 569. DOI: 10.3390/educsci14060569

Lytvynova, S. H., Rashevska, N. V., & Proskura, S. L. (2024). The use of artificial intelligence in teaching students programming languages. In Proceedings of the IX International Workshop on Professional Retraining and Life-Long Learning using ICT: Person-oriented Approach (3L-Person 2024) co-located with 19th International Conference on ICT in Education, Research, and Industrial Applications (No. 3781, pp. 10-29). CEUR Workshop Proceedings

Ma, A. (2024). AI vs. human translation: Shaping the future of language learning through AI-generated bilingual captions. *SHS Web of Conferences*, *199*, 01023. https://doi.org/DOI: 10.1051/shsconf/202419901023

Maatuk, A. M., Elberkawi, E. K., Aljawarneh, S., Rashaideh, H., & Alharbi, H. (2022). The COVID-19 pandemic and E-learning: Challenges and opportunities from the perspective of students and instructors. *Journal of Computing in Higher Education*, *34*(1), 21–38. PMID: 33967563

Mageira, K., Pittou, D., Papasalouros, A., Kotis, K., Zangogianni, P., & Daradoumis, A. (2022). Educational AI chatbots for content and language integrated learning. *Applied Sciences (Basel, Switzerland)*, *12*(7), 3239. DOI: 10.3390/app12073239

Maghsudi, S., Lan, A., Xu, J., & Van Der Schaar, M. (2021). Personalized education in the Artificial intelligence era: What to expect next. *IEEE Signal Processing Magazine*, *38*(3), 37–50. DOI: 10.1109/msp.2021.3055032

Mahat-Shamir, M., Neimeyer, R. A., & Pitcho-Prelorentzos, S. (2019). Designing in-depth semi-structured interviews for revealing meaning reconstruction after loss. *Death Studies*, *45*(2), 83–90. DOI: 10.1080/07481187.2019.1617388 PMID: 31116652

Majumdar, A. (2021). Thematic analysis in qualitative research. In *IGI Global eBooks* (pp. 604–622). https://doi.org/DOI: 10.4018/978-1-6684-3881-7.ch031

Makaryan, M. (2024, August 6). Policymakers should capitalize on positive public opinion to promote beneficial AI use. *Center for Data Innovation*. https://datainnovation.org/2024/08/policymakers-should-capitalize-on-positive-public-opinion-to-promote-beneficial-ai-use/

Manikandan, G., Bhuvaneswari, G., & Joel, M. R. (2023). Artificial intelligence to the assessment, monitoring, and forecasting of drought in developing countries. In *2023 International Conference on Circuit Power and Computing Technologies (ICCPCT)* (pp. 886–892). IEEE. https://doi.org/DOI: 10.1109/ICCPCT58313.2023.10245072

Manoharan, G., Ashtikar, S. P., & Nivedha, M. (2024). Integrating Artificial Intelligence in Library Management: An Emerging Trend. *AI-Assisted Library Reconstruction*, 144-157.

Manoharan, G., & Ashtikar, S. P. (2024). A Theoretical Framework for Emotional Intelligence in Academic Leadership in Higher Education. In *Building Organizational Resilience with Neuroleadership* (pp. 96–112). IGI Global.

Manoharan, G., & Ashtikar, S. P. (2024). Nexus between Leadership and Effective Communication: Implications for Educational Institutions. In *Neuroleadership Development and Effective Communication in Modern Business* (pp. 274–291). IGI Global.

Manoharan, G., Ashtikar, S. P., Rao, C. G., & Nivedha, M. (2024). A Pedagogical Landscape: Narrative Study on Emerging Artificial Intelligence Trends in Education. In *Inclusive Educational Practices and Technologies for Promoting Sustainability* (pp. 22–41). IGI Global.

Mapp, T. (2008). Understanding phenomenology: The lived experience. *British Journal of Midwifery*, *16*(5), 308–311. DOI: 10.12968/bjom.2008.16.5.29192

Market. us. (2024). *EdTech market size, share, trends | CAGR of 13.9%* [Data set].

Marshall, B., Cardon, P., Poddar, A., & Fontenot, R. (2013). Does sample size matter in qualitative research?: A review of qualitative interviews in IS research. *Journal of Computer Information Systems*, *54*(1), 11–22.

Matellio Inc. (2023, October 13). A guide to IoT use cases in education: Unlocking the future of learning. *Matellio*. https://www.matellio.com/blog/iot-use-cases-in-education/

Matthiesen, S., & Nelius, T. (2018). Managing assumptions during analysis-study on successful approaches of design engineers. In *DS 91: Proceedings of NordDesign 2018*, Linköping, Sweden, 14th–17th August 2018.

McAlister, A. R., Alhabash, S., & Yang, J. (2024). Artificial intelligence and ChatGPT: Exploring Current and potential future roles in marketing education. *Journal of Marketing Communications*, *30*(2), 166–187.

McCook, A. (2017). *Newly released AI software writes papers for you—What could go wrong*. Retraction Watch.

McCusker, K., & Gunaydin, S. (2015). Research using qualitative, quantitative or mixed methods and choice based on the research. *Perfusion*, *30*(7), 537–542. PMID: 25378417

McDonald, N., Johri, A., Ali, A., & Collier, A. H. (2025). Generative artificial intelligence in higher education: Evidence from an analysis of institutional policies and guidelines. Computers in Human Behavior. *Artificial Humans*, *3*, 100121. DOI: 10.1016/j.chbah.2025.100121

McInnis-Domínguez, M. (2023). An AI Solution: Using ChatGPT to Counter Plagiarism and Boost Enrollments in Hispanic Literature Courses. *Middle Atlantic Review of Latin American Studies*, *7*(2).

McKinsey & Company. (2022, August 19). Machine learning meets higher learning. https://www.mckinsey.com/featured-insights/sustainable-inclusive-growth/charts/machine-learning-meets-higher-learning

McMurtrie, B. (2022, December 13). AI and the future of undergraduate writing. *The Chronicle of Higher Education*. https://www.chronicle.com/article/ai-and-the-future-of-undergraduate-writing

McTighe, J., & Wiggins, G. (2013). *Essential questions: Opening doors to student understanding*. Association for Supervision and Curriculum Development.

Meganck, S., Smith, J., & Guidry, J. (2020). The skills required for entry-level public relations: An analysis of skills required in 1,000 PR job ads. *Public Relations Review*, *46*(5), 101973. DOI: 10.1016/j.pubrev.2020.101973 PMID: 32952274

Melkonyan, A., & Matevosyan, A. (2020). Technology-assisted foreign language learning (TALL) in the digital age. *SHS Web of Conferences, 88*, 02005. https://doi .org/DOI: 10.1051/shsconf/20208802005

Metz, A. (2022). "6 Exciting Ways to Use Chatgpt – From Coding to Poetry". TechRadar. htt ps://www.techradar.com/features/6- exciting- ways- to- use- chatgpt -from-coding-to -poetry.

Mezirow, J. (1991). *Transformative dimensions of adult learning*. Jossey-Bass.

Michel-Villarreal, R., Vilalta-Perdomo, E., Salinas-Navarro, D. E., Thierry-Aguilera, R., & Gerardou, F. S. (2023). Challenges and Opportunities of Generative AI for Higher Education as Explained by ChatGPT. *Education Sciences, 13*(9), 856. DOI: 10.3390/educsci13090856

Miller, R. E. (2024). Pandora's can of worms: A year of generative AI in higher education. *Portal (Baltimore, Md.)*, *24*(1), 21–34. DOI: 10.1353/pla.2024.a916988

MobyMax. (2024). Find and Fix Learning Gaps. https://www.mobymax.com/

Mollick, E. R., & Mollick, L. (2023). Assisting, Augmenting, and Evaluating Creativity with Generative AI. https://ssrn.com/abstract=4375796

Mondal, H., & Mondal, S. (2023). ChatGPT in academic writing: Maximizing its benefits and minimizing the risks. *Indian Journal of Ophthalmology*, *71*(12), 3600–3606. PMID: 37991290

Moorhouse, B. L., & Kohnke, L. (2024). The effects of generative AI on initial language teacher education: The perceptions of teacher educators. *System*, *122*, 103290. DOI: 10.1016/j.system.2024.103290

Morgan, D. L. (2023). Exploring the use of artificial intelligence for qualitative data analysis: The case of ChatGPT. *International Journal of Qualitative Methods*, *22*, 1–10. DOI: 10.1177/16094069231211248

Morrison-Smith, S., & Ruiz, J. (2020). Challenges and barriers in virtual teams: A literature review. *SN Applied Sciences*, *2*(6), 1–33.

Murray, M. D. (2023). Generative and AI authored artworks and copyright law. *Hastings Communications & Entertainment Law Journal, 45*(1), 27–44. DOI: 10.2139/ssrn.4152484

Naeem, M., Ozuem, W., Howell, K., & Ranfagni, S. (2023). A Step-by-Step process of thematic analysis to develop a conceptual model in qualitative research. *International Journal of Qualitative Methods, 22.* Advance online publication. DOI: 10.1177/16094069231205789

Nagarro. (2021). AI & ML in education: Real-life use cases. https://www.nagarro.com/en/blog/ai-ml-education-real-life-use-cases

Namous, A., & Bouigha, K. (2024). *Teachers' and Students' Perception about the Effects of Using ChatGPT, Grammarly, and Quillbot on Students' Writing Skills* (Doctoral dissertation, university center of abdalhafid boussouf-MILA).

Nathani, Y. (2025, January 16). AI in education: The quiet revolution India needs. *Times of India Voices.* https://timesofindia.indiatimes.com/blogs/voices/ai-in-education-the-quiet-revolution-india-needs/

Nath, H. K., & Liu, L. (2017). Information and communications technology (ICT) and services trade. *Information Economics and Policy, 41*, 81–87. DOI: 10.1016/j.infoecopol.2017.06.003

Nativi, S., Mazzetti, P., & Craglia, M. (2021). Digital ecosystems for developing digital twins of the earth: The destination earth case. *Remote Sensing, 13*(11), 2119.

Nazer, L. H., Zatarah, R., Waldrip, S., Ke, J. X. C., Moukheiber, M., Khanna, A. K., Hicklen, R. S., Moukheiber, L., Moukheiber, D., Ma, H., & Mathur, P. (2023). Bias in artificial intelligence algorithms and recommendations for mitigation. *PLOS Digital Health, 2*(6), e0000278. DOI: 10.1371/journal.pdig.0000278 PMID: 37347721

Nero, V. (2024). We Tested 20+ AI PR Tools, So You Don't Have To. https://www.buzzstream.com/blog/pr-ai-tools/

Ng, D. T. K., Leung, J. K. L., Chu, S. K. W., & Qiao, M. S. (2021). Conceptualizing AI literacy: An exploratory review. *Computers and Education: Artificial Intelligence, 2*, 100041. DOI: 10.1016/j.caeai.2021.100041

Nguyen, G. T. B. S. (2024). *An exploration of Faculty and Students' Self-Reported Awareness and use of Blackboard Ally for online course accessibility* (By R. M. Aye Ed. D., A. Catterson Ph. D., & C. McDuffie Ph. D.). https://www.bakeru.edu/images/pdf/SOE/EdD_Theses/Nguyen_Gaileen.pdf

Nguyen, M. (2024). Artificial Intelligence Chatbots in Telecommunications: Transforming Customer Service in the Digital Age.

Norton, B., & Toohey, K. (2011). Identity, language learning, and social change. *Language Teaching*, *44*(4), 412–446. DOI: 10.1017/S0261444811000309

Nostrum, E. (2024, July 20). AI tools democratizing education for less privileged students. https://erasmusnostrum.org/ai-tools-democratize-education/

Nuraeni, C., Carolina, I., Supriyatna, A., Widiati, W., & Bahri, S. (2020). Mobile-Assisted Language Learning (MALL): Students' Perception and Problems towards Mobile Learning in English Language. *Journal of Physics: Conference Series*, *1641*(1), 012027. DOI: 10.1088/1742-6596/1641/1/012027

Nusivera, E., Hikmat, A. & Ghani, A. A. R. (2025). Integration of Chat-GPT Usage in Language Learning Model to Improve Argumentation Skills, Complex Comprehension Skills, and Critical Thinking Skills. *International Journal of Learning, Teaching and Educational Research*, 24, No. 2, 375-390, February 2025. https://doi.org/. Received Dec 12, 2024; Revised Feb 3, 2025; Accepted Feb 19, 2025DOI: 10.26803/ijlter.24.2.19

O'Neil, C. (2016). *Weapons of Math Destruction: How Big Data Increases Inequality and Threatens Democracy*. Crown Publishing Group.

Obenza, B. N., Salvahan, A., Rios, A. N., Solo, A., Alburo, R. A., & Gabila, R. J. (2023). University students' perception and use of ChatGPT: Generative artificial intelligence (AI) in higher education. *International Journal of Human-Computer Studies*, *5*(12), 76–107. DOI: 10.31149/ijhcs.v5i12.5033

OECD. (2021). *OECD digital education outlook 2021: Pushing the frontiers with artificial intelligence, blockchain and robots*. OECD Publishing., DOI: 10.1787/589b283f-

Okon, S. U., Olateju, O., Ogungbemi, O. S., Joseph, S. A., Olisa, A. O., & Olaniyi, O. O. (2024). Incorporating Privacy by Design Principles in the Modification of AI Systems in Preventing Breaches across Multiple Environments, Including Public Cloud, Private Cloud, and On-prem. SSRN *Electronic Journal*. https://doi.org/DOI: 10.2139/ssrn.4945564

Okonkwo, C. W., & Ade-Ibijola, A. (2021). Chatbots applications in education: A systematic review. *Computers and Education: Artificial Intelligence*, *2*, 100033. DOI: 10.1016/j.caeai.2021.100033

Olari, V., & Romeike, R. (2021) Addressing AI and data literacy in teacher education: A review of existing educational frameworks. *The 16th Workshop in Primary and Secondary Computing Education*, USA, 1-2. https://doi.org/DOI: 10.1145/3481312.3481351

Oliver, N. (2022). Artificial intelligence for social good-the way forward. Science, Research and Innovation Performance of the EU 2022 Report, 604-707.

Omar, M., Sorin, V., Agbareia, R., Apakama, D. U., Soroush, A., Sakhuja, A., & Klang, E. (2025). Evaluating and addressing demographic disparities in medical large language models: A systematic review. *International Journal for Equity in Health*, *24*(1), 57. PMID: 40011901

Omar, R., Kaliappen, N., Khamis, K. A., & Sulisworo, D. (2021). Blended learning approach in graduate studies: A bibliometric analysis from 1997-2021. *International Journal of Information and Education Technology (IJIET)*, *11*(11), 546–552.

Omona, K. (2024). *Global Perspectives on Micro-learning and Micro-credentials in Higher Education*. IGI Global.

Onwuegbuzie, A. J., & Abrams, S. S. (2021). Nonverbal communication analysis as mixed analysis. In *The Routledge reviewer's guide to mixed methods analysis* (pp. 239–258). Routledge.

Ooi, K. B., Tan, G. W. H., Al-Emran, M., Al-Sharafi, M. A., Capatina, A., Chakraborty, A., & Wong, L. W. (2023). The Potential of Generative Artificial Intelligence Across Disciplines: Perspectives and Future Directions. *Journal of Computer Information Systems*, *65*(1), 1–32. DOI: 10.1080/08874417.2023.2261010

Oppenlaender, J. (2022). The creativity of text-to-image generation. *Proceedings of the 25th International Academic Mindtrek Conference*, 192–202. DOI: 10.1145/3569219.3569352

Oravec, J. A. (2023). Artificial intelligence implications for academic cheating: Expanding the dimensions of responsible human-AI collaboration with ChatGPT. *Journal of Interactive Learning Research*, *34*(2), 213–237.

Orchard, T., & Tasiemski, L. (2023). The rise of Generative AI and possible effects on the economy. *Economics and Business Review*, *9*(2), 9–26. DOI: 10.18559/ebr.2023.2.732

Ouyang, F., Wu, M., Zheng, L., Zhang, L., & Jiao, P. (2023). Integration of artificial intelligence performance prediction and learning analytics to improve student learning in online engineering course. *International Journal of Educational Technology in Higher Education*, *20*(1), 4. PMID: 36683653

Ovcharuk, O., Ivaniuk, I., Soroko, N., Gritsenchuk, O., & Kravchyna, O. (2020). The use of digital learning tools in the teachers' professional activities to ensure sustainable development and democratization of education in European countries. *Information Technologies and Learning Tools*, *75*(1), 163–176. DOI: 10.33407/itlt.v75i1.3533

Palea, A., & Buciuman, C. (2024). The Impact of Artificial Intelligence (AI) on Teaching Public Relations (PR). *Emerging Technologies, Challenges and Opportunities in Education and Research,* 11.

Pandey, K. K., & Shukla, D. (2020). Stratified sampling-based data reduction and categorization model for big data mining. In *Communication and Intelligent Systems* [Springer Singapore.]. *Proceedings of ICCIS, 2019*, 107–122.

Papakostas, C., Troussas, C., & Sgouropoulou, C. (2024). Review of the Literature on AI-Enhanced Augmented Reality in Education. *Special Topics in Artificial Intelligence and Augmented Reality: The Case of Spatial Intelligence Enhancement*, 13-50.

Parcel Pending. (2024, February 4). 8 examples of IoT applications in universities. *Parcel Pending*. https://www.parcelpending.com/en-us/blog/iot-applications-in-university/

Parks, C. (2017). Beyond compliance: Students and FERPA in the age of big data. *Journal of Intellectual Freedom & Privacy*, *2*(2), 23–33.

Pasca, M. G., & Arcese, G. (2023). ChatGPT between opportunities and challenges: an empirical study in Italy. *The TQM Journal*, (ahead-of-print).

Pasquinelli, M. (2023). *The eye of the master: A social history of artificial intelligence*. Verso Books.

Patel, S., & Kumar, P. (2023). Optimizing Support Vector Machine parameters for big data analysis in social media sentiment analysis. *Big Data Research*, *22*(2), 158–171. DOI: 10.1016/j.bdr.2023.01.003

Paul, R., & Elder, L. (2014). *The miniature guide to critical thinking concepts and tools* (7th ed.). Foundation for Critical Thinking.

Pavlik, J. V. (2023). Collaborating with ChatGPT: Considering the implications of generative artificial intelligence for journalism and media education. *Journalism & Mass Communication Educator*, *78*(1), 84–93. DOI: 10.1177/10776958221149577

Pavlova, O., & Kuzmin, A. (2024). Analysis of artificial intelligence based systems for automated generation of digital content.

Pellas, N. (2023). The influence of sociodemographic factors on students' attitudes toward AI-generated video content creation. *Smart Learning Environment, 10*(57). Advance online publication. DOI: 10.1186/s40561-023-00276-4

Pérez, J., Daradoumis, T., & Puig, J. (2020). Rediscovering the use of chatbots in education: A Systematic literature review. *Computational Applications in Engineering Education,* 28, 1–https://www.semanticscholar.org/paper/ Rediscovering-the-use-of-chatbots-in-education%3A-A-P%C3%A9rez Daradoumis/6f07a03d6a96e943bee-b3cad641c700f124c5cf7

Personalized education in the Artificial intelligence era: What to expect next. (2021, May 1). IEEE Journals & Magazine | IEEE Xplore. https://ieeexplore.ieee.org/abstract/document/9418572

Pesovski, I., Santos, R., Henriques, R., & Trajkovik, V. (2024). Generative AI for customizable learning experiences. *Sustainability, 16*(7), 3034. DOI: 10.3390/su16073034

Piaget, J. (1970). Piaget's theory. In Mussen, P. (Ed.), *Carmichael's manual of child psychology* (3rd ed., pp. 703–732). Wiley.

Pittman, J., Severino, L., DeCarlo-Tecce, M. J., & Kiosoglous, C. (2021). An action research case study: Digital equity and educational inclusion during an emergent COVID-19 divide. *Journal for Multicultural Education, 15*(1), 68–84.

Pokrivcakova, S. (2023). Pre-service teachers' attitudes towards artificial intelligence and its integration into EFL teaching and learning. *Journal of Language and Cultural Education, 11*(3), 100–114. DOI: 10.2478/jolace-2023-0031

Popenici, S. A. D., & Kerr, S. (2017). Exploring the impact of artificial intelligence on teaching and learning in higher education. *Research and Practice in Technology Enhanced Learning, 12*(22), 1–13. DOI: 10.1186/s41039-017-0062-8 PMID: 30595727

Porter, B., & Grippa, F. (2020). A platform for AI-enabled real-time feedback to promote digital collaboration. *Sustainability, 12*(24), 10243. DOI: 10.3390/su122410243

Portugal INCoDe. 2030 (2017). Iniciativa Nacional Competências Digitais e.2030, Portugal INCoDe.2030. https://www.incode2030.gov.pt/

Portugal INCoDe. 2030 (2019). Estratégia Nacional de Inteligência Artificial (National Strategy for Artificial Intelligence). https://www.incode2030.gov.pt/aip-2030/

Prasad, R., & Makesh, D. (2024). *Impact of AI on Media & Entertainment Industry. Media & Journalism Transformations-Emerging Trends and Paradigm Shifts.* Emerald Publications.

Pratschke, B. M. (2024). *Generative AI and Education: Digital Pedagogies, Teaching Innovation and Learning Design*. Springer.

Purushottamashtikar, S., & Manoharan, G. (2024, June). Emotional intelligence on higher education educators: A systematic literature review. In *AIP Conference Proceedings* (Vol. 2971, No. 1). AIP Publishing.

Qadir, J. 2023. Engineering Education in the Era of ChatGPT: Promise and Pitfalls of Generative AI for Education. *IEEE Global Engineering Education Conference (EDUCON)*, Kuwait, 1-9. DOI: 10.1109/EDUCON54358.2023.10125121

Radanliev, P., De Roure, D., Novitzky, P., & Sluganovic, I. (2024). Accessibility and inclusiveness of new information and communication technologies for disabled users and content creators in the Metaverse. *Disability and Rehabilitation. Assistive Technology*, *19*(5), 1849–1863. PMID: 37585705

Rafa, A. T. (2024, February 18). Paving way for a more inclusive Bangladesh. *The Daily Star*. https://www.thedailystar.net/anniversary-supplement-2024/innovate-educate-elevate/news/paving-the-way-more-inclusive-bangladesh-3545126

Rahiman, H. U., & Kodikal, R. (2023). Revolutionizing education: Artificial intelligence empowered learning in higher education. *Cogent Education*, *11*(1). Advance online publication. DOI: 10.1080/2331186x.2023.2293431

Rahimi, R., Jones, J., & Bailey, C. (2024). Exploring contract cheating in further education: Student engagement and academic integrity challenges. *Ethics and Education*, *19*(1), 38–58.

Rajabi, P., Taghipour, P., Cukierman, D., & Doleck, T. (2023). Exploring ChatGPT's impact on post-secondary education: A qualitative study. *Proceedings of the 25th Western Canadian Conference on Computing Education*, 1–6. https://doi.org/DOI: 10.1145/3593342.3593360

Raji, I. D., Kumar, I. E., Horowitz, A., & Selbst, A. (2022). The fallacy of AI functionality. *2022 ACM Conference on Fairness, Accountability, and Transparency*, 959–972. https://doi.org/DOI: 10.1145/3531146.3533158

Ramaul, L., Ritala, P., & Ruokonen, M. (2024). Creational and conversational AI affordances: How the new breed of chatbots are revolutionizing the knowledge industries. *Business Horizons*.

Rane, N., Choudhary, S., & Rane, J. (2023). Education 4.0 and 5.0: Integrating Artificial Intelligence (AI) for personalized and adaptive learning. SSRN *Electronic Journal*. https://doi.org/DOI: 10.2139/ssrn.4638365

Rane, N. (2024). Enhancing the quality of teaching and learning through ChatGPT and similar large language models: Challenges, future prospects, and ethical considerations in education. *TESOL and Technology Studies*, *5*(1), 1–6. DOI: 10.48185/tts.v5i1.1000

Rane, N., Choudhary, S., & Rane, J. (2024). Artificial intelligence, natural language processing, and machine learning to enhance e-service quality on e-commerce platforms. Available at *SSRN* 4847952.

Rastrollo-Guerrero, J. L., Gomez-Pulido, J. A., & Duran-Domınguez, A. (2020). Analyzing and predicting students' performance by means of machine learning: A review. *Applied Sciences (Basel, Switzerland)*, *10*(3), 1042. DOI: 10.3390/app10031042

Razak, A., Nayak, M. P., Manoharan, G., Durai, S., Rajesh, G. A., Rao, C. B., & Ashtikar, S. P. (2023). Reigniting the power of artificial intelligence in education sector for the educators and students competence. In *Artificial Intelligence and Machine Learning in Smart City Planning* (pp. 103–116). Elsevier.

Reddy, V., & Shah, A. (2022). Optimizing K-Means clustering for financial fraud detection: A comparative study with SVM and Random Forest. *Journal of Financial Data Analysis*, *14*(1), 34–48. DOI: 10.1016/j.finanal.2022.03.005

Reed, K. M., & Allen, J. A. (2022). *Suddenly hybrid: Managing the modern meeting*. John Wiley & Sons.

Ren, Y., Ruan, Y., Tan, X., Qin, T., Zhao, S., Zhao, Z., & Liu, T. Y. (2019). Fastspeech: Fast, robust and controllable text to speech. In *Advances in Neural Information Processing Systems, 32*.

Rettig, C., & Mickeleit, T. (2023). There is no shortcut to AI. Or is there? How German communications professionals are navigating the AI revolution: Insights from a focus group discussion of the members of AG CommTech. In Adi, A. (Ed.), *Artificial Intelligence in Public Relations and Communications: cases, reflections, and predictions* (pp. 63–72). Quadriga University of Applied Sciences.

Riapina, N. (2024). Teaching AI-Enabled Business Communication in Higher Education: A Practical Framework. *Business and Professional Communication Quarterly*, *87*(3), 511–521. DOI: 10.1177/23294906231199249

Right Question Institute. (n.d.). *Question formulation technique (QFT)*. Retrieved from https://rightquestion.org/qft/

Rios, J. A., Ling, G., Pugh, R., Becker, D., & Bacall, A. (2020). Identifying critical 21stcentury skills for workplace success: A content analysis of job advertisements. *Educational Researcher*, *49*(2), 80–89. DOI: 10.3102/0013189X19890600

Robles, M. M. (2012). Executive Perceptions of the Top 10 Soft Skills Needed in Today's Workplace. *Business Communication Quarterly*, *75*(4), 453–465.

Romero-Rodríguez, J. M., Alonso-García, S., Marín-Marín, J. A., & Gómez-García, G. (2020). Considerations on the implications of the Internet of Things in Spanish universities: The usefulness perceived by professors. *Future Internet*, *12*(8), 123. DOI: 10.3390/fi12080123

Rosman, M. R. M., Alias, N. R., Arshad, I. H., Hamid, H. A., & Idris, Z. (2022). Assessing Students' Perceived Engagement and Perceived Performance for E-Learning in East Coast Malaysia: A Partial Least Square Structural Equation Modeling Approach. *IEEE Engineering Management Review*, *51*(1), 63–75.

Rospigliosi, P. (2023). Artificial intelligence in teaching and learning: What questions should we ask of ChatGPT? *Interactive Learning Environments*, *31*(1), 1–3. DOI: 10.1080/10494820.2023.2180191

Roy, G., Babu, R., Kalam, M. A., Yasmin, N., Zafar, T., & Nath, S. R. (2021). Response, readiness and challenges of online teaching amid COVID-19 pandemic: The case of higher education in Bangladesh. *The Educational and Developmental Psychologist*, *40*(1), 40–50. DOI: 10.1080/20590776.2021.1997066

Rudolph, J., Tan, S., & Tan, S. (2023). ChatGPT: Bullshit spewer or the end of traditional assessments in higher education? *Journal of Applied Learning and Teaching*, *6*(1), 342–363.

Rukmini, S., Sreenivasulu, Y., Raghu, T., Nagatulasi, K., & Manoharan, G. (2024, June). English language teaching in technological and management studies in India: An edu-techno approach. In *AIP Conference Proceedings* (Vol. 2971, No. 1). AIP Publishing.

Russell, S. J., & Norvig, P. (2016). *Artificial intelligence: a modern approach*. Pearson.

Russell, S. J., & Norvig, P. (2022). *Artificial Intelligence: A Modern Approach* (4th ed.). Pearson.

Ruzgar, N. S., & Chua-Chow, C. (2023). Perception of students on online exams and how sequential exams and the lockdown browser affect student anxiety and performance. *WSEAS Transactions on Computer Research, 11*, 92–110.

Ryan, R. M. (2017). *Self-determination theory: Basic psychological needs in motivation, development, and wellness*. Guilford Press.

Sabraz Nawaz, S., Fathima Sanjeetha, M. B., Al Murshidi, G., Mohamed Riyath, M. I., Mat Yamin, F. B., & Mohamed, R. (2024). Acceptance of ChatGPT by undergraduates in Sri Lanka: A hybrid approach of SEM-ANN. *Interactive Technology and Smart Education*. Advance online publication. DOI: 10.1108/itse-11-2023-0227

Sadler, D. R. (1989). Formative assessment and the design of instructional systems. *Instructional Science, 18*(2), 119–144. DOI: 10.1007/BF00117714

Sahu, S. K., & Mazumdar, K. (2024). Exploring security threats and solutions techniques for Internet of Things (IoT): From vulnerabilities to vigilance. *Frontiers in Artificial Intelligence*, *7*, 1397480. Advance online publication. DOI: 10.3389/frai.2024.1397480 PMID: 38845684

Sajja, R., Sermet, Y., Cikmaz, M., Cwiertny, D., & Demir, I. (2024). Artificial intelligence-enabled intelligent assistant for personalized and adaptive learning in higher education. *Information (Basel)*, *15*(10), 596.

Sajja, R., Sermet, Y., Cikmaz, M., Cwiertny, D., & Demir, I. (2024). Artificial Intelligence-Enabled Intelligent Assistant for Personalized and Adaptive Learning in Higher Education. *Information (Basel)*, *15*(10), 596. DOI: 10.3390/info15100596

Salas-Pilco, S. Z., Xiao, K., & Oshima, J. (2022). Artificial Intelligence and New Technologies in Inclusive Education for Minority Students: A Systematic Review. *Sustainability*, *14*(20), 13572. DOI: 10.3390/su142013572

Saldaña, J. (2021). Coding techniques for quantitative and mixed data. *The Routledge reviewer's guide to mixed methods analysis*, pp.151-160.

Sallam, M. (2023). The utility of ChatGPT as an example of large language models in healthcare education, research and practice: Systematic review on the future perspectives and potential limitations. *MedRxiv*.

Salleh, M. (2020). Teacher Learning Outcomes on Post COVID-19: A Review Based on Malaysia and other Asian Countries Perspective. *International Journal of Academic Research in Business & Social Sciences*, *10*(11), 164–173. DOI: 10.6007/IJARBSS/v10-i11/8276

Sandhu, R., Channi, H. K., Ghai, D., Cheema, G. S., & Kaur, M. (2024). An Introduction to Generative AI Tools for Education 2030. Integrating Generative AI in Education to Achieve Sustainable Development Goals, 1-28.

Sanusi, I. T., Olaleye, S. A., Agbo, F. J., & Chiu, T. K. F. (2022). The role of learners' competencies in artificial intelligence education. *Computers and Education: Artificial Intelligence*, *3*, 100098. Advance online publication. DOI: 10.1016/j.caeai.2022.100098

Saunders, B., Sim, J., Kingstone, T., Baker, S., Waterfield, J., Bartlam, B., & Jinks, C. (2018). Saturation in qualitative research: Exploring its conceptualization and operationalization. *Quality & Quantity*, *52*, 1893–1907. PMID: 29937585

Sawyer, R. K. (2022). 33 The Learning Sciences in the 2020s: Implications for Schools and Beyond.

Schiff, D. (2022). Education for AI, not AI for Education: The Role of Education and Ethics in National AI Policy Strategies. *International Journal of Artificial Intelligence in Education*, *32*, 527–563. DOI: 10.1007/s40593-021-00270-2

Schneider, T. (2020). An in-depth analysis of SVM and K-Means clustering: Strengths, limitations, and comparative performance. Medium. https://medium.com/%40taylorschneider_61189/svm-k-means-clustering-939532b65e49

Schön, D. A. (1983). *The reflective practitioner: How professionals think in action*. Basic Books.

SchooLinks. (2024). A College & Career Platform for Modern Students. https://www.schoolinks.com/

Schwarz, A. (2024). Instructional Risk and Crisis Communication at Higher Education Institutions during COVID-19: Insights from Practitioners in the Global South and North. *Journal of International Crisis and Risk Communication Research*, *7*(1), 1–47.

Schweyer, A. (2018). Predictive analytics and artificial intelligence in people management. Incentive Research Foundation, 1–18.

Sebesta, J., & Davis, V. L. (2023, June 30). *Supporting Instruction and Learning* through Artificial Intelligence: A Survey of Institutional Practices & Policies. WICHE Cooperative for Educational Technologies. wcet.wiche.edu/resources/wcet-report-supporting-instruction-learning-through-artificial-intelligence-a-survey-of-institutional-practices-policies/

Selvi, R., Athinarayanan, S., Devi, V., Gobinath, M., & Shanthakumar, P. (2024). Combining neural and semantic features in the analysis of being supportive in online feedback from customers. *ITEGAM-JETIA*, *10*(48), 8–13.

Selwyn, N. (2019). *Should robots replace teachers? AI and the Future of Education*. Polity Press.

ercan, E., & Voicu, B. (2022). Patterns of Academic Integrity Definitions among BA Romanian Students'. The Impact of Rising Enrolments. *Revista de Cercetare si Interventie Sociala*, *78*, 87–106.

Shaik, T., Tao, X., Li, Y., Dann, C., McDonald, J., Redmond, P., & Galligan, L. (2022). A review of the trends and challenges in adopting natural language processing methods for education feedback analysis. *IEEE Access : Practical Innovations, Open Solutions*, *10*, 56720–56739.

Sharples, M. (2022). New AI tools that can write student essays require educators to rethink teaching and assessment. London School of Economics Blog. https://blogs.lse.ac.uk/impactofsocialsciences/2022/05/17/new-aitools-that-can-write-student-essays-require-educators-torethink-teaching-and-assessment/

Shaun, R., De Baker, J., & Inventado, P. S. (2014). *Educational Data Mining and Learning Analytics*.

Shemshack, A., & Spector, J. M. (2020). A systematic literature review of personalized learning terms. *Smart Learning Environments*, *7*(1), 33. DOI: 10.1186/s40561-020-00140-9

Shoaib, M. R., Wang, Z., Ahvanooey, M. T., & Zhao, J. (2023). Deepfakes, Misinformation, and Disinformation in the Era of Frontier AI, Generative AI, and Large AI Models. In *Unmasking DeepFake Visual Content with Generative AI*. https://doi.org/DOI: 10.1109/icca59364.2023.10401723

Shohel, M. M. C., Roy, G., Ashrafuzzaman, M., & Babu, R. (2022). Teaching and Learning in Higher Education in Bangladesh during the COVID-19 Pandemic: Learning from the Challenges. *Education Sciences*, *12*(12), 857. DOI: 10.3390/educsci12120857

Sholokhova, S., Bizzari, V., & Fuchs, T. (2022). Exploring phenomenological interviews: Questions, lessons learned and perspectives. *Phenomenology and the Cognitive Sciences*, *21*(1), 1–7. DOI: 10.1007/s11097-021-09799-y

Siddiquah, A., & Salim, Z. (2017). The ICT facilities, skills, usage, and the problems faced by the students of higher education. *Eurasia Journal of Mathematics, Science and Technology Education*, *13*(8), 4987–4994.

Singh, D., Makkar, S., Manoharan, G., Durai, S., Purushottamashtikar, S., & Alexrajesh, G. (2024, June). The impact of information technology enabler and organizational learning on performance: A systematic literature review. In *AIP Conference Proceedings* (Vol. 2971, No. 1). AIP Publishing.

Singh, M. (2023). Maintaining the integrity of the SOUTH AFRICAN university: The impact of chatgpt on plagiarism and scholarly writing. *South African Journal of Higher Education, 37*(5), 203–220. DOI: 10.20853/37-5-5941

Sinokki, S. (2024). A Day in the Life of a Technical Support Specialist.

Sivakumaran, A. R., Shanthakumar, P., & Joel, M. R. (2024). IoMT-based smart intelligent healthcare system using optimization-driven deep residual network for brain tumor detection. *International Journal of Pattern Recognition and Artificial Intelligence, 38*(15), 2457011.

Slimi, Z., & Carballido, B. V. (2023). Navigating the Ethical Challenges of Artificial Intelligence in Higher Education: An Analysis of Seven Global AI Ethics Policies. TEM Journal, 12(2), 590-602. https://doi.org/DOI: 10.18421/TEM122-02

Smith, J., & Williams, L. (2022). Using Support Vector Machines for predictive analytics in student performance: A case study in higher education. *International Journal of Education and Data Science, 8*(3), 45–61. DOI: 10.1080/0123456789

Smolansky, A., Cram, A., Raduescu, C., Zeivotos, S., Huber, E., & Kizilcec, R. F. (2023). Educator and student perspectives on the impact of generative AI on assessments in higher education. *Proceedings of the Tenth ACM Conference on Learning @ Scale*, 378–382. https://doi.org/DOI: 10.1145/3573051.3596191

Smyrnova-Trybulska, E., Morze, N., & Varchenko-Trotsenko, L. (2022). Adaptive learning in university students' opinions: Cross-border research. *Education and Information Technologies, 27*(5), 6787–6818. PMID: 35095326

Sok, S., & Heng, K. (2023). ChatGPT for education and research: A review of benefits and risks. *Cambodian Journal of Educational Research, 3*(1), 110–121. DOI: 10.62037/cjer.2023.03.01.06

Southworth, J., Migliaccio, K., Glover, J., Glover, J., Reed, D., McCarty, C., Brendemuhl, J., & Thomas, A. (2023). Developing a model for *AI Across the curriculum*: Transforming the higher education landscape via innovation in AI literacy. *Computers and Education: Artificial Intelligence, 4*, 100127. DOI: 10.1016/j.caeai.2023.100127

Sprintzeal. (n.d.). IoT security challenges and best practices: Risk and solution. https://www.sprintzeal.com/blog/iot-security-challenges

Sriram, K. P., Sujatha, P. K., Athinarayanan, S., Kanimozhi, G., & Joel, M. R. (2024, July). Transforming agriculture: A synergistic approach integrating topology with artificial intelligence and machine learning for sustainable and data-driven practice. In *2024 2nd International Conference on Sustainable Computing and Smart Systems (ICSCSS)* (pp. 1350–1354). IEEE.

Stahl, B. C., & Eke, D. (2024). The ethics of ChatGPT–Exploring the ethical issues of an emerging technology. *International Journal of Information Management*, *74*, 102700.

Stake, R. E. (1995). *The art of case study research*. Sage Publications.

Stanier, J. (2022). An introduction to engaged phenomenology. *JBSP : the Journal of the British Society for Phenomenology. British Society for Phenomenology*, *53*(3), 226–242. DOI: 10.1080/00071773.2022.2081533 PMID: 35813180

Stöhr, C., Ou, A. W., & Malmström, H. (2024). Perceptions and usage of AI chatbots among students in higher education across genders, academic levels and fields of study. *Computers and Education Artificial Intelligence*, *7*, 100259. DOI: 10.1016/j.caeai.2024.100259

Stokel-Walker, C. (2022). AI text generators could help write student essays. *Nature*, *611*(7935), 227–228. PMID: 36344616

Stone, A. (2014). New Directions in ASL-English Bilingual Ebooks. *Critical Inquiry in Language Studies*, *11*(3), 186–206. DOI: 10.1080/15427587.2014.936242

Susnjak, T. (2022). ChatGPT: The end of online exam integrity? *arXiv preprint* arXiv:2212.09292.

Susnjak, T. (2022). ChatGPT: The End of Online Exam Integrity? *arXiv, 2212.09292*. DOI: 10.48550/arXiv.2212.09292

Svalberg, A. M.-L. (2007). Language awareness and language learning. *Language Teaching*, *40*(4), 287–308. DOI: 10.1017/S0261444807004491

Swan, K. (2021). The Community of Inquiry Framework, Online and Blended Learning, and the i2Flex Classroom Model. In *Handbook of Research on K-12 Blended and Virtual Learning Through the i²Flex Classroom Model* (pp. 1-17). IGI Global.

Swargiary. (2024). *Navigating the Digital Frontier: Case Studies in Online Learning for Career Advancement*. Scholars' Press

Swiatek, L., & Galloway, C. (2022). Artificial intelligence and public relations: Growing opportunities, questions, and concerns. In *The Routledge Companion to Public Relations* (pp. 352–362). Routledge.

Swiecki, Z., Khosravi, H., Chen, G., Martinez-Maldonado, R., Lodge, J. M., Milligan, S., Selwyn, N., & Gasevic, D. (2022). Assessment in the age of artificial intelligence. *Computers and Education: Artificial Intelligence*, *3*, 100075. DOI: 10.1016/j.caeai.2022.100075

Świerczyński, M., & Więckowski, Z. (2023). Liability for damages caused by artificial intelligence systems – main challenges to be addressed by the European Union conflict-of-laws regulations. *Prawo w Działaniu*, *54*, 200–216. DOI: 10.32041/pwd.5407

Taha, J. A. B. A., Hanid, M. F. B. A., & Said, M. N. H. M., bin Hassan, R., & Yik, L. H. (2020). Effectiveness of using augmented reality application in the subject of educational technology for undergraduate students. *Journal of Critical Reviews*, *7*(15), 1845–1850. DOI: 10.31838/jcr.07.15.337

ală, M. L., Müller, C. N., Năstase, I. A., State, O., & Georghe, G. (2024). Exploring university students' perceptions of generative artificial intelligence in education. *Amfiteatru Economic Journal*, *26*(65), 71–88. DOI: 10.24818/EA/2024/ 65/71

Talukder, M. B., & Kumar, S. (2024). The Development of Human Capital in The Hospitality Business. In S. Taneja, P. Kumar, Reepu, B. Balusamy, K. Sood, & S. Grima (Eds.), *Contemporary Studies in Economic and Financial Analysis* (pp. 21–38). Emerald Publishing Limited. https://doi.org/DOI: 10.1108/S1569-375920240000114002

Tan, J., & Zhang, Z. (2023). SVM and K-Means clustering for predicting COVID-19 vaccine acceptance among different demographics. *Journal of Public Health*, *45*(4), 324–337. DOI: 10.1093/pubmed/fdz002

Tanyildizi, N. I., & Yıldız, I. (2024). The Use of Artificial Intelligence in Health Communication: A Research on ChatGPT. In *Machine Learning and Generative AI in Smart Healthcare* (pp. 117–138). IGI Global.

Tawalbeh, L., Miuheidat, F., Tawalbeh, M., & Quwaider, M. (2020). IoT privacy and security: Challenges and solutions. *Applied Sciences (Basel, Switzerland)*, *10*(11), 4102. DOI: 10.3390/app10114102

Taylor, C. L., Said-metwaly, S., Camarda, A., & Barbot, B. (2023). Gender differences and variability in creative ability: A systematic review and meta-analysis of the greater male variability hypothesis in creativity. *Journal of Personality and Social Psychology*, •••, 1–19. DOI: 10.1037/pspp0000484

Técnico Lisboa. (November 2023). Sobre a utilização de IA nos métodos de ensino e de avaliação de conhecimentos (On the use of AI in teaching methods and knowledge assessment) https://conselhopedagogico.tecnico.ulisboa.pt/files/sites/32/ferramentas-de-ai-no-ensino-v8-1.pdf

Terzopoulos, G., & Satratzemi, M. (2020). Voice assistants and smart speakers in everyday life and in education. *Informatics in Education*, *19*(3), 473–490.

Tharp, R. G. (2008). Effective pedagogy in culturally responsive classrooms. *International Journal of Educational Development.*

Thomas, J. W. (2000). *A review of research on project-based learning*. Retrieved from https://www.bie.org/files/researchreviewPBL_2000.pdf

Thongprasit, J., & Wannapiroon, P. (2022). Framework of artificial intelligence learning platform for education. *International Education Studies*, *15*(1), 76–86. DOI: 10.5539/ies.v15n1p76

Thorp, H. H. (2023). ChatGPT is fun, but not an author. *Science*, *379*(6630), 313–313. PMID: 36701446

Timotheou, S., Miliou, O., Dimitriadis, Y., Sobrino, S. V., Giannoutsou, N., Cachia, R., Monés, A. M., & Ioannou, A. (2023). Impacts of digital technologies on education and factors influencing schools' digital capacity and transformation: A literature review. *Education and Information Technologies*, *28*, 6695–6726. DOI: 10.1007/s10639-022-11431-8 PMID: 36465416

Tlili, A., Shehata, B., Adarkwah, M. A., Bozkurt, A., Hickey, D. T., Huang, R., & Agyemang, B. (2023). What if the devil is my guardian angel: ChatGPT as a case study of using chatbots in education. *Smart Learning Environments*, *10*(1), 15. DOI: 10.1186/s40561-023-00237-x

Tomei, L. A., Maine, J., Moussa, K., Holler, M. B., Hobbs, B., & Austin, S. (2024). The top 12 technologies for teaching and learning in the post-pandemic era. In *Exploring technology-infused education in the post-pandemic era* (pp. 1–95). IGI Global.

Topping, K. J. (2009). Peer assessment. *Theory into Practice*, *48*(1), 20–27. DOI: 10.1080/00405840802577569

Toufaily, E., Zalan, T., & Dhaou, S. B. (2021). A framework of blockchain technology adoption: An investigation of challenges and expected value. *Information & Management*, *58*(3), 103444. DOI: 10.1016/j.im.2021.103444

Townsend, D., & Hunt, R. (2019). Entrepreneurial action, creativity, & judgment in the age of artificial intelligence. *Journal of Business Venturing Insights, 11*, e00126. DOI: 10.1016/j.jbvi.2019.e00126

Tugui, A., Jeflea, F-V., Opariuc, C., Filipeanu, D., Agheorghiesei, D-T. (2022). Societal Transformations in Romanian Society: Humanity's Interaction with Artificial Intelligence towards the Technological Singularity. *Transformations in Business & Economics, 21* (2A /56A), 435-461.

Tuomi, I., Punie, Y., Vuorikari, R., & Cabrera, M. (2018). *The impact of Artificial Intelligence on learning, teaching, and education.* European Commission: Joint Research Centre. Publications Office of the European Union.

Tuomi, I., Cachia, R., & Villar-Onrubia, D. (2023). *On the Futures of Technology in Education: Emerging Trends and Policy Implications.* Joint Research Center. *Publications Office of the European Union., JRC134308.* Advance online publication. DOI: 10.2760/079734

Tyack, D., & Cuban, L. (1995). *Tinkering toward Utopia: A century of public school reform.* Harvard University Press.

Tzimas, D., & Demetriadis, S. (2021). Ethical issues in learning analytics: A review of the field. *Educational Technology Research and Development, 69*(2), 1101–1133. DOI: 10.1007/s11423-021-09977-4

UNESCO Education Sector. (2021). *AI and education: guidance for policymakers.* UNESCO. https://books.google.com.bd/books?hl=en&lr=&id=yyE7EAAAQBAJ&oi=fnd&pg=PA3&dq=there+is+still+a+long+way+to+go+in+terms+of+addressing+these+concerns,+it+is+important+for+educators+and+policymakers+to+work+together&ots=cBj9D3zrK5&sig=FbdHaZLejkpn-IA1G8G7AoBupVk&redir_esc=y#v=onepage&q&f=false

UNESCO. (2021). *AI and education: Guidance for policy-makers.* https://unesdoc.unesco.org/ark:/48223/pf0000376709

UNESCO. (2023). *Guidance for generative AI in education and research.* https://unesdoc.unesco.org/ark:/48223/pf0000386693

UNICEF. (2021). *Policy guidance on AI for children.* Retrieved March 19, 2023, from https://www.unicef.org/globalinsight/media/1171/file/UNICEF-Global-Insight-policy-guidance-AI-childr

University of Sydney. (n.d.). Artificial intelligence in education: Democratising policy. https://www.sydney.edu.au/arts/our-research/research-projects/artificial-intelligence-in-education-democratising-policy.html

Usher, M. (2025). Generative AI vs. instructor vs. peer assessments: A comparison of grading and feedback in higher education. *Assessment & Evaluation in Higher Education*, •••, 1–16. DOI: 10.1080/02602938.2025.2487495

Uttamchandani, S., & Quick, J. (2022). An introduction to fairness, absence of bias, and equity in learning analytics. In *Handbook of Learning Analytics* (pp. 205–212).

Vakrats, D., & Wang, X. (2020). Artificial intelligence in advertising creativity. *Journal of Advertising*, *50*(1), 39–51. DOI: 10.1080/00913367.2020.1843090

Valavanidis, A. (2023). Artificial Intelligence (AI) Applications. Department of Chemistry, National and Kapodistrian University of Athens, University Campus Zografou, 15784.

Valverde-Berrocoso, J., Fernández-Sánchez, M. R., Revuelta Dominguez, F. I., & Sosa-Díaz, M. J. (2021). The educational integration of digital technologies preCovid-19: Lessons for teacher education. *PLoS One*, *16*(8), e0256283. PMID: 34411161

Van Dis, E. A. M., Bollen, J., Zuidema, W., van Rooij, R., & Bockting, C. L. (2023). ChatGPT: Five priorities for research. *Nature*, *614*(7947), 224–226. PMID: 36737653

Van Maanen, J. (1988). *Tales of the field: On writing ethnography*. University of Chicago Press.

Van Manen, M. (2017). Phenomenology in its original sense. *Qualitative Health Research*, *27*(6), 810–825. DOI: 10.1177/1049732317699381 PMID: 28682720

van Niekerk, J., Delport, P. M. J., & Sutherland, I. (2025). Addressing the use of generative AI in academic writing. *Computers and Education: Artificial Intelligence*, *8*, 1–11. DOI: 10.1016/j.caeai.2024.100342

Van Roy, V., Vertesy, D., & Vivarelli, M. (2018). Technology and employment: Mass unemployment or job creation? Empirical evidence from European patenting firms. *Research Policy*, *47*(9), 1762–1776. DOI: 10.1016/j.respol.2018.06.008

Velagaleti, S. B., Choukaier, D., Nuthakki, R., Lamba, V., Sharma, V., & Rahul, S. (2024). Empathetic Algorithms: The Role of AI in Understanding and Enhancing Human Emotional Intelligence. *Journal of Electrical Systems*, *20*(3s), 2051–2060.

Venkatesh, V., Brown, S. A., & Sullivan, Y. W. (2016). Guidelines for conducting mixed-methods research: An extension and illustration. *Journal of the Association for Information Systems*, *17*(7), 2.

Vetrivel, V. P., & Arun. (2024). The role of AI in transforming assessment practices in education. In *Advances in Educational Marketing, Administration, and Leadership* (pp. 43–70). IGI Global

Vettleson-Trutza, S., Yang, Y., Snyder, M., & Jazdzewski, D. (2023). B-138 Skewed demographics of patient population contributes to selection biases in clinical study population. *Clinical Chemistry*, *69*(Supplement_1), hvad097–472.

Vincent-Lancrin, S., & van der Vlies, R. (2020, April 8). *Trustworthy artificial intelligence (AI) in education: Promises and challenges*. OECD Education Working Papers. https://doi.org/DOI: 10.1787/a6c90fa9-en

Vitale, C., Bowyer, D., & Bayerlein, L. (2020). Developing and Presenting a Framework for Meeting Industry, Student and Educator Expectations in University Degrees. *E-Journal of Business Education & Scholarship of Teaching*, *14*(1), 57–65.

Viterouli, M., Belias, D., Koustelios, A., Tsigilis, N., & Papademetriou, C. (2024). Time for Change: Designing Tailored Training Initiatives for Organizational Transformation. In *Organizational Behavior and Human Resource Management for Complex Work Environments* (pp. 267–307). IGI Global

Vlasenko, Y., Zhyliak, N., Voloshchuk, M., Humeniuk, I., & Storozhuk, N. (2023). Socio-psychological and socio-cultural features of communication in an inclusive educational space and in the conditions of multiculturalism. *Iaroslava Levchenko, Anton Kholodov*, 104.

Vygotsky, L. S. (1978). *Mind in society: The development of higher psychological processes*. Harvard University Press.

Wach, K., Duong, C. D., Ejdys, J., Kazlauskaitė, R., Korzynski, P., Mazurek, G., & Ziemba, E. (2023). The dark side of generative artificial intelligence: A critical analysis of controversies and risks of ChatGPT. *Entrepreneurial Business and Economics Review*, *11*(2). Advance online publication. DOI: 10.15678/EBER.2023.110201

Walczak, K., & Cellary, W. (2023). Challenges for higher education in the era of widespread access to generative AI. Economics and Business Review/The Poznań University of Economics Review, 9(2), 71-100. https://doi.org/DOI: 10.18559/ebr.2023.2.743

Walford, G. (2008). *How to do educational ethnography*. Tufnell Press.

Wang, S., Wang, F., Zhu, Z., Wang, J., Tran, T., & Du, Z. (2024). Artificial intelligence in education: A systematic literature review. *Expert Systems with Applications*, *252*(A), 124167. DOI: 10.1016/j.eswa.2024.124167

Wang, C., Chen, X., Yu, T., Liu, Y., & Jing, Y. (2024). Education reform and change driven by digital technology: A bibliometric study from a global perspective. *Humanities & Social Sciences Communications*, *11*(1). Advance online publication. DOI: 10.1057/s41599-024-02717-y

Wang, H., Dang, A., Wu, Z., & Mac, S. (2024). Generative AI in higher education: Seeing ChatGPT through universities' policies, resources, and guidelines. *Computers and Education: Artificial Intelligence*, *7*, 100326. DOI: 10.1016/j.caeai.2024.100326

Wang, L., Chen, Y., & Zhang, F. (2021). Support vector machines in cancer genomic classification: Identifying subtypes for personalized treatment. *Frontiers in Oncology*, *11*, 635210. DOI: 10.3389/fonc.2021.635210

Wang, R., & Zhan, H. (2023). Deliberate misinterpretation from the perspective of socio-cognitive pragmatics. *Humanities & Social Sciences Communications*, *10*(1), 1–8.

Wang, T., Lund, B. D., Marengo, A., Pagano, A., Mannuru, N. R., Teel, Z. A., & Pange, J. (2023). Exploring the potential impact of artificial intelligence (AI) on international students in higher education: Generative AI, chatbots, analytics, and international student success. *Applied Sciences (Basel, Switzerland)*, *13*(11), 6716. DOI: 10.3390/app13116716

Wang, Y.-M., Wei, C.-L., Lin, H.-H., Wang, S.-C., & Wang, Y.-S. (2022). What drives students' AI learning behavior: A perspective of AI anxiety. *Interactive Learning Environments*, *32*(6), 2584–2600. DOI: 10.1080/10494820.2022.2153147

Watermeyer, R., Phipps, L., Lanclos, D., & Knight, C. (2023). Generative AI and the automating of academia. *Postdigital Science and Education*, *6*(2), 446–466. DOI: 10.1007/s42438-023-00440-6

Weizenbaum, J. (1966). ELIZA – A computer program for the study of natural language communication between man and machine. *Communications of the ACM*, *10*(8), 36–45. DOI: 10.1145/365153.365168

Wenden, A. L. (2002). Learner Development in Language Learning. *Applied Linguistics*, *23*(1), 32–55. DOI: 10.1093/applin/23.1.32

Wenger, D., Hossain, M. S., & Senseman, J. R. (2024). *AI and the Impact on Journalism Education*. Journalism & Mass Communication Educator., DOI: 10.1177/10776958241296497

Wertsch, J. V. (1988). *Vygotsky and the social formation of mind*. Harvard university press.

Whitaker, A. (2016). *Art Thinking: How to Carve Out Creative Space in a World of Schedules, Budgets, and Bosses* (1st ed.). HarperBus.

Whittaker, T., & Jenkins, R. (2024, September 12). AI literacy on the agenda: EU, UK and US. Society for Computers and Law. https://www.scl.org/ai-literacy-on-the-agenda-eu-uk-and-us/

Williams, B. M., & Martin, G. (2021). Exploring the rhetoric of social class among first-generation, low-income college students in US higher education. *Higher Education Research & Development*, *41*(6), 2094–2107. DOI: 10.1080/07294360.2021.1967885

Williamson, B., & Piattoeva, N. (2019). Objectivity as standardization in data-scientific education policy, technology and governance. *Learning, Media and Technology*, *44*(1), 64–76. DOI: 10.1080/17439884.2018.1556215

Willingham, D. T. (2007). Critical thinking: Why is it so hard to teach? *American Educator*, *31*(1), 8–19.

Winchester, M. K., & Winchester, T. M. (2012). If you build it will they come? Exploring the student perspective of weekly student evaluations of teaching. *Assessment & Evaluation in Higher Education*, *37*(6), 671–682.

Windels, K., Mallia, K. L., & Broyles, S. J. (2013). Soft Skills: The Difference between Leading and Leaving the Advertising Industry? *Journal of Advertising Education*, *17*(2), 17–27. DOI: 10.1177/109804821301700204

Winkler, R., & Söllner, M. (2020). *Personalization in Artificial Intelligence: How the AI Revolution is Reshaping Education and Learning*. Springer.

Woerner, J. H. R., Turtova, A. P., & Lang, A. S. I. D. (2024). *Transformative Potentials and Ethical Considerations of AI Tools in Higher Education: Case Studies and Reflections*. IEEE., DOI: 10.1109/SoutheastCon52093.2024.10500042

Woinaroschy, A. (2020). Personal considerations about creativity and artificial intelligence. *Journal of Engineering Sciences and Innovation*, *5*(1), 63–68. DOI: 10.56958/jesi.2020.5.1.7

Wong, G., Ma, X., Dillenbourg, P., & Huan, J. (2020). Broadening artificial intelligence education in K-12: Where to start? *ACM Inroads*, *11*(1), 20–29. DOI: 10.1145/3381884

Wong, Y., Fan, S., Guo, Y., Xu, Z., Stephen, K., Sheoran, R., & Kankanhalli, M. (2022). Compute to tell the tale: Goal-driven narrative generation. In *Proceedings of the 30th ACM International Conference on Multimedia* (pp. 6875–6882), Lisboa, Portugal.

Woo, J. H., & Choi, H. (2021). *Systematic Review for AI-based Language Learning Tools* (Version 1). arXiv. https://doi.org/DOI: 10.48550/ARXIV.2111.04455

Woodruff, A., Shelby, R., Gage Kelley, P., Rousso-Schindler, S., Smith-Loud, J., & Wilcox, L. (2024). How Knowledge Workers Think Generative AI Will (Not) Transform Their Industries. In *Proceedings of the CHI Conference on Human Factors in Computing Systems (CHI '24),* May 11–16, 2024, Honolulu, HI, USA. ACM, New York, NY, USA. DOI: 10.1145/3613904.3642700

Woods, P. (1996). *Researching the art of teaching: Ethnography for educational use*. Routledge.

Wu, Y. & Goldman School of Public Policy, University of California, Berkeley. (2023). Data Governance and Human Rights: An algorithm Discrimination Literature review and Bibliometric analysis. *Journal of Humanities, Arts and Social Science*. https://doi.org/DOI: 10.26855/jhass.2023.01.018

Wu, J., & Gu, Y. (2022). Analysis of Online Classroom Education on the Learning Patterns for College Students Using Human-Computer Interaction. *International Journal of Human-Computer Interaction*, *41*(3), 1829–1840. DOI: 10.1080/10447318.2022.2115640

Wu, X. Y. (2024). Exploring the effects of digital technology on deep learning: A meta-analysis. *Education and Information Technologies*, *29*(1), 425–458.

Wu, X., Duan, R., & Ni, J. (2023). Unveiling security, privacy, and ethical concerns of ChatGPT. *Journal of Information and Intelligence*, *2*(2), 102–115. DOI: 10.1016/j.jiixd.2023.10.007

Xia, Q., Chiu, T. K., Lee, M., Sanusi, I. T., Dai, Y., & Chai, C. S. (2022). A self-determination theory (SDT) design approach for inclusive and diverse artificial intelligence (AI) education. *Computers & Education*, *189*, 104582. DOI: 10.1016/j.compedu.2022.104582

Xie, F., & Derakhshan, A. (2021). A conceptual review of positive teacher interpersonal communication behaviors in the instructional context. *Frontiers in Psychology*, *12*, 708490. PMID: 34335424

Xu, B., Chen, N. S., & Chen, G. (2020). Effects of teacher role on student engagement in WeChat-Based online discussion learning. *Computers & Education*, *157*, 103956.

Xu, H., & Hamari, J. (2022). How to improve creativity: A study of gamification, money, and punishment. *Behaviour & Information Technology*. Advance online publication. DOI: 10.1080/0144929X.2022.2133634

Yang, A. (2024). Preparing Public Relations' Practitioners for the AI Era: Advancing Pedagogical Principles in Public Relations' Artificial Intelligence Education. *Journalism & Mass Communication Educator*, 10776958241277682.

Yang, E., & Beil, C. (2024). Ensuring data privacy in AI/ML implementation. *New Directions for Higher Education, 2024*(207), 63–78. DOI: 10.1002/he.20509

Yang, J. (2023). Preparing for the New Era of Artificial Intelligence: My Experience of Teaching "Artificial Intelligence in Advertising". *Journal of Advertising Education, 27*(2), 101–116.

Yang, X., Zhang, M., Zhao, Y., Wang, Q., & Hong, J.-C. (2022). Relationship between creative thinking and experimental design thinking in science education: Independent or related: Independent or related. *Thinking Skills and Creativity, 46*, 101183. https://doi.org/https://doi.org/10.1016/j.tsc.2022.101183

Yaxley, H. (2017). *Career strategies in public relations: constructing an original tapestry paradigm* (Doctoral dissertation). Bournemouth University.

Yim, I. H. Y., & Wegerif, R. (2024). Teachers' perceptions, attitudes, and acceptance of artificial intelligence (AI) educational learning tools: An exploratory study on AI literacy for young students. *Future in Educational Research, 2*, 313–345. DOI: 10.1002/fer3.65

Yin, R. K. (2009). *Case Study Research. Design and Methods* (4th ed.). Sage.

Yin, R. K. (2018). *Case study research and applications: Design and methods* (6th ed.). Sage Publications.

Yi, Y. (2021). Establishing the concept of AI literacy: Focusing on competence and purpose. *JAHR – European. Journal of Bioethics, 12*(2), 353–368. DOI: 10.21860/j.12.2.8

Yoder-Himes, D. R., Asif, A., Kinney, K., Brandt, T. J., Cecil, R. E., Himes, P. R., & Ross, E. (2022, September). Racial, skin tone, and sex disparities in automated proctoring software. [). Frontiers Media SA.]. *Frontiers in Education, 7*, 881449.

Youvan, D. (2024, January). The role of AI in revolutionizing academic publishing and knowledge dissemination.

Yudiono, H., Maulana, S., Wijaya, M. B. R., Aprianto, R., & Karsan, K. (2021). Product-based learning model through the alignment of mechanical engineering competencies with industry. *Jurnal Pendidikan Teknologi dan Kejuruan, 27*(1), 74-80. DOI: 10.21831/jptk.v27i1.28832

Yusuf, S. O., Abubakar, J. E., Durodola, R. L., Ocran, G., Paul-Adeleye, A. H., & Yusuf, P. O. (2024). Impact of AI on continuous learning and skill development in the workplace: A comparative study with traditional methods.

Yuwono, E. I., Tjondronegoro, D., Riverola, C., & Loy, J. (2024). Co-creation in action: Bridging the knowledge gap in artificial intelligence among innovation champions. *Computers and Education: Artificial Intelligence*, *7*, 1–16. DOI: 10.1016/j.caeai.2024.100272

Zajko, M. (2022). Artificial intelligence, algorithms, and social inequality: Sociological contributions to contemporary debates. *Sociology Compass*, *16*(3). Advance online publication. DOI: 10.1111/soc4.12962

Zarzycki, M., Morrison, V., Bei, E., & Seddon, D. (2023). Cultural and societal motivations for being informal caregivers: A qualitative systematic review and meta-synthesis. *Health Psychology Review*, *17*(2), 247–276. PMID: 35081864

Zawacki-Richter, O. (2018). *Theories of Distance Education and AI in Learning*. Routledge.

Zawacki-Richter, O. (2019). The role of artificial intelligence in education: Current insights and future research directions. *Educational Technology Research and Development*, *67*(4), 745–773. DOI: 10.1007/s11423-019-09764-7

Zawacki-Richter, O., Marín, V. I., Bond, M., & Gouverneur, F. (2019). Systematic review of research on artifcial intelligence applications in higher education—Where are the educators? *International Journal of Educational Technology in Higher Education*, *16*(1), 1–27. DOI: 10.1186/s41239-019-0171-0

Zeb, A., Ullah, R., & Karim, R. (2024). Exploring the role of ChatGPT in higher education: Opportunities, challenges and ethical considerations. *The International Journal of Information and Learning Technology*, *41*(1), 99–111.

Zhai, X. (2022). ChatGPT user experience: Implications for education. *Available at SSRN* 4312418.

Zhai, X., Chu, X., Chai, C. S., Jong, M. S. Y., Istenic, A., Spector, M., & Chen, Y. (2021). A review of artificial intelligence (AI) in education from 2010 to 2020. *Complexity. Article ID, 8812542*. Advance online publication. DOI: 10.1155/2021/8812542

Zhai, X., Chu, X., Chai, C. S., Jong, M. S. Y., Istenic, A., Spector, M., & Li, Y. (2021). A Review of Artificial Intelligence (AI) in Education from 2010 to 2020. *Complexity*, *2021*(1), 8812542.

Zhang, M., & Li, J. (2021). A commentary of GPT-3 in MIT Technology Review 2021. *Fundamental Research (Beijing)*, *1*(6), 831–833. DOI: 10.1016/j.fmre.2021.11.011

Zhang, X., & Cao, Z. (2021). A framework of an intelligent education system for higher education based on deep learning. *International Journal of Emerging Technologies in Learning*, *16*(7), 233–248. DOI: 10.3991/ijet.v16i07.22123

Zhang, Y., Liu, T., & Wang, J. (2020). Applications of Support Vector Machines in healthcare data analysis: A comprehensive review. *Journal of Health Informatics*, *45*(3), 215–227. DOI: 10.1016/j.jhi.2020.05.007

Zhang, Y., Xu, T., & Wang, X. (2024). Distance-based kernel for SVM classification to improve accuracy. *Frontiers in Artificial Intelligence*, *7*, 1287875. https://www.frontiersin.org/articles/10.3389/frai.2024.1287875/full PMID: 38469159

Zhao, J., & Gallant, D. J. (2012). Student evaluation of instruction in higher education: Exploring issues of validity and reliability. *Assessment & Evaluation in Higher Education*, *37*(2), 227–235.

Zhou, Y., & Zhang, W. (2024). Using K-Means clustering and SVM for improving email spam classification accuracy. *Journal of Artificial Intelligence*, *58*(3), 204–217. DOI: 10.1002/jai.2024

Ziemba, E., & Wątróbski, J. (Eds.). (2024). *Adoption of Emerging Information and Communication Technology for Sustainability*. CRC Press.

Zohar, A., & Dori, Y. J. (2003). Higher order thinking skills and low-achieving students: Are they mutually exclusive? *Journal of the Learning Sciences*, *12*(2), 145–181. DOI: 10.1207/s15327809jls1202_1

Zou, D. (2019). A comparative study of Support Vector Machines and Spectral Embedding methods for classification and clustering. *Proceedings of the International Conference on Data Science and Technology*, 254-263. https://arxiv.org/abs/1902.05724

About the Contributors

Alexandre Duarte has a PhD in Communication Sciences (specialization in Organizational and Strategic communications) from the University of Minho, is a Professor at NOVA University of Lisbon, researcher at ICNOVA/UNL and Invited Professor at Catholic University of Portugal, where he coordinates the Postgraduate Courses in Communication and Advertising Creativity, and Service Design. Having worked in several multinational advertising agencies for more than 20 years as a Senior Creative Copywriter, he was Tutor of the Young Marketers Academy of the EUROBEST Festival, CEO of RESTART – Institute of Arts and Creativity and advisor to SUPERBRANDS Portugal. Since 2021, is a member of the Research Committee of EDCOM - European Institute for Commercial Communications Education, and from 2024, assumed the Coordination of the Advertising Working Group of the Portuguese Association of Communication Sciences - SOPCOM.

José Gabriel Andrade is a researcher and professor on media, marketing and communication at the University of Minho. José holds a European PhD in Communication Sciences from the Catholic University of Portugal with the support of the Portuguese Foundation for Science and Technology, Fundação para a Ciência e a Tecnologia (FCT) and a Master in Communication Sciences: Communication, Organization and New Technologies from the Portuguese Catholic University, Universidade Católica Portuguesa - UCP, with the support of the high level scholarship Program of the European Union for Latin America (Alban). He coordinated the Master in Digital Communication and integrated the structure responsible for quality management, internships, communication and interface with the University community, actively participating in the professional and personal development of students. He is the director of the Casa do Conhecimento Cultural Unit of the University of Minho.

Patrícia Dias is Assistant Professor of the Faculty of Human Sciences (FCH) at the Catholic University of Portugal (UCP), where she coordinates the

Post-graduate course Social Brands – Communication and Marketing in the Digital Environment. She is a member of the Executive Board of the Research Centre on Peoples and Cultures (CEPCEP), integrated researcher at the Research Centre for Communication and Culture (CECC), and collaborator at the Católica Research Centre on Psychological, Family and Social Wellbeing. Holding a PhD in Communication Sciences, her research interests are the use of digital media by children and families, mobile communication, digital marketing and communication strategies, and emergent technologies within the scope of the Internet of Things. She is the author of "Smarketing - How Mobile Marketing is Changing Portugal" (2020), "Living in the Digital Society" (2014) and of "The Mobile Phone and Daily Life" (2008).

***

Shivasharana A is an Associate Professor at the REVA Business School, REVA University. He has altogether 35 years of experience that includes both Industry and Teaching. In the field of Academics (Teaching), he has worked in various capacities as a Lecturer, Sr. Lecturer, Reader, Assistant Professor, and Head of the Department. He is a Doctorate in the field of Management (Specialized in Operations and Systems). He has taught various subjects and in continuation too. He has published/presented papers at national and international conferences. He is a self-directed, action-oriented professional with over 25 years of experience in education. His educational qualifications are M.Sc. (Mathematics'), MBA (Operations and Systems'), M.Phil. (Management), PGCCA (Computers), Masters in Induction Programming, and Ph.D. (Logistics and Supply Chain Management).

Thamotharan A currently working as an Associate Professor in REVA Business School, REVA University, and Bengaluru. He has a total teaching experience of 15 years. Received MBA from Annamalai University in 2007. Received his Ph.D. in Management from Manonmaniam Sundharanar University, Tamil Nadu in 2017. His research interests include financial markets, financial services, investments and capital markets. He has conducted various workshops, seminar and faculty development programs on derivatives market. He is also a member of BOE, BOS at institutions of repute. He chaired national and international level conferences. Supported research scholars, students and faculty members for data analysis using SPSS and AMOS. He has also guided M.Phil., scholars in their research work and currently guiding Ph.D. scholar in the field of finance. Published research papers in Scopus indexed journals and UGC approved journals.

Alifennesa Alif is an undergraduate researcher at the DIU Centre for Social Media. Her primary focus is on conducting impactful research to develop innovative strategies and solutions that drive Sustainable Development Goals and enhance organizational growth. She is also passionate about Public Relations, Development Management and Communication.

Harani B currently serving as a Professor at REVA Business School, REVA University Bengaluru, she is engaged in both academic teaching and content development for undergraduate and postgraduate management programs. She has authored numerous articles in international and national journals, contributed chapters to books, and presented research papers at various prestigious conferences worldwide. In addition to her academic responsibilities, she has successfully organized national and international conferences, faculty development programs, panel discussions, and expert talks, all while serving as the research coordinator. Her involvement in multiple academic roles highlights her commitment to enhancing the institution's research profile. As a research guide, she has supervised three scholars who have earned their Ph.D. in areas such as Green Management, Integrated Accounting, and Economics. She is currently guiding five additional research scholars in topics including Sustainable Agricultural Practices, Green Banking, and Consumer Behavior. In her current role as the Ph.D. Program Coordinator at the Faculty of Commerce, Management, and REVA Business School, she continues to support and guide the academic and research endeavours of the faculty and students.

Elizabeth Bridgen is Head of Academic Improvement (Partner Provision) at Buckinghamshire New University, UK. Her research mostly explores the lived experience of public practitioners with a focus on those who are often excluded from mainstream scholarship. She is co-editor with Sarah Williams of Women's Work in Public Relations (2024), to which she also contributed a chapter 'Just like any other: Public Relations Careers in the Adult Industries' and co-author with Ileana Zeler of Race, Diversity and Social Mobility in the Public Relations Industry (2025). She is also co-editor with Dejan Verčič of Experiencing Public Relations: International Voices and recently contributed chapters to the books Towards a New Understanding of Masculine Habitus: Women in Leadership in Public Relations (Topic, 2023) and Gender and Freelancing in the Communication Industries: Experiences, practices, discourses (Anton and Moise, 2025). She has published in academic journals including Journal of Communication Management, PRism, and Journal of Media Practice and Education.

Nurul Ain Chua Binti Abdullah is a Senior Lecturer at Universiti Malaysia Terengganu (UMT), where she focuses on teaching Mandarin as a foreign language to non-native learners. She is actively involved in research related to Mandarin language acquisition and educational technology in language learning. Dr. Nurul Ain has over 30 years of experience in education and has taught at various levels, from primary to tertiary. She has presented her research at numerous national and international conferences. Her research interests include technology-enhanced language learning, language pedagogy, and differentiated instruction.

Camelia Cu nir is Senior Lecturer in the Department of Cultural Anthropology and Communication of the Faculty of Journalism and Communication Sciences, University of Bucharest. She has a PhD in Communication Sciences with the published thesis "Media discourse of Romanian public intellectuals after 1989" (2017) followed by a co-authored L'Harmattan volume "Intellectuels et médias à l'ère numérique" /Public intellectuals and media in the digital era (2021). Her research interests include Sociology of intellectuals, Social Media Influencers, Discourse Analysis, Digital Communication and Semiotics.

Aftab Hossain is an Assistant Professor and Head of the Department of Journalism, Media and Communication, Daffodil International University. Also, he completed his PhD from the School of Communication, Universiti Sains Malaysia. His research interests include social media, media framing, online harassment and bullying, media biases and cinema.

M. Robinson Joel received the Doctorate Ph.D degree in Computer and Information Technology from the Manonmaniam Sundaranar University, Tirunelveli in March 2019. He completed his M.Tech in Manonmaniam Sundaranar University, Tirunelveli 2002. He is currently working as an Associate Professor in the Department of Computer Science and Engineering, KCG College of Technology, Chennai. He has 16 years of teaching experience.

Tereza Klabíková Rábová is Vice-Dean for External Relations at the Faculty of Social Sciences, Charles University, since 2022. She has worked at the Department of Marketing Communication and Public Relations since 2012 as an Assistant Professor. Her research and education focuses on media and institutional communication, discourse analysis, and science communication. She co-authored a global study on trust in scientists published in Nature Human Behaviour and co-organized the Science Communication 360° conference. Tereza holds a Ph.D. in Media and Communication Studies and completed a doctoral research fellowship at EHESS in Paris. She is also a long-standing lecturer in the University of the Third Age program, where she shares her expertise with lifelong learners.

Sanjeev Kumar is an accomplished expert in Food and Beverage. He currently holds the positions of Professor in Lovely Professional University, Punjab, India. With over a decade of experience in the field, food Service Industry, his research focuses on Alcoholic beverages, Event management and Sustainable Management Practices, Metaverse, AI Machine Learning and Artificial Intelligence. He has published more than 60 research papers, articles and chapters in Scopus Indexed, UGC Approved and peer reviewed Journals and books. Dr. Sanjeev Kumar participated and acted as resource person in various National and International conferences, seminars, session chair, research workshops and industry talks and his work has been widely cited.

Mayyer Ling is a lecturer for the English Studies programme at Universiti Brunei Darussalam. Her research interests are metadiscourse, teaching and learning in higher education, including the use of artificial Intelligence, and digital discourse analysis. As an early career academic, she has published widely in corporate communication, educational strategies, language learning, and socio-cultural studies. She was awarded the Wellington Doctoral Scholarship in 2019 and obtained her PhD in Applied Linguistics in 2023. She is an advocate for equity in education. She volunteers for the Sultan Haji Hassanal Bolkiah Foundation and the Brunei Darussalam National Association of the Blind (BDNAB) where she can align her advocacy with her passion and professional values.

Ashok M is a pioneering figure in the field of Computer Science and Engineering (CSE), with a particular focus on Artificial Intelligence (AI) and Machine Learning (ML). Throughout his illustrious career, Ashok has been a dedicated advocate for technological advancements and the practical application of AI in various domains. Born with an innate curiosity for the potential of machines to mimic human cognitive functions, Ashok embarked on his academic journey by pursuing a degree in Computer Science and Engineering. His academic prowess was evident from the outset, as he delved deep into understanding algorithms, data structures, and programming languages.Ashok's fascination with AI and ML emerged during his postgraduate studies, where he specialized in cutting-edge techniques that mimic human cognition to solve complex problems. He became engrossed in the concept of creating intelligent machines capable of learning, reasoning, and problem-solving.

Geetha Manoharan is currently working in Telangana as an assistant professor at SR University. She is the university-level PhD program coordinator and has also been given the additional responsibility of In Charge Director of Publications and Patents under the Research Division at SR University.

Mădălina Moraru is an Associate Professor PhD., Director of the Advertising and Digital Communication Master Program at the University of Bucharest, and Vice-Dean of the Faculty of Journalism and Communication Science, Romania. She holds a PhD in Communication sciences and has over 16 years of experience teaching advertising. Mrs. Moraru is a member of Edcom – EACA, ECREA, and ESA. From 2010 to 2013 she received postdoctoral fellowships at the University of Oklahoma, US, and Staffordshire University and Buckinghamshire New University, UK. Between 2010 and 2013 she conducted a strategic European grant on the glocalization topic. During her activity, she authored many chapters, over 20 research articles, as well as two books focusing on myth, storytelling, and planning in advertising. She is active by getting involved in the Romanian industry's projects and being invited to the most important events: Advertising Day, Fibra award, member in Romanian Effie Juries.

Hana Moravcová, Ph.D., is an assistant professor at the Institute of Communication Studies and Journalism at Charles University from 2022. Dr. Moravcová received her Ph.D. in economics and finance at Charles University in 2020. Her research fields are institutional economics, law and economics, economic history, and business history. She specializes in topics such as the economic history of authors´ rights, state interventions toward creative industries, and communication of socioeconomic policies. Before her academic career, from 2011 to 2015, she worked at the Ministry of Finance and Czech National Bank as an expert in the regulation of financial markets.

Menard Musendekwa, (PhD) is a distinguished scholar in Theology, specializing in the Old Testament, and a dedicated Minister of Religion. His academic journey spans across multiple disciplines, reflecting his versatile expertise in areas such as Church History, Theology, Gender Studies, Education, and Climate Change, among others. With a rich portfolio of publications in esteemed journals and numerous contributions to book chapters, he has made significant scholarly contributions that resonate across academic circles. Dr. Musendekwa's commitment to academic excellence is further demonstrated through his active engagement in various academic conferences, where he shares insights and collaborates with fellow scholars. Currently serving as the Chair of Theology at Reformed Church University in Zimbabwe and holding the position of Vice-Principal at Murray Theological College, he brings a wealth of experience to his roles. With a profound dedication to university education, Dr. Musendekwa continues to inspire and mentor the next generation of scholars, shaping the future of theological studies and beyond.

Arpita Nayak is currently serving as an Assistant Professor, offering courses in management. She completed her Ph.D. in management from the KIIT School of Management. Her MBA and strong interest in Human Resource Management (HRM) led her to pursue further studies in HRM. Her passion for talent management inspired her doctoral research on "A Comparative Study on Talent Management in Private and Public Manufacturing Industries in Odisha." Dr. Nayak has presented research papers at both national and international conferences and has published articles in SCOPUS-listed journals. Over the years, she has taught a variety of subjects, including Human Resource Management, Principles of Management, Business Studies Management, Tribal Entrepreneurship, and Organizational Behaviour. In addition to her academic career, she also has several years of corporate work experience.

K. Fouzia Sulthana working as Professor in Artificial Intelligence and Data Science at Rajalakshmi Institute of Technology, chembarabakkam

Romina Surugiu is Associate Professor of Journalism and Media Studies, and Dean of the Faculty of Journalism and Communication Studies, University of Bucharest. She holds a PhD in Philosophy from the University of Bucharest (2006), and worked as a postdoctoral researcher in Communication Studies at the University of Bucharest (2010-2013), and at the Uppsala University (2012). She has published/coordinated research on journalism practice and specialist journalism, on the dynamics of work and gender in the media, and on the history of the European television. She is a member of the board of RN 18 Sociology of Communications and Media Research (European Sociological Association). Currently, she is the project director of "L'impact de l'IA sur les pratiques professionnelles dans l'enseignement universitaire de communication et médias – IACOM", financed by Agence Universitaire de la Francophonie. Recent publications: Media si Inteligenta Artificiala (Media and AI, coordinated with Antonio Momoc, Tritonic Books, 2024), Hybrid Work Organisation and Well-Being Strategies in Advertising Agencies During the COVID-19 Pandemic (coauthor Mădălina Moraru, IGI Global, 2023), Mapping Gender Employment Inequality in the Media Sector in Romania (Mediascapes, 2023)

Narayanaswamy T is currently working as an Associate Professor (Finance Domain) at REVA Business School, REVA University, Bengaluru. He has a total teaching experience of 13 years and an industry experience of 2 years. He received a B.Tech from Anna University, Tamil Nadu in 2007, and an MBA from the same University in 2010. He received his Ph.D. in Management from Bharathiar University, Tamil Nadu in 2017. His research interests span financial productivity, financial services, investments and capital markets. He has conducted several workshops and faculty development programs on financial analysis using Excel, data analysis using SPSS and Outcome Based Education for the students and faculty members. Also, he has guided more than 100 MBA students and a few PhD scholars in their research work. He has published various articles in Scopus indexed journals. He is also having an experience in handling IQAC and accreditation activities of management programs. He is also one of NISM certified Securities Market Trainers (SMARTs) which is an educational initiative of SEBI (Securities and Exchange Board of India). As a part of this initiative, he regularly conducts Investor Awareness Programs for the students, faculty members and the public. He has recently completed his Post Graduate Program in Data Science and Business Analytics offered by Great lakes Executive Learning Academy.

Sarah Williams, PFHEA, MCIPR, MCIM, CMgr, is Pro-Vice Chancellor, External Collaborations at Buckinghamshire New University, UK. She is co-editor with Elizabeth Bridgen of Women's Work in Public Relations, to which she also contributed three chapters, 'Just Because We Don't See It, Doesn't Mean It Doesn't Happen', 'Performing Professionalism: A Story in Three Acts', and 'Using Ethnography to Explore Women's Work in Public Relations'. She is also a contributor to Experiencing Public Relations: International Voices, edited by Bridgen, E. and Verčič, D. She is also a co-editor with Nikos Stylos, Roya Rahimi and Bendegul Okumus of Generation Z Marketing and Management Tourism and Hospitality and contributed a chapter to 'Promotional Strategies and New Service Opportunities in Emerging Economies' edited by Nadda, V., Dadwal, S. & Rahimi, R and published in 2017. She has had work published in the Asia Pacific Journal of Public Relations, and Advances in Hospitality and Tourism and is writing a book chapter which investigates the lived experiences of female PR freelancers in the UK for a forthcoming book on gender and freelancing in the communication industries (edited by Anca Anton and Raluca Moise). Her research explores the lived experience of PR practitioners with a focus on professionalism and professionalisation, and is currently working on a research project on the lived experience of female freelancers in PR communities. Sarah is a senior examiner for the Chartered Institute of Marketing and sits on the Midlands regional committee of the Chartered Institute of Public Relations in the United Kingdom.

Goh Ying Soon is a senior lecturer and he currently teaches Mandarin as the third language to non-native learners in MARA University of Technology, Malaysia. He is a member of the International Society for Chinese Language Teaching. He has experiences in teaching Mandarin at primary, secondary and tertiary level for more than 25 years. He has been actively presenting papers in national and international conferences. His research interests are on the use of educational technology in Mandarin teaching and learning, web-based instruction, translation, and etc.

Index

A

B

C

D

E

F

G

H

I

L

M

N

T

U

V

www.ingramcontent.com/pod-product-compliance
Lightning Source LLC
LaVergne TN
LVHW062341300926
849161LV00007B/1776
* 9 7 9 8 3 3 7 3 6 0 1 8 8 *